FERN HECKBURN

Financial Accounting Theory

fourth edition

william r. scott

UNIVERSITY OF WATERLOO
QUEEN'S UNIVERSITY

PEARSON

Prentice
Hall

Toronto

Library and Archives Canada Cataloguing in Publication

Scott, William R. (William Robert), 1931–

Financial accounting theory / William R. Scott. — 4th ed.

Includes bibliographical references and index.
ISBN 0-13-129491-1

1. Accounting. I. Title.

HF5635.S36 2006   657'.044   C2005-903084-4

ISBN 0-13-129491-1

Vice-President, Editorial Director: Michael J. Young
Executive Editor: Samantha Scully
Sponsoring Editor: Lori Will
Executive Marketing Manager: Cas Shields
Associate Editor: Stephen Broadbent
Production Editor: Cheryl Jackson
Copy Editor: Shirley Corriveau
Proofreader: Cat Haggert
Production Coordinator: Patricia Ciardullo
Page Layout: Carolyn E. Sebestyen
Cover and Interior Design: Jennifer Stimson
Cover Image: Getty Images/Don Carstens

10 9 8 7 6   10 09 08 07

Printed and bound in United States of America

Permission to reprint Section 1000.15 (in part), Section 3480.02, and Section 1505.04 of the *CICA Handbook* granted by The Canadian Institute of Chartered Accountants.

To Mary Ann, Julie, Martha, Kathy, Paul, and Cary

Contents

Preface

This book began as a series of lesson notes for a financial accounting theory course of the Certified General Accountants' Association of Canada. The lesson notes grew out of a conviction that we have learned a great deal about the role of financial accounting and reporting in our society from securities markets and information economics-based research conducted over many years, and that financial accounting theory comes into its own when we formally recognize the information asymmetries that pervade business relationships.

The challenge was to organize this large body of research into a unifying framework and to explain it in such a manner that professionally oriented students would both understand and accept it as relevant to the financial accounting environment and ultimately to their own professional careers.

This book seems to have achieved its goals. In addition to being part of the CGA program of professional studies for a number of years, it has been extensively class-tested in financial accounting theory courses at the University of Waterloo, Queen's University, and several other universities, both at the senior undergraduate and professional Master's levels. I am encouraged by the fact that, by and large, the students comprehend the material and, indeed, are likely to object if the instructor follows it too closely in class. This frees up class time to expand coverage of areas of interest to individual instructors and/or to motivate particular topics by means of articles from the financial press and professional and academic literature.

Despite its theoretical orientation, the book does not ignore the institutional structure of financial accounting and standard setting. It features considerable coverage of financial accounting standards. Many important standards, such as reserve recognition accounting, management discussion and analysis, employee stock options, post-employment benefits, financial instruments, ceiling tests, hedge accounting, and comprehensive income are described and critically evaluated. The structure of standard-setting bodies is also described, and the role of structure in helping to engineer the consent necessary for a successful standard is evaluated. While the text discussion concentrates on relating standards to the theoretical framework of the book, the coverage provides students with the occasion to learn the contents of the standards themselves.

I have also used this material in Ph.D. seminars. Here, I concentrate on the research articles that underlie the text discussion. Nevertheless, the students appreciate the framework of the book as a way of putting specific research papers into perspective. Indeed, the book proceeds in large part by selecting important research papers for description and commentary, and provides extensive references to other research papers underlying the text discussion. Assignment of the research papers themselves could be especially useful for instructors who wish to dig into methodological issues that, with some exceptions, are downplayed in the book itself.

In this fourth edition, I have added references and discussion of recent research articles, updated the coverage of financial accounting standards, and generally revised the exposition as a result of comments received and experience in teaching from earlier editions. The major change is an updating of the theory of agency in Chapter 9, with related updating of executive compensation and earnings management topics in Chapters 10 and 11. Other changes include incorporating effects of the Enron and WorldCom financial reporting scandals into the text discussion, introduction of Theory in Practice vignettes to better illustrate the relevance of the theory, expanding discussion of international accounting standards convergence, and updating much of the problem material. I have also expanded the number of optional sections for those who do not wish to delve too deeply into certain topics.

Despite these changes, the book largely retains the structure, organization, and markets-oriented outlook of the earlier editions, although I have introduced some discussion of ethical behaviour. Ethical behaviour has always been implicit in this book, although primarily cast in terms of full disclosure, usefulness, cooperative behaviour, and reputation. This edition makes this connection more explicit. While coverage of securities market inefficiencies is updated, the book retains the view that investor rationality and efficient securities market theory are still the most useful theories to guide accountants in their disclosure decisions, and that the motivation and monitoring of responsible managerial performance is an equally important role of financial reporting as the providing of useful information to investors.

Supplements

Instructor's Resource CD-ROM (ISBN 0-13-201728-8)

This resource CD includes the following instructor supplements:

- **Instructor's Manual** The Instructor's Manual includes suggested solutions to the end-of-chapter Questions and Problems, including a number of new problems added in this edition. It also offers learning objectives for each chapter and suggests teaching approaches that could be used. In addition, it comments on other issues for consideration, suggests supplementary references, and contains some additional problem material.
- **PowerPoints** PowerPoint presentations offer a comprehensive selection of slides covering theories and examples presented in the text. They are designed to organize the delivery of content to students and stimulate classroom discussion.

Acknowledgments

I have received a lot of assistance in writing this book. First, I thank CGA Canada for their encouragement and support over a number of years. Much of the material in the questions and problems has been reprinted or adapted from the *Accounting Theory I* course and examinations of the Certified General Accountants' Association of Canada. These are acknowledged where used.

At Pearson Education Canada I would like to thank Lori Will, Stephen Broadbent, Cheryl Jackson, Shirley Corriveau, Cat Haggert, Michelle Hodgson, Anita Smale, Trish Ciardullo, Carolyn Sebestyen, and Jennifer Stimson. I extend my thanks and appreciation to the following reviewers as well: Maureen P. Gowing, Concordia University; J. Roderick Tilley, Mount Saint Vincent University; Dr. Ian Hutchinson, Acadia University; Irene Wiecek, University of Toronto at Mississauga; Dr. A. L. Dartnell, FCGA; Kathryn Pedwell, University of Ottawa; and David Senkow, University of Regina. I acknowledge the financial assistance of the Ontario Chartered Accountants' Chair in Accounting at the University of Waterloo, which has enabled teaching relief and other support in the preparation of the original manuscript. Financial support of the School of Business of Queen's University is also gratefully acknowledged.

I also thank numerous colleagues and students for advice and feedback. These include Sati Bandyopadhyay, Phelim Boyle, Dennis Chung, Len Eckel, Haim Falk, Steve Fortin, Jennifer Kao, David Manry, Patricia O'Brien, Bill Richardson, Gordon Richardson, Dean Smith, and Dan Thornton. Special thanks to Dick VanOfferen for helpful comments on earlier editions.

I thank the large number of researchers whose work underlies this book. As previously mentioned, numerous research papers are described and referenced. However, there are many other worthy papers that I have not referenced. This implies no disrespect or lack of appreciation for the contributions of these authors to financial accounting theory. Rather, it has been simply impossible to include them all, both for reasons of space, and the boundaries of my own knowledge.

I am grateful to Carolyn Holden for skilful, timely, and cheerful typing of the original manuscript in the face of numerous revisions, and to Jill Nucci for research assistance.

Finally, I thank my wife and family who, in many ways, have been involved in the learning process leading to this book.

William Scott

Chapter 1

Introduction

FIGURE 1.1 ORGANIZATION OF THE BOOK

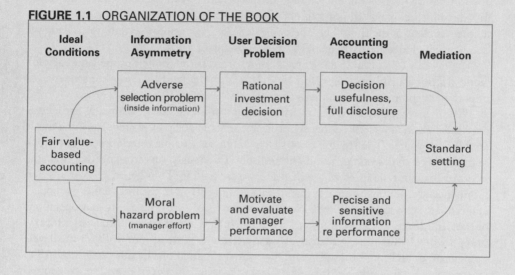

1.1 The Objective of This Book

This book is about accounting, not how to account. It argues that accounting students, having been exposed to the methodology and practice of accounting, need at least one course that critically examines the broader implications of financial accounting for the fair and efficient operation of our economy. Its objective is to give the reader an understanding of the current financial accounting and reporting environment, taking into account the diverse interests of both external users and management.

1.2 Some Historical Perspective

Accounting has a long history. The first complete description of the double entry book-keeping system appeared in 1494, authored by Luca Paciolo, an Italian monk/mathematician.[1] Paciolo did not invent this system—it had developed over a long period of time. Segments that developed first included, for example, the collection of an account receivable. "Both sides" of such a transaction were easy to see, since cash and accounts receivable have a physical and/or legal existence, and the amount of the increase in cash was equal to the decrease in accounts receivable. The recording of other types of transactions, such as the sale of goods or the incurring of expenses, however, took longer to develop. In the case of a sale, it was obvious that cash or accounts receivable increased, and that goods on hand decreased. But, what about the difference between the selling price and the cost of the goods sold? There is no physical or legal representation of the profit on the sale. For the double entry system to handle transactions such as this, it was necessary to create *abstract* concepts of income and capital. By Paciolo's time, a complete double entry system quite similar to the one in use today was in place. Indeed, it was the abstract nature of the system, including the properties of capital as the accumulation of income and income as the rate of change of capital[2], that attracted the attention of mathematicians of the time. The "method of Venice," as Paciolo's system was called, was frequently included in mathematics texts in subsequent years.

Following 1494, the double entry system spread throughout Europe, and Paciolo's work was translated into English in 1543. It was in England that another sequence of important accounting developments took place.

By the early eighteenth century, the concept of a joint stock company had developed in England to include permanent existence, limited liability of shareholders, and transferability of shares. Transferability of shares led in turn to the development of a stock market where shares could be bought and sold. Obviously, investors needed financial information about the firms whose shares they were trading. Thus began a long transition for financial accounting, from a system to enable a merchant to control his/her own operations to a system to inform investors who were not involved in the day-to-day operations of the firm. It was in the joint interests of the firm and investors that financial information provided by the firm was trustworthy, thereby laying the groundwork for the development of an auditing profession and government regulation. In this regard, the 1844 Companies Act was notable. It was in this act that the concept of providing an audited balance sheet to shareholders first appeared in the law, although this requirement was dropped in subsequent years[3] and not reinstated until the early 1900s. During the interval, voluntary provision of information was common, but its effectiveness was hampered by a lack of accounting principles. This was demonstrated, for example, in the controversy of whether amortization of capital assets had to be deducted in determining income available for dividends (the courts ruled it did not).

In the twentieth century, major developments in financial accounting shifted to the United States, which was growing rapidly in economic power. The introduction of a corporate income tax in the United States in 1909 provided a major impetus to income measurement, and, as noted by Hatfield (1927, p. 140), was influential in persuading business managers to accept amortization as a deduction from income.

Nevertheless, accounting in the United States continued to be relatively unregulated, with financial reporting and auditing largely voluntary. However, the stock market crash of 1929 and resulting Great Depression led to major changes. The most noteworthy was the creation of the Securities and Exchange Commission (SEC) by the Securities Act of 1934, with a focus on protecting investors by means of a disclosure-based regulatory structure.

Merino and Neimark (1982) (MN) examined the conditions leading up to the creation of the SEC. In the process, they reported on some of the securities market practices of the 1920s and prior. Apparently, voluntary disclosure was widespread, as also noted by

Benston (1973). However, MN claim that such disclosure was motivated by big business's desire to avoid regulations to enhance "potential competition."

Full disclosure regulations would enhance competition by enabling potential entrants to identify high-profit industries. Presumably, big business felt that voluntary disclosure would avoid pressure for regulation but provide enough leeway that high profitability could be disguised. Thus, informing investors was not the main motivation of disclosure. Instead, investors were "protected" by a "two-tiered" market structure whereby prices were set by knowledgeable insiders, subject to a self-imposed "moral regulation" to control misleading reporting. Unfortunately, moral regulation was not always effective, and MN refer to numerous instances of manipulative financial reporting and other abuses, which were widely believed to be major contributing factors to the 1929 crash.

The 1934 securities legislation can then be regarded as a movement away from a potential competition rationale for disclosure towards the supplying of better-quality information to investors as a way to control manipulative financial practices.[4]

One of the practices of the 1920s that received criticism was the frequent appraisal of capital assets, the values of which came crashing down in 1929. A major lesson learned by accountants as a result of the Great Depression was that values were fleeting. The outcome was a strengthening of the historical cost basis of accounting. This basis received its highest expression in the famous Paton and Littleton monograph, *An Introduction to Corporate Accounting Standards*, of 1940. This document elegantly and persuasively set forth the case for historical cost accounting, based on the concept of the firm as a going concern. This concept justifies important attributes of historical cost accounting such as waiting to recognize revenue until objective evidence of realization is available, the matching against realized revenues of the allocated costs of earning those revenues, and the deferral of unrealized gains and losses on the balance sheet until the time came to match them with revenues. As a result, the income statement reliably shows the current "installment" of the firm's earning power. The income statement replaced the balance sheet as the primary focus of financial reporting.

It is sometimes claimed that the Paton and Littleton monograph was too persuasive, in that it shut out exploration of alternative bases of accounting. As we shall see in this book, historical cost is still the primary basis of accounting and it has only relatively recently begun to yield to **fair value** accounting and the renewed importance of the balance sheet. The term "fair value" is a general expression for the valuation of any asset or liability on the basis of its market value, the discounted present value of its future receipts, or in some cases by means of a mathematical model.[5]

Another lesson learned by accountants was how to survive in the new SEC-regulated environment. The SEC has the power to establish the accounting standards and procedures used by firms under its jurisdiction. If the SEC chose to use this power, the prestige and influence of the accounting profession would be greatly eroded, possibly to the point where financial reporting becomes a process of "manual thumbing" with little basis for professional judgement and little influence on the setting of accounting standards. However, the SEC chose (and still chooses) to delegate most standard setting to the profession.[6] To retain this delegated authority, however, the accounting profession must retain the SEC's confidence that it is doing a satisfactory job of creating and maintaining a financial reporting environment that protects and informs investors and encourages the proper operation of capital markets. Thus began the search for accounting principles, those underlying truths on which the practice of accounting is, or should be, based. This was seen as a way to improve practice by reducing inconsistencies in choice of accounting policies across firms and enabling the accounting for new reporting challenges[7] to be deduced from basic principles rather than developing in an ad hoc and inconsistent way.

Accountants have laboured long and hard to find these basic principles, but with relatively little success.[8] Indeed, they have never agreed on a definition of what accounting principles are, let alone a list of them.

As a result, accounting theory and research up to the late 1960s consisted largely of a priori reasoning as to which accounting principles and practices were "best." For example, should the effects of changing prices and inflation on financial statements be taken into account, and, if so, how? This debate can be traced back at least as far as the 1920s. Some accountants argued that the fair values of specific assets and liabilities held by the firm should be recognized, with the resulting unrealized holding gains and losses included in net income. Other accountants argued that inflation-induced changes in the purchasing power of money should be recognized. During a period of inflation, the firm suffers a purchasing power loss on monetary assets such as cash and accounts receivable, since the amounts of goods and services that can be obtained when they are collected and spent is less than the amounts that could have been obtained when they were created. Conversely, the firm enjoys a purchasing power gain on monetary liabilities such as accounts payable and long-term debt. Separate reporting of these gains and losses would better reflect real firm performance, it was argued. Still other accountants argued that the effects of *both* specific and inflation-induced changes in prices should be taken into account. Others, however, often including firm management, resisted these suggestions. One argument, based in part on experience from the Great Depression, was that estimates of fair values and measurements of inflation were unreliable, so that taking them into account would not necessarily improve the measurement of the firm's (and the manager's) performance.

Nevertheless, standard setters in numerous countries did require some disclosures of the effects of changing prices. In Canada, for example, Section 4510 of the *CICA Handbook*, issued in 1982, required disclosure in the notes to the financial statements of the fair values of inventories and capital assets, and of purchasing power gains and losses resulting from inflation. Section 4510 was subsequently withdrawn. However, this withdrawal was due more to the decline in inflation in the years following introduction of the section rather than to the debate having been settled.

The basic problem with debates such as the accounting for changing prices debate was that there was little theoretical basis for choosing among the various alternatives, particularly since, as mentioned, accountants were unable to agree on a set of basic accounting principles.

During this period, however, major developments were taking place in other disciplines. In particular, a theory of rational decision-making under uncertainty developed as a branch of statistics. This theory prescribes how individuals may revise their beliefs upon receipt of new information. The theory of efficient securities markets developed in economics and finance. The Possibility Theorem of Arrow (1963) led to the realization that there was no such thing as true net income or perfect accounting standards, implying that the search for the best accounting principles and practices was a "will-o'-the-wisp."

These theories, which began to show up in accounting theory in the latter half of the 1960s, generated the concept of decision—useful (in place of true) financial statement information. This concept first appeared in the American Accounting Association (AAA)[9] monograph, *A Statement of Basic Accounting Theory*, in 1966. Current statements of basic accounting principles, most notably the Conceptual Framework of the Financial Accounting Standards Board (FASB), are based on decision usefulness.

Equally important was the development of the economics of imperfect information, a branch of economics that formally recognizes that some individuals have an information advantage over others. This led to the development of the theory of agency, which has greatly increased our understanding of the legitimate interests of business management in financial reporting and standard setting.

These theories suggest that the answer to which way to account, if any, for changing prices outlined above will be found in the extent to which they lead to good investment decisions. Furthermore, any resolution will have to take the concerns of management into account.

In Canada, the development of financial accounting and reporting has proceeded differently, although the end result is basically similar to that of the United States. Financial reporting requirements in Canada were laid down in federal and provincial corporations acts, along the lines of the English corporations acts referred to above. The ultimate power to regulate financial reporting rests with the legislatures concerned. However, in 1946, the Committee on Accounting and Auditing Research, now the Accounting Standards Board (AcSB), of the Canadian Institute of Chartered Accountants (CICA) began to issue bulletins on financial accounting issues. These were intended to guide Canadian accountants as to best practices, and did not have force of law. In 1968, these were formalized into the *CICA Handbook*. At first, adherence to these provisions was voluntary but, given their prestigious source, they were difficult to ignore. Over time, the *Handbook* gained recognition as the authoritative statement of Generally Accepted Accounting Principles (GAAP) in Canada. Ultimately, provincial securities commissions and the corporations acts formally recognized this authority. For example, in 1975, for federally regulated companies, the Canada Business Corporations Act required adherence to the *CICA Handbook* to satisfy reporting requirements under the act. The end result, then, is similar to that in the United States in that the body with ultimate authority to set accounting standards has delegated this function to a private professional body.[10]

More recently, several notable events have had a major impact on financial accounting and reporting. These followed from the stock market boom in the late 1990s and its collapse in the early 2000s. During the collapse, share prices of many firms, especially those in the "hi-tech" industry, fell precipitously. For example, while the share price of General Electric Corp. fell from a high of about $55 U.S. in August 2000 to a low of about $21 in October 2002, that of telecommunications firm Nortel Networks fell from a high of about $82 U.S. to a low of 44 cents over the same period.

A contributing factor to the market collapse was the revelation of numerous financial reporting irregularities. Frequently, these involved revenue recognition, which has long been a problem in accounting theory and practice. Palmose and Scholz (2004), in a study of 492 U.S. corporations that reported restatements of prior years' incomes during 1995–1999, report that revenue restatements were the single most common type of restatement in their sample. In part, this problem is due to the vagueness and generality of revenue recognition criteria under GAAP. For example, revenue can be recognized when the significant risks and rewards of ownership have been transferred to the buyer and collection is reasonably assured.

During the boom of the late 1990s and early 2000s, many firms, especially newly established ones with little or no history of profits, attempted to impress investors and enhance their stock prices by reporting a rapidly growing stream of revenue. Subsequently, when the boom collapsed, much recognized revenue proved to be premature and had to be reversed.

Numerous other, even more serious, failures of financial reporting have also come to light. Two of these are particularly notable. Enron Corp. was a large U.S. corporation with initial interests in natural gas distribution. Following substantial deregulation of the natural gas market in the United States during the 1980s, Enron successfully expanded its operations to become an intermediary between natural gas producers and users, thereby enabling them to manage their exposures to fluctuating natural gas prices. For example, it offered long-term fixed-price contracts to public utilities and natural gas producers. Subsequently, Enron extended this business model to a variety of other trading activities, including steel, natural gas, electricity, and weather futures. Its stock market performance was dramatic, rising to a high of about $90 U.S. per share in late 2000. To finance this rapid expansion, and support its share price, Enron needed both large amounts of capital and steadily increasing earnings. Meeting these needs was complicated by the fact that its forays into new markets were not always profitable, creating a temptation to disguise losses.[11]

In the face of these challenges, Enron resorted to devious tactics. One tactic was to create various special purpose entities (SPEs). These were limited partnerships formed for

Theory in Practice 1.1

In July, 2002, Qwest Communications International Inc., a large provider of Internet-based communications services, announced that it was under investigation by the SEC. Its share price immediately fell by 32%. In February, 2003, the SEC announced fraud charges against several senior Qwest executives, alleging that they had inflated revenues during 2000 and 2001 in order to meet revenue and earnings projections.

One tactic used was to separate long-term sales of equipment and services into two components. Full revenue was immediately recognized on the equipment component despite the obligation to honour the service component over an extended period. A related tactic was to price services at cost, putting all profit into the equipment component, which was immediately recognized as revenue despite a continuing obligation to protect the customer from risk of obsolescence on the equipment "sold." Yet another tactic was to recognize revenue from the sale of fibre-optic cable despite an ability of the purchaser to exchange the cable at a later date. In retrospect, Qwest's revenue recognition practices were premature, to say the least.

In June 2004, the SEC announced settlements with some of the officers charged. One officer, for example, repaid $200,000 of "ill-gotten gains," plus a penalty of $150,000, and agreed to "cease and desist" from any future violations.

specific purposes, and effectively controlled by senior Enron officers. These SPEs were financed largely by Enron's contributions of its own common stock, in return for notes receivable from the SPE. The SPE could then borrow money using the Enron stock as security, and use the borrowed cash to repay its note payable to Enron. In this manner, much of Enron's debt did not appear on its balance sheet—it appeared on the books of the SPEs instead.

In addition, Enron received fees for management and other services supplied to its SPEs, and also investment income. This investment income is particularly worthy of note. By applying fair value accounting to its holdings of Enron stock, the SPE included increases in the value of this stock in its income. As an owner of the SPE, Enron included its share of the SPE's income in its own earnings. In effect, Enron was able to include increases in the value of its own stock in its reported earnings!

Of course, if the SPEs had been consolidated with Enron's financial statements, as they should have been, the effects of these tactics would disappear. The SPE debt would then show on Enron's consolidated balance sheet, fees billed would be offset against the corresponding expense recorded by the SPE, and Enron's investment in its SPEs would have been deducted from its shareholders' equity.

However, the SPEs were not consolidated, seemingly with the agreement of Enron's auditor. However, in late 2001, Enron announced that it would now consolidate, apparently in response to an inquiry from the SEC. This resulted in an increase in its reported debt of some $628 million, a decrease in its shareholders' equity of $1.1 billion, and large reductions in previously reported earnings. Investors quickly lost all confidence in the company. Its share price fell to almost zero and it filed for bankruptcy protection in December, 2001.

A second major abuse was relatively less complex. WorldCom Inc. was a large U.S. telecommunications carrier. During the years 1999 to 2002, the company overstated its earnings by about $11 billion. Almost $4 billion of this amount arose from capitalization of network maintenance and other costs that should have been charged to expense as incurred—a tactic that overstated both reported earnings and operating cash flow. Another $3.3 billion of overstatement arose from reductions in the allowance for doubtful accounts. Again, when these abuses came to light, investor confidence collapsed and WorldCom applied for bankruptcy protection in 2002.

These, and numerous other, reporting abuses took place regardless of the fact that the financial statements of the companies involved were audited and certified as in accordance with GAAP. As a result, public confidence in financial reporting and the operation of capital markets was severely shaken.

One result of this collapse of confidence was increased regulation. The most notable example is the Sarbanes-Oxley Act, passed by the U.S. Congress in 2002. This wide-ranging act is designed to restore public confidence by reducing the likelihood of accounting horror stories such as those just described. The act does this by improving corporate governance and tightening the audit function. One of its major provisions is to create the Public Company Accounting Oversight Board. This agency has the power to set auditing standards and to inspect and discipline auditors of public companies. The act also restricts several of the non-audit services offered by auditing firms to their clients, such as information systems and valuation services. Furthermore, the auditor now reports to the audit committee of the client's board of directors, rather than to management. The audit committee must be composed of directors independent of the company.

Other provisions of Sarbanes-Oxley include a requirement that firms' financial reports shall include "all material correcting adjustments," and disclose all material off-balance-sheet loans and other relations with "unconsolidated entities." Furthermore, the Chief Executive Officer and Chief Financial Officer must certify that the financial statements present fairly the company's results of operations and financial position.

The standard setting bodies themselves are also moving to restore public confidence. For example, in Canada, the Accounting Standards Board (AcSB) has implemented two new accounting standards that, presumably, are intended to reduce the likelihood of Enron and WorldCom-style reporting failures. Section 1100 of *CICA Handbook*, adopted in 2003, clarifies the meaning of Canadian GAAP and removes the ability of a firm to depart from GAAP. Prior to Section 1100, firms had some room to adopt accounting policies that departed from GAAP by claiming that use of GAAP would result in misleading financial statements. Section 1400 of the *Handbook,* adopted at the same time, requires that financial statements present fairly the firm's financial position and results of operations, and asserts that fair presentation includes the provision of sufficient information about significant transactions that their effects on the financial statements can be understood. These requirements of Section 1400 are similar to some of the requirements of the Sarbanes-Oxley Act outlined above.

Earlier in this section, we noted that one of the effects of the stock market crash of 1929 was a strengthening of the historical cost basis of accounting. This raises the question of whether the recent stock market crash and revelation of abuses of fair value accounting will result in a similar movement back to a more conservative basis of accounting in the 2000s. Basu (1997) defines conservatism as the requiring of a higher standard of verification to record gains than to record losses, resulting in persistent understatement of net assets relative to their fair values. By this definition, historical cost accounting contains conservative elements. For example, inventories are understated relative to the amount of cash they are expected to generate, since they are carried at cost rather than fair value. This is because historical cost accounting avoids recognizing increases in fair value of assets until objective evidence (such as a sale) is available. However, it is less likely to avoid recognizing decreases as, for example, in the lower of cost or market rule for inventories. Nevertheless, there is little evidence of a movement back to historical cost in the years following the 2000 crash, as accounting standard setters continue to bring fair value-oriented standards on line.[12] Nevertheless, we shall see later that academic accountants have begun to give renewed attention to conservatism as a desirable way to account. The full impact on financial accounting and reporting of the recent horror stories remains to be seen.

These various developments set the stage for the current financial accounting and reporting environment that is the subject of this book.

1.3   A Note on Ethical Behaviour

The collapse of Enron and WorldCom, and subsequent collapse of public confidence in financial reporting, raise questions about how to restore this confidence. One response is increased regulation, as in the Sarbanes-Oxley Act described above. However, **ethical behaviour** by accountants and auditors is also required, since numerous accountants designed, were involved in, or at least knew about, the reporting irregularities. Also, the financial statements of the firms involved were certified by their auditors as being in accordance with GAAP.

By ethical behaviour, we mean that accountants and auditors should "do the right thing." In our context, this means that accountants must behave with integrity and independence in putting the public interest ahead of the employer's and client's interests should these conflict.

It is important to realize that there is a social dimension to integrity and independence. That is, a society depends on shared beliefs and common values. This notion goes back to Thomas Hobbes, a seventeenth century philosopher, in his book *The Leviathan*. Hobbes argued that if people acted solely as selfish individuals, society would collapse to the point where force, or the threat of force, would prevail—there would be no cooperative behaviour. He also argued that rules, regulations, and the courts were not enough to restore cooperative behaviour, since no set of rules could possibly anticipate all human interaction. What is needed, in addition, is that people must recognize that it is in their joint interests to cooperate.

Clearly, the force of Hobbes' arguments can be seen in the Enron and WorldCom disasters. We have a set of rules governing financial reporting (e.g., GAAP). However, GAAP was not followed and/or was bent so as to conform to its letter but not its intent. Cooperative behaviour broke down because certain individuals behaved in a manner that broke the rules—they did not behave with integrity and independence. This was good for them, at least in the short run, but bad for society. Hobbes' prediction is that increased regulation will not suffice to prevent a repetition of these reporting disasters. What is also needed is ethical behaviour.

Note, however, that there is a time dimension to ethical behaviour. An accountant can act in his/her own self-interest and still behave ethically. This is accomplished by taking a longer-run view of the consequences of one's actions. For example, suppose that an accountant is instructed to understate a firm's environmental liabilities. In the short run, doing so will benefit the accountant through job retention, promotion, and higher compensation. In the longer run, though, future generations will suffer through increased pollution, shareholders will suffer from reduced share price when the extent of environmental liability becomes known, and investors as a whole will suffer when reduced public confidence in financial reporting lowers the prices of all shares. The accountant will suffer through dismissal, professional discipline or expulsion, and reduced compensation due to reduced stature of all accountants. By taking account of these longer-run costs, the accountant is motivated to behave ethically. In effect, in the longer run, self-interested behaviour and ethical behaviour merge.

In this book, we will often cast our discussion in terms of full disclosure, usefulness of financial statements, cooperative behaviour, and reputation, all of which benefit society. However, in acting so as to meet these desirable characteristics of financial reporting, the accountant is also acting ethically.

1.4 The Complexity of Information in Financial Accounting and Reporting

The environment of accounting is both very complex and very challenging. It is complex because the product of accounting is **information**—a powerful and important commodity.

One reason for the complexity of information is that individuals are not unanimous in their reaction to it. For example, a sophisticated investor may react positively to the valuation of certain firm assets and liabilities at fair value on the grounds that this will help to predict future firm performance.[13] Other investors may be less positive, perhaps because they feel that fair value information is unreliable, or simply because they are used to historical cost information. Furthermore, managers, who will have to report the fair values, might react quite negatively. Management typically objects to inclusion of unrealized gains and losses resulting from changes in fair values in net income, arguing that these items introduce excessive volatility into earnings, do not reflect their performance, and should not be included when evaluating the results of their efforts. These arguments may be somewhat self-serving, since part of management's job is to anticipate changes in fair values and take steps to protect the firm from adverse effects of these changes. For example, management may hedge against increases in prices of raw materials and changes in interest rates. Nevertheless, managements' objections remain. As a result, accountants quickly get caught up in whether reported net income should fulfill a role of facilitating the prediction of firm performance, or a role of reporting on management's stewardship of the firm's resources.

Another reason for the complexity of information is that it does more than affect individual decisions. In affecting decisions it also affects the operation of markets, such as securities markets and managerial labour markets. It is important to the efficiency and fairness of the economy itself that these markets work well.

The challenge for financial accountants, then, is to survive and prosper in a complex environment characterized by conflicting pressures from different groups with an interest in financial reporting. This book argues that the prospects for survival and prosperity will be enhanced if accountants have a critical awareness of the impact of financial reporting on investors, managers, and the economy. The alternative to awareness is simply to accept the reporting environment as given. However, this is a very short-term strategy, since environments are constantly changing and evolving.

1.5   The Role of Accounting Research

A book about accounting theory must inevitably draw on accounting research, much of which is contained in academic journals. There are two complementary ways that we can view the role of research. The first is to consider its effects on accounting practice. For example, a decision usefulness approach underlies Section 1000 of the *CICA Handbook*, and the Conceptual Framework of the FASB in the United States. The essence of this approach is that investors should be supplied with information to help them make good investment decisions. One has only to compare the current annual report of a public company with those issued in the 1960s and prior to see the tremendous increase in disclosure over the 25 years or so since decision usefulness formally became an important concept in accounting theory.

Yet, this increase in disclosure did not "just happen." It, as outlined in Section 1.2, is based on fundamental research into the theory of investor decision-making and the theory of capital markets, which have guided the accountant in what information is useful. Furthermore, the theory has been subjected to extensive empirical testing, which has established that, on average, investors use financial accounting information much as the theory predicts.

Independently of whether it affects current practice, however, there is a second important view of the role of research. This is to improve our *understanding* of the accounting environment, which we argued above should not be taken for granted. For example, fundamental research into models of conflict resolution, in particular agency theory models, has improved our understanding of managers' interests in financial reporting, of the role of executive compensation plans in motivating and controlling management's operation of the firm, and of the ways in which such plans use accounting information. This in turn leads to an improved understanding of managers' interests in accounting policy choice and why they may want to bias or otherwise manipulate reported net income, or, at least, to have some ability to manage the "bottom line." Research such as this enables us to understand the boundaries of management's legitimate role in financial reporting, and why the accountant is frequently caught between the interests of investors and managers. In this book, we use both of the above views. Our approach to research is twofold. In some cases, we choose important research papers, describe them intuitively, and explain how they fit into our overall framework of financial accounting theory and practice. In other cases, we simply refer to research papers on which our discussion is based. The interested reader can pursue the discussion in greater depth if desired.

1.6   The Importance of Information Asymmetry

This book is based on information economics. This is a unifying theme that formally recognizes that some parties to business transactions may have an information advantage over others. When this happens, the economy is said to be characterized by **information asymmetry**. We shall consider two major types of information asymmetry.

The first is **adverse selection**. For our purposes, adverse selection occurs because some persons, such as firm managers and other insiders, will know more about the current condition and future prospects of the firm than outside investors. There are various ways that managers and other insiders can exploit their information advantage at the expense of outsiders. For example, managers may behave unethically by biasing or otherwise managing the information released to investors, perhaps to increase the value of stock options they hold. They may release information early to selected investors or analysts, enabling insiders to benefit at the expense of ordinary investors. Such tactics reduce the ability of ordinary investors to make good investment decisions. Then, investors' concerns about the possibility of biased information release and favouritism will make them wary of buying firms' securities, with the result that capital markets will not function as well as they should. We can then think of financial accounting and reporting as a mechanism to control adverse selection by timely and credible conversion of inside information into outside information.

> *Adverse selection is a type of information asymmetry whereby one or more parties to a business transaction, or potential transaction, have an information advantage over other parties.*

The second type of information asymmetry is **moral hazard**. Moral hazard exists in many situations. For example, a trustee for a bond issue may shirk his/her duties, to the disadvantage of the bondholders. In our context, moral hazard occurs because of the separation of ownership and control that characterizes most large business entities. It is effectively impossible for shareholders and creditors to observe directly the extent and quality of top manager effort on their behalf. Then, the manager may be tempted to shirk on effort, blaming any deterioration of firm performance on factors beyond his or her control. Obviously, if this happens, there are serious implications both for investors and for the efficient operation of the economy. We can then view accounting net income as a measure of managerial performance, or stewardship. This helps to control moral hazard in two complementary ways. First, net income can serve as an input into executive compensation contracts to motivate manager performance. Second, net income can inform the managerial labour market, so that a manager who shirks will suffer a decline in income, reputation, and market value in the longer run.

> *Moral hazard* is a type of information asymmetry whereby one or more parties to a business transaction, or potential transaction, can observe their actions in fulfillment of the transaction but other parties cannot.

1.7 The Fundamental Problem of Financial Accounting Theory

It turns out that the most useful measure of net income to inform investors, that is, to control adverse selection, need not be the same as the best measure to motivate manager performance, that is, to control moral hazard. This was recognized by Gjesdal (1981). Investors' interests are best served by information that enables better investment decisions and better-operating capital markets. Providing it is reasonably reliable, fair value accounting fulfils this role, since it provides up-to-date information about assets and liabilities, hence of future firm performance, and reduces the ability of insiders to take advantage of changes in fair values.

Managers' interests are best served by information that is highly informative about their effort in running the firm, since this enables efficient compensation contracts and better operation of managerial labour markets. But fair value accounting may be very volatile in its impact on reported earnings and may be more subject to bias and manipulation than historical cost-based information. Both of these effects reduce the informativeness of earnings about manager effort. Thus, from a managerial perspective, a less volatile and more conservative income measure, such as one based on historical cost, may better fulfil a role of reporting on manager effort.

Given that there is only one bottom line, the fundamental problem of financial accounting theory is how to reconcile these different roles for accounting information.

1.8 Regulation as a Reaction to the Fundamental Problem

There are two basic reactions to the fundamental problem. One is, in effect, to ask, "What problem?" That is, why not let market forces determine how much and what kinds of information firms should produce? We can think of investors and other financial statement users as demanders of information and of managers as suppliers. Then, just as in markets for apples and automobiles, the forces of demand and supply can determine the quantity produced.

This view argues, in effect, that market forces can sufficiently control the adverse selection and moral hazard problems so that investors are protected, and managerial labour markets and securities markets will work reasonably well. Indeed, as we shall see, there are a surprising number of ways whereby managers can credibly supply information, including accounting information. Furthermore, investors as a group are surprisingly sophisticated in ferreting out the implications of information for future firm performance. Consequently, according to this view, unregulated market prices reasonably reflect firm and manager value.

The second reaction is to turn to **regulation** to protect investors, on the grounds that information is such a complex and important commodity that market forces alone fail to adequately control the problems of moral hazard and adverse selection. This leads directly to the role of standard setting, which is viewed in this book as a form of regulation that lays down generally accepted accounting principles.

Of course, consistent with the arguments of Hobbes (Section 1.3), we cannot expect regulation to completely protect investors. Consequently, the rigorous determination of the right amount of regulation is an extremely complex issue of social choice. At the present time we simply do not know which of the above two reactions to the fundamental problem is on the right track. Certainly, we witness lots of regulation in accounting, and there appears to be no slowing down in the rate at which new standards are coming on line. Consequently, it may seem that society has resolved the question of extent of regulation for us.

Yet, we live in a time of deregulation. Recent years have witnessed substantial deregulation of major industries such as transportation, telecommunications, financial services, and electric power generation, where deregulation was once thought unthinkable. The reason it is important to ask whether similar deregulation should take place in the information "industry" is because regulation has a cost—a fact often ignored by standard setters. Again, the answer to the question of whether the benefits of regulation outweigh the costs is not known. However, we shall pursue this issue later in the book.

1.9   The Organization of This Book

Figure 1.1 summarizes how this book operationalizes the framework for the study of financial accounting theory outlined above. There are four main components of the figure, and we will outline each in turn.

1.9.1   Ideal Conditions

Before considering the problems introduced into accounting by information asymmetry, it is worthwhile to consider what accounting would be like under ideal conditions. This is depicted by the leftmost box of Figure 1.1. By ideal conditions we mean an economy characterized by perfect and complete markets or, equivalently, by a lack of information asymmetry and other barriers to fair and efficient market operation. Such conditions are also called "first best." Then, asset and liability valuation is on the basis of expected present values of future cash flows. Arbitrage ensures that present values and market values are equal. Investors and managers would have no scope for disagreement over the role of financial reporting and no incentives to call for regulation.

Unfortunately, or perhaps fortunately, ideal conditions do not prevail in practice. Nevertheless, they provide a useful benchmark against which more realistic, "second best" accounting conditions can be compared. For example, we will see that there are numerous instances of the actual use of fair value-based accounting techniques in financial reporting. Reserve recognition accounting for oil and gas companies is an example. Furthermore, the use of such techniques is increasing, as in recent standards requiring fair value accounting for financial instruments. A study of accounting under ideal conditions is useful not only because practice is moving to increased use of fair values, but more importantly, it helps us to see what the real problems and challenges of fair value accounting are when the ideal conditions that they require do not hold.

1.9.2 Adverse Selection

The top three boxes of Figure 1.1 represent the second component of the framework. This introduces the adverse selection problem. As discussed in Section 1.6, this is the problem of communication from the firm to outside investors. Here, the accounting role is to provide a "level playing field" through full disclosure of useful and cost-effective information to investors and other financial statement users.

To understand how financial accounting can help to control the adverse selection problem, it is desirable to have an appreciation of how investors make decisions. This is because knowledge of investor decision processes is essential if the accountant is to know what information they need. The study of investment decision making is a large topic, since investors undoubtedly make decisions in a variety of ways, ranging from intuition to "hot tips" to random occurrences such as a sudden need for cash to sophisticated computer-based models.

The approach we will take in this book is to assume that most investors are **rational**, that is, they make decisions so as to maximize their expected utility, or satisfaction, from wealth. This theory of rational investment decision has been widely studied. In making the rationality assumption we do not imply that all investors make decisions this way. Indeed, there is increasing recognition that many investors do not behave rationally in the sense of maximizing their expected utility of wealth. We do claim, however, that the theory captures the average behaviour of those investors who want to make informed investment decisions, and this claim is backed up by substantial empirical evidence.

The reporting of information that is useful to rational investors is called the **decision usefulness** approach. As suggested in Section 1.2, this approach underlies the pronouncements of major standard setting bodies, such as the Conceptual Framework of the FASB.

There are two versions of decision usefulness. One is called the **information perspective**. This perspective takes the view that the form of disclosure does not matter—it can be in notes, or in supplementary disclosures such as reserve recognition accounting and management discussion and analysis, in addition to the financial statements proper.[14] Rational investors are regarded as sufficiently sophisticated on average that they can digest the implications of public information from any source.

Recent years, however, have seen a considerable increase in the use of fair values, including for leases, pensions, other postretirement benefits, and financial instruments. This version is called the **measurement perspective** on decision usefulness. Under this perspective, accountants expand their approach to decision usefulness by taking more responsibility for incorporating measurements of fair values into the financial statements proper. Whether this means that accountants have forgotten the lessons of the 1920s and 1930s, or whether improvements in measurement tools, such as statistical analysis of large databases and the use of mathematical models to estimate fair values, and new regulations such as Sarbanes-Oxley, will help to avoid the recent abuses of fair values discussed in Section 1.2, is difficult to say. Only time will tell if these reporting failures will slow down or reverse the measurement perspective.

1.9.3 Moral Hazard

The bottom three boxes of Figure 1.1 represent the third component of the book. Here, the information asymmetry problem is moral hazard, arising from the unobservability of the manager's effort in running the firm. That is, the manager's decision problem is to decide on how much effort to devote to running the firm on behalf of the shareholders. Since effort is unobservable, the manager may be tempted to shirk on effort. However, since net income reflects manager performance, it operates as an indirect measure of the manager's effort decision. Consequently, the user decision problem is how to use financial reporting to motivate and evaluate manager performance. To be informative about performance, net income should be a precise and sensitive measure of this performance.

1.9.4 Standard Setting

We can now see the source of the fundamental problem of financial accounting theory more clearly. Fair values of assets and liabilities are of greater interest to investors than their historical costs, since fair values provide the best available indication of future firm performance and investment returns. However, as mentioned, managers may feel that gains and losses from adjusting the carrying values of assets and liabilities to fair value do not reflect *their own* performance. Accounting standard setters quickly get caught up in mediation between the conflicting interests of investors and managers. This is depicted by the rightmost box in Figure 1.1.

1.10 Relevance of Financial Accounting Theory to Accounting Practice

The framework just described provides a way of organizing our study of financial accounting theory. However, this book also recognizes an obligation to convince you that the theory is relevant to accounting practice. This is accomplished in two main ways. First, the various theories and research underlying financial accounting are described and explained in plain language, and their relevance is demonstrated by means of numerous references to accounting practice. For example, Chapter 3 describes how investors may make rational investment decisions, and then goes on to demonstrate that this decision theory underlies the Conceptual Framework of the FASB. Also, the book contains numerous instances where accounting standards are described and critically evaluated. In addition to enabling you to learn the contents of these standards, you can better understand

and apply them when you have a grounding in the underlying reasoning on which they are based. The second approach to demonstrating relevance is through assignment problems. A concentrated attempt has been made to select relevant problem material to illustrate and motivate the concepts.

Recent years have been challenging, even exciting, times for financial accounting theory. We have learned a tremendous amount about the important role of financial accounting in our economy from the information economics research outlined above. If this book enables you to better understand and appreciate this role, it will have attained its objective.

Notes

1. For some information about Paciolo, a translation of his bookkeeping treatise, and a copy of an Italian version, see *Paciolo on Accounting*, by R. Gene Brown and Kenneth S. Johnston (1963).

2. Readers with a mathematical background will recognize these relationships as related to the fundamental theorem of calculus.

3. The dropping of these requirements did not mean that firms should not supply information to shareholders, but that the amount and nature of information supplied was a matter between the firm and its shareholders. In effect, it was felt that market forces, rather than legal requirement, were sufficient to motivate information production.

4. Actually, MN pose a much deeper question. Widespread share ownership had long been seen as a way of reconciling increasingly large and powerful corporations with the popular belief in individualism, property rights, and democracy, whereby the "little guy" could take part in the corporate governance process. With the 1929 crash and subsequent revelation of manipulative abuses, a new approach was required that would both restore public confidence in securities markets and be acceptable to powerful corporate interest groups. MN suggest that the creation of the SEC was an embodiment of such a new approach.

5. Fair value is defined in *CICA Handbook* Section 3860.05, with respect to financial instruments, as the amount of the consideration that would be agreed upon in an arm's-length transaction between knowledgeable, willing parties who are under no compulsion to act. The term originated with the Financial Accounting Standards Board, the current U.S. accounting standard setter, as, for example, in Statement of Financial Accounting Standards (SFAS) 87 (1986) with respect to pension assets and in SFAS 107 (1992) with respect to financial instruments.

6. This is not to say that the SEC stands aloof from accounting standards. If it perceives that standards as set by the profession are straying too far from what it wants, the SEC can bring considerable pressure to bear short of taking over the process. In this regard, see Note 7.

7. The controversy over the investment tax credit in the United States provides an excellent example. The 1962 Revenue Act provided firms with a credit against taxes payable

of 7% of current investment in capital assets. The controversy was whether to account for the credit as a reduction in current income tax expense or to bring all or part of it into income over the life of the capital assets to which the credit applied. The Accounting Principles Board (the predecessor body to the FASB) issued APB2, requiring the latter alternative. The SEC, however, objected and issued its own standard, allowing greater flexibility in accounting for the credit. The Accounting Principles Board backed down and issued APB4 in 1964 allowing either alternative. The basic problem, as seen by the standard setters, was the lack of a set of basic accounting principles from which the correct accounting for the credit could be deduced.

8. For a detailed description of the search for accounting principles in the United States from the inception of the SEC to the present, see Storey and Storey (1998).

9. The American Accounting Association is an association of academic accountants. It does not have standard setting authority like the FASB. Nevertheless, professional accountants later picked up on the decision usefulness concept. See *Study Group on the Objectives of Financial Statements* (1973), also called the Trueblood committee report.

10. Strictly speaking, the AcSB is sponsored by the CICA, whereas the FASB is a privately funded body separate from The American Institute of Certified Public Accountants, the professional accounting body analogous to the CICA in Canada.

11. For further discussion of Enron's business model, see Healy and Palepu (2003).

12. It should be noted, however, that many of these standards involve writing assets down to fair value but not writing up to fair value, as, for example, in ceiling tests for capital assets and goodwill. This asymmetric treatment of unrealized fair value gains and losses can be regarded as a stronger form of conservatism than historical cost accounting.

13. If markets work well, market value is equally likely to rise or fall. Thus current market price is the best predictor of future value, hence of future firm performance.

14. Strictly speaking, the term "financial statements" includes the notes to the statements. When we refer to disclosure within the financial statements themselves, we will use the term "financial statements proper." Thus, if a firm values an asset at fair value in its accounts and reports the resulting number on the balance sheet, it reports fair value in the financial statements proper. If it discloses the fair value only in a note, this would be reported in the financial statements but not in the financial statements proper.

Chapter 2

Accounting Under Ideal Conditions

FIGURE 2.1 ORGANIZATION OF CHAPTER 2

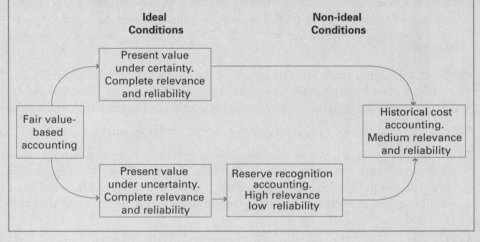

2.1 Overview

We will begin our study of financial accounting theory by considering the present value model. This model provides the utmost in **relevant information** to financial statement users. In this context we define relevant information as information about the firm's future economic prospects, that is, its dividends, cash flows, and profitability.

Our concern is with the conditions under which relevant financial statements will also be reliable, where we define **reliable information** as information that is precise and free from bias. We will also explore the conditions under which market values of assets and liabilities can serve as indirect measures of value. This will be the case under ideal conditions (to be defined later). If conditions are not ideal (which is usually the case), fundamental problems are created for asset valuation and income measurement. Figure 2.1 outlines the organization of this chapter.

2.2 The Present Value Model Under Certainty

The present value model is widely used in economics and finance and has had considerable impact on accounting over the years. We first consider a simple version of the model under conditions of certainty. By "certainty" we mean that the future cash flows of the firm and the interest rate in the economy are publicly known with certainty. We denote these as **ideal conditions**.

EXAMPLE 2.1

THEORETICAL ILLUSTRATION OF THE PRESENT VALUE MODEL UNDER CERTAINTY

Consider P.V. Ltd., a one-asset firm with no liabilities. Assume that the asset will generate end-of-year cash flows of $100 each year for two years and then will have zero value. Assume also that the risk-free interest rate in the economy is 10%. Then, at time 0 (the beginning of the first year of the asset's life), the present value of the firm's future cash flows, denoted by PA_0, is:

$$PA_0 = (\$100 \div 1.10) + (\$100 \div (1.10)^2)$$
$$= \$90.91 + \$82.64$$
$$= \$173.55$$

We can then prepare a present value opening balance sheet as follows:

P.V. Ltd.
Balance Sheet
As at Time 0

Capital asset, at present value $173.55	Shareholders' equity	$173.55

Now, move on to time 1, one year later. At that time, the present value of the remaining cash flows from the firm's asset is:

$$PA_1 = \$100 \div 1.10$$
$$= \$90.91$$

The firm's income statement for year 1 is:

P.V. Ltd.
Income Statement
For Year 1

Cash flow	$100.00
Amortization expense	82.64
Net income	$ 17.36

Amortization expense is calculated as $173.55 − $90.91 = $82.64—that is, the decline in the present value of the future receipts from the asset over the year. This way of calculating amortization differs from the way that accountants usually calculate it. Nevertheless, it is the appropriate approach under the ideal conditions of this example, namely, future cash flows known with certainty and a fixed risk-free interest rate.

Then, the end-of-year-1 balance sheet is:

P.V. Ltd. Balance Sheet As at End of Year 1				
Financial Asset			**Shareholders' Equity**	
Cash		$100.00	Opening value	$173.55
Capital Asset			Net income	17.36
Opening value	$173.55			
Accumulated amortization	82.64	90.91		
		$190.91		$190.91

This assumes that the firm pays no dividend. A dividend can be easily incorporated by reducing cash and shareholders' equity by the amount of the dividend.

Note the following points about Example 2.1:

1. The net book value of the capital asset at any year-end is equal to its fair value (see the definition of fair value in Section 1.2), where fair value is here determined as the present value of the future cash flows from that asset, discounted at 10%. Amortization expense is the change in present value over the year.

2. Net income for the year is equal to the year's cash flow of $100 less the $82.64 decline in the present value of the asset. Note that it is also equal to $PA_0 \times 10\% = \$173.55 \times 10\% = \$17.36$. This amount is called **accretion of discount**. It is the opening present value multiplied by the interest rate. The term arises because the stream of cash receipts is one year closer at the end of the year than it was at the beginning. The $17.36 is also referred to as *ex ante* or **expected net income** since, at time 0, the firm expects to earn $17.36. Of course, because all conditions are known with certainty, the expected net income will equal the *ex post* or **realized net income**.

3. **Relevant** financial statements are defined as those that give information to investors about the firm's future economic prospects. The information in Example 2.1 is entirely relevant. To see this, note first that, fundamentally, economic prospects are defined by the firm's stream of future dividends—it is dividends that provide a payoff to investors, the present value of which serves to establish firm value.

Then, it might seem that the firm's dividend policy will affect its value, since the timing of dividends will affect their present value. However, under ideal conditions, this would not be the case, and is called **dividend irrelevancy**.

To see why dividend policy does not matter under ideal conditions, note that as long as investors can invest any dividends they receive at the *same rate* of return as the firm earns on cash flows *not* paid in dividends, the present value of an investor's overall interest in the firm is independent of the timing of dividends. This holds in our example since there is only one interest rate in the economy. In effect, the firm's cash flows establish the size of the "pot" that is ultimately available to investors and it does not matter if this pot is distributed sooner or later. If it is distributed during the current year, investors can earn 10% on the distributions. If it is distributed in a subsequent year, the firm earns 10% on amounts not distributed, but this accrues to investors through an increase in the value of their investment. The present value to the investor is the same either way.

Under dividend irrelevancy, cash flows are just as relevant as dividends, because cash flows establish the firm's dividend-paying ability. As a result, the financial statements under Example 2.1 are entirely relevant.

4. As an accountant, you might be wondering why the firm's net income seems to play no role in firm valuation. This is quite true—it doesn't, under ideal conditions of certainty. The reason is that future cash flows are known and hence can be discounted to provide balance sheet valuations. Net income is then quite trivial, being simply accretion of discount as pointed out above. In effect, under ideal conditions, the balance sheet contains all the relevant information and the income statement contains none.[1] Even though net income is "true and correct," it conveys no information because investors can always figure it out by multiplying the opening balance sheet value by the interest rate. To put this another way, there is no information in the current net income that helps investors predict future economic prospects of the firm. These are already known to investors by assumption. This is an important point and we shall return to it later. For now, suffice it to say that when ideal conditions do not hold, the income statement assumes a much more significant role.

5. Define **reliable** financial statements as being precise and free from bias. The information in Example 2.1 is entirely reliable, since we have assumed that future cash flows and the interest rate are known with certainty. Note that there are *two components* of reliability. One is precision, the extent to which the financial statements are free of random error, or noise. Noise can arise from errors in the firm's accounting system, and from errors in estimates. Noise can also be present even in the absence of errors. This can occur if the quantity being estimated is subject to wide variation. For example, suppose that present value, or current market value, is used in the financial statements as a measure of the fair value of an asset. Even if they are not biased, these volatile measures of value may be proved wrong by subsequent events, such as changing market prices, if conditions are not ideal. Of course, under ideal conditions of certainty, this would not occur.

The second component of reliability is freedom from bias or manipulation. Lack of reliability harms investors in two related ways. First, information that is imprecise will need revision later. This can adversely affect investors' current decision calculations. Second, managers may bias or otherwise manipulate financial statement information, which can also adversely affect investor decisions. When information is perfectly reliable, neither of these problems can arise.

In sum, noise is absent under ideal conditions of certainty, since future cash flows and the interest rate are publicly known. As a result, present value and market value cannot be proven wrong by later events. Also, any errors, or attempts by management to bias the financial statements, would be immediately detected.

6. Under the ideal conditions of future cash flows known with certainty and the economy's risk-free interest rate given, the market value of the asset will be equal to its present value. To see this, consider the following argument: Given an interest rate of 10%, no one would be willing to pay more than $173.55 for the asset at time 0—if they did, they would be earning less than 10%. Also, the owners of the asset would not sell it for less than $173.55—if offered less than $173.55, they would be better off to retain it and earn 10%. If they needed the money they could borrow at 10% against the asset as security. Thus, the only possible equilibrium market price is $173.55. This argument is a simple example of the principle of **arbitrage**. If market prices for identical goods and services are such that it is possible to make a profit by simply buying in one market and selling in another, these are called arbitrage profits. However, it seems reasonable to expect that, if future cash flows and the risk-free rate are publicly known, the scramble of self-interested individuals to make these quick profits would eliminate any price discrepancies.[2]

7. Arbitrage means that there are two ways to determine asset fair value. We can calculate the discounted present value of future cash flows, as in Example 2.1. We will call this the **direct approach**. Alternatively, we can use market value. We will call this the **indirect approach**. Under ideal conditions, the two approaches yield identical results.

8. As P.V. Ltd. owns only one asset and has no liabilities, the firm's market value would also be $173.55 at time 0, being the sum of the financial assets[3] and the present value of future cash receipts from the capital asset. Thus, the total market value of P.V.'s shares outstanding would be $173.55. In more general terms, if a firm has more than one asset, the market value of the firm would be the sum of the value of its financial assets plus the value of the joint future receipts from its capital assets, including intangibles, less the present value of any liabilities. At points in time after time 0, the firm's market value continues to equal the sum of its financial assets plus capital assets, net of liabilities. Note, however, that dividend policy affects the amount of financial assets. To the extent that the firm does not pay out all of its profits in dividends, it will earn a return on reinvested assets. Question 2, at the end of this chapter, illustrates this point. See also the discussion of dividend irrelevancy above.

2.2.1 Summary

The purpose of Example 2.1 is to demonstrate that under the ideal conditions of future cash flows known with certainty and a fixed risk-free interest rate in the economy, it is possible to prepare relevant financial statements that are also reliable. The process of arbitrage ensures that the market value of an asset equals the present value of its future cash flows. The market value of the firm is then the value of its financial assets plus the value of its capital assets (less any liabilities).

Net income for the period equals cash flow plus or minus the change in the value of its financial and capital assets during the period or, equivalently, the firm's opening market value multiplied by the interest rate. However, even though net income can be perfectly calculated, it has no information content, because investors can easily calculate it for themselves. All of the "action" is on the balance sheet, which shows the value of the firm. Because of dividend irrelevancy, all of these conclusions are independent of the firm's dividend policy.

2.3 The Present Value Model Under Uncertainty

It is instructive to extend the present value model to the presence of uncertainty. With one major exception, most of the concepts carry over from Example 2.1. Again, we will proceed by means of an example.

EXAMPLE 2.2

THEORETICAL ILLUSTRATION OF THE PRESENT VALUE MODEL UNDER UNCERTAINTY

Let us continue Example 2.1 taking into account that the economy can be in a "bad" state or a "good" state during each year. If it is in the bad state, cash flows will be $100 for the year. If it is in the good state, however, cash flows will be $200 for the year. Assume that during each year the bad state and the good state each occur with probability 0.5. This assumption implies that the state realizations are independent over the two years of the example. That is, the state realization in year 1 does not affect the probabilities[4] of state realization in year 2.

Uncertain future events such as the state of the economy are called **states of nature**, or **states** for short. Thus the states in this example are, for each year:

> **State 1:** Economy is bad.
>
> **State 2:** Economy is good.

Note that no one can control which of the states is realized—this is why they are called states of *nature*. Other examples of states that affect cash flows are weather, government policies, strikes by suppliers, equipment breakdowns, etc. In any realistic situation there will be a large number of possible states. However, our two-state example is sufficient to convey the idea—states of nature are a conceptual device to model those uncertain, uncontrollable future events whose realization affect the cash flows of the firm.

While at time 0 no one knows which state will occur, we assume that the *set* of possible states is publicly known and complete. That is, every possible future event that can affect cash flows is known to everyone. Thus, while no one knows for sure which state will occur, it is known that whatever state does happen must be an element of the set. Furthermore, we assume that the state realization is publicly observable—everyone will know which state actually happens. Finally, we assume that the state probabilities are **objective**, and publicly known. By objective we mean that if we imagine a long-run sequence of repetitions of our economy, the bad state will occur with relative frequency 0.5 (or whatever other state probability we were to assume). Think by analogy with rolling a pair of fair dice. We know that the probability of a seven, say, is 1/6, and that if we were to roll the dice a large number of times a seven will appear with relative frequency 1/6. Note that an implication of objective probabilities here is that the outcome of any particular roll tells us nothing about the true state of the dice—we already know that the true state is that they are fair. Thus, the probability of a seven on the next roll remains at 1/6, and similarly for the probability of any other outcome.

These assumptions extend the concept of ideal conditions, also called "first-best" conditions, to take uncertainty into account. To summarize[5]

Ideal conditions under uncertainty are characterized by: (1) a given, fixed interest rate at which the firm's future cash flows are discounted, (2) a complete and publicly known set of states of nature, (3) state probabilities objective and publicly known, and (4) state realization publicly observable.

Another way to think about ideal conditions here is that they are similar to conditions of certainty except that future cash flows are known *conditionally* on the states of nature. That is, *if* state 1 happens, *then* cash flows will be $200, etc. We will assume that P.V. Ltd.'s future cash flows are discounted at 10%.

Given these ideal conditions, we can now calculate the **expected present value** of P.V.'s future cash flows at time 0:

$$PA_0 = 0.5 \left(\frac{\$100}{1.10} + \frac{\$200}{1.10} \right) + 0.5 \left(\frac{\$100}{1.10^2} + \frac{\$200}{1.10^2} \right)$$
$$= (0.5 \times \$272.73) + (0.5 \times \$247.93)$$
$$= \$136.36 + \$123.97$$
$$= \$260.33$$

We can then prepare P.V.'s opening balance sheet as:

P.V. Ltd. Balance Sheet As at Time 0			
Capital asset, at expected present value	$260.33	Shareholders' equity	$260.33

It is worthwhile to ask whether the time 0 market value of the asset, and hence of the firm, would be $260.33, as per the balance sheet. It is tempting to answer yes, since this is the firm's expected value given dividend irrelevance. But, uncertainty introduces an additional consideration not present in the certainty model of Section 2.2. This is that investors may be averse to risk. While the *expected* value of the firm is $260.33 at time 0, it is shown below that the expected value of the firm at the *end* of year 1 will be $236.36 or $336.36 depending on whether the bad state or the good state happens in that year. Ask yourself whether you would be indifferent between having $260.33 in your pocket or a 50/50 gamble of $236.36 or $336.36 The present value of the 50/50 gamble is:

$$
\begin{aligned}
PA_0 \quad &= 0.5 \times \frac{\$236.36}{1.10} + 0.5 \times \frac{\$336.36}{1.10} \\
&= (0.5 \times \$214.87) + (0.5 \times \$305.78) \\
&= \$107.44 + \$152.89 \\
&= \$260.33
\end{aligned}
$$

the same as the sure thing. But, most people would prefer the sure thing, because it is less risky. Then, the market value of the firm will be less than $260.33, since to the extent that investors are collectively risk-averse they will value the risky firm at less than its present value.

In this chapter, we will ignore this complication by assuming that investors are risk-neutral. That is, they are indifferent between the sure thing and the 50/50 gamble above. Then, the firm's market value will be $260.33 at time 0. This assumption of risk-neutral investors will be relaxed later, since accountants have a role to play in informing investors about the firm's riskiness as well as its expected value. The concept of a risk-averse investor is introduced in Section 3.4 and the impact of risk on firm valuation is shown in Section 4.5. For now, suffice it to say that the expected value of future cash flows or, more generally, future firm performance, is relevant for investors irrespective of their attitudes to risk.

Given risk-neutral valuation, the arbitrage principle will ensure that the market value of the firm's asset, and of the firm itself, is $260.33. The arbitrage principle would still hold if investors were averse to risk but the market value would be driven to an amount less than $260.33.

To return to the example, you should verify that *expected* net income for year 1— also called accretion of discount—is $0.10 \times \$260.33 = \$26.03$, analogous to the certainty case (see question 3).

Now, at the end of year 1 the expected present value of the remaining cash flows from the asset is:

$$
PA_1 = 0.5 \left(\frac{\$100}{1.10} + \frac{\$200}{1.10} \right) = \$136.36
$$

Assuming that the year 1 state realization is bad economy, P.V.'s year 1 *realized* income statement is:

P.V. Ltd. Income Statement (bad economy) For Year 1	
Cash flow	$100.00
Amortization expense ($260.33 − $136.36)	123.97
Net loss	$23.97

The year-end balance sheet is:

P.V. Ltd.
Balance Sheet
(bad economy)
As at End of Year 1

Financial Asset			**Shareholders' Equity**	
Cash		$100.00	Opening value	$260.33
Capital Asset			Net loss	23.97
Opening value	$260.33			
Accumulated amortization	123.97	136.36		
		$236.36		$236.36

Again, arbitrage ensures that the market value of the asset is $136.36 and of the firm is $236.36 at time 1. We continue the assumption that the firm pays no dividend. Ideal conditions ensure that it makes no difference whether the firm pays a dividend or not, as in the certainty case. In other words, dividend irrelevancy continues to hold. Question 4 pursues this point.

The major difference between the uncertainty and certainty cases is that *expected net income and realized net income need not be the same under uncertainty.* To analyze this further, consider the following alternative calculation of net income given state 1:

P.V. Ltd.
Alternative Income Statement
(bad economy)
For Year 1

Accretion of discount (0.10 × $260.33)		$26.03
Less: Abnormal earnings, as a result of bad-state realization:		
Expected cash flows (0.5 × $100 + 0.5 × $200)	$150	
Actual cash flows	100	50.00
Net loss		$23.97

Note that the negative $50 of unexpected cash flows results in a $50 "shock" to earnings for the year. The negative $50 earnings shock is called **abnormal earnings**, or, equivalently, **unexpected earnings**, since it reduces expected earnings of $26.03 to a loss of $23.97. Under this calculation, net income consists of *expected* net income less the abnormal earnings for year 1 resulting from the bad-state realization of $50.

It should be noted that in our example abnormal earnings do not **persist**. That is, their effect dissipates completely in the year in which they occur. In general, this need not be the case. For example, if the bad-state realization was due to, say, a tax increase that affected economic activity, the abnormal effect on earnings may persist for several periods. We ignore this possibility here to keep the example simple. However, we will return to the concept of persistence in Chapters 5 and 6.

Yet another way to calculate income, familiar from introductory accounting, is to calculate the change in balance sheet net assets for the year, adjusted for capital transactions. In this example, we have:

$$\text{Net income} = \$236.36 - \$260.33 - \$0 = -\$23.97$$

where capital transactions are zero. Thus, knowing the present values of all assets and liabilities enables one to calculate present value-based net income.

Now, let's consider the accounting if the state realization is a good economy. At the end of year 1, the present value of the remaining cash flows is still $136.36, and the year 1 income statement is:

P.V. Ltd.
Income Statement
(good economy)
For Year 1

Cash flow	$200.00
Amortization expense ($260.33 – $136.36)	123.97
Net income	$76.03

Under the alternative calculation of net income, we have:

P.V. Ltd.
Alternative Income Statement
(good economy)
For Year 1

Accretion of discount	$26.03
Add: Abnormal earnings, as a result of good-state realization ($200 – $150)	50.00
Net income	$76.03

The abnormal earnings of $50 is the difference between actual and expected cash flows for year 1, and these abnormal earnings increase expected earnings up to a profit of $76.03.

The year-end balance sheet is:

			P.V. Ltd. Balance Sheet (good economy) As at End of Year 1		
Financial Asset			**Shareholders' Equity**		
Cash		$200.00	Opening value		$260.33
Capital Asset			Net income		76.03
Opening value	$260.33				
Accumulated amortization	123.97	136.36			
		$336.36			$336.36

Again, arbitrage ensures that the firm's market value at time 1 will be $336.36, given risk-neutral investors.

Note the following points about Example 2.2:

1. It continues to be the case that financial statements are both completely relevant and completely reliable. They are relevant because balance sheet values are based on expected future cash flows, and dividend irrelevancy holds. They are reliable because ideal conditions ensure that present value calculations are precise and free of bias— a complete set of states of nature plus objective state probabilities, together with a given, fixed interest rate, enable a present value calculation that is incapable of error, or of being manipulated by management. All relevant future states are anticipated and, since state probabilities are objective and publicly known, the expected present value cannot be proven wrong by subsequent events. Of course, reliability here is in an *ex ante* sense. Expected time 1 value calculated at time 0 will generally not equal actual value at time 1, depending on which state is realized. Nevertheless, for investor decision-making purposes, beginning-of-period present value is what is needed, and this is completely reliable in our example.

2. Like the certainty case, there are still two ways of calculating balance sheet fair values: we can calculate expected present values directly or we can use market values. Under ideal conditions, arbitrage forces the two ways to yield identical results.

3. Despite the fact that expected and realized net income need not be equal, the income statement still has no information content when abnormal earnings do not persist. Investors have sufficient information to calculate for themselves what realized net income will be, once they know the current year's state realization. This calculation is programmable and no accounting policy decisions are needed.

4. At the risk of getting ahead of ourselves, let us see how the income statement *can* be informative. For this, we need only relax the assumption that state probabilities are objective. This puts us into the realm of **subjective probabilities**, which are for-

mally introduced in Chapter 3. Then, investors no longer have "ready-made" state probabilities available to them for purposes of calculating expected future firm performance. Rather, they must assess these probabilities themselves, using whatever information is available. There is no longer any guarantee that in a long-run sequence of repetitions of the economy, the bad and good states will occur with the same relative frequencies as the probabilities assigned by the investor. The reason, of course, is that individuals are limited in their knowledge and forecasting ability. Note that if state probabilities are subjective, so are the resulting expected values. That is, the value of the firm is also subjective.

Subjective probabilities are a more reasonable assumption than objective probabilities, because the future performance of a business entity is much more complex and difficult to predict than a simple roll of fair dice. Since investors know that their predictions are subject to error, they will be alert for information sources that enable them to revise their probability assessments. The income statement is one such source. When state probabilities are subjective, the income statement can provide information about what these probabilities are. For example, observing a net income of $76.03 this year in Example 2.2 may cause you to increase your probability of the good state in future years. This would improve your ability to predict firm cash flows and profitability.

If this argument is unclear to you, return to the analogy of rolling dice, but now assume that you do not know whether the dice are fair. What is your probability of rolling a seven? Obviously, this probability is no longer objective, and you must assess it on the basis of whatever information and prior experience you have. However, rolling the dice (analogous to observing the income statement) provides information, and after a few rolls you should have a better idea whether their true state is fair or not fair. For example, if you rolled five times and a seven came up each time, you would probably want to increase from 1/6 your subjective probability of rolling a seven. Just as improved knowledge of the true state of the dice will help you to predict future rolls, improved knowledge of the true state of the firm will help you to predict future firm performance and investment returns. In Chapter 3 we will show how investors can use financial statement information to revise their subjective probabilities of future firm performance.

2.3.1 Summary

The purpose of Example 2.2 is to extend the present value model to formally incorporate uncertainty, using the concepts of states of nature and objective probabilities. The definition of ideal conditions must be extended to include a complete and publicly known set of states of nature, with future cash flows known *conditionally* on state realization. Also, ideal conditions now specify objective state probabilities and that the state realization be publicly observable. The logic of the present value model under certainty then carries over, except that market values are based on *expected* cash flows, assuming investors are risk-neutral.

The major difference between the certainty and uncertainty cases is that *expected* and *realized* net income need no longer be the same under uncertainty, and the difference is called abnormal earnings. Nevertheless, financial statements based on expected present values continue to be both relevant and reliable. They are relevant because they are based on expected future cash flows. They are reliable because financial statement values objectively reflect these expected future cash flows and, as in the certainty case, management manipulation is not possible. All of these conclusions are independent of the firm's dividend policy, since dividend irrelevancy continues to hold.

2.4   Reserve Recognition Accounting (RRA)

2.4.1   An Example of RRA

By now, you probably want to point out that the real world is *not* characterized by ideal conditions. This is quite true. Nevertheless, accounting practice is moving strongly towards increased use of fair values for major classes of assets and liabilities. For example, defined post-employment benefits to retirees, such as pensions, healthcare, and disability are accounted for on the basis of expected future benefit payments under Section 3461 of the *CICA Handbook* and the FASB's Statement of Financial Accounting Standards (SFAS) 87 and 106 in the United States. Also, SFAS 133 requires that all derivative financial instruments be measured at fair value, and similar requirements are proposed in Canada. These and other examples of the measurement perspective are reviewed in Chapter 7.

Despite the moves towards fair value, the present value model encounters serious reliability problems when we try to apply it without ideal conditions. To illustrate these problems, we now consider reserve recognition accounting for oil and gas companies.

In 1982, the FASB issued SFAS 69, which requires supplemental disclosure of certain information about the operations of publicly traded oil and gas companies. An interesting aspect of SFAS 69 is that disclosure of the estimated present value of future receipts from a company's proved oil and gas reserves is required. The estimate is known as the "standardized measure." The intent, presumably, is to provide investors with more relevant information about future cash flows than that contained in the conventional, historical cost-based financial statements. Oil and gas companies, it can be argued, particularly need to give this type of supplementary disclosure because the historical cost of oil and gas properties may bear little relationship to their value.

It can hardly be said that oil and gas companies operate under conditions of certainty. Consequently, we shall consider SFAS 69 in relation to our present value model under uncertainty, which was illustrated in Example 2.2. Present value accounting applied to oil and gas reserves is known as **reserve recognition accounting (RRA)**.

Consider first Table 2.1, adapted from the 2000 *Annual Report* of Chieftain International, Inc., a Canadian corporation with shares traded on the Toronto Stock Exchange and on the American Stock Exchange in the United States. Note that the undiscounted future net cash flows are shown, and also the present value of these cash flows, discounted at 10%. When estimating future cash flows, SFAS 69 requires that the present value calculations use year-end oil and gas prices (as opposed to prices expected to be in effect when the reserves are lifted and sold). No information is given about the riskiness of the estimates. That is, no states of nature and probabilities are given, only the end results of the expectation calculation.

TABLE 2.1 CHIEFTAIN INTERNATIONAL, INC. PRESENT VALUE OF ESTIMATED FUTURE NET CASH FLOWS (millions of dollars)

December 31	2000	1999	1998
Future cash inflows	$2,096	$677	$402
Future production and development costs	(329)	(274)	(186)
Future income taxes	(544)	(63)	–
Future net cash flows	1,223	340	216
10% discount factor	(374)	(115)	(63)
Standardized measure	$ 849	$225	$153

SOURCE: 2000 *Annual Report* of Chieftain International, Inc. Reprinted by permission.

This disclosure seems to conform fairly well to our theoretical Example 2.2. The $849 is the amount that would appear on Chieftain's December 31, 2000 present value-based balance sheet for the asset "proved oil and gas reserves" if one was prepared. It corresponds to the $136.36 valuation of the capital asset at time 1 in Example 2.2. It should be noted, however, that the 10% discount rate used by Chieftain is not the single known rate in the economy. Rather, this rate is mandated by SFAS 69, presumably for comparability across firms. Also, as mentioned, the figures apply only to proved reserves and not all of Chieftain's assets.

Table 2.2 gives changes in the standardized measure.

TABLE 2.2 CHIEFTAIN INTERNATIONAL, INC. CHANGES IN THE STANDARDIZED MEASURE OF DISCOUNTED FUTURE NET CASH FLOWS (millions of dollars)

	2000	1999	1998
Standardized measure, beginning of year	$225	$153	$200
Changes result from:			
Sales, net of production costs	(103)	(61)	(45)
Net change in prices and production costs	710	83	(80)
Extensions and discoveries, net of costs	224	83	30
Change in estimated future development costs	(39)	(23)	(16)
Development costs incurred during the year	28	10	23
Revisions to quantity estimates	88	(8)	(17)
Accretion of discount	22	15	20
Purchase of reserves in place	11	–	3
Changes in timing and other	14	15	(4)
Net change in income taxes	(331)	(42)	39
Standardized measure, end of year	$849	$225	$153

SOURCE: 2000 *Annual Report* of Chieftain International, Inc. Reprinted by permission.

To understand this statement, we rework Example 2.2 in Table 2.3 to show the changes in the book value of the capital asset during the year, assuming state 2 (good economy) is realized (a similar analysis applies to state 1).

TABLE 2.3 EXAMPLE 2.2: CHANGE IN BOOK VALUE OF CAPITAL ASSET DURING THE YEAR (state 2 realized)

Present value of capital asset, beginning of year (time 0)		$260.33
Less: Sales in year 1 (cash flow from operations)		200.00
		60.33
Add:		
Accretion of discount	$26.03	
Unexpected cash flows	50.00	76.03
BV of capital asset, end of year (time 1)		$136.36

Now, we rework Chieftain's Changes in the Standardized Measure in Table 2.2 into a format consistent with Table 2.3, as shown in Table 2.4.

TABLE 2.4 CHIEFTAIN INTERNATIONAL, INC. REWORKED STANDARDIZED MEASURE FOR THE YEAR ENDED DECEMBER 31, 2000 (millions of dollars)

Present value of standardized measure at beginning of year			$225
Less: Sales (i.e., cash flow from operations) in year			103
			122
Add:			
Accretion of discount		$ 22	
Present value of additional reserves added during year (224 + 11)		235	
Development costs incurred during year		28	
Unexpected items—changes in value of previous-year reserves:			
Net change in prices and production costs	$710		
Revisions to quantity estimates	88		
Change in future development costs	(39)		
Changes in timing and other	14		
Net change in income taxes	(331)	442	727
Present value of standardized measure at end of year			$849

Check each of these numbers from the original Chieftain International statement in Tables 2.1 and 2.2. The $28 of development costs incurred during the year represents the increase in present value resulting from the expenditure of some of the development costs allowed for in the beginning-of-year present value.

The changes in estimates of $442 should be considered carefully. Note, in particular, that there are a number of changes, including revisions of quantities, prices, and costs as well as related income taxes. Note also that the amounts are quite material. For example, the net change in prices and production costs of $710 is 3.16 times the present value at the beginning of 2000. The number and magnitude of these changes are the main differences between our Example 2.2, which assumed ideal conditions, and the "real world" environment in which Chieftain operates. We shall return to this point shortly.

Note that the accretion of discount is 10% of beginning-of-year present value, as it was in Example 2.2.

Finally, what would Chieftain's 2000 present value-based net income from proved oil and gas reserves be? This can be quite simply calculated as in Table 2.5.

TABLE 2.5 CHIEFTAIN INTERNATIONAL, INC. INCOME STATEMENT FOR 2000 FROM PROVED OIL AND GAS RESERVES (millions of dollars)

Cash flow from operations	$103
Development costs incurred in year	(28)
Amortization "expense" (increase in present value of reserves during the year (849 – 225)	624
Net income from proved oil and gas reserves	$699

Or, in the alternative format:

Expected net income—accretion of discount		$22
Abnormal Earnings:		
Present value of additional reserves added during year	235	
Unexpected items—changes in value of previous-year reserves	442	677
Net income from proved oil and gas reserves		$699

Again, the material impact on net income of changes in estimates is apparent. These amount to almost 31 times expected net income. Note also that amortization expense is negative for the year. This can happen under present value accounting, and simply means that present value increased over the year.

2.4.2 Summary

The procedures used by Chieftain International to account for the results of its oil and gas operations under RRA seem to conform to the theoretical present value model under uncertainty, except that it is necessary to make material changes to previous estimates.

2.4.3 Critique of RRA

Management's Reaction This necessity to make changes in estimates seems to be the Achilles' heel of RRA. Oil company managers, in particular, tend to regard RRA with reservation and suspicion. As an example, the following statement appears in Chieftain's 2000 RRA disclosure:

> *The inexactness associated with estimating reserve quantities, future production streams, and future development and production expenditures, together with the assumptions applied in valuing future production, substantially diminish the reliability of this data. The values so derived are not considered to be estimates of fair market value. We therefore caution against simplistic use of this information.*

One might ask why Chieftain reports RRA information at all, since SFAS 69 is a U.S. accounting standard. However, since its shares are traded on the American Stock Exchange, it must meet U.S. reporting requirements. Also, it may want to report information with which U.S. investors are familiar. Since the RRA information has been prepared, it can also be reported to Canadian shareholders at little additional cost.

Usefulness to Investors   While it is clear that management is cautious about RRA, this does not necessarily mean that it does not provide useful information to investors. Certainly, RRA is more relevant than historical cost information, so it has the potential to be useful. To see the potential for relevance, compare the present value-based 2000 net income from Table 2.5 with Chieftain's historical cost-based earnings from oil and gas[6] summarized in Table 2.6.

TABLE 2.6   CHIEFTAIN INTERNATIONAL, INC.
EARNINGS FROM OIL AND GAS PRODUCING ACTIVITIES FOR THE YEAR ENDED DECEMBER 31, 2000 (millions of dollars)

RESULTS OF OPERATIONS			
December 31	**2000**	**1999**	**1998**
Total sales to customers	$117	$75	$62
Production expenses	(17)	(19)	(18)
Depletion and depreciation	(44)	(68)	(48)
Income taxes	(20)	6	2
Results of operations	$ 36	$ (6)	$ (2)

SOURCE: 2000 *Annual Report* of Chieftain International, Inc. Reprinted by permission.

Comparison of net income under the two bases is complicated by the fact that the present value calculations relate only to proved reserves. However, let us take the $36 total results of operations for 2000 in Table 2.6 as the historical cost analogue of the $699 present value-based income in Table 2.5. This seems reasonable since, if oil and gas has been sold, the reserves it came from are obviously proved.

We see that the present value-based earnings are *much* higher than their historical cost-based counterpart. What accounts for the difference? The difference can be explained by different bases of **revenue recognition**. Under RRA, revenue is recognized as reserves are proved, and changes in the current market value of proved reserves are included in income as they occur. Note, from Table 2.2, that the present value of proved reserves increased by $624 during 2000. The reason for the increase is primarily the major rise in oil and gas prices during the year (also increase in quantities). This rise in prices increased the present value of proved reserves by $710 (less income taxes of $331), which explains most of the excess of RRA net income over historical cost. Under historical cost accounting, as you know, this increase in the value of the proved reserves would not show up in the income statement until the proved reserves were produced and sold. In effect, the present value-based income statement recognizes the increase sooner. Thus, present value information has the potential for usefulness because of this greater relevance.

Revenue recognition and asset valuation are two sides of the same coin. We can discuss the timing of revenue recognition (the credit side of the coin), as in the previous paragraph. Or, we can discuss whether reserves should be valued at present value, as in RRA, or whether they should be valued at cost, as in historical cost accounting (the debit side of the coin). The same tradeoff between relevance and reliability applies. From the revenue side, recognizing revenue sooner increases relevance, since the investor receives an earlier reading on future cash flows. However early recognition decreases reliability, since there is a greater chance that revenue estimates will have to be revised. From the asset side, valuing reserves at present value increases relevance, but decreases reliability as evidenced by the major revisions to reserve estimates emphasized in Section 2.4.1. Similarly, Examples 2.1 and 2.2 concentrated on the valuation of assets at present value. However, we could have equivalently emphasized that under ideal conditions revenue is recognized when capital assets are acquired, since future cash flows (i.e., revenues) are inputs into the present value calculations.

Regardless of whether investors focus on revenue recognition or asset valuation, we should observe some reaction in the price of Chieftain's shares to the release of RRA information if RRA is in fact useful. Empirical evidence on the usefulness of RRA is reviewed in Chapter 5. For now, suffice it to say that it has been difficult to find evidence of usefulness.

Discussion Management's concerns, as quoted above, suggest that something is amiss. Why would management be concerned about information that has considerable relevance for investors? The main point to realize is that Chieftain does not operate under the ideal conditions of Examples 2.1 and 2.2. Consider the difficulties that Chieftain's accountants face in applying ideal conditions. First, interest rates in the economy are not fixed, although SFAS 69 deals with this by requiring a fixed, given rate of 10% for the discounting. Second, the set of states of nature affecting the amounts, prices, and timing of future production is much larger than the simple two-state set in Example 2.2, due to the complex environment in which oil and gas companies operate. SFAS 69 reduces some of this complexity by requiring that reserves be valued using year-end prices. However, reserve quantity states, and the timing of their extraction, are still needed. Third, it is unlikely that the state realization would be publicly observable. Events like equipment breakdowns, production problems, and minor oil spills would most likely be inside information of the firm. As a result, outsiders have no way of knowing whether the changes in estimates are precise and unbiased, particularly since RRA is unaudited.[7]

A fourth problem is more fundamental. Objective state probabilities are not available. Consequently, subjective state probabilities need to be assessed by Chieftain's engineers and accountants, with the result that the standardized measure is itself a subjective estimate.

Theory in Practice 2.1

The subjectivity of reserve quantity estimates is illustrated by the case of Royal Dutch/Shell. Long a respected company, Shell's reputation suffered a severe blow when, in January 2004, it reduced its "proved" reserves by 20%, reclassifying them as "probable." This was followed by several smaller reductions. Apparently, the company had been overstating its proved reserves as far back as 1997 to disguise falling behind its competitors in replacing its reserves. Such overstatements were enabled by relatively vague SEC rules (which Shell purported to follow) that require "reasonable certainty" of recovery under existing economic and operating conditions to classify reserves as proved. Also, the reserve quantities were unaudited.

This scandal, which resulted in the dismissals of its chairman and head of exploration and development, and a preliminary fine by the SEC of $150 million U.S., led to a major drop in Shell's share price as investors revised downwards their probabilities of Shell's future performance. The relevance of Shell's reserve information was overwhelmed by low reliability introduced by manager bias.

Because of these difficulties in applying ideal conditions, the reliability of RRA information is severely compromised. This shows up in the number and materiality of quantity and price revisions to estimates, as shown in Table 2.4. It is not that estimates of expected future cash flows cannot be made. After all, RRA is on line. Rather, lacking objective probabilities, these estimates become subject to revisions that threaten reliability to the point where the benefit of increased relevance is compromised. The important point is that, without ideal conditions, complete relevance and reliability are no longer jointly attainable. One must be traded off against the other.

2.4.4 Summary

RRA represents a valiant attempt to convey relevant information to investors. On the surface, the present value information conforms quite closely to the theoretical present value model under uncertainty. If one digs deeper, however, serious problems of estimation are revealed. This is because oil and gas companies do not operate under the ideal conditions assumed by the theoretical model. As a result, reserve information loses reliability, as evidenced by the need for substantial annual revisions, as it gains relevance. It seems necessary to trade off these two desirable information qualities.

2.5 Historical Cost Accounting Revisited

As our discussion of RRA in Section 2.4 points out, as a practical matter it seems impossible to prepare financial statements that are both completely relevant and completely reliable. Consequently, relevance and reliability must be traded off. The historical cost basis of accounting can be thought of as one such tradeoff. Recall that under historical cost accounting the primary basis of valuation for several major asset categories, such as inventories, long-term portfolio investments, and capital assets including intangibles, is *cost*, or cost less amounts written off as amortization. On the liability side, long-term debt is also valued at cost, in the sense that the carrying value of such debt is based on interest rates in effect when the debt was issued—carrying value is not adjusted for subsequent interest rate changes.

Historical cost accounting is relatively reliable because the cost of an asset or liability to a firm is usually an objective number that is less subject to errors of estimation and bias than are present value calculations. Unfortunately, however, historical costs may lack relevance. While historical cost, market value, and present value may be similar as at the date of acquisition, market values and present values will change over time as market conditions change. Nevertheless, accountants continue to use the historical cost basis of accounting for major asset types because they are willing to trade off a considerable amount of relevance to obtain reasonable reliability. Consequently, historical cost accounting represents a particular tradeoff between the two.

2.5.1 The Challenge of Historical Cost Accounting

The essential difference between present value-based accounting such as RRA and historical cost-based accounting (or any other basis of accounting, for that matter) is one of *timing* of recognition of changes in asset value. Present value accounting is a balance sheet approach to accounting, also called a **measurement perspective**. That is, increases (or decreases) in asset and liability values are recognized (measured) as they occur, by discounting future cash flows (the essence of value) and capitalizing them on the balance sheet. Income is then essentially the net change in present values for the period.

Historical cost accounting, however, is an income statement approach, also called an **information perspective**. Under this perspective, unrealized increases in value are not recognized on the balance sheet, and net income lags behind real economic performance, a characteristic that we shall call **recognition lag**. That is, the accountant waits until increases in value are validated through realization as increased sales or cash flows. Income is then a process of matching of revenues with the costs of earning those revenues. The income statement assumes a more important role, since it provides information on the current "installment" of the value created by the firm.[8]

When conditions are not ideal, the question then is, does historical cost-based accounting provide better information about the firm's *future* economic prospects (the primary interest of investors) than present value-based accounting? Accountants have debated this question for many years, and we return to it in Chapter 6. For now, suffice it to say that arguments can be made in favour of the income statement approach. One argument is the relative reliability of historical cost, as mentioned above. More fundamentally, historical cost accounting is a way to "smooth out" current period cash flows into a measure of the longer-run or persistent earning power that is implied by those cash flows. Persistent earning power then provides the basis for an assessment of future economic prospects.

To smooth out current period cash flows, the accountant has to calculate **accruals**, that is, to match costs and revenues. However, at this point, historical cost accounting faces a major challenge. There is usually no unique way to match costs with revenues. This complicates the ability of historical cost-based earnings to reveal persistent earning power. To illustrate, we now consider three examples.

Amortization of Capital Assets A major problem with matching is the amortization of capital assets. The matching principle deems it necessary to deduct amortization of capital assets from revenue for the period to arrive at net income. Yet, it does not state *how much* amortization should be accrued except for a vague indication that it should be systematic and rational. For example, paragraph 3061.28 of the *CICA Handbook* states that amortization should be recognized in a rational and systematic manner appropriate to the nature of a capital asset with a limited life and its use by the firm.

As a result of this vagueness, a variety of amortization methods are acceptable for use in practice, such as straight-line, declining-balance, and so on.

If it were possible to value capital assets on a present value basis for the financial statements, we would need only *one* amortization method—the change in the present value of the future receipts from the assets during the period, as illustrated in Examples 2.1 and 2.2. As it is not usually possible to reliably value capital assets this way, the door is opened to a variety of amortization methods. This complicates the comparison of profitability across firms, because we must ascertain the amortization methods firms are using before making comparisons. It also means that firm managers have some room to manage their reported profitability through choice of amortization method or through changes to the method used. Thus, while one can argue, as we have above, that historical cost financial statements may be more reliable than those prepared on a present value or market value basis, this reliability may be eroded to the extent that managers can choose between alternative historical cost-based accounting policies to manage reported net income for their own purposes. In other words, while historical cost accounting may be more reliable than value-based methods, it is by no means completely reliable.

Future Income Tax Liability A major accounting controversy in Canada arose in 1953 when the Income Tax Act was amended to allow firms to choose the method of amortization they wanted for their reported financial statements, while claiming maximum capital cost allowance on their tax returns. Prior to this, firms could not claim more capital cost allowance than the amortization they recorded in their financial statements. Most firms responded to the 1953 amendment by using straight-line amortization for financial reporting while claiming maximum capital cost allowance for tax purposes. Since capital cost allowance is a form of declining-balance amortization, this created an income tax accounting problem. Taxes saved by claiming maximum capital cost allowance in the early years of an asset's life did not necessarily represent a permanent saving but instead created a liability to repay the taxes in later years, when maximum capital cost allowance was less than straight-line amortization for capital assets.

The controversy was whether to record the tax liability (and resulting higher income tax expense) on the firm's financial statements. Some argued that these should be recorded, because the matching principle of historical cost accounting required that income tax expense should be matched with the amount of amortization actually recorded on the financial statements. Others, however, felt that the recording of a liability was not required by the matching principle. In most cases (for example, if a firm was growing, in which case capital cost allowance would tend to remain greater than straight-line amortization), the possibility that the taxes saved would have to be repaid in some future year was remote. It does not make sense, they argued, to match costs that are unlikely to be paid with revenue. The controversy continued until 1963, when the *CICA Handbook* required recording of the liability.

Currently, paragraph 3465.10 of the *CICA Handbook* states that the firm shall recognize a future income tax liability whenever recovery or settlement of the carrying amount of an asset or liability would result in future income tax payments.

Note that the essential source of the future tax liability question is the multiplicity of acceptable amortization methods under historical cost accounting. The problem arises because the method firms use on their financial statements usually differs from the method allowed for tax purposes. If there was only one amortization method, as under present value accounting with ideal conditions, firms' book and tax figures would be the same and the tax liability problem for amortization would not arise.

Full-Cost Versus Successful-Efforts in Oil and Gas Accounting Under historical cost accounting, we need to know the *cost* of assets, so that they can be amortized (matched) against revenues over their useful lives. We suggested earlier in this section that the cost of assets is usually reliably determinable. However, in some cases, even the cost of assets is not clear. Oil and gas accounting provides an interesting and important example.

There are two basic methods of determining the cost of oil and gas reserves. The **full-cost method** capitalizes all costs of discovering reserves (subject to certain exceptions), including the costs of unsuccessful drilling. The argument is that the cost of successful wells includes the costs of dry holes drilled in the search for the successful ones. The **successful-efforts method** capitalizes only the costs of successful wells and expenses dry holes, the rationale being that it is difficult to regard a dry hole in the ground as an asset.

Clearly, these two approaches can produce materially different recorded costs for oil and gas reserves, with the result that amortization expense can also be materially different. In turn, this complicates the comparison of the reported net incomes of oil and gas firms, because different firms may use different methods for determining the cost of their reserves. For our purposes, however, simply note that the historical cost basis of accounting cannot settle the question of which method is preferable. The historical cost basis requires only that a cost of oil and gas reserves be established. It does not require a particular method for establishing what the cost should be. In fact, both methods are allowed in Canada and the United States.

Notice that use of RRA in the firm's accounts would eliminate the full-cost versus successful-efforts controversy. RRA values oil and gas reserves at their present values. It is *not* a cost-based approach, so the question of how to determine cost does not arise. Under RRA, amortization expense is the change in the present value of oil and gas reserves during the period.

2.5.2 Accountants' Reaction to the Challenge

Since it seems impossible to prepare a complete set of present value-based financial statements with sufficient reliability, the historical cost accounting framework will likely be with us for a long time to come. Consequently, the major accounting bodies have reacted to the challenge of historical cost-based accounting by retaining its framework, but turning their attention to making financial statements more *useful*, within that framework. This is not to say that certain assets and liabilities cannot be reported on a present value or market value basis. Indeed, use of fair values in the financial statements is increasing, as will be discussed in Chapters 6 and 7. Nevertheless, since major asset and liability categories, such as capital assets, intangibles, and long-term debt, continue to be accounted for primarily on the historical cost basis, we can still say that this is the basic framework of accounting.

To increase the usefulness of historical cost accounting, accountants have adopted a strategy of *full disclosure*. Disclosure of accounting policies used enables investors to at least be aware of the particular policies the firm has chosen out of the multiplicity of policies that are available for most assets and liabilities. Also, **supplementary information** is given to help investors project current performance into the future. The RRA disclosure discussed in Section 2.4 is an example of such supplementary information.

2.5.3 Summary

The continued use of historical cost accounting in financial reporting can be thought of as a consequence of the impossibility of preparing reliable financial statements on a present value basis. The use of historical cost accounting represents a particular tradeoff between relevance and reliability. Complete relevance is not attained, because historical cost-based asset values need bear little resemblance to discounted present values of future cash flows. However, complete reliability is not attained either, since the possibility of imprecision and bias remains. The measurement of net income becomes a process of matching, rather than a simple calculation of accretion of discount, and the matching principle usually allows different ways of accounting for the same item. Frequently, accounting standard-setting bodies step in to impose uniform accounting policies to reduce the multiplicity of policy choices.

Given the continuing use of historical cost-based accounting in practice, accountants have tried to make the historical cost framework more useful. One way of increasing usefulness is to retain the historical cost framework but expand disclosure in the annual report, so as to help investors to make their own estimates of future economic prospects.

2.6 The Non-Existence of True Net Income

To prepare a complete set of financial statements on a present value basis, recall that it is necessary to value *all* of the firm's assets and liabilities this way, with net income being the change in the firm's present value during the period (adjusted for capital transactions such as dividends). Yet, we saw with RRA that severe problems arise when we try to apply the present value approach to even a single type of asset. These problems would be compounded if the approach was extended to all other assets and liabilities.

This leads to an important and interesting conclusion, namely that under the real-world conditions in which accounting operates, *net income does not exist as a well-defined economic construct*. As evidence, simply consider Chieftain International's 2000 RRA net income of $699 in Table 2.5. How can we take this as well-defined, or "true," income when we know that next year there will be another flock of unanticipated changes to the estimates that underlie the 2000 income calculation?

A fundamental problem is the lack of objective state probabilities. With objective probabilities, present values of assets and liabilities correctly reflect the uncertainty facing the firm, since present values then take into account all possible future events and their probabilities. In this case, accounting information is completely relevant as well as completely reliable and true economic income exists.

An indirect approach to true economic income of basing the income calculation on changes in market values rather than present values runs into the problem that market values need not exist for all firm assets and liabilities, a condition known as **incomplete markets**. For example, while there may be a market price for a barrel of crude oil, what is the market value of Chieftain's reserves? In the face of uncertainties over quantities, prices, and lifting costs, an attempt to establish their market value runs into the same estimation problems as RRA. As a result, a ready market value is not available. If market values are not available for all firm assets and liabilities, an income measure based on market values is not possible. Beaver and Demski (1979) give formal arguments to show that income is not well defined when markets are incomplete.[9]

Lacking objective probabilities, the door is opened for subjective estimates of future firm performance. These estimates can be subject to both lack of precision and possible bias. As a result, accounting estimates based on present value lose reliability as they strive to maintain relevance.

Thus, a second conclusion is that accountants feel that historical cost-based accounting for major classes of operating assets and liabilities represents a more useful way to account, since we observe historical cost accounting for these classes strongly rooted in practice. Some relevance is lost, but hopefully this is more than made up for by increased reliability.

You may be bothered by the claim that true net income does not exist. Should we devote our careers to measuring something that doesn't exist? However, we should be glad of the impossibility of ideal conditions. If they existed, no one would need accountants! As discussed in Examples 2.1 and 2.2, net income has no information content when conditions are ideal. The present value calculations and related income measurement could then be programmed in advance. All that is needed is the set of states, their probabilities, and knowledge of which state is realized, and accountants would not be needed for this. Thus, we can say of income measurement, "If we can solve it, we don't need it."

This lack of a theoretically correct concept of income is what makes accounting both frustrating and fascinating at the same time. It is frustrating because of the difficulty of agreeing on accounting policies. Different users will typically want different tradeoffs between relevance and reliability. As a result, there are often several ways of accounting for the same thing. It is fascinating because the lack of a well-defined concept of net income means that a great deal of *judgement* must go into the process of asset valuation and income measurement. It is judgement that makes accounting valuable and, indeed, provides the very basis of a profession.

2.7 Conclusion to Accounting Under Ideal Conditions

Instead of dwelling on questions of existence of net income, accountants turned their efforts to making historical cost-based financial statements more useful. We will now proceed to study decision usefulness.

Questions and Problems

1. Prepare the income statement for year 2 and the balance sheet at the end of year 2 for P.V. Ltd. in Example 2.1 under the assumption that P.V. Ltd. pays no dividends. (CGA-Canada)

2. Show that an owner of P.V. Ltd. in Example 2.1 would not care whether P.V. Ltd. paid any dividend at the end of year 1. State precisely why this is the case. (CGA-Canada)

3. Calculate the expected net income for P.V. Ltd. for years 1 and 2 in Example 2.2. Explain why expected net income is also called "accretion of discount." (CGA-Canada)

4. Show that an owner of P.V. Ltd. in Example 2.2 would not care whether P.V. Ltd. paid any dividend at the end of year 1. Assume that the good-economy state was realized in year 1. (CGA-Canada)

5. In Example 2.2, assume that P.V. Ltd. pays no dividends over its life, until a liquidating dividend is paid at the end of year 2 consisting of its cash on hand at that time.

   Required

   Verify that the market value of P.V. Ltd. at time 0 based on the present value of dividends equals $260.33, equal to P.V.'s market value based on expected future cash flows.

6. A simple example of the difference between ideal and non-ideal conditions is the rolling of a die.

   Required
   a. Calculate the expected value of a single roll of a fair die.
   b. Now suppose that you are unsure whether the die is fair. How would you then calculate the expected value of a single roll?
   c. Now roll the die four times. You obtain 6, 4, 1, 3. Does this information affect your belief that the die is fair? Explain.

7. Explain why, under ideal conditions, there is no need to make estimates when calculating expected present value.

8. Explain why estimates are required to calculate expected present value when conditions are *not* ideal. (CGA-Canada)

9. Do you think that the market value of an oil and gas firm will be affected when RRA information is presented in addition to historical cost-based earnings from oil and gas producing activities? Explain why or why not.

10. Explain why, under non-ideal conditions, it is necessary to trade off relevance and reliability. Define these two terms as part of your answer. (CGA-Canada)

11. Why do you think Chieftain International's management expresses severe reservations about RRA?

12. The text discussion of RRA is in terms of the relevance and reliability of the asset valuation of oil and gas reserves. RRA can also be evaluated in terms of the criteria for revenue recognition. The *CICA Handbook*, Section 3400, states that revenue involving the sale of goods should be recognized when the seller has transferred to the buyer the significant risks and rewards of ownership, and reasonable assurance exists regarding the measurement of the consideration that will be received.

Required

   a. At what point in their operating cycle do most industrial and retail firms regard revenue as having been earned (i.e., realized)? Use the two *CICA Handbook* criteria above to explain why.

   b. Suppose that X Ltd. is an oil and gas producer. X Ltd. uses RRA on its books and prepares its financial statements on this basis. When (i.e., at what point in the operating cycle) is revenue recognized under RRA? Does this point meet the criteria for revenue recognition under GAAP as given in the *CICA Handbook* above? Explain why or why not.

13. Inventory is another asset for which there is a variety of ways to account under historical cost accounting, including first-in, first-out; last-in, first-out; average cost; etc.

   a. How would inventory be accounted for under ideal conditions? In your answer, consider both balance sheet and revenue recognition perspectives.

   b. Give reasons why inventory is usually accounted for on a historical cost basis. Is accounting on this basis completely reliable? Why?

14. Sure Corp. operates under ideal conditions of certainty. It acquired its sole asset on January 1, 2005. The asset will yield $500 cash at the end of each year from 2005 to 2007, inclusive, after which it will have no market value and no disposal costs. The interest rate in the economy is 6%. Purchase of the asset was financed by the issuance of common shares. Sure Corp. will pay a dividend of $50 at the end of 2005 and 2006.

Required

   a. Prepare a balance sheet for Sure Corp. as at the end of 2005 and an income statement for the year ended December 31, 2005.

   b. Prepare a balance sheet for Sure Corp. as at the end of 2006 and an income statement for the year ended December 31, 2006.

   c. Under ideal conditions, what is the relationship between present value and market value? Why? Under the real conditions in which accountants operate, to what extent do market values provide a way to implement fair value accounting? Explain.

   d. Under real conditions, present value calculations tend to be of low reliability. Why? Does this mean that present value-based accounting for assets and liabilities is not decision useful? Explain.

Note: In the following problem, the capital asset is financed in part by means of interest-bearing bonds.

15. P Ltd. operates under ideal conditions. It has just bought a capital asset for $3,100, which will generate $1,210 cash flow at the end of one year and $2,000 at the end of the second year. At that time, the asset will be useless in operations and P Ltd. plans to go out of business. The asset will have a known salvage value of $420 at the end of the second year. The interest rate in the economy is constant at 10% per annum.

    P Ltd. finances the asset by issuing $605 par value of 12% coupon bonds to yield 10%. Interest is payable at the end of the first and second years, at which time the bonds mature. The balance of the cost of the asset is financed by the issuance of common shares.

    Required
    a. Prepare the present value-based balance sheet as at the end of the first year. P Ltd. plans to pay no dividends in this year.
    b. Give two reasons why ideal conditions are unlikely to hold.
    c. If ideal conditions do not hold, but present value-based financial statements are prepared anyway, is net income likely to be the same as you calculated in part **a**? Explain why or why not. (CGA-Canada)

16. Rainy Ltd. operates under ideal conditions of uncertainty. Its cash flows depend crucially on the weather. On January 1, 2005, Rainy acquired equipment to be used in its operations. The equipment will last two years, at which time its salvage value will be zero. Rainy financed the equipment purchase by issuing common shares.

    In 2005, net cash flows will be $700 if the weather is rainy and $200 if it is dry. In 2006, cash flows will be $900 if the weather is rainy and $300 if it is dry. Cash flows are received at year-end. In each year, the probability that the weather is rainy is 0.3 and 0.7 that it is dry. The interest rate in the economy is 6% in both years.

    Rainy pays a dividend of $50 at the end of 2005.

    Required
    a. In 2005, the weather is rainy. Prepare a balance sheet as at the end of 2005 and an income statement for 2005. Prepare the income statement under both the "sales less amortization" and "alternative" formats.
    b. If we attempt to apply the present value model under uncertainty to the more realistic conditions under which accountants operate, the expected present value calculations become unreliable. Explain why.
    c. Explain why well-defined (i.e., "true") net income does not exist under the realistic conditions under which accountants operate. In place of true net income, what criterion have accountants adopted to guide their financial accounting and reporting decisions?

Note: In the following problem, state probabilities are not independent over time. Part **c** requires calculations not illustrated in the text.

17. Conditional Ltd. operates under ideal conditions of uncertainty. It has just purchased a new machine, at a cost of $3,575.10, paid for entirely from the proceeds of a stock issue. The interest rate in the economy is 8%. The machine is expected to last for two years, after which time it will have zero salvage value.

    The new machine is an experimental model, and its suitability for use in Conditional's operations is not completely known. Conditional assesses a 0.75 probability that there will be a major machine failure during the first year of operation, and a 0.25 probability that the machine will operate as planned. If there is a major failure, cash flow for the year will be $1,000. If the machine operates as planned, cash flow will be $3,000 for the year. If there is no major failure in the first year, the probability of a major failure in the second year, and resulting cash flows of $1,000, falls to 0.60. If there is no major failure in the second year, cash flows for that year will again be $3,000. However, if there is a major failure in the first year, the lessons learned from correcting it will result in only a 0.10 probability of failure in the second year.

    It turns out that there is no major failure in the first year.

    Required
    a. Verify that the cost of $3,575.10 for the machine is correct.
    b. Prepare the income statement for year 1 under the "sales less amortization" format.
    c. Prepare the income statement for year 1 under the "alternative" format.
    d. Prepare a balance sheet as at the end of the first year.

18. On January 1, 2005, ABC Ltd. started its business by purchasing a productive oil well. The proved oil reserves from the well are expected to generate $7,000 cash flow at the end of 2005, $6,000 at the end of 2006, and $5,000 at the end of 2007. Net sales is gross revenues less production costs. Net sales equals cash flows. On January 1, 2008, the oil well is expected to be dry, with no environmental liabilities. The management of ABC Ltd. wishes to prepare financial statements based on RRA in accordance with SFAS 69. The following information is known about the well at the end of 2005.
    - Actual cash flows in 2005 amounted to $6,500, that is, $500 less than expected.
    - Changes in estimates: Due to improved recovery (of oil from the well), cash flows in 2006 and 2007 are estimated to be $6,500 and $6,000 respectively.

    Required
    a. Prepare the income statement of ABC Ltd. for 2005 from its proved oil reserves.
    b. Managements of some firms have expressed serious concerns about the reliability of the RRA information. Outline two of these concerns.

19. The following RRA information is taken from the December 31, 2000, *Annual Report* of FX Energy, Inc.

FX Energy, Inc.
Changes In the Standardized Measure of Discounted Future Cash Flows
For the year ended December 31, 2000
($ thousands)

Present value at January 1, 2000	$5,460
Sales of oil produced, net of production costs	(1,172)
Net changes in prices and production costs	(159)
Extensions and discoveries, net of future costs	2,511
Changes in estimated future development costs	(53)
Previously estimated development costs incurred during the year	202
Revisions in previous quantity estimates	(31)
Accretion of discount	546
Changes in rates of production and other	116
Present value at December 31, 2000	$7,420

Required

a. Prepare income statements, similar to Table 2.5, in both the "sales less amortization" format and the "alternative" format.

b. Explain why amortization expense for 2000 is negative. FX Energy reports elsewhere in its *Annual Report* an (historical cost-based) operating loss from exploration and production for 2000 of $7,245. While all of this amount may not derive from proved reserves, take this operating loss as a reasonable historical cost-based analogue of the RRA income you calculated in part **a**. Also explain why RRA income for 2000 is different from the $7,245 loss under historical cost.

c. The standardized measure is applied only to proved reserves under SFAS 69, using year-end oil and gas prices. Explain why.

d. SFAS 69 mandates a discount rate of 10% for the RRA present value calculations, rather than allowing each firm to choose its own rate. Why? Can you see any disadvantages to mandating a common discount rate?

Note: The item "extensions and discoveries, net of future costs" represents additional reserves proved during the year. Treat it as a separate abnormal earnings item in the alternative income statement. The item "changes in rates of production and other" represents changes in timing of extraction from the timing that was expected at the beginning of 2000.

21. The text states that matching of costs and revenues is a major challenge of historical cost accounting. Another challenge is revenue recognition, that is, when to recognize revenue as realized, or earned. Most firms recognize revenue as earned at the point of sale. More generally, revenue from sale of goods should be recognized when the significant risks and rewards of ownership are transferred to the buyer, and reasonable assurance exists with respect to the amount of consideration to be received. For services and long-term contracts, revenue should be recognized as the work is performed, providing there is reasonable assurance of the amount of consideration that will be received from the service or contract (see *CICA Handbook*, Section 3400).

It is often not clear just when these general criteria are met. Furthermore, firms with no earnings history (e.g., startup firms) and firms that are incurring significant losses or declines in earnings have an incentive to record revenue as early as possible, so as to improve the appearance of their financial statements. Consider the case of Lucent Technologies Inc. In December 2000, Lucent restated its revenue for its fiscal year ended September 30, 2000, reducing the amounts originally reported as follows:

Vendor Financing	$199 (millions)
Partial shipments	28
Distribution partners	452
Total	$679

The vendor financing component of the restatement represents previously unrecorded credits granted by Lucent to customers, to help them finance purchases of Lucent products. That is, the customer sales were originally recorded gross, rather than net, of the credits. The distribution partners' component represents product shipped to firms with which Lucent did not deal at arm's length, but which was not resold by these firms at year end. These firms included certain distributors in which Lucent had an ownership interest. The practice of overshipping to distributors is called "stuffing the channels."

In its 2000 *Annual Report*, Lucent reported net income of $1,219 million, compared to $4,789 million for 1999 and $1,065 million for 1998.

On May 17, 2004, the SEC announced charges against Lucent and several of its officers for overstating revenues by $1,148 million in 2000 in order to meet sales targets. The company's share price fell by 5.5% on that day. Tactics used, the SEC claimed, included the granting of improper credits to customers to encourage them to buy company products, and invoicing sales to customers that were subject to renegotiation in subsequent periods.

Subsequently, Lucent paid a fine of $25 million for "lack of cooperation." In addition, the company, and some of the executives charged, settled the allegations by paying penalties, without admitting or denying guilt.

Required

a. What is the most relevant point of revenue recognition? The most reliable? Explain.

b. Do you feel that Lucent's original recognition of the above components as revenue was consistent with the general revenue recognition criteria given above? Explain why or why not. In your answer, consider the tradeoff between relevance and reliability.

c. What additional revenue recognition questions arise when the vendor has an ownership interest in the customer?

22. Refer to the revenue recognition practices of Qwest Communications outlined in the Theory in Practice vignette in Section 1.2.

Required

a. Use the concept of relevance to argue that firms should record revenue as earned as early as possible in their operating cycles. Was Qwest's revenue recognition policy relevant? Explain.

b. Use the concept of reliability to argue that firms should wait until the significant risks and rewards of ownership are transferred to the buyer, and there is reasonable assurance of collection, before recording revenue. Was Qwest's revenue recognition policy reliable? Explain.

c. When is revenue recognized under ideal conditions? Why?

23. National Instrument 51-101 of the Canadian Securities Administrators (a forum of 13 provincial and territorial securities regulators), effective September 30, 2003, lays down disclosure requirements for Canadian oil and gas firms. These requirements include:

   ■ Proved reserve quantities, defined as reserves that can be estimated with a high degree of certainty (operationalized as at least 90% probability) to be recoverable.

   ■ Probable reserve quantities, defined as additional reserves such that there is at least a 50% probability that the amounts actually recovered will exceed the sum of estimated proved and probable reserves.

   ■ Future net revenues from proved reserves and changes therein, discounted at 10% and undiscounted, using

      i) year-end prices and costs

      ii) forecasted prices and costs

   ■ Future net revenues from probable reserves, discounted at 5%, 10%, 15%, and 20%, and undiscounted, using forecasted prices and costs.

   In addition, reserves data must be verified by a qualified independent professional and reviewed by the board of directors.

   Required

   a. Evaluate the relevance of National Instrument 51-101 disclosures in comparison to those of SFAS 69 and the SEC definition of proved reserves, which is that there must be "reasonable certainty" of recovery under existing economic and operating conditions.

   b. Evaluate the reliability of National Instrument 51-101 disclosures in comparison to those of SFAS 69 and the SEC definition of proved reserves.

24. "A theoretically correct measure of income does not exist in the real world in which accountants must operate."

   Required

   a. What is meant by the phrase "a theoretically correct measure of income"?

   b. Why does a theoretically correct measure of income not exist in the real world? Discuss.

   c. Discuss how the historical cost basis of accounting trades off relevance against reliability.

   d. Give two examples of problems or weaknesses associated with historical cost accounting. (CGA-Canada)

Notes

1. This argument can be turned around. We could argue that if the firm's future income statements were known with certainty, in conjunction with the interest rate, then they would contain all relevant information and the balance sheet could be easily deduced. In effect, each statement contains all the information needed for the other. We view the balance sheet as more fundamental under ideal conditions of certainty, however.

2. To illustrate arbitrage, assume a share of ABC Ltd. is selling in Toronto for $10, and the same share is selling in New York for $10.50 (in Canadian dollars). Ignoring commissions, ABC shares could be purchased on the Toronto market for $10 and sold in New York for $10.50, for a profit of $0.50 per share. However, share price will quickly rise in Toronto because of greater demand, and will just as quickly fall in New York because of greater supply. This change in the supply/demand relationship will bring the market prices into equality in the two markets.

3. Here, the only financial item is cash. Generally, financial assets are assets whose values are fixed in terms of money, such as accounts receivable and investments with a fixed face value, such as bonds. Certain other assets, such as investments in shares, are also regarded as financial assets if a ready market value is available. Financial liabilities, such as accounts payable, bank loans, and bonds issued, are defined similarly.

4. The independence assumption is not crucial to the example. With slight added complexity we could allow for conditional probabilities, where the probability of state realization in year 2 depends on the state realization in year 1. For example, if the good state happened in year 1, this might increase the probability that the good state would also happen in year 2. See problem 17.

5. Somewhat weaker conditions than these would be sufficient to give a first-best economy. Our purpose here, however, is only to give a set of conditions sufficient to ensure that net income is well defined and without information content.

6. SFAS 69 also requires the reporting of historical cost-based results of operations for oil and gas producing activities.

7. Note, however, from Table 2.2, that changes to estimates are separately reported under RRA. A manager who may be tempted to prepare careless or biased estimates knows that resulting errors will be brought out in following years.

8. For an extensive discussion of the balance sheet versus income statement approaches, and the inability of the income statement approach to resolve the question of how to match costs and revenues, see Storey and Storey (1998).

9. For a counterargument, see Ohlson (1987).

Chapter 3

The Decision Usefulness Approach to Financial Reporting

FIGURE 3.1 ORGANIZATION OF CHAPTER 3

3.1 Overview

In Chapter 2 we concluded that the present value model faces some severe problems in practice. It is doubtful that a complete set of financial statements on this basis is feasible. This inability to value the whole firm on a present value basis means that a theoretically well-defined concept of net income does not exist in the complex, real world in which accountants operate.

In this chapter we will begin our study of how to tackle this problem. In Chapter 2 we suggested that historical cost accounting makes more sense perhaps than many give it credit for, particularly when we recognize that it produces reliable information, even though historical cost information is not as relevant as market or present value-based approaches to fair value.

Given historical cost accounting for major classes of assets and liabilities, the next question is: How can financial statements based on historical costs be made more *useful?* This leads to an important concept in accounting—the concept of **decision usefulness**. To properly understand this concept, we need to consider other theories (that is, other than the present value model) from economics and finance. We, as accountants, cannot proceed to make financial statements more useful until we know just what usefulness means. We also need a precise definition of information. Decision theories and capital market theories assist in conceptualizing the meaning of useful financial statement information.

The main purpose of this chapter is to introduce you to some of these theories and to discuss their relevance to accounting. As we shall see, major accounting standard-setting bodies have picked up on these theories, to such an extent that they underlie many of the accounting standards and pronouncements issued by these bodies. Figure 3.1 outlines the organization of this chapter.

3.2 The Decision Usefulness Approach

As we can infer from Section 2.5, the decision usefulness approach to accounting theory takes the view that "if we can't prepare theoretically correct financial statements, at least we can try to make historical cost-based statements more useful." First enunciated in 1966,[1] and reinforced by the influential 1973 report of the Trueblood Commission,[2] this simple observation has had major implications for accounting theory and practice. In particular, we must now pay much closer attention than we did in Chapter 2 to financial statement users and their decision needs, since under non-ideal conditions it is not possible to read the value of the firm directly from the financial statements.

Decision usefulness is contrasted with another view of the role of financial reporting, namely stewardship, whereby the role is to report on management's success, or lack thereof, in managing the firm's resources. As stated in Chapter 1, we regard each role as equally important. In this chapter, we begin our discussion of decision usefulness. Discussion of the second role begins in Chapter 8.

In adopting the decision usefulness approach, two major questions must be addressed. First, who are the users of financial statements? Clearly, there are many users. It is helpful to categorize them into broad groups, such as investors, lenders, managers, unions, standard setters, and governments. These groups are called **constituencies** of accounting.

Second, what are the decision problems of financial statement users? By understanding these decision problems, accountants will be better prepared to meet the information needs of the various constituencies. Financial statements can then be prepared with these information needs in mind. In other words, tailoring financial statement information to the specific needs of the users of those statements will lead to improved decision-making. In this way, the financial statements are made more *useful*.

Of course, determining the specific decision needs of users is by no means an obvious process. For example, what information does a holder of the firm's long-term debt need to make a rational decision about whether to sell certain holdings? Would this decision be helped or hindered by including future income tax liabilities on the balance sheet?

In the face of difficult questions like these, accountants have turned to various theories in economics and finance for assistance. In this chapter we consider the single-person

theory of decision. This theory is a good place to begin to understand how individuals may make rational decisions under uncertainty.

The theory enables us to appreciate the concept of information, which enables decision-makers to update their subjective beliefs about future payoffs from their decisions.

We also consider the **theory of investment**, a specialization of decision theory to model the decision processes of a rational investor. In particular, the theory of investment helps us to understand the nature of *risk* in a portfolio investment context.

These theories are important to accountants because they have been adopted by major professional accounting standard-setting bodies. An examination of some of the pronouncements of the Conceptual Framework project of the FASB (Section 3.8) shows that the above theories lurk just under the surface. Consequently, an understanding of the theories enables a deeper understanding of the pronouncements themselves.

3.2.1 Summary

Accountants have adopted a decision usefulness approach to financial reporting as a reaction to the impossibility of preparing theoretically correct financial statements. However, the decision usefulness approach leads to the problems of identifying the users of financial statements and the information they need to make good decisions. Accountants have decided that investors are a major constituency of users and have turned to various theories in economics and finance—in particular, to theories of decision and investment— to understand the type of financial statement information investors need.

3.3 Single-Person Decision Theory

Single-person decision theory takes the viewpoint of an individual who must make a decision under conditions of uncertainty.[3] It recognizes that state probabilities are no longer objective, as they are under ideal conditions, and sets out a formal procedure whereby the individual can make the best decision, by selecting from a set of alternatives. This procedure allows additional information to be obtained to revise the decision-maker's subjective assessment of the probabilities of what might happen after the decision is made (i.e., the probabilities of states of nature). Decision theory is relevant to accounting because financial statements provide additional information that is useful for many decisions, as illustrated in Example 3.1.

3.3.1 Decision Theory Applied

EXAMPLE 3.1
A TYPICAL INVESTMENT DECISION

Bill Cautious has $10,000 to invest for one period. He has narrowed down his choice to two investments: shares of X Ltd. or government bonds yielding 2 1/4%. We will denote the act of buying the shares by a_1, and the bonds by a_2.

If he buys the shares, Bill faces risk. That is, the future performance of X Ltd. is not known when Bill makes his decision. Consequently, he defines two states of nature:

State 1: X Ltd. future performance high

State 2: X Ltd. future performance low

We can think of X Ltd.'s future performance in terms of its cash flows or earnings. If X Ltd. is in state 1, Bill's net return on the X shares will be $1,600, where net return is calculated as:

Net return = End-of-period market value + Dividends in period − Original investment

If X Ltd. is in state 2, assume that Bill's net return will be zero.

If Bill buys the bonds, he receives interest of $225 next period, regardless of the state of nature. That is, the bond investment is treated as riskless.

The amounts to be received from a decision are called **payoffs**, which we can summarize by a **payoff table** as shown in Table 3.1.

TABLE 3.1 PAYOFF TABLE FOR DECISION THEORY EXAMPLE 3.1

Act	State	
	High	**Low**
a₁ (buy shares)	$1,600	$0
a₂ (buy bonds)	$225	$225

Now consider the state probabilities. Bill subjectively assesses the probability of state 1 (the high-performance state) as $P(H) = 0.30$. The probability of state 2 is then $P(L) = 0.70$. These probabilities incorporate all that Bill knows about X Ltd. to this point in time. These are called **prior probabilities**. He could base these probabilities, for example, on an analysis of X Ltd.'s past financial statements. Instead, or in addition, he could study the current market price of X Ltd. shares. If share price is low, it would indicate an unfavourable market evaluation of X's future prospects, and Bill might also take this into account when assessing his state probabilities.

Bill is risk-averse. Let us assume that the amount of utility, or satisfaction, he derives from a payoff is equal to the square root of the amount of the payoff.[4] Thus, if he receives a payoff of $1,600, his utility is 40. This assumption of risk aversion is not necessary to our example. We could just as easily assume Bill was risk-neutral and evaluate the expected *dollar* amounts of the various payoffs. However, investors are generally risk-averse, so we will work in utilities rather than dollars. Section 3.4 considers risk aversion in greater detail.

In view of our discussion of ethical issues in Section 1.3, a complete evaluation of the utility of an act requires Bill to evaluate any effects of his decision on others. Here, however, Bill's decision is relatively self-contained. That is, whether he buys the shares or the bonds will have little or no effect on anyone else. Consequently, we evaluate his utility in terms of its effect on his own wealth. In other decision problems, for example whether to buy the shares of a firm that is a heavy polluter, Bill may reduce the utility of his payoffs to recognize the adverse social effects of his decision.

Figure 3.2 gives a decision tree diagram for this decision problem. The leftmost numbers in parentheses in the middle column of the figure are the probabilities of the states, the second column from the right shows the dollar amounts of the payoffs, and the rightmost column gives Bill's utility for each amount.

FIGURE 3.2 DECISION TREE FOR BILL'S CHOICE

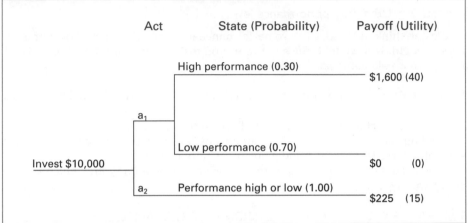

The decision theory tells us that, if he must decide now, Bill should choose the act with the highest **expected utility**. We will denote the expected utility of act a_1 by $EU(a_1)$, and so on.

$$EU(a_1) = (0.30 \times 40) + (0.70 \times 0) = 12$$
$$EU(a_2) = 1.00 \times 15 = 15$$

Therefore, it appears that Bill should choose a_2 and buy the bonds. (A possible alternative would be to diversify, that is, buy some of each type of security. We will rule this out for now by assuming that the brokerage fees for buying small amounts are prohibitive.)

However, Bill has another alternative: to obtain *more information* before deciding. Accordingly, let's assume that he decides to become more informed. The annual report of X Ltd. is to be released within the next few days and Bill decides to wait for it, since it provides readily available and cost-effective evidence about the state of the firm. When the annual report comes, Bill notes that net income is quite high. In effect, the current financial statements show "good news" (GN).

On the basis of extensive experience in financial statement preparation and analysis, Bill knows that if X Ltd. really is a high-state firm, there is an 80% probability that the current year's financial statements will show GN and 20% probability that they will show bad news (BN). Denote these conditional probabilities by $P(GN/H) = 0.80$ and $P(BN/H) = 0.20$ respectively. Note that even if the firm is in the high state, there is still a 20% probability that the financial statements show BN. This is because the financial statements are not completely relevant and reliable.

Bill also knows that if X Ltd. is a low-state firm, it is still possible that the financial statements show GN, Again, this is because the financial statements are not completely relevant and reliable. Assume that if X Ltd. really is in a low state, the probability that the current year's financial statements will show GN is 10%, giving a 90% probability that they will show BN. Denote these conditional probabilities by $P(GN/L) = 0.10$ and $P(BN/L) = 0.90$ respectively.

Now, armed with the GN evidence from the current financial statements and the above conditional probabilities, Bill can use Bayes' theorem to calculate his **posterior state probabilities** (that is, posterior to the financial statement evidence). The posterior probability of the high-performance state is:

$$P(H/GN) = \frac{P(H)\ P(GN/H)}{P(H)\ P(GN/H) + P(L)\ P(GN/L)}$$

$$= \frac{0.30 \times 0.80}{(0.30 \times 0.80) + (0.70 \times 0.10)}$$

$$= 0.77$$

where:

P(H/GN) is the (posterior) probability of the high state given the good-news financial statement

P(H) is the prior probability of the high state

P(GN/H) is the probability that the financial statements show good news given that the firm is in the high state

P(L) is the prior probability of the low state

P(GN/L) is the probability that the financial statements show good news given that the firm is in the low state

Then, the posterior probability P(L/GN) of X Ltd. being in the low-performance state is $1.00 - 0.77 = 0.23$. Recall that if the state is high, the payoff from Bill's share investment will be high ($1,600), and if it is low, the payoff will be low ($0).

Bill can now calculate the expected utility of each act on the basis of his posterior probabilities:

$$EU(a_1/GN) = (0.77 \times 40) + (0.23 \times 0) = 30.8$$
$$EU(a_2/GN) = 1.00 \times 15 = 15$$

Thus, the GN current financial statement information has caused Bill's optimal decision to change to a_1—he should buy the shares of X Ltd.

3.3.2 The Information System

It is important to understand why financial statement information is useful here. To be useful, it must help predict future investment returns. Under historical cost accounting, the financial statements do not show expected future performance directly (as they did under the ideal conditions of Examples 2.1 and 2.2, where future cash flows were discounted to the present). Nevertheless, financial statements will still be useful to investors to the extent that the good or bad news they contain will persist into the future. Think of a progression, from current good or bad earnings news to future expected firm performance to future expected investment returns.

To return to our example, the good news was that current earnings were high. This information enabled Bill to predict high future performance with probability 0.77, and this is also the probability of the high payoff on his investment. Of course, such information is a double-edged sword. Had the financial statements contained bad news, Bill's probability of high payoff would have been lowered just as surely as it was raised by good news.

We may conclude that financial statements can still be useful to investors even though they do not report directly on future cash flows by means of present value-based calculations. Here, it is the lack of ideal conditions that gives the income statement its information content—recall that there was really no information in net income in Examples 2.1 and 2.2. While Examples 2.2 and 3.1 both allow for uncertainty, the fundamental difference between them is that state probabilities were objective in Example 2.2, but subjective here. This opens a role for information to help the decision-maker update subjective state probabilities and predict investment returns.

The heart of the linkage between current financial statement information and future firm performance is the conditional probabilities P(GN/H) and P(BN/L). These probabilities are called an **information system**, which can be summarized by a table such as Table 3.2. Recall that, in our example, the probability that the current financial statements of X Ltd. show good news, conditional on the firm being in the high performance state, is 0.80. The probability they show bad news conditional on the low performance state is 0.90. The 0.80 and 0.90 probabilities are called **main diagonal probabilities**; the others are called **off-main diagonal probabilities**.

*An **information system** is a table giving, conditional on each state of nature, the objective[5] probability of each possible financial statement evidence item.*

TABLE 3.2 INFORMATION SYSTEM FOR DECISION THEORY EXAMPLE 3.1

		Current Financial Statement Evidence	
		GN	BN
	High	0.80	0.20
State			
	Low	0.10	0.90

Note that financial statements are not perfect, or "true"—this would be the case only under ideal conditions. As mentioned above, there is a 20% probability that even if the firm is in the high state the financial statements would show BN, and a 10% probability that if it is in the low state the financial statements would show GN. This weakening of the relationship between current financial statement information and future firm performance is sometimes described as **noise** or as low **earnings quality** in the financial statements. Nevertheless, the information system is **informative**, since it enables Bill to update his prior probabilities to reflect what he now knows, thereby affecting his decision. For cases of fully informative and non-informative information systems, see question 1 at the end of this chapter.

Note also that the extent of informativeness depends on the relevance and reliability of the financial statements. For example, suppose X Ltd. was to switch to fair value from historical cost[6] for its capital assets. The resulting increase in relevance would tend to increase the main diagonal probabilities of the information system and lower the off-main diagonal ones. This is because fair values, for example, current market values, of assets are better predictors of their future values (and hence of future firm performance) than are historical costs of capital assets. However, the use of fair values would also decrease reliability, because market values are volatile and, if current market values are not readily available, subject to possible managerial bias. This would have the opposite effect on the main diagonal probabilities. Thus, it is difficult to say whether such an accounting policy change would increase or decrease the informativeness of the information system.

However, if it were possible to increase relevance without sacrificing reliability or vice versa, the result would be to increase financial statement usefulness. One way to accomplish this would be to present **supplementary fair value information**, as in RRA. This increases relevance for those who want to use supplemental information. However, the historical cost-based primary statements are still available for those who want the somewhat greater reliability of historical cost.

The concept of informativeness of an information system is useful in understanding the role of information in decision-making. The higher the main diagonal probabilities relative to the off-main diagonal ones, the more informative the system—or, equivalently, the higher its quality. Consequently, the more informative an information system, the more decision useful it is. It enables better predictions of relevant states of nature and resulting payoffs. In an investment context, these payoffs are returns on investments.

While thinking of financial statements as a table of conditional probabilities may take some getting used to, the concept of an information system is one of the most powerful and useful concepts in financial accounting theory. It is a powerful concept because it captures the information content of financial statements, thereby determining their value for investor decision-making. It is a useful concept because many practical accounting problems can be framed in terms of their impact on the information system. We pointed out above that if a move to fair value accounting for capital assets is to be decision useful, the increase in relevance (which increases the main diagonal probabilities) must outweigh the decrease in reliability (which decreases them). Similar reasoning can be applied to new or proposed accounting standards. Standards requiring fair value accounting for financial instruments, for example, will be decision useful only if the increased relevance of reporting is not outweighed by decreased reliability. Since most financial accounting debates can be cast in terms of relevance versus reliability, the information system provides a useful framework for evaluation.

The quality of an information system can be estimated empirically. For example, Easton and Zmijewski (1989) (EZ) examined Value Line analysts' revisions of future quarterly earnings forecasts following the GN or BN in firms' current quarterly earnings. Future quarterly earnings are analogous to the states of nature in Table 3.2 (Value Line predicts future performance in terms of earnings), and the GN or BN in current quarterly earnings constitutes the financial statement evidence in that table. Value Line provides forecasts for a large number of firms, and these forecasts are revised quarterly.

For a sample of 150 large U.S. corporations followed by Value Line over the period 1975–1980, EZ found that for every $1 of GN or BN in reported earnings, the Value Line analysts increased or decreased next quarter's earnings forecast by about 34 cents on average. This implies that the information systems underlying the sample firms' financial statements are informative, that is, analysts use current financial statement information to revise their beliefs about future firm performance. EZ called the effect of current financial statement information on analysts' next quarter earnings forecast a "revision coefficient." This coefficient is a proxy for earnings quality.

EZ also found that the higher a firm's revision coefficient is (recall that the 34 cents above is an average), the stronger was the effect of the GN or BN in current earnings on the market price of the firm's shares. This is consistent with investors accepting the analysts' evaluation of the information system, bidding share price up or down more strongly the higher the quality of the system.

EZ's results are consistent with the decision theory model of Example 3.1. Empirical studies of the response of share price to financial statement information are considered in greater detail in Chapter 5.

Theory in Practice 3.1

Decision theory methods are finding applications in several areas other than accounting. Consider, for example, the evaluation of new medical discoveries. Suppose that a drug company has developed a new, expensive, test for a deadly disease. It has administered the test to a sample of persons and has compiled the test's success rates (correct identification of persons who do and do not have the disease) and failure rates (incorrect identification). The success rates correspond to the main diagonal probabilities of the information system in Table 3.2, and the failure rates correspond to the off-main diagonal probabilities. The higher the main diagonal probabilities relative to off-main diagonal, the better the test discriminates (i.e., predicts future performance) between persons who do and do not have the disease.

The company is now trying to decide whether to proceed with marketing the test. Commercial success will be assured if the test is demanded by a large number of people. That is, the test will be popular if persons with low prior probability of having the disease (i.e., most persons) will want to take it. The drug company uses Bayes' theorem to calculate the posterior probability of having the disease for a person with an assumed low prior probability. If it finds the posterior probability to be high (indicating that the test discriminates very well), such persons will be likely to want to take the expensive test. Consequently, the drug company may decide to proceed.

3.3.3 Information Defined

Decision theory and the concept of informativeness give us a precise way to define information:

> **Information** is evidence that has the potential to affect an individual's decision.

Notice that this is an *ex ante* definition. We would hardly expect an individual to gather evidence if he or she didn't expect to learn enough so as to possibly affect a decision. Bayes' theorem is simply a device to process what has been learned. The crucial requirement for evidence to constitute information is that for at least some evidence that might be received, beliefs will be sufficiently affected that the optimal decision will change.

Also, the definition is individual-specific. As pointed out in Chapter 1, individuals may differ in their reaction to the same information source. For example, their prior probabilities may differ, so that posterior probabilities, and hence their decisions, may differ even when confronted with the same evidence.

The definition should really be interpreted net of cost. An information source may have the potential to affect an individual's decision but, if it is too costly, it is not information because it will not be used. It can be argued, however, that financial statements are a cost-effective information source because of the large number of potential users.

Finally, it should be emphasized that an individual's receipt of information and subsequent belief revision is really a continuous process. We can think of the individual as using Bayes' theorem every time a new information item comes along. Example 3.1 concentrated on belief revision following receipt of the annual report, but obviously there are many other information sources, such as newspapers, speeches and announcements, statistical reports, etc. that can also affect decisions. Hopefully, by supplying relevant and reliable information, financial statements will continue their role as an important source of information.

3.3.4 Summary

Decision theory is important because it helps us to understand why information is such a powerful commodity—it can affect the actions taken by investors. Accountants, who prepare much of the information required by investors, need to understand this powerful role.

3.4 The Rational, Risk-Averse Investor

In decision theory, the concept of a rational individual simply means that in making decisions, the chosen act is the one that yields the highest expected utility.[7] This implies that the individual may search for additional information relating to the decision, using it to revise state probabilities by means of Bayes' theorem.

Of course, whether individuals actually make decisions this way is difficult to say. Nevertheless, in thinking about questions of decision usefulness, it is helpful to assume that they do. As we will discuss in Section 6.2, we do not mean to imply that all individuals make decisions as the theory suggests, but only that the theory captures the average behaviour of investors who want to make good investment decisions. Alternatively, we can argue that if investors want to make good decisions this is how they *should* proceed. If individuals do not make decisions in some rational, predictable manner it is difficult for accountants, or anyone else, to know what information they find useful. At any rate, implications of the theory have been subjected to much empirical testing, as we shall see in Chapter 5. To the extent that predictions of the theory are confirmed empirically, our confidence that the decision theory model is a reasonable one is strengthened.

It is also usually assumed that rational investors are **risk-averse**.[8] To see the intuition underlying this concept, think of yourself as an investor who is asked to flip a fair coin with your university or college instructor—suppose the coin is a penny. You would probably be willing to flip for pennies, if for no other reason than to humour the instructor. If the ante were raised, you would probably be willing to flip for dimes, quarters, even dollars.

However, there would come a point where you would refuse—say, flipping for $100,000 (if you didn't refuse, the instructor would).

Remind yourself that the expected payoff of flipping a fair coin is zero, regardless of the amount at stake, since you have a 50% chance of winning and a 50% chance of losing in all cases. Thus, your increasing nervousness as the stakes are raised means that another effect, beyond the expected value of the gamble, is operating. This is risk aversion.

Note also that risk-averse individuals trade off expected return and risk. For example, if the coin was biased in your favour—say you have a 75% chance of winning—you would probably be willing to flip for higher stakes than if the coin was fair. In effect, you are now willing to bear more risk in exchange for a higher expected value—the expected payoff of your gamble is now $0.50 per dollar rather than 0.

To model risk aversion, decision theorists use the device of a **utility function**, which relates payoff amounts to the decision-maker's utility for those amounts.

To portray a utility function, consider Figure 3.3. The solid line shows the utility function of Bill Cautious in Example 3.1. Bill's utility function is:

$$U(x) = \sqrt{x}, \ x \geq 0$$

Where x is the amount of the payoff, $x \geq 0$. Note that the utility function of a risk-averse individual is concave.

FIGURE 3.3 RISK-AVERSE UTILITY FUNCTION

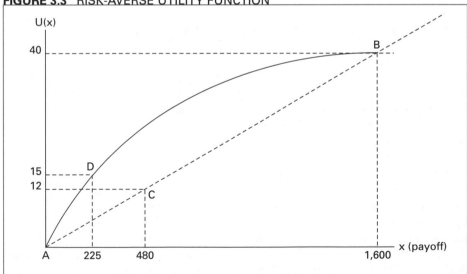

Based on his prior probabilities, Bill's expected payoff for act a_1 is $(0.3 \times \$1,600) + (0.7 \times 0) = \$480$. The expected *utility* of the payoff is at point C on the dotted line joining A and B. This expected utility of $(0.3 \times 40) + (0.7 \times 0) = 12$ is less than the utility of 15 for the risk-free investment at point D on Figure 3.3. Consequently, Bill's rational decision is to choose the risk-free investment, if he were to act on the basis of his prior probabilities. This is the case even though the expected payoff of the risky investment ($480) is greater than the risk-free payoff ($225). This demonstrates that Bill is averse to risk.

To see how Bill's decision may change if the risky investment were less risky, assume that the possible payoffs are now $200 (with probability 0.7) and $1,133.33 (with probability 0.3) instead of the earlier $0 and $1,600. You should verify that the expected payoff is still $480 but the expected utility rises to 20.[9] Then, Bill's rational decision, a priori, is to buy the risky investment. The reduction in risk raises expected utility, even though the expected payoff has not changed.

Despite the intuitive appeal of risk aversion, it is sometimes assumed that decision-makers are **risk-neutral**. This means that they evaluate risky investments strictly in terms of expected payoff—risk itself does not matter per se. We made this assumption in Example 2.2. Figure 3.4 shows the utility function of a risk-neutral decision-maker. A typical risk-neutral utility function is $U(x) = bx$, where b is the slope of the line. Here, utility is simply a linear function of the payoff.

FIGURE 3.4 RISK-NEUTRAL UTILITY FUNCTION

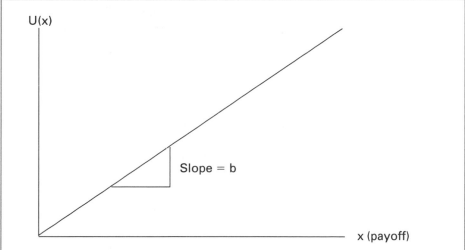

Risk neutrality may be a reasonable assumption when the payoffs are small. However, risk aversion is the more realistic assumption in most cases. The concept of risk aversion is important to accountants, because it means that investors need information concerning the risk, as well as the expected value, of future returns.

* 3.5 The Principle of Portfolio Diversification

In Section 3.4, we stated that individual investors were typically assumed to be risk-averse. Consequently, for a given expected payoff from investments the rational investor

---

*Sections 3.5, 3.6, and 3.7 can be ignored with little loss of continuity. However, diversification and beta are referred to frequently in subsequent chapters. Readers with no previous exposure to these concepts should read at least Sections 3.5 and 3.7.1.

wants the lowest possible risk or, equivalently, for a given risk, will want the highest possible expected payoff. In effect, the investor adopts a tradeoff between risk and return; greater risk will be borne only if expected return is higher and vice versa.

One way investors can lower risk for a given expected return is to adopt a strategy of diversification, that is, to invest in a portfolio of securities. The principle of portfolio diversification shows us that some, but not all, risk can be eliminated by appropriate investment strategy. This principle has important implications for the nature of the risk information that investors need. The risk reported on by many common accounting-based risk measures, such as times interest earned or the current ratio, can be reduced or eliminated a priori by appropriate diversification.

Before illustrating the diversification principle, we return briefly to our risk-averse investor. Note that before we can calculate an individual's expected utility for different investment acts, we need to know what that individual's utility function looks like. For example, Bill Cautious' utility function in Example 3.1 was $U(x) = \sqrt{x}$, $x \geq 0$. With this utility function and payoff probabilities, Bill's expected utilities for different acts were calculated and compared.

One might reasonably ask, "How do we know what an individual's utility function is?" To avoid this question, we shall now assume **mean-variance utility**:

$$U_i(a) = f_i(\bar{x}_a, \sigma_a^2)$$

where symbol a represents an investment act. For example, investment act a could be an investment in a riskless government bond, or in a firm's shares, as in Example 3.1. Alternatively, it could be an investment in a portfolio of securities.

The equation states that the utility of an investment act a to investor i is a function f_i of the expected rate of return from that act $\bar{x}_a$ and the risk as measured by its variance σ_a^2. We assume that f_i is increasing in $\bar{x}_a$ and decreasing in σ_a^2. A specific example of a mean variance utility function is:

$$U_i(a) = 2\bar{x}_a - \sigma_a^2$$

which can be seen to increase in $\bar{x}_a$ and decrease in σ_a^2. Individuals will have different tradeoffs between expected rate of return and risk—for example, a more risk-averse investor might have $-2\sigma_a^2$ rather than $-\sigma_a^2$ as shown above. It is not true in general that the utility of an act depends only on its mean and variance. However, investigation of this is beyond our scope.

The significance of a mean-variance utility assumption to accountants is that it makes investors' decision needs more explicit—all investors need information about the expected values and riskiness of returns from investments, regardless of the specific forms of their utility functions. Without such an assumption, specific knowledge of investors' utility functions would be needed to fully deduce their information requirements.

With this background in mind, we now illustrate the principle of portfolio diversification by means of two examples.

Suppose that a risk-averse investor (Toni Difelice) has $200 to invest and is considering investing all of it in the shares of firm A, currently trading for $20. Assume that Toni assesses a 0.74 probability [10] that the shares will increase in market value to $22 over the coming period and a 0.26 probability that they will decrease to $17. Assume also that A will pay a dividend of $1 per share at the end of the period (we could also make the dividend uncertain, but this would just add complexity without affecting the point to be made).

EXAMPLE 3.2
THE PRINCIPLE OF PORTFOLIO DIVERSIFICATION (PART 1)

As in our decision theory Example 3.1, Toni's subjective probabilities could be posterior to her analysis of firm A's financial statements and the resulting application of Bayes' theorem. Alternatively, they could be her prior probabilities based on whatever other information is at her disposal. For present purposes, the extent to which Toni may have become informed does not matter. The important point is that she has assessed probabilities.

The payoffs from Toni's proposed investment are as follows:

If shares increase: $22 × 10 shares + $10 dividend = $230
If shares decrease: $17 × 10 shares + $10 dividend = $180

TABLE 3.3 CALCULATING EXPECTED RATE OF RETURN AND VARIANCE

Payoff	Rate of Return	Probability	Expected Rate of Return	Variance
$230	$\frac{230 - 200}{200} = 0.15$	0.74	0.1110	$(0.15 - 0.0850)^2 \times 0.74 = 0.0031$
$180	$\frac{180 - 200}{200} = -0.10$	0.26	-0.0260	$(-0.10 - 0.0850)^2 \times 0.26 = 0.0089$
			$\overline{x}_a = 0.0850$	$\sigma_a^2 = 0.0120$

Table 3.3 shows the calculation of the expected rate of return and variance of this investment. Henceforth, we will work with the *rate* of return. As can be seen from Table 3.3, this just involves dividing net returns by the amount of original investment ($200). The division by original investment is a standardization device—rates of return can be directly compared across securities while amounts of returns cannot. Also, rate of return fits in nicely with the assumption of mean-variance utility, which is in terms of the expected value and variance of rate of return.

The variance of return is 0.0120. The variance of an investment return serves as a measure of its riskiness. Since Toni is risk-averse, increasing riskiness will lower her utility, other things equal.

Assume that Toni's utility function is:

$$U_i(a) = 2\overline{x}_a - \sigma_a^2$$

as given above. Then, her utility for this investment is:

$$(2 \times 0.0850) - 0.0120 = 0.1580$$

Toni now has to decide whether to take this investment act. If she feels that this utility is not sufficiently high, further search would be necessary to find a more attractive investment, or some other use for the $200 of capital.

EXAMPLE 3.3
THE PRINCIPLE OF PORTFOLIO DIVERSIFICATION (PART 2)

It turns out that Toni would not be rational to accept the above investment—a more attractive investment can be found. It is possible to find another investment decision that has the same expected return but lower risk. This is because of the **principle of portfolio diversification**.

To illustrate, assume that shares of firm B are also traded on the market, with a current market value of $10. These shares also pay a dividend of $1. Assume there is a 0.6750 probability that firm B's shares will increase in market value to $10.50 at the end of the period, and a 0.3250 probability that they will decrease to $8.50.

Now suppose that Toni decides to invest $200 in six shares of firm A at $20 and eight shares of firm B at $10. We must calculate Toni's expected utility for the portfolio consisting of six shares of firm A and eight shares of firm B. Notice that the same amount ($200) is invested, but that it is now spread over two different securities.

Four possible payoffs now exist from the portfolio: both shares increase in market value, one share increases and the other decreases, or both shares decrease. The amounts of the payoffs and their assumed probabilities are as follows:

TABLE 3.4 PAYOFFS AND THEIR PROBABILITIES

A		B		Dividends		Total Payoff	Probability
132	+	84	+	14	=	$230	0.5742
132	+	68	+	14	=	$214	0.1658
102	+	84	+	14	=	$200	0.1008
102	+	68	+	14	=	$184	0.1592
							1.0000

Recall that six shares of firm A and eight shares of firm B are held, and that the high payoff is $22 per share for firm A and $10.50 for firm B, plus a $1 dividend from each share. This gives the $230 payoff on the first line of the table. The other payoffs are similarly calculated.

Now let us consider more closely the probabilities we have assumed for the four possible payoffs. The returns from shares of firm A and firm B are correlated in our example. To see this, consider the first row in Table 3.4 with a total payoff of $230. This payoff will be realized if both shares A and B realize their high-payoff values. On the basis of our assumption about the probabilities of the individual payoffs of shares A and B, the probabilities of these two payoffs, when each share is considered separately, are 0.74 for A and 0.6750 for B. If the payoffs of shares A and B were independent, the probability of both shares realizing their high payoffs would be $0.74 \times 0.6750 = 0.4995$.

However, in any economy, there are states of nature, also called factors, which affect the returns of *all* shares, such as levels of interest rates, foreign exchange rates, the level of economic activity, and so on. These are called **market-wide** or **economy-wide factors**. Their presence means that if the return on one share is high, it is more likely that the returns on most other shares in the economy will also be high—more likely, that is, than would be the case if the returns on shares were independent. Thus, we have assumed that the probability that both shares A and B realize their high payoffs is 0.5742, greater than the 0.4995 that we would obtain under independence, to reflect these underlying common factors.

Similar reasoning applies to the last row of Table 3.4 with a payoff of $184. Here we have assumed that the joint probability of both firm A and firm B realizing their low payoffs is 0.1592, greater than the (0.26 × 0.3250 = 0.0845) probability under independence. If market-wide state realizations are such that they work against high returns (that is, if the economy is performing poorly), then the probability that both shares realize low payoffs is greater than what would be expected under independence.

Of course, while share returns may be correlated because of common factors, they will not be perfectly correlated. It is still possible that one firm realizes a high return and another a low return—witness the two middle rows of Table 3.4. This is because, in addition to economy-wide factors, there are also **firm-specific factors** that affect the return of one firm only. Examples include the quality of a firm's management, new patents, strikes, machine breakdowns, and so on. Thus, the second row of the table represents a situation where firm A realizes a high return (say, because of a new invention it has just patented) and firm B realizes a low return (say, because of a critical machine failure in its assembly line). However, because of the presence of economy-wide factors, the probabilities for these high/low payoff realizations will also be different than under independence. This is true of Example 3.3.

It should be pointed out that the preceding argument assumes that the *only* source of correlation between returns on firms' shares is market-wide factors. In effect, we have partitioned states of nature that can affect share returns into two components—economy-wide and firm-specific. This is a simplification, since, for example, industry-wide factors could introduce additional returns correlation. However, the simplification is a widely used one and is sufficient for our purposes. It leads to an important measure of share riskiness (beta), which we will discuss shortly. For now, you should realize that the assumption implies that if *all* factors were economy-wide, returns on firms' shares would be perfectly correlated. If *all* factors were firm-specific, returns would be independent. As is usually the case, the truth lies somewhere in between. Consequently, the probabilities given in Table 3.4 assume that both types of factors are present.

The expected rate of return and variance of Toni's portfolio of A and B shares are calculated in Table 3.5 using the correlated probabilities. Thus, the expected rate of return of the portfolio is 0.0850, as before (we have forced this result by appropriate choice of the probabilities, to facilitate comparison), but the variance has decreased to 0.0074, from 0.0120. Since Toni is risk-averse, she would be better off buying the portfolio of A and B shares rather than just A, because the expected return is the same, but the risk is lower.

TABLE 3.5 CALCULATING EXPECTED RATE OF RETURN AND VARIANCE

Payoff	Rate of Return		Probability	Expected Rate of Return	Variance
$230	$\dfrac{230 - 200}{200} =$	0.15	0.5742	0.0861	$(0.15 - 0.0850)^2 \times 0.5742 = 0.0024$
$214	$\dfrac{214 - 200}{200} =$	0.07	0.1658	0.0116	$(0.07 - 0.0850)^2 \times 0.1658 = 0.0000$
$200	$\dfrac{200 - 200}{200} =$	0.00	0.1008	0.0000	$(0.00 - 0.0850)^2 \times 0.1008 = 0.0007$
$184	$\dfrac{184 - 200}{200} =$	−0.08	0.1592	− 0.0127	$(-0.08 - 0.0850)^2 \times 0.1592 = 0.0043$
				$\overline{x}_a = 0.0850$	$\sigma_a^2 = 0.0074$

In fact, her utility now is:

$$U_i(a) = (2 \times 0.0850) - 0.0074$$
$$= 0.1626$$

up from 0.1580 for the single-share investment.

3.5.1 Summary

Risk-averse investors can take advantage of the principle of portfolio diversification to reduce their risk, by investing in a portfolio of securities. This is because realizations of firm-specific states of nature tend to cancel out across securities, leaving economy-wide factors as the main contributors to portfolio risk.

While individual attitudes to risk may differ, we can see investors' decision needs with particular clarity if we assume mean-variance utility. Then, regardless of the degree of risk aversion, we know that utility increases in expected rate of return and decreases in variance of the portfolio.

* 3.6   The Optimal Investment Decision

If a portfolio of two shares is better than one, then a three-share portfolio should be better than two, and so on. Indeed, this is the case and, assuming there are no transaction costs such as brokerage fees, Toni should continue buying until the portfolio includes some of every security traded on the market. This is called "holding the market portfolio." Note again that the total amount invested remains at $200, but is spread over a greater number of securities.

*This section can be omitted without loss of continuity.

Be sure you understand *why* the same amount invested in a portfolio can yield lower risk than if it were invested in a single firm for the same expected rate of return. The reason is simply that when more than one risky investment is held, *the firm-specific risks tend to cancel out*. If one share realizes a low return, there is always the chance that another share will realize a high return. [11] The larger the number of different firms' shares in the portfolio, the more this effect can operate. As a result, the riskiness of returns is reduced, which we have illustrated above by means of our variance calculations. Of course, in the presence of economy-wide risk, there is not a complete cancelling out. At a minimum, that is, when the market portfolio is held, the economy-wide factors will remain to contribute to portfolio risk, and this risk cannot be diversified away. Such non-diversifiable risk is called **systematic risk**.

Conceptually, the market portfolio includes all assets available for investment in the economy. As a practical matter, the market portfolio is usually taken as all the securities traded on a major stock exchange. The return on the market portfolio can then be proxied by the return on a market index for that exchange, such as the Dow Jones Industrial Average index of the New York Stock Exchange, the S&P/TSX Composite Index, etc.

Now return to our investor, Toni Difelice. Toni decides to buy the market portfolio after hearing about the benefits of diversification. Her first task is to assess the expected return and variance of the market portfolio. She subjectively assesses a 0.8 probability that the S&P/TSX Composite index will increase by 10% for the coming period and a 0.2 probability that it will increase by $2\frac{1}{2}$%. Then, denoting the expected return and variance of the market portfolio by $\bar{x}_M$ and σ_M^2 respectively:

$\bar{x}_M$ $= (0.10 \times 0.8) + (0.0250 \times 0.2) = 0.0850$
$\sigma_M^2 = [(0.10 - 0.0850)^2 \times 0.8] + [(0.0250 - 0.0850)^2 \times 0.2]$
$\quad\quad = 0.0002 + 0.0007$
$\quad\quad = 0.0009$

This gives Toni a utility of:

$2\bar{x}_M - \sigma_M^2 = 0.1700 - 0.0009$
$\quad\quad\quad = 0.1691$

which is greater than the 0.1626 utility of the two-share portfolio in Example 3.3.

The question now is: Is this Toni's optimal investment decision? The answer is probably not. If Toni were quite risk-averse, she might prefer a portfolio with lower risk than 0.0009, and would be willing to have a lower expected return as a result.

One strategy she might follow would be to sell some of the high-risk stocks in her portfolio. But, if she does this, she is no longer holding the market portfolio, so some of the benefits of diversification are lost. How can Toni adjust portfolio risk to her desired level without losing the benefits of diversification?

The answer lies in the **risk-free asset**. If a risk-free asset, such as treasury bills yielding, say, 4%, is available, an investor could sell some of the market portfolio (that is, sell some of each security, so that the market portfolio is still held but total investment in it is lower) and use the proceeds to buy the risk-free asset. This strategy is depicted in Figure 3.5 as a move from M, where only the market portfolio is held, to Y. Risk is lower at Y, but so is expected return, compared to M. However, if the investor is quite risk-averse this could raise utility.

FIGURE 3.5 THE OPTIMAL PORTFOLIO INVESTMENT DECISION

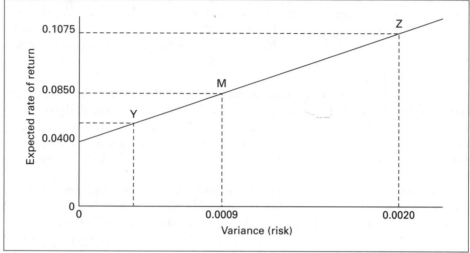

Conversely, if Toni were less risk-averse, she may prefer to borrow at the risk-free rate and buy more of the market portfolio, thereby moving to Z, with higher expected return and risk.

In this way, each investor can secure a desired risk-return tradeoff while continuing to enjoy the maximum risk-reduction effects of diversification.

To illustrate, suppose that Toni borrows $100 at a rate of 0.04 and buys an additional $100 of the market portfolio. Toni now has $300 of market portfolio, on which she expects to earn 0.0850, and owes $100 at 4% interest. But her own investment is still $200. Consequently, her expected return is now:

$$\bar{x}_a = \left(\frac{300}{200} \times 0.0850\right) - \left(\frac{100}{200} \times 0.0400\right)$$

$$= (0.1275 - 0.0200)$$

$$= 0.1075$$

The variance of her return also increases, since she now has $300 at risk on an investment of $200. There is no variance attached to the $100 borrowed, of course, since interest and principal payments are fixed. The variance of her return is now:

$$\sigma_a^2 = (300/200)^2 \times 0.0009$$

$$= 0.0020$$

yielding utility of $(2 \times 0.1075) - 0.0020 = 0.2130$. This yields Toni a higher utility than simply holding the market portfolio (0.1691). Toni will continue to borrow until the amount borrowed and reinvested yields an $\bar{x}_a$ and σ_a^2 that maximizes her utility. In fact, if she can borrow all she wants at 4%, she would borrow $9,800, which would yield her utility of 2.33.

3.6.1 Summary

When transaction costs are ignored, a risk-averse investor's optimal investment decision is to buy that combination of market portfolio and risk-free asset that yields the best tradeoff between expected return and risk. This tradeoff is individual-specific—it depends on the investor's utility function. Some investors may wish to reduce their investment in the market portfolio and buy the risk-free asset with the proceeds. Others may wish to borrow at the risk-free rate and increase their investment. Either way, all investors can enjoy the full benefits of diversification while at the same time attaining their optimal risk-return tradeoff.

* 3.7 Portfolio Risk

3.7.1 Calculating and Interpreting Beta

The principle of diversification leads to an important risk measure of a security in the theory of investment. This is **beta**, which measures the co-movement between changes in the price of a security and changes in the market value of the market portfolio. To illustrate, we will calculate the betas of shares of firms A and B in Example 3.3, in relation to the market portfolio M given in Section 3.6.

Beta is an important and useful concept in financial accounting. As we shall see in Chapter 5, a stock's beta is a crucial component of empirical studies of the usefulness to investors of financial accounting information. Also, it is a "launching pad" for reporting on firm risk. Reporting on risk is discussed in Section 7.5. Consequently, an understanding of what a stock's beta is and what it tells us about firm risk is an important part of an accountant's knowledge base.

EXAMPLE 3.4
CALCULATING BETA

The beta of A shares, denoted by β_A, is given by:

$$\beta_A = \frac{Cov(A,M)}{Var(M)}$$

where Cov(A,M) is the covariance of the returns on A with the returns on the market portfolio M. In effect, β_A measures how strongly the return on A varies as the market varies. For example, a high-beta security would undergo wide swings in

---

*This section can be omitted without loss of continuity.

rate of return as market conditions change. Shares of airlines and aircraft manu-
facturers are examples, since these industries are sensitive to economic conditions.
Shares of electric utilities and fast food firms would be low-beta, since the returns
of such firms are less subject to the state of the economy.

Division by Var(M) is simply a standardization device, to express Cov(A,M) in units
of market variance. For example, if the returns on the Toronto and New York Stock
Exchanges have different variances, standardization by the variance of returns on
the respective exchanges enables betas of Canadian and U.S. firms to be compared.

To calculate the beta of security A, assume that the conditional payoff probabilities of A are as follows:

- When return on M is high:

  Probability that return on A is high = 0.90
  Probability that return on A is low = 0.10

- When return on M is low:

  Probability that return on A is high = 0.10
  Probability that return on A is low = 0.90

These probabilities could be estimated by examining past data on the returns
on A shares in relation to the returns on M. Cov(A,M) is calculated in Table 3.6.

TABLE 3.6 CALCULATION OF COVARIANCE

Returns		Joint		
A	M	Probabilities		
High	High	$(0.15 - 0.0850)(0.10 - 0.0850) \times 0.72$	=	0.0007
High	Low	$(0.15 - 0.0850)(0.0250 - 0.0850) \times 0.02$	=	−0.0001
Low	High	$(-0.10 - 0.0850)(0.10 - 0.0850) \times 0.08$	=	−0.0002
Low	Low	$(-0.10 - 0.0850)(0.0250 - 0.0850) \times 0.18$	=	0.0020
		Cov(A,M)	=	0.0024

In the first row of the table, the values 0.15 and 0.0850 are the high return and the
expected return respectively of A (see Table 3.3). Similarly 0.10 and 0.0850 are the
high return and the expected return of M (see Section 3.6). The joint probability
that both A and M pay off high is:

Prob(A high and M high) = Prob(M high) Prob(A high/M high)
$$= 0.8 \times 0.9$$
$$= 0.72$$

You should verify the remaining rows in the table.

Then, recalling from Section 3.6 that $\sigma_M^2 = Var(M) = 0.0009$, we obtain:

$$\beta_A = \frac{0.0024}{0.0009} = 2.6667$$

For security B in Example 3.3, assume that the conditional payoff probabilities are:

■ When return on M is high:

Probability that return on B is high = 0.7917
Probability that return on B is low = 0.2083

■ When return on M is low:

Probability that return on B is high = 0.2083
Probability that return on B is low = 0.7917

Then, similar calculations give:

$$\beta_B = \frac{0.0014}{0.0009} = 1.5556$$

You should verify this calculation.[12]

Because β_B is lower than β_A, an investor who buys only B shares is more insulated from the ups and downs of the stock market than if he/she buys only A shares. This is the sense in which a low-beta security has low risk.[13]

3.7.2 Portfolio Expected Value and Variance

Since risk-averse investors with mean-variance utility functions need to know the expected value and variance of their investment portfolios, we give here formulae for their calculation. In the process, we shall see that beta measures the amount of systematic risk contributed by a security to a portfolio.

The expected value of return on a portfolio P is calculated as a weighted average of the expected returns on the securities in the portfolio:

$$\bar{x}_P = k_1 \bar{x}_1 + k_2 \bar{x}_2 + \dots + k_n \bar{x}_n$$

where $\bar{x}_P$ is the expected return on P, $\bar{x}_1$ is the expected return on security 1, etc., k_1 is the proportion of total portfolio investment in security 1, etc., and there are n securities in the portfolio.

In Example 3.3, n = 2, k_1 = \$120/\$200 = 0.6, k_2 = (1 − k_1) = 0.4, and the expected returns on the two securities A and B in Toni's portfolio were both 0.0850. Then, the formula gives:

$$\bar{x}_{A+B} = (0.6 \times 0.0850) + (0.4 \times 0.0850) = 0.0850$$

which, of course, agrees with the direct calculation in Table 3.5.

For the variance of portfolio return, we have the following standard formula for the variance of a sum of random variables:

$$\text{Var}(P) = \sigma_P^2 = k_1^2\sigma_1^2 + k_2^2\sigma_2^2 + \dots + k_n^2\sigma_n^2 + 2k_1k_2 \, \text{Cov}(x_1,x_2) + 2k_1k_3 \, \text{Cov}(x_1,x_3)$$
$$+ \dots + 2k_{n-1}k_n \, \text{Cov}(x_{n-1},x_n)$$

That is, the variance of P is the weighted sum of the variances of the individual securities in P plus the weighted sum of covariances of all the pairs of securities in P.

In Example 3.3, the formula reduces to:

$$\text{Var}(A + B) = k_1^2\,\text{Var}(A) + (1 - k_1)^2\,\text{Var}(B) + 2k_1(1 - k_1)\,\text{Cov}(A,B)$$

The main point here is that portfolio variance depends not only on the variances of the component securities, but also, if the security returns are correlated, on the covariance between them (if the returns on A and B are uncorrelated, $\text{Cov}(A,B) = 0$).

In an investment context, the returns on A and B are most definitely correlated because of economy-wide factors. In fact, we have assumed that economy-wide factors are the *only* source of correlation between security returns. Then, we can write the covariance between A and B in terms of their covariances with the market portfolio M:

$$\text{Cov}(A,B) = \frac{\text{Cov}(A,M)\,\text{Cov}(B,M)}{\text{Var}(M)}$$

$$= \text{Var}(M)\beta_A\beta_B$$

The portfolio variance becomes:[14]

$$\begin{aligned}
\text{Var}(A + B) &= 0.6^2\,\text{Var}(A) + 0.4^2\,\text{Var}(B) + 2 \times 0.6 \times 0.4\,\text{Var}(M)\beta_A\beta_B \\
&= (0.36 \times 0.0120) + (0.16 \times 0.0088) + (0.48 \times 0.0009 \times 2.6667 \times 1.5556) \\
&= 0.0043 + 0.0014 + 0.0017 \\
&= 0.0074
\end{aligned}$$

which agrees with the direct calculation in Table 3.5. Thus, we see that securities A and B contribute systematic risk of 0.0017 to the portfolio variance of 0.0074, or about 23%.

3.7.3 Portfolio Risk as the Number of Securities Increases

A contribution of 23% may not seem like much, but this results from the presence of only two securities in the portfolio. Consider what happens as the number of securities in the portfolio increases. Let there now be n securities in portfolio P. To simplify a bit, we will assume that an equal amount is invested in each security, so that the proportion of each security in P is $1/n$ of the total amount invested. Then:

$$\begin{aligned}
\text{Var}(P) &= \frac{1}{n^2}\sigma_1^2 + \frac{1}{n^2}\sigma_2^2 + \dots + \frac{1}{n^2}\sigma_n^2 + \frac{2}{n^2}\,\text{Cov}(x_1,x_2) + \frac{2}{n^2}\,\text{Cov}(x_1,x_3) + \dots + \frac{2}{n^2}\,\text{Cov}(x_{n-1},x_n) \\
&= \frac{1}{n^2}\left[\sigma_1^2 + \sigma_2^2 + \dots + \sigma_n^2\right] + \frac{2}{n^2}\,\text{Var}(M)\left[\beta_1\beta_2 + \beta_1\beta_3 + \dots + \beta_{n-1}\beta_n\right]
\end{aligned}$$

There are n variance terms in the formula. However, the number of covariance terms goes up quite quickly relative to n. In fact, there are $n(n - 1) \div 2$ covariance terms. For example, if n = 10, there are 10 variance terms but 45 covariance terms.

This means that, even for portfolios that contain a modest number of securities, *most of the risk is systematic risk*, from the covariance terms. For example, for n = 10, the coefficient of the variance terms is only 1/100, so that the variances of the 10 securities contribute only 10% of their average variance to the portfolio variance. However, while the coefficient of the systematic risk terms is only 2/100, there are 45 terms, so the covariances contribute fully 90% of their average covariance to the portfolio variance. In other words, *most of the benefits of diversification can be attained with only a few securities in the portfolio.* This is fortunate, since brokerage and other transactions costs would prevent most investors from buying the market portfolio.[15] From an accounting standpoint, this means that for most investors, useful information is that which helps them assess securities' expected returns and betas.

3.7.4 Summary

When transactions costs are not ignored, a risk-averse investor's optimal investment decision is to buy relatively few securities, rather than the market portfolio. In this way, most of the benefits of diversification can be attained, at reasonable cost.

Information about securities' expected returns and betas is useful to such investors. This enables them to estimate the expected return and riskiness of various portfolios that they may be considering. They can then choose the portfolio that gives them their most preferred risk-return tradeoff, subject to the level of transactions costs that they are willing to bear.

3.8 The Reaction of Professional Accounting Bodies to the Decision Usefulness Approach

It is interesting to note that major professional accounting bodies have adopted the decision usefulness approach. For example, Section 1000 of the *CICA Handbook* states (paragraph 1000.15), in part:

> *The objective of financial statements is to communicate information that is useful to investors, members, contributors, creditors and other users ... in making their resource allocation decisions and/or assessing management stewardship.*

However, the earliest and most complete statement of this adoption comes from the FASB in its Conceptual Framework project. The Conceptual Framework specifically mentions investors' needs for information about the uncertainty of future investment returns as well as their expected values. While Section 1508 of the *CICA Handbook* lays down conditions for disclosure of measurement uncertainty, Section 1000 does not mention risk. In view of our demonstration above that rational investors need information about risk as well as expected value of returns, we shall concentrate here on the Conceptual Framework.

According to *Statement of Financial Accounting Concepts* (1978) (SFAC 1), the purpose of the concepts project is "to set forth fundamentals on which financial accounting and reporting standards will be based." SFAC 1 gives a series of objectives of financial reporting. Its first objective of financial reporting is to:

> *provide information that is useful to present and potential investors and creditors and other users in making rational investment, credit, and similar decisions.*

FASB = Fin Acc Std Board

Note particularly the use of the word "rational" in this objective. This is the tie-in to the economic decision theory. As pointed out in Section 3.4, decision-makers who proceed in accordance with the theory, that is, those who make decisions so as to maximize their expected utility, are referred to as rational.

Note also that a variety of constituencies are included in this most general objective (present and potential investors and creditors and other users) and also that a wide variety of decisions are contemplated (investment, credit, and similar decisions). This immediately raises the question of what particular decision-makers and decisions are involved. Thus, SFAC 1 states that the second objective of financial reporting is to:

> *provide information to help present and potential investors and creditors and other users in assessing the amounts, timing, and uncertainty of prospective cash receipts from dividends or interest and the proceeds from the sale, redemption, or maturity of securities or loans.*

Thus, we can see that the primary decision addressed in SFAC 1 is the investment decision in firms' shares or debt. Specifically, cash receipts from dividends or interest are *payoffs*, similar to those in the payoff table (Table 3.1) of Example 3.1. Note that these investment decisions apply to potential investors as well as present ones. This means that financial statements must communicate useful information to the market, not just to existing investors in the firm.

Note also that the second objective is future-oriented—it calls for information about "prospective" cash receipts from dividends or interest. There is a clear recognition that investors need information to help them estimate *future* payoffs from their investments. In particular, the second objective states that investors need to assess "the amounts, timing, and uncertainty" of prospective returns. While the terms used are somewhat different, these will be recognized as relating to the expected value and risk of future returns. Thus, the second objective also contains a clear recognition that (risk-averse) investors will want information about risk of returns as well as their expected amounts, just as the theory of investment predicts.

The question now arises: How can historical cost-based financial statements be useful in predicting future returns? This is probably the major difficulty that the FASB's Conceptual Framework has faced. Given that historical cost accounting is fixed in practice, it is necessary to establish some linkage between past firm performance and future prospects. Without such linkage, the decision-oriented objectives of SFAC 1 would not be attainable.

We can see the linkage clearly, however, by drawing on the decision theory model. In particular, refer to the information system (Table 3.2) for Example 3.1. The table provides a probabilistic relationship between current financial statement information (GN or BN) and the future-oriented states of nature (high or low performance), that will determine future investment payoffs. In effect, current financial statement information and future returns are linked via the conditional probabilities of the information system.

Consistent with the information system linkage, SFAC 1 states:

> *Although investment and credit decisions reflect investors' and creditors' expectations about future enterprise performance, those expectations are commonly based at least partly on evaluations of past enterprise performance.*

This is the crucial argument that enables the Conceptual Framework to maintain that past-oriented, historical cost-based financial statement information can be useful to forward-looking investors. It is consistent with the decision usefulness approach, which purports that information is useful if it helps investors make their own estimates of future returns.

In SFAC 2, the FASB goes on to consider the characteristics that are necessary if financial statement information is to be useful for investor decision-making. This is another crucial and delicate aspect of the whole conceptual framework—how can financial statement information be presented so as to be of maximum use to investors in predicting future returns? Once again, the answer lies in the concepts of **relevance** and **reliability**.

In Chapter 2, we defined relevant financial statements as those that give information to investors about the firm's future economic prospects. The SFAC 2 definition is somewhat broader:

> *Relevant accounting information is capable of making a difference in a decision by helping users to form predictions about the outcomes of past, present, and future events or to confirm or correct prior expectations. Information can make a difference to decisions by improving decision makers' capacities to predict or by providing feedback on earlier expectations. Usually, information does both at once, because knowledge about the outcomes of actions already taken will generally improve decision makers' abilities to predict the results of similar future actions. Without a knowledge of the past, the basis for a prediction will usually be lacking. Without an interest in the future, knowledge of the past is sterile.*

The essence of the SFAC 2 definition is that information is relevant if it helps financial statement users to form their own predictions of events (such as future performance and resulting payoffs). Again, this is consistent with the decision usefulness approach. Thus, we can say that under the ideal conditions of Chapter 2, relevant financial statement information consists of (the discounted present values of) future payoffs, or expected future payoffs. Under less-than-ideal conditions, relevant financial statement information consists of information that helps investors form *their own* expectations of future payoffs. By extending the definition of relevance to include information that can help investors form their own payoff estimates, the scope for information to be relevant is greatly enlarged.

It is also worth noting that the FASB notion of relevance is consistent with the definition of information in decision theory. Recall that information is that which has the potential to change individual decisions, that is, it can "make a difference." In effect, evidence is not really information unless it is capable of affecting user decisions. This role of information comes across with particular clarity in Bayes' theorem. Recall that Bayes' theorem provides a vehicle for investors to update their prior beliefs about relevant states of nature on the basis of new information, as illustrated in Example 3.1.

Another desirable information characteristic in SFAC 2 is reliability. In Chapter 2 we defined reliable information as information that is precise and free from bias. According to SFAC 2:

> *To be reliable, information must have representational faithfulness and it must be verifiable and neutral.*

This characteristic can be reconciled with our definition. We can equate representational faithfulness and neutrality with freedom from bias. For example, if financial statement information is biased due to managerial misrepresentation towards a predetermined result, that information would be neither representationally faithful nor neutral.

Also, the precision of financial statement information can be equated with representational faithfulness and verifiability. We saw in Section 2.4 that a major problem with RRA was the imprecision of the discounted reserves' valuation, with the consequence that major adjustments of prior years' valuations were frequently required. In effect, the estimates were not sufficiently precise for purposes of estimating an oil company's future cash flows; hence, they were not representationally faithful to the resources or events those numbers purport to represent. In addition, they would lack verifiability in the sense that independent measurers would be likely to achieve different RRA estimates under similar circumstances.

SFAC 2 continues on to explore other desirable characteristics of useful financial statement information. One of these is **timeliness**, which is best thought of as a constraint on relevance. That is, if a manager delays the release of information, it loses any relevance it may have had if it had been released promptly.

As previously mentioned, the main point to realize is that, to be useful for investment decision purposes, financial statement information need not necessarily involve a direct prediction of future firm payoffs. Rather, if the information has certain desirable characteristics, such as relevance, reliability, and timeliness, it can be an informative input to help investors form their own predictions of these payoffs.

3.8.1 Summary

The FASB's SFAC 1 represents an important adaptation of decision theory to financial accounting and reporting. Furthermore, this theory is oriented in SFAC 1 to the theory of decision-making for investors, which has been much studied in economics and finance.

SFAC 2 operationalizes the decision usefulness approach by developing the characteristics that accounting information should have in order to be useful. In essence, accounting information should provide an informative information system that links current financial statements with future state realizations and payoffs. Two major informative characteristics are *relevance* and *reliability*. Relevant information is information that has the capacity to affect investors' beliefs about future returns, and it should be released in a timely manner. Reliable information faithfully represents what it purports to measure. It should be precise and free from bias.

3.9 Conclusions on Decision Usefulness

Following from the pioneering *ASOBAT* and Trueblood Committee reports, the decision usefulness approach to financial reporting implies that accountants need to understand the decision problems of financial statement users. Single-person decision theory and its specialization to the portfolio investment decision provide an understanding of the needs of rational, risk-averse investors. This theory tells us that such investors need information to help them assess securities' expected returns and the riskiness of these returns. In the theory of investment, beta is an important risk measure, being the standardized covariance of a security's return with the return on the market portfolio. This covariance risk is the main component of the riskiness of a diversified portfolio, even if the portfolio contains only a relatively few securities.

Historical cost-based financial statements are an important and cost-effective source of information for investors, even though they do not report directly on future investment payoffs. They provide an information system that can help investors to predict future firm performance, which, in turn, predicts future investment returns. This predictive role is enhanced to the extent that financial statements are relevant and reliable.

Major accounting standard-setting bodies such as the CICA and the FASB have adopted the decision usefulness approach. This is evidenced by their conceptual frameworks, which show a clear recognition of the role of financial reporting in providing relevant and reliable information for investors.

Questions and Problems

1. Refer to Table 3.2, the information system table for Example 3.1. Prepare a similar table for a **perfect**, or **fully informative**, information system, that is, an information system that perfectly reveals the true state of nature. Do the same for a **non-informative** information system, that is, one that reveals nothing about the true state.

   Use the probabilities from the two tables you have prepared to revise state probabilities by means of Bayes' theorem, using the prior probabilities and GN message given in Example 3.1. Comment on the results. (CGA-Canada)

2. What would the utility function of a **risk-taking** investor look like? What sort of portfolio would such an individual be likely to invest in? What information would the investor need? (CGA-Canada)

3. An investor's utility function is:

   $$U_i(a) = 3\bar{x} - \frac{1}{2}\,\sigma_x^2$$

   Act a_1 has $\bar{x} = 0.88$, $\sigma_x^2 = 0.512$, yielding $U_i(a_1) = 2.384$. Act a_2 has $\bar{x} = 0.80$.

   What σ_x^2 would this act require to yield the same utility as a_1? Comment on the result with regard to risk and expected return. (CGA-Canada)

4. Refer to Figure 3.5. Suppose Toni's utility function is:

   $$U_i(a) = \frac{1}{2}\bar{x} - 16\sigma_x^2$$

   Calculate Toni's utility at point Z on Figure 3.5 and compare it with her utility at point M. Which act does Toni prefer? Explain. (CGA-Canada)

5. What is the beta of:
   a. The market portfolio
   b. The risk-free asset
   c. Portfolio A + B in Example 3.3 and Section 3.7 (CGA-Canada)

6. Explain why most of the benefits of diversification can be attained with only a rel-atively few securities in the portfolio. Assume that an equal amount is invested in each security. Does the riskiness of the return on a diversified portfolio approach zero as the number of securities in the portfolio gets larger? Explain. (CGA-Canada)

7. The FASB states in SFAC 1:

   Information about enterprise earnings based on accrual accounting generally provides a better indicator of an enterprise's present and continuing ability to generate favourable cash flows than information limited to the financial effects of cash receipts and payments.

   In other words, the FASB is arguing that net income is a better predictor of future cash flows than current cash flows themselves. This may seem surprising.

   Why do you think the FASB makes this argument? (CGA-Canada)

8. Verify the statement made at the end of Section 3.6 that if Toni Difelice can borrow all she wants at 4% she would borrow $9,800, yielding utility of 2.33.

9. Give some reasons why the off-main diagonal probabilities of an information system such as that depicted in Table 3.2 are non-zero. Use the concepts of relevance and reli-ability in your answer. Explain why an information system is more useful the lower the off-main diagonal probabilities are.

10. a. State the decision usefulness approach to accounting theory.
    b. What two questions arise once the decision usefulness approach is adopted?
    c. What primary constituency of financial statement users has been adopted by the major professional accounting bodies as a guide to the reporting of decision-useful financial information?
    d. According to the FASB Conceptual Framework's second objective of financial reporting, what information is needed by the constituency of users that you have identified in part **c**?
    e. Explain why information about the riskiness of securities is useful to investors. (CGA-Canada)

11. Mr. Smart is an investor with $15,000 to invest. He has narrowed his choice down to two possible investments:

    ■ Mutual fund
    ■ Common shares in Buyme Corporation

    Mr. Smart is risk-averse. The amount of utility he derives from a payoff is:

    Utility = 2ln(payoff)

    where ln denotes natural logarithm. The decision tree for Mr. Smart's problem appears in Figure 3.6.

Because of a planned major purchase, Mr. Smart intends to sell his investment one year later. The payoffs represent the proceeds from the sale of the investment and receipt of any dividends, net of initial investment. The probabilities represent Mr. Smart's prior probabilities about the state of the economy (good or bad) over the coming year.

FIGURE 3.6 DECISION TREE FOR MR. SMART'S PROBLEM

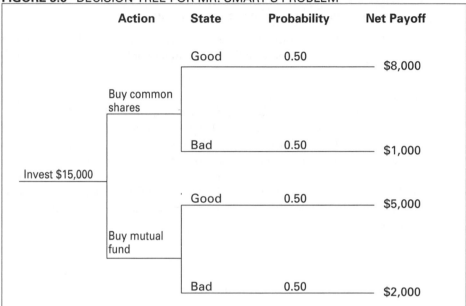

Action	State	Probability	Net Payoff
	Good	0.50	$8,000
Buy common shares			
	Bad	0.50	$1,000
Invest $15,000			
	Good	0.50	$5,000
Buy mutual fund			
	Bad	0.50	$2,000

Required

a. Calculate Mr. Smart's expected utility for each action and indicate which action he would choose if he acted on the basis of his prior information.

b. Now, suppose Mr. Smart decides that he would like to obtain more information about the state of the economy rather than simply accepting that it is just as likely to be good as bad. He decides to take a sample of current annual reports of major corporations. Every annual report shows that its firm is doing well, with increased profits over the previous year. The probability that there would be such healthy profits if the state of the economy actually was good is 0.75. The probability of such healthy profits is only 0.10 if the state of the economy actually was bad.

Use Bayes' theorem to calculate Mr. Smart's posterior probabilities of the high and low states of the economy. Will he change his decision?

Note: Round your calculations to two decimal places.

12. John Save plans to invest $5,000 in one of the following instruments:

- Bonds of J Ltd., yielding 12%
- Canada Savings Bonds, yielding 8%

On the basis of his knowledge of current economic conditions and the outlook for the industry of J Ltd., John assesses the prior probability that J Ltd. will go bankrupt as 0.05. If this happens, John will lose both principal and interest and receive no money at the end of the year. If J Ltd. does not go bankrupt, John plans to sell the bonds, plus interest, at the end of one year.

Of course, the probability that the Canada Savings Bonds will fail to pay off is zero. John also plans to sell these, plus interest, one year later.

John is risk-averse, and decides to choose that investment that yields the highest expected utility. Assume that John's utility for an amount of $x is given by $\sqrt{x}$, where x is the gross payoff.

Required
a. On the basis of his prior probabilities, which investment should John choose?
b. Rather than choosing on the basis of his prior probabilities, assume that John decides to analyze the current financial statements of J Ltd. These financial statements can look "good" (G) or "bad" (B). After his analysis, John realizes that the statements look good. On the basis of his extensive understanding of financial statement analysis, he knows that the probability that the financial statements would look good given that the firm was actually heading for bankruptcy is 0.10, that is:

$$P(G/S_1) = 0.10$$

where S_1 denotes the state of heading for bankruptcy.

Similarly, John knows that:

$$P(G/S_2) = 0.80$$

where S_2 denotes the state of not heading for bankruptcy.

Advise John as to which investment he should now take. Use Bayes' theorem.

Note: Round your calculations to four decimal places. (CGA-Canada)

13. Consider the common stock of A Ltd. and the common stock of B Ltd. These two common stocks have the same expected return and the same variance of return.

You are a risk-averse investor and have a fixed sum of money to invest. You are considering the following two choices:

a. Investing the entire sum of money in common stock of A Ltd.
b. Investing in a portfolio with the investment equally distributed between common stock of A Ltd. and common stock of B Ltd.

Required

Discuss whether you would choose alternative **a** or **b** or whether you are indifferent between them. Explain your choice. (CGA-Canada)

14. "It is possible to reduce risk in a portfolio by diversification."

    Required
    a. Do you agree with this statement? If so, why? Explain.
    b. Can the risk of a portfolio be reduced to zero by diversification? Explain.
    c. Why is beta the most relevant measure of risk in a diversified portfolio?

15. Marie has $1,000 that she wishes to invest for one year. She has narrowed her choices down to one of the following two actions:

    a_1: Buy bonds of Risky Mining Ltd. These pay 14.4% interest, unless Risky goes bankrupt, in which case Marie will lose her principal and interest.

    a_2: Buy Canada Savings bonds, paying 6.4% interest.

    Marie assesses her prior probability of Risky Mining Ltd. going bankrupt as 0.40. Marie's utility for money is given by the square root of the amount of her gross payoff. That is, if she buys the Canada Savings Bonds her payoff is $1,064, etc. Marie is a rational decision-maker.

    Required
    a. Based on her prior probabilities, which action should Marie take? Show your calculations.
    b. Before making a final decision, Marie decides she needs more information. She obtains Risky Mining's current financial statements and examines its debt-to-equity ratio. This ratio can be either "HI" or "LO." Upon calculating the ratio, Marie observes that it is LO. On the basis of her prior experience in bond investments, Marie knows the following conditional probabilities:

	DEBT-TO-EQUITY RATIO Future State	
	LO	HI
NB (Not Bankrupt)	0.50	0.50
B (Bankrupt)	0.05	0.95

    Which action should Marie now take? Show your calculations, taken to two decimal places.

    c. The Accounting Standards Board adopts a major new standard affecting Risky Mining Ltd.'s financial statements. Pension liabilities and other post-employment benefits must now be measured in the financial statements at their expected discounted present values, instead of the previous pay-as-you-go accounting.

    Evaluate the likely impact of the new standard on the main diagonal probabilities of the information system in part **b**.

16. A rational investor has $1,000 to invest. She is contemplating investing the full amount in shares of Company A (a_1) or investing it in a risk-free government bond (a_2).

The investor identifies two states of nature:

State H: Company A has high future performance.
State L: Company A has low future performance.

On the basis of her prior information about Company A, the investor assesses the following subjective prior probabilities.

State H: 0.2
State L: 0.8

The following is the payoff table for these two investments. Payoffs are net of (i.e., they exclude) the original investment.

		State	
		H	L
Act	a_1	$324	$0
	a_2	$36	$36

The investor is risk-averse, with utility equal to the square root of the net dollar payoff.

Required
a. On the basis of her prior probabilities, which act should the investor take? Show calculations.
b. Instead of acting now, the investor decides to obtain more information about Company A, by careful reading of its annual report. The investor, who is an expert in financial accounting and reporting standards, knows that they are based primarily on historical cost accounting and the lower-of-cost-or-market rule. The quality of financial statements prepared according to these standards is expressed in the following information system.

Current Annual Report Evidence			
		GOOD	BAD
State	H	0.6	0.4
	L	0.1	0.9

Good evidence means that a company reports increased profits and adequate working capital. Bad evidence means that the company's profits are down and working capital is low.

Upon reading the current annual report, the investor finds it is Good.

Which act should the investor take now? Show calculations.

c. Assume that the accounting standards are revised to require fair value accounting for major asset classes. Evaluate, in words, the impact of this revision on the quality of the information system.

17. Ajay is a rational, risk-averse investor with $5,000 to invest for one year. He has decided to invest this amount in a high-technology firm, and has narrowed his choice down to either AB Ltd. or XY Ltd. AB is a highly speculative firm with good prospects but no established products. XY is a well-established firm with stable performance. The returns (net of amount invested) for each firm depend on its next year's performance, as follows:

		Return	
		AB Ltd.	XY Ltd.
	High	$1,089	$324
Next Year's Performance			
	Low	$0	$196

For each firm, Ajay assesses prior probabilities of 0.5 for the high- and low-performance states. His utility for his investment return is equal to the square root of the amount of net payoff received.

Required

a. On the basis of his prior probabilities, should Ajay invest in AB Ltd. (a_1) or XY Ltd. (a_2)? Show calculations.

b. XY Ltd. has just released its annual report. Ajay decides to analyze it before investing. His analysis shows "good news" (GN). He consults Al, an expert in financial reporting standards, who is quite critical of the quality of current GAAP. Al advises that based on current GAAP, the information system for firms' annual reports is as follows:

		Financial Statement Information	
		GN	BN
	High	0.6	0.4
Next Year's Performance			
	Low	0.5	0.5

The annual report of AB Ltd. is not due for some time, and nothing else has happened to cause Ajay to change his prior probabilities of AB's next year performance. Which investment should Ajay make now? Show calculations.

c. Concerned by several recent financial reporting failures, the regulatory authorities decide to act. They quickly introduce several new accounting standards, including tighter controls over revenue recognition and greater conservatism in asset valuation. New corporate governance regulations and restrictions on the ability of auditors to engage in non-audit services for their clients are also implemented. Al advises Ajay that the information system for annual reports following these new standards and regulations is as follows:

		Financial Statement Information	
		GN	BN
	High	0.8	0.2
Next Year's Performance			
	Low	0.2	0.8

Instead of the information system in b., Al advises Ajay to use this information system to revise his prior probabilities of XY Ltd.'s next year performance based on the GN in its annual report. AB Ltd. still has not reported and Ajay's prior probabilities of its performance are unchanged. Which act should Ajay now take? Show calculations.

18. The following problem is designed to encourage your consideration of Bayes' theorem. It shows how unaided judgement about probabilities can often be far off the mark. The problem is adapted from one appearing in an article in *The Economist*, "Getting the goat," February 20, 1999, p. 72. This article discusses how people who guess at probabilities can frequently be wrong:

A disease is present in the population at the rate of one person per thousand. A test for the disease becomes available. The drug company that is marketing the test randomly selects you to take the test. You agree, and the test results are positive. If the disease is present, the test always shows a positive result. However, the test has a 5% probability of showing a positive result when in fact the disease is not present. What is the probability that you have the disease?

Notes

1. As mentioned in Section 1.2, decision usefulness was the focus of the 1966 AAA monograph, *A Statement of Basic Accounting Theory* (*ASOBAT*).

2. The Trueblood Commission was a study group of the American Institute of Certified Public Accountants, which, in its 1973 report, *Objectives of Financial Statements*, accepted the decision usefulness approach of *ASOBAT*. The significance of this acceptance is that the AICPA is a professional accounting body, whereas the AAA is an association of academics.

3. For a formal development of the concepts of decision theory, including utility theory, the information system, and the value of information, see Laffont (1989), especially Chapters 1, 2, and 4. See also Demski (1972), especially Chapters 1 to 3. For an excellent intuitive development of the theory, see Raiffa (1968).

4. We define utility here in terms of the net payoff. Conceptually, utility should be defined in terms of the investor's total wealth. However, we opt for the simplest presentation in this example. Note also that the payoff for square root utility must be positive. If a negative (net) payoff is possible, we could work with gross payoffs or assume some other measure of utility, such as the log of the payoff.

5. While the decision-maker's prior and posterior probabilities are subjective, the information system probabilities are objective. As explained below, these objective probabilities are determined by the quality of the financial statements. For the distinction between objective and subjective probabilities, see Example 2.2.

6. The main diagonal probabilities of the information system in Table 3.2 are chosen to be consistent with the concept of conservatism. Recall from our discussion in Section 1.2 that conservatism is defined as the requiring of a higher standard of verification to record gains than to record losses. That is, the firm waits to record gains until there is objective evidence of their realization, but anticipates losses by writing assets down (or liabilities up) if a loss is expected. In Section 1.2, we used the lower-of-cost-or-market rule for inventories as an example of this latter tendency. Now if the firm is in the low state, losses are anticipated, by definition. Similarly, gains are anticipated in the high state. Consequently, since anticipated losses are recognized in the accounts but anticipated gains are not, the financial statements are more likely to show bad news when the firm is in the low state than they are to show good news if the firm is in the good state, assuming reasonable reliability of the loss estimate. This is captured in Table 3.2 by the BN/low-state probability (0.90) being higher than the GN/high state probability (0.80). Historical cost accounting, which is regarded as conservative but reasonably reliable, could produce such a pattern, for example. Loosely speaking, we can say that conservative financial statements are more informative about the bad state than about the good state.

7. Strictly speaking, choosing the act that maximizes expected utility is a *consequence* of rationality, not rationality itself. Savage (1954) defines a set of axioms of rational behaviour under uncertainty with subjective probabilities. If an individual behaves according to these axioms, it can be shown that that individual will prefer one act to another if and only if its expected utility is higher than the other, where the expectation is with respect to the individual's subjective state probabilities. See, for example, Laffont (1989, pp. 14-17) for a demonstration.

8. For a formal development and analysis of risk aversion, see Pratt (1964), or Laffont (1989), Chapter 2.

9. The expected payoff is:

$$(0.7 \times \$200) + (0.3 \times \$1,133.33) = \$480$$

Expected utility is:

$$(0.7 \times \sqrt{200}) + (0.3 \times \sqrt{1,133.33}) = (0.7 \times 14.14) + (0.3 \times 33.66)$$
$$= 9.90 + 10.10$$
$$= 20$$

10. Note that we have suppressed the set of states of nature in this example. That is, Toni assesses payoff probabilities directly, rather than routing them through states. Thus, instead of saying "The probability that firm A is in high-performance state is 0.74 and if A really is in this state the payoff will be \$230," we simply say "The probability of the \$230 payoff is 0.74." This simplification has certain analytical advantages and is frequently used.

11. The risk we are referring to here is *ex ante* risk. That is, the investor is in the process of an investment decision and is looking ahead. This is not to say that if a firm in the portfolio realizes, say, a low return because some unfortunate firm-specific risk factor has happened, the investor will not be angry *ex post*.

12. The expected return of B is:

$$\left(0.6750 \times \frac{92 - 80}{80}\right) + \left(0.3250 \times \frac{76 - 80}{80}\right)$$

$$= (0.6750 \times 0.15) + (0.3250 \times -0.05) = 0.0850$$

(See Example 3.3.)

Cov(B,M) is calculated as:

Returns		Joint Probabilities	
B	**M**		
High	High	$(0.15 - 0.085)(0.10 - 0.085) \times 0.6333 =$	0.0006
High	Low	$(0.15 - 0.085)(0.025 - 0.085) \times 0.0417 =$	−0.0002
Low	High	$(-0.05 - 0.085)(0.10 - 0.085) \times 0.1667 =$	−0.0003
Low	Low	$(-0.05 - 0.085)(0.025 - 0.085) \times 0.1583 =$	0.0013
		Cov(B,M) $=$	0.0014

The joint probability of B high and M high is given by $0.8 \times 0.7917 = 0.6333$. You should now verify the remaining lines.

13. Note that A shares have the same expected return as B shares (0.085), but higher risk since $\beta_A = 2.6667$ while $\beta_B = 1.5556$. Then, it might seem that Toni should buy only B shares. However, this not the case—Toni will still want to hold both A and B shares in her portfolio. If she invests all of her \$200 in B, her expected return is 0.085 and variance of return is 0.0088 (see Note 14), giving expected utility of 0.1612, which is less than expected utility of 0.1626 from holding both A and B. In this case, the benefits of diversification outweigh the fact that B shares by themselves have lower risk.

14. $\text{Var(B)} = \sigma_B^2 = [0.6750 \times (0.15 - 0.0850)^2] + [0.3250 \times (-0.05 - 0.0850)^2]$
    $= 0.0029 + 0.0059$
    $= 0.0088$

15. An alternative to buying the market portfolio is to invest in an index fund. This is a fund that tracks the rate of return on a stock market index. This attains the benefits of full diversification, but with lower transactions costs. However, unless he/she buys every stock in the index, the manager of such a fund would be crucially interested in stocks' expected returns and betas.

Chapter 4

Efficient Securities Markets

FIGURE 4.1 ORGANIZATION OF CHAPTER 4

4.1 Overview

In this chapter, we consider the interaction of investors in a securities market. The theory of efficient securities markets predicts that the security prices that result from this interaction have some appealing properties. In essence, these prices "fully reflect" the collective knowledge and information-processing expertise of investors. The process by which prices do this is quite complex and not fully understood. Nevertheless, the general outlines of the process are easy to see, and we shall concentrate on these.

Securities market efficiency has important implications for financial accounting. One implication is that it leads directly to the concept of *full disclosure*. Efficiency implies that it is the information content of disclosure, not the form of disclosure itself, that is valued by the market. If so, information can be released as easily in notes and supplementary disclosures as in the financial statements proper. The theory also affects how the accountant should think about reporting on firm risk.

In efficient markets theory, accounting is viewed as being in competition with other information sources such as news media, financial analysts, and even market price itself. As a vehicle for informing investors, accounting will survive only if it is relevant, reliable, timely, and cost-effective, relative to other sources.

Efficient securities market theory also alerts us to what is the primary reason for the existence of accounting, namely information asymmetry. When some market participants know more than others, pressure arises to find mechanisms whereby the better informed, who wish to do so, can credibly communicate their information to others, and whereby those with information disadvantage can protect themselves from possible exploitation by the better informed. Insider trading is an example of such exploitation.

We can then think of accounting as a mechanism to enable communication of useful information from inside the firm to outside. In addition to enabling better investor decisions, this has social benefits through improving the operation of securities markets.

As mentioned in Section 1.2, accounting theorists began to realize the importance of securities market efficiency in the late 1960s. Since that time, the theory has guided much accounting research and has had major implications for accounting practice. By and large, financial accounting standard-setting bodies and regulators have accepted the full disclosure and decision usefulness implications of securities market efficiency. To illustrate this, we will examine management discussion and analysis (MD&A), an important disclosure standard, from an informational perspective.

Finally, it should be emphasized that efficiency is a *model* of how a securities market operates. Like any model, it does not capture the full complexity of such a market. Indeed, recent years have seen an increasing number of questions about whether investors are as rational as the model assumes. We will explain some of these questions in Chapter 6, and evaluate their implications for financial accounting. The real question, however, is whether the efficient securities market model captures *enough* of the real market that accountants can be guided by its predictions. In Chapter 6 we conclude that it does. We also conclude that to the extent securities markets are not fully efficient, this further increases the importance of financial reporting. Figure 4.1 outlines the organization of this chapter.

4.2 Efficient Securities Markets

4.2.1 The Meaning of Efficiency

In Chapter 3 we studied the optimal investment decisions of rational investors. Now consider what happens when a large number of rational individuals interact in a securities market. Our interest is in the characteristics of the market prices of securities traded in the market, and how these prices are affected by new information.

If information was free, it is apparent that investors would want to take advantage of it. For instance, under the ideal conditions of Example 2.2, investors would want to know which state of nature was realized, since this affects the future share price and dividends of the firm. By assumption, information is free under ideal conditions since state realization is publicly observable. Thus, all investors would use this information, and the process of arbitrage ensures that the market value of the firm then adjusts to reflect the revised cash flow expectations that result, as illustrated in Example 2.2.

Unfortunately, information is not free under non-ideal conditions. Investors have to decide how much accounting expertise and information to acquire, and then to form their own subjective estimates of firms' future performance. Furthermore, these estimates will need revision as new information comes along. Each investor then faces a cost-benefit tradeoff with respect to how much information to gather. There is a variety of relevant information sources—the financial press, tips from friends and associates, changes in economic conditions, advice from analysts and brokers, etc. We can think of rational investors as continuously revising their subjective state probabilities as such information is received. From our standpoint, of course, a major source of cost-effective information is firms' quarterly and annual reports. Probability revision arising from financial statement information was illustrated in Example 3.1.

At least some investors spend considerable time and money to use these information sources to guide their investment decisions. Such expert investors are called **informed**. Bill Cautious, in Example 3.1, is an example of such an investor.

It should be apparent that informed investors will want to move *quickly* upon receipt of new information. If they do not, other investors will get there first and the market value of the security in question will adjust so as to reduce or eliminate the benefit of the new information.

When a sufficient number of investors behave this way, the market becomes **efficient**. There are several definitions of an efficient securities market. The definition that we shall use here is the **semi-strong form**.

> An **efficient securities market** is one where the prices of securities traded on that market at all times fully reflect all information that is publicly known about those securities.

Three points are particularly noteworthy. First, market prices are efficient with respect to *publicly known* information. Thus, the definition does not rule out the possibility of inside information. Persons who possess inside information, in effect, know more than the market. If they wish to take advantage of their inside information, insiders may be able to earn excess profits on their investments at the expense of outsiders. This is because the market prices of these investments, reflecting only outside or publicly available information, do not incorporate the knowledge that insiders possess. Not every insider is "bad," of course. Some managers may seek ways to credibly communicate their inside information to the market, perhaps to bolster their firms' share price, and their reputations. Nevertheless, investors will still be worried about the *possibility* of insider trading.

A second, related, point is that market efficiency is a *relative* concept. The market is efficient relative to a stock of publicly available information. There is nothing in the definition to suggest that the market is omniscient and that market prices always reflect real underlying firm value. Market prices can certainly be wrong in the presence of inside information, for example.

The definition of efficiency does imply, however, that once new or corrected information becomes publicly available, the market price will quickly adjust to it. This adjustment occurs because rational investors will scramble to revise their beliefs about future performance as soon as new information, from whatever source, becomes known. As a result, the expected returns and risk of their existing portfolios will change and they will enter the market to restore their optimal risk/return tradeoffs. The resulting buy-and-sell decisions will quickly change security prices to fully reflect the new information.

A third implication is that investing is **fair game** if the market is efficient. This means that investors cannot expect to earn excess returns on a security, or portfolio of securities, over and above the normal expected return on that security or portfolio, where the normal expected return allows for risk. One way to establish a normal return benchmark is by means of a capital asset pricing model, as will be illustrated in Section 4.5.

Finally, given market efficiency, a security's market price should fluctuate randomly over time. That is, there should be no serial correlation of share returns. Thus, if a firm reports GN today, its share price should rise to reflect this news the same day. If, in the absence of any further news, its price continues to rise during succeeding days, this is evidence of inefficiency. The reason why price fluctuations are random is that anything about a firm that can be *expected*, such as the seasonal nature of its business, the retirement of its chief executive, or the expected profit on a major new contract, will be fully reflected in its security price by the efficient market as soon as the expectation is formed. That is, the market's expectation of the effect of such events on the value of the firm is on average *unbiased*. The only reason that prices will change is if some relevant, but *unexpected*, information comes along. By definition, unexpected events occur randomly. For example, an accident may change the expected profit on a contract, and share price will quickly respond to reflect this random event. Thus, if we examine the time series formed by the sequence of price changes for a particular security, this series should fluctuate randomly over time according to market efficiency theory. A time series that exhibits such serially uncorrelated behaviour is sometimes called a **random walk**.[1]

4.2.2 How Do Market Prices Fully Reflect All Available Information?

We now consider *how* market prices fully reflect all available information. This process is by no means obvious or transparent. As described previously, rational, informed investors will demand information about securities. However, there is no guarantee that all individuals will react identically to the same information. For example, they may have different prior beliefs. Some may have superior expertise to analyze financial statement information. In a sense, the decision theory model is like an automobile. It provides a vehicle to process information, but nothing guarantees that everyone's driving habits are identical or that they all take the same route to a destination.

As a result, it is quite likely that different investors will react to the same information differently, even though they all proceed rationally. Yet, investors interact in a market, each making buy/sell decisions about various securities. Since the market price of a security is the result of the demand for and supply of the security by investors, how can the market price fully reflect all available information when the individuals making the demand and supply decisions are different?

An interesting insight into this question can be gained from an example in Beaver (1989, p. 150, Table 6-1). The example relates to forecasting the results of football games. The *Chicago Daily News*, during 1966–1968, printed weekly the predictions of each of its sports staff as to who would win that weekend's college football games. Table 4.1, taken from Beaver, summarizes the outcomes of these predictions.

Note the following points from Table 4.1. First, there were a number of different forecasters (15–16) and a large number of forecasts were made (619 over the three years). Second, no one individual forecaster dominated in terms of forecasting ability. The best forecasters in 1966 were well down the list in subsequent years, and vice versa. Third, note the consistent performance of the consensus forecast. The consensus forecast was also published weekly by the *Chicago Daily News* and, for each game, consisted of the team favoured to win by the majority of those forecasting. It is clear that the consensus forecast has a quality that transcends the forecasting ability of the individual forecasters from which the consensus is derived.

TABLE 4.1 FORECASTING OUTCOMES OF FOOTBALL GAMES

	1966	1967	1968
Total forecasters (including consensus)	15	15	16
Total forecasts made per forecaster	180	220	219
Rank of consensus*	1 (tie)	2	2
Median rank of forecasters	8	8	8.5
Rank of best forecasters:			
J. Carmichael (1966)	1 (tie)	8	16
D. Nightingale (1966)	1 (tie)	11	5
A. Biondo (1967)	7	1	6
H. Duck (1968)	8	10	1

*When all three years are combined, the consensus outperforms every one of the forecasters (that is, ranks first).

Source: William H. Beaver, *Financial Reporting: An Accounting Revolution* ® 1981, p. 162, Table 6-1. Reprinted by permission of Prentice-Hall Inc., Upper Saddle River, New Jersey. Data are from "Here's How Our Staff Picks 'Em," *Chicago Daily News*, November 25, 1966 (p. 43), November 24, 1967 (p. 38), and November 29, 1968 (p. 43). Reprinted with special permission from the *Chicago Sun-Times* © 1999.

To translate the example into a securities market context, we can think of the forecasters as investors in a security and the forecasts as their various buy/sell decisions. The consensus forecast is analogous to the market price, since it is a type of average of the various individual forecasting decisions.

The rationale behind the example is not hard to see. It appears that the differences in forecasting ability of individual forecasters tend to cancel out when the consensus is formed, leaving a "market price" that outperforms the ability of any of the market participants.

Of course, just because a consensus forecast outperforms individual forecasters of football games does not by itself mean that the same phenomenon carries over to security prices. Essentially, what is required is that investors' estimates of security values must on average be unbiased. That is, the market does not systematically misinterpret the valuation implications of a stock of information, but rather puts a valuation on securities that is *on average* correct or unbiased. As mentioned, this does not mean that any individual investor will necessarily be correct, but it does mean that *on average* the market uses all available information. This is the meaning of the term "fully reflects" in the definition of securities market efficiency given above.

It should be emphasized that this argument assumes that individual decisions are independent, so that individual differences cancel out in their effect on price. If this is not the case, efficiency arguments break down.[2] Thus, if our football forecasters got together to work out and agree on a consensus forecast, their forecasts would not be independent if they reflected the views of, say, a dominant and persuasive member of the group. Similarly, if a sufficient number of investors display a collective bias in their reaction to new information about a firm, the resulting share price will be biased. For example, a firm may have reported a pattern of increasing earnings. If investors expect future earnings growth to continue simply because of growth in the past, share price momentum may develop. Then, share prices may be "too high," driven by past price increases rather than by rational evaluation of information by independent investors. We will return to this point in Chapter 6, where we discuss whether securities markets are fully efficient.

Theory in Practice 4.1

Prof. Burton Malkiel, in his 1973 book *A Random Walk Down Wall Street*, argued that randomly throwing darts at a list of shares traded on the New York Stock Exchange would earn just as high a return as the returns earned by professional money managers. His argument drew on efficient markets theory, which predicts that, since share price always fully reflects all publicly available information, there are no "bargain" stocks. Then, professional money managers cannot do better than a strategy of random stock choice.

During the 1990s, *The Wall Street Journal* tested this argument. It sponsored a monthly series of contests, whereby four investment analysts each picked a favoured stock. The return on each stock over the next six months was tallied and compared with the return on a randomly chosen stock for the same period. For the first 100 contests, the pros earned an average six-months return of 10.9% while the darts earned a 4.5% return. The average six-months return of the Dow Jones index was 6.8%.

When asked to explain these results, Prof. Malkiel defended the efficiency theory, arguing that the results could be explained by risk differences. He also pointed out that stock market performance during the 1990s was driven by very large firms. But, since there are many more relatively small firms on the market than large firms, the probability that a randomly thrown dart would pick a small firm was quite high. Also, as investors learned of the stocks picked by the pros they would revise upwards their opinions of these stocks. The resulting increase in demand would raise their prices and returns relative to the randomly chosen stocks.

4.2.3 Summary

In an efficient securities market, prices fully reflect all available information, and the price changes on such a market will behave randomly over time. Efficiency is defined relative to a stock of information. If this stock of information is incomplete, say because of inside information, or wrong, security prices will be wrong. Thus, market efficiency does not guarantee that security prices fully reflect real firm value. It does suggest, however, that prices are unbiased relative to publicly available information and will react quickly to new or revised information.

The quantity and quality of publicly available information will be enhanced by prompt and full reporting. However, individual investors may have different prior beliefs and/or may interpret the same information differently. Nevertheless, roughly speaking, we can think of these differences as averaging out, so that the market price has superior quality to the quality of the information processing of the individuals trading on the market. This argument assumes, however, that investors evaluate new information independently.

4.3 Implications of Efficient Securities Markets for Financial Reporting

4.3.1 Implications

An early examination of the reporting implications of efficient securities markets appeared in an article by W. H. Beaver, "What Should Be the FASB's Objectives?" (1973). Here, we will outline Beaver's arguments.

According to Beaver, the first major implication is that accounting policies adopted by firms do not affect their security prices, as long as these policies have no differential cash flow effects, the particular policies used are disclosed, and sufficient information is given so that the reader can convert across different policies. Thus, Beaver would regard accounting disputes such as a firm's choice of amortization method, the accounting for future tax liabilities, and the full-cost versus successful-efforts approach for oil and gas firms as, essentially, "tempests in a teapot." Notice that a firm's choice between different accounting policies in each of these disputes involves only "paper" effects. The policy chosen will affect reported net income, but will not directly affect future cash flows and dividends. For example, an oil and gas firm's proceeds from sale of crude and refined products will not depend directly on whether it uses full-cost or successful-efforts accounting. In particular, the amount of income tax the firm must pay will not be affected by its accounting policy choice in any of these three disputed areas since the tax department has its own way of calculating expenses and income in each area, independent of how the firm accounts for them on its books. If investors are interested in future cash flows and dividends and their impact on security returns, and if choosing between accounting policies does not directly influence these variables, the firm's choice between accounting policies should not matter.

Thus, the efficient market argument is that as long as firms disclose their selected policy, and any additional information needed to convert from one method to another, investors are able to make the necessary calculations to see through to the resulting differences in reported net income. That is, the market can see through to the ultimate cash flow and dividend implications regardless of which accounting policy is actually used for reporting. Thus, the efficient market is not "fooled" by differing accounting policies when comparing different firms' securities. This suggests that management should not care about which particular accounting policies they use as long as those policies have no direct cash flow effects.

We thus see that full disclosure extends to disclosure of the firm's accounting policies. This is recognized by standard setters. For example, the *CICA Handbook*, paragraph 1505.04, states:

> *A clear and concise description of the significant accounting policies of an enterprise should be included as an integral part of the financial statements.*

A second implication follows—namely, efficient securities markets go hand in hand with full disclosure. If a firm's management possesses relevant information about the firm and if this can be disclosed at little or no cost, management should then disclose this information on a timely basis unless it is certain that the information is already known to investors from other sources. More generally, management should develop and report information about the firm as long as the benefits to investors exceed the costs. The reasons are twofold. First, market efficiency implies that investors will use all available, relevant information as they strive to improve their predictions of future returns, so that additional information will not be wasted. Second, the more information a firm discloses about itself, the greater is investors' confidence in the securities market, since there is less inside information to worry about.

Third, market efficiency implies that firms should not be overly concerned about the naive investor—that is, financial statement information need not be presented in a manner so simple that everyone can understand it. The reasoning, from Fama (1970), is that if *enough* investors understand the disclosed information, the market price of a firm's shares is the same as it would be if all investors understood it. This is because informed investors will engage in buy/sell decisions on the basis of the disclosed information, moving the market price towards its efficient level. Also, naive investors can hire their own experts, such as financial analysts or investment fund managers, to interpret the information for them, or can mimic the buy/sell decisions of informed investors. As a result, any information advantage that informed investors have is quickly dissipated. In other words, naive investors can *trust* the efficient market to price securities so that they always reflect all that is publicly known about the firms that have issued them, even though these investors may not have complete knowledge and understanding themselves. This is referred to as investors being **price-protected** by the efficient market.

Since Beaver's paper, accountants have recognized that there is a variety of reasons for trading securities. For example, some investors may make a rational decision to rely on market price as a good indicator of future payoffs, rather than incur the costs of becoming informed. Others may trade for a variety of non-portfolio reasons—perhaps an unexpected need for cash has arisen. Consequently, "naive" may not be the best word to describe uninformed investors. This is considered further in Section 4.4.

A final implication is that accountants are in competition with other providers of information, such as financial analysts, media, disclosures by company officials, and so on. That is, belief revision is a continuous process, as pointed out in Section 3.3.3. Thus, if accountants do not provide useful, cost-effective information, the role of the accounting function will decline over time as other information sources take over—accountants have no *inherent* right to survive in the competitive marketplace for information. However, survival will be more likely if accountants recognize that the ultimate responsibility of their profession is to society. This longer run point of view is encouraged by standards that promote useful information, by penalties for individuals who abuse public trust for short-term gain, and by encouragement of ethical behaviour.

Beaver's paper was published in 1973. Consequently, it predates SFAC 1 (issued in 1978) and SFAC 2 (1980) by several years. However, it provides a good example of the early enthusiasm of accounting theorists for efficient securities markets. It also highlights the type of disclosure-oriented thinking that led to the formal statement of the usefulness criterion by the FASB in SFAC 1.

4.3.2 Summary

Beaver argues that securities market efficiency has several implications for financial reporting. First, managers and accountants should not be concerned about which accounting policies firms use unless different accounting policies have direct cash flow effects. Many accounting policy alternatives, about which accountants have argued long and hard, do not have such cash flow effects. Second, firms should disclose as much information about themselves as is cost-effective—the fact of disclosure and not the form it takes is what is important. The efficient market will prefer the least costly form of disclosure, other things equal. One can argue, however, that financial statements are a cost-effective disclosure medium. Third, firms need not be concerned about the naive investor when choosing disclosure policies and formats. Such persons are price-protected, because efficient security prices fully reflect all that is publicly known about those securities. Furthermore, there is a variety of mediums, such as financial analysts and investment funds, whereby investors can take advantage of sophisticated information without needing to fully understand it themselves. Finally, the efficient market is interested in useful information from any source, not just accounting reports.

4.4   The Informativeness of Price

4.4.1 A Logical Inconsistency

The careful reader may have noticed an inconsistency in our discussion of efficient securities markets to this point. Recall that efficiency implies that the market price of a security at all times fully reflects all that is publicly known about that security. What is it that drives market price to have this "fully reflects" characteristic? It is the actions of informed investors who are always striving to obtain and process information so as to make good buy/sell decisions.

However, by the definition of market efficiency, all available information is already reflected in market price. That is, the price is **fully informative**.[3] Since information acquisition is costly, and investors could not expect to beat the market when the market price already reflects all publicly known information, investors would simply stop gathering information and rely on market price as the best indicator of future security returns. For example, a simple decision rule would be to buy and hold a diversified investment portfolio, changing its composition only if the risk/return tradeoff of the portfolio gets out of line.

The logical inconsistency, then, is that if prices fully reflect available information, there is no motivation for investors to acquire information; hence, prices will not fully reflect available information. In terms of football forecasting, the forecasters would stop putting effort into their forecasts because they can't beat the consensus forecast, but then the consensus forecast would lose its superior forecasting ability. Technically speaking, the problem here is that stable equilibrium prices do not exist, as shown by Grossman (1976).

This has potentially serious implications for accounting theory, since a lack of equilibrium makes it problematic whether financial statement information is useful to investors. Also, it is contrary to what we observe. SFAC 1 (Section 3.8) certainly implies that investors find financial reporting useful, for example.

However, there is an easy way out of the inconsistency. This is to recognize that there are other sources of demand and supply for securities than the buy/sell decisions of rational informed investors. For example, people may buy or sell securities for a variety of unpredictable reasons—they may decide to retire early, they may need money to pay gambling debts, they may have received a "hot tip," etc. Such persons are called **liquidity traders** or **noise traders**. Their buy/sell decisions will affect a security's market price, but the decisions come at random—they are not based on a rational evaluation of information.

To illustrate how market price is affected by the presence of noise trading, suppose that a rational investor observes a security's price to be higher than he/she had expected based on all the information currently possessed by that investor. Now, our investor knows that other rational investors also have their own information about the security and that this information may well be more favourable. These other investors may be buying and driving up the security's price. As a result, our investor is inclined to raise his/her expectation of the security's value. While the investor does not know what information other investors have, it is rational to believe that the information is favourable and this may be what is driving up the security's price.

However, our investor also knows that the higher-than-expected security price may simply be due to noise trading. Perhaps someone has temporarily invested a large cash windfall in a randomly chosen portfolio of securities, including the security in question. If so, our investor would *not* want to increase his/her expectation of the security's value. Since each scenario is possible, the investor will increase his/her expectation of the security's value, but to an amount *less than* the security's current market price. That is, the rational investor responds by putting some weight on each possibility. In effect, the current share price conveys *some* information about share value but not *all* information as in the fully informative case.

For our purposes, an important point to note is that investors now have an incentive to update their beliefs by gathering more information. If they can find out which explanation is the correct one, this can quickly be turned into a profitable investment opportunity. For example, if further investigation reveals that the firm is undervalued, the investor will buy. If, instead, investigation reveals that the share price is temporarily high due to noise trading, the investor will sell short. The efforts of investors to do this will then drive share price towards its efficient value. Presumably, at least some of this additional information will come from analysis of financial statements.

When investors behave as just described, they are said to have **rational expectations**. Security prices are said to be **partially informative** in the presence of noise trading and rational expectations. Note that market prices are still efficient in the presence of noise trading, but in an *expected value* sense, since noise has expectation zero. That is, the investor expects that a security's market price fully reflects all publicly available information, but further investigation may reveal that this is not the case.

The extent to which investors gather additional information depends on a number of factors, such as how informative price is, the quality of financial statement information, and the costs of analysis and interpretation. These factors lead to empirical predictions about how security market prices respond to financial statement information. For example, we might expect that price will be more informative for large firms, since they are more "in the news" than small firms, hence their market price will incorporate considerable information. This reduces the ability of financial statements to add to what is already known about such firms. Thus, we would predict that security prices respond less to financial statement information for large firms than for small firms.

Furthermore, note that firm management has an incentive to cater to the desire of investors to ferret out information. For example, management may have inside information that leads it to believe the firm is undervalued. To correct this, management may engage in **voluntary disclosure**, that is, disclosure of information beyond the minimum requirement of GAAP and other reporting standards. Such disclosure can have credibility, even if unaudited, since legal liability imposes discipline on managers' reporting decisions. Unfortunately, there are limitations on voluntary disclosure, not only because the legal system may be unable to completely enforce credibility but because management will not want to reveal information that would give away competitive advantage.

However, voluntary disclosure is much more complex and subtle than simply disclosing information. Management can signal inside information by its choice of accounting policies and, indeed, by the nature and extent of voluntary disclosure itself. For example, instead of directly revealing good news about a secret research program, a firm that feels it is undervalued could choose very conservative accounting policies. This reveals inside information about the firm's future performance since management would not likely adopt conservative policies unless it felt that future cash flows and earnings would be high enough to absorb the resulting conservative "hit." Realizing this, rational investors would respond to these conservative policies by bidding up the firm's share price. This means that there are potential rewards to investors, and analysts, for careful and complete analyses of firms' annual reports. Such analyses may identify mispricing and can quickly be turned into profitable investment decisions.

Also, an increase in the quality of financial statement information, other things equal, should lead investors to increase their utilization of financial statement information relative to price. For example, the requirement by securities commissions that firms include **management discussion and analysis (MD&A)** in their annual reports may increase market price reactions to annual reports. Annual reports should have higher information content with MD&A than without it. MD&A is discussed in Section 4.8.

We conclude that the term "fully reflects" in the efficient securities market definition has to be interpreted with care. It does not mean that security prices are fully informative with respect to available information at all points in time. Indeed, if it did, this would have adverse implications for the usefulness of financial statements. Rather, the term should be interpreted as reflecting a tension between the level of informativeness allowed by noise and liquidity traders, and the ability of investors and analysts to identify mispriced securities through analysis of the financial statements proper, supplementary disclosures, accounting policy choice, the nature and extent of voluntary disclosure, and, indeed, of all other available information. With this interpretation in mind, it is important to point out that the implications of security market efficiency as outlined by Beaver in Section 4.3 continue to apply. In particular, the importance of full disclosure remains.

4.4.2 Summary

While the ability of a market price to *average out* individual differences in information processing, as we saw in the football forecasting example, is on the right track, the process of price formation in securities markets is much more complex than this. Through consideration of ways that rational investors can become more informed by careful analysis of managers' disclosure decisions, and by allowing for other sources of demand and supply for securities than from rational, informed investors, accountants are beginning to understand the role of information in price. The presence of non-rational traders does not necessarily mean that the efficient securities market concept that share prices "fully reflect" information is invalid, but rather that this concept must be interpreted with care.

Improved understanding of the process of price formation leads to empirical predictions of how security prices respond to accounting information and, ultimately, enables accountants to prepare more useful financial statements.

4.5 A Capital Asset Pricing Model

We are now in a position to formalize the relationship between the efficient market price of a security, its risk, and the expected rate of return on a security. We shall do so by means of the well-known Sharpe-Lintner capital asset pricing model (CAPM) (Sharpe, 1964; Lintner, 1965).

First, we need some preliminaries. Define R_{jt}, the net rate of return on the shares of firm j for time period t, as:

$$R_{jt} = \frac{P_{jt} + D_{jt} - P_{j,t-1}}{P_{j,t-1}} = \frac{P_{jt} + D_{jt}}{P_{j,t-1}} - 1 \tag{4.1}$$

where:

P_{jt} is the market price of firm j's shares at the end of period t

D_{jt} is dividends paid by firm j during period t

$P_{j,t-1}$ is the market price of firm j's shares at the beginning of period t

This is the return concept used in Examples 3.1, 3.2 and 3.3. It is a *net* rate of return given that the opening market price is subtracted in the numerator. We can also define a *gross rate of return* as $1 + R_{jt}$, where:

$$1 + R_{jt} = \frac{P_{jt} + D_{jt}}{P_{j,t-1}}$$

Since the only difference between the two rates of return concepts is the 1, we can use them interchangeably. In fact, to conform to common practice, we will usually refer to both net and gross rates of return as simply **returns**.

We can think of returns as either *ex post* or *ex ante*. *Ex post*, we are at the end of period t and looking back to calculate the return actually realized during the period, as in Equation 4.1. Alternatively, we can stand at the beginning of period t (i.e., at time t-1) and think of an *ex ante* or expected return as:

$$E(R_{jt}) = \frac{E(P_{jt} + D_{jt})}{P_{j,t-1}} - 1 \tag{4.2}$$

That is, expected return for period t is based on the expected price at the end of the period plus any dividends expected during the period, divided by the current price.

Now, consider an economy with a large number of rational, risk-averse investors. Assume that there is a risk-free asset in the economy, with return R_f. Assume also that security markets are efficient and transaction costs are zero. Then, the Sharpe-Lintner CAPM shows that:

$$E(R_{jt}) = R_f(1 - \beta_j) + \beta_j E(R_{Mt}) \tag{4.3}$$

where β_j is the beta of share j and R_{Mt} is the return on the market portfolio for period t.

Note that the model is in terms of the market's *expected* returns. Equation 4.3 states that at the beginning of period t the expected return for the period equals a constant $R_f(1 - \beta_j)$ plus another constant β_j times the expected return on the market portfolio.

Strictly speaking, markets do not have expectations—individuals do. One way to think of the market's expectations is that the price of a share behaves *as if* the market holds a certain expectation about its future performance. More fundamentally, the market price of a share includes a sort of average of the expectations of all informed investors, much like the consensus forecast in the Beaver football example (Section 4.2.2) includes an average expectation of the forecasters.

It is not difficult to see the intuition of the model. Since rational investors will fully diversify when transactions costs are zero, the only risk measure in the formula is β_j. Firm-specific risk does not affect share price because it disappears in fully diversified portfolios. Also, note that the higher is β_j the higher is expected return, other things equal. This is consistent with risk aversion, since risk-averse investors will require a higher expected return to compensate for higher risk.

Note also the role of the current market price $P_{j,t-1}$ in the model. The return demanded by the market on share j for period t, that is, $E(R_{jt})$ in Equation 4.3, is a function only of R_f, R_{Mt}, and β_j. The current market price does not appear. However, in Equation 4.2, given expected end-of-period price P_{jt} and dividends D_{jt}, we see that $P_{j,t-1}$ in the denominator will adjust so that the right-hand side of Equation 4.2 equals $E(R_{jt})$. That is, a share's current price will adjust so that its expected return equals the return demanded by the market for that share as given by Equation 4.3.

We can now see how new information affects firm j's share price. Suppose that at time t-1 (now) some new firm-specific information comes along that raises investors' expectations of P_{jt} (and possibly also of D_{jt}), without affecting R_f, β_j or $E(R_{Mt})$. This will throw Equation 4.2 out of balance, since $E(R_{jt})$ from Equation 4.3 does not change. Thus, $P_{j,t-1}$, the current price, must rise to restore equality. This, of course, is consistent with market efficiency, which states that the market price of a security will react immediately to new information.

For our purposes, there are three main uses for the CAPM formula. First, it brings out clearly how share prices depend on investors' expectations of future share price and dividends. If these expectations change (the numerator of Equation 4.2), current price $P_{j,t-1}$ (the denominator) will immediately change to reflect these new expectations. For a given change in expectations, and given R_f and $E(R_{Mt})$, the amount of the change in current price depends only on the share's beta. To put this another way, the larger the change in expectations, the larger the change in price, other things equal.

Second, by reverting to an *ex post* view of returns, the CAPM provides us with a way of separating the realized return on a share into expected and unexpected components. To see this, consider the following version of the model, where we are now at the end of period t and looking back:

$$R_{jt} = \alpha_j + \beta_j R_{Mt} + \epsilon_{jt} \tag{4.4}$$

This version of CAPM is called the **market model**. It states that the realized return R_{jt} for the period is the sum of the beginning-of-period *expected* return ($\alpha_j + \beta_j R_{Mt}$) and the *unexpected* or **abnormal**[4] return ϵ_{jt}. The expected return comes from the CAPM, with $\alpha_j = R_f(1 - \beta_j)$. The ϵ_{jt} captures the impact on R_{jt} of all those events during period t that were not expected at the beginning of the period. By definition in an efficient market, $E(\epsilon_{jt}) = 0$, since new information comes along randomly. But, in any period t the *realized* value of ϵ_{jt} need not be zero. Its realized value will depend on just what information did come along. Thus, the market model enables an *ex post* separation of the realized return R_{jt} into expected ($\alpha_j + \beta_j R_{Mt}$) and unexpected or abnormal (ϵ_{jt}) components.

Third, the market model provides a convenient way for researchers and analysts to estimate a stock's beta. Notice that the market model is presented in the form of a regression equation. By obtaining past data on R_{jt} and R_{Mt}, the coefficients of the regression model can be estimated by least-squares regression. If we assume that the market is able to form unbiased expectations of R_{Mt} (so that R_{Mt} is a good proxy for $E(R_{Mt})$, which is unobservable), and if we assume that β_j is stationary over time, then the coefficient of R_{Mt} from least-squares regression is a good estimate[5] of β_j. Furthermore, the reasonableness of the estimation can be checked by comparing the estimated coefficient α_j with $(1 - \beta_j)R_f$—the two should be the same.

As we will see in Chapter 5, much empirical research in accounting has required an accurate estimate of beta, and we will return to its estimation in Section 7.5.1. For now, it is important to realize that the CAPM provides an important and useful way to model the market's expectation of a share's returns, and that the model depends crucially on securities market efficiency. Also, it shows clearly how new information affects current share price.

For later reference, it should be noted that the CAPM and market model do not consider information asymmetry. For example, outside investors face the risk that insiders may profit at their expense, and this risk cannot be diversified away. To compensate for the additional risk, called **estimation risk**, investors will demand higher expected return than given by the CAPM. Thus, while it is a good place to start, the CAPM may understate cost of capital for many firms. As we point out in the next section, estimation risk is important for accountants, since it may be reduced by full and timely disclosure.

4.6 Information Asymmetry

4.6.1 A Closer Look at Information Asymmetry

In this section, we take a closer look at the notion of "publicly available" information in the efficient securities market definition. This leads directly to what is undoubtedly the most important concept of financial accounting theory—*information asymmetry*. Frequently, one type of participant in the market (sellers, for example) will know something about the asset being traded that another type of participant (buyers) does not know. When this situation exists, the market is said to be characterized by information asymmetry. As mentioned in Section 1.6, there are two major types of information asymmetry—adverse selection and moral hazard. We now consider these in greater detail.

First, note that information asymmetry is an important reason for market incompleteness (Section 2.6). That is, in extreme cases, a market may collapse, or fail to develop in the first place, as a result of information asymmetry. To illustrate, consider the market for insurance policies. You may wish to buy insurance against the possibility of failing to attain your university or college degree or professional accounting designation. You would be better off with such a policy, at least if the cost was fair. Serious illness or accident may prevent your completion of the course of studies, and you could eliminate this risk if you had a policy that reimbursed you for your loss of the present value of the increased future income that would follow the attainment of your degree or designation. However, issuance of such a policy would create severe difficulties for the insurance company. One difficulty is that people who were sick would flock to enroll in educational programs (called an **adverse selection** problem, because people whose health is adverse to the insurance company's best interests self-select themselves to buy insurance). Then, when their illness led to their failure, they could collect on their policies and still enjoy the monetary fruits of a degree.

Another problem is that if you owned such a policy, you would probably shirk your studies, even if you were perfectly healthy. Why put in all the time and effort to complete your course of studies when, by merely failing, you could receive equivalent compensation from your insurance policy? This is called a **moral hazard** problem, for you are tempted to cheat the company by shirking your studies. Note that requiring a medical certificate would not be of much use here, because of the difficulty in establishing that it was the illness that led to the failure.

As a result, no insurance company would sell you a policy that would reimburse you for your full income loss if you failed to attain your degree. The problem is information asymmetry. You have a major information advantage over the company, because the company can only observe whether you fail, not whether your illness, accident, or shirking caused you to fail.

Faced with information disadvantages of this magnitude, the company responds by not writing insurance policies of the type described. That is, no market develops.

In other cases, information asymmetry is not so severe as to prevent the market from developing. Nevertheless, the market does not work as well as it might. This situation was studied by Akerlof (1970). An example of a market characterized by information asymmetry is the used car market. The owner of a car will know more about its true condition, and hence its future stream of benefits, than would a potential buyer. This creates an adverse selection problem, since the owner may try to take advantage of this inside information by bringing a "lemon" to market, hoping to get more than it is worth from an unsuspecting buyer. However, buyers will be aware of this temptation and, since they don't have the information to distinguish between lemons and good cars, will lower the price they are willing to pay for any used car. As a result, many cars—the good ones—will have a market value that is less than the real value of their future stream of benefits. The arbitrage effect, whereby cars of similar service potential must sell for similar prices, operates less effectively when it is difficult to know exactly what the service potential of a used car is. Thus, owners of good cars are less likely to bring them to market. In other words, the market for used cars does not work as well as it might—purchasers cannot always buy a car of the exact type and condition they want.

It is interesting to note the variety of devices that markets use to reduce the effects of information asymmetry. Thus, used car markets are characterized by guarantees, safety certificates, test drives, dealers who attempt to establish a good reputation, and so on.

Insurance markets are characterized by medical examinations for life and health insurance, co-insurance and deductible clauses for fire insurance, premium reductions for good driving records, and so on. However, because they are costly, these devices do not completely eliminate the problem. Nevertheless, they may be sufficiently effective to at least allow the market to operate, albeit not as well as it would in the absence of information asymmetry.

One of the reasons why information asymmetry is of such importance to accounting theory is that *securities markets* are subject to information asymmetry problems, such as insider information and insider trading. Even if security market prices fully reflect all publicly available information, it is still likely that insiders know more than outsiders about the true state of the firm. If so, they may take advantage of their information to earn excess profits by biasing, delaying, or withholding its public release while they buy or sell shares on the basis of this information. This is another example of the adverse selection problem, since insiders will be attracted by these opportunities, which are *adverse* to the interests of investors. Of course, investors will be aware of this estimation risk and will lower the amounts that they would otherwise be willing to pay for all shares, to reflect their expected losses at the hands of insiders. Just like the used car market, the efficient securities market does not work as well as it might.

The collapse of Enron and WorldCom outlined in Section 1.2 is an example of the adverse effects of information asymmetry on securities markets. As a result of these and other financial reporting failures, investors realized that the shares of many firms were lemons. As a result, they lost confidence in the financial statements of all firms. A major fall in share prices took place as investors withdrew from the market.

It may seem strange that markets can be efficient but yet investor confidence can collapse. However, we can reconcile these seemingly conflicting notions by introducing the concept of the **fundamental value** of a share:

> The **fundamental value** of a share is the value it would have in an efficient market if there is no inside information. That is, all information about the share is publicly available.

Obviously, prior to their collapse, the market prices of Enron and WorldCom shares did not reflect fundamental value, even though the market may have been efficient relative to the information about these firms that *was* publicly available. As a result of these and other such episodes, investors realized that many other firms' shares may have the same problem, leading to a general loss of confidence.

Of course, fundamental value is a theoretical ideal. We would not expect that inside information can be completely eliminated. It may not be cost effective for a firm to directly reveal strategic information about research in process or plans for a takeover bid, for example.

The steps taken by governments and accounting bodies to restore public confidence following the Enron and WorldCom collapses, outlined in Section 1.2, can be regarded as attempts to reduce adverse selection. Many of these steps involve improving policies of full disclosure, to expand the set of information that is publicly available and reduce biases. Also, timeliness of reporting will reduce the ability of insiders to profit from their information advantage. Thus, we can think of financial reporting as a device to control the adverse selection problem, thereby reducing estimation risk. This improves the operation of securities markets and reduces incompleteness.

4.6.2 Summary

Under ideal conditions, the firm's market value fully reflects *all* information. That is, price equals fundamental value. When conditions are not ideal, market value fully reflects all *publicly available* information, if security markets are efficient.

The difference between these two information sets includes **inside information**. The ability of insiders to profit from their information advantage is an example of the adverse selection problem. Full and timely disclosure will reduce this problem, thereby improving the working of securities markets. Since reporting of all inside information is too costly, however, the adverse selection problem will still be present.

4.7 The Social Significance of Securities Markets That Work Well

In a capitalist economy, securities markets are the primary vehicle whereby capital is raised and allocated to competing investment needs. Consequently, it is socially desirable that these markets work well in the sense that security prices provide correct values to guide the flow of investment funds. For example, a firm that has high-expected-value capital projects will be encouraged to invest in them if it receives a high price for its securities, and investment should be discouraged in firms that do not have high-expected-value capital projects. This will happen to the extent that security prices reflect fundamental value. Of course, this is what society wants, since investment capital is in scarce supply. Social welfare will be enhanced if scarce capital goes to the most productive alternatives.

However, as mentioned, security prices will not fully reflect fundamental value due to the costs of eliminating inside information. Investors will be aware of the estimation risk resulting from adverse selection and insider trading. Then, a "lemons" phenomenon comes into play. Investors recognize that the market is not a "level playing field" and either withdraw from the market or lower the amount they are willing to pay for *any* security. Then, firms with high-quality investment projects will not receive a high price for their securities, and the market is not working as well as it should. A related problem is that if too many investors withdraw, the market becomes **thin** or, equivalently, it loses **depth**. Then, potential investors may not be able to buy or sell all they want of a security at the market price, which further hampers investment.

Empirical evidence on the importance of markets that work well for efficient capital allocation is provided by Wurgler (2000). He estimates the efficiency of capital allocation for 65 countries over the years 1963–1995 and finds that countries with more firm-specific information incorporated into share prices (relative to industry- and economy-wide information, which affects all share prices) enjoy greater capital allocation efficiency.[6] Note that more firm-specific information incorporated into share prices is just another way of saying that the market is working better, or, equivalently, that there is less inside information.

Of course, developed capitalist economies have a variety of mechanisms for promoting the operation of securities markets. One such approach is to impose **penalties** on the market. Thus, we witness government securities commissions such as the Ontario Securities Commission (OSC) in Ontario and the SEC in the United States. These agencies create and enforce regulations to, for example, control insider trading and promote prompt disclosure of significant events, with penalties for violation.

However, the efficient market can provide **incentives** for the release of inside information even in the absence of penalties for abuse. A variety of mechanisms are available whereby firms with high-quality investment projects can credibly communicate this to the market, thereby enhancing reputation and the price they obtain for their securities. **Signalling** is one such mechanism—for example, insiders may retain a substantial equity position in new projects, thereby signalling to the market their beliefs in their high-quality project. The higher the project quality, the greater the incentive to signal. Signals will be considered in greater detail in Chapter 12.

For present purposes, a related incentive mechanism is full disclosure. Firms have an incentive to engage in full disclosure in their financial reports.[7] If such disclosures are credible, investors will remove them from the "lemons" category and will, as a result, be willing to pay higher prices for their securities than they otherwise would.

Obviously, penalty-based and incentive-based mechanisms are not mutually exclusive—we witness both in our economy. The penalty approach is like a "stick" and requires regulation to enforce it. The need for regulation will be reduced, however, to the extent that "carrots" are available to enable firms that wish to do so to credibly reveal their information, thereby enabling them to receive a fair price for their securities.

We may conclude that the social benefits of securities markets that work reasonably well will be attained if the following two conditions are met:

- All useful information is in the public domain, at least up to the ability of penalties and incentives to cost-effectively motivate the release of inside information.

- Securities market prices are efficient relative to this information.

4.8   An Example of Full Disclosure

4.8.1 Introduction

In this section, we consider an important full disclosure accounting standard. Specifically, we outline and illustrate **management discussion and analysis (MD&A)**. This is a standard that requires firms to provide a narrative explanation of company performance, financial condition, and future prospects. The intent is to assist investors to interpret the firm's financial statements.

While of interest in its own right, this standard also provides an important illustration of how the amount of useful information in the public domain can be increased. The MD&A standard lies between the carrot-and-stick approaches to information release. While all public companies have to provide MD&A, there is some latitude in the extent to which they meet the letter of its disclosure requirements. For example, while some firms may provide what is mainly a rehash of information already available from the financial statements, others may go beyond the minimum requirements by releasing inside information about, for example, future business strategies, plans, and prospects.

4.8.2 Management Discussion and Analysis

Objectives of MD&A   Our coverage of MD&A is based on the requirements of National Instrument NI 51-102 of the OSC, effective in 2004. Similar requirements are laid down in other jurisdictions, such as that of the SEC in the United States. Also, through the Canadian Securities Administrators (a forum of 13 provincial and territorial securities regulators), harmonized MD&A regulations now apply across Canada.

MD&A is a narrative explanation, through the eyes of management, of company performance, financial condition, and future prospects. It is to be written in language that investors are able to understand. Its objectives include:

- To help current and prospective investors understand the financial statements.
- To discuss information not fully reflected in the financial statements.
- To discuss important trends and risks.
- To provide information about the quality, and potential variability, of earnings and cash flow, to help investors determine if past performance is indicative of future performance.

To implement these objectives, specific disclosure requirements include:

- Discuss overall firm performance, and revenue, asset, and liability items. Explain factors that have caused period-to-period variations, such as acquisitions and dispositions. Indicate with which set of accounting principles the financial statements are consistent.
- Discuss the firm's ability to meet short- and long-term liquidity needs.
- Discuss important commitments and off-balance-sheet arrangements.
- Discuss changes in accounting policies.
- Explain and discuss trends, risks and uncertainties that are expected to affect future performance. Describe how financial instruments are used to manage risks. Explain needed changes to forward-looking information previously provided that is now known to be in error because of subsequent developments.

Several aspects of these requirements should be noted:

- The MD&A standard has a clear forward-looking orientation. For example, known trends affecting future performance should be discussed. This orientation is consistent with the FASB's conceptual framework, outlined in Section 3.8, which asserts investors' interests in assessing prospective cash receipts from their investments.
- The concept of an information system is implicit in the MD&A standard. As discussed in Section 3.3.2, the information system specifies the relationship between current financial statement evidence and future firm performance. This is recognized in the standard's objective of helping investors to determine if past firm performance is indicative of future performance.
- Also consistent with its future orientation, the standard tilts towards relevance in the relevance/reliability tradeoff. That is, there is less need to wait until objective evidence is available than in the financial statements. However, MD&A does not completely ignore reliability considerations. For example, NI 51-102 requires that the firm's MD&A be approved by its board of directors. Presumably, this is to reduce the likelihood of manager manipulation and bias. Also, reminiscent of the adjustments of previous estimates in RRA, the firm is required to discuss any needed changes to for-

ward-looking information provided in previous MD&A that is now known to be in error as a result of further developments. This requirement helps with reliability since the manager knows that errors or biases in estimates will have to be explained later.

- The MD&A standard seems reasonably consistent with the theories of rational investor decision-making and market efficiency. For example, it emphasizes full disclosure and recognizes that investors need forward-looking information and information about risk. Indeed, the standard can be regarded as an attempt to make securities markets work better by providing a vehicle for management to disclose inside information. This consistency with theory is not complete, however. For example, the emphasis is on firm-specific risk disclosure. Yet, the theory of investment suggests that much of this risk can be diversified away. Also, MD&A is to be written in plain language. While this is difficult to disagree with, it is not consistent with the argument of Beaver (Section 4.3) that firms need not be too concerned about the naïve investor, due to the price protection characteristic of efficient market prices.

With this background in mind, we now illustrate some of these considerations by means of the MD&A of a large Canadian corporation.

An Example of MD&A Disclosure Exhibit 4.1 reproduces portions of the MD&A and related disclosures in the 2003 *Annual Report* of Canadian Tire Corporation, Limited, including all of its risk management discussion. Canadian Tire won the Award of Excellence in Annual Reporting of the 2003 CICA Corporate Reporting Awards as well as the award for the best overall annual report for its industry category.

Canadian Tire's MD&A begins with an overview of the business, then describes its strategic plan, including the performance indicators it uses to monitor its financial goals. Recent performance relative to these goals is also disclosed. The firm also provides extensive discussion of current operations and financial conditions, but this is not reproduced here.

Canadian Tire discusses the performance and prospects of its major divisions, including its retail division reproduced in the exhibit. The discussion covers market trends, how Canadian Tire positions itself in its markets, and market opportunities. Note, in particular, its focus on the scope for growth.

With respect to its discussion of risk management, note the variety of risks Canadian Tire faces. These range from the risk to its profitability resulting from the actions of competitors, to the seasonal nature of its business, to credit risks arising from failure of contracting parties to fulfil their obligations, to price risks such as changes in foreign exchange rates and interest rates. The steps that Canadian Tire takes to control these risks, such as its hedging policies, and credit granting and collection policies, are outlined. There is also a candid admission that some risks cannot be controlled, such as the weather, and credit risk resulting from economic downturns.

Discussion MD&A represents a major step taken by securities commissions to set standards that go beyond the requirements of GAAP. The reason why securities commissions become involved in MD&A disclosure regulation, presumably, is that the accounting recommendations of the *CICA Handbook* relate to the financial statements, whereas the concern of the OSC and other securities regulators is with the disclosures by management contained elsewhere in the annual report, to which the *CICA Handbook* does not apply.

Exhibit 4.1 MD&A Extracts, from 2003 Annual Report, Canadian Tire Corporation, Limited

1. Corporate Overview

1.1 Overview of the business

Canadian Tire is a growing, innovative network of interrelated businesses that includes:

> Canadian Tire Retail (CTR);

> Canadian Tire Petroleum (Petroleum);

> Mark's Work Wearhouse (Mark's); and

> Canadian Tire Financial Services (Financial Services).

CTR is Canada's leading hard goods retailer with a network of Canadian Tire stores that are operated by Associate Dealers, as well as a chain of specialty automotive hard parts stores that are run by franchisees and operate under the name of PartSource. Petroleum is Canada's largest independent retailer of gasoline with an agent-run chain of gas bars, convenience stores and kiosks, car washes and propane stations. Mark's is one of Canada's largest specialty footwear and apparel retailers, specializing in industrial work wear and business casual apparel with corporate and franchise stores operating under the Mark's Work Wearhouse and Work World banners, and L'Équipeur in the province of Quebec. Financial Services markets the Canadian Tire retail card, *Options* MasterCard, insurance products, commercial credit cards, various warranties and an emergency roadside assistance service called Canadian Tire Auto Club. Canadian Tire Bank, a federally regulated bank that forms part of Financial Services, manages and finances credit card accounts related to customers' use of their *Options* MasterCards and Canadian Tire retail cards.

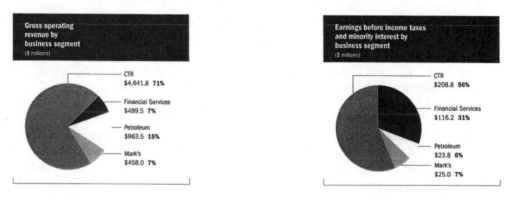

Gross operating revenue by business segment ($ millions)
- CTR $4,641.8 **71%**
- Financial Services $489.5 **7%**
- Petroleum $963.5 **15%**
- Mark's $458.0 **7%**

Earnings before income taxes and minority interest by business segment ($ millions)
- CTR $208.8 **56%**
- Financial Services $116.2 **31%**
- Petroleum $23.8 **6%**
- Mark's $25.0 **7%**

1.2 Strategic Plan objective

Canadian Tire's Strategic Plan (the Plan) was introduced in 2001 as a roadmap for the Company's growth over the 2001 to 2005 Plan period. The Plan's primary objective was, and continues to be, to achieve long-term top-quartile performance among North American retailers in total return to shareholders.[1] Since the beginning of the Plan period on December 31, 2000 to January 3, 2004, Canadian Tire's annualized total return to shareholders was 29.9 percent, which ranked Canadian Tire in the first quartile of North American retailers with respect to this metric.

[1] Total return to shareholders is measured by the change in stock price during the period plus dividends, all of which is then divided by the stock price at the beginning of the period. The comparison group includes North American retailers listed in the major consumer product indices on the Toronto Stock Exchange, The NASDAQ Stock Market and the New York Stock Exchange.

1.3 Strategic Plan performance indicators

Management set out five financial goals with the adoption of the Plan. Management believes the Company will continue to deliver top-quartile total return to shareholders over the 2001 to 2005 Plan period through successful execution of its Plan and achievement of its financial goals. Periodic fluctuations in the Company's performance or its stock price may, however, occur.

The following table shows how the Company has performed against its long-term objectives and also illustrates how the Company's 2003 performance has contributed to the accomplishment of those objectives. The right-hand column of the table shows the Company's 2003 performance with certain adjustments to meet the needs of some analysts and investors who regard these adjusted figures as more meaningful measures of operating results. The adjustments include a $6.8 million charge related to an automotive parts supply chain restructuring in the fourth quarter of 2002 and gains and losses arising from the sales of credit charge receivables and dispositions of property and equipment.

Management's Discussion and Analysis

Strategic Plan key metrics	Annual Strategic Plan goals 2001 to 2005	Beginning of fiscal 2001 to the end of fiscal 2003 performance	2003 year-over-year performance	2003 year-over-year performance, excluding non-operating Items[1]
Comparable store sales[2]	3 to 4%[3]	2.8%[3]	4.7%	4.7%
Gross operating revenue	at least 10%[4]	8.0%[4]	10.2%	10.2%
EBITDA[5] and minority interest	10 to 15%[4]	9.8%[4]	10.4%	9.9%
Earnings per share	12 to 15%[4]	17.4%[4]	19.5%	16.5%
After-tax return on invested capital	at least 10%[3]	8.3%[3]	9.0%	8.6%

[1] Non-operating items include gains and losses on the sales of credit charge receivables and the dispositions of property and equipment and a charge resulting from agreements with NAPA Canada made in the fourth quarter of 2002 which did not repeat in 2003.

[2] Represents sales growth at CTR only.

[3] Average of 2003, 2002 and 2001 percentages.

[4] Plan goals and performance for these metrics are expressed in terms of a compound annual growth rate (CAGR).

[5] Earnings before interest, income taxes, depreciation and amortization. See note on non-GAAP measures at the end of this MD&A.

Retail

"Canadian Tire Retail (CTR) is regaining earnings momentum with new opportunities for growth as we develop our customer relationships, enhance our unique product offering and look to the future with our new Concept 20/20 stores."

Mark Foote, President, Canadian Tire Retail

Market Trends   Competition in Canada's retail market and in the sectors served by Canadian Tire has intensified over the past decade, with the aggressive expansion in Canada of both national and international retailers. But we have also seen consolidation in the marketplace with the demise of department stores, unfocused retailers, and many independents. To grow in this market, retailers must have a winning value proposition and respond to the changing demographics and lifestyles of Canadian consumers who demand an optimum combination of choice, convenience, value and service.

Unique Positioning   Canadian Tire's unique positioning springs from our unique product offering – an offering that resonates among Canadians because it has evolved from the realities of this country's geography, climate, changing seasons and lifestyles. No other retailer replicates this product offering, although we face plenty of competition in almost every category we serve. Through the strength of our brand - an icon that is an indispensable part of the lives of millions of Canadians – and of our hugely popular Canadian Tire 'Money' loyalty program, we have built and maintained market leadership in the automotive, hardware, houseware, sporting goods and lawn and garden segments. We participate in 83 different retail categories in these segments, and we are the market leader in over half of those categories. Most significantly, we have become known as an innovator through our focus on introducing Exciting, New and Exclusive (ENE) Products. The vast majority of Canadians are customers of Canadian Tire, and over half shop in our stores at least monthly – a compelling competitive advantage.

Market Opportunities   Our huge customer base and market leadership in core retail segments raises an obvious question: where do we grow from here? We see plenty of scope for growth - through basic market growth of the segments we serve, through market share gains which we can achieve in every category, and through development of new product categories in response to the changing needs of our customers. Realizing these opportunities rests on our ability to strengthen customer relationships - encouraging more visits to our stores and greater sales per visit. To achieve these goals we have been moving forward on all fronts - effectively pursuing strategies to build leadership in merchandising, promotions, store development, product line enhancements, service and customer fulfillment.

Annual
CTR
retail sales
($ billions)

6.3

5.0 5.2 5.6 5.8

99 00 01 02 03

Factors contributing to higher total retail sales in 2003 include improved execution of basic merchandising and special promotions. Total retail sales for CTR for the 14-week fourth quarter of 2003 were $1.86 billion, up 12.2 percent compared to $1.66 billion of sales in the 13-week fourth quarter of 2002. On a more comparable 13-week basis, total sales in 2003 were $1.76 billion, up 6.4 percent over 2002 sales. Several factors contributed to the increase in sales, including special events and promotions, such as flyers and television advertising for innovative products. Seasonal products and a planned shift to higher margin goods did not deliver the expected sales performance in the fourth quarter of 2002, further improving the comparison to sales in the fourth quarter of 2003.

The strongest categories in the fourth quarter of 2003 were sporting goods (up 15.5 percent), hardware (up 13.4 percent) and automotive (up 13.1 percent).

On an annual basis, total retail sales for CTR for the 53 weeks of 2003 were $6.25 billion, up 7.0 percent compared to the $5.84 billion of sales in the 52-week period of 2002. On a more comparable 52-week basis, total sales in 2003 were $6.16 billion, up 5.3 percent over 2002 sales. The strongest categories in 2003 were lawn and garden (up 10.6 percent), automotive (up 7.1 percent) and sporting goods (up 7.3 percent).

The following table shows retail sales in each of CTR's major product divisions for 2003, all of which had higher sales compared to 2002.

Retail sales by product division[1]

($ in millions)	2003	2002	Change
Home	$ 2,615.6	$ 2,469.6	5.9%
Leisure	1,682.2	1,548.2	8.7%
Automotive	1,650.2	1,538.0	7.3%
Total retail	$ 5,948.0	$ 5,555.8	7.1%

[1] To directly compare the performance of sales divisions in the stores, the above figures exclude online sales and the labour portion of auto service sales.

Other common measures of the performance of retailers include average sales per store and average sales per square foot. Canadian Tire's performance on these metrics is shown in the following tables.

Average retail sales per Canadian Tire store[1]

($ in millions)	2003	2002	2001
Traditional stores	$ 8.2	$ 8.2	$ 8.3
New-format stores	15.2	15.0	15.1

[1] Retail sales are shown on a comparable 52-week basis in each year and exclude online sales and the labour portion of auto service sales.

Comparable store sales growth in new-format stores continues to outpace sales growth in traditional stores. The larger size, more convenient layout and substantially greater selection in new-format stores create a more enjoyable shopping experience for customers. The result is more customer visits and much higher average spending per visit.

Average sales per square foot of Canadian Tire retail space[1,2]

($)	2003	2002	2001
Traditional stores	$ 499	$ 495	$ 498
New-format stores	423	419	421

[1] Retail sales are shown on a comparable 52-week basis in each year and exclude online sales and the labour portion of auto service sales.
[2] Retail space excludes warehouse, garden centre and auto service areas.

As expected, average sales per square foot in new-format stores has been lower than in traditional stores due to the larger retail square footage.

Management's Discussion and Analysis

3.4 Funding costs

The following table summarizes the Company's total funding costs excluding those of GCCT and including the impact of interest rate swaps, part of Canadian Tire's risk management program, which is discussed below.

Interest expense[1]

($ in millions)	2003	2002
Long-term interest expense	$ 82.4	$ 80.3
Short-term interest expense	2.6	2.7
Total	$ 85.0	$ 83.0
Effective blended cost of debt	6.8%	6.3%

[1] Interest expense is increased or decreased by the interest rate differentials paid or received on interest swap contracts.

The effective average blended cost of debt increased from 2002 to 2003 largely due to the maturity of lower cost debt and the marking to market of an interest rate swap contract in 2003.

4. Risk Management

Canadian Tire approaches the management of risk strategically in keeping within its objective to improve total return to shareholders. To ensure that it has an effective risk management strategy, the Company has embarked upon the development of an enterprise risk management (ERM) framework.

The ERM framework sets out principles, processes and tools for evaluating and mitigating risks across the organization in an effective and consistent manner. The ERM process will help the business managers focus on those risks that are most likely to threaten the achievement of strategic and operating objectives. Once fully implemented, an effective ERM program mitigates risk and protects assets, cash flow, earnings and shareholder value.

ERM is a disciplined and integrated Company-wide approach to managing risks. The first step in ERM is to develop a perpetual process for the identification and assessment of the Company's principal risks. Management expects to have the initial risk assessment completed during 2004 and to reflect the findings of this review in the MD&A for the 2004 annual report.

4.1 Business risk

Canadian Tire is exposed to a number of risks in the normal course of its business that have the potential to affect its operating performance.

Retail competitive risk. Canadian Tire competes against international, national and regional retailers such as department stores, mass merchandisers, home-improvement warehouse operators, petroleum retailers and specialty marketers which currently operate in one or more of the Company's business segments. These retailers represent a competitive risk to the Company's ability to attract customers and operate successfully in its markets.

The Company actively monitors and analyzes competitive and economic developments in its markets to determine its competitiveness within each market or business segment. Canadian Tire has unique assets that provide advantages within its markets, including: brand equity, significant real estate investments, a strong loyalty program, MasterCard credit offering for its customers, a best-in-class customer call centre, a highly efficient distribution system and solid vendor relationships.

Canadian Tire also has core strengths that reduce competitive risk. Foremost is the network of Associate Dealers, agents and franchisees whose investment and commitment to their retail operations provide a significant competitive advantage. In addition, another key strength is the convenient location of the 452 Canadian Tire stores, 322 Mark's Work Wearhouse stores, 232 Petroleum stations, 39 PartSource stores and 47 car washes.

Internal and independent consumer surveys indicate that customers have exceptionally high awareness of, and loyalty to, CTR. In addition, Canadian Tire stores hold strong market-share positions in many product categories. This is particularly evident in automotive and hardware lines and in selected seasonal and sporting goods categories.

The strengths discussed above are reinforced by continuous strategic and operational reviews of core product categories, providing a comprehensive and up-to-date awareness of CTR's market position, opportunities and threats. This knowledge facilitates ongoing innovation at Canadian Tire, such as new-format stores, new merchandising concepts, PartSource and the development of CTR's online offering, CT Direct, all of which are expected to contribute to long-term growth in revenues, market share and profitability.

Specific initiatives designed to enhance CTR's competitive position, and thus reduce the Company's retail competitive risk, have been described in the discussion of CTR that begins on page 32 of this report.

Environmental risk.   Environmental risk at Canadian Tire is primarily associated with the handling of gasoline, oil and propane within the Company's Petroleum business and with the handling and recycling of certain materials, such as paint, oil and lawn chemicals, sold in Canadian Tire and PartSource stores. Responsible companies establish and follow comprehensive environmental policies and practices to avoid putting their reputations and their licence to operate at risk. Canadian Tire's management believes that its environmental protection programs are in the forefront of the retail industry. The Company's procedures for the identification and mitigation of environmental risk, as well as its record of accomplishment in this area, have enabled it to purchase environmental insurance coverage at very favourable premiums.

In 2003, the Company continued to ensure that management systems were in place to address environmental issues, policies and procedures. The Canadian Tire Board of Directors and its Audit and Social Responsibility Committees receive quarterly and annual reports on environmental, health and safety issues, policies and procedures.

Canadian Tire carries out regular assessments of facilities and procedures to determine whether its operations meet regulatory and corporate requirements. In addition, the Company has initiated many proactive programs that set new standards of environmental management. These programs are discussed in more detail under "Environmental, Health and Safety Stewardship" on page 82 of this report.

Commodity price risk.   The operating performance of any non-integrated petroleum retailer can be affected by the fluctuations of the refiner-driven commodity cost of gasoline. CTR and Petroleum are directly affected by this risk. During the past five years, Petroleum has significantly reduced its operating costs, making it less vulnerable to these fluctuations and, thus, more profitable. Petroleum also has a very competitive contract with a major supplier to purchase gasoline.

Seasonality risk.   Businesses that derive a significant amount of their revenues from the sale of seasonal merchandise have a degree of risk from unseasonable weather patterns.

CTR's offering features many seasonal products and as a result, CTR experiences seasonal variances in its business. In most years the Company records stronger gross operating revenues and consolidated earnings before income taxes in the second and fourth quarters. Revenue and earnings in the first quarter are typically the lowest. To lessen these variances, CTR works with its suppliers to plan the timing of shipments and, where possible, to shorten lead times on product orders. Nevertheless, it is impossible to entirely remove the risks and uncertainties associated with the seasonal nature of CTR's product offering.

Similarly, Mark's business remains very seasonal, with the fourth quarter typically producing about 40 percent of total annual retail sales and most of the annual profits, resulting from the general increase in consumer apparel spending in that period. Detailed sales reporting and merchandise planning modules assist Mark's in mitigating the risk and uncertainties associated with seasonal programs, but cannot remove them completely, as inventory orders, especially for a significant portion of merchandise purchased offshore, must be placed well ahead of the season.

Dealer contracts.   The success of Canadian Tire, particularly the CTR division, is closely tied to the success of Canadian Tire stores. Associate Dealers (Dealers) operate the retail business of these stores. The relationship between the Company and the Dealers combines the flexibility of an independent business with the advantages of a central marketing and purchasing organization. The combined experience of the Dealers is a valuable source of assistance to fellow Dealers and to the Company as it develops and implements new merchandising and marketing concepts. Most importantly, the Company depends on the Dealers to successfully execute retail programs and strategies.

To maintain controls over the brand and the quality and range of products and services offered at Canadian Tire stores, each Dealer agrees to purchase merchandise from, or approved by, the Company. In addition, each Dealer agrees to comply with the policies, marketing plans and operating standards prescribed by the Company. These obligations are specified under Dealer contracts, which expire at various times for individual Dealers. Certain schedules of the contracts expire in June 2004.

CTR and the Associate Dealers reached an agreement in principle in September 2003 that will guide the establishment of a new commercial contract between the parties covering important financial, strategic and operational changes. The agreement defines a new contract that would result in a positive contribution to the future earnings of the Company while continuing to offer an attractive incentive for Associate Dealers to build, maintain and grow the business of their stores. Most terms of the new commercial contract will extend for a 10-year period beginning July 2004, although the financial terms will be reviewed after five years.

4.2 Capital management risk

It is important to note that, in implementing financial strategies to reduce risk, Canadian Tire's treasury department does not operate as a profit centre. Controls are in place to detect and prevent speculative activity.

Financial products risk.   It is the Company's policy to identify and manage currency, interest-rate and commodity-price risk proactively and conservatively.

There are typically two parties to a financial transaction. The successful completion of the transaction and the mitigation of risk depend on the ability of both parties to meet their financial commitments in the transaction. In the case of Canadian Tire, counterparty credit risk is considered to be negligible as the Company restricts the counterparties that it deals with to highly rated financial institutions. The Company also ensures that there is no undue concentration with any single counterparty.

Management's Discussion and Analysis

Foreign exchange risk.   As a significant importer of foreign goods and services, the Company has a proactive and conservative policy to mitigate the risk of sudden fluctuations in currency exchange rates. The Company's policy is to hedge a minimum of 75 percent of expected purchases of foreign goods and services on a rolling four- to six-month basis. As management deems appropriate, the Company extends its currency hedging a further six months or even longer. This hedging program has the effect of reducing any near term impact of favourable or detrimental fluctuations in exchange rates. The impact of fluctuations in exchange rates on the cost of goods sold is also reduced by a financial arrangement with Associate Dealers to share margin with the Company.

Credit charge receivables risk.   Canadian Tire, through its Financial Services business, grants credit to its customers on Canadian Tire and *Options* MasterCard credit cards to increase the loyalty of these customers and the Company's profitability. With the granting of credit, the Company assumes certain credit risks.

Financial Services has minimized those credit risks in the following three areas of the credit process, improving the quality of its credit charge portfolio:

> When granting credit, sophisticated automated credit scoring models are used to determine the creditworthiness of each customer. These credit scoring processes are constantly improved based on new information;

> When monitoring the credit charge portfolio, Financial Services uses the latest technology to make more accurate credit decisions for each customer account, thereby limiting credit risk exposure; and

> When collecting credit charge receivables, Financial Services has adopted a collection modelling technology that has significantly improved the effectiveness of the collection process.

The Financial Services card base comprises more than 4.3 million cardholders across Canada, with about 70 percent in Ontario and Quebec.

Financial Services has used securitization as a source of funding over the past several years as a normal part of financing growth in credit charge receivables. At the end of 2003, Financial Services had securitized about 77 percent of the net managed portfolio of credit charge receivables. Securitization involves the sale of credit charge receivables to Glacier Credit Card Trust (GCCT), and is an important source of funding for Canadian Tire.

Securitization risk.   Securitization protects shareholders from risk associated with the portfolio of credit charge receivables as a result of any significant unexpected changes, such as an economic downturn. However, should such changes occur, further securitization could become more difficult and costly.

Interest rate risk.   The Company's sensitivity to movements in interest rates is substantially limited to its cash and short-term investments, commercial paper and medium term notes. A 1 percent change in interest rates would not materially affect the Company's earnings, cash flow or financial position.

All of the Company's long-term debt has been issued at fixed rates and, as described in Note 6 to the Consolidated Financial Statements, is not sensitive to interest rate movements. From time to time the Company enters into interest rate swaps to manage its current and anticipated exposure to fluctuations in interest rates and market liquidity. The Company monitors, on an ongoing basis, market conditions and the impact of interest rate fluctuations on its fixed to floating interest rate exposure mix.

The Company also reviews interest rate sensitivity by business unit. Most of Financial Services' revenue is not interest rate sensitive as it is generated from the *Options* MasterCard and Canadian Tire's retail cards, each of which carries fixed interest rates appropriate to customer groups with common credit ratings. Financial Services' funding requirements were reduced during 2003 primarily by the sale of credit charge receivables through the securitization program described on page 49. However, the balance of Financial Services' funding requirements in 2003 was met with the issuance of floating rate debt, which makes the business results somewhat sensitive to changes in interest rates. Canadian Tire constantly monitors the potential impact of interest rate fluctuations on its fixed/floating rate exposure and has managed its overall balance between fixed and floating rate debt to reduce the magnitude of this exposure. As the success of Financial Services is dependent upon its ability to access capital markets at favourable rates, and given the rapid growth of the managed portfolio of credit charge receivables, maintaining the quality of the securitized receivables is a priority of Financial Services.

Canadian Tire's MD&A seems to fully meet the objectives and requirements of the standard given above. Indeed, its disclosures exceed a minimal rehashing of financial statement information and vague gestures to future prospects. The information provided goes well beyond what can be learned from the financial statements themselves. In particular, the discussion is from management's perspective, and contains considerable forward-looking information to assist investors to assess the probabilities of future firm performance.

It is interesting to speculate why some firms go beyond minimal reporting requirements, particularly due to the potential for lawsuits if the forward-looking disclosures are not met. One possibility is that the Canadian reporting environment may be less litigious than others, such as the United States. Another is that by building investor confidence through reducing estimation risk, the firm's cost of capital will be reduced. This is discussed in Chapter 12. Yet another possibility is that a full disclosure reputation may also affect customer, as well as investor, confidence.

4.9 Conclusions on Efficient Securities Markets

Efficient securities market theory has major implications for financial accounting. One of these is that supplementary information in financial statement notes or elsewhere is just as useful as information in the financial statements proper. Another is that efficiency is defined relative to a stock of publicly known information. Financial reporting has a role to play in improving the amount, timing, and accuracy of this stock, thereby enabling capital markets to work better and improve the operation of the economy.

MD&A is an important example of a full disclosure standard. This standard has the potential to convey information beyond that contained in the conventional historical cost-based financial statements. This potential is not only in the information contained in the disclosure per se. The extent to which the firm goes beyond minimal MD&A requirements tells the market something more. Superior disclosure signals a confident, well-planned management approach (otherwise, why release the information?), suggesting that good performance in the face of changing opportunities, risks, and uncertainties will continue.

Full disclosure has two main benefits, which can be attained simultaneously. One is to enable investors to make better decisions. The other is to improve the ability of securities markets to direct investment to its most productive uses. The reason why these benefits are attained simultaneously, of course, is that better information enables more-informed buy/sell decisions, and helps share price to reflect fundamental firm value. Share price, in turn, affects the firm's investment decisions.

Another implication of efficient securities market theory appears in Beaver's 1973 analysis. This is that the specific accounting policies adopted by firms do not matter as long as they have no differential cash flow effects across those policies, full disclosure is made of the particular policies used, and investors have sufficient information to convert from one policy to another. The reason, according to efficient markets theory, is that investors as a whole will *look through* reported net income to its underlying implications for future cash flows. In so doing, they will take into account the specific accounting policies used in calculating net income. Thus, firms' choices of amortization policy, of successful-efforts or full-cost accounting for oil and gas exploration, of accounting for future tax liabilities, and so on, will not affect the efficient market prices of their securities, providing the specific accounting policies they are using are fully disclosed. Thus, we see that the full-disclosure principle extends to disclosure of accounting policies.

Accountants are improving their understanding of the role of information in determining price. In essence, market price aggregates the collective information processing and decision-making expertise of investors. Thus, market price itself has considerable information content, which individuals may use as input into their decisions. A "buy and hold" investment strategy is an example of a decision that relies on the information content of market price.

This aggregation of information into market price contains a logical contradiction, however. If price is fully informative, no one would bother to collect additional, costly, information. In effect, market price contains within it the seeds of its own destruction. However, we can identify two factors to prevent this from happening:

- Noise and liquidity traders introduce a random component to market price, which prevents market price from being fully informative about future value.

- Information asymmetry, in particular the presence of inside information, means that not all relevant information is in the public domain. Then, investors have the potential to earn extra profits if they can ferret out some of this inside information. Improved disclosure, as in MD&A, provides investors with some help in this regard.

As Beaver (1973) put it, accountants are in competition with other information sources. We now know that market price is one of these other sources. Think of market price as aggregating all relevant "other" information up to the time of release of the financial statements. The question then is: Is it cost-effective for rational investors to inform themselves by utilizing the financial statements?

Again, the accountants' answer is the concept of full disclosure. By increasing the information content of financial reporting, including supplementary information in notes and MD&A, not only do accountants help preserve their competitive advantage, they also improve social welfare by reducing the adverse impacts of inside information.

If investors do in fact find accounting information useful, this should show up as a response of security prices to this information. In the next chapter, we will examine empirical evidence in this regard.

Questions and Problems

1. Two firms, of the same size and risk, release their annual reports on the same day. It turns out that they each report the same amount of net income. Following the release, the share price of one firm rose strongly while the other rose hardly at all.

   Explain how it is possible for the market to react positively to one firm's annual report and hardly at all to the other when the firms are similar in size, risk, and reported profitability.

2. Shares of firm A and firm B are traded on an efficient market. The two firms are of the same size and risk. They both report the same net income. However, you see in the financial statement notes that firm A uses the LIFO inventory method and declining-balance amortization for capital assets, while firm B uses the FIFO inventory method and straight-line amortization.

   Which firm's shares should sell at the higher price-to-earnings ratio, all other things being equal? Explain. Assume a period of rising prices. (CGA-Canada)

3. Using the concept of information asymmetry, answer the following questions:
   a. You observe that used cars sold by new car dealers sell for a higher price, for models of same make, year, and condition, than used cars sold by used car dealers. Why?
   b. Why would a fire insurance policy contain a $150 deductible provision?
   c. Why would a life insurance company require a medical examination before approving applications for new policies?
   d. A firm plans to raise additional capital by means of a new issue of common shares. Before doing so, it hires a well-known investment house to help design and market the issue, and also switches auditors from a small, local firm to a "Big Four" firm. Why? (CGA-Canada)

4. To what extent might the financial press provide a relevant source of information for investors? Would this information source conflict with or complement financial statement information? Explain. (CGA-Canada)

5. On January 21, 1993, *The Wall Street Journal* reported that General Electric Co.'s fourth-quarter 1992 earnings rose 6.2% to $1.34 billion or $1.57 a share, setting a new record and bringing the earnings for 1992 to $4.73 billion or $5.51 a share. After adjusting for extraordinary items, 1992 earnings from continuing operations were up about 10% from the previous year.

   The *Journal* also reported that forecasts made by analysts averaged $1.61 per share for the fourth quarter of 1992, and from $5.50 to $5.60 per share for the whole year. One analyst was quoted as saying that 1992 "wasn't a bad year for GE" despite the downturn in the stock market on the day of the earnings announcement.

   Yet, on the same day the fourth-quarter earnings were announced, General Electric Co.'s stock price fell $1.50 to $82.625 on the New York Stock Exchange.

   Required
   a. Give three reasons to explain why this could happen.
   b. Use the Sharpe-Lintner CAPM (Equations 4.2 and 4.3) to explain how the new information caused the current price slip. Calculations are not required.

6. Atlas Ltd. is a listed public company. It is in a volatile industry. The market price of its shares is highly sensitive to its earnings. The company's annual meeting is to be held soon, and the president is concerned, expecting to be attacked strongly by a dissident group of shareholders.

One issue the dissidents are expected to focus on is the company's amortization policy. They will claim that the annual declining-balance amortization charges are excessive—that the company's conservative amortization policy seriously understates annual earnings per share, causing the shares' market price to be artificially low. Threats have even been made of suing management and the board of directors to "recover the resulting loss in market value, relative to shareholders in companies with less conservative amortization policies, suffered by Atlas shareholders."

The president has asked you to help prepare a defence against the expected attack on the company's amortization policy.

Required

Write a memo summarizing how you would recommend the president respond to this attack. (CGA-Canada)

7. The article "GM to Take Charge of $20.8-Billion" here reproduced from *The Globe and Mail* (February 2, 1993) describes the potential impact of SFAS 106, "Accounting for Postretirement Benefits Other Than Pensions," on General Motors and Ford. For example, it appears that General Motors will be required to record a liability of $20.8 billion, reducing its shareholders' equity from $27.8 billion to $7 billion, about a 75% reduction.

GM to Take Charge of $20.8-Billion

Atlanta—General Motors Corp. will take a $20.8-billion (U.S.) charge against 1992 earnings to account for a new way of estimating retiree health care costs, the auto maker's directors decided yesterday.

The charge, which will not affect the struggling auto maker's cash flow, will leave GM with the largest annual loss of any U.S. corporation, eclipsing the company's 1991 loss of $4.45-billion, which was a record at that time.

Including accounting changes, other charges and losses on its North American operations, GM's 1992 loss could approach $23-billion.

The $20.8-billion is a non-cash charge. It reduces GM's net worth to about $7-billion, still sufficient to pay stock dividends under the laws of Delaware, where GM is incorporated.

Separately, GM said it would take a $744-million fourth-quarter restructuring charge for its National Car Rental Systems business. In a recent U.S. Securities and Exchange Commission filing, GM estimated that charge at about $300-million.

The accounting change, required by the Financial Accounting Standards Board of all publicly traded U.S. companies, has had a major effect on each of the Big Three U.S. auto makers.

Ford Motor Co. said it would take a $7.5-billion charge against 1992 earnings to account for the change. Chrysler Corp. said it has not decided whether to take its $4.7-billion charge as a lump sum in the first quarter or spread it over 20 years, as the standard allows.

continued ➜

> GM had estimated its charge for adopting the new accounting standard at $16-billion to $24-billion. The $20.8-billion actual charge includes its workers, GM Hughes Electronics Corp. and its financial subsidiary, General Motors Acceptance Corp.
>
> The company's EDS Corp. subsidiary does not pay health benefits, so it was exempt.
>
> *Source:* The Globe and Mail, *February 2, 1993. Reprinted by permission of The Associated Press.*

Required

Describe and explain how you would expect the efficient securities market to react to this information.

8. You have just obtained inside information about a firm that employs you and in which you own shares. The information is that the current quarter's earnings will be substantially below forecast. Should you sell your shares before the bad news becomes publicly known? Outline arguments for and against this temptation.

9. A major reason for the rarity of formal financial forecasts in annual reports is the possibility of lawsuits if the forecast is not met, particularly in the United States. On November 17, 1995, *The Wall Street Journal* reported that the SEC was supporting a bill before the U.S. Senate to provide protection from legal liability resulting from forecasts, providing that "meaningful cautionary statements" accompanied the forecast.

Required
a. To the extent that firms are discouraged from providing financial forecasts by the prospect of litigation, how could this lead to a negative impact on the operation of securities markets? Can you give an argument that a litigious environment might actually help the operation of securities markets?
b. Explain how the passage of a bill such as that mentioned above might benefit investors.
c. Explain how passage might benefit firms.

10. Refer to the dart-throwing vignette in section 4.2.2.

Required
a. Use efficient securities market theory to explain how "dart-throwing" may be a desirable investment strategy.
b. Explain Prof. Malkiel's argument that risk differences may be driving the superior average returns earned by the pros and the Dow Jones index. How would you determine whether risk differences were affecting the results?
c. Explain another possible reason, not mentioned by Prof. Malkiel, for the superior returns earned by the pros.

11. For companies with no history of positive earnings, such as startup companies, growth of revenues provides an alternative performance measure and indicator of

possible future earning power. This is particularly the case if the new company incurs high R&D costs, advertising, and other startup expenditures that delay the advent of reported earnings. Without reported earnings, such companies may inflate reported revenues to impress investors. In an article in *The Globe and Mail*, December 30, 2000, Janet McFarland discusses some of these practices. They include:

- Recognizing full revenue even though products or systems can be returned, or when there are future obligations such as servicing the products and systems sold.

- Recording revenue on long-term contracts in advance of billings to the customer (billings may be delayed as a form of vendor financing to the customer, a practice frequently used to attract business from cash-short firms).

- Recording revenue from gross sales when the company is an agent rather than a principal.

Examples of such practices include Imax Corp., which reported the (discounted) full amounts of minimum royalties due under 10-year or more leases of its theatre systems (in accordance with GAAP for long-term leases), leaving itself open to the possibility that customers may default on payments due in future. JetForm Corp. recognized revenue from consulting contracts on the percentage-of-completion method, although amounts billed to customers were less. Bid.Com, a firm that conducted on-line auctions as agent for the seller, included the purchase price, rather than its commission on the purchase, as revenue.

One of the problems surrounding reporting of revenue is that while a firm's revenue recognition policy must be disclosed, the disclosure standards in Canada are vague. Thus companies typically state that revenue is recognized as goods are shipped or services rendered, or that revenues on long-term contracts are recognized on a percentage-of-completion basis. These statements are sufficiently general that practices such as the above may be unknown to the market.

Required

a. To what extent can revenue growth substitute for net income as a predictor of future earning power? Explain. Use efficient securities market concepts in your answer, and consider the requirement under GAAP for immediate writeoff of research and startup costs.

b. Use the concept of relevance to defend the revenue recognition policies outlined above.

c. Use the concept of reliability to criticize the revenue recognition policies outlined above.

d. To the extent that investors are aware of the possible use of revenue recognition policies that overstate revenues (even though, for a specific firm, they may not know the extent to which that firm is using such policies), what is the effect on the operation of the capital market? Explain.

Notes

1. More generally, the random fluctuation could be about a trend line. For example, the price of a security may have an upward trend over time.

2. This phenomenon, that the collective judgements of a large group can be surprisingly accurate, has been documented in numerous contexts. Surowiecki (2004) gives four conditions needed for the effect to operate: diversity of information, independence, decentralization, and aggregation.

3. In Section 3.3.2, we applied the term "informative" to the information system. An informative information system leads the decision-maker to revise his/her prior probabilities. In that context, a *fully* informative information system perfectly reveals the state of nature (see question 1 of Chapter 3). In the context of this chapter, "fully informative" applies to share price rather than to an information system, but the reasoning is similar—current share price fully reflects or, equivalently, perfectly reveals all publicly available information. Note that if share price is fully informative, the information system formed by financial statements is non-informative—it reveals nothing new about the firm since share price already reveals all. Hence the logical inconsistency—if share prices are fully informative, no one would use financial statements. But, if no one used financial statements, share prices would no longer be fully informative.

4. This abnormal return should not be confused with abnormal earnings of P.V. Ltd. in Example 2.2. While the idea is the same, abnormal security return here refers to a *market* return, whereas abnormal earnings refer to *accounting* net income.

5. Estimating beta by least-squares regression is not inconsistent with the calculation of beta described in Section 3.7.1. The regression approach merely provides a convenient framework to carry out the estimation. To see this, note the definition of the coefficient of an independent variable in a regression model—it is the amount of change in the dependent variable (R_{jt}) for a unit change in the independent variable (R_{Mt}). This is exactly the definition of beta. As explained in Section 3.7.1, beta measures the strength of the variation in a security's return as the market return varies.

6. Wurgler estimates a country's efficiency of capital allocation by the relationship between its growth in investment and its growth in output—more output from a unit of growth in investment implies higher capital allocation efficiency. He estimates the amount of firm-specific information in a country's share prices by their **synchronicity** (the extent to which share prices move together)—less synchronicity implies more firm-specific information relative to industry- and economy-wide information.

7. This argument assumes that the disclosure is truthful. Truthful disclosure can be encouraged by, for example, an audit.

Chapter 5

The Information Perspective on Decision Usefulness

FIGURE 5.1 ORGANIZATION OF CHAPTER 5

5.1 Overview

There is a saying that "the proof of the pudding is in the eating." If the efficient markets theory and the decision theories underlying it are reasonable descriptions of reality on average, we should observe the market values of securities responding in predictable ways to new information.

This leads to an examination of empirical research in accounting. Despite the difficulties of designing experiments to test the implications of decision usefulness, accounting research has established that security market prices do respond to accounting information. The first solid evidence of this, security market reaction to earnings announcements, was provided by Ball and Brown in 1968. Since then, a large number of empirical studies have documented additional aspects of securities market response.

On the basis of these studies, it does seem that accounting information is useful to investors in helping them estimate the expected values and risks of security returns. One has only to contemplate the use of Bayes' theorem in Example 3.1 to see that if accounting information did not have information content there would be no revision of beliefs upon receipt, hence no triggering of buy/sell decisions. Without buy/sell decisions, there would be no trading volume or price changes. In essence, information is useful if it leads investors to change their beliefs and actions. Furthermore, the degree of usefulness for investors can be measured by the extent of volume or price change following release of the information.

This equating of usefulness to information content is called the **information perspective** on decision usefulness of financial reporting, an approach that has dominated financial accounting theory and research since 1968, and has only within the last few years begun to yield to a measurement perspective, to be discussed in Chapters 6 and 7. As we have seen in Sections 3.8 and 4.8, the information perspective has been adopted by major accounting standard setting bodies. This perspective takes the view that investors want to make *their own* predictions of future security returns (instead of having accountants do it for them, as under ideal conditions) and will "gobble up" all useful information in this regard. As mentioned, empirical research has shown that at least some accounting information is perceived as useful. Furthermore, the information approach implies that empirical research can help accountants to further increase usefulness by letting market response guide them as to what information is and is not valued by investors.

*The **information perspective** on decision usefulness is an approach to financial reporting that recognizes individual responsibility for predicting future firm performance and that concentrates on providing useful information for this purpose. The approach assumes securities market efficiency, recognizing that the market will react to useful information from any source, including financial statements.*

One must be careful, however, when equating usefulness with the extent of security price change. While investors, and accountants, may benefit from useful information, it does *not* follow that *society* will necessarily be better off. Information is a very complex commodity and its private and social values are not the same. One reason is *cost*. Financial statement users do not generally pay directly for this information. As a result, they may find information useful even though it costs society more (in the form of higher product prices to help firms pay for generating and reporting the information) than the increased usefulness is worth. Furthermore, information affects people differently, requiring complex cost-benefit tradeoffs to balance the competing interests of different constituencies.

These social considerations do not invalidate the information perspective. Accountants can still strive to improve their competitive position in the information marketplace by providing useful information. And, it is still true that securities markets will do a better job of allocating scarce capital to the extent that security prices provide good indicators of investment opportunities. However, what accountants cannot do is claim that the "best" accounting policy is the one that produces the greatest market response. Figure 5.1 outlines the organization of this chapter.

5.2 Outline of the Research Problem

5.2.1 Reasons for Market Response

We begin by reviewing the reasons why we would predict that the market price of a firm's shares will respond to its financial statement information. For most of this chapter we will confine financial statement information to reported net income. The information content of net income is a topic that has received extensive empirical investigation. Information content of other financial statement components will be discussed in Section 5.7 and in Chapter 7.

Consider the following predictions about investor behaviour, in response to financial statement information:

1. Investors have prior beliefs about a firm's future performance, that is, its cash flows and earnings, since these affect the expected returns and risk of the firm's shares. These prior beliefs will be based on all available information, including market price, up to just prior to the release of the firm's current net income. Even if they are based on publicly available information, these prior beliefs need not all be the same, because investors will differ in the amount of information they have obtained and in their abilities to interpret it.

2. Upon release of current year's net income, certain investors will decide to become more informed, by analyzing the income number. For example, if net income is high, or higher than expected, this may be good news. If so, investors, by means of Bayes' theorem, would revise upward their beliefs about future firm performance. Other investors, who perhaps had overly high expectations for what current net income should be, might interpret the same net income number as bad news.

3. Investors who have revised their beliefs about future firm performance upward will be inclined to buy the firm's shares at their current market price, and vice versa for those who have revised their beliefs downward. Investors' evaluations of the riskiness of these shares may also be revised.

4. We would expect to observe the volume of shares traded to increase when the firm reports its net income. Furthermore, this volume should be greater the greater are the differences in investors' prior beliefs and in their interpretations of the current financial information. If the investors who interpret reported net income as good news (and hence have increased their expectations of future performance) outweigh those who interpret it as bad news, we would expect to observe an increase in the market price of the firm's shares, and vice versa.

Beaver (1968), in a classic study, examined trading volume reaction. He found a dramatic increase in volume during the week of release of earnings announcements. Further details of Beaver's findings are included in question 9 of this chapter. In the balance of this chapter we will concentrate on market price reaction. Market price reaction may provide a stronger test of decision usefulness than volume reaction. For example, the model of Kim and Verrecchia (1997) suggests that volume is noisier than price change as a measure of decision usefulness of financial statement information.

You will recognize that the preceding predictions follow the decision theory and efficient markets theory of Chapters 3 and 4 quite closely. If these theories are to have relevance to accountants, their predictions should be borne out empirically. An empirical researcher could test these predictions by obtaining a sample of firms that issue annual reports and investigating whether the volume and price reactions to good or bad news in earnings occur as the theories lead us to believe. This is not as easy as it might seem, however, for a number of reasons, as we will discuss next.

5.2.2 Finding the Market Response

1. Efficient markets theory implies that the market will react quickly to new information. As a result, it is important to know *when* current year's reported net income first became publicly known. If the researcher looked for volume and price effects even a few days too late, no effects may be observed even though they had existed.

   Researchers have solved this problem by using the date the firm's net income was reported in the financial media such as *The Wall Street Journal*. If the efficient market is going to react, it should do so in a **narrow window** of a few days surrounding this date.

2. The good or bad news in reported net income is usually evaluated relative to what investors *expected*. If a firm reported net income of, say, $2 million, and this was what investors had expected (from quarterly reports, speeches by company officials, analysts' predictions, forward-looking information in MD&A and, indeed, in share price itself), there would hardly be much information content in reported net income. Investors would have already revised their beliefs on the basis of the earlier information. Things would be different, however, if investors had expected $2 million and reported net income was $3 million. This good news would trigger rapid belief revision about the future prospects of the firm. This means that researchers must obtain a proxy for what investors expected net income to be.

3. There are always many events taking place that affect a firm's share volume and price. This means that a market response to reported net income can be hard to find. For example, suppose a firm released its current year's net income, containing good news, on the same day the federal government first announced a substantial decrease in the deficit. Such a public announcement would probably affect prices of all or most securities on the market, which in turn might swamp the price impact of the firm's earnings release. Thus, it is desirable to separate the impacts of market-wide and firm-specific factors on share returns.

5.2.3 Separating Market-Wide and Firm-Specific Factors

As described in Section 4.5, the market model is widely used to *ex post* separate market-wide and firm-specific factors that affect security returns. Figure 5.2 gives a graphical illustration of the market model for firm j for period t, where we take the length of the period as one day. Longer time periods, such as a week, month, or year, and even shorter periods, are also used by researchers.

FIGURE 5.2 SEPARATING MARKET-WIDE AND FIRM-SPECIFIC SECURITY RETURNS USING THE MARKET MODEL

R_{Mt} = Return on market portfolio for period t

R_{jt} = Return on firm j's shares for period t

The figure shows the relationship between the return on firm j's shares and the return on the market portfolio (proxied, for example, by the Dow Jones Industrial Average index or the S&P/TSX Composite index).

Consider the equation of the market model, repeated here from Section 4.5 (Equation 4.4):

$$R_{jt} = \alpha_j + \beta_j R_{Mt} + \epsilon_{jt}$$

As described in Section 4.5, the researcher will obtain past data on R_{jt} and R_{Mt} and use regression analysis to estimate the coefficients of the model. Suppose that this yields $\alpha_j = 0.0001$ and $\beta_j = 0.80$, as shown in the figure.[1]

Now, armed with this estimate of the market model for firm j, the researcher can consult *The Wall Street Journal* to find the day of the firm's current earnings announcement. Call this day "day 0." Suppose that for day 0 the return on the Dow Jones Industrial index was 0.001.[2] Then, the estimated market model for firm j is used to predict the return on firm j's shares for this day. As shown in Figure 5.2, this expected return[3] is 0.0009. Now assume that the *actual* return on firm j's shares for day 0 is 0.0015. Then, the difference between actual and expected returns is 0.0006 (that is, $\epsilon_{jt} = 0.0006$ for this day). This 0.0006 is an estimate of the abnormal, or firm-specific, return on firm j's shares for that day.[4] This abnormal return is also interpreted as the rate of return on firm j's shares for day 0 *after removing* the influence of market-wide factors. Note that this interpretation is consistent with Example 3.3, where we separated the factors that affect share returns into market-wide and firm-specific categories. The present procedure provides an operational way to make this separation.

5.2.4 Comparing Returns and Income

The empirical researcher can now compare the abnormal share return on day 0 as calculated above with the unexpected component of the firm's current reported net income. If this unexpected net income is good news (that is, a positive unexpected net income) then, given securities market efficiency, a positive abnormal share return constitutes evidence that investors on average are reacting favourably to the unexpected good news in earnings. A similar line of reasoning applies if the current earnings announcement is bad news.

To increase the power of the investigation, the researcher may wish to similarly compare a few days on either side of day 0. It is possible, for example, that the efficient market might learn of the good or bad earnings news a day or two early. Conversely, positive or negative abnormal returns may continue for a day or two after day 0 while the market digests the information, although market efficiency implies that any excess returns should die out quickly. Consequently, the summing of abnormal returns for a three-to-five-day narrow window around day 0 seems more reasonable than examining day 0 only. It also helps protect against the possibility that the date of publication of current earnings in the financial media may not be a completely accurate estimate of the date of their public availability.

If positive and negative abnormal returns surrounding good or bad earnings news are found to hold across a sample of firms, the researcher may conclude that predictions based on the decision theory and efficient securities market theory are supported. This would in turn support the decision usefulness approach to financial accounting and reporting, because, if investors did not find the reported net income information useful, a market response would hardly be observed.

Of course, this methodology is not foolproof—a number of assumptions and estimations have to be made along the way. One complication is that other firm-specific information frequently comes along around the time of a firm's earnings announcement. For example, if firm j announced a stock split or a change in its dividend on the same day that it released its current earnings, it would be hard to know if a market response was due to one or the other. However, researchers can cope with this by simply removing such firms from the sample.

Another complication is the estimation of a firm's beta, needed to separate market-wide and firm-specific returns as in Figure 5.2. As mentioned, this estimation is usually based on a regression analysis of past data using the market model. Then, the estimated beta is the slope of the regression line. However, as we will discuss in Section 6.2.3, a firm's beta may change over time, for example as it changes its operations and/or its capital structure. If the estimated beta is different from the true beta, this affects the calculation of abnormal return, possibly biasing the results of the investigation.

There is a variety of ways to cope with this complication. For example, it may be possible to get a "second opinion" on beta by estimating it from financial statement information rather than from market data. (This is considered in Section 7.5.1.) Alternatively, beta may be estimated from a period after the earnings announcement and compared with the estimate from a period before the announcement.

Also there are ways to separate market-wide and firm-specific returns that ignore beta. For example, we can estimate firm-specific returns by the difference between firm j's stock return during period 0 and the average return on its shares over some prior period. Or, we can take the difference between firm j's return during period 0 and the return on the market portfolio for the same period. Alternatively, as in Easton and Harris (1991), we can simply work with total share returns and not factor out market-wide returns at all.

The rationale for these simpler procedures is that there is no guarantee that the market model adequately captures the real process generating share returns—the impact of estimation risk and securities market inefficiencies on share returns is discussed in Chapter 6. To the extent it does not, use of the market model may introduce more error in estimating beta and abnormal returns than it reduces by removing market-wide returns and controlling for risk. A further complication is that there is a variety of market portfolio return indices available, of which the Dow Jones Industrial Average is only one. Which one should be used?

These issues were examined by Brown and Warner (1980) in a simulation study. Despite modelling and measurement problems such as those mentioned above, Brown and Warner concluded that, for monthly return windows, the market model-based procedure outlined in Section 5.2.3 performed reasonably well relative to alternatives such as those mentioned above. Consequently, this is the procedure we will concentrate on.

Using this procedure, it does appear that the market reacts to earnings information much as the theories predict. We will now review the first solid evidence of this reaction, the famous 1968 Ball and Brown study.

5.3 The Ball and Brown Study

5.3.1 Methodology and Findings

In 1968, Ball and Brown (BB) began a tradition of empirical capital markets research in accounting that continues to this day. They were the first to provide convincing scientific evidence that firms' share returns respond to the information content of financial statements. This type of research is called an **event study**, since it studies the securities market reaction to a specific event, in this case a firm's release of its current net income. A review of the BB paper is worthwhile because its basic methodology, and adaptations and extensions of it, continues to be used. Their paper continues to provide guidance, as well as encouragement, to those who wish to better understand the decision usefulness of financial reporting.

BB examined a sample of 261 New York Stock Exchange (NYSE) firms over nine years from 1957 to 1965. They concentrated on the information content of earnings, to the exclusion of other potentially informative financial statement components such as liquidity and capital structure. One reason for this, as mentioned earlier, was that earnings for NYSE firms were typically announced in the media prior to actual release of the annual report so that it was relatively easy to determine when the information first became publicly available.

BB's first task was to measure the information content of earnings, that is, whether reported earnings were greater than what the market had expected (GN), or less than expected (BN). Of course, this requires a proxy for the market's expectation. One proxy they used was last year's actual earnings, from which it follows that unexpected earnings is simply the change in earnings.[5] Thus, firms with earnings higher than last year's were classified as GN, and firms with earnings lower than last year were classified as BN.

The next task was to evaluate the market return on the shares of the sample firms near the time of each earnings announcement. This was done according to the abnormal returns procedure illustrated in Figure 5.2. The only difference was that BB used monthly returns (daily returns were not available on databases in 1968).

Analogously to Figure 5.2, suppose that firm j reported its 1957 earnings in February 1958, and that these earnings were GN. Suppose also that the return on the NYSE market portfolio in February 1958 was 0.001, yielding an expected firm j return of 0.0009. BB would then calculate the actual return on firm j shares for February 1958. Suppose this was 0.0015, yielding an abnormal return for February of 0.0006. Since firm j's 1957 earnings were reported in February 1958 and since its shares earned 0.0006 over and above the market in this month, one might suspect that the reason for the positive abnormal return was that investors were reacting favourably to the GN information in earnings.

The question then was: Was this pattern repeated across the sample? The answer was yes. If we take all the GN earnings announcements in the sample (there were 1,231), the *average* abnormal security market return in the month of earnings release was strongly positive. Conversely, the average abnormal return for the 1,109 bad news earnings announcements in the sample was strongly negative. This provides substantial evidence that the market did respond to the good or bad news in earnings during a narrow window consisting of the month of earnings announcement release.

An interesting and important aspect of the BB study was that they repeated their abnormal security market returns calculation for a **wide window** consisting of each of the 11 months prior to and the 6 months following the month of earnings release (month 0). BB calculated average abnormal returns for each month of this 18-month window. The results are shown in Figure 5.3, taken from BB.

The upper part of Figure 5.3 shows cumulative average abnormal returns for the GN earnings announcement firms in the sample; the bottom part shows the same for the BN announcement firms. As can be seen, the GN firms strongly outperformed the total sample (which approximates the market-wide return), and the BN firms strongly underperformed, over the 11 month period leading up to the month of earnings release.

5.3.2 Causation Versus Association

Note that the returns are *cumulative* in the diagram. While there was a substantial increase (for GN) and decrease (for BN) in average abnormal returns in the narrow window consisting of month 0, as described above, Figure 5.3 suggests that the market began to *anticipate* the GN or BN as much as a year early, with the result that returns accumulated steadily over the period. As can be seen, if an investor could have bought the shares of all GN firms one year before the good news was released and held them until the end of the month of release, there would have been an extra return of about 6% over and above the market-wide return. Similarly, an abnormal loss of over 9% would have been incurred on a portfolio of BN firms bought one year before the bad news was released.[6]

This leads to an important distinction between narrow and wide window studies. If a security market reaction to accounting information is observed during a narrow

FIGURE 5.3 ABNORMAL RETURNS FOR GN AND BN FIRMS

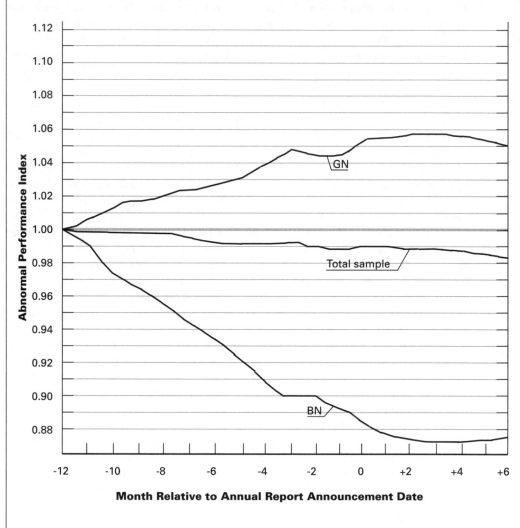

Source: Ray Ball and P. Brown, "An Empirical Evaluation of Accounting Income Numbers," Journal of Accounting Research (Autumn 1968), p. 169. Reprinted by permission.

window of a few days (or, in the case of BB, a month) surrounding an earnings announcement, it can be argued that the accounting information is the *cause* of the market reaction. The reason is that during a narrow window there are relatively few firm-specific events other than net income to affect share returns. Also, if other events do occur, such as stock splits or dividend announcements, the affected firms can be removed from the sample, as mentioned. Thus, a narrow-window association between security returns and accounting information suggests that accounting disclosures are the *source* of new information to investors.

Evaluation of security returns over a wide window, however, opens them up to a host of other value-relevant events. For example, a firm may have discovered new oil and gas reserves, be engaged in promising R&D projects, and have rising sales and market share. As the market learns this information from more timely sources, such as media articles, firm announcements, conditions in the economy and industry, quarterly reports, etc, share price would begin to rise. This reflects the partly informative nature of security prices since, in an efficient market, security prices reflect all available information, not just accounting information. Thus, firms that in a real sense are doing well would have much of the effect on their share prices anticipated by the efficient market before the GN appears in the financial statements. That is, *prices lead earnings* over a wide window.

Clearly, this effect was taking place in the BB study. As a result, it cannot be claimed that reported net income *causes* the abnormal returns during the 11 months leading up to month 0. The most that can be argued is that net income and returns are *associated*. That is, for wide windows, it is the real, underlying, economic performance of the firm that generates the association, since both share price and (with a lag) net income reflect real performance.

To pursue this "prices lead earnings" effect, suppose that we continue to widen the window, perhaps up to several years. We will find that the association between share returns and earnings increases as the window widens. While historical cost-based net income tends to lag behind the market in reflecting value-relevant events, as the window is widened the relative effect of the lag decreases. Over a long period of time the sum of net incomes reported over that period captures more of the effects of economic factors such as those described above, even though there may be a lag in their initial recognition. This effect was studied by Easton, Harris, and Ohlson (1992), who found that the association between security returns and historical cost-based earnings improved as the window was widened, up to 10 years. A similar effect was observed by Warfield and Wild (1992), who found that the association between security returns and earnings for annual reporting periods averaged over 10 times the association for quarterly periods.

In the long run, the total income earned by the firm, regardless of the basis of accounting, will approach total income under ideal conditions (on this point, see question 16). But a narrow window association, as BB found for month 0, provides stronger support for decision usefulness, since it suggests that it is the accounting information that actually causes investor belief revision and hence security returns.

5.3.3 Outcomes of the BB Study

One of the most important outcomes of BB was that it opened up a large number of additional usefulness issues. A logical next step is to ask whether the *magnitude* of unexpected earnings is related to the *magnitude* of the security market response—recall that BB's analysis was based only on the *sign* of unexpected earnings. That is, the information content of earnings in BB's study was classified only into GN or BN, a fairly coarse measure.

The question of magnitude of response was investigated, for example, by Beaver, Clarke, and Wright (BCW) in 1979. They examined a sample of 276 NYSE firms with December 31 year-ends, over the 10-year period from 1965 to 1974. For each sample firm, for each year of the sample period, they estimated the unexpected earnings changes.

They then used the market model procedure described in Sections 4.5 and 5.2.3 to estimate the abnormal security returns associated with these unexpected earnings changes.

Upon comparison of unexpected earnings changes with abnormal security returns, BCW found that the greater the change in unexpected earnings, the greater the security market response. This result is consistent with the CAPM (Section 4.5) and with the decision usefulness approach, since the larger are unexpected earnings changes the more investors on average will revise upwards their estimates of future firm performance and resulting returns from their investments, other things equal.

Also, since 1968, accounting researchers have studied securities market response to net income on other stock exchanges, in other countries, and for quarterly earnings reports, with similar results. The approach has been applied to study market response to the information contained in new accounting standards, auditor changes, etc. Here, however, we will concentrate on what is probably the most important extension of BB, earnings response coefficients. This line of research asks a different question than BCW, namely, for a *given* amount of unexpected earnings, is the security market response greater for some firms than for others?

5.4 Earnings Response Coefficients

Recall that the abnormal securities market returns identified by BB were *averages*, that is, they showed that on average their GN firms enjoyed positive abnormal returns, and negative for their BN firms. Of course, an average can conceal wide variation about the average. Thus, it is likely that some firms' abnormal returns were well above average and others' were well below.

This raises the question of *why* the market might respond more strongly to the good or bad news in earnings for some firms than for others. If answers to this question can be found, accountants can improve their understanding of how accounting information is useful to investors. This, in turn, could lead to the preparation of more useful financial statements.

Consequently, one of the most important directions that empirical financial accounting research took since the BB study is the identification and explanation of differential market response to earnings information. This is called **earnings response coefficient (ERC)** research.[7]

> An **earnings response coefficient** *measures the extent of a security's abnormal market return in response to the unexpected component of reported earnings of the firm issuing that security.*

5.4.1 Reasons for Differential Market Response

A number of reasons can be suggested for differential market response to historical cost-based earnings. We will review these in turn.

Beta The riskier is the sequence of a firm's future expected returns, the lower will be its value to a risk-averse investor, other things equal. For a diversified investor, the relevant risk measure of a security is its beta, explained in Section 3.7. Since investors look to current earnings as an indicator of future firm performance and share returns, the riskier these future returns are the lower investors' reactions to a given amount of unexpected earnings will be.

To illustrate, think of a typical risk-averse, rational investor whose utility increases in the expected value and decreases in the risk of the return on his or her portfolio. Suppose that the investor, upon becoming aware that a portfolio security has just released GN earnings information, revises upwards the expected rate of return on this security, and decides to buy more of it. However, if this security has high beta, this will increase portfolio risk.[8] Consequently, the investor would not buy as much more as if the security was low beta. In effect, the high beta acts as a brake on the investor's demand for the GN security. Since all risk-averse, rational informed investors will think this way, the demand for the GN firm's shares will be lower the higher is its beta, other things equal. Of course, lower demand implies a lower increase in market price and return in response to the GN, hence, a lower ERC.

Empirical evidence of a lower ERC for higher-beta securities has been found by Collins and Kothari (1989) and by Easton and Zmijewski (1989).

Capital Structure For highly levered firms, an increase, say, in earnings (before interest) adds strength and safety to bonds and other outstanding debt, so that much of the good news in earnings goes to the debtholders rather than the shareholders. Thus, the ERC for a highly levered firm should be lower than that of a firm with little or no debt, other things equal. Empirical evidence of a lower ERC for more highly levered firms has been reported by Dhaliwal, Lee, and Fargher (1991).

Persistence We would expect that the ERC will be higher the more the good or bad news in current earnings is expected to **persist** into the future. Thus, if current GN is due to the successful introduction of a new product or vigorous cost-cutting by management, the market response should be higher than if the GN was due to, say, an unanticipated gain on disposal of plant and equipment. In the latter case, the firm's market value increases dollar-for-dollar with the amount of the gain, since there is no reason to expect the unusual gain to recur. This implies a relatively low ERC. In the new product and cost-cutting cases, the ERC should be higher, since the revenue increases or cost savings will persist, to benefit future income statements as well. Evidence that ERCs are higher the higher the persistence of unexpected current earnings changes is presented by Kormendi and Lipe (1987).

Persistence is a challenging and useful concept. One reason, advanced by Ramakrishnan and Thomas (1991) (RT) is that different components of net income may have different persistence. For example, suppose that in the same year a firm successfully introduces a new product it also reports a gain on disposal of plant and equipment. Then, the persistence of earnings is an average of the differing persistence of the components of earnings. RT distinguish three types of earnings events:

- Permanent, expected to persist indefinitely
- Transitory, affecting earnings in the current year but not future years
- Price-irrelevant, persistence of zero

The ERCs per dollar of unexpected earnings for these are $(1 + R_f)/R_f$ (where R_f is the risk-free rate of interest under ideal conditions), 1, and 0 respectively.[9]

In effect, there are three ERCs, all of which may be present in the same income statement. RT suggest that instead of trying to estimate an average ERC, investors should attempt to identify the three types separately and assign different ERCs to each. In so doing, they can identify the firm's permanent, or persistent, earning power. This implies that accountants should provide lots of classification and detail on the income statement.

To understand the ERC for permanent earnings, note that it can be written as $1 + 1/R_f$. Thus, under ideal conditions, the market response to $1 of permanent earnings consists of the current year's installment of 1 plus the present value of the perpetuity of future installments of $1/R_f$. (This ignores riskiness of the future installments, which is appropriate if investors are risk-neutral or the permanent earnings are firm-specific.) Writing the ERC this way also shows that when earnings persist beyond the current year, the magnitude of the ERC varies inversely with the interest rate.

Another aspect of ERCs is that their persistence can depend on the firm's accounting policies. For example, suppose that a firm uses fair value accounting, say for a capital asset, and that the fair value of the asset increases by $100. Assume that the increase results from an increase in the price of the product produced by the asset. Then, assuming that changes in fair value are included in income, net income for the period will include[10] GN of $100. Since unexpected changes in fair value occur randomly, by definition, the market will not expect the $100 to persist. Thus, the ERC is 1.

Suppose instead that the firm uses historical cost accounting for the asset and that the annual increase in contribution margin is $9.09. Then there will be only $9.09 of GN in earnings this year. The reason, of course, is that under historical cost accounting the $100 increase in fair value is brought into income only as it is realized. The efficient market will recognize that the current $9.09 GN is only the "first installment." [11] If it regards the value increase as permanent and $R_f = 10\%$, the ERC will be 11 (1.10/0.10).

Zero-persistence income statement components can result from choice of accounting policy. Suppose, for example, that a firm capitalizes a large amount of organization costs. This could result in GN on the current income statement, which is freed of the costs because of their capitalization. However, assuming the organization costs have no salvage value, the market would not react to the "GN," that is, its persistence is zero. As another example, suppose that a firm writes off research costs currently in accordance with section 3450 of the *CICA Handbook*. This could produce BN in current earnings. However, to the extent the market perceives the research costs as having future value, it would not react negatively to this BN so that persistence is zero or negative. The possibility of zero or negative persistence suggests once more the need for detailed income statement disclosure, including a statement of accounting policies.

Earnings Quality   Intuitively, we would expect a higher ERC for higher-quality earnings. Recall from Section 3.3.2 that we define the quality of earnings by the magnitude of the main diagonal probabilities of the associated information system. The higher these probabilities, the higher we would expect the ERC to be, since investors are better able to infer future firm performance from current performance.

As a practical matter, measurement of earnings quality is less clear, since information system probabilities are not directly observable. One approach, discussed in Section 3.3.2, is to infer earnings quality by the magnitude of analysts' earnings forecast revisions following earnings announcements.

Another approach is suggested by DeChow and Dichev (2002).They point out that net income is composed of:

Net income = cash flow from operations ± net accruals

where net accruals, which can be positive or negative, include changes in non-cash working capital accounts such as receivables, allowance for doubtful accounts, inventories, accounts payable, etc., as well as amortization expense. They then argue that earnings quality depends primarily on the quality of working capital accruals, since cash flow from operations is relatively less subject to errors and manager bias.

To measure accrual quality, DeChow and Dichev suggest that to the extent current period working capital accruals show up as cash flows next period, those accruals are of high quality. For example, if accounts receivable at the end of the current period are $1,000, less an allowance for doubtful accounts of $100, and if $900 is collected next period, then the accounts receivable and doubtful accounts accruals are of high quality since they match perfectly with the cash subsequently collected. However, if only $800 is subsequently collected, the accruals are of lower quality since there has been an error in their estimation or, perhaps, deliberate net overstatement by management so as to increase current reported net income.

A similar argument applies to last period's accruals. Suppose, for example, that accounts receivable last period were $700, less an allowance for doubtful accounts of $60, and that they realized $600 in the current period. This lowers the quality of current accruals and earnings since current bad debts expense includes the $40 underprovision, which really belongs to last period.

To test their concept of accrual quality, DeChow and Dichev suggest estimating the following regression equation:

$$\Delta WC_t = b_0 + b_1 CFO_{t-1} + b_2 CFO_t + b_3 CFO_{t+1} + \varepsilon_t$$

where ΔWC_t is the change in net working capital for the firm in question for period t, that is, total working capital accruals. For example, in our illustration above, if accounts receivable and allowance for doubtful accounts are the only working capital items, working capital has increased by $\Delta WC_t = \$240$ (900 − 640) in period t. This is an accrual because net income includes this amount (assuming the firm recognizes income at point of sale) but it has not yet been received in cash.

CFO_{t-1} is cash flow from operations in period t − 1, etc., b_0, b_1 and b_2 are constants to be estimated, and ε_t is the residual error term, that is, the portion of total accruals not explained by cash from operations.

Accrual quality, hence earnings quality, is measured by the magnitude of ε_t, that is high ε_t indicates a poor match between current accruals ΔWC_t and actual operating cash flow realizations. Evidence that firm's share prices respond positively to accrual quality as measured by this procedure is reported by Francis, LaFond, Olsson, and Schipper (2004).

Growth Opportunities For reasons related to the above persistence and earnings quality arguments, the GN or BN in current earnings may suggest future growth prospects for the firm, and hence a higher ERC. One might think that historical cost-based net income really cannot say anything about the future growth of the firm. However, this is not necessarily the case. Suppose that current net income reveals unexpectedly high profitability for some of the firm's recent investment projects. This may indicate to the market that the firm will enjoy strong growth in the future. One reason, of course, is that to the extent the high profitability persists, the future profits will increase the firm's assets. In addition, success with current projects may suggest to the market that this firm is also capable of identifying and implementing additional successful projects in future, so that it becomes labelled as a growth firm. Such firms can easily attract capital and this is an additional source of growth. Thus, to the extent that current good news in earnings suggests growth opportunities, the ERC will be high.

To illustrate, extend the persistence example above by assuming that the $9.09 of current permanent earnings increase is expected to grow by 5% per year. The present value at 10% of a perpetuity that increases by 5% per year is $1/(0.10 - 0.05) = 20$, greater than $1/0.10 = 10$ under no-growth. Thus, the ERC is 21 rather than 11 as before.

Evidence that the ERC is higher for firms that the market regards as possessing growth opportunities is shown by Collins and Kothari (1989). They use the ratio of market value of equity to book value of equity as a measure of growth opportunities, the rationale being that the efficient market will be aware of the growth opportunities before they are recognized in net income and will bid up share price accordingly. Collins and Kothari find a positive relationship between this measure and the ERCs of their sample firms.

The Similarity of Investor Expectations Different investors will have different expectations of a firm's next-period earnings, depending on their prior information and the extent of their abilities to evaluate financial statement information. However, these differences will be reduced to the extent that they draw on a common information source, such as analysts' consensus forecasts, when forming their expectations. Consider a firm's announcement of its current earnings. Depending on their expectations, some investors will regard this information as GN, others as BN, hence some will be inclined to buy and some to sell. However, to the extent that investors' earnings expectations were "close together," they will put the same interpretation on the news. For example, if most investors base their earnings expectation on the analysts' consensus forecast, and current earnings are less than forecast, they will all regard this as BN and will be inclined to sell rather than buy. Thus, the more similar the earnings expectations the greater the effect of a dollar of abnormal earnings on share price. In effect, the more precise are analysts' forecasts the more similar are investors' earnings expectations and the greater the ERC, other things equal. For an analysis of conditions under which the ERC is increasing in the precision of analysts' earnings forecasts and how this precision is affected by factors such as earnings quality and number of analysts forecasting the firm, see Abarbanell, Lanen, and Verrecchia (1995).

The Informativeness of Price We have suggested on several previous occasions that market price itself is partially informative about the future value of the firm. In particular, price is informative about (i.e., leads) future earnings. Recall that the reason is that market price aggregates all publicly known information about the firm, much of which the accounting system recognizes with a lag. Consequently, the more informative is price, the less will be the information content of current accounting earnings, other things equal, hence the lower the ERC.

A proxy for the informativeness of price is *firm size*, since larger firms are more in the news. However, Easton and Zmijewski (1989) found that firm size was not a significant explanatory variable for the ERC. The reason is probably that firm size proxies for other firm characteristics, such as risk and growth, as much as it proxies for the informativeness of share price. Once these factors are controlled for, any significant effect of size on the ERC seems to go away. Collins and Kothari (1989) dealt with size by moving the wide window over which security returns were measured earlier in time for large firms, on the grounds that share price is more informative for such firms. They found that this substantially improved the relationship between changes in earnings and security returns, since a more informative share price implies that the market anticipates changes in earning power sooner. Once this time shifting was done, size appeared to have no explanatory power for the ERC.

5.4.2 Implications of ERC Research

Be sure that you see the reason *why* accountants should be interested in the market's response to financial accounting information. Essentially, the reason is that improved understanding of market response suggests ways that they can further improve the decision usefulness of financial statements. For example, lower informativeness of price for smaller firms implies that expanded disclosure for these firms would be useful for investors, contrary to a common argument that larger firms should have greater reporting responsibilities.

Also, the finding that ERCs are lower for highly levered firms supports arguments to expand disclosure of the nature and magnitude of financial instruments, including those that are off-balance-sheet. If the relative size of a firm's liabilities affects the market's response to net income, then it is desirable that all liabilities be disclosed.

The importance of growth opportunities to investors suggests, for example, the desirability of disclosure of segment information, since profitability information by segments would better enable investors to isolate the profitable, and unprofitable, operations of the firm. Also, MD&A enables the firm to communicate its growth prospects, as illustrated in Section 4.8.2.

Finally, the importance of persistence and quality of earnings to the ERC means that disclosure of the *components* of net income is useful for investors. In sum, lots of detail in the income statement, the balance sheet, and in supplemental information helps investors interpret the current earnings number.

5.4.3 Measuring Investors' Earnings Expectations

As mentioned previously, researchers must obtain a proxy for expected earnings, since the efficient market will only react to that portion of an earnings announcement that it did not expect. If a reasonable proxy is not obtained, the researcher may fail to identify a market reaction when one exists, or may incorrectly conclude that a market reaction exists when it does not. Thus, obtaining a reasonable estimate of earnings expectations is a crucial component of information perspective research.

Under the ideal conditions of Example 2.2, expected earnings is simply accretion of discount on opening firm value. When conditions are not ideal, however, earnings expectations are more complex. One approach is to project the time series formed by the firm's past reported net incomes, that is, to base future expectations on past performance. A reasonable projection, however, depends on earnings persistence. To see this, consider the extremes of 100% persistent earnings and zero persistent earnings. If earnings are completely persistent, expected earnings for the current year are just last year's actual earnings. Then, unexpected earnings are estimated as the *change* from last year. This approach was used by Ball and Brown, as described in Section 5.3. If earnings are of zero persistence, then there is no information in last year's earnings about future earnings, and all of current earnings are unexpected. That is, unexpected earnings are equal to the *level* of current year's earnings. This approach was used by Bill Cautious in Example 3.1.

Which extreme is closer to the truth? This can be evaluated by the degree of correlation between security returns and the estimate of unexpected earnings, a question examined by Easton and Harris (1991). Using regression analysis of a large sample of U.S. firms over the period 1969–1986, they documented a correlation between one-year security returns and the change in net income, consistent with the approach of Ball and Brown. However, there was an even stronger correlation between returns and the level of net income. Furthermore, when both earnings changes and levels were used, the two variables combined did a significantly better job of predicting returns than either variable separately. These results suggest that the truth is somewhere in the middle, that is, both changes in and levels of net income are components of the market's earnings expectations, where the relative weights on the two components depend on earnings persistence.

The foregoing discussion is based solely on a time series approach, however. Another source of earnings expectations is analysts' forecasts. These are now widely available for most large firms. If analysts' forecasts are more accurate than time series forecasts, they provide a better estimate of earnings expectations, since rational investors will presumably use the most accurate forecasts. Evidence by Brown, Hagerman, Griffin, and Zmijewski (1987), who studied the quarterly forecasting performance of one forecasting organization (Value Line), suggests that analysts outperform time series models in terms of accuracy. O'Brien (1988) also found that analysts' quarterly earnings forecasts were more accurate than time series forecasts. These results are what we would expect, since analysts can bring to bear information beyond that contained in past earnings when making their earnings projections.

When more than one analyst follows the same firm, it seems reasonable to take the consensus, or average, forecast as the proxy for the market's earnings expectation, following the reasoning underlying the football forecasting example of Section 4.2.2. O'Brien pointed out, however, that the age of a forecast has an important effect on its accuracy. She found that the single most recent earnings forecast provided a more accurate earnings prediction in her sample than the average forecast of all analysts following the firm, where the average ignored how old the individual forecasts were. This suggests that the timeliness of a forecast dominates the cancelling-out-of-errors effect of the average forecast.

Despite evidence that analysts' forecasts tend to be more accurate than forecasts based on time series, other evidence, discussed by Kothari (2001), suggests that analysts' forecasts are optimistically biased, although the bias may have decreased in recent years. Nevertheless, recent studies of the information content of earnings tend to base earnings expectations on analysts' forecasts.

Theory in Practice 5.1

Cisco Systems Inc. is a large provider of networking equipment, based in San Jose, California. In August 2004, it released financial results for the quarter ended July 30, 2004. Its revenues increased by 26% over the same quarter of 2003. Its net income for the quarter was $1.4 billion or 21 cents per share, a 41% increase over the same quarter of 2003, and 5% in excess of the average analysts' forecast of 20 cents.

Yet, Cisco's share price fell almost 18% to $18.29 following the announcement. This fall in price seems contrary to the results of Ball & Brown and subsequent researchers, who have documented a positive market response to good earnings news. However, certain balance sheet and supplemental information was not so favourable. For example, inventory turnover declined to 6.4 from 6.8 in 2003, gross margin declined slightly, order backlog was down and, while revenue was growing, its rate of growth appeared to be declining. Also, several analysts commented on an increase in inventories, suggesting lower accrual quality to the extent these inventories would be slow in selling. Furthermore, Cisco's CEO, commenting on the quarter's results, mentioned that the firm's customers were becoming more cautious about spending.

These negative signals implied low quality and negative persistence for the good earnings news, probably compounded by very similar investor expectations. The result was a negative ERC.

5.4.4 Summary

The information content of reported net income can be measured by the extent of security price change or, equivalently, by the size of the abnormal market return, around the time the market learns the current net income. This is because rational, informed investors will revise their expectations about future firm performance and share returns on the basis of current earnings information. Revised beliefs trigger buy/sell decisions, as investors move to restore the risk/return tradeoffs in their portfolios to desired levels. If there was no information content in net income there would be no belief revision, no resulting buy/sell decisions, and hence no associated price changes.

For a given amount of unexpected net income, the extent of security price change or abnormal returns depends on factors such as firm size, capital structure, risk, growth prospects, persistence, the similarity of investor expectations, and earnings quality.

Following the pioneering study of Ball and Brown, empirical research has demonstrated a differential market response depending on most of these factors. These empirical results are really quite remarkable. First, they have overcome substantial statistical and experimental design problems. Second, they show that the market is, on average, very sophisticated in its ability to evaluate accounting information. This supports the theory of securities market efficiency and the decision theories that underlie it. Finally, they support the decision usefulness approach to financial reporting.

Indeed, the extent to which historical cost-based net income can provide "clues" about future firm performance may seem surprising. The key, of course, is the information system probabilities, as shown in Table 3.2. In effect, the higher the main diagonal probabilities, the greater we would expect the ERC to be. This supports the FASB's contention in its Conceptual Framework that investors' expectations are based "at least partly on evaluations of past enterprise performance" (Section 3.8). As accountants gain a better understanding of investor response to financial statement information, their ability to provide useful information to investors will further increase.

5.5 Unusual, Non-recurring, and Extraordinary Items

In Section 5.4.1, we mentioned Ramakrishnan and Thomas' (1991) suggestion that investors separately estimate permanent, transitory, and price-irrelevant components of earnings. An interesting example of the importance of earnings persistence can be found in the reporting of events that are unusual and/or infrequent. Since these items may not recur regularly, their persistence will be transitory or price-irrelevant. This means that they must be fully disclosed; otherwise, the market may get an exaggerated impression of earnings persistence.

The reporting of **extraordinary items** is specified by Section 3480 of the *CICA Handbook*. In 1989, Section 3480 was revised to introduce greater consistency in the reporting of extraordinary items on the income statement. According to paragraph 3480.02:

> *Extraordinary items are items which result from transactions or events that have all of the following characteristics:*
>
> (a) *they are not expected to occur frequently over several years;*
> (b) *they do not typify the normal business activities of the entity; and*
> (c) *they do not depend primarily on decisions or determinations by management or owners.*

The last characteristic in the definition was added in the 1989 revision. Prior to that time, only the first two characteristics applied. The result was to eliminate a large number of former extraordinary items such as, for example, gains or losses on disposals of capital assets. After 1989 such unusual and non-recurring gains or losses would be included *before* income from continuing operations, because management controls the timing of such transactions.

This revision seems to resolve the issue of **classificatory smoothing**, whereby management could smooth (or otherwise manage) earnings from continuing operations by choosing to classify unusual items above or below the operating earnings line. Evidence that managers in the United States, prior to 1989, behaved as if they smoothed earnings from continuing operations by means of classificatory smoothing was reported by

Barnea, Ronen, and Sadan (1976). By requiring those unusual items whose amounts and/or timing could be controlled by management to be consistently reported as part of operating income, the 1989 revision effectively eliminated the ability to engage in classificatory smoothing. It therefore appeared that the new Section 3480 represented an improvement in financial reporting.

However, the nature of the improvement can be questioned, based on the ERC research outlined in Section 5.4. Specifically, unusual items have low persistence. For example, a gain on sale of capital assets would have persistence of 1 or less. Other unusual items could have persistence as low as zero, to the extent that they are not value-relevant at all.

The impact of the 1989 revisions to Section 3480 caused a number of low-persistence unusual and non-recurring items to move from extraordinary items up to the operating section of the income statement. The income statement format following from Section 3480 is summarized as follows (we ignore income taxes for simplicity):

Net income before unusual and non-recurring items,
    also called core earnings   x x

Unusual and non-recurring items   <u>x x</u>

Income from continuing operations,
    also called operating income   x x

Extraordinary items   <u>x x</u>

Net income   <u>x x</u>

Core earnings represents the persistent component of income, and is the basis of investors' estimates of future earning power. Unusual and non-recurring items are items that do not qualify as extraordinary items under Section 3480. As mentioned, they are of low persistence, by definition.

We can now see two related problems arising from the 1989 revisions to Section 3480. First, if unusual and non-recurring items are not fully disclosed, investors may overestimate the persistence of operating income, although Section 1520 and, more recently, Section 1400, of the *Handbook* do require disclosure of these items. Second, and of greater concern, the amounts and timing of the recording of unusual and non-recurring items are subject to strategic manipulation by management. For example, if management chooses to recognize an unusual loss currently, income from continuing operations is reduced. Furthermore, if the loss had been building up for some time, earnings of previous periods are, in retrospect, overstated. More serious, management may overstate the amount of the loss—the amounts of many losses, such as a writedown of goodwill from acquisitions, are highly subjective and difficult for investors to verify. Then, by excessively relieving *future* periods of charges for amortization, core earnings in future years are overstated. There is no requirement under current GAAP to separate out the effects of prior writedowns from core earnings.[12] Thus, the accounting for unusual and non-recurring items has the potential to confuse the matching of costs and revenues that is at the heart of historical cost-based accounting and, at the very least, complicates the evaluation of earnings persistence.

These issues were investigated by Elliott and Hanna (1996), who found a significant decline in the core earnings ERC in quarters following the reporting of a large unusual item (usually, these were losses rather than gains). Furthermore, the ERC declined further if the firm reported numerous large special items over time. This latter evidence is consistent with the market interpreting the frequency of recording of unusual and non-recurring items as a proxy for their potential misuse. We will return to the impact of extraordinary, unusual, and non-recurring items on core earnings in our discussion of earnings management in Chapter 11.

Thus, the question appears to be open whether Section 3480 actually succeeded in improving financial reporting. From our standpoint, however, Section 3480 represents an interesting example of how theory can be brought to bear to reexamine an issue that was thought resolved.

Theory in Practice 5.2

As a result of the September 11 terrorist attacks in the United States, numerous companies incurred substantial expenses and revenue losses. For example, airlines were unable to fly for two days.

In the United States, accounting standards for extraordinary items are similar to those given above for Canada. In a 2001 news release, the FASB decided against allowing costs resulting from the attacks to be treated as extraordinary items. The FASB had originally considered allowing at least some costs as extraordinary, but came to the conclusion that it would be impossible to reliably separate direct costs (e.g., airlines' losses of revenue during the two-day shutdown) from indirect costs (e.g., continuing loss of customers from public concerns about safety, and general loss of business and consumer confidence). Also, some of these costs would be recovered through insurance and government assistance. Consequently, the FASB concluded that all costs resulting from September 11 be classified as part of income from continuing operations, with any government assistance also reported in continuing operations, as a separate line item.

In this regard, *The Globe and Mail*, in an October 29, 2001 article, quoted Patricia O'Malley, a prominent Canadian accountant and member of the International Accounting Standards Board, as saying "given the world we live in, it would be hard to call them extraordinary."

5.6 A Caveat About the "Best" Accounting Policy

To this point, we have argued that accountants can be guided by securities market reaction in determining usefulness of financial accounting information. From this, it is tempting to conclude that the "best" accounting policy is the one that produces the greatest market price response. For example, if net income reported by oil and gas firms under successful-efforts accounting produces a greater market reaction than net income reported under full-cost accounting, successful-efforts should be used, because investors find it more useful.

However, we must be extremely careful about this conclusion. Accountants may be better off to the extent that they provide useful information to investors, but it does not follow that *society* will necessarily be better off.

The reason is that information has characteristics of a **public good**. A public good is a good such that consumption by one person does not destroy it for use by another. Consumption of a **private good**—such as an apple—eliminates its usefulness for other consumers. However, an investor can use the information in an annual report without eliminating its usefulness to other investors. Consequently, suppliers of public goods may have trouble charging for these products, so that we often witness them being supplied by governmental or quasi-governmental agencies—roads and national defence, for example. If a firm tried to charge investors for its annual report, it would probably not attract many customers, because a single annual report, once produced, could be downloaded to many users. Instead, we observe governments through securities legislation and corporations acts, *requiring* firms to issue annual reports.

Of course, firms' annual reports are not "free." Production of annual reports is costly. Other, more significant, costs include the disclosure of valuable information to competitors and the likelihood that manager operating decisions will be affected by the amount of information about those decisions that has to be released. For example, managers may curtail plans for expansion if too much information about them has to be disclosed. Investors will eventually pay for these costs through higher product prices. Nevertheless, investors perceive annual reports as free, since the extent to which they use them will not affect the product prices they pay. Also, investors may incur costs to inform themselves, either directly, or indirectly by paying for analyst or other information services. Nevertheless, the basic "raw material" is perceived as free and investors will do what any other rational consumer will do when prices are low—consume more of it. As a result, *investors may perceive accounting information as useful even though from society's standpoint the costs of this information outweigh the benefits to investors.*

Also, as mentioned in Chapter 1, information affects different people differently. Thus, information may be useful to potential investors and competitors but current shareholders may object to supplying it. As a result, the social value of such information depends on both the benefits to potential investors and competitors, and the costs to shareholders. Such cost-benefit tradeoffs are extremely difficult to make.

Think of information as a commodity, demanded by investors and supplied by firms through accountants. Because of the public-good aspect of information, we cannot rely on the forces of demand and supply to produce the socially "right" or first-best amount of production, as we can for private goods produced under competition. The essential reason is that the price system does not, and probably cannot, operate to charge investors the full costs of the information they use. Consequently, from a social perspective we cannot rely on the extent of security market response to tell us which accounting policies should be used (or, equivalently, "how much" information to produce). Formal arguments to support this conclusion were given by Gonedes and Dopuch (1974).

We will return to the question of regulation of information production in Chapters 12 and 13. For now, the point to realize is that it is still true that accountants can be guided by market response to maintain and improve their competitive position as suppliers to the marketplace for information. It is also true that securities markets will work better to the extent security prices provide good indications of underlying real investment opportunities. However, these social considerations do suggest that, as a general rule, accounting standard-setting bodies should be wary of using securities market response to guide their decisions.

Interestingly, an exception to this rule seems to have occurred with respect to standard setters' decisions to eliminate current cost accounting for capital assets. SFAS 33, which required U.S. firms to report supplemental current cost information for certain assets, was discontinued in 1986. Discontinuance was based in part on the influential study by Beaver and Landsman (1983), who failed to find any incremental securities market reaction to current cost information over and above the information content of historical cost-based net income.[13] In Canada, Hanna, Kennedy, and Richardson (1990) recommended the discontinuance of Section 4510 of the *CICA Handbook*, which laid down procedures for supplemental current cost disclosures for capital assets. They were unable to find evidence of usefulness of this information and the section was withdrawn in 1992. It is difficult to disagree with decisions to cease production of information that no one finds useful. Nevertheless, from a social perspective, no one knows whether this decision was correct, due to the difficulties of measuring social costs and benefits.

5.7 The Information Content of RRA

In this section we depart from our concentration on the information content of historical cost-based net income in order to consider the informativeness of other financial statement information. Specifically, we will consider whether RRA information has additional information content over historical cost net income and book value. Recall from Section 2.4 that SFAS 69 requires oil and gas firms to report supplementary present value information about proved reserves.

A priori, we would expect that if supplemental fair value-oriented information is going to be useful for investors, it would be in the oil and gas industry. One could argue, for example, that historical cost and fair value are especially likely to diverge in this industry—a lucky firm might, at low cost, find a bonanza. More importantly, we pointed out the implications of inside information in Section 4.6. Since so much of the value of an exploring/producing oil company depends on its reserves, shares of such a firm seem especially susceptible to the problems of information asymmetry, as illustrated by the reserve problems of Royal Dutch/Shell outlined in Section 2.4.3. Consequently, the market should be particularly interested in reserves information. However, RRA reserves information will only be useful to investors if it enables better predictions of firm performance. Indeed, we will see that empirical tests of RRA decision usefulness are not clear-cut.

The theoretical and empirical ability of RRA to explain the market's evaluation of oil and gas reserves was extensively investigated by Magliolo (1986), in tests conducted on a sample of firms over 1979–1983, inclusive. In one set of tests, Magliolo compared the undiscounted value of net reserves reported in RRA to an estimate of the market's valuation of those reserves. This RRA information did not perform according to theory in its ability to explain market value. Indeed, RRA was outperformed by reserve information provided by an investment service. This service makes a number of adjustments to the current operating data of oil and gas firms to arrive at an economic estimate of revenues and costs. The implication is that RRA, in addition to concerns about reliability, may not be as relevant as competing sources of reserves information.

Magliolo also examined the ability of the elements of an RRA-based income statement (see Table 2.5 for such a statement) to explain *changes* in the market's valuation of reserves. He found that additional reserves proved during the year had significant explanatory power, although some of it appeared to be anticipated by the market, which suggests that other, more timely information sources are available to investors. Other components of the RRA income statement had little explanatory ability. Magliolo concluded that, overall, RRA does not measure the market values of oil and gas reserves as theory would predict.

Other researchers have also investigated the information content of RRA. Doran, Collins, and Dhaliwal (1988) (DCD) studied a sample of 173 producing oil and gas firms over the six-year period 1979–1984. They studied the sub-periods 1979–1981 and 1982–1984 separately.[14]

For each sample observation, DCD calculated monthly abnormal returns as in Figure 5.2 for a 12-month period ending on the firm's year-end (December 31), and summed them for each observation to give a 12-month abnormal return. The question then was, to what extent did RRA information have incremental ability, in addition to the change in historical cost net income, to explain the abnormal return? You will recognize that this approach is similar to that discussed in Sections 5.2 and 5.3, except that now two variables are being used to explain abnormal security returns, rather than one. To the extent that the two-variable model does a better job of explaining abnormal returns than a model using only historical cost-based net income, it can be argued that the supplemental RRA information is useful for investors, in the sense that it has information content about future share returns over and above the information content of historical cost net income.

Using regression analysis, DCD showed that during 1979–1981 *both* historical cost and RRA information had significant explanatory power, supporting the incremental usefulness of RRA. However, during 1982–1984, *neither* variable had significant explanatory power. Thus, their results were mixed. DCD attributed this to the fact that oil and gas market prices were much more volatile during the earlier period. Consequently, investors would be particularly interested in information about reserves and expected market prices during 1979–1981.

Nevertheless, the fact that they also found historical cost-based net income not to have significant explanatory power for abnormal returns during 1982–1984 is puzzling, since this conflicts with the wealth of evidence about the usefulness of income discussed in Sections 5.3 and 5.4. DCD attribute this result to the fact that the market was expecting an oil glut during 1982–1984 and that the effects of this expectation on oil company share prices swamped the impact of reported net income.[15]

Despite these explanations, DCD's results provide, at best, fairly weak evidence in favour of RRA. This lack of strong results also shows up in other studies. For example, Harris and Ohlson (1987) (HO) examined the ability of RRA information to explain the market value of the oil and gas assets[16] of producing firms, rather than abnormal returns as in DCD. Using a sample of 273 observations over the five-year period from 1979 to 1983, they found that the book value of oil and gas assets[17] had significant explanatory power for the market value of these assets. RRA information also had some explanatory power, but less than historical cost.

HO also examined the usefulness of reserve quantity information. SFAS 69 also requires that quantities of proved oil and gas reserves, and changes in the quantities during the year, be disclosed. HO found that quantity information had no incremental explanatory power beyond RRA. In other words, when both quantity information and RRA information are available it seems that investors go for RRA.

It should be pointed out that the DCD study was "wide window," that is, security returns were measured over a 12-month period. Thus, even if a significant association between security returns and RRA was found, this does not mean that the RRA information *causes* abnormal security returns. The most that can be said is that security market price and RRA both reflect the underlying value of future returns from oil and gas properties. This does not necessarily mean that RRA information is not useful, since, knowing that RRA reflects underlying value, investors may use this information in their investment decisions. It does mean, however, that RRA competes with information from other sources. For example, Ghicas and Pastena (1989) also examined the incremental information content of RRA. However, they introduced financial analyst forecasts of oil company values as a *third* explanatory variable. They found that when recent analyst information was available any ability that RRA had to explain oil company value disappeared. Thus, a further constraint on the decision usefulness of RRA is that its potential relevance may be superseded by other, more timely sources of information, consistent with Magliolo's finding.

Even if we ignore the question of timeliness, however, the difficulty that empirical research has had to demonstrate decision usefulness of RRA is surprising. Given the apparent sophistication of security market reaction to reported net income, one would expect a similar reaction to relevant balance sheet and supplementary information.

Several reasons can be suggested for the weak results for RRA. One is reliability, as mentioned. Perhaps RRA is too imprecise to be useful. We saw in Section 2.4.3 that management is lukewarm about the usefulness of RRA, claiming low reliability. Second, the research faces more severe methodological difficulties than it does in finding a market reaction to net income. One problem is in finding the point in time that the market first becomes aware of the RRA information. For net income, media publication of the earnings announcement provides a reasonable event date. However, given the inside nature of oil and gas reserves information and its importance to firm value, analysts and others may work particularly hard to ferret it out in advance of the annual report. If a reasonable event date for the release of reserve information cannot be found, return studies must use wide windows, which are open to a large number of influences on price in addition to accounting information.

A third reason may be that historical cost-based information about oil and gas reserves may be more value-relevant than implied by our discussion above. HO suggest that oil companies will not throw money away on exploration and development but, rather, will only spend it if the expected benefits at least equal the costs. This means that the higher is the book value of an oil company's oil and gas properties, the more the company thinks they are worth (allowing for risk), and vice versa. If this argument that book value makes economic sense is combined with the greater reliability of historical cost information than RRA, it is not surprising that the market may find historical cost book value more useful.

In a followup study, Harris and Ohlson (1990) (HO) investigated the information content of historical cost reserves information more closely. They continued to find that historical cost dominated RRA. Furthermore, their results suggest that the market, if anything, underuses the information content of historical cost reserves information. This finding is of interest because it raises the alternative possibility that securities markets may not be as efficient as the information perspective assumes.

However, one must be cautious in accusing the market of a lack of sophistication. Instead of searching for a direct link between other financial statement information and abnormal security returns, as the above studies have done, there is an indirect approach that links other information to the quality of earnings. To illustrate, suppose that an oil company reports high earnings this year, but supplemental oil and gas information shows that its reserves have declined substantially over the year. An interpretation of this information is that the firm has used up its reserves to increase sales in the short run. If so, the quality of current earnings is reduced, since they contain a non-persistent component that will dissipate if new reserves are not found. Then, the market's reaction to the bad news in the supplemental reserve information may be more easily found in a low ERC than in a direct reaction to the reserve information itself. A higher ERC would be expected if reserves had increased.

While their study was not specifically oriented to oil and gas firms, this approach was used by Lev and Thiagarajan (1993) (LT). They identified 12 "fundamentals" used by financial analysts in evaluating earnings quality. For example, one fundamental was the change in inventories, relative to sales. If inventories increase, this may suggest a decline in earnings quality—the firm may be entering a period of low sales, or simply be managing its inventories less effectively. Other fundamentals include change in capital expenditures, order backlog, and, in the case of an oil and gas company, the change in its reserves.

For each firm in their sample, LT calculated a measure of earnings quality by assigning a score of 1 or 0 to each of that firm's 12 fundamentals, then adding the scores. For example, for inventories, a 1 is assigned if that firm's inventories, relative to sales, are down for the year, suggesting higher earnings quality, and a 0 score is assigned if inventories are up.

When LT added these fundamental scores as an additional explanatory variable in an ERC regression analysis, there was a substantial increase in ability to explain abnormal security returns beyond the explanatory power of unexpected earnings alone. This suggests that the market, aided perhaps by analysts, is quite sophisticated in its evaluation of earnings, using balance sheet and supplementary information to augment the information content of the earnings announcement itself.

5.8   Conclusions on the Information Perspective

The empirical literature in financial accounting is vast, and we have looked only at certain parts of it. Nevertheless, we have seen that, for the most part, the securities market response to reported net income is impressive in terms of its sophistication. Results of empirical research in this area support the efficient markets theory and related decision theories.

What is puzzling, however, is that the market does not seem to respond to non-earnings information as strongly as it does to earnings information. RRA was examined as an example of non-earnings information where, a priori, a strong market response would be expected. The extent to which the lack of strong market response to non-earnings information such as RRA is due to methodological difficulties, to its low reliability, to availability of alternative information sources, or to failure of efficient markets theory itself is not fully understood at the present time, although it may be that investors route their reaction to such information, at least partly, through their perceptions of earnings quality.

As stated earlier, the approach to financial accounting theory that equates the extent of security price change with information content and hence with decision usefulness, is known as the information perspective. The essence of this approach is that investors are viewed as attempting to predict future returns from their investments. They seek all relevant information in this regard, not just accounting information. To maximize their competitive position as suppliers of information, accountants may then seek to use the extent of security market response to various types of accounting information as a guide to its usefulness to investors. This motivates their interest in empirical research on decision usefulness. Furthermore, the more information accountants can move from inside to outside the firm, the better can capital markets guide the flow of scarce investment funds.

Despite these considerations, accountants must be careful of concluding that the accounting policies and disclosures that produce the greatest market response are the best for society. This is not necessarily true, due to the public-good nature of accounting information. Investors will not necessarily demand the "right" amount of information, since they do not bear its full costs. These concerns limit the ability of decision usefulness research to guide accounting standard setters.

Nevertheless, until recently, the information perspective has dominated financial accounting theory and research since the Ball and Brown paper of 1968. It has led to a tremendous amount of empirical investigation that has enriched our understanding of the decision usefulness of accounting information for investors.

Questions and Problems

1. Explain the information perspective on financial reporting. Does it rely on the historical cost basis of accounting? (CGA-Canada)

2. Refer to the separation of market-wide and firm-specific security returns as shown in Figure 5.2. What factors could reduce the accuracy of the estimate of abnormal returns? (CGA-Canada)

3. Explain why the market might begin to anticipate the GN or BN in earnings as much as a year in advance, as Ball and Brown found in Figure 5.3. (CGA-Canada)

4. Give examples of components of net income with:
   a. High persistence
   b. Persistence of 1
   c. Persistence of 0 (CGA-Canada)

5. Explain why it is desirable to find the exact time that the market first became aware of an item of accounting information if any security price reaction to this information is to be detected. Can such a time always be found? Explain why or why not. What can researchers do when the exact time cannot be isolated? (CGA-Canada)

6. Is a negative ERC possible? Explain why or why not.

7. A researcher finds evidence of a security price reaction to an item of accounting information during a narrow window of three days surrounding the date of release of this information and claims that it was the accounting information that caused the security price reaction. Another researcher finds evidence of security price reaction to a different item of accounting information during a wide window beginning 12 months prior to the release of the financial statements containing that item. This researcher does not claim that the accounting information caused the security price reaction but only that the information and the market price reaction were associated.

Explain why one can claim causation for a narrow window but not for a wide window. Which price reaction constitutes the stronger evidence for usefulness of accounting information? Explain.

8. XYZ Ltd. is a large retail company listed on a major stock exchange, and its reported net income for the year ended December 31, 2005 is $5 million. The earnings were announced to the public on December 31, 2005.

Financial analysts had predicted the company's net income for 2005 to be $7 million. The financial analysts' prediction of $7 million net income was in effect up until the release of the 2005 earnings on December 31, 2005.

Assumptions

- No other news about XYZ Ltd. was released to the public on December 31, 2005.
- No significant economy-wide events affecting share prices occurred on December 31, 2005.
- Financial analysts' forecasts about XYZ Ltd.'s net income represented the market's expectations about XYZ Ltd.'s income.

Required
a. Would you expect a change in price of XYZ Ltd.'s common stock on December 31, 2005? If so, why? Explain.
b. Consider the two situations below:

    i. The deviation of forecasted earnings from actual earnings of $2 million ($7 million − $5 million) is completely accounted for by the closing down of a number of its retail outlets.

    ii. The deviation of the forecasted earnings from actual earnings of $2 million is completely accounted for by a fire in XYZ Ltd.'s largest retail outlet, which had caused the outlet to be closed temporarily for six months.

In which of these two scenarios would you expect the price change of XYZ Ltd.'s common stock to be greater? Explain.

9. In a classic study, Beaver (1968) examined the trading volume of firms' securities around the time of their earnings announcements. Specifically, he examined 506

annual earnings announcements of 143 NYSE firms over the years 1961–1965 inclusive (261 weeks).

For each earnings announcement, Beaver calculated the average daily trading volume (of the shares of the firm making that announcement) for each week of a 17-week window surrounding week 0 (the week in which the earnings announcement was made). For each firm in the sample, he also calculated the average daily trading volume outside its 17-week window. This was taken as the normal trading volume for that firm's shares.

For each week in the 17-week window, Beaver averaged the trading volumes over the 506 earnings announcements in the sample. The results are shown in Figure 5.4 below. The dotted line in the figure shows the average normal trading volume outside the 17-week window.

As can be seen from the figure, there was a dramatic increase in trading volume, relative to normal, in week 0. Also, volume is below normal during most of the weeks leading up to week 0.

FIGURE 5.4 VOLUME ANALYSIS

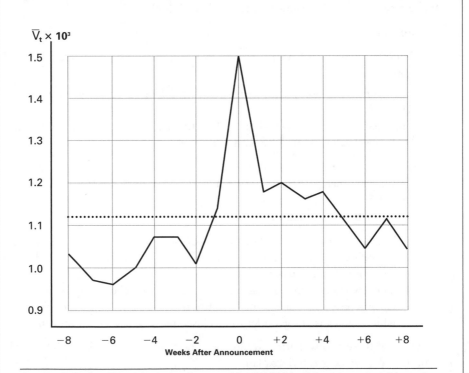

Source: W. Beaver, "The Information Content of Annual Earnings Announcements," Journal of Accounting Research, Supplement, 1968: 67–92. Reprinted by permission.

Required

a. Why do you think trading volume increased in week 0?

b. Why do you think trading volume was below normal in the weeks leading up to week 0?

c. Do Beaver's volume results support the decision usefulness of earnings information? Explain.

d. Which is the better indicator of decision usefulness, the abnormal return measure (Figure 5.2) or the volume measure? Explain. (CGA-Canada)

10. Discuss the impact of firm size on the ERC.

11. X Ltd. is a growth firm that uses very conservative accounting policies. Y Ltd. is growing more slowly and uses fair value accounting for its capital assets and related amortization.

Otherwise, X Ltd. and Y Ltd. are quite similar. They are the same size, and have similar capital structures and similar betas.

Required

a. Both X Ltd. and Y Ltd. report the same GN in earnings this year. Which firm would you expect to have the greater security market response (ERC) to this good earnings news? Explain.

b. Suppose that X Ltd. had a much higher debt-to-equity ratio and beta than Y Ltd. Would your answer to part **a** change? Explain.

12. On the basis of the empirical evidence presented in this chapter, do you feel the FASB is correct in its claim in SFAC 1 (see Section 3.8) that investors' expectations about future enterprise performance "are commonly based at least partly on evaluations of past enterprise performance?" Explain.

13. By defining extraordinary items to be infrequent, not typical of normal business activities, and not depending on management decision, Section 3480 of the *CICA Handbook* greatly increases the need for adequate disclosure of the components of reported net income. Explain why.

14. Explain why financial statement information has characteristics of a public good. Include a definition of a public good in your answer. What does this imply about using the *extent* of security market reaction to accounting information to guide accountants? Standard setters?

15. You estimate empirically the ERC of firm J as 0.38. Firm K is identical to firm J in terms of size, earning power, persistence of earnings, and risk. Unlike firm J, however, firm K includes a high-quality financial forecast in its MD&A. You estimate firm K's ERC as 0.57. Which firm's net income report appears to be more useful to investors? Explain. Does this mean that all firms should be required to prepare high-quality financial forecasts? Explain.

16. It is important to realize that different bases of accounting, such as present value accounting and historical cost-based accounting, do not affect total earnings over the life of the firm, but only the timing of the recognition of those earnings. In effect, over the life of the firm, the firm "earns what it earns," and different bases of accounting will all produce earnings that add up to this total.

If this is so, then we would expect that the greater the number of time periods over which we aggregate a firm's historical cost earnings, the closer the resulting total will be to economic earnings, that is, the earnings total that would be produced over the same periods under ideal conditions.

This was studied by Easton, Harris, and Ohlson (1992) (EHO) and by Warfield and Wild (1992) (WW). EHO proxied economic income by the return on the firm's shares on the securities market. When this return was aggregated over varying periods of time (up to 10 years) and compared with historical cost-based earnings returns for similar periods, the comparison improved as the time period lengthened. WW studied a similar phenomenon for shorter periods. They found, for example, that the association between economic and accounting income for quarterly time periods was on average about 1/10 of their association for an annual period, consistent with historical cost-based net income lagging behind economic income in its recognition of relevant economic events.

Required

a.   In Example 2.1, calculate net income for years 1 and 2 assuming that P.V. Ltd. used straight-line amortization for its capital asset, while retaining all other assumptions. Verify that total net income over the two-year life of P.V. Ltd. equals the total net income that P.V. Ltd. would report using present value amortization.

b.   Do the same in Example 2.2, assuming that the state realization is bad and good in years 1 and 2 respectively.

c.   Use the fact that accruals reverse to explain why total net income over the two years in **a** and **b** above are the same under economic and straight-line amortization. Are these results consistent with the empirical results of EHO and WW outlined above?

17. On May 8, 2001, the *Financial Post* reported "The Street Turns Against Canadian Tire." Canadian Tire Corporation, Limited's share price had risen by $0.75 to $24.90 on May 2, 2001, following a news release in which Wayne Sales, president and CEO at the time, said "We are pleased with our ability to deliver double digit growth . . . ." Canadian Tire's reported earnings of $0.37 per share exceeded analysts' expectations.

The market soon learned, however, that reported earnings included an $8 million one-time gain on sale of certain Canadian Tire assets. Without this gain, earnings were $0.29 per share, 6% below earnings for the same quarter of 2000. Canadian Tire's share price quickly fell back to $22.95.

The *Post* reported that "Passing off" a one-time gain as part of operating earnings "didn't fool or impress analysts" and is something they "hoped not to see again."

Required

a.   Use efficient securities market theory to explain the rise in Canadian Tire's share price on May 2, 2001, and the rapid subsequent fall in share price.

b.   Was Canadian Tire correct in including the $8 million one-time gain in operating income? Explain.

c. Evaluate the persistence of Canadian Tire's reported net income of $0.37 per share (no calculations required). Does the fact of Mr. Sale's ignoring of this item in his press release affect your evaluation? Explain why or why not.

18. On October 19, 2000, *The Globe and Mail* reported on Imperial Oil Ltd.'s earnings for the third quarter ended on September 30, 2000, released on October 18. Net income was a record $374 million, up from $191 million for the same quarter of the previous year. Return on equity was 25.7%, up from 10.1% a year earlier. Earnings for the quarter included a $60 million gain on Imperial's sale of its Cynthia pipeline and other assets. Cash flow for the quarter was $433 million, up from $270 million in the previous year's third quarter. The reported profit of $374 million was in line with analysts' expectations.

On October 18, the TSE oil and gas index rose by 0.6%, as the market anticipated higher prices for oil and gas. Yet, Imperial's share price fell on the day by $1.25, to close at $37.35. *The Globe and Mail* also reported analysts' comments about a widening discount for heavy crude oil, relative to light crude. Imperial is Canada's biggest producer of heavy crude. Also, Imperial's production from its oil sands projects declined in the quarter, due to maintenance and temporary production problems.

Required
a. Calculate the abnormal return, relative to the TSE oil and gas index, on Imperial Oil's shares for October 18, 2000. Imperial Oil's beta is approximately 0.65.
b. Is the abnormal decline in Imperial's share price on October 18 consistent with efficient securities market theory? Explain why or why not. Consider earnings persistence in your answer.
c. In what section of the income statement should the $60 million gain on the sale of the Cynthia pipeline be reported? Explain.

19. Refer to the Theory in Practice 5.2 in Section 5.5 concerning the September 11 terrorist attacks in the United States.

Required
a. Do you agree that the costs resulting from September 11 are not extraordinary items? Explain why or why not.
b. Evaluate the persistence (in words—no calculations required) of these costs.
c. From the standpoint of efficient markets theory, how should these costs be disclosed? Does it matter whether or not they are classified as extraordinary?

20. On October 21, 2004, Abitibi-Consolidated Inc., a large Canadian-based newsprint and groundwood producer, reported income from continuing operations for its third quarter, 2004, of $182 million, or $0.41 per share. This compares with a net loss from continuing operations for the same quarter of 2003 of $70 million, or $0.16 per share. Sales for the quarter were $1,528 million, and core earnings (i.e., excluding unusual and non-recurring items) were $82 million. The analyst forecast for the third quarter, 2004, was a loss of $0.06 per share.

Unusual and non-recurring items included a gain of $239 million from foreign exchange conversion. Much of the company's long-term debt is denominated in U.S. dollars. The foreign exchange gain arose because of the rising value of the Canadian dollar, relative to the U.S. dollar, during the quarter.

Comparable figures for the third quarter of 2003 were: sales of $1,340 million, a core loss of $32 million, and foreign exchange conversion gain of $13 million.

There is no mention of R&D costs in the company's third quarter report. Its 2003 annual report mentions R&D only in passing, with reference to forest conservation. Presumably, R&D expenditures are relatively low.

Abitibi-Consolidated's share price rose $0.59 to $7.29 on the Toronto stock exchange on October 21, 2004. The S&P/TSX index gained 59 points to close at 8847 on the same day. According to media reports, the increases were driven by a "red-hot" materials and energy sector (including Abitibi-Consolidated). In a conference call accompanying its third quarter report, Abitibi-Consolidated's CEO complained that investors were too pessimistic about the company. The company's beta, according to Yahoo! Finance, is 0.779.

Required

a. Evaluate (in words only) the persistence of Abitibi-Consolidated's operating income for the third quarter of 2004.

b. The company reported no extraordinary items in its third quarter report. Do you feel that the foreign exchange gain of $239 million should have been reported as extraordinary, rather than as unusual and non-recurring? Explain why or why not.

c. Do you feel that the increase in Abitibi-Consolidated's share price on October 21 was consistent with efficient securities market theory or do you agree with the CEO? Explain, and show any calculations.

Notes

1. As mentioned in Section 4.5, this estimate of α_j should equal $(1 - \beta_j)R_f$, where R_f is the risk-free rate of interest. Here, $\alpha_j = 0.0001$ implies $R_f = 0.0005$ per day.

2. The market return for day 0 is calculated as follows:

$$R_{M0} = \frac{\text{Level of DJ Index, end of day 0} + \text{Dividends on DJ Index on day 0}}{\text{Level of DJ Index, beginning of day 0}} - 1$$

Sometimes, because of data problems, the dividends are omitted.

3. Calculated as:

$$E(R_{jt}) = \alpha_j + \beta_j R_{M0}$$
$$= 0.0001 + (0.80 \times 0.001)$$
$$= 0.0009$$

4. Again, this abnormal return should not be confused with abnormal earnings of P.V. Ltd. in Example 2.2. While the idea is the same, abnormal return here refers to a *market* return, whereas abnormal earnings refer to *accounting* net income.

5. Other ways to estimate investor expectations are discussed in Section 5.4.3.

6. Note that the loss on bad news firms can be converted into a gain by selling short the shares of the bad news firms.

7. For reasons explained in Section 5.3.2, the interpretation of a narrow-window ERC is different from a wide-window ERC. Here we will refer, somewhat loosely, to both types as simply ERCs.

8. Recall from Section 3.7 that in reasonably diversified portfolios, most of the portfolio risk stems from the betas of the securities in the portfolio. Thus, if the investor were to buy more shares of a security whose beta is greater than the average beta of the securities presently in the portfolio, this will raise the average, hence increasing portfolio risk.

9. These are "market value" ERCs, where the market's response to GN or BN is expressed in terms of the abnormal change in market value, rather than the abnormal return as in our ERC definition. To convert a market value ERC to a rate of return ERC, divide it by opening firm value.

10. This is analogous to the inclusion of unexpected oil and gas price changes in income under RRA. See the alternative format in Table 2.5.

11. This assumes that the market knows that the increase in market value is $100. Possibly, this would be known from sources other than the financial statements. If not, considerable onus is put on the firm for full disclosure. Perhaps MD&A provides a vehicle for management to reveal this information.

12. Note that under RRA, adjustments to prior period estimates are reported separately. Perhaps this approach could be adopted for the effects of current write-offs on future core earnings. If so, this would constitute a major extension of full disclosure. We will return to this possibility in Section 11.6.3.

13. A number of reasons other than lack of usefulness can be suggested for these results. First, the market may value the information but is able to estimate it from other sources. Second, the information may be relevant but unreliable, since a large number of assumptions and estimates go into its preparation. Third, the market may have reacted to the information but the research methodology was not sufficiently powerful to find it. For example, the Beaver and Landsman (1983) study was criti-

cized by Bernard (1987) on methodological grounds. Indeed, some evidence of securities market reaction has been found in studies subsequent to Beaver and Landsman. Thus, Bernard and Ruland (1987) found some information content for current cost information, at least in certain industries.

14. SFAS 69 came into effect in 1982. However, the SEC required disclosure of information similar to RRA information from 1979 to 1981.

15. Note that the procedure to separate economy-wide returns and abnormal returns illustrated in Figure 5.2 does *not* remove industry-wide returns. These will be buried in abnormal returns under the Figure 5.2 procedure, because all firms in DCD's sample were in the oil and gas industry. This illustrates one of the difficulties of working with data from a single industry in empirical studies.

16. HO estimated the market value of oil and gas assets by subtracting the book value of net non-oil and gas assets from the market value of the firm's capital stock and marketable debt.

17. HO's significant result held for both book value on a successful-efforts basis and on a full-cost basis.

Chapter 6

The Measurement Perspective on Decision Usefulness

FIGURE 6.1 ORGANIZATION OF CHAPTER 6

6.1 Overview

The measurement perspective on decision usefulness implies greater usage of fair values in the financial statements proper. Following from our discussion in Section 2.5.1, greater use of fair values suggests a balance sheet approach to financial reporting, as opposed to the income statement approach that underlies the research described in Chapter 5.

We define the measurement perspective as follows:

*The **measurement perspective** on decision usefulness is an approach to financial reporting under which accountants undertake a responsibility to incorporate fair values into the financial statements proper, providing that this can be done with reasonable reliability, thereby recognizing an increased obligation to assist investors to predict firm value.*

Of course, if a measurement perspective is to be useful, it must not be at the cost of a substantial reduction in reliability. While it is unlikely that a measurement perspective will *replace* the historical cost basis of accounting, it is the case that the relative balance of cost-based versus fair value-based information in the financial statements is moving in the fair value direction. This may seem strange, given the problems that techniques such as RRA accounting have experienced. However, a number of reasons can be suggested for the change in emphasis.

One such reason involves securities market efficiency. Despite the impressive results outlined in Chapter 5 in favour of the decision usefulness of reported net income, recent years have seen increasing theory and evidence suggesting that securities markets may not be as efficient as originally believed. This suggestion has major implications for accounting. To the extent that securities markets are not fully efficient, the reliance on efficient markets to justify historical cost-based financial statements supplemented by much supplementary disclosure, which underlies the information perspective's approach to decision usefulness, is threatened. For example, if investors collectively are not as adept at processing information as rational decision theory assumes, perhaps usefulness would be enhanced by greater use of fair values in the financial statements proper. Furthermore, while beta is the only relevant risk measure according to the CAPM, perhaps accountants should take more responsibility for reporting on firm risk if markets are not fully efficient.

Other reasons derive from a low proportion of share price variability explained by historical cost-based net income, from the Ohlson clean surplus theory that provides support for increased measurement, and from the legal liability to which accountants are exposed when firms become financially distressed.

In this chapter we will outline and discuss these various reasons. Figure 6.1 outlines the organization of this chapter.

6.2 Are Securities Markets Efficient?

6.2.1 Introduction

In recent years, increasing questions have been raised about the extent of securities market efficiency. These questions are of considerable importance to accountants since, if they are valid, the practice of relying on supplementary information in notes and elsewhere to augment the basic historical cost-based financial statements may not be completely effective in conveying useful information to investors. Furthermore, if securities markets are not fully efficient, improved financial reporting may be helpful in reducing inefficiencies, thereby improving the operation of securities markets. In this section, we will outline and discuss the major questions that have been raised about market efficiency.

The basic premise of these questions is that average investor behaviour may not correspond with the rational decision theory and investment models outlined in Chapter 3. For example, individuals may have **limited attention**. That is, they may not have time and ability to process all available information. Then, they will concentrate on information that is readily available, such as the "bottom line," and ignore information in notes and elsewhere in the annual report. Furthermore, investors may be biased in their reaction to information, relative to how they should react according to Bayes' theorem. For example, psychological evidence suggests that individuals tend to be **overconfi-**

dent—they overestimate the precision of information they collect themselves (see, for example, the discussion in Odean (1998)). If an individual's information collecting activities reveal GN, for example, he or she will revise their subjective probability of high future performance by more than they should according to Bayes' theorem. If a significant proportion of investors behave this way, share price will overreact to the GN, at least in the short run.

Another attribute of many individuals is **self-attribution bias**, whereby individuals feel that good decision outcomes are due to their abilities, whereas bad outcomes are due to unfortunate realizations of states of nature, hence not their fault. Suppose that following an overconfident investor's decision to purchase a firm's shares, its share price rises (for whatever reason). Then, the investor's faith in his or her investment ability rises. If share price falls, faith in ability does not fall. If enough investors behave this way, share price **momentum** will develop. That is, reinforced confidence following a rise in share price leads to the purchase of more shares, and share price rises further. Confidence is again reinforced, and the process feeds upon itself, that is, it gains momentum. Daniel, Hirshleifer and Subrahmanyam (1998) present a model whereby momentum develops when investors are overconfident and self-attribution biased. Daniel and Titman (1999), in an empirical study, report that over the period 1968–1997 a strategy of buying portfolios of high-momentum shares and short-selling low-momentum ones earned high and persistent abnormal returns (i.e., higher than the return from holding the market portfolio), consistent with the overconfidence and momentum arguments.[1]

Self-attribution bias and momentum are, of course, inconsistent with securities market efficiency and underlying decision theory. According to the CAPM, higher returns can only be earned if higher beta risk is borne. Yet Daniel and Titman report that the average beta risk of their momentum portfolios was less than that of the market portfolio. Furthermore, share price momentum implies positive serial correlation of returns, contrary to the random walk behaviour of returns under market efficiency.

The study of behavioural-based securities market inefficiencies is called **behavioural finance**. For a comprehensive review of the theory and evidence of behavioural finance, see Hirshleifer (2001). We now review several other questions about efficiency that have been raised in this theory.

6.2.2 Prospect Theory

The **prospect theory** of Kahneman and Tversky (1979) provides a behavioural-based alternative to the rational decision theory described in Section 3.3. According to prospect theory, an investor considering a risky investment (a "prospect") will separately evaluate prospective gains and losses. This separate evaluation contrasts with decision theory where investors evaluate decisions in terms of their effects on their total wealth (see Chapter 3, Note 4). Separate evaluation of gains and losses about a reference point is an implication of the psychological concept of **narrow framing**, whereby individuals analyze problems in too isolated a manner, as a way of economizing on the mental effort of decision making. This mental effort may derive from limited attention, as mentioned above. As a result, an individual's utility in prospect theory is defined over deviations from zero for the prospect in question, rather than over total wealth.

Figure 6.2 shows a typical investor utility function under prospect theory.

FIGURE 6.2 PROSPECT THEORY UTILITY FUNCTION

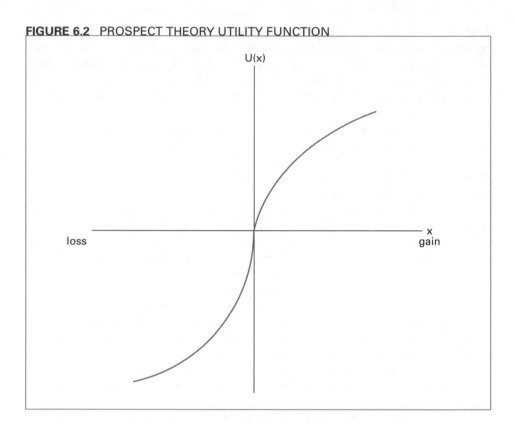

The investor's utility for gains is assumed to exhibit the familiar risk-averse, concave shape as illustrated in Figure 3.3. However, prospect theory assumes **loss aversion**, a behavioural concept whereby individuals dislike even very small losses. Thus, beginning at the point where the investment starts to lose in value, the investor's rate of utility loss is greater than the rate of utility increase for a gain in value.[2] Indeed, the utility for losses is assumed to be convex rather than concave, so that the investor exhibits risk taking behaviour with respect to losses. This leads to a **disposition effect**, whereby the investor holds on to losers and sells winners, and, indeed, may even buy more of a loser security. The disposition effect was studied by Shefrin and Statman (1985). They identified a sample of investors whose rational decision was to sell loser securities before the end of the taxation year. They found, however, that the investors tended to avoid selling, consistent with the disposition effect.

Prospect theory also assumes that when calculating the expected value of a prospect, individuals "weight" their probabilities. This weighting is a ramification of overconfidence. Thus, evidence (e.g., GN) that a state (e.g., high future performance) is likely to happen will be underweighted, particularly if the evidence is abstract, statistical, and highly relevant. In effect, by underweighting evidence that a state is likely to happen, the main diagonal probabilities of the information system are perceived by the overconfident investor as lower than they actually are. As a result, the individual's posterior probability of the state is also too low. However, individuals tend to overweight salient, anecdotal, and extreme evidence (e.g., a media article claiming that a stock is about to take off), even though realization of the state "taking off" is a rare event.

These tendencies lead to "too low" posterior probabilities on states that are likely to happen, and "too high" on states that are unlikely to happen. The posterior probabilities need not sum to one.

The combination of separate evaluation of gains and losses and the weighting of probabilities can lead to a wide variety of "irrational" behaviours. For example, fear of losses may cause investors to stay out of the market even if prospects have positive expected value according to a decision theory calculation. Also, they may underreact to bad news by holding on to "losers" so as to avoid realizing a loss and, as mentioned above, may even buy more of a loser stock, thereby taking on added risk. Thus, under prospect theory, investor behaviour depends in a complex way on the levels of payoff probabilities, risk aversion with respect to gains, and risk taking with respect to losses.

Theory in Practice 6.1

A number of experiments have tested the predictions of prospect theory. In one experiment (Knetsch (1989)), a group of student subjects was each given a chocolate bar and another group each given a mug. The 2 items (i.e., prospects) were of roughly equal monetary value. The subjects were then allowed the option of trading with other subjects. For example, a student who had received a chocolate bar but who preferred a mug could exchange with someone who wanted a chocolate bar. Since the 2 items were of equal value, and were assigned randomly to the subjects, rationality predicts that about half of them would trade. However, only about 10% traded.

These results are consistent with prospect theory. This can be seen from Figure 6.2. Since the rate at which investor utility decreases for small losses is greater than the rate at which it increases for small gains, disposing of ("losing") an item already owned creates a larger utility loss than the utility gained by acquiring another item of equal value. As a result, the subjects tended to hold on to the item they had been given.

Subsequent experiments by List (2003) cast these results in a different light, however. List conducted experiments in real markets, rather than in simulated markets with student subjects as above. A distinguishing feature of real markets is that they contain traders with varying degrees of experience. List found that as their experience increased, the behaviour of market participants converged towards that predicted by rational decision theory. He also showed how more experienced traders could buy and sell from less sophisticated ones so as to drive market prices towards their efficient levels.[3] Consequently, List's results tend to support the rational decision theory over prospect theory.

There are few empirical accounting tests of prospect theory. However, one such test was conducted by Burgstahler and Dichev (1997). In a large sample of U.S. firms from 1974–1976, these researchers documented that relatively few firms in their sample reported small losses. A relatively large number of firms reported small positive earnings. Burgstahler and Dichev interpreted this result as evidence that firms that would otherwise report a small loss manipulate cash flows and accruals to manage their reported earnings upwards, so as to instead show small positive earnings (techniques of earnings management are discussed in Chapter 11).

As Burgstahler and Dichev point out, this result is consistent with prospect theory. To see why, note again from Figure 6.2 that the rate at which investor utility decreases for small losses is greater than the rate at which it increases for small gains. This implies a relatively strong negative investor reaction to a small reported loss. Managers of firms that would otherwise report a small loss thus have an incentive to avoid this negative investor reaction, and enjoy a positive reaction, by managing reported earnings upwards. (Of course, managers of firms with *large* losses have similar incentives, but as the loss increases it becomes more difficult to manage earnings sufficiently to avoid the loss. Also, the incentive to manage earnings upwards declines for larger losses since the rate of negative investor reaction is not as great.)

However, Burgstahler and Dichev suggest that their evidence is also consistent with rational behaviour. Lenders will demand better terms from firms that report losses, for example. Also, suppliers may cut the firm off, or demand immediate payment for goods shipped. To avoid these consequences, managers have an incentive to avoid reporting losses if possible. Also, firms in a loss position may be eligible for income tax refunds, which could put them into a small profit position even without deliberate earnings management. As a result, the extent to which Burgstahler and Dichev's findings support prospect theory is unclear.

6.2.3 Is Beta Dead?

As mentioned in Section 4.5, an implication of the CAPM is that a stock's beta is the sole firm-specific determinant of the expected return on that stock. If the CAPM reasonably captures rational investor behaviour, share returns should be increasing in βj and should be unaffected by other measures of firm-specific risk, which are diversified away. However, in a large sample of firms traded on major U.S. stock exchanges over the period 1963–1990, Fama and French (1992) found that beta, and thus the CAPM, had little ability to explain stock returns. Instead, they found significant explanatory power for the book-to-market ratio (B/M) (ratio of book value of common equity to market value). They also found explanatory power for firm size. Their results suggest that rather than looking to beta as a risk measure, the market acts as if firm risk increases with book-to-market and decreases with firm size.

Fama and French's findings are not necessarily inconsistent with rational investor behaviour and efficient securities markets. For example, investors may purchase shares of low B/M firms to protect themselves against undiversifiable risk of, say, a downturn in the economy that would lead many firms into financial distress. Purchasing shares of low B/M firms provides such protection since one reason that the market assigns high market value, relative to book value, to a firm is that the firm is unlikely to become financially distressed. The $E(R_{Mt})$ term of the market model (see Section 4.5) may not fully capture the risk of financial distress since it is an average across all firms in the market. As a result, rational investors will look to other risk measures, such as book-to-market, when making their portfolio decisions.

The Fama and French results do threaten the CAPM, however, since they imply that beta is not the only relevant risk measure. The low explanatory power for beta documented by Fama and French has led some to suggest that beta is "dead."

Somewhat different results are reported by Kothari, Shanken, and Sloan (1995), however. They found that over a longer period of time (1941–1990) beta *was* a significant predictor of return. Book-to-market also predicted return, but its effect was relatively weak. They attributed the difference between their results and those of Fama and French to differences in methodology and time period studied.

Behavioural finance, however, provides a different perspective on the validity of the CAPM and beta. That is, share return behaviour inconsistent with the CAPM is viewed as evidence of market inefficiency. In this regard, Daniel, Hirshleifer, and Subrahmanyam (2001) present a model that assumes two types of investors—rational and overconfident. Because of rational investors, a stock's beta is positively related to its returns, as in the CAPM. However, overconfident investors overreact as they gather information. This drives share price too high or low, driving the firm's book-to-market ratio too low or high. Over time, share price reverts towards its efficient level as the overconfidence is revealed. As a result, both beta and book-to-market ratio are positively related to future share returns. However, in the Daniel, Hirshleifer, and Subrahmanyam model, the positive book-to-market relation to future share returns found by Fama and French is not driven by rational investors protecting themselves against financial distress. Rather, it is driven by overconfidence, a behavioural effect inconsistent with rationality and efficiency.

The status of the CAPM and its implications for beta thus seem unclear. A possible way to rescue beta is to recognize that it may change over time. Our discussion in Section 4.5 assumed that beta was **stationary**. However, events such as changes in interest rates and firms' capital structures, improvements in firms' abilities to manage risk, and development of global markets may affect the relationship between the return on individual firms' shares and the marketwide return, thereby affecting the value of firms' betas. If so, evidence of share return behaviour that appears to conflict with the CAPM could perhaps be explained by shifts in beta.

If betas are non-stationary, rational investors will want to know when and by how much they have changed. This is a difficult question to answer in a timely manner, and different investors will have different opinions. This introduces differences in their investment decisions, even though they all have access to the same information and proceed rationally with respect to their estimate of what beta is. In effect, an additional source of estimation risk (see section 4.5), beyond the uncertainty resulting from random states of nature and possible insider trading, is introduced into the market. This arises from the mistakes investors make in evaluating new values of non-stationary share price parameters. As a result, additional volatility is introduced into share price behaviour but beta remains as a variable that explains this behaviour. That is, the CAPM implication that beta is an important risk variable is reinstated, with the proviso that beta is non-stationary. Models that assume rational investor behaviour in the face of non-stationarity [4] are presented by Kurz (1997). Evidence that non-stationarity of beta explains much of the apparent anomalous behaviour of share prices is provided by Ball and Kothari (1989).[5]

From an accounting standpoint, to the extent that beta is not the only relevant firm-specific risk measure, this can only increase the role of financial statements in reporting useful risk information (the book-to-market ratio is an accounting-based variable, for example). Nevertheless, in the face of the mixed evidence reported above, we conclude that beta is not dead. However, it may change over time and may have to "move over" to share its status as a risk measure with accounting-based variables.

6.2.4 Excess Stock Market Volatility

Further questions about securities market efficiency derive from evidence of excess stock price volatility at the market level. Recall from the CAPM that, holding beta and the risk-free interest rate constant, a change in the expected return on the market portfolio, $E(R_{Mt})$, is the only reason for a change in the expected return of firm j's shares. Now the fundamental determinant of $E(R_{Mt})$ is the aggregate expected dividends across all firms in the market—the higher are aggregate expected dividends the more investors will invest in the market, increasing demand for shares and driving the stock market index up (and vice versa). Consequently, if the market is efficient, changes in $E(R_{Mt})$ should not exceed changes in aggregate expected dividends.

This reasoning was investigated by Shiller (1981), who found that the variability of the stock market index was several times greater than the variability of aggregate dividends. Shiller interpreted this result as evidence of market inefficiency.

Subsequently, Ackert and Smith (1993) pointed out that while expected future dividends are the fundamental determinant of firm value, they should be defined broadly to include all cash distributions to shareholders, such as share repurchases and distributions following takeovers, as well as ordinary dividends. In a study covering the years 1950–1991, Ackert and Smith showed that when these additional items were included, excess volatility disappeared.

However, despite Ackert and Smith's results, there are reasons why excess volatility may exist. One reason, consistent with efficiency, derives from non-stationarity, as outlined in the previous section. Other reasons derive from behavioural factors. The momentum model of Daniel, Hirshleifer, and Subrahmanyam (2001) implies excess market volatility as share prices overshoot and then fall back. A different argument is made by DeLong, Shleifer, Summers, and Waldmann (1990). They assume a capital market with both rational and positive feedback investors. Positive feedback investors are those who buy in when share price begins to rise, and vice versa. One might expect that rational investors would then sell short, anticipating the share price decline that will follow the price run-up caused by positive feedback buying. However, the authors argue that rational investors will instead "jump on the bandwagon," to take advantage of the price run-up while it lasts. As a result, there is excess volatility in the market.

In sum, it seems that the question of excess market volatility raised by Shiller is unresolved. The results of Ackert and Smith suggest it does not exist if dividends are defined broadly. Even if excess volatility does exist, it can possibly be explained by rational models based on non-stationarity. Alternatively, volatility may be driven by behavioural factors, whereby prices overreact then fall back as the overreaction is revealed, inconsistent with market efficiency.

6.2.5 Stock Market Bubbles

Stock market bubbles, wherein share prices rise far above rational values, represent an extreme case of market volatility. Shiller (2000) investigates bubble behaviour with specific reference to the surge in share prices of technology companies in the United States in the years leading up to 2000. Bubbles, according to Shiller, derive from a combination of biased self-attribution and resulting momentum, positive feedback trading, and to "herd" behaviour reinforced by optimistic media predictions of market "experts." These reasons underlie Federal Reserve Board Chairman Greenspan's famous "irrational exuberance" comment on the stock market in a 1996 speech.

Shiller argues that bubble behaviour can continue for some time, and that it is difficult to predict when it will end. Eventually, however, it will burst because of growing beliefs of, say, impending recession or increasing inflation.

6.2.6 Efficient Securities Market Anomalies

We conclude this section with evidence of market inefficiency that specifically involves financial accounting information. Recall that the evidence described in Chapter 5 generally supports efficiency and the rational investor behaviour underlying it. There is, however, other evidence suggesting that the market may not respond to information exactly as the efficiency theory predicts. For example, share prices sometimes take some time to fully react to financial statement information, so that abnormal security returns persist for some time following the release of the information. Also, it appears that the market may not always extract all the information content from financial statements. Cases such as these that appear inconsistent with securities market efficiency are called **efficient securities market anomalies**. We now consider two such anomalies.

Post-announcement Drift Once a firm's current earnings become known, the information content should be quickly digested by investors and incorporated into the efficient market price. However, it has long been known that this is not exactly what happens. For firms that report good news in quarterly earnings, their abnormal security returns tend to drift upwards for at least 60 days following their earnings announcement. Similarly, firms that report bad news in earnings tend to have their abnormal security returns drift downwards for a similar period. This phenomenon is called **post-announcement drift**. Traces of this behaviour can be seen in the Ball and Brown study reviewed in Section 5.3—see Figure 5.3 and notice that abnormal share returns drift upwards and downwards for some time following the month of release of GN and BN, respectively.

Reasons for post-announcement drift have been extensively studied. For example, Foster, Olsen, and Shevlin (1984) examined several possible explanations for its existence. Their results suggested that apparent post-announcement drift may be an artifact of the earnings expectation model used by the researcher. As outlined in Chapter 5, most studies of securities market response to earnings announcements measure their information content by some proxy for unexpected earnings, on the grounds that the market will only respond to that portion of a current earnings announcement that it did not expect. When these authors proxied unexpected earnings by the change in earnings from the same quarter last year, they found strong evidence of post-announcement drift.

However, with other proxies for unexpected earnings, there appeared to be no such drift. Since we do not know which earnings expectation model is the correct one, or, for that matter, even whether unexpected earnings is the best construct for measuring investor reaction (see Section 5.4.3), the Foster, Olsen, and Shevlin results tended to leave the existence of post-announcement drift up in the air, so to speak.

Be sure you see the significance of post-announcement drift. If it exists, investors could earn arbitrage profits, at least before transactions costs and before taking risk into account, by buying shares of good news firms on the day they announced their earnings and selling short shares of bad news firms. But, if investors scrambled to do this, the prices of good news firms' shares would rise right away, and those of bad news firms' shares would fall, thereby eliminating the post-announcement drift.

Bernard and Thomas (1989) (BT) further examined this issue. In a large sample of firms over the period 1974–1986, they documented the presence of post-announcement drift in quarterly earnings. Indeed, an investor following the strategy of buying the shares of GN firms and selling short BN on the day of earnings announcement, and holding for 60 days, would have earned an average return of 18%, over and above the marketwide return, before transactions costs, in their sample.

An explanation is that *investors appear to underestimate the implications of current earnings for future earnings*. As BT point out, it is a known fact that quarterly seasonal earnings changes are positively correlated. That is, if a firm reports, say, GN this quarter, in the sense that this quarter's earnings are greater than the same quarter last year, there is a greater than 50% chance that its next-quarter earnings will also be greater than last year's. Rational investors should anticipate this and, as they bid up the price of the firm's shares in response to the *current* GN, they should bid them up some more due to the increased probability of GN in *future* periods. However, BT's evidence suggests that this does not happen. The implication is that post-announcement drift results from the market taking considerable time to figure this out, or at least that it underestimates the magnitude of the correlation (Ball and Bartov, 1996). In terms of the information system given in Table 3.2, BT's results suggest that Bill Cautious evaluates the main diagonal probabilities as less than they really are.

Researchers continue to try to solve the post-announcement drift puzzle. For example, Bartov, Radhakrishnan, and Krinsky (2000) point out that the market contains sophisticated and unsophisticated investors. They find that post-announcement drift is less if a greater proportion of a firm's shares is held by institutional investors. To the extent that institutions are a good proxy for sophisticated investors, their results suggest that post-announcement drift is driven by unsophisticated investors who, presumably, do not comprehend the full information in current quarterly earnings. Also, Brown and Han (2000) find that post-announcement drift holds, in their sample, only for firms with poor information environments (small firms, firms with little analyst following, and firms with few institutional investors).

While studies such as these increase our understanding of post-announcement drift, they do not fully explain why it continues to exist. Thus, post-announcement drift continues to represent a serious and important challenge to securities market efficiency.

Market Response to Accruals

Sloan (1996), for a large sample of 40,769 annual earnings announcements over the years 1962–1991, separated reported net income into operating cash flow and accrual components. This can be done by recalling the formula introduced in Section 5.4.1:

Net income = cash flow from operations ± net accruals

where net accruals include amortization expense and net changes in non-cash working capital such as receivables, allowance for doubtful accounts, inventories, accounts payable, etc.

Sloan points out that, other things equal, the efficient market should react more strongly to a dollar of good news in net income if that dollar comes from operating cash flow rather than from accruals. The reason is familiar from elementary accounting—accruals reverse. Thus, looking ahead, a dollar of operating cash flow this period is more likely to be repeated next period than a dollar of accruals, since the effects of accruals on earnings reverse in future periods. In other words, cash flow is more persistent. Sloan estimated separately the persistence of the operating cash flows and accruals components of net income for the firms in his sample, and found that operating cash flows had higher persistence than accruals. That is, consistent with the above "accruals reverse" argument, next year's reported net income was more highly associated with the operating cash flow component of the current year's income than with the accrual component.

If this is the case, we would expect the efficient market to respond more strongly to the GN or BN in earnings the greater is the cash flow component relative to the accrual component in that GN or BN, and vice versa. Sloan found that this was not the case. While the market did respond to the GN or BN in earnings, it did not seem to "fine-tune" its response to take into account the cash flow and accruals composition of those earnings. Indeed, by designing an investment strategy to exploit the market mispricing of shares with a high or low accruals component in earnings, Sloan demonstrated a one-year return of 10.4% over and above the market return.

Sloan's results raise further questions about securities market efficiency.

Discussion of Efficient Securities Market Anomalies

Numerous investigators have tried to explain anomalies without abandoning efficient securities market theory. One possibility is risk. If the investment strategies that appear to earn anomalous returns identify firms that have high betas, then what appear to be arbitrage profits are really a reward for holding risky stocks.[6] The authors of the anomaly studies were aware of this possibility, of course, and conducted tests of the riskiness of their investment strategies. In all cases, they concluded that risk effects were not driving their results, although these conclusions have received extensive investigation by others.

Another possible explanation for the anomalies is transactions costs. The investment strategies required to earn arbitrage profits may be quite costly in terms of investor time and effort, requiring not only brokerage costs but continuous monitoring of earnings announcements, annual reports, market prices; overcoming any behavioural biases, and development of the required expertise.[7] Bernard and Thomas (1989) present some evidence that transactions costs limit the ability of investors to exploit post-announcement drift. Thus, their 18% annual return, and Sloan's 10.4% may appear to be anomalous only because the costs of the investment strategies required to earn them are at least this high.

If we accept this argument, securities market efficiency can be reconciled with the anomalies, at least up to the level of transactions costs. To put it another way, we would hardly expect the market to be efficient with respect to more information than it is cost-effective for investors to acquire.

The problem with a transactions cost-based defence of efficiency, however, is that any apparent anomaly can be dismissed on cost grounds. If cost is used to explain everything, then it explains nothing. That is, unless we know what the costs of an investment strategy *should* be, we do not know whether the profits earned by that strategy are anomalous. We conclude that the efficient securities market anomalies continue to raise challenging questions about the extent of securities market efficiency.

6.2.7 Implications of Securities Market Inefficiency for Financial Reporting

To the extent that securities markets are not fully efficient, this can only increase the importance of financial reporting. To see why, let us expand the concept of noise traders introduced in Section 4.4.1, as suggested by Lee (2001). Specifically, now define noise traders to also include investors subject to the behavioural biases outlined above. An immediate consequence is that noise no longer has expectation zero. That is, even in terms of expectation, share prices may be biased up or down relative to their fundamental values. Over time, however, rational investors, including analysts, will discover such mispricing and take advantage of it, driving prices towards fundamental values.

Improved financial reporting, by giving investors more help in predicting fundamental firm value, will speed up this arbitrage process. Indeed, by reducing the costs of rational analysis, better reporting may reduce the extent of investors' behavioural biases. In effect, securities market inefficiency supports a measurement perspective.

6.2.8 Conclusions About Securities Market Efficiency

Collectively, the theory and evidence discussed in the previous sections raise serious questions about the extent of securities market efficiency. Fama (1998), however, evaluates much of this evidence and concludes that it does not yet explain the "big picture." That is, while there is evidence of market behaviour inconsistent with efficiency, there is not a unified alternative theory that predicts and integrates the anomalous evidence. For example, Fama points out that apparent overreaction of share prices to information is about as common as underreaction. Thus, post-announcement drift involves underreaction to accounting information whereas the Sloan accruals anomaly involves overreaction to the accrual component of net income. What is needed to meet Fama's concern is a theory that predicts when the market will overreact and when it will underreact.

This lack of a unified theory may be changing. The theoretical models of Daniel, Hirshleifer, and Subrahmanyam (see Sections 6.2.1 and 6.2.3) incorporate behavioural variables into rigorous economic models of the capital market. They generate predictions of momentum, volatility, and drift that are consistent with many of the empirical observations. More recently, Hirshleifer and Teoh (2003) present a model in which some investors are fully rational but others have limited ability to process publicly available information. Limited ability implies that the *form* of presentation, as opposed simply to its information content, affects investors' interpretations of the information. For example, consider the question of expensing of executive stock options (ESOs), versus showing ESO cost in the notes to the financial statements (this controversy will be discussed in Sections 7.3.3 and 8.3). The Hirshleifer and Teoh model predicts that failure to expense ESOs results in overvaluation of the firm. This is because investors with limited ability to process information concentrate on reported net income, ignoring the ESO cost information buried in the notes. Expensing ESOs makes it easier for these investors to realize that ESOs have a cost, and that the firm is less profitable than it may appear. This prediction is in stark contrast to efficient securities market theory, which predicts that whether or not ESOs are expensed makes no difference to firm value as long as the cost is disclosed somewhere.

With respect to the empirical studies that support behavioural finance, Fama criticizes their methodology, arguing that many of the anomalies tend to disappear with changes in how security returns are measured. Kothari (2001) gives an extensive discussion of these issues, cautioning that much apparent inefficiency may instead be the result of methodological problems. Consideration and evaluation of these problems is beyond our scope here.

Studies that claim to show market inefficiencies are often disputed on the grounds that the "smart money," that is, rational investors, will step in and immediately arbitrage away any share mispricing. In the process, investors that are not fully rational will suffer losses and will be forced out of the market. Defenders of behavioural finance argue that this is not necessarily the case. One argument is that rational, risk averse investors will be unsure of the extent of irrational investor behaviour, and will not be sure how long momentum and bubbles will last. As a result of this added risk, they hesitate to take positions that fully eliminate mispricing. Another argument (DeLong, Shleifer, Summers, and Waldmann (1990)—see Section 6.2.4) is that rational investors may jump on the bandwagon to take advantage of momentum-driven price rises while they last. In effect, behavioural finance argues that "irrational" behaviour may persist.

There is evidence that biased investor behaviour and resultant mispricing is strongest for firms for which financial evaluation is difficult, such as firms with a large amount of unrecorded intangible assets, growth firms and, generally, firms where information asymmetry between insiders and outsiders is high. For example, Daniel and Titman (1999)—see Section 6.2.1—found greater momentum in stocks with low book-to-market ratios than in stocks with high ratios. Firms with low book-to-market ratios include growth firms and firms with unrecorded intangibles. This suggests that greater use of a measurement perspective for intangible assets, such as goodwill (to be discussed in Section 7.4), has a role to play in reducing investor biases and controlling market inefficiencies. Kothari (2001) cautions, however, that studies that claim to find evidence of inefficiencies for firms in poor information environments are particularly subject to methodological problems, since, by definition, data on such firms are less reliable.

Finally, notwithstanding the title of this section, whether securities markets are or are not efficient is really not the right question. Instead, the question is one of the extent of efficiency. The evidence described in Chapter 5, for example, suggests considerable efficiency. To the extent that markets are reasonably efficient, the rational decision theory which underlies efficiency continues to provide guidance to accountants about investors' decision needs. A more important question for accountants is the extent to which a measurement perspective will increase decision usefulness, thereby reducing any securities market inefficiencies that exist. For example, if behavioural factors cause share prices to depart from efficient values, a measurement perspective may speed up their reversion to these values.

We conclude that the efficient securities market model is still the most useful model to guide financial reporting, but that the theory and evidence of inefficiency has accumulated to the point where it supports a measurement perspective, even though this may involve a sacrifice of some reliability for increased relevance.

6.3 Other Reasons Supporting a Measurement Perspective

A number of considerations come together to suggest that the decision usefulness of financial reporting may be enhanced by increased attention to measurement. As just discussed, securities markets may not be as efficient as previously believed. Thus, investors may need more help in assessing probabilities of future firm performance than they obtain from historical cost statements. Also, we shall see that reported net income explains only a small part of the variation of security prices around the date of earnings announcements, and the portion explained may be decreasing. This raises questions about the relevance of historical cost-based reporting.

From a theoretical direction, the clean surplus theory of Ohlson shows that the market value of the firm can be expressed in terms of income statement and balance sheet variables. While the clean surplus theory applies to any basis of accounting, its demonstration that firm value depends on fundamental accounting variables is consistent with a measurement perspective.

Finally, increased attention to measurement is supported by more practical considerations. In recent years, auditors have been subjected to major lawsuits. In retrospect, it appears that net asset values of failed firms were seriously overstated. Accounting standards that require marking-to-market, ceiling tests, and other fair value-based techniques may help to reduce auditor liability in this regard.

We now review these other considerations in more detail.

6.4 The Value Relevance of Financial Statement Information

In Chapter 5 we saw that empirical accounting research has established that security prices do respond to the information content of net income. The ERC research, in particular, suggests that the market is quite sophisticated in its ability to extract value implications from financial statements prepared on the historical cost basis.

However, Lev (1989) pointed out that the market's response to the good or bad news in earnings is really quite small, even *after* the impact of economy-wide events has been allowed for as explained in Figure 5.2. In fact, only 2 to 5% of the abnormal variability of narrow-window security returns around the date of release of earnings information can be attributed to earnings itself.[8] The proportion of variability explained goes up somewhat for wider windows—see our discussion in Section 5.3.2. Nevertheless, most of the variability of security returns seems due to factors other than the change of earnings. This finding has led to studies of the **value relevance** of financial statement information, that is, the extent to which financial statement information has a material effect on share returns and prices.

An understanding of Lev's point requires an appreciation of the difference between **statistical significance** and **practical significance**. Statistics that measure value relevance such as R^2 (see Note 8) and the ERC can be significantly different from zero in a statistical sense, but yet can be quite small. Thus, we can be quite sure that there *is* a security market response to earnings (as opposed to *no* response) but at the same time we can be disappointed that the response is not larger than it is. To put it another way, suppose that, on average, security prices change by $1 during a narrow window of three or four days around the date of earnings announcements. Then, Lev's point is that only about two to five cents of this change is due to the earnings announcement itself, even after allowing for market-wide price changes during this period.

Indeed, value relevance may be deteriorating. Brown, Lo, and Lys (1999), for a large sample of U.S. stocks, conclude that R^2 has decreased over the period 1958–1996. They also examined the trend of the ERC over the same period—recall from Section 5.4.2 that the ERC is a measure of the usefulness of earnings. Brown, Lo, and Lys found that the ERC also had declined over 1958–1966. Lev and Zarowin (1999), in a study covering 1978–1996, found similar results of declining R^2 and ERC. A falling ERC is more ominous than a falling R^2, since a falling R^2 perhaps due to an increased impact over time of other information sources on share price, rather than a decline in the value relevance of accounting information. The ERC, however, is a direct measure of accounting value relevance, regardless of the magnitude of other information sources.

Contrasting evidence, however, is provided by Landsman and Maydew (2002), for a sample of quarterly earnings announcements over 1972–1988. Instead of R^2 and ERC, they measured the information content of earnings by the resulting abnormal security return, that is, by the residual of the market model (Section 4.5). Recall from Section 5.2.3 that the residual term of the market model measures the firm-specific information content of an earnings announcement. By this measure, Landsman and Maydew found that the information content of earnings had *increased* over the period they studied.

This raises the question, how can the R^2 and ERC fall but abnormal return increase? A reconciliation is suggested by Francis, Schipper and Vincent (2002). They point out an increasing tendency for large firms to report other information, such as sales, unusual and non-recurring items, and forward-looking information at the same time as they make their earnings announcements. Thus, while the share price response to net income as such (measured by R^2 and ERC) may be falling, the response to the earnings announcement taken as a whole (measured by abnormal return) is increasing. Francis, Schipper and Vincent present evidence consistent with this argument.

Of course, we would never expect net income to explain *all* of a security's abnormal return, except under ideal conditions. Historical cost accounting and conservatism means that net income lags in recognizing much economically significant information, such as the value of intangibles. Recognition lag lowers R^2 by waiting longer than the market before recognizing value-relev̄   ̄ ̄
Even if accountants were   ˄ᵐation to the market, our discus-
sion of the informativeness of   ˜ ᵑeed to recognize the
presence of noise and liquidit   ̄ᵗ explain
all of abnormal return vari   ɔeta

(Section 6.2.3) and excess volatility introduced by non-rational investors (Section 6.2.4) further increase the amount of share price volatility to be explained.

Nevertheless, a "market share" for net income of only 2 to 5% and falling seems low, even after the above counterarguments are taken into account. Lev attributed this low share to poor earnings quality, leading to a suggestion that earnings quality could be improved by introducing a measurement perspective into the financial statements. At the very least, evidence of low-value relevance of earnings suggests that there is still plenty of room for accountants to improve the usefulness of financial statement information.

6.5 Ohlson's Clean Surplus Theory

6.5.1 Three Formulae for Firm Value

The Ohlson **clean surplus theory** provides a framework consistent with the measurement perspective, by showing how the market value of the firm can be expressed in terms of fundamental balance sheet and income statement components. The theory assumes ideal conditions in capital markets, including dividend irrelevancy.[9] Nevertheless, it has had some success in explaining and predicting actual firm value. Our outline of the theory is based on a simplified version of Feltham and Ohlson (1995) (FO). The clean surplus theory model is also called the **residual income** model.

Much of the theory has already been included in earlier discussions, particularly Example 2.2 of P.V. Ltd. operating under ideal conditions of uncertainty. You may wish to review Example 2.2 at this time. In this section we will pull together these earlier discussions, and extend the P.V. Ltd. example to allow for earnings persistence. The FO model can be applied to value the firm at any point in time for which financial statements are available. For purposes of illustration, we will apply it at time 1 in Example 2.2, that is, at the end of the first year of operation.

FO begin by pointing out that the fundamental determinant of a firm's value is its dividend stream. Assume, for P.V. Ltd. in Example 2.2, that the bad-economy state was realized in year 1 and recall that P.V. pays no dividends, until a liquidating dividend at time 2. Then, the expected present value of dividends at time 1 is just the expected present value of the firm's cash on hand at time 2:

$$PA_1 = \frac{0.5}{1.10}(\$110 + \$100) + \frac{0.5}{1.10}(\$110 + \$200)$$

$$= \$95.45 + \$140.91$$

$$= \$236.3$$

Recall th ... the bad state happens and $200 for the
good state. 7 ... cash on hand at time
1 invested a
   Given ... pressed in terms of its
future cash ... happened in period 1:

$$PA_1 = \$100 + \left(0.5 \times \frac{\$100}{1.10}\right) + \left(0.5 \times \frac{\$200}{1.10}\right)$$

$$= \$100 + \$136.36$$

$$= \$236.36$$

where the first term is cash on hand at time 1, that is, the present value of $100 cash is just $100.

The market value of the firm can also be expressed in terms of financial statement variables. FO show that:

$$PA_t = bv_t + g_t \tag{6.1}$$

at any time t, where bv_t is the net book value of the firm's assets per the balance sheet and g_t is the expected present value of future abnormal earnings, also called **goodwill**. For this relationship to hold it is necessary that all items of gain or loss go through the income statement, which is the source of the term "clean surplus" in the theory.

To evaluate goodwill for P.V. Ltd. as at time t = 1, we look ahead over the remainder of the firm's life (1 year in our example).[10] Recall that **abnormal earnings** are the difference between actual and expected earnings. Using FO's notation, define ox_2 as earnings for year 2 and ox_2^a as abnormal earnings for that year.[11] From Example 2.2, we have:

If the bad state happens for year 2, net income for year 2 is

$$(100 \times 0.10) + 100 - 136.36 = -\$26.36,$$

where the bracketed expression includes interest earned on opening cash.

If the good state happens, net income is

$$10 + 200 - 136.36 = \$73.64$$

Since each state is equally likely, expected net income for year 2 is

$$E\{ox_2\} = (0.5 \times -26.36) + (0.5 \times 73.64) = \$23.64$$

Expected abnormal earnings for year 2, the difference between expected earnings as just calculated and accretion of discount on opening book value, is thus

$$E\{ox_2^a\} = 23.64 - (0.10 \times 236.36) = \$0$$

Goodwill, the expected present value of future abnormal earnings, is then

$$g_1 = 0/1.10 = 0$$

Thus, for P.V. Ltd. in Example 2.2 with no persistence of abnormal earnings, goodwill is zero. This is because, under ideal conditions, arbitrage ensures that the firm expects to earn only the given interest rate on the opening value of its net assets. As a result, we can read firm value directly from the balance sheet:

$$PA_1 = \$236.36 + \$0$$
$$= \$236.36$$

Zero goodwill represents a special case of the FO model called **unbiased accounting**, that is, all assets and liabilities are valued at fair value. When accounting is unbiased, and abnormal earnings do not persist, all of firm value appears on the balance sheet. In effect, the income statement has no information content, as we noted in Example 2.2.

Unbiased accounting represents the extreme of the measurement perspective. Of course, as a practical matter, firms do not account for all assets and liabilities this way. For example, if P.V. Ltd. uses historical cost accounting for its capital asset, bv_1 may be biased downwards relative to fair value. FO call this **biased accounting**. When accounting is biased, the firm has *unrecorded* goodwill g_t. However, the clean surplus formula (6.1) for PA_t holds for any basis of accounting, not just unbiased accounting under ideal conditions. To illustrate, suppose that P.V. Ltd. uses straight-line amortization for its capital asset, writing off $130.17 in year 1 and $130.16 in year 2. Note that year 1 present value-based amortization in Example 2.2 is $123.97. Thus, with straight-line amortization, earnings for year 1 and capital assets as at the end of year 1 are biased downwards relative to their ideal conditions counterparts. We now repeat the calculation of goodwill and firm value as at the end of year 1, continuing the assumption of bad state realization for year 1.

With straight-line amortization, expected net income for year 2 is:

$$E\{ox_2\} = (100 \times 0.10) + 0.5(100 - 130.16) + 0.5(200 - 130.16) = \$29.84$$

Expected abnormal earnings for year 2 is:

$$E\{ox_2{}^a\} = 29.84 - (0.10 \times 230.16) = \$6.82,$$

where $230.16 is the firm's book value at time 1, being $100 cash plus the capital asset book value on a straight-line basis of $130.16.

Goodwill is then

$$g_1 = 6.82/1.10 = \$6.20,$$

giving firm market value of

$$PA_1 = 230.16 + 6.20$$
$$= \$236.36,$$

the same as the unbiased accounting case.

While firm value is the same, the goodwill of $6.20 is unrecorded on the firm's books. This again illustrates the point made in Section 2.5.1 that under historical cost accounting net income lags real economic performance. Here, historical cost-based net income for year 1 is \$100 − \$130.17 = −\$30.17, less than net income of −\$23.97 in Example 2.2. Nevertheless, if unrecorded goodwill is correctly valued, the resulting firm value is also correct.

This ability of the FO model to generate the same firm value regardless of the accounting policies used by the firm has an upside and a downside. On the upside, an investor who may wish to use the model to predict firm value does not have to be concerned about the firm's choice of accounting policies. If the firm manager biases reported net income upwards to improve apparent performance, or biases net income downwards by means of a major asset writedown, the firm value as calculated by the model is the same.[12] The reason is that changes in unrecorded goodwill induced by accounting policy choice are offset by equal but opposite changes in book values. The downside, however, is that the model can provide no guidance as to what accounting policies *should* be used.

We now see the sense in which the Ohlson clean surplus theory supports the measurement perspective. Fair value accounting for P.V.'s assets reduces the extent of biased accounting. In doing so, it moves more of the value of the firm onto the balance sheet, thereby reducing the amount of unrecorded goodwill that the investor has to estimate. While the sum of book value and unrecorded goodwill is the same in theory, whether or not the firm uses fair value accounting, in practice the firm can presumably prepare a more accurate estimate of fair value than can the investor. If so, and if the estimate is reasonably reliable, decision usefulness of the financial statements is increased, since a greater proportion of firm value can simply be read from the balance sheet. This is particularly so for investors who may not be fully rational, and who may need more help in determining firm value than they receive under the information perspective.

* 6.5.2 Earnings Persistence

FO then introduce the important concept of *earnings persistence* into the theory. Specifically, they assume that abnormal earnings are generated according to the following formula:

$$ox_t^a = \omega ox_{t-1}^a + \upsilon_{t-1} + \widetilde{\epsilon}_t \qquad\qquad (6.2)$$

FO call this formula an **earnings dynamic**. The $\widetilde{\epsilon}_t$ are the effects of state realization in period t on abnormal earnings, where the "~" indicates that these effects are random, as at the beginning of the period. As in Example 2.2, the expected value of state realization is zero and realizations are independent from one period to the next.

The ω is a persistence parameter, where $0 \leq \omega < 1$. For $\omega = 0$, we have the case of Example 2.2, that is, abnormal earnings do not persist. However, $\omega > 0$ is not unreasonable. Often, the effects of state realization in one year will persist into future years. For example, the bad-state realization in year 1 of Example 2.2 may be because of a rise in interest rates, the economic effects of which will likely persist beyond the current year. Then, ω captures the proportion of the \$50 abnormal earnings in year 1 that would continue into the following year.

---

*Section 6.5.2 can be skipped without loss of continuity.

However, note that $\omega < 1$ in the FO model. That is, abnormal earnings of any particular year will die out over time. For example, the effects of a rise in interest rates will eventually dissipate. More generally, forces of competition will eventually eliminate positive, or negative, abnormal earnings, at a rate that ultimately depends on the firm's business strategy.

Note also that persistence is related to its empirical counterpart in the ERC research. Recall from Section 5.4.1 that ERCs are higher the greater the persistence in earnings. As we will see in Example 6.1 below, this is exactly what clean surplus theory predicts—the higher ω is, the greater the impact of the income statement on firm value.

The term v_{t-1} represents the effect of other information becoming known in year $t - 1$ (i.e., other than the information in year $t - 1$'s abnormal earnings) that affects the abnormal earnings of year t. When accounting is unbiased, $v_{t-1} = 0$. To see this, consider the case of R&D. If R&D was accounted for on a fair value basis (i.e., unbiased accounting) then year $t - 1$'s abnormal earnings includes the change in value brought about by R&D activities during that year. Of this change in value, the proportion ω will continue into next year's earnings. That is, if R&D is valued at fair value, there is no relevant other information about future earnings from R&D—current earnings includes it all.

When accounting is biased, v_{t-1} assumes a much more important role. Thus, if R&D costs are written off as incurred, year $t - 1$'s abnormal earnings contain no information about future abnormal earnings from R&D activities. As a result, to predict year t's abnormal earnings it is necessary to add in as other information an outside estimate of the abnormal earnings in year t that will result from the R&D activities of year $t - 1$. That is, v_{t-1} represents next period's earnings from year $t - 1$'s R&D.

In sum, the earnings dynamic models current year's abnormal earnings as a proportion ω of the previous year's abnormal earnings, plus the effects of other information (if accounting is biased), plus the effects of random state realization.

Finally, note that the theory assumes that the set of possible values of $\tilde{\epsilon}_t$ and their probabilities are known to investors, consistent with ideal conditions. It is also assumed that investors know ω. If these assumptions are relaxed, rational investors will want information about $\tilde{\epsilon}_t$ and ω and can use Bayes' theorem to update their subjective state probabilities. Thus, nothing in the theory conflicts with the role of decision theory that was explained in Chapter 3.

EXAMPLE 6.1
PRESENT VALUE MODEL UNDER UNCERTAINTY AND PERSISTENCE

We now extend Example 2.2 to allow for persistence. Continue all the assumptions of that example and add the further assumption $\omega = 0.40$. Since ideal conditions imply unbiased accounting, $v_{t-1} = 0$. Recall that abnormal earnings for year 1 are –$50 or $50, depending on whether the bad state or good state happens. Now, 40% of year 1 abnormal earnings will persist to affect operating earnings in year 2.

We begin with the amortization schedule for P.V.'s capital asset, based on the expected decline in the asset's present value as at time 0. This amortization schedule is the same as in Example 2.2, that is:

Amortization, year 1 = \$260.33 − \$136.36 = \$123.97
Amortization, year 2 = \$136.36 − 0 $\quad$ = \$136.36
$$\overline{\underline{\$260.33}}$$

Now, assume that the bad state happens in year 1. (A similar analysis applies if the good state happens.) Then, we calculate P.V.'s market value at time 1. We begin with the formula based on expected future dividends.

$$PA_1 = \frac{0.5}{1.10} [(\$110 - (0.40 \times \$50) + \$100)] + \frac{0.5}{1.10} [(\$110 - (0.40 \times \$50) + \$200)]$$

$$= \left(\frac{0.5}{1.10} \times \$190 \right) + \left(\frac{0.5}{1.10} \times \$290 \right)$$

$$= \$86.36 + \$131.82$$

$$= \$218.18$$

Note the effect of persistence—40% of year 1 abnormal earnings will persist to reduce year 2 cash flows. Otherwise, the calculation is identical with Example 2.2. We see that the effect of persistence of the bad state is to reduce the time 1 firm value by 236.36 − 218.18 = \$18.18, the present value of the \$20 of reduced future cash flows.

Now, moving from the dividends formula to the clean surplus formula for firm value (6.1), FO use the earnings dynamic equation (6.2) to show that that the firm's goodwill g_t can be expressed in terms of the current year's abnormal earnings, giving a market value of:

$$PA_t = bv_t + (\alpha \times ox_t^a) \tag{6.3}$$

where $\alpha = \omega/(1 + R_f)$ is a capitalization factor.[13] Note, as mentioned above, that the higher is the persistence parameter ω the higher is the impact of current earnings information on share price PA_t. In our example, for t = 1:

Cash on hand $\qquad$ = \$100.00
Book value of asset, based on
$\quad$ amortization schedule, \$260.33 − \$123.97 = \$136.36
bv_t $\qquad$ = \$236.36

This gives:

$$PA_t = bv_t + (\alpha \times ox_t^a)$$

$$= \$236.36 + \left(\frac{0.40}{1.10} \times -\$50 \right)$$

$$= \$236.36 - \$18.18$$

$$= \$218.18$$

which agrees with the market value based on expected future dividends.

The implications of the FO model with persistence are twofold. First, even under ideal conditions, *all the action is no longer on the balance sheet*. The income statement is important too, because it reveals the current year's abnormal earnings, 40% of which, in this case, will persist into future periods. Thus, we can regard abnormal earnings as 40% persistent in this example.

Second, the formula (6.2) implies that investors will want information to help them assess persistent earnings, since these are important to the future performance of the firm. Our discussion of extraordinary items in Section 5.5 showed how accountants can help in this regard by appropriate classification of items with low persistence. Also, the formula is consistent with the empirical impact of persistence on the ERC as outlined in Section 5.4.1, where we saw that greater persistence is associated with stronger investor reaction to current earnings.[14]

6.5.3 Estimating Firm Value

The FO model can be used to estimate the value of a firm's shares. This can then be compared to the actual market value, to indicate possible over- or undervaluation by the market, and to aid in investment decisions. The following example applies the model to Canadian Tire Corporation, Limited. The methodology used in this example is based on the procedures outlined in Lee (1996).

EXAMPLE 6.2
ESTIMATING THE VALUE OF COMMON SHARES OF CANADIAN TIRE

From Canadian Tire's 2003 *Annual Report* (not reproduced here), we take 2003 net income (NI_{2003}) as $255.3, before minority interest (all dollar figures are in millions), its book value as $1,806.9 at December 28, 2002 and $2,033.3 at December 31, 2003 (bv_{2003}) (both including minority interest). This gives Canadian Tire's 2003 return on opening equity (ROE_{2003}) as 0.14. Somewhat arbitrarily, we assume that this return will continue for the next seven years, after which return will equal Canadian Tire's cost of capital. We will return to this assumption shortly.

Dividends totalled $32.5 for 2003, giving a dividend payout ratio of 32.5/255.3 = 0.13. We assume that this ratio will also continue for seven years.

To estimate Canadian Tire's cost of equity capital, we use the CAPM (Section 4.5):

$$E(R_{jt}) = R_f(1 - \beta_j) + \beta_j E(R_{Mt}),$$

where firm j is Canadian Tire and t is March 2004. That is, we assume the market became aware of Canadian Tire's 2003 *Annual Report* during March 2004. $E(R_{jt})$ thus represents the rate of return demanded by the market for Canadian Tire shares at that time or, equivalently, its cost of capital. We take the risk-free rate of interest as $R_f = 0.0425$ per annum, the bank prime rate in March 2004. To this rate, we add a market risk premium[15] of 4%, to estimate the expected annual rate of return on the market portfolio as 0.0825. To estimate beta, we use the formula from Section 3.7:

$$\beta = \frac{Cov(j,M)}{Var(M)} = \frac{0.00208}{0.00169} = 1.23$$

where Cov (j, M) and Var (M) are estimated from returns data[16] for Canadian Tire and the S&P/TSX 300 index for March 2004. Then, our estimate of the firm's cost of equity capital is:

$$E(R_{jt}) = 0.0425(1 - 1.23) + (1.23 \times 0.0825)$$

$$= 0.09$$

We assume that this 9% cost of capital will stay constant.

Next, we evaluate Canadian Tire's unrecorded goodwill. As stated earlier, goodwill is the present value of expected future abnormal earnings, which we evaluate over a seven-year horizon from December 2003. First, we use the clean surplus relation to project end-of-year book values:

$$bv_{2004} = bv_{2003} + NI_{2004} - d_{2004}$$

where d is dividends. Using the relationship $d_t = kNI_t$, where k is the dividend payout ratio, this becomes:

$$bv_{2004} = bv_{2003} + (1 - k)NI_{2004}$$

$$= bv_{2003} [1 + (1 - k)ROE]$$

$$= 2033.3 [1 + (0.87 \times 0.14)]$$

$$= 2033.3 \times 1.12$$

$$= \$2,277$$

Similar calculations give:

$$bv_{2005} = \$2,550$$
$$bv_{2006} = \$2,856$$
$$bv_{2007} = \$3,199$$
$$bv_{2008} = \$3,583$$
$$bv_{2009} = \$4,013$$

Now abnormal earnings are defined as the difference between actual earnings and accretion of discount. Accretion of discount is cost of capital times opening book value. Actual earnings for a given year are projected as ROE times opening book value. Thus expected abnormal earnings for 2004 are:

$$ox^a_{2004} = [ROE - E(R_j)]bv_{2003}$$

$$= (0.14 - 0.09)2033.3$$

$$= 0.05 \times 2033.3$$

$$= \$102$$

Similar calculations give:

$ox^a_{2005} = \$114$

$ox^a_{2006} = \$128$

$ox^a_{2007} = \$143$

$ox^a_{2008} = \$160$

$ox^a_{2009} = \$179$

$ox^a_{2010} = \$201$

The present value of these abnormal earnings, that is, goodwill, at December 31, 2003, discounted at Canadian Tire's cost of capital, is

$$g_{2003} = \frac{102}{1.09} + \frac{114}{1.09^2} + \frac{128}{1.09^3} + \frac{143}{1.09^4} + \frac{160}{109^5} + \frac{179}{1.09^6} + \frac{201}{1.09^7}$$

$$= \$710$$

Finally, we add in December 31, 2003 book value (i.e., bv_{2003}):

$$PA_{2003} = 2,033.3 + 710$$

$$= \$2,743.3$$

Canadian Tire had 80.605607 million common shares outstanding[17] as at December 31, 2003, giving an estimated value per share of $34.03.

Canadian Tire's actual share price around the end of March 2004 was $58, considerably more than our estimate. While one could adjust estimates of the risk-free interest rate, dividend payout ratio, and cost of capital, reasonable changes to these estimates would not affect the calculation significantly.

Consequently, the discrepancy between estimated and actual share price in Example 6.2 seems rather large. One possible explanation is that Canadian Tire's shares may be affected by the momentum behaviour described in Section 6.2.1. However, while share prices in general were recovering strongly during March 2004 from their lows of the previous two years, this recovery may not have developed to the point where momentum behaviour would be expected.

Another possibility lies with the ROE used in our earnings projections. We have assumed that Canadian Tire's ROE stays constant at 0.14. Perhaps the market expects that ROE will increase. That is, our estimate may not have fully used all available information. Dechow, Hutton, and Sloan (1999), in a large sample of U.S. firms over the period 1976–1995, report that estimates of firm value based on the FO model that ignored other information were too low. To gain some insight into this possibility, consider analysts' forecasts of Canadian Tire earnings. We have used only information from the 2003 financial statement in our estimates, whereas analysts can bring considerably more information to bear. From Globeinvestor.com on June 12, 2004, we note that Canadian Tire's 2003 earnings per share was $3.06, and that the average of analysts' earnings per share forecast was $3.29 for 2004 and

$3.74 for 2005. These forecasts represent annual earnings increases of 7.5% and 14%, respectively, for a 22% increase over the two years. These compare with an annual increase of (ROE $\times$ (1 − k)) approximately 12% implicit in our analysis, or about 25% over 2 years. Thus, our ROE estimate seems reasonably consistent with analysts' estimates.

Another earnings-related concern arises from recognition lag. For example, firms that conduct R&D will have their reported net income and net worth biased downwards relative to share values, since the market will look through these biased amounts to the expected value of the R&D. To the extent that R&D will increase *future* earnings, we may wish to increase our projected ROE by adding back to reported earnings all or part of R&D expense. This would increase our estimate of share value. However, as a practical matter, estimating the future value of R&D is difficult, and, in the case of Canadian Tire, there is little R&D to add back.

Yet another possibility for the discrepancy is the persistence of abnormal earnings. We have assumed that Canadian Tire generates abnormal earnings of (0.14 − 0.09) 0.05 for seven years and zero thereafter. That is, current abnormal earnings are assumed to be completely persistent for seven years and then immediately fall to zero. Other persistence assumptions are possible. Since Canadian Tire is well established in a stable industry, perhaps abnormal earnings will persist longer. If we were to extend the number of years, this would increase the estimated share value in our example. For example, an assumption that ROE of 14% will continue for 14 and 21 years, with other assumptions unchanged, raises estimated share value to $44.68 and $57.54, respectively. However, it is not clear that this should be done. Even for well-established firms, competitive pressures operate to eliminate abnormal earnings over time. Supporting this refusal, Dechow, Hutton, and Sloan (1999) present tentative evidence that investors may not fully anticipate the extent to which future abnormal earnings decline.

In sum, the most likely explanation for the excess of market value over our estimate is that the market expects abnormal earnings to persist considerably longer than our assumption of seven years.

Despite discrepancies such as this between estimated and actual share value, the FO model can be useful for investment decision making. To see how, suppose that you carry out a similar analysis for another firm—call it Firm X—and obtain an estimated share value of $25. Which firm would you sooner invest in if they were both trading at $58? Canadian Tire, with estimated share value of $34.03, may be the better choice, since it has a higher ratio of model value to actual share value. That is, more of its actual share value is "backed up" by book value and expected abnormal earnings. Indeed, Frankel and Lee (1998), who applied the methodology of Example 6.2 to a large sample of U.S. firms during 1977–1992, found that the ratio of estimated market value to actual market value was a good predictor of share returns for two to three years into the future. Thus, for the years following 2003, Frankel and Lee's results suggest that Canadian Tire's share return should outperform that of Firm X.

We conclude that while our procedure to estimate Canadian Tire's share price is on the right track, the market seems to have considerably higher earnings expectations than ours. This leads to an examination of empirical studies of the ability of the clean surplus approach to predict earnings and share price.

6.5.4 Empirical Studies of the Clean Surplus Model

Clean surplus theory has generated much empirical research. One aspect of this research compares the relative predictive ability of the dividend, cash flow, and residual income models. Recall from Section 6.5.1 that under ideal conditions all three models produce identical valuations. However, when conditions are not ideal, the model that produces the best predictions is an empirical matter. For example, it is often argued that the clean surplus model has an advantage because it uses balance sheet information and, as a result, has to project only abnormal or residual income. Cash flow and dividend models must predict total future flows. Thus, the clean surplus model has "less" to predict and is thereby less subject to error. It is also argued that the clean surplus model is more convenient to apply than the cash flow model. It uses readily available financial statement information and does not have to back cash flows out of accrual accounting-based reports.

A major practical problem in applying all three models is the choice of forecast horizon, and what value, if any, to assign to flows beyond the horizon (called terminal value). Our Canadian Tire estimate used a forecast horizon of seven years, with a terminal value of zero on the grounds that competitive pressures are expected to eliminate abnormal returns beyond that time. Of course, this zero terminal value assumption is rather arbitrary. Perhaps a better (but still arbitrary) assumption is that Canadian Tire's abnormal earnings would not fall to zero, but rather start to decline after seven years. Then, terminal value is greater than zero, which would increase our value estimate.

An alternative assumption is to base terminal value on analysts' long-range forecasts. In this regard, Courteau, Kao, and Richardson (2001), for a sample of U.S. firms over the period 1992–1996, studied the relative predictive ability of the three models, using analysts' predictions of earnings and a five-year forecast horizon. They found that predictions using arbitrary terminal value assumptions, as we did for Canadian Tire, substantially underestimated share market prices. When terminal values were based on analysts' long-range forecasts, predictions were much more accurate. Furthermore, the three models were then roughly equal in their forecasting ability, consistent with our theoretical expectation.

A second type of empirical clean surplus research studies the prediction of future earnings, since future earnings are a main input into the goodwill estimate. In particular, this research examines how other information can improve earnings and share price predictions. This represents a significant change in emphasis from research under the information perspective, which studies the association between financial statement information and share returns. As an example of this change in emphasis, consider the study of Abarbanell and Bushee (1997). In an extension of the approach used by Lev and Thiagarajan (1993) (Section 5.7), they showed how certain "fundamental signals" from the current financial statements, such as changes in sales, accounts receivable, inventories, gross margin, and capital expenditure could improve the prediction of next year's earnings changes. They went on to show that analysts appeared to underuse the fundamental signals when predicting earnings, suggesting that their earnings forecasts would benefit from greater attention to the full information potential of financial statements. Myers (1999) adds order backlog as other information in the earnings dynamic, but finds this does not remove a tendency for under-prediction of firm value by the clean surplus model. Begley and Feltham (2002) add analysts' forecasts and current capital expenditures as other information. They find that these variables significantly improve prediction of unrecorded goodwill for their sample firms. Overall, these results suggest considerable promise for the usefulness of financial statement information, beyond the information in current earnings, in improving earnings and share price predictions.

Finally, another use of the theory is to estimate a firm's cost of capital. In Example 6.2, note that any four of the five variables—share price, book value, expected future earnings, risk-free interest rate, and cost of capital—can be used, in principle, to solve for the other one. Thus, the clean surplus model provides an alternative to the CAPM for cost of capital estimation.

6.5.5 Summary

Clean surplus theory has had a major impact on financial accounting theory and research. By demonstrating that firm value can equally well be expressed in terms of financial accounting variables as in terms of dividends or cash flows, it has led to increased research attention to earnings prediction. Much of this research explores how current financial statement information can be used to improve this prediction. Better earnings prediction enables better estimates of unrecorded goodwill, leading to better predictions of firm value and hence better investment decisions.

The theory also leads to a measurement perspective, since the more fair values are reported on the balance sheet the less the proportion of firm value included in unrecorded goodwill, hence the less the potential for investor mistakes in estimating this complex component of firm value. This can improve investor decision-making and proper securities market operation, particularly if securities markets are not as fully efficient as once believed.

6.6 Auditors' Legal Liability

Perhaps the main source of pressure for the measurement perspective, however, comes as a reaction to spectacular failures of large firms. Many such events have taken place in the United States. During the early 1980s, numerous financial institutions, specifically savings and loan associations, failed.[18] While these failures preceded the Enron and WorldCom financial reporting disasters (see Section 1.2), they remain important because they generated many of the pressures leading to the measurement perspective.

Typically, these savings and loan failures involved overstatement of net assets on the audited balance sheets, with resultant overstatements of earnings. Auditors are often under considerable pressure from management to bend or "stretch" GAAP, so that legal capital requirements, earnings targets and/or analysts' forecasts will be met. Indeed, such stretching was a major contributing factor to the savings and loans failures. But, yielding to such pressure can result in substantial legal liability. For example, an article in *The Wall Street Journal* (March 11, 1994, p. A2) reported lawsuits against the audit firm of Deloitte and Touche totalling $1.85 billion. The charges arose from alleged clean audit opinions issued to savings and loan associations that, in retrospect, were insolvent. The article described a proposed settlement of these lawsuits in excess of $300 million. While considerably less than the amounts at suit, this was the second-largest liability settlement surrounding the savings and loan debacle. (The largest was a $400-million settlement by Ernst and Young for similar charges.)

How can auditors protect themselves against pressures and potential liabilities such as these? One response, of course, is ethical behaviour, recognizing that the long-run interests of the accounting/auditing profession are served by not yielding to inappropriate management pressures to stretch GAAP.

Ethical behaviour, however, can be bolstered by conservative accounting. As pointed out in Section 1.2, historical cost accounting contains conservative elements, due to a reluctance to recognize gains in fair value but less reluctance to recognize declines. As we have mentioned previously, the lower-of-cost-or-market rule for inventories is a long-standing example of conservative accounting.

Nevertheless, despite the lower-of-cost-or-market rule for inventories, GAAP did not at the time of the savings and loan failures require recognition of fair value decreases for major classes of assets and liabilities if the firm intended to hold them to maturity. Examples include certain long-term investments, capital assets, intangibles, and long-term debt. Retention of these items at cost or amortized cost was justified by the going concern assumption of historical cost accounting. But, as mentioned above, overvaluation of net assets was a major criticism of financial reporting following the savings and loan failures.

It seemed that a stronger form of conservatism, requiring an extension of lower-of-cost-or-market thinking, was needed. Standard setters have implemented several standards of this nature in the years following the savings and loan debacle, such as **ceiling tests** for capital assets and goodwill. These tests represent a partial application of the measurement perspective. They require the auditor to estimate the fair value of these assets. If fair value is greater than book value, there is no writeup. However, if fair value is less than book value, book value is written down. Then, perhaps, the fact that such writedowns are required by GAAP will help auditors resist management pressure to overstate net assets. Furthermore, auditors can reduce their liability exposure by pointing out that, with ceiling tests, the financial statements proper *anticipate* the negative value changes leading to bankruptcy, merger, downsizing, environmental liabilities, etc. Of course, determination of fair value requires greater use of estimates and judgement but, because of legal liability, the relevance/reliability tradeoff may have shifted towards greater relevance.

The incidence of conservatism in the United States was investigated by Basu (1997). He measured the conservativeness of financial reporting using the correlation between net income and share returns. As Basu argues, the efficient securities market will bid up the share prices of firms that are performing well and bid down the prices of firms that are performing poorly. Under conservative accounting, the earnings of firms that are performing well *will not* include the unrealized increases in assets that characterize a firm that is doing well. However, the earnings of firms that are performing poorly *will* include decreases in the values of their assets. It follows that the correlation between share returns and earnings will be higher for firms that are performing poorly than for firms that are performing well. As Basu puts it, earnings are more timely in their recognition of poor performance than of good performance. The difference between these two correlations can thus be viewed as evidence of conservative accounting. In a large sample of firms over the years 1963–1990, Basu found significantly higher correlation for firms in his sample that were doing poorly than for firms that were doing well, consistent with his argument.

Using this measurement approach, Basu went on to examine the period 1983–1990. This period has been identified as a period of high growth in litigation against auditors, and corresponds roughly to the aftermath of the savings and loan failures described above.

He found that conservatism increased in this period relative to earlier periods of low lit-igation growth. This suggests that standard setters reacted to auditors' legal difficulties by increasing conservatism, as in the ceiling test standards referred to above. For further discussion of these litigation and regulation-based explanations for conservatism, see Watts (2003).

These explanations for conservatism can also be supported by the decision theory out-lined in Chapter 3. To see this, consider the following example.

* **EXAMPLE 6.3**

ASYMMETRY OF INVESTOR LOSSES

Bill Cautious, a rational investor, has a $10,000 investment in the shares of X Ltd. He plans to use this investment to live on over the next two years. After that time, he will have graduated and will have a high-paying job. Consequently, he is not concerned right now about planning beyond two years. His goal is to maximize his total utili-ty over this period. For simplicity, we assume that X Ltd. pays no dividends over these two years. Bill is risk-averse, with utility in each year equal to the square root of the amount he spends in that year.

It is easy to see that Bill's total utility will be maximized if he spends the same amount each year. That is, he will sell $5,000 of his shares now and sell the remain-ing $5,000 at the beginning of the second year.[19]

Suppose, however, that at the end of the first year, Bill finds that his opening wealth was misstated, due to an error by the X Ltd. auditor. A writeoff of $2,000 should have been recognized by X Ltd. at the beginning of the first year, but was not recognized until the end of the year. That is, the auditor has made an overstate-ment error, so that Bill's shares were overvalued at the beginning of the first year by $2,000. As a result, Bill realizes that his opening wealth was really $8,000, and that he should have spent only $4,000 in that year. However, he has already spent $5,000 of his shares, leaving $3,000 for year 2.

Now calculate Bill's utility for the two years, evaluated as at the end of the first year:

$$EU^a \ (Overstatement) = \sqrt{5,000} + \sqrt{3,000}$$

$$= 70.71 + 54.77$$

$$= 125.48$$

where EU^a denotes Bill's actual utility, being the utility of the $5,000 he has already spent plus the utility to come next year from his remaining asset.

If Bill had known at the beginning of the first year that his wealth was only $8,000, he would have planned to spend $4,000 each year. His expected utility would have been:

---

*Example 6.3 can be skipped without loss of continuity.

$$EU^a \ (Overstatement) = \sqrt{4,000} + \sqrt{4,000}$$

$$= 63.24 + 63.25$$

$$= 126.49$$

Thus Bill has lost utility of 126.49 – 125.48 = 1.01 as a result of the auditor's overstatement error.

Now assume instead that the auditor makes a $2,000 understatement error. Thus, Bill finds out at the end of the first year that his opening wealth was really $12,000, and that he should have spent $6,000 in the first year. His actual utility over the two years is thus:

$$EU^a \ (Understatement) = \sqrt{5,000} + \sqrt{7,000}$$

$$= 70.71 + 83.67$$

$$= 154.38$$

Whereas, if Bill had known his wealth was $12,000:

$$EU^a \ (Understatement) = \sqrt{6,000} + \sqrt{6,000}$$

$$= 77.46 + 77.46$$

$$= 154.92$$

Thus, Bill has lost utility of 154.92 – 154.38 = 0.54 as a result of the auditor's understatement error. Note that even though Bill finds out that his wealth was $2,000 higher than he had originally thought, he still suffers a loss of utility from the audit error. This is because the error has cost him the opportunity to optimally plan his spending over time.

The main point of the example is that while the audit error was $2,000 in each case, Bill's loss of utility for an overstatement error is almost twice the loss for an understatement of the same amount. Bill will be upset in either case, but he is more upset about an overstatement. Consequently, the auditor is more likely to be sued for overstatement errors. For a more formal model to demonstrate this asymmetry, see Scott (1975).

Anticipating loss asymmetry, the auditor reacts by being conservative. Writing assets down to fair value but not writing them up decreases the likelihood of an overstatement error and increases the likelihood of an understatement error. This, in turn, decreases the likelihood of being sued since conservative accounting means the investor is less likely to suffer a wealth overstatement. Standard setters, who would also like to see fewer investor lawsuits, will encourage conservatism with new accounting standards. Experimental evidence consistent with auditors' greater avoidance of overstatement errors relative to understatement errors is reported by Barron, Pratt, and Stice (2001).

This effect, which is driven by the concavity of a risk-averse investor's utility function, may underlie the litigation and regulation explanations for conservatism, and the increase in conservatism documented by Basu (1997).

In sum, one way that accountants and auditors can bolster ethical behaviour and protect themselves against legal liability is to expand accounting conservatism. Note that since conservatism requires measurement of fair values, we can regard it as a (one-sided) version of the measurement perspective.

6.7 Conclusions on the Measurement Perspective on Decision Usefulness

Recall that the information perspective on financial reporting is content to accept the historical cost basis of accounting, and rely on full disclosure to enhance usefulness to investors. The form of disclosure does not matter, since it is assumed that there are enough rational, informed investors to quickly and correctly incorporate any reasonable form into the efficient market price. Empirical research has confirmed that the market finds net income information at least to be useful. In effect, empirical research under the information perspective tends to accept the efficient market price and to evaluate the usefulness of accounting information in terms of its association with this market price.

However, there are a number of questions about the information perspective. First, securities markets may not be as fully efficient as had previously been believed, suggesting that investors might need some help in figuring out the full implications of accounting information for future returns. Some of this help may be supplied by moving fair value information from financial statement notes into the financial statements proper. Second, a market share of 2 to 5% for net income seems low and, despite theoretical support, it has been difficult to find much direct market reaction at all to non-earnings accounting information. In addition, legal liability may force accountants to increase conservatism in the financial statements by adopting a one-sided version of fair value measurement.

The measurement perspective is reinforced by the development of the Ohlson clean surplus theory, which emphasizes the fundamental role of financial accounting information in determining firm value. This theory implies a more basic role for financial statements in reporting on firm value than the information perspective, which views accounting information as one of many information sources competing for the attention of the efficient market. Thus, the clean surplus theory leads naturally to the measurement perspective.

Of course, the measurement perspective runs into problems of reliability. Consequently, we do not expect the measurement perspective to extend to a complete set of financial statements on a fair value basis. Rather, the question is one of degree—to what degree will fair values supplant costs in financial reporting? Consequently, in the next chapter we review GAAP from a valuation perspective. There always has been a substantial present value and market value component to the financial statements. But, as we shall see, recent years have witnessed a number of new fair value standards.

Questions and Problems

1. Why does a measurement perspective on decision usefulness suggest more value-relevant information in the financial statements proper, when efficient securities market theory implies that financial statement notes or other disclosure would be just as useful?

2. What will be the impact on relevance, reliability, and decision usefulness of financial statement information as accountants adopt the measurement perspective?

3. Explain in your own words what "post-announcement drift" is. Why is this an anomaly for securities market efficiency?

4. Explain in your own words why the market response to accruals, as documented by Sloan (1996), is an anomaly for securities market efficiency.

5. An investor considers two mutual funds. Based on past experience, the first fund has expected return of 0.08 and standard deviation of 0.05. The second fund has expected return of 0.07 and standard deviation of 0.06. There is no reason to assume that future performance of these funds will differ from past performance. However, the second fund has a guarantee attached that return in any year will not be negative.

   The investor buys the second fund. Use prospect theory to explain why.

6. Lev, in his article "On the Usefulness of Earnings" (1989), points out the low ability of reported net income to explain variations in security prices around the date of release of earnings information. Lev attributes this low explanatory power to low earnings quality.

   Required
   a. Define earnings quality. Relate your answer to the concept of an information system in single-person decision theory.
   b. What other reasons might there be for the low explanatory power of earnings?
   c. How might an increased measurement perspective in financial statements increase earnings quality, and hence the impact of earnings on security prices?

7. In Section 6.4, the concept of value relevance of net income is introduced. It appears that the value relevance of reported earnings, as measured by R^2 or ERC, is low, and falling over time. Use single person decision theory to explain why value relevance of reported earnings can be measured by R^2 or ERC. Is it possible for abnormal share return to increase but R^2 and ERC to fall? Explain.

8. For what reasons might transactions costs, including investors' time to figure out and operate strategies that appear to beat the market, not be a completely adequate explanation for the apparent efficient securities market anomalies?

9. Reproduced on page 189 is the Economic Value Added (EVA) disclosure from the MD&A section of the 1996 *Annual Report* of Domtar, Inc. Some of the uses of EVA are outlined in Domtar's discussion in the disclosure. Of interest here is the close relationship between the EVA measurement formula and the clean surplus-based valuation procedure outlined in Example 6.2. Note that the EVA for a given year

is equivalent to abnormal earnings (ox_t^a) for that year in our example. Recall that goodwill is calculated as the present value of expected future abnormal earnings.

Domtar continues to use EVA, and its 2003 *Annual Report* contains a brief summary. However, 1996 was the last year it gave details of its EVA calculation. Consequently, we will continue with its 1996 disclosure.

Economic Value Added (EVA)

At the end of 1995, the Corporation adopted a new management system known as Economic Value Added, or EVA®, to ensure that the decision-making process at Domtar is aligned with the objective of increasing shareholder value.

In 1996, this concept was implemented throughout the Corporation and is being used for measuring performance, evaluating investment decisions, improving communication and for incentive compensation. EVA® training courses were developed and are being provided to a large number of employees in on-going efforts to develop a value creation culture at Domtar.

The EVA® measurement formula is as follows:

EVA® = NOPAT[1] – Capital Charge[2]

[1] Net operating profit after tax
[2] Capital employed × Cost of capital for the Corporation

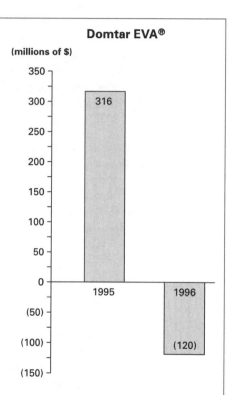

This simple formula highlights the notion that in order to create value for Domtar shareholders, every business unit must generate returns at least equal to its cost of capital, including both debt and shareholders' equity.

Following a record year in 1995 when $316 million of EVA® was created, EVA® for Domtar in 1996 was $120 million negative, due to the decline in selling prices.

	EVA®	=	NOPAT	–	Capital Charge
1995	316	=	539	–	223
1996	(120)	=	88	–	208

Domtar remains committed to creating long-term shareholder value and will intensify its efforts in 1997, especially in areas under its control, such as productivity, costs, customer service, and capital management. Domtar will also benefit from an overall lower cost of capital going forward as a result of its debt management program completed in 1996.

Required

a. Evaluate the usefulness of this approach to communicating information to investors. Consider both relevance and reliability issues.

b. If you were the top manager of a company using EVA, would its use encourage or discourage you from initiating major, capital intensive expansion projects? Explain why or why not.

c. You are an investor in a fast-growing, high-tech company that reports EVA. The assets of the company are primarily intangible (patents, skilled workforce) and are unrecorded on the company's books, hence not included in the EVA capital charge. How would the unrecorded, intangible nature of the assets of such a company affect your interpretation of its EVA? Explain.

d. Note that reporting of EVA is voluntary. Domtar reports this information for 1996 even though its EVA is negative. Does Domtar's willingness to report this information add credibility to its claim that it "will intensify its efforts in 1997?" Explain.

10. A firm is expected to earn $100 net income for next year, at the end of which time the firm will be wound up. The $100 expected earnings includes gains and losses from disposals of assets and liabilities, and all other winding up costs. The firm's book value at the beginning of the year is $500, and its cost of capital is 14%. What is the firm's market value as at the beginning of the year?

a. $526.32

b. $570.00

c. $587.72

d. $600.00

11. You are the senior accountant of a large, publicly traded company that is experiencing a decline of business that management feels is temporary. To meet earnings projections given in its previous year's MD&A, management asks you to find an additional $5 million of reported earnings for the current year. After some study, you determine that to increase earnings by this magnitude, it is necessary to recognize additional revenue on contracts in process, even though the contracts are far from completion and it is questionable whether or not any profits will actually be realized. A careful study of accounting standards relating to revenue recognition leads you to the conclusion that to recognize $5 million of profits at this stage would not be in accordance with GAAP. Consequently, the auditors will be expected to object.

You report this to management, but are instructed to proceed anyway. Management assures you that next year's business will be much better and the premature revenue recognition will never be noticed. Furthermore, management is sure it can convince the auditor of this as well.

Required

What will you do in response to this ethical dilemma? Give reasons for and against your decision.

12. Recent years have seen considerable litigation against auditors in the United States. A major source of this litigation arises from the pressure firms feel to meet analysts' earnings expectations. To avoid reporting lower-than-expected earnings, firms sometimes use earnings management, such as premature revenue recognition and other devices, to raise reported net income. To avoid a qualified audit report, the firm may pressure its auditor to "stretch" GAAP. This puts the auditor in a difficult ethical position. The auditor's primary responsibility is to the shareholders. However, it is management that influences the audit committee and pays for auditor appointments. If the auditor does not go along, he/she may lose the audit client, and also any non-audit services also provided. Furthermore, he/she will inevitably be drawn into lawsuits when the earnings management becomes known (as it eventually must, since accruals reverse).

For example, Waste Management Inc. overstated its earnings during a five-year period in the 1990s, using a variety of earnings management devices such as lengthening the useful life of capital assets, increasing their estimated salvage value, and understating liabilities for rehabilitating contaminated waste disposal sites. In December 1998, Waste Management's auditor, Arthur Andersen, offered $220 million to settle class action lawsuits following revelation of these practices. In March 2002, the SEC announced that it had filed suit against the founder and five senior managers of Waste Management for "massive fraud." In October 2004, one of these managers, the former vice-president of finance, agreed to pay over $800,000 U.S. to settle his charges. He was also barred from serving as a director or officer of a public company.

One can sympathize with company managers for wanting to meet earnings expectations. The market will severely penalize their stock price if they do not. For example, in 1997, Eastman Kodak announced that revenue would not meet expectations due to the high value of the U.S. dollar, and analysts reduced their estimate of first quarter, 1997, earnings from $0.90 per share to $0.80. Kodak's share price fell by $9.25 to $79 in heavy trading. Subsequently, Kodak reported earnings per share for the quarter of $0.81, and share price rose $2.25 to $75.37.

This market reaction has been repeated many times since. An article in *The Wall Street Journal* in April 2000 quoted a prominent investment manager as saying that the market is "overdiscounting" changes in earnings expectations and that it is "reacting too much."

Required

a. Why might an auditor be tempted to go along with client pressure to manage reported earnings so as to meet analysts' expectations? What are some of the possible longer-run costs to the auditor if he/she goes along?

b. To what extent would increased use of a measurement perspective in financial reporting reduce auditor exposure to client pressure and lawsuits?

c. Use concepts from behavioural finance to explain why the market may "overreact" to changes in earnings expectations.

   d. Is the $9.25 reduction in Kodak's share price reported above inconsistent with
       efficient securities market theory? Explain why or why not.

13. In its third quarter, 2004 report, TD Bank Financial Group (TD) reports **econom-
    ic profit** of $259 million. Its calculation of economic profit is summarized as fol-
    lows (millions of dollars):

Average common shareholders' equity for the quarter	$12,195
Add goodwill amortized to date	2,894
Average invested capital before goodwill amortization	$15,089
Capital charge at 10.7% per annum, estimated using CAPM	$ 405
Net income applicable to common shareholders ($565) plus amortization of intangibles ($99)	664
Economic profit	$ 259
Economic return on average invested capital	17.5%

   Required
   a. What is the relationship between TD's calculation of economic profit and the
       calculation of firm value illustrated in Example 6.2?
   b. Does TD have unrecorded goodwill? Explain why or why not.
   c. As a common shareholder of TD, which earnings number, net income or eco-
       nomic profit, do you find more useful in evaluating the bank's performance?
       Explain.

Notes

1. It should be noted that Daniel and Titman's investment strategy used hindsight to
   pick stocks with high and low momentum. The strategy would not be implementable
   in real time.

2. In mathematical terms, the utility function is continuous but not differentiable at zero.

3. This supports the argument of Fama (1970) (see Section 4.3.1) that a sufficient
   number of sophisticated investors can drive the efficient market security price.

4. Non-stationarity provides an alternative to noise trading, discussed in Section 4.4.1,
   for the non-collapse of share prices on an efficient market. When share price parameters, such as beta, are non-stationary, investors will have differing opinions as to
   whether current share prices reflect their current beta values, and will trade on the basis
   of these opinions.

5. While it does not apply directly to beta, further CAPM support is provided by
   Durnev, Morck, Yeung, and Zarowin (2003) (DMYZ). Recall from Section 4.5
   (Equation 4.4) that the residual term ε_{jt} of the market model includes the firm-
   specific portion of share return (whereas the $\alpha_j + \beta_j R_{Mt}$ term captures the market- and

industry-wide portion). DMYZ found that the variance of the market model residual is positively related to amounts of future abnormal earnings. Now the variance of ε_{jt} can be interpreted as an inverse measure of **synchronicity**, that is, the residual variance captures the amount of firm-specific information, relative to the amount of industry- and economy-wide information, incorporated into share price—relatively more firm-specific information generates a bigger variance, or lower synchronicity. Later (since net income lags in recognizing many relevant events), this information shows up as gains and losses in net income. In effect, the market anticipates GN and BN in earnings and capitalizes it into share price before the earnings are reported. This result supports the CAPM and the efficient markets theory on which it is based, because, as originally suggested by Roll (1988), the low ability of the CAPM to explain share returns may be due in part to the large amount of firm-specific information constantly being developed by investors, rather than just to the CAPM leaving out important risk variables. DMYZ found no support for an alternative interpretation of the variance of ε_{jt} as simply the result of noise trading or investor limited attention.

6. For example, firms' betas may shift when they announce good or bad earnings news. If the beta shifts were positive for GN firms and negative for BN, this could explain post-announcement drift as simply an artifact of the higher (for GN firms) and lower (for BN) returns that investors would demand to compensate for the changes in risk, since, as discussed in Sections 3.4, 3.5, and 3.6, investors trade off risk and return. While BT present evidence that, following earnings announcements, betas do shift in the manner described above, the magnitude of the shifts is much smaller than what would be required to explain the magnitude of the post-announcement drift.

7. Suppose that transactions costs were 5% of the amount invested. Then, if it was possible to gross 5% by a strategy of buying GN firms and selling short BN firms, transactions costs would consume the 5% profit, so investors would not bother. Thus, what might appear to be a profitable investment strategy may merely reflect the level of transactions costs required to earn those profits.

8. The proportion of variability is measured by the R^2 statistic from the regression of abnormal security returns on unexpected earnings.

9. The clean surplus model can be extended to allow for some information asymmetry, although under restrictive conditions. See Feltham and Ohlson (1996).

10. In the FO model, the firm's life is assumed infinite.

11. The "o" stands for "operating." If the firm has financial assets, such as cash or securities, these are assumed to earn the risk-free rate of interest. Consequently, financial assets do not contribute to goodwill, which is the ability to earn *abnormal* earnings.

12. The investor may wonder *why* the manager chose these particular accounting policies, however. That is, the manager's choice of accounting policies may itself reveal inside information to the market. Then, it is not completely correct to say that the investor need not be concerned about accounting policy choice. This is considered in Chapter 11.

13. Our expression for α differs slightly from that of FO. They assume that the firm has an infinite life, whereas our assumption is that P.V. Ltd. has a two-year life.

14. The persistence parameter ω can be related to the three types of earnings events distinguished by Ramakrishnan and Thomas (1991) (RT) (Section 5.4.1), namely permanent, transitory, and price-irrelevant, with ERCs of $(1 + R_f)/R_f$, 1, and 0, respectively. First, consider a $1 permanent abnormal earnings event occurring in year t for a firm with an infinite life. This will increase bv_t, in FO notation, by $1. In addition, ω of this will persist to year t + 1, $ω^2$ to year t + 2, etc. Thus, the total effect, discounted at the rate R_f, of the $1 of year t abnormal earnings on PA_t, that is, the ERC, is

$$ERC = 1 + \frac{ω}{1 + R_f} + \frac{ω^2}{(1 + R_f)^2} + \frac{ω^3}{(1 + R_f)^3} + \dots$$

$$= \frac{1 + R_f}{1 + R_f - ω}$$

In RT terms, permanent abnormal earnings have an ERC of $(1 + R_f)/R_f$. To express this ERC in terms of ω, we have

$$\frac{1 + R_f}{1 + R_f - ω} = \frac{1 + R_f}{R_f},$$

which holds for ω = 1.

Thus permanent abnormal earnings have ω = 1. Note that this is outside the range of ω in the earnings dynamic (6.2). That is, for an infinite firm horizon the FO model is not defined for permanent earnings.

RT transitory abnormal earnings have an ERC of 1. Thus

$$\frac{1 + R_f}{1 + R_f - ω} = 1,$$

which holds for ω = 0. Thus, transitory earnings have an ω of zero.

For price-irrelevant abnormal earnings, with ERC of 0, we have

$$\frac{1 + R_f}{1 + R_f - ω} = 0,$$

which is satisfied only in the limit as $ω → ± ∞$. Since this is again outside the allowed range for ω, the FO model is not defined for price-irrelevant abnormal earnings.

15. The market risk premium is the additional return, over and above the risk-free rate, demanded by investors to compensate them for bearing the systematic risk of the mar-

ket portfolio. The 4% estimate of this premium is taken from Palepu, Healy, and Bernard (2000), page 13–9.

16. I am unable to find a free web site that reports beta for Canadian Tire. Consequently, I have calculated beta from its formula, as given. Specifically, Cov (j, M) and Var (M) are calculated from daily returns data for Canadian Tire and the S&P/TSX 300 index for March 2004 (22 observations).

17. Canadian Tire Corporation, Limited has two classes of common shares outstanding—voting and non-voting, with most of the shares non-voting. For purposes of this example, we combine the two classes.

18. For further information about the 1980s savings and loan debacle, see Zeff (2003, pp. 272–273), and the references therein.

19. To verify this, Bill's utility from spending the same amount in each year is

$$\sqrt{5,000} + \sqrt{5,000} = 70.71 + 70.71 = 141.42$$

Any other spending allocation has lower utility. For example, if he spends $4,500 in year 1 and $5,500 in year 2, his utility is

$$\sqrt{4,500} + \sqrt{5,500} = 67.08 + 74.16 = 141.24$$

For simplicity, we assume that Bill has zero time preference for consumption. That is, a dollar of spending in year 1 has the same utility as in year 2, and vice versa.

Chapter 7

Measurement Perspective Applications

FIGURE 7.1 ORGANIZATION OF CHAPTER 7

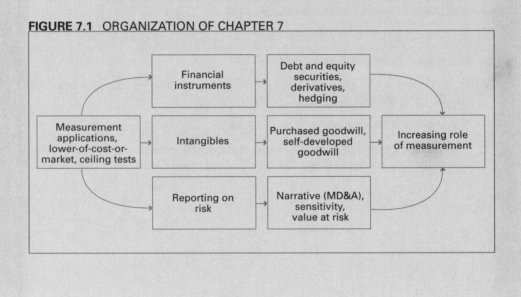

FIGURE 7.1 ORGANIZATION OF CHAPTER 7

7.1 Overview

Despite the pressures for a measurement perspective discussed in Chapter 6, the movement of accounting practice in this direction encounters two formidable obstacles. The first is reliability. The decision usefulness of fair value-based financial statements will be compromised if too much reliability is sacrificed for greater relevance. Second, management's skepticism about RRA that we saw in Section 2.4.3 carries over to fair value accounting in general, particularly since the measurement perspective implies that fair values are incorporated into the financial statements proper. Management's concerns are further enhanced if unrealized gains and losses from changes in fair values are included in net income.

Nevertheless, recent years have seen major new measurement-oriented standards, with more on the horizon. In this chapter, we review and evaluate some of these standards. Figure 7.1 outlines the organization of this chapter.

7.2   Longstanding Measurement Examples

Even though financial statements are conventionally referred to as based on historical cost, they contain a substantial fair value component. To preface a discussion of recent measurement-oriented standards, we will review some common longstanding instances of market and present value-based valuations.

7.2.1 Accounts Receivable and Payable

For most firms, current accounts receivable (net of allowance for doubtful accounts) and accounts payable are valued at the expected amount of cash to be received or paid. Since the length of time to payment is short, the discount factor is negligible, and this basis of valuation approximates present value.

7.2.2 Cash Flows Fixed by Contract

There are numerous instances where cash flows are fixed by contract. Then, valuation is based on present value if the contract provides reliable estimates of amounts and timing of future cash flows and interest rate. For example, if a firm issues long-term debt and uses the compound interest method to amortize any premium or discount, it can be shown that the resulting net book value of the debt equals the present value of the future interest and principal payments, discounted at the effective rate of interest of the debt established at the time of issue.

As another example, Section 3065 of the *CICA Handbook* requires capital lease contracts and related leased assets to be valued at the present value of minimum lease payments, using the lower of the interest rate implicit in the lease and the lessee's current borrowing rate.

It should be noted, however, that if market interest rates change during the life of the contract, present values of outstanding debt or leases are not adjusted. As far as interest rates are concerned, the accounting for leases and debt is still on a historical cost basis. Consequently, the accounting for long-term debt and leases is only a partial application of the measurement perspective.

7.2.3 The Lower-of-Cost-or-Market Rule

The lower-of-cost-or-market rule is another long-established example of a measurement perspective. Under this rule, when the market value of a temporary investment falls below its carrying value, Section 3010 of the *CICA Handbook* requires a writedown to market value. A similar rule is traditionally applied to inventories. Also, if the value of a long-term investment falls below its carrying value, and the decline in value is not temporary, it should be written down under Section 3050 of the *Handbook*.

Note that while asset values are written down under lower-of-cost-or-market, they are not written up. Indeed, once an asset is written down, the written-down value becomes the new "cost," which may not be written up again.

The lower-of-cost-or-market rule is usually justified in terms of conservatism. It is more difficult to justify in terms of decision usefulness, however, since one would think that if market value information is useful, it would be useful when value is greater than cost as well as when it is less than cost. However, as argued in Section 6.6, conservatism reduces the likelihood of overstatement errors, and auditors feel, with some justification, that their exposure to legal liability is greater for an asset overstatement than for an equivalent amount of understatement. Consequently, the rule remains as only a partial application of the measurement perspective.

7.2.4 Push-Down Accounting

When one firm acquires all, or virtually all, of another firm in an arm's-length transaction, Section 1625 of the *CICA Handbook* allows (but does not require) the assets and liabilities of the acquired firm to be comprehensively revalued, with the resulting values recorded on the books of the acquired firm. This is called **push-down accounting**. The result is that the assets and liabilities are recorded on the books of the acquired firm at their fair values as established in the acquisition transaction. In addition, Section 1625 requires comprehensive revaluation following a financial reorganization, provided that the reorganization is significant enough to result in a substantial realignment of interests. Thus, Section 1625 constitutes another major example of the measurement perspective.

7.2.5 Ceiling Test for Property, Plant and Equipment

Section 3063 of the *CICA Handbook* imposes a **ceiling test** for long-lived assets, such as property, plant and equipment. While the primary basis of accounting for these assets continues to be historical cost, Section 3063 requires a writedown when their net carrying value exceeds the net recoverable amount.

The calculation of the net recoverable amount (i.e., the ceiling) requires the estimation of future direct net cash flows from use of the long-lived assets. These cash flows are essentially future operating cash inflows less related cash outflows, including any removal and site restoration costs, plus residual or salvage value. A similar ceiling test also applies to the costs of oil and gas exploration where these are accounted for under the full-cost method (see Section 2.5.1).

Section 3063 lays down a two-step ceiling test procedure. First, it is determined if the long-lived asset is **impaired**. This is the case if book value exceeds the sum of *undiscounted* expected future direct net cash flows. If an asset is deemed impaired, the second step is to determine its **fair value**. Fair value can be measured by means of quoted market prices, if available. Otherwise, fair value can be measured as the *discounted* expected present value of the asset's future direct net cash flows.

However, the ceiling test is one-sided. That is, subsequent writeup of impaired assets is not allowed if fair value rises. Consequently, like the lower-of-cost-or-market rule, the ceiling test is only a partial application of the measurement perspective. Ceiling tests (similar provisions are laid down by SFAS 144 in the United States) help protect the auditor from legal liability, and contribute to the increase in conservatism documented by Basu (1997), as discussed in Section 6.6.

Nevertheless, despite the partial nature of its application, ceiling tests represent an important extension of the measurement perspective to major classes of assets.

7.2.6 Pensions and Other Post-employment Benefits

Defined benefit pension plans[1] are accounted for on a present value basis under Section 3461 of the *CICA Handbook*—pension liabilities are based on expected present value of pension benefits earned by the employee to date, taking into account projected compensation to expected retirement. Pension fund assets are valued at fair value. Pension expense for a period includes service cost—the expected present value of benefits earned by employees under the plan for the period, including projected increases in earnings, plus accretion of discount on opening pension liability, reduced by earnings on pension plan assets.

Effective in 2001, Section 3461 also applies to other post-employment benefits (OPEBs), such as health care and insurance provided to current and retired employees. Section 3461 regards OPEBs as a form of deferred compensation that, like pensions, should be recorded as employee services are rendered. The accumulated OPEB liability is based on service cost—the expected present value of benefits to be paid on behalf of current and retired employees. The expense for the period includes service cost and accretion of discount, less any expected return on plan assets. Similar provisions in the United States were laid down in 1990 by SFAS 106.

Prior to the effective dates of SFAS 106 and Section 3461, most firms accounted for OPEBs on a pay-as-you-go basis, recognizing an expense only as cash payments were made. Thus, adoption of fair value accounting usually results in the recording of a substantial liability to catch up on accumulated OPEB obligations to current and retired employees. These standards allow the offsetting charge to go directly to retained earnings (retroactive application) or to be amortized over future years (prospective application), thus avoiding a substantial earnings hit in the year of adoption.

For firms that used the retroactive option, the amount of the writeoff was often surprisingly large. For example, *The Globe and Mail* (February 2, 1993) reported a $20.8 billion one-time charge by General Motors Corp. to record its OPEB obligation upon adoption of SFAS 106 (see Chapter 4, Question 7). This reduced its shareholders' equity by about 75%!

For our purposes, the important aspect of pension and OPEB accounting is its use of discounted present value to calculate expense and accumulated liabilities. Indeed, SFAS 106 and Section 3461 go further in a measurement perspective than lower-of-cost-or-market and ceiling tests, since changes in plan assumptions and interest rates require revisions to liability and expense calculations.

As we would expect, accounting for pensions and OPEBs on a present value basis entails a loss of reliability, due to the many assumptions and estimates that have to be made, including the choice of a discount rate. Recall that low reliability is a possible explanation for the apparent lack of decision usefulness of RRA, as discussed in Section 5.7. The usefulness of OPEB information was investigated by Amir (1993), who studied the impact on firms' share prices of the estimated amounts of their OPEB liabilities. For a 1992 sample of 231 U.S. firms, Amir documented a negative relationship, suggesting that investors used OPEB information in their decision-making. Presumably, in contrast to RRA, the contractual nature of most pension and OPEB plans endows their future cash flows with sufficient certainty that increased relevance is not negated by lower reliability. Consequently, the accounting for employee future benefits is a major example of the measurement perspective in financial accounting.

7.2.7 Impaired Loans

Section 3025 of the *CICA Handbook*, released in 1994, relates to impaired loans. This standard requires that loans be written down by the lender to their **estimated realizable amount** when they become impaired or restructured. This amount is based on the expected future cash flows to be derived from the loans, discounted at the rate of interest implicit in the loan transaction. Any loss resulting from such a writedown is to be recorded in current income. Furthermore, the net carrying value of impaired loans is generally adjusted for subsequent changes in the estimated realizable amount, with the resulting charge or credit reflected in the income statement.

It is this latter provision, which allows subsequent writeup if loan quality improves, that is of particular interest, suggesting a movement away from the partial measurement approaches of the lower-of-cost-or-market rule and ceiling test. Thus, the impaired loans standard indicates a clear extension of the valuation approach by standard setters. This is confirmed in *Handbook* paragraph 3025.49, which states that disclosure of the net charge or credit to income resulting from loan impairment allows users of financial statements to assess the effect on net income of changes in expectations of the amounts and timing of future cash flows from loans.

7.2.8 Summary

The above is only a partial listing of longstanding fair value-based measurements in generally accepted accounting principles. For a more complete discussion, see Weil (1990). For our purposes, the main point to realize is that a considerable amount of measurement perspective is already inherent in financial statements, even though those statements are regarded as primarily historical cost-based.

The foregoing examples, however, understate the extent of measurement perspective in current GAAP. We now turn to a consideration of more recent fair value-oriented accounting standards.

7.3 Financial Instruments

7.3.1 Introduction

In Canada, accounting for **financial instruments** is laid down by Section 3860 of the *CICA Handbook*, issued in 1995. Section 3860 deals primarily with the definition and supplementary disclosure of financial instruments. It does not specify how they should be valued in the financial statements proper. Consequently, this standard is more in keeping with the information perspective than with application of the measurement perspective, the topic of this chapter. Nevertheless, we will include it in our discussion here for continuity.

Financial instruments are defined in Section 3860 as follows:

A financial instrument is any contract that gives rise to both a financial asset of one party and a financial liability or equity instrument of another party.

Financial assets and liabilities are defined quite broadly. Thus, Section 3860 defines a financial asset as:

(i) cash;

(ii) a contractual right to receive cash or another financial asset from another party;

(iii) a contractual right to exchange financial instruments with another party under conditions that are potentially favourable; or

(iv) an equity instrument of another entity.

Similarly, a financial liability is any liability that is a contractual obligation:

(i) to deliver cash or another financial asset to another party; or

(ii) to exchange financial instruments with another party under conditions that are potentially unfavourable.

Thus, financial assets and liabilities include items such as accounts and notes receivable and payable, debt and equity securities held by the firm, and bonds outstanding. These are referred to as primary instruments. Also included are **derivative instruments**, to be discussed in Section 7.3.3.

As mentioned, Section 3860 is information perspective-oriented. For example, it requires disclosure of fair values of financial instruments as supplementary information. Thus, it does not lay down rules for financial instrument valuation in the accounts, although the valuation of certain types of primary financial instruments, such as receivables, impaired loans, and capital leases are prescribed in other sections. However, a measurement perspective for financial instruments has developed much further in the United States. While Canadian standard setters are moving to adopt similar fair value accounting standards, these are not expected to be in place until at least 2006. In the meantime, it is instructive to look at U.S. developments to see some of the problems that must be overcome in moving to fair value financial instrument accounting.

7.3.2 Valuation of Debt and Equity Securities

SFAS 115 of the FASB applies to investments in debt securities and to investments in equity securities with readily determinable fair values. It requires that these assets be classified at acquisition into one of three categories:

- **Held-to-Maturity** Debt securities for which the entity has a "positive intent and ability" to hold to maturity
- **Trading Securities** Held for a short time for the purpose of selling them
- **Available-for-Sale** All other securities to which SFAS 115 applies

While held-to-maturity securities are valued at amortized cost, both trading and available-for-sale securities are valued at fair value. For trading securities, unrealized gains and losses from such valuations are included in income. For available-for-sale securities, unrealized gains and losses are included in other comprehensive income.

A statement of **other comprehensive income** is required in the United States by SFAS 130. Other comprehensive income includes gains and losses from adjustments to fair value of available-for-sale securities, foreign currency translation adjustments, and several other types of unrealized gains and losses. Other comprehensive income is reported after net income, or as a component of a statement of changes in shareholders' equity. As these gains and losses are realized, they are transferred to net income. The sum of net income and other comprehensive income is called **comprehensive income** by SFAS 130. SFAS 130 is discussed in Section 13.6.2.

To understand SFAS 115's seemingly inconsistent juxtaposition of accounting policies, two major problems need to be pointed out. The first problem is **gains trading**, also called "cherry picking." This is a practice that financial institutions, including those involved in the savings and loan debacle discussed in Section 6.6, have been suspected of using as a way to manage their reported earnings. Gains trading can be employed when investment portfolios are valued at cost or amortized cost, and when at least some securities have risen in value. Then, the institution can realize a gain by selling securities that have risen in value, while continuing to hold securities that may have fallen in value. No loss is recognized on these latter securities, because they continue to be carried at cost on grounds that they will be held to maturity.

Note that gains trading is not possible if securities are valued at fair value, with unrealized gains and losses included in net income—if changes in fair value are recorded as they occur, then there is no gain or loss on disposal. Thus, the firm has no discretion to cherry pick (but see problem 7). However, it is interesting to note that SFAS 115 has the potential to make the problem of gains trading worse rather than better. When securities are transferred from held-to-maturity to trading, SFAS 115 requires that the transfer be accounted for at fair value, with any gain or loss included in net income. Thus, to gains trade, the firm need only reclassify held-to-maturity securities as trading—no sale of securities is needed.

However, SFAS 115 protects against this possibility by placing stringent conditions on transfers into and out of held-to-maturity. For example, if a firm intends to hold a debt security for an indefinite period, this does not qualify as held-to-maturity. Also, transfers out of held-to-maturity require events that are "isolated, nonrecurring, and unusual for the reporting enterprise that could not have been reasonably anticipated. . . ." Indeed, SFAS 115 stipulates that the whole category may be reclassified as available-for-sale if any held-to-maturity securities are disposed of prior to maturity.

The second problem is one of volatility of reported net income. SFAS 115 applies only to financial assets. However, financial institutions and other firms may coordinate the duration and other characteristics of their financial assets and liabilities in order to create a **natural hedge** of changes in values. For example, a firm with long-term debt issued at a fixed interest rate may purchase fixed interest-bearing securities of similar amount and maturity. If interest rates, say, go down, the real value of the firm goes down due to the increase in the market value of the debt. However, this will be offset by the increase in the value of the interest-bearing securities. It then seems reasonable that if financial assets are carried at fair values so should financial liabilities. Otherwise, the volatility of net income that results from recognizing unrealized gains and losses from only financial assets is greater than the real volatility the firm has chosen through its natural hedging activities. It is for this reason, presumably, that SFAS 115 stipulates that certain securities (held-to-maturity) need not be carried at fair value and that gains and losses on others (available-for-sale) are excluded from net income. If unrealized gains and losses on these financial assets do not enter into net income, they cannot contribute to excess volatility.

One might ask why SFAS 115 does not simply require that financial liabilities also be carried at fair value, rather than going through the contortions just described.[2] The difficulty is that financial institutions are a major industry affected by SFAS 115 and that, to date, a generally accepted method of fair-valuing the demand deposit liabilities of financial institutions does not exist. It may seem reasonable to value demand deposits at their face value, since this is the amount that depositors can demand. This is the way demand deposits are currently valued. However, this basis of valuation ignores the value of **core deposit intangibles**. These can arise from customers' acceptance of a lower-than-market rate of interest on their deposits, due to goodwill, habit, location, etc. As a simple example, suppose that a bank pays 1% interest on a customer's $100 deposit but lends the customer's money at 5%. Then, as long as the customer keeps the $100 on deposit, the bank's $100 deposit liability is offset by a core deposit intangible asset that will generate $4 per year. The face amount of deposit liabilities should be reduced by this intangible asset for a fair valuation. Yet this introduces problems of reliably estimating the timing of withdrawals and discounting, which are currently unresolved. In the face of these difficulties, SFAS 115 opts not to require fair value accounting for any financial liabilities, and to control resulting excess volatility of net income by retention of historical cost accounting for held-to-maturity securities, and exclusion of unrealized gains and losses on available-for-sale securities from net income. While retention of historical cost for held-to-maturity securities does not eliminate the possibility of gains trading, the FASB must feel that the stringent controls over transfers between categories will keep the problem within bounds.

Despite these compromises, SFAS 115 represents a clear extension of the measurement perspective beyond the realm of supplemental disclosure and into the financial statements proper. Major classes of financial assets are to be fair-valued with unrealized gains and losses included either in net income or other comprehensive income.

7.3.3 Derivative Instruments

Derivative instruments are contracts, the value of which depends on some **underlying** price, interest rate, foreign exchange rate, or other variable. A common example is an option, such as a call option, that gives the holder a right to buy, say, 100 shares of a firm's common stock for $20 each during, or at the end of, some specified period. The notional amount of the contract is 100 (shares). The underlying is the market price of the shares. The higher the market price, the higher the value of the option, other things equal. Other examples of derivatives include futures, forward and swap contracts, interest rate caps and floors, and fixed-rate loan commitments. Generally, these instruments convey a benefit to the holder if there is a favourable movement in the underlying. If the underlying moves unfavourably, there may or may not be a loss to the holder.

A characteristic of derivative instruments is that they generally require or permit settlement in cash—delivery of the asset associated with the underlying need not take place. Thus, the option contract above need not involve the holder actually buying the shares, but only receiving the value of the option in cash at time of settlement. As another example, suppose a firm needs to borrow a large sum of money in six months time. It is concerned that interest rates may rise over this period. It buys a bond futures contract giving it the right to sell government bonds at a specified price on a settlement date six months hence. If interest rates go up, the underlying market value of the bonds goes down, and the value of the futures contract rises to offset the higher borrowing cost. If this contract had to be settled physically, the firm would have to enter the bond market on the settlement date, buy the requisite amount of government bonds, and sell them to the party on the other side of the contract at the contract price to realize the value of the contract. With cash settlement, the firm can simply receive a cash payment equal to the value of the contract, thereby saving both sides the costs of physical buying and selling. The ability to settle derivative instruments in cash has contributed to the great increase in their use over the past number of years.

Derivative instruments may or may not require an initial net investment. For example, a firm may enter into an interest rate swap contract that requires no cash outlay. If an initial investment is required, it is for less than the notional amount times the underlying. In the option example above, if the current share price is, say, $18, the cost to the holder of the option contract will certainly be less than $1,800, the amount that would be required to buy the shares outright. This is reasonable, because while the holder of the option will participate in any price increase of the shares during the option term, other rights of ownership, such as dividends, are excluded. In effect, the option holder is buying only the rights to future appreciation in value over some time period, not the shares themselves. In our bond futures contract example, the firm could also have protected itself by borrowing now, to lock in the current interest rate. But, this would require an additional interest cost for six months on the full amount needed.

These three examples illustrate the leverage aspect of derivatives—a lot of protection can be acquired at relatively low cost. Leverage is another reason for the great increase in the use of derivatives in recent years. Of course, leverage is a two-edged sword. If derivatives are used to speculate on the underlying price rather than to manage risk, the amount that can be lost, for a low initial investment, can be very large indeed.[3] This low initial investment characteristic of derivatives is a reason why accountants have found them difficult to deal with under historical cost accounting. Since there is little or no cost to account for, all or part of the contract is off-balance sheet.

For this reason, standard-setting bodies have required supplementary disclosure of information about financial instruments, including derivatives. As mentioned, Section 3860 of the *CICA Handbook* requires fair value information to be disclosed for financial instrument assets and liabilities, both recognized and unrecognized, as well as details of their terms and conditions. Information about **credit risk** of financial assets is also required, where credit risk is the risk that the other party to the contract will not fulfill its obligations. Related requirements are now contained in SFAS 107 of the FASB.

The accounting for derivative instruments has moved substantially towards a measurement perspective, however, by SFAS 133 of the FASB. This standard requires that all derivatives be measured at fair value for balance sheet purposes. If a derivative is traded on a market that works reasonably well, fair value is measured by its market value. If it is not traded, models of derivative value can be used. A Canadian standard similar to SFAS 133 is awaiting implementation. In the meantime, we will concentrate on SFAS 133.

How can we model the fair value of an option? To illustrate, consider our example of a call option to purchase 100 shares at $20, where the current market price is $18 per share. Assume that the option can be exercised at the end of two months. Assume also that the shares change their price only at the end of each month, and that these price changes follow a random walk (see Section 4.2.1). Specifically, assume that share price will increase each month by $2 with probability 0.5 or decrease by $2 with probability 0.5. This price behaviour is depicted in Figure 7.2.

Looking ahead from time 0 (now), at the end of the first month the 100 shares will have a market value of $2,000 with probability 0.5, and a value of $1,600 with probability 0.5. At the end of the second month (the expiry date of the option) their market value will be $2,200 with probability 0.25 (i.e., 0.5 × 0.5), $1,800 with probability 0.5 (0.25 + 0.25) or $1,400 with probability 0.25.

FIGURE 7.2 A SIMPLE OPTION PRICING MODEL

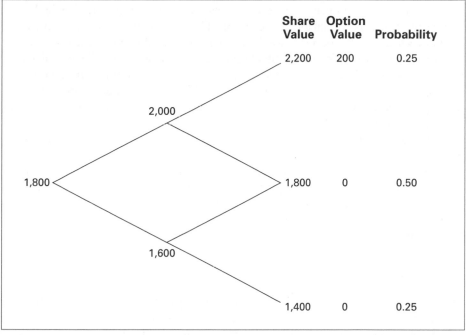

	Share Value	Option Value	Probability
	2,200	200	0.25
2,000			
1,800	1,800	0	0.50
1,600			
	1,400	0	0.25

Now the option will only be exercised if the value of the shares is $2,200. Since the exercise price is $20 per share, or $2,000 in total, the value of the option is then $200. For the other two possible share values, the option will not be exercised, so that its value is then $0.

The question then is, what is the fair value of the option at time 0, its date of issuance? If we assume that the risk-free interest rate in the economy is zero, this fair value is simply $200 × 0.25 = $50, the expected value of the option at maturity.[4]

Of course, our assumption that the share price changes only at the end of each month is unrealistic. In reality, many share prices change almost continuously. This can be modelled in our example by increasing the number of times that price changes in Figure 7.2 (but holding the time to expiration constant at two months). As the number of times the price changes goes to infinity (i.e., share price varies continuously) the fair value of the option is given by the famous Black/Scholes (1973) option pricing formula,[5] which values the option as a function of the following five variables:

- Current market price of the share—$18
- Variability of return of the share
- Exercise price of option—$20
- Time to expiration
- Risk-free interest rate

The first two of these inputs to the formula are characteristics of the underlying share price. Thus, given values for the last three variables, we see how the value of the option derives from the current market price and return variability of the share. The higher the current price, the more valuable is the option. The greater the variability of the price, the more valuable is the option since there is a greater likelihood that the price will rise by the expiry date (there is also a greater likelihood that the price will fall but, in that case, the option need not be exercised). Since Black/Scholes, models to value other, more complex derivative instruments have been developed. Thus, under appropriate conditions, models provide a way to implement the fair value calculations required by Section 3860, SFAS 107, and SFAS 133.

Changes in fair value of derivative instruments are recognized in net income under SFAS 133, except for certain hedging contracts, which we will discuss in Section 7.3.4.

It is noteworthy that SFAS 133 applies only to derivatives, not to all financial instruments. Debt and equity securities continue to be accounted for in the United States under SFAS 115, discussed in Section 7.3.2. Implementation of fair-value accounting for all financial instruments will require dealing with problems of core deposit intangibles and income volatility that were discussed in that section.

7.3.4 Hedge Accounting

Firms issue or acquire financial instruments for a variety of reasons. For example, they may manage their capital structure by means of convertible debt. They may manage their cash flows by issuing zero-coupon debt. Interest rate swaps and bond futures contracts may enable lower financing costs. Perhaps the major reason why firms deal in financial instruments, however, is to *manage risk*.[6] It is this role of financial instruments that we concentrate on here.

The term "manage" risk is used advisedly. The goal of risk management is to produce a desired level of firm-specific risk, not necessarily to reduce it to zero. Zero risk may be too costly, or not even possible. Indeed, it may not even be desirable, since investors can reduce firm-specific risk for themselves through portfolio diversification.

As mentioned in Section 7.3.2, firms are, to some extent, protected against risks by natural hedging. While we will consider only hedging by means of derivative instruments, it should be noted that natural hedges are ultimately a management decision and any evaluation of a firm's susceptibility to risk should also consider natural hedging. Here, we simplify by viewing hedging by means of derivative instruments as a way of reducing *specific* risks, such as the risk of interest rate changes on floating-rate debt, or foreign exchange risk on anticipated future sales. Natural hedging is viewed as reducing *total*, or non-specific, firm risk. In effect, hedging with derivative instruments takes over where natural hedging leaves off.

As suggested above, a variety of complex financial instruments has been developed to enable firms to better manage risks. Many of these risks are **price risks**, arising from changes in interest rates, commodity prices, and foreign exchange rates. Other risks arise from credit risk. The accounting for these complex instruments involves difficult issues of recognition and valuation, which standard-setting bodies are currently addressing.

Derivative instruments designated as hedges of recognized assets and liabilities are called **fair value hedges**. The essence of such a hedge is that if a firm owns, say, a risky asset, it can hedge this risk by acquiring a **hedging instrument**—some other asset or liability whose value moves in the direction opposite to that of the **hedged item**. Accounting for hedges of transactions that take place entirely within the current period is relatively straightforward. The gain or loss on the hedged item and the loss or gain on the hedging instrument can both be recorded in current net income, which then includes a realized loss or gain only to the extent the hedge is not completely effective. Hedges may not be completely effective because there may not exist a hedging instrument that will completely offset the hedged item's gain or loss. For example, a bank may have trouble finding a perfect hedge for the risk of changing interest rates on its deposit liabilities. The risk resulting from the absence of a perfectly effective hedge is called **basis risk**.

Frequently, however, hedging transactions do not take place entirely within the current period. For example, suppose that during the year a firm hedges its price risk on its finished goods inventory by entering into a forward contract to sell the inventory at its current market price. Thus, the inventory is the hedged item and the forward contract is the hedging instrument. Suppose that, at year-end, the inventory is still on hand and its market price has fallen. As a result, the fair value of the forward contract has risen.

Under SFAS 133, gains and losses on fair value hedges are included in current earnings. The related loss or gain on the hedged item is also included in current earnings. Thus, our firm writes its inventory down to fair value and writes the forward contract up, so that net income is affected only to the extent that the hedge is not completely effective. However, the value of the forward contract is added to the inventory, contrary to the traditional lower-of-cost-or-market rule (Section 7.2.3). In effect, the firm can circumvent lower-of-cost-or-market and, more generally, ceiling tests (Section 7.2.5), by appropriate hedging strategy.

Firms also may hedge *anticipated* transactions. Such contracts are called **cash flow hedges**. Under SFAS 133, cash flow hedges are fair-valued, with unrealized gains and losses included in other comprehensive income until the transactions affect net income. Then, any accumulated gain or loss is transferred into net income for that period. For example, an oil and gas producer may wish to hedge next period's sales. These cash receipts are risky because of fluctuations in oil and gas prices and, if the oil and gas is sold in foreign markets, fluctuations in foreign exchange rates. Including unrealized gains and losses on cash flow hedges in other comprehensive income reduces the volatility problem by delaying their effect on net income until the next period, when the anticipated cash flows are realized.

An instrument must meet certain criteria if it is to be eligible for hedge accounting under SFAS 133. Non-derivative instruments are generally prohibited from being eligible. This rules out hedge accounting for natural hedges. Also, options issued as stock-based compensation are excluded. For instruments that are eligible, management must **designate** the instrument as a hedge at the inception of the hedge, identify the hedged item and document the nature of the risk being hedged. The rationale is that reported net income would lose reliability if management had the discretion to designate a hedging instrument at any time it wanted. For example, faced with a major loss on derivatives not held as a hedge, management could decide to retroactively designate them as cash flow hedges of forecasted transactions. Then, the loss could be put into other comprehensive income, thereby at least delaying its impact on net income.

Note that if a derivative cannot be designated, it does not enjoy the benefits of hedge accounting, such as offsetting of gains or losses on the derivative by fair-valuing the hedged item (fair value hedge) or delaying loss recognition to other comprehensive income (cash flow hedge). Another benefit is that if the hedged item is subject to the ceiling test (e.g., oil and gas reserves), ceiling test writedowns may be avoided. Denial of these benefits increases the volatility of reported earnings. High earnings volatility can have adverse effects on firms with high debt loads by increasing the probability of financial distress, and on growth firms who may want to hedge their risks but may have relatively few hedgeable items. Such firms would need to rely on natural hedges. In effect, SFAS 133 enables hedge accounting for specific risks, but does not facilitate the reduction of total firm risk which, as mentioned, would benefit highly levered and high-growth firms. For further discussion of these issues, see Guay (1999).

Another criterion for designation as a hedge is that the derivative instrument must be "highly effective" in offsetting changes in the fair value of the hedged item. SFAS 133 does not lay down rules for determining high effectiveness except that management's documentation of hedge effectiveness should be consistent with the entity's established risk management strategy. However, highly effective essentially means that there is high negative correlation between the fair values of the hedging instrument and the hedged item.

One way of estimating this correlation is the *cumulative dollar offset* method. For example, suppose that a firm borrows at a variable interest rate. It hedges its cash flow risk by purchasing a treasury bill futures contract, whereby it undertakes to sell a given number of treasury bills at some future date at a fixed price. Suppose that, due to rising interest rates, its interest payments increase by $1,500, and the fair value of its treasury bill futures contract rises by $1,300. Then the ratio of loss to gain is $-1,500/+1,300 = -1.15$. Since this is reasonably close to a perfect ratio of -1, this supports continuing the designation of the futures contract as a hedge.

Theory in Practice 7.1

Whether an instrument is regarded as a hedge or not can have significant effects on the financial statements. A case in point is El Paso Corporation, a large Texas-based producer and distributor of natural gas. During 1999–2002, El Paso Production Co., a subsidiary, entered into forward contracts to lock in the price it received for its future gas production. These forward contracts were with El Paso Merchant Energy, another El Paso subsidiary. Merchant Energy then entered into a set of similar contracts with outside third parties. Since outside parties were now involved, the corporation as a whole was, at this point, protected against future natural gas price changes. El Paso accounted for these forward contracts as cash flow hedges under SFAS 133. As a result, unrealized gains and losses on these derivatives were included in other comprehensive income.

continued ➜

However, Merchant Energy then entered into a second set of similar, but opposite, forward contracts with third parties, thereby effectively unwinding the company's price protection. Nevertheless, it continued to designate the original set of contracts between Production and Merchant Energy as hedges under SFAS 133.

During 2001, the price of natural gas had fallen to the point where the ceiling test applied, and El Paso's gas reserves would normally have had to be written down to fair value. However, since the original contracts were designated as hedges, a writedown was not made since the hedges protected the firm against natural gas price declines.

In 2004, El Paso announced that following a review by the company and its auditors, and investigation by regulatory authorities, it had decided that its cash flow hedges did not qualify for hedge accounting under SFAS 133 presumably because of the unwinding referred to above. As a result, the ceiling test for 2001 kicked in retroactively, and El Paso was forced to write its reserves down by $1.6 billion—the amount that should have been written off in 2001. (While the price of natural gas has risen considerably since 2001, recall that the ceiling test does not allow for subsequent writeup if fair value increases.)

The stock market reacted calmly to these events, perhaps due to the company's emphasis that cash flows were not affected, and that future depletion expense would be reduced. On August 10, 2004, the date the company announced it was discontinuing hedge accounting, El Paso's share price fell by only 6 cents, to $7.65. On August 23, the date it announced that the writedown was $1.6 billion, share price rose by 24 cents to $8.05.

Prior to SFAS 133 (and still in Canada until a new standard similar to SFAS 133 comes on line in 2006), unrealized gains and losses recognized on designated hedging instruments were deferred to the balance sheet until the offsetting transactions took place. The rationale of these deferrals is not hard to see—the matching concept of historical cost accounting is violated if gains or losses on hedged items and related hedging instruments are recognized in different periods. Deferral gets them into the same period. This is consistent with the income statement approach that underlies the information perspective and historical cost accounting—deferred gains and losses can be included on the balance sheet, since they are "by-products" of matching of costs and revenues. Under the measurement perspective, however, with its focus on the balance sheet, deferred gains and losses are not assets and liabilities, since they do not involve future economic benefits or payments. Instead, unrealized gains and losses are included in income, or other comprehensive income. By eliminating such deferrals from the balance sheet, SFAS 133 represents a substantial step towards the measurement perspective.

7.4 Accounting for Intangibles

7.4.1 Introduction

Intangible assets are capital assets that do not have physical substance, such as patents, trademarks, franchises, good workforce, location, restructurings, information technology, Internet site names, and, more generally, goodwill.

Some intangibles are accounted for much like property, plant, and equipment. If they are purchased, or self-developed with reasonable certainty of future benefits, they are valued at cost and amortized over their useful lives. If they are acquired in a business combination and meet certain conditions, cost is equal to their fair value at acquisition. Such intangibles are subject to the ceiling test described in Section 7.2.5.

Intangible assets are important assets for many firms and, for some firms, comprise most of firm value. However, unless they satisfy the criteria of the previous paragraph, their fair values, and even their costs, are difficult to establish reliably, particularly if they are self-developed. This is because the costs of intangibles may be spread over many years and, as these costs are incurred, it may not be known whether they will ever produce future benefits. An example is the costs of research and development, which can lead to many of the intangibles mentioned above. Since it is so difficult to predict future payoffs from these costs, it is not reliably known whether they will be recovered, let alone what their fair value is. As a result, Section 3450 of the *CICA Handbook* requires that research costs not appear on the balance sheet at all—they are charged to expense as incurred. Costs of developing a product or process resulting from research may be capitalized only if their future benefits are reasonably certain. In the United States, SFAS 2 requires that all R&D costs be written off in the year they are incurred. Consequently, self-developed intangibles resulting from the firm's research will not appear on the balance sheet.

However, it is important to realize that intangibles are "there" even if they are not on the balance sheet. Instead, due to recognition lag, they appear through the income statement. That is, since historical cost accounting waits until value is realized as sales and earnings, the income statement contains the current "installment" of the value of intangibles. If these installments are positive, the firm has goodwill.[7] That is, goodwill exists if the firm earns more than its cost of capital on its net assets, including any separately identified intangibles. This mirrors exactly our procedure in Section 6.5.3, where Canadian Tire's unrecorded goodwill was calculated as the present value of expected future abnormal earnings.

The question then is, should goodwill remain off the balance sheet, with the implication that the income statement reports on it as realized, or should its fair value be measured and reported on the balance sheet? Reporting the fair value of goodwill has potential for increased decision usefulness, since this may reveal management's inside information about future expected earning power (which is what creates the goodwill), and it is management that has the best information about what this earning power is. But, reporting the fair value of goodwill creates serious problems of reliability.

At this point, it is helpful to distinguish between self-developed goodwill and purchased goodwill. We first consider purchased goodwill.

7.4.2 Accounting for Purchased Goodwill

When one firm acquires another in a business combination, the **purchase method** of accounting for the transaction requires that the tangible and identifiable intangible assets, and the liabilities of the acquired company be valued at their fair values for purposes of the consolidated financial statements.[8] Goodwill is then the difference between the net amount of these fair values and the total purchase price paid by the acquiring company. We illustrate the traditional accounting for purchased goodwill with an example.

EXAMPLE 7.1

ACCOUNTING FOR PURCHASED GOODWILL

JDN Ltd. is a rapidly expanding "hi-tech" firm. As at January 1, 2005, it had 100 shares outstanding, trading at $10. Its balance sheet was as follows:

JDN Ltd.			
Balance Sheet			
As at January 1, 2005			
Capital Assets	$500	Liabilities	$100
		Shareholders' Equity	400
	$500		$500

S Ltd. is also growing rapidly, and is in a business similar to that of JDN. Its balance sheet as at January 1, 2005 was as follows:

S Ltd.			
Balance Sheet			
As at January 1, 2005			
Capital Assets	$300	Liabilities	$140
		Shareholders' Equity	160
	$300		$300

On January 1, 2005, JDN purchases all the 160 outstanding shares of S Ltd. in exchange for 40 shares of JDN's stock valued at $10 each, for a total purchase price of $400. The balance sheet of JDN immediately after the acquisition was:

JDN Ltd.			
Balance Sheet (Post-Acquisition)			
As at January 1, 2005			
Capital Assets, excluding		Liabilities	$100
Investment in S	$500		
Investment in S	400	Shareholders' Equity	800
	$900		$900

As mentioned, the identifiable assets and liabilities of the purchased company must be valued at their fair values for purposes of preparing a consolidated balance sheet, with any excess of the purchase price over net fair value reflected as goodwill. Assume that as at the date of acquisition the fair value of S Ltd.'s capital assets was estimated as $340, and of its liabilities as $140. The consolidated balance sheet of JDN and its wholly owned subsidiary S Ltd. as at date of acquisition was thus:

JDN Ltd. and Subsidiary
Consolidated Balance Sheet
As at January 1, 2005

Capital Assets,		Liabilities	$240
excluding goodwill	$840		
Goodwill	200	Shareholders' Equity	800
	$1,040		$1,040

Goodwill is determined as the amount paid for S Ltd. ($400) less the fair value of net assets acquired ($200).

Until 2001 in Canada and the United Stares, this goodwill was amortized over its useful life, consistent with the matching concept of historical cost accounting. Management strongly complained about goodwill amortization, however, since it forced down consolidated net income following the acquisition, making it more difficult to demonstrate that the acquisition was a successful business strategy. Obviously, management has an incentive to demonstrate, through increased earnings, its good business judgement in entering into a business combination.

In response, many managers attempted to circumvent the effects of goodwill amortization by emphasizing **pro-forma income** (also called cash income[9]) rather than GAAP net income, where pro-forma income is defined as net income before goodwill amortization, restructuring charges, and a variety of other unusual, non-recurring, and extraordinary items selected by management. Under this tactic, the GAAP income statement itself is not affected. However, pro-forma income is emphasized in earnings announcements, messages to shareholders, MD&A, etc. In this way, management seeks to convince investors that goodwill amortization and related items do not matter, in the sense that they are not relevant to the evaluation of the performance of the consolidated entity.

A criticism of pro-forma income was that to the extent management succeeded in convincing investors that this is a better profit measure than GAAP net income, there was less discipline for managers to avoid overpaying in business acquisitions. The excessive goodwill amortization that results from overpaying was simply ignored. Another criticism is that it may mislead investors, since there are no standards to determine just what items are excluded from GAAP income. This is of particular concern if securities markets are not fully efficient.

Theory in Practice 7.2

As an illustration of pro-forma income, consider the 2000 *Annual Report* of The Toronto-Dominion Bank (TD Bank). In its MD&A, TD Bank reported operating cash basis net income of $2,018, $1,472, and $1,183 ($million) for 2000, 1999, and 1998, respectively, explaining that these amounts exclude items that are not "part of our normal operations." The bank's reported GAAP net incomes for

continued ➡

these three years as per its consolidated income statement were $1,025, $2,981, and $1,138, respectively. For 2000, the difference is due to the after-tax effects of $1,203 amortization of goodwill arising from TD Bank's acquisition of Canada Trust in that year, plus $475 of restructuring costs from the same transaction. Clearly, the two earnings sequences give different impressions of TD Bank's operations.

As another illustration, JDS Uniphase Corporation reported a preliminary GAAP net loss for its fiscal year ended June 30, 2001 of $50.558 billion, reportedly the largest loss ever incurred by a North American corporation. This loss included a writedown of purchased goodwill of $44.774 billion,[10] in addition to amortization of remaining purchased goodwill of $5.475 billion. Nevertheless, in a news announcement accompanying the release of its 2001 preliminary loss, JDS reported a pro forma profit of $67.4 million (see problem 9).

In response to tactics such as these, standard setters have eliminated the amortization of goodwill. This was accomplished in the United States by SFAS 142, effective in July 2001. In Canada, Section 3062 of the *CICA Handbook* contains similar requirements. These standards constitute a substantial movement towards the measurement perspective. Specifically, goodwill is retained on the consolidated balance sheet at its value established at time of purchase, unless there is evidence of impairment, in which case a ceiling test is to be applied to write goodwill down to its new fair value. Since goodwill amortization was a major management complaint, it will be interesting to see the extent to which its elimination reduces emphasis on pro-forma income.

7.4.3 Self-Developed Goodwill

Unlike purchased goodwill, no readily identifiable transactions exist to determine the cost of self-developed goodwill. Consequently, costs that may create goodwill, such as R&D, are usually written off as incurred. As mentioned, any goodwill that develops from these costs shows up in subsequent income statements. This recognition lag is a major reason why share price responds to earnings announcements, as documented in Chapter 5. The market watches net income carefully for clues as to future earning power.

Nevertheless, the proportion of abnormal share return explained by net income is low, and seems to be declining over time, as discussed in Section 6.4. Reasons for this low market share were examined by Lev and Zarowin (1999) (LZ). Recall that their study was introduced in Section 6.4, where we noted their findings of declining earnings value relevance over time. Here, we consider LZ's investigation into reasons for this falling market share. They argue that this is due primarily to a failure to account properly for self-developed intangibles.

LZ's argument is easy to see. Consider a firm's current R&D expenditures. Since they are expensed, these costs force net income down. However, an efficient market will not penalize the firm for the resulting lower reported earnings to the extent it expects positive results from the R&D, and may even reward it with a higher stock price. Obviously, if the firm's share price responds positively to costs that force current net income down, this will show up as a low association between abnormal share return and net income, and a low, possibly negative, ERC. Furthermore, LZ suggest, most firms' expenditures on self-developed intangibles increase over time, driven by deregulation, innovation, and competition. If so, the low association intensifies. In effect, current accounting for R&D results in a *mismatch* of the costs of intangibles with the revenues generated by those intangibles. These effects, LZ argue, are a prime contributor to low and declining R^2s and ERCs.

To investigate this argument, LZ examine a sample of U.S. firms with high research intensity, that is, firms whose R&D costs have grown at an increasing rate. While R&D is only one intangible, they focus on it on grounds that R&D is a major contributor to self-developed goodwill. LZ find a significantly lower association between share returns and reported earnings for this sample than for a second sample of firms with low R&D intensity, consistent with their argument.

The question then is, what might be done to improve the accounting for intangibles? One suggestion made by LZ is for a type of successful efforts accounting for R&D. They propose that the costs of R&D be capitalized if they pass a feasibility test, such as a working model or a successful clinical trial. Capitalization at this point, they argue, provides a reasonable tradeoff between relevance and reliability, and reveals inside information about the success of R&D efforts to the market. The capitalized costs would then be amortized over their estimated useful life.

7.4.4 The Clean Surplus Model Revisited

Another approach to valuing goodwill is to use the clean surplus model discussed in Section 6.5. Recall that our valuation of the share value of Canadian Tire Corporation, Limited in Section 6.5.3 resulted in a goodwill estimate of $710 (million). Perhaps this amount could be formally incorporated into the financial statements as the fair value of Canadian Tire's goodwill. While we discussed at the time some of the reliability issues surrounding this estimate, if the estimate was to be prepared by management it would convey relevant information about Canadian Tire's expected future earning power.[11]

Alternatively, the clean surplus goodwill calculation could possibly serve as a ceiling test for purchased goodwill. If, in the case of Canadian Tire, the book value of its purchased goodwill exceeds $710, this suggests that purchased goodwill should be written down so as not to exceed this value.[12, 13] Such a procedure, however, clouds the distinction between purchased and self-developed goodwill. For example, the purchased goodwill might be worthless, in which case it should be written down to zero, and the $710 would then be entirely self-developed. For further discussion of the possible use of the clean surplus model to account for goodwill, see AAA Financial Accounting Standards Committee (2001).

7.4.5 Summary

Accounting for intangibles is the ultimate test of the measurement perspective. Application of the measurement perspective to accounting for goodwill creates severe reliability problems. These problems may be somewhat mitigated for purchased goodwill, since at least a cost figure is available. Yet, even for purchased goodwill, amortization was essentially arbitrary due to the difficulty of establishing useful life. Furthermore, management disliked being charged for goodwill amortization and took steps to avoid it. Standard setters have moved towards a measurement perspective to purchased goodwill by introducing new standards to write it down only if there is evidence of impairment. The clean surplus model may provide a framework to structure the estimation of the fair value of goodwill.

When goodwill is self-developed, further reliability problems arise, and standard setters usually react by requiring immediate expensing of the costs of intangibles that underlie self-developed goodwill. However, this creates problems of matching of costs and revenues, and, arguably, is the root cause of low value-relevance of reported earnings. A suggestion to improve the accounting for self-developed goodwill is capitalization and amortization of successful research projects.

7.5 Reporting on Risk

7.5.1 Beta Risk

In SFAC 1 and Section 3860 of the *CICA Handbook*, professional accounting bodies recognize that investors need risk information. The theory underlying the CAPM suggests (Section 4.5) that a stock's beta is the sole firm-specific risk measure for a rational investor's diversified portfolio. The usual way to estimate beta is by means of a regression analysis based on the market model.

These considerations suggest there is little role for reporting of firm risk. However, this is not the case. One reason, discussed in Section 6.2, is that investors may not always behave as the rational decision theory leading to the CAPM predicts. Another, pointed out in Sections 4.5 and 6.2.3, derives from estimation risk and the role of financial reporting in reducing it. Yet another reason is the possibility, raised in Section 7.3.3, that managers may use derivatives to speculate. Then, disclosure of the firm's risk management strategies, the fair values of its various derivatives, and their unrealized gains and losses, is crucial. Consequently, even if beta is not dead, accounting-based risk disclosures are useful for investors.

Given that beta remains an important risk measure, if it is not stationary (Section 6.2.3), investors will want to know when and by how much it has changed. The financial statements may be of help here, since beta and various accounting-based risk measures are correlated. Financial statement-based risk measures may indicate the direction and magnitude of a change in beta sooner than the market model, which would require several periods of new data for re-estimation.

Beaver, Kettler, and Scholes (1970) (BKS) were the first to examine formally the relationship between beta and financial statement-based risk measures. For a sample of 307 New York Stock Exchange firms over two time periods, 1947–1956 and 1957–1965, they used a market model regression analysis to estimate betas for their sample firms for each time period. Then they calculated various financial statement-based risk measures for the same periods. The correlations between three of these risk measures and betas were as shown in Table 7.1.

TABLE 7.1 CORRELATION COEFFICIENTS BETWEEN ACCOUNTING RISK MEASURES AND BETA, FOR FIVE-SECURITY PORTFOLIOS

ACCOUNTING RISK MEASURES	PERIOD 1	PERIOD 2
	1947–56	1957–65
Dividend payout	−0.79	−0.50
Leverage	0.41	0.48
Earnings variability	0.90	0.82

Source: BKS, Table 5. Reprinted by permission.

Dividend payout is the ratio of common share cash dividends to net income. Leverage is the ratio of senior debt securities to total assets. Earnings variability is the standard deviation of the firm's price/earnings ratio over the period.

Notice that the signs of the correlations are what we would expect (for example, the higher the dividend payout, the lower the risk, since a firm facing significant risks would likely retain its earnings for protection rather than pay them out) and that most of the correlations are quite high. Furthermore, there is reasonable consistency between Period 1 and 2. Indeed, BKS report that their most highly correlated accounting variable was a better predictor of a stock's beta than its current beta, supporting our suggestion above that accounting-based risk measures may provide timely indications of shifts in beta.

These correlation results may seem surprising since, a priori, it is not obvious why a market-based risk measure has anything to do with accounting variables. However, Hamada (1972) showed that, under ideal conditions, there is a direct relationship between debt-to-equity and beta. Lev (1974) showed a direct relationship, also under ideal conditions, between operating leverage and beta (operating leverage is the ratio of fixed to variable operating costs). BKS' results suggest that these relationships carry over at least in part to non-ideal conditions. The rationale for these results is not hard to see. The higher a firm's financial and operating leverage, the more it will benefit if business conditions improve, and suffer if they deteriorate, since high leverage means a high proportion of fixed costs in the firm's cost structure, hence high sensitivity of earnings to changes in the level of activity. The efficient market will be aware of this and, the higher the leverage, the more it will bid up share price when business conditions improve, and vice versa. The stock market index will also rise and fall with business conditions. Since beta measures how strongly the firm's share price varies as the market varies, the greater the leverage the higher is beta.

BKS' findings have financial reporting implications. Hamada's study implies that off-balance-sheet liabilities should be brought onto the balance sheet at fair value to maximize correlation of debt-to-equity with beta. Section 3065 of the *CICA Handbook*, which requires present value accounting for capital leases, is a longstanding partial example. SFAS 133, described in Section 7.3.4, requires derivative instruments, many of which were previously off-balance-sheet, to be recorded at fair value.

Lev's study implies that firms should separate fixed and variable operating costs, if investors are to infer beta from the financial statements. Surprisingly, financial reporting seems of little help here. Indeed, Ryan (1997) points out that absorption cost accounting, which includes fixed operating costs in inventory, actually increases the difficulty of evaluating operating leverage.

7.5.2 Stock Market Reaction to Other Risks

In view of questions raised about the CAPM and beta, however, the relevance for investors of firm-specific risk information requires empirical investigation. This investigation has been aided because, over the past few years, standard setters have been requiring increased risk-related information in annual reports. We have already seen in Section 4.8.2 that MD&A requires a discussion of risks and uncertainties, particularly with respect to downside risk. Also, many of the disclosures required by Section 3860 and SFASs 107 and 133 (see Section 7.3.4) are risk-related. These include supplementary information about exposures to market and credit risks and about the firm's risk management policies, for example.

Much of the empirical research in this area relates to financial institutions. For such firms, financial assets and liabilities comprise most of book value, and it is to financial assets and liabilities that many of the risk-related disclosure standards relate. Barth, Beaver, and Landsman (1996) (BBL) examined the effects of supplemental SFAS 107 fair-value disclosures on the market value of equity for a sample of 136 U.S. banks for 1992 and 1993. They found a market response to the fair values of banks' loans portfolios, suggesting that the relevance of fair-value reporting of these assets outweighs reliability difficulties in measuring loan value. This result extended the finding by Barth (1994) that fair values of banks' investment securities (another major class of bank assets) also is related to the market value of banks' shares.

Interestingly, BBL found that the market response to fair value of loans was smaller for banks in lower-than-average financial condition (measured by their regulatory capital ratios). This implies that the market evaluates such banks as riskier—a bank in poor financial condition is less likely to be around to realize the unrealized gains and losses on its loan portfolio. BBL also found that banks' share values were negatively affected by amounts of non-performing loans and interest-sensitive liabilities, and positively affected by amounts of interest-sensitive assets. This means that these sources of risk were not fully hedged, consistent with our discussion of the costs of hedging in Section 7.3.4.

Schrand (1997) studied the effect on interest rate risk of derivatives-based hedging activities, for a sample of 208 savings and loans associations during 1984–1988. She measured the interest rate sensitivity of her sample firms by their one-year "maturity gap," the amount of their interest-sensitive assets maturing in one year less their interest-sensitive liabilities maturing in one year. The greater the gap, the greater the sensitivity of their share returns to unexpected changes in interest rates.

Note that maturity gap corresponds to the concept of natural hedging introduced in Section 7.3.2—the narrower the gap the more the institution is coordinating the maturities of its on-balance-sheet, interest-sensitive assets and liabilities so as to reduce its interest rate risk. For most of her sample firms, Schrand found that the gap was negative. That is, consistent with BBL, Schrand's firms were not completely eliminating their risk by means of natural hedging (if they were, the gap would be zero). For each sample firm, Schrand then evaluated the effect of the firm's (off-balance-sheet) derivatives hedging activities on its one-year maturity gap. She found that the more a firm reduced its gap in this way, the less sensitive its share price was to unexpected interest rate changes, particularly for the larger institutions in her sample (which were more active users of derivatives).

Collectively, the results of BBL and Schrand suggest that the stock market is sensitive to interest rate risk, over and above its sensitivity to beta. Furthermore, both the firm's on-balance-sheet natural hedging as well as its off-balance-sheet derivatives hedging (Schrand's study predates SFAS 133) affect the magnitude of the market response.

We would expect that if other sources of risk than beta were to be useful for investors, it would be for interest rate risk of financial institutions. However, firms in other industries also face price risks, raising the question of whether the market is also sensitive to these. Wong (1998) examined the foreign exchange risk of a sample of 145 manufacturing firms during 1994–1996. He found that, for some firms in his sample, share price was sensitive to foreign currency exposure. However, unlike Schrand, neither the fair value nor the notional amount (i.e., face value) of firms' foreign exchange derivatives positions explained the magnitude of the sensitivity. One possible explanation is that investors sufficiently diversify their holdings that they are not sensitive to firms' foreign exchange risks. However, Wong attributed the lack of results to shortcomings of hedging disclosures in annual reports (much of Schrand's data was taken from regulatory filings, which would not be available for industrial firms). He recommended more disaggregated disclosures in annual reports of notional amounts, fair values, long and short positions, and maturities by class of instrument.

7.5.3 A Measurement Perspective on Risk Reporting

The disclosures discussed in the previous section are primarily oriented to the information perspective—they involve the communication of information to enable investors to make their own risk evaluations. However, like valuations of assets and liabilities, reporting on risk is also moving towards a measurement perspective.

In this regard, consider the risk disclosure requirements laid down by the SEC (1997), as described by Linsmeier and Pearson (1997). These include quantitative price risk disclosures, which can take the following forms: (1) a **tabular presentation** of fair values and contract terms sufficient to enable investors to determine a firm's future cash flows from financial instruments by maturity date; (2) a **sensitivity analysis** showing the impact on earnings, cash flows, or fair values of financial instruments, resulting from changes in relevant commodity prices, interest rates, and foreign exchange rates; or, (3) **value at risk**, being the loss in earnings, cash flows, or fair values resulting from future price changes sufficiently large that they have a specified low probability of occurring.

Much of this risk information is reported as part of MD&A—see our discussion of Canadian Tire's risk disclosures in Section 4.8.2. While the tabular presentation is oriented to an information perspective, the latter two alternatives are of interest because they are measurement-oriented. The firm, rather than investors, prepares the quantitative risk assessments. We would expect that it is the firm that has the most accurate estimates of its own risks. Hence, these latter two risk measures have the greater potential for decision usefulness.

Table 7.2 shows a sensitivity disclosure from the 2003 *Annual Report* of Suncor Energy, Inc. The table shows the impact on cash flows and earnings of relevant commodity price, interest rate, and foreign exchange rate risks.

TABLE 7.2 SENSITIVITY ANALYSIS[1] FROM SUNCOR ENERGY'S 2003 ANNUAL REPORT

	2003 Average	Change	Approximate Change in Pretax Cash Flow from Operations	After-tax Earnings
Oil Sands				
Price of crude oil ($/barrel)[2]	$37.19	US$1.00	64	42
Sweet/sour differential ($/barrel)	$7.92	US$1.00	27	17
Sales (bpd)	218 300	1 000	12	8
Natural Gas				
Price of natural gas ($/mcf)[2]	$6.42	0.10	5	3
Production of natural gas (mmcf/d)	187	10	15	8
Energy Marketing and Refining— Canada				
Retail gasoline margins cents per litre (cpl)	6.6	0.1	2	1
Refining/wholesale margin (cpl)[2]	6.5	0.1	5	3
Refining and Marketing—U.S.A.				
Retail gasoline margins (cpl)	5.6	0.1	—	—
Refining/wholesale margin (cpl)	5.9	0.1	2	1
Consolidated				
Exchange rate: Cdn$/US$	0.72	0.01	44	35

1 The sensitivity analysis shows the main factors affecting Suncor's annual pretax cash flow from operations and after-tax earnings based on actual 2003 operations. The table illustrates the potential financial impact of these factors applied to Suncor's 2003 results. A change in any one factor could compound or offset other factors.

2 Includes the impact of hedging activities.

Reprinted by permission of Suncor Energy Inc.

Note that oil, gas, and Canadian gasoline price sensitivities are given net of hedging activities, while U.S. gasoline and exchange rate sensitivities are not. Presumably, the after-hedging sensitivities are of greater relevance, which raises the question of why the latter two risks are reported before hedging. One possibility is that these latter risks are not hedged. For example, Suncor reports in its financial statement notes that no foreign exchange risk on its U.S. dollar-denominated petroleum and natural gas revenues is hedged. Presumably, Suncor relies on natural hedging to protect itself here—it reports in its MD&A that the negative earnings impact of a strengthening Canadian dollar is partially offset by foreign exchange gains on its U.S. dollar-denominated debt and preferred shares.

Sensitivity estimates are subject to relevant range problems. Thus, if the price of oil were to change by, say, $3/bbl, it is unlikely that the impact on earnings would be three times the impact of the $1/bbl change given in the table. Another problem is with co-movements in prices, as Suncor points out in note 1 to the table. It is unlikely, for example, that changes in the prices of crude oil and natural gas are independent. Yet, each change estimate in Table 7.2 holds the other prices constant. Finally, nothing is said about the probabilities of price changes. These would have to be assessed by the investor.

The value at risk approach addresses some of these problems. Consider, for example, a firm's portfolio of financial instruments at year-end. To calculate value at risk, the firm first needs to assess a joint probability distribution of the various price risks that affect the fair value of the portfolio over some holding period, say 90 days. This, in turn, is converted into a distribution of the changes in the fair value of the portfolio. The value at risk is then the loss in fair value that has only a 5% (or some other low probability) chance of occurring over the 90-day holding period. In effect, a loss greater than the value at risk is a rare event. The approach can also be extended to cash flow and earnings value at risk.

Microsoft Corporation is a well-known user of value at risk. It faces foreign currency, interest rate, and securities price risks, which it hedges by means of options and other derivatives. Microsoft does not fully hedge these risks; this is likely to be too costly. However, it uses value at risk to estimate its unhedged exposure, and reports the results in its annual report. Presumably, Microsoft adjusts the extent of its hedging activities so as to attain the level of price risk it is willing to bear.

Microsoft's 2003 *Annual Report* discloses that there is a $97^{1}/_{2}$% probability that the loss on its assets subject to interest rate, currency, and equity price risks would not exceed $987 million over a 20-day holding period (thus, only a $2^{1}/_{2}$% probability of a loss greater than this amount).

As Microsoft points out, a prolonged market decline extending for more than 20 days could result in a larger loss. Nevertheless, given Microsoft's 2003 reported net income of $9,993 million, the investor knows that a loss due to price risks of more than 10% of earnings is unlikely.

While primarily geared to downside risk, there appears to be no reason why value at risk could not be applied to upside risk as well. Thus we might reasonably expect that Microsoft is unlikely to gain more than $987 million over 20 days if price risks move in its favour.

A challenging aspect of value at risk, however, is the need to assess the joint price distribution, including correlations between the price risks. Keeping track of past price changes is one way to do this. Nevertheless, if there are, say, 10 price risks faced by a portfolio, then 10 expected values, 10 variances and 45 correlations need to be estimated. Microsoft explains that it bases its calculations on the past behaviour of relevant market prices, but cautions that the distribution of past prices may change, reducing the reliability of the value at risk calculations.

7.5.4 Summary

We conclude that information about firm risk, in addition to beta, is valued by the stock market, particularly for financial institutions. This is documented by the sensitivity of share returns of these institutions to risk exposures and to the impact of hedging on these exposures. Financial reporting has responded by increased reporting of fair values for financial instruments, supplemented by discussion of risks and how they are managed, and by disclosure of financial instrument contract information. This enables investors to better evaluate the amounts, timing, and uncertainty of returns on their investments. It can be suggested that increased disaggregation of financial instrument information would further assist investors in this regard.

Financial reporting is also moving towards providing investors with quantitative risk information, such as sensitivity analyses and value at risk. Despite methodological challenges, these represent important steps in moving risk disclosures towards a measurement perspective.

7.6 Conclusions on Measurement Perspective Applications

There are numerous instances of the use of fair values in financial reporting, and the list is growing. Many uses involve only partial application of a measurement perspective, as in lower-of-cost-or-market, long-term debt, ceiling tests, and push-down accounting. Thus, under lower-of-cost-or-market and ceiling tests, written-down assets are not written up again if value increases. Also, under current GAAP, the present value of long-term debt is not adjusted for changes in interest rates, and once subsidiary asset values are pushed down they are not revalued subsequently. Nevertheless, partial applications of fair value have the potential to be decision useful to the extent they reveal a material change in the firm's financial position and prospects.

However, several standards extend the measurement perspective so as to periodically measure both value increases and decreases. Thus, under Section 3025 of the *CICA Handbook*, impaired loans may be written up if impairment is reduced. Furthermore, pensions and OPEBs are reported at present value each period in Canada and the United States. Under SFAS 115, in the United States, trading and available-for-sale securities are fair-valued each period. While the information is supplemental, Section 3860, as well as SFAS 107 in the United States, require periodic disclosure of fair value and risk information for a variety of financial instruments. Even the accounting for business combinations and purchased goodwill is becoming measurement-oriented, as witnessed by standards which apply a ceiling test to purchased goodwill. Also, SEC regulations require disclosure of quantitative risk measures.

Certainly, it appears that decision usefulness is moving more and more into the arena of measurement. Reasons for this were suggested in Chapter 6. They include the low value relevance of historical cost-based net income, reactions to theory and evidence that securities markets may not be as fully efficient as originally believed, increasing acceptance of a theory that expresses firm value in terms of accounting variables, and auditor legal liability resulting from abuses of the historical cost system. The combined effect of these factors seems to have convinced accounting standard setters that striving for greater relevance is worthwhile, even at the cost of some sacrifice of reliability.

Whether the recent measurement-oriented standards described in this chapter will increase the market share of financial accounting information in explaining share returns, and will reduce auditor liability, remains to be seen. Furthermore, only time will tell whether the downturn in economic activity triggered in 2000 by the collapse of share prices of many technology firms will slow down or accelerate the measurement perspective. On the one hand, this collapse may remind accountants of the lesson from the Great Depression of the 1930s, that values are fleeting, thereby reinforcing the historical cost basis. On the other hand, the measurement perspective may be reinforced, as accountants strive to ensure that new, lower values for assets such as purchased goodwill are promptly and fully reported.

Questions and Problems

1. Under generally accepted accounting principles, certain current assets such as cash, accounts receivable, and marketable securities (when fair value is below cost) are carried at present value and/or market value. Does this violate the historical cost basis of accounting? Explain.

   Note: A good answer will consider the point in the operating cycle at which revenue is realized.

2. Explain why the reporting of deferred assets and liabilities on the balance sheet is inconsistent with the measurement perspective.

3. Explain why a firm may not necessarily reduce its price risks to zero by means of hedging transactions. (CGA-Canada)

4. On August 31, 1999, an article in *The Globe and Mail*, "2000: New year, new accounting, new costs," anticipated the introduction of Section 3461 of the *CICA Handbook*, requiring accrual accounting for OPEBs. The article noted that firms have the option of recording the accumulated OPEB liability as a direct charge to retained earnings, or to defer the amount of the liability over the next several years and amortize it. The article quotes Mr. Ken Vallillee, a partner of a large accounting firm, as saying "Most companies will opt for the one-time charge if they can." The article also points out that Section 3461 replaces the previous method of accounting for OPEBs, charging cash payments for OPEBs to expense as they are made.

   Required
   a. Explain the extent to which the new standard will increase the decision usefulness of financial statements for investors. Consider both issues of relevance and reliability in your answer.
   b. Do you agree with Mr. Vallillee that most firms will opt for the one-time charge? Explain why or why not.
   c. What effects will the reporting of the OPEB liability have on the market value of affected firms' shares? Will the effect depend on how the firm chooses to record the liability? In your answer, consider situations where share price might fall, remain unchanged, or rise. Assume in your answer that securities markets are efficient.

5. Refer to the El Paso Corporation vignette (Theory in Practice 7.1) in Section 7.3.4.

Required

a. Why are unrealized gains and losses on derivative instruments designated as cash flow hedges included in other comprehensive income under SFAS 133?

b. Explain why effective cash flow hedging of future production can reduce or avoid ceiling test writedowns.

c. Use the "highly effective" criterion for a hedge to evaluate whether El Paso's decision that its cash flow hedges of its oil and gas production were not valid was a correct one.

d. Suppose that El Paso did not revise its cash flow hedge accounting. That is, suppose that it continued to designate these hedges as effective cash flow hedges. Suppose also that media reports began to question whether El Paso's natural gas reserves were correctly stated. Outline some possible consequences for El Paso of this questioning.

e. Do you feel that the management of El Paso, and its auditor, behaved ethically during this episode? Explain why or why not.

6. Share prices of many "high-tech" firms are quite volatile relative to the stock market index. In an article in *The Wall Street Journal* (reprinted in *The Globe and Mail*, May 16, 2001), Greg Ip discusses a reason why. He points out that high-tech firms have high fixed costs, consisting mainly of R&D driven by rapid technological progress. They also have low variable costs, since the direct production costs of their products tend to be very low. In effect, high-tech firms have high operating leverage.

For example, Yahoo Inc. incurred a drop in revenue of 42% in the first quarter of 2001, but its costs barely dropped. It reported an operating loss of $33 million for the quarter, compared to a profit of $87 million in the last quarter of 2000.

Required

a. Use high operating leverage to explain high stock price variability.

b. Use the argument that beta is non-stationary (Section 6.2.3) to explain high stock price volatility.

c. Use the behavioural finance concepts of momentum and bubbles to explain high stock price volatility.

d. Are these three sources of volatility mutually exclusive? Explain.

7. Under SFAS 115, most loan assets held by U.S. banks are held in the held-to-maturity category, where they are valued at amortized cost. Of course, if the fair value of a loan should fall below this amount, the impaired loans standard requires a writedown. The same is true in Canada, where Section 3025 of the *CICA Handbook* requires writedown of impaired loans. Following the 2000 economic downturn, investors watched loan writedowns with particular care. Major writedowns will likely result in a decline in the bank's share price, as investors interpret the writedown as a sign of loan quality problems to come. For example, in Canada, *The Globe and Mail*, March 7, 2001, reports "Scotiabank profit overshadowed by impaired loans." The bank reported a substantial increase in first quarter, 2001 net income. However, it also reported a 44% increase in impaired loans. Its share price on the Toronto Stock Exchange fell by $3.46, closing at $42.44.

Faced with reactions such as these, banks may wish to disguise the extent of major loan writedowns. An article in *The Economist*, March 22, 2001, "Shell game," describes how some U.S. banks have responded.

The trick, according to *The Economist*, is to transfer problem loans to the available-for-sale category from held-to-maturity. Under SFAS 115, available-for-sale securities are valued at their fair value. Thus, the transferred loans must be written down. However, the writedown will be buried in larger totals and the market would not know how much of the total adjustment to fair value belongs to the loans transferred. Furthermore, unrealized gains and losses from fair valuing available-for-sale securities are included in other comprehensive income under SFAS 115, so that writedowns do not affect net income. Another consequence is that the book value of held-to-maturity loans on the balance sheet is reduced, so that any existing loan loss allowance will appear more adequate.

Whether banks actually sell the transferred problem loans is an open question. *The Economist* points out that the dollar amount of secondary trading has risen dramatically in recent years. However, the length of time that banks can hold loans in the available-for-sale category without selling them is a "grey area." Presumably, the banks' auditors will be aware of these practices and will take steps to discourage them. However, *The Economist* quotes an official of the Office of the Comptroller of the Currency (a U.S. banking regulator) as saying auditors "too often side with their clients" in grey areas.

Required
a. What is the likely effect on banks' share prices and on the operation of capital markets of the above practice? Explain.
b. Why does SFAS 115 allow held-to-maturity loans to be valued at cost, or amortized cost, instead of at fair value like trading and available-for-sale securities? Explain. To what extent would amending SFAS 115 to require fair value accounting for all financial instruments eliminate the practice? Explain.
c. If you were the auditor of a bank engaging in the above practice, would you qualify your audit report if the bank refused your request to stop? Discuss why or why not. In your answer, consider both principles of ethical behaviour and your own reputation and economic well-being.

8. On March 11, 2000, *The Globe and Mail* reported "Ballard losses double." The reference was to Ballard Power Systems Inc., a Canadian developer of fuel cell technology. On March 10, 2000, Ballard reported an operating loss of $26 million for the fourth quarter of 1999, bringing its loss for the year to $75.2 million on revenues of $33.2 million. Its loss for 1998 was $36.2 million on revenues of $25.1 million. The reason for the increased loss in 1999, according to Ballard, was a huge increase in R&D spending for its fuel cell technology.

On March 10, 2000, Ballard's share price closed at $189 on the Toronto Stock Exchange, up $14 on the day for an increase of 8%.

Required
a. Does the increase in Ballard's share price on March 10, 2000, on the same day that it reported an increased loss, imply a high or low R^2 and ERC for the rela-

tionship between the return on Ballard's shares and abnormal earnings? Explain, using the arguments of Lev and Zarowin (1999). Assume that the increase in the TSE 300 index on March 10, 2000, was less than 8%.

b. How do Lev and Zarowin propose to improve the accounting for R&D? Explain how this proposal could affect R^2 and the ERC.

c. Does Ballard's share price behaviour on March 10, 2000, suggest securities market efficiency or inefficiency? Explain.

9. As mentioned in Section 7.4.2, JDS Uniphase Corporation reported a preliminary loss of $50.558 billion for the year ended June 30, 2001. In a July 26, 2001, news release accompanying its financial statements, JDS also presented a "pro-forma" income statement that showed a profit for the year of $67.4 million. The difference is summarized as follows ($ million):

Net loss, as reported	$50,558.0
Add:	
Write off of purchased goodwill	$44,774.3
Write off of tangible and intangible assets from acquisitions	5,939.2
Losses on equity investments	1,453.3
Gain on sale of subsidiary	(1,768.1)
Non-cash stock option compensation	385.6
Income tax	(158.9)
	50,625.4
Pro-forma net income	$ 67.4

Required

a. The purchased goodwill arose primarily from business acquisitions paid for in shares of JDS Uniphase. In *The Globe and Mail*, July 27, 2001, Fabrice Taylor stated that in JDS' case, "most of the goodwill on the books comes from over-valued stock." In a separate article, Showwei Chu quotes a senior technology analyst as "They paid what the companies were worth at the time." While currently trading in the $4 range, JDS' shares were trading between $100 and $200 when most of the acquisitions were made.

i) Assume securities markets are fully efficient. Does the $44,774.3 writeoff of purchased goodwill represent a real loss to JDS Uniphase and its shareholders, given that no cash is involved? If so, state precisely the nature of the loss and who ultimately bears it.

ii) Would your answer change if securities markets are subject to momentum and bubble behaviour? Explain.

b. What additional information is added to the publicly available information about JDS Uniphase as a result of the supplementary pro-forma income disclosure?

c. Why did JDS Uniphase management present the pro-forma income disclosure?

    d.   To the extent that investors accept pro-forma income as a measure of management performance, how might this affect management's propensity to overpay for future acquisitions? Explain.

10. Refer to the sensitivity analysis of Suncor Energy Inc. reproduced in Table 7.2. The analysis discloses the potential effects of changes in oil sands, natural gas, and other products, and of changes in the Can./U.S. dollar exchange rate, on 2003 cash flows and earnings.

Required
    a.   Evaluate the relevance and reliability of this method of disclosing risk information.

    b.   The analysis indicates that the sensitivity of its natural gas production is net of hedging activities. As an investor, would you find sensitivity information net of hedging, or before hedging, more useful? Explain.

    c.   Suncor's price risks arise from changes in the market prices of crude oil, natural gas, and refined products, with associated foreign exchange risk because market prices are largely based on the U.S. dollar. Suncor reports elsewhere in its MD&A (not reproduced) that its board of directors has approved hedging of up to 35% of its 2004 crude oil production against price risks. Why would Suncor's board impose this limitation on management's ability to manage risk? Give reasons based on internal control, cost, and investor diversification considerations.

11. EnCana Corp. a large Canadian oil and gas company, reported net income of $393 million U.S. (EnCana reports in U.S. dollars) for its third quarter, 2004. This compares with net income of $290 million for the same quarter of 2003. However, third quarter, 2004 earnings would have been even higher but for a $321 million after tax unrealized loss on hedges of future oil and gas sales charged against operations. EnCana accounts for such financial instruments at fair value, with unrealized gains and losses included in net income. The loss was due to the dramatic increase in oil prices during 2004, and illustrates that while hedging may protect the firm from losses if product prices decline, it also shuts them out of gains if prices increase.

Required
    a.   Explain why EnCana reported a loss on its hedging activities.

    b.   Canada does not yet have in place accounting standards similar to SFAS 130 and SFAS 133. Assuming that its hedges qualified for hedge accounting under SFAS 133, how would EnCana's unrealized hedging loss have been accounted for under these standards?

    c.   Give reasons why firms such as EnCana typically hedge at least part of their price risk of future anticipated sales.

Notes

1. A defined benefit pension plan specifies the benefits to be received by an employee, such as 75% of salary at time of retirement. This type of plan is distinguished from

a defined contribution plan, where the contribution to be made by the employer is specified. In a defined contribution plan, the pension benefits received by the employee depend on the amounts contributed and the earnings of the plan assets. For a defined benefit plan, the employer bears the risk of fluctuations in the value of plan assets. For a defined contribution plan, this risk is borne by the employee.

2. In Section 7.3.1, we mentioned that fair value-based accounting standards similar to those of the FASB are awaiting implementation in Canada. An important difference between these standards and SFAS 115, however, is that financial *liabilities* held for trading are included in this category under the Canadian standard. Then, changes in the fair value of these liabilities are included in net income. This greater breadth of application is noteworthy because it helps to reduce the problem of excess earnings volatility that arises if financial assets are fair valued but financial liabilities are not.

3. Examples of speculation using derivatives that resulted in bankruptcy or near bankruptcy include Orange County, California; Barings Bank; and Long-term Capital Management. For accounts of these disasters, see Boyle & Boyle (2001), Chapter 8.

4. If the risk-free interest rate is greater than zero, the option fair value is more complex. Also, options are usually fair-valued by an equivalent approach, called a **replicating portfolio**. This is a portfolio consisting of an investment in the underlying share plus a short position in a risk-free asset, where the amounts of each security are determined each period so that the replicating portfolio yields the same return as the option for each possible end-of-period value of the option. Since the underlying share and the risk-free asset have readily available market values, and since the return on the option is the same as that of the replicating portfolio, arbitrage forces the fair value of the option to equal the value of the replicating portfolio. For details, see Boyle & Boyle (2001), Chapter 4.

5. Boyle & Boyle (2001), Chapter 5, page 89, call this formula the Black/Scholes/Merton formula, due to important contributions by Robert Merton (1973).

6. It should be apparent that risk goes both ways. That is, assets (and liabilities) may decrease or increase in value. Thus, if an asset is fully hedged against price risk, the firm will not suffer from a decline in asset value but will not enjoy an increase in value either (see problem 11). This is a statistical notion of risk. Nevertheless, we will sometimes use the term risk in the sense of downside risk only. Credit risk, for example, is the risk of loss from the failure of the other party to a contract to fulfil its obligations.

7. The abnormal earnings installments could also be negative. This simply means that the firm is expected to earn less than its cost of capital, that is, it has "badwill."

8. These fair values may or may not be pushed down to the books of the acquired company. See Section 7.2.4.

9. Of course, this is not really "cash" income since it includes other accruals, such as sales on credit. It is not known where the term originated.

10. The company's preliminary net loss for the year was increased by further goodwill writedowns of $5.3 billion reported in its audited financial statements for the year.

11. Management may not be willing to reveal this estimate, on grounds that it may reveal important information to competitors.

12. This requires that purchased goodwill be excluded from opening book value for purposes of the clean surplus goodwill calculations.

13. Canadian Tire reports purchased goodwill and other intangibles of $90.6 million in its 2003 *Annual Report*.

Chapter 8

Economic Consequences and Positive Accounting Theory

FIGURE 8.1 ORGANIZATION OF CHAPTER 8

8.1 Overview

You may have noticed that there has been little discussion of management's interests in financial reporting to this point other than several references to management skepticism about fair value accounting. As mentioned earlier, a thesis of this book is that motivation of responsible manager performance is an equally important role of financial accounting as the provision of useful information to investors. If so, it is necessary that accountants understand and appreciate management's interests in financial reporting.

This will involve us in a new line of thought that, at first glance, differs sharply from the investor decision-based and efficient market-oriented theories discussed earlier. Our first task is to understand the concept of **economic consequences**. In the process, we will also learn about some of the accounting problems in two major areas of accounting policy choice—stock-based compensation and costs of oil and gas exploration.

Economic consequences is a concept that asserts that, despite the implications of efficient securities market theory, accounting policy choice can affect firm value.

Essentially, the notion of economic consequences is that firms' accounting policies, and changes in policies, *matter*. Primarily, they matter to management. But, if they matter to management, accounting policies matter to the investors who own the firms, because managers may well change the actual operation of their firms due to changes in accounting policies. An example would be changes in accounting policies relating to oil and gas company reserves. Changes in such accounting policies, according to economic consequences arguments, may alter managers' exploration and development activities, which in turn may affect firm value. If these changes are potentially negative and if many investors are affected, investors may bring pressure to bear on their elected representatives. Indeed, managers will lobby these same representatives if they feel that a proposed accounting standard negatively affects their interests. Consequently, politicians will also be interested in firms' accounting policies and in the standard-setting bodies that determine them.

It is important to point out that the term "accounting policy" refers to *any* accounting policy, not just one that affects a firm's cash flows. Suppose that a firm changes from declining-balance to straight-line amortization. This will not in itself affect the firm's cash flows. Nor will there be any effect on income taxes paid, since tax authorities have their own capital cost allowance regulations. However, the new amortization policy will certainly affect reported net income. Thus, according to economic consequences doctrine, the accounting policy change will matter, despite the lack of cash flow effects. Under efficient markets theory the change will not matter (although the market may ask *why* the firm changed the policy) because future cash flows, and hence the market value of the firm, are not directly affected.

An understanding of the concept of economic consequences of accounting policy choice is important for two reasons. First, the concept is interesting in its own right. Many of the most interesting events in accounting practice derive from economic consequences. Second, a suggestion that accounting policies do not matter is at odds with accountants' experience. Much of financial accounting is devoted to discussion and argument about which accounting policies should be used in various circumstances, and many debates and conflicts over financial statement presentation involve accounting policy choice. Economic consequences are consistent with real-world experience.

The presence of economic consequences raises the question of why they exist. To begin to answer this question, we introduce **positive accounting theory**. This theory is based on the contracts that firms enter into, in particular executive compensation contracts and debt contracts. These contracts are frequently based on financial accounting variables, such as net income and the ratio of debt to equity. Since accounting policies affect the values of these variables, and since management is responsible for the firm's contracts, it is natural that management be concerned about accounting policy choice. Indeed, management may choose accounting policies so as to maximize the firm's interests, or its own interests, relative to these contracts. Positive accounting theory attempts to predict what accounting policies managers will choose in order to do this. Figure 8.1 outlines the organization of this chapter.

8.2   The Rise of Economic Consequences

One of the most persuasive accounts of the existence of economic consequences appears in an early article by Stephen Zeff (1978) entitled "The Rise of 'Economic Consequences.'" The basic questions that it raises are still relevant today.

Zeff defines economic consequences as "the impact of accounting reports on the decision-making behaviour of business, government and creditors." The essence of the definition is that accounting reports can *affect* the real decisions made by managers and others, rather than simply *reflecting* the results of these decisions.

Zeff documents several instances in the United States where business, industry associations, and governments attempted to influence, or did influence, accounting standards set by the Accounting Principles Board (predecessor to the FASB) and its predecessor, the Committee on Accounting Procedure (CAP).

This "third-party intervention," as Zeff calls it, greatly complicated the setting of accounting standards. If accounting policies did not matter, choice of such policies would be strictly between the standard-setting bodies and the accountants and auditors whose task was to implement the standards. If only these parties were involved, the traditional accounting model, based on well-known concepts such as matching of costs and revenues, realization, and conservatism, could be applied and no one other than the parties involved would care what specific policies were used. In other words, accounting policy choice would be *neutral* in its effects.

As an example of an economic consequences argument, Zeff discusses the attempts by several U.S. corporations to implement replacement cost accounting during 1947 to 1948, a period of high inflation. Here, the third-party constituency that intervened was management, who, unlike their more recent scepticism about fair value accounting, argued in favour of replacement cost amortization to bolster arguments for lower taxes and lower wage increases, and to counter a public perception of excess profitability. The efficient market argument would be that such intervention was unnecessary because the market would see through the high reported net incomes produced by historical cost amortization during inflation. If so, it should not be necessary to remind users by formal adoption of replacement cost amortization. It is interesting to note that the CAP held its ground in 1948 and reaffirmed historical cost accounting.

Zeff goes on to outline the response of standard-setting bodies to these various interventions. One response was to broaden the representation on the standard-setting bodies themselves; for example, the Financial Accounting Foundation (the body that oversees the FASB) includes not only professional accountants but also members from management, the securities industry, and academe. Also, the use of exposure drafts of proposed new standards became common as a device to allow a variety of constituencies to comment on proposed accounting policy changes.

As Zeff puts it, standard-setting bodies face a dilemma. To retain credibility with accountants, they need to set accounting policies in accordance with the financial accounting model and its traditional concepts of matching and realization (recall that Zeff is describing practices prior to the increased emphasis on the measurement perspective). Yet, as we have seen in Section 2.5, such historical cost-based concepts seldom lead to a unique accounting policy choice. That is, since net income does not exist as a well-defined economic construct under non-ideal conditions, there is no theory that clearly prescribes what accounting policies should be used, other than a vague requirement that some trade-off between relevance and reliability is necessary. This opens the door for various other constituencies to get into the act and argue for their preferred accounting policies. In short, standard-setting bodies must operate not only in the accounting theory domain, but also in the political domain. Zeff refers to this as a "delicate balancing act." That is, without a theory to guide accounting policy choice, we must find some way of reaching a consensus on accounting policies. In a democratic setting, this implies involvement in the political domain. While a need for delicate balancing complicates the task of standard setters, it makes the study of the standard-setting process, and of accounting theory in general, much more challenging and interesting.

8.2.1 Summary

Despite the implications of efficient market theory, it appears that accounting policy choices have economic consequences for the various constituencies of financial statement users, even if these policies do not directly affect firm cash flows. Furthermore, different constituencies may prefer different accounting policies. Specifically, management's preferred policies may be at odds with those that best inform investors.

Economic consequences complicate the setting of accounting standards, which require a delicate balancing of accounting and political considerations. Standard setting bodies have responded by bringing different constituencies onto their boards and by issuing exposure drafts to give all interested parties an opportunity to comment on proposed standards.

8.3 Employee Stock Options

We now examine two areas where economic consequences have been particularly apparent. The first of these is accounting for stock options issued to management and, in some cases, to other employees, giving them the right to buy company stock over some time period. We will refer to these options as **ESO**s.

Accounting for ESOs in the United States has traditionally been based on the 1972 Opinion 25 of the Accounting Principles Board (APB 25). This standard requires firms issuing fixed[1] ESOs to record an expense equal to the difference between the market value of the shares on the date the option was granted to the employee (the **grant date**) and the exercise, or strike, price of the option. This difference is called the **intrinsic value** of the option. Most firms granting ESOs set the exercise price equal to the grant date market value, so that the intrinsic value is zero. As a result, no expense for ESO compensation need be recorded. For example, if the underlying share has a market value of $10 on the grant date, setting the exercise price at $10 triggers no expense recognition, whereas setting the exercise price at $8 triggers an expense of $2 per ESO granted.

In the years following issuance of APB 25, this basis of accounting became widely recognized as inadequate. Even if there is no intrinsic value, an option has a **fair value** on the grant date, since the price of the underlying share may rise over the term to expiry (the **expiry date**) of the option. Thus failure to record an expense understates the firm's compensation cost and overstates its net income. Furthermore, a lack of earnings comparability across firms results, since different firms have different proportions of options in their total compensation packages. These problems worsened as a result of a dramatic increase in the use of ESO compensation since 1972, particularly for small, start-up, high-tech firms. These firms particularly like the non-cash-requiring aspect of ESOs and their motivational impact on the workforce, as well as the higher reported profits that result compared to other forms of compensation.

Also during this period, executive compensation came under political scrutiny, due to the high amounts of compensation that top executives received. Firms were perhaps motivated to award seemingly excessive amounts of ESO compensation since such compensation was "free." Charging the fair value of ESOs to expense would, some felt, help investors to see the real cost to the firm of this component of compensation. Indeed, in February 1992, a bill was introduced into the U.S. Congress requiring ESOs to be valued and expensed.

One of the reasons why the APB had not required fair value accounting for ESOs was the difficulty of establishing this value. This situation changed somewhat with the advent of the Black/Scholes option pricing formula (see Section 7.3.3). However, several aspects of ESOs are not captured by Black/Scholes. For example, the model assumes that options can be freely traded, whereas ESOs cannot be exercised until the **vesting date**, which is typically one or more years after they are granted. Also, if the employee leaves the firm prior to vesting the options are forfeited or, if exercised, there may be restrictions on the employee's ability to sell the acquired shares. In addition, the Black/Scholes formula assumes that the option cannot be exercised prior to expiry (a European option), whereas ESOs are American (can be exercised prior to expiry). Nevertheless, it was felt by many that Black/Scholes provided a reasonable basis for estimation of ESO fair value.

Consequently, in June 1993, the FASB issued an exposure draft of a proposed new standard. The exposure draft proposed that firms record compensation expense based on the fair value at the grant date of ESOs issued during the period. Fair value could be determined by Black/Scholes or other option pricing formula, with adjustment for the possibility of employee retirement prior to vesting and for the possibility of early exercise. Early exercise was dealt with by using the *expected* time to exercise, based, for example, on past experience, rather than the time to expiry, in the Black/Scholes formula.

The exposure draft attracted extreme opposition from business, which soon extended into the Congress. Concerns were expressed about the economic consequences of the lower reported profits that would result. These claimed consequences included lower share prices, higher cost of capital, a shortage of managerial talent, and inadequate manager and employee motivation. This would particularly disadvantage small start-up companies that, as mentioned, were heavy options users. To preserve their bottom lines, firms would be forced to reduce ESO usage, with negative effects on cash flows, motivation, and innovation. This, it was claimed, would threaten the competitive position of American industry. Business was also concerned that the draft proposal was politically motivated. If so, opponents of the proposal would feel justified in attacking it with every means at their disposal.

Another series of questions related to the ability of Black/Scholes to reliably measure ESO fair value. To see these concerns, we first need to consider just what the costs to the firm of ESOs are, since, unlike most costs, ESOs do not require a cash outlay. Essentially, the cost is borne by the firm's existing shareholders through dilution of their proportionate interests in the firm. Thus, if an ESO is exercised at a price of, say, $10 when the market value of the share is $30, the *ex post* cost to the firm and its shareholders is $20. By admitting the new shareholder at $10, the firm foregoes the opportunity to issue the share at the market price of $30. That is, the $20 opportunity cost measures the dilution of the existing shareholders' interests. The fair value of the ESO at the grant date, hence the cost to the firm, is then the expected present value of this opportunity cost.[2] Reporting this cost increases relevance, since future dividends will be reduced to the extent they are diluted over a larger number of shares. The reduction in earnings from expensing ESOs anticipates these lower dividends, thereby helping investors to better predict future cash flows from their investments.

However, this ESO cost is very difficult to measure reliably. As mentioned, the employee may exercise the option at any time after vesting up to expiry. The *ex post* cost to the firm will then depend on the difference between the market value of the share and the exercise price at that time. In order to know the fair value of the ESO it is necessary to know the employee's optimal exercise strategy.

This strategy was modelled by Huddart (1994). As Huddart pointed out, determining the employee's strategy requires knowledge of the process generating the firm's future stock price, the employee's wealth and utility function (in particular the degree of risk aversion), whether the employee holds or sells the acquired shares (many firms require senior officers to hold large amounts of company stock) and, if sold, what investment alternatives are available. Matters are further complicated if the firm pays dividends on its shares and if the motivational impact of the ESO affects share price.

By making some simplifying assumptions (including no dividends, no motivational impact), Huddart showed that the Black/Scholes formula with ESOs held to expiry date can substantially overstate the fair value of an ESO at the grant date. To see why, we first note three option characteristics:

1. The expected return from holding an option exceeds the expected return on the underlying share. This is because the option cannot be worth less than zero, but the share price can fall below the option's exercise price. As a result, a risk-neutral employee would not normally exercise an ESO before maturity.

2. The "upside potential" of an American option (its propensity to increase in value) increases with the time to maturity. The longer the time, the greater the likelihood that during this interval the underlying share price will take off, making the option more valuable. Early exercise sacrifices some of this upside potential.

3. If an option is "deep-in-the-money," that is, if the value of the underlying share greatly exceeds the exercise price, the set of possible payoffs from holding the option and their probabilities closely resembles the set of payoffs and probabilities from holding the underlying share. This is because for a deep-in-the-money option the probability of share price falling below exercise price is low. Then, every realization of share price induces a similar realization in the option value. As a result, if the employee is required to hold the shares acquired, he or she might as well hold the option to maturity. The payoffs are the same and, due to the time value of money, paying the exercise price at expiry dominates paying it sooner.

The question then is, are there circumstances where the employee will exercise the option early? Huddart identifies two. First, if the ESO is only slightly in-the-money (substantial risk of zero payoff), the time to maturity is short (little sacrifice of upside potential), and the employee is required to hold the shares acquired, risk aversion can trigger early exercise. Since there is substantial risk of zero return, the risk-averse employee (who trades off risk and return) may feel that the reduction in risk from exercising the option now rather than continuing to hold it outweighs the lower expected return from holding the share.

The second circumstance occurs when the ESO is deep-in-the-money, the time to expiry is short, and the employee can either hold the acquired share or sell it and invest the proceeds in a riskless asset. If the employee is sufficiently risk averse, the riskless asset is preferred to the share. Because the option is deep-in-the-money, the payoffs and their probabilities are similar for the share and ESO. Thus the employee is indifferent to holding the ESO or the share. Since holding the riskless asset is preferred to holding the share, it is also preferred to holding the option. Then, the employee will exercise the option, sell the share, and buy the riskless asset.

In a follow-up empirical study to test the early exercise predictions, Huddart and Lang (1996) examined the ESO exercise patterns of the employees of eight large U.S. corporations over a ten-year period. They found that early exercise was common, consistent with Huddart's risk aversion assumption. They also found that the variables that explained empirically the early exercises, such as time to expiration and extent to which the ESO was in-the-money, were "broadly consistent" with the predictions of the model.

The significance of early exercise is that the fair value of ESOs at grant date is less than the value determined by Black/Scholes which, as mentioned, assumes the option is held to expiry. This is particularly apparent for the first early exercise scenario outlined above. If the ESO is barely in-the-money, the *ex post* cost of the option to the employer (share price less exercise price) is low. While the cost savings from the second circumstance are less, the cost to the employer is still less than Black/Scholes, as Huddart shows.

Subsequent research has tended to confirm the tendency of Black/Scholes to overstate *ex post* ESO cost. Hall and Murphy (2002), using a different approach than Huddart, also demonstrate a substantial probability of early exercise, and show that this significantly reduces the firm's ESO cost below Black/Scholes. Their analysis also suggests considerable variability in employees' exercise decisions.

Early exercise, presumably, is the reason the FASB exposure draft proposed using expected time to exercise, rather than expiry date, in the Black/Scholes formula.

However, as Huddart points out, use of expected time to exercise reduces the overstatement of ESO cost, but does not eliminate it, as also demonstrated by Hemmer, Matsunaga, and Shevlin (1994) (HMS).[3] In an empirical study, Marquardt (2002) examined the accuracy of the Black/Scholes formula based on expected time to exercise. In a sample of 966 option grants by 57 large U.S. companies over 1963–1984, she found that Black/Scholes tended to produce positively biased estimates of *ex post* ESO cost, consistent with the analyses of Huddart and HMS. She also found that the accuracy of this estimated cost varied widely for different firms.

We conclude that ESO cost estimates tend to be unreliable, due both to upward bias and wide variability of employees' early exercise decisions

As one can imagine, theory and evidence suggesting that the exposure draft, if implemented, may not produce reliable estimates of ESO cost would be seized upon by critics, particularly if the estimates tended to be too high. As a result, in December 1994, the FASB announced that it was dropping the exposure draft, on the grounds that it did not have sufficient support. Instead, the FASB turned to supplementary disclosure. In

SFAS 123, issued in 1995, it urged firms to use the fair value approach suggested in the exposure draft, but allowed the APB 25 intrinsic value approach provided the firm gave supplementary disclosure of ESO expense, determined by amortizing over their vesting periods the fair value of awarded ESOs based on expected time to exercise.

As an example of supplementary disclosure under SFAS 123, consider the following summary from the 2003 *Annual Report* of Microsoft Corporation:

Net income as reported ($ millions)	$9,993
Add back stock-based employee compensation expense included in reported net income, net of tax	52
Deduct employee stock-based compensation expense determined under fair value-based method, net of tax	(2,514)
Net income as per SFAS 123	$7,531
Earnings per share, as reported	$0.93
Earnings per share, SFAS 123	$0.70

SFAS 123 amounts are based on the Black/Scholes formula with an expected time to exercise of 7 years. The decline in net income and earnings per share is about 25%. This material effect on income is even greater than the results of Botosan and Plumlee (2001), who found, in a 1998 sample of 100 fastest-growing U.S. firms, that earnings were reduced on average by about 14% on application of SFAS 123.

Above, we outlined Huddart's result that early ESO exercise can be triggered by risk aversion. This, however, is not the only possible explanation for early exercise. Aboody and Kasznik (2000) (AK) studied the information release practices of CEOs around ESO grant dates. They confined their study to CEOs because it is the CEO that controls the firm's release of information. Their results are based on a sample of 4,426 ESO awards to CEOs of 1,264 different U.S. firms during 1992–1996. Of these awards, 2,039 were by firms with *scheduled* grant dates. That is, awards were made on the same dates each year.[4] Thus, CEOs of these firms knew when the ESO awards were coming.[5]

AK found that, on average, CEOs of firms with scheduled ESOs used a variety of tactics to manipulate share price downwards just prior to the grant date, and to manipulate price up shortly after. One tactic was to make an early announcement of an impending BN quarterly earnings report, but to make no such announcement for an impending GN report. Other tactics included influencing analysts' earnings forecasts and selective timing of release of their own forecasts.

Since the exercise price of an ESO is usually set equal to share price on the grant date to avoid expense recognition under APB 25, a low share price on this date increases the extent to which the ESO will be in the money during the exercise period. This increases the expected value of the award to the CEO. It also increases the likelihood of early exercise since, according to Huddart's analysis, deep-in-the-money ESOs are more likely to be exercised early. Furthermore, if implementation of the FASB exposure draft would cause compensation committees to reduce usage of ESOs, the ability of CEOs to engage in this opportunistic behaviour would be reduced, further increasing the intensity of their objections.

Since the 1993 exposure draft was abandoned, we do not know whether its economic consequences would have been as severe as its critics claimed. The firm's cash flows would not be directly affected by the recording of an expense for stock options. Nevertheless, despite the prediction of efficient securities market theory that accounting policy changes without cash flow effects will not affect share price if the change is fully disclosed, business *did* perceive economic consequences. Otherwise, it would not have opposed the exposure draft to the extent it did.

More recently, financial reporting scandals such as Enron and WorldCom (see Section 1.2) have led to renewed pressure to expense ESOs. In retrospect, it seems that manipulations of stock price by these and other companies were often driven by senior executives' attempts to increase the values of their ESOs. Then, these executives would cash them in (sometimes in a manner to disguise the transaction) and, presumably, invest the proceeds in less risky securities. This behaviour is predicted by Huddart for deep-in-the-money ESOs. Expensing of ESOs, it is argued, will reduce usage of ESO compensation, thereby lowering the temptation of management to engage in this "pump and dump" behaviour.

Theory in Practice 8.1

Bartov and Mohanram (2004) tested a sample of 1,218 U.S. companies with large ESO exercises by senior executives, during 1992–2001. They found a significant decrease in average abnormal share price and earnings in the two years following such exercises, relative to a control sample of similar firms with no large ESO exercises. They also show evidence of abnormally large income-increasing accruals in the two years prior to exercise. The authors concluded that the senior managers in their test sample were aware of deteriorating profitability, and pumped up earnings and share price to delay the market's awareness of the deterioration. They then exercised their ESOs and, presumably, dumped the acquired shares immediately so as to maximize their cash proceeds. The lower earnings and share prices in the two years following exercise were driven by the reversal of the prior accruals and the market's belated awareness of the declining profitability.

In Canada, accounting standards now require expensing of ESOs, effective, for most firms, for fiscal years beginning on or after January 1, 2004. The International Accounting Standards Board has a similar standard in place. In the United States, accounting standards require expensing for fiscal years beginning after June 15, 2005, despite the raising of economic consequences and reliability concerns similar to those expressed over the 1993 exposure draft.

8.4 Stock Market Reaction to Successful-Efforts Accounting in the Oil and Gas Industry

Our second illustration of economic consequences has a somewhat different focus. The previous example was concerned with management and regulator reaction to accounting policies. Here we will look at investor reaction. Recall again that under the efficient markets theory developed in Chapter 4, there should be no effect on the market price of firms' shares arising from a change in accounting policy if that policy change does not influence cash flows. Consequently, if a share price reaction is observed following a change in accounting policy that has no cash flow effects, such an observation would raise further questions about efficient securities market theory and/or reinforce economic consequences arguments. It should by no means be taken for granted that such a share price reaction would be observed, however. Empirical research is needed to investigate this issue.

Our coverage here is based on an article by Lev, "The Impact of Accounting Regulation on the Stock Market: The Case of Oil and Gas Companies" (1979). Lev's study concerned SFAS 19, issued in 1977. That statement required that all U.S. oil and gas firms account for their exploration costs using the successful-efforts (SE) method. Recall that we discussed SE in relation to the alternative full-cost (FC) method in Section 2.5.1; you may wish to review the discussion at this time. While use of successful efforts is no longer required under GAAP, Lev's article is still relevant today, because it remains one of the few studies to document a market response to an accounting policy change that had no cash flow effects.

Since the choice of accounting policy for oil and gas exploration costs represents a policy choice with no direct cash flow effects, efficient securities market theory predicts that there should be no managerial objections to the use of SE. Yet, economic consequence arguments were very much in evidence with respect to SFAS 19. In particular, there were concerns about possible adverse impacts on competition in the oil and gas industry and on oil and gas exploration. The source of these concerns was that most small oil and gas firms used FC. Since SE tended to produce lower reported net income than FC, especially for actively exploring firms,[6] it was feared that the lower reported net incomes would make it more difficult for small firms to raise capital, thus reducing competition and extent of exploration.

Consequently, Lev set out to determine whether the security prices of oil and gas firms were affected by the imposition of SE. If the concerns about SE expressed by the smaller oil and gas firms were well founded, the answer should be yes, strengthening the economic consequences argument.

While the publication of an earnings announcement in the financial press works well as an estimate of the date on which the market becomes aware of current earnings, it can be much more difficult to establish the comparable date for a non-earnings event study. Lev took the event date as July 18, 1977, the date that the FASB issued the exposure draft for SFAS 19. It was always possible that some other event occurring around this date could trigger oil stock price changes, rather than the event of interest. However, Lev carefully examined news reports surrounding July 18 that might have related to oil and gas and concluded that this was not the case.

Lev secured a sample of 49 FC firms (firms that had been using FC and hence would be required to switch to SE under SFAS 19) and a control sample of 34 SE firms. The daily stock returns for these firms were examined for a seven-day period surrounding July 18, using the same abnormal returns procedure that was described in Section 5.2 and used by Ball and Brown and in ERC studies.

He found a significant average negative, abnormal return for the shares of the 49 sample FC firms on the day following the release of the exposure draft. For the 34 sample firms that were already using SE, and were relatively unaffected by the exposure draft, there was little average negative return.

Lev reran his analysis using the "raw" returns, that is, the total daily share returns without separation into economy-wide and firm-specific components. He found roughly similar results, consistent with no major economy-wide events taking place on or about July 18, 1977.

Other researchers have also investigated security price reaction to changes in accounting standards. With respect to oil and gas, Dyckman and Smith (1979) and Kross (1982) found no significant reaction, while Lys (1984) did. It is instructive to contemplate possible reasons for market reaction. As discussed by Lev, one possibility is securities market inefficiency—perhaps this is another anomaly. In view of the questions raised in Section 6.2 about the extent of securities market efficiency, this is a possibility. However, other reasons can be suggested. One is that FC firms may run into difficulties raising capital and/or may reduce their exploration activities once they were forced to use SE. Another reason is that the reduction in reported net income and shareholders' equity following a switch to SE might affect management bonuses and debt covenant ratios. The market could have been reacting to possible dysfunctional manager response to problems such as these. In the final analysis, however, we simply do not know why the market reacted as it did in Lev's study.

Nevertheless, while we may not know the reason, Lev's result does suggest that the market did react to an accounting event with no cash flow implications. Consequently, it is evidence that mandated accounting policy changes can have security price effects, thereby strengthening the economic consequences argument.

8.5 The Relationship Between Efficient Securities Market Theory and Economic Consequences

At this point, we may have another anomaly. Efficient securities market theory predicts no price reaction to accounting policy changes that do not impact underlying profitability and cash flows. If there is no securities price reaction (implying no change in firms' costs of capital), it is unclear why management and regulators should be particularly concerned about the accounting policies that firms use. In other words, efficient markets theory implies the importance of full disclosure, including disclosure of accounting policies. However, once full disclosure of accounting policies is made, the market will interpret the value of the firm's securities in the light of the policies used and will not be fooled by variations in reported net income that arise solely from differences in accounting policies.

Yet, in two important areas of accounting policy choice, we have seen that two major constituencies of financial statement users—management and investors—have indeed reacted to paper changes in accounting policy. The strength of management reaction seems particularly surprising, even involving appeals to government authority to intervene on its behalf. These various reactions are summarized in the concept of economic consequences. That is, accounting policy choice can matter even in the absence of cash flow effects.

Thus, accounting policies have the potential to affect real management decisions, including decisions to intervene either for or against proposed accounting standards. This "tail wagging the dog" aspect of economic consequences is all the more interesting in view of the empirical results described in Chapter 5. These results are remarkable in the sophistication they document of the market's response to financial accounting information. The question then is, does the existence of economic consequences reinforce the theory and evidence that securities markets are not fully efficient, as discussed in Section 6.2, or can efficient securities markets and economic consequences be reconciled?

Our next task is to do what any discipline does when confronted with observations, specifically, economic consequences, that are inconsistent with existing theory. We search for a more general theory that may include the existing theory but that also has the potential to explain the inconsistent observations. This brings us to positive accounting theory.

8.6 The Positive Theory of Accounting

8.6.1 Outline of Positive Accounting Theory

For our purposes, the term "positive" refers to a theory that attempts to make good predictions of real-world events. Thus:

> **Positive accounting theory (PAT)** *is concerned with predicting such actions as the choices of accounting policies by firm managers and how managers will respond to proposed new accounting standards.*

For example, can we predict which oil and gas firm managers will choose the successful-efforts accounting policy for their exploration costs and which will choose full-cost? Can we predict which managers will react favourably to fair value accounting standards for financial instruments, and which will be opposed?

PAT takes the view that firms[7] organize themselves in the most efficient manner, so as to maximize their prospects for survival[8]— some firms are more decentralized than others, some firms conduct activities inside while other firms contract out the same activities, some firms finance more with debt than others, etc. The most efficient form of organization for a particular firm depends on factors such as its legal and institutional environment, its technology, and the degree of competition in its industry. Taken together, these factors determine the set of investment opportunities available to the firm, and hence its prospects.

A firm can be viewed as a **nexus of contracts**, that is, its organization can be largely described by the set of contracts it enters into. For example, contracts with employees (including managers), with suppliers, and with capital providers are central to the firm's operations. The firm will want to minimize the various **contracting costs** associated with these contracts. These include costs of negotiation, costs arising from moral hazard and monitoring of contract performance, costs of possible renegotiation or contract violation should unanticipated events arise during the term of the contract, and expected costs of bankruptcy and other types of financial distress. Contracting costs also affect the firm's cost of capital, since bonds and shares represent contracts between the firm and its capital providers. Contracts with the lowest contracting costs are called **efficient contracts**.

Many of these contracts involve accounting variables. Thus, employee promotion and remuneration may be based on accounting-based performance measures such as net income, or the meeting of preset individual targets, such as cost control. Contracts with suppliers may depend on liquidity and financing variables. Lenders may demand protection in the form of maintenance of certain financial ratios such as debt-to-equity or times interest earned, or minimum levels of working capital or equity.

PAT argues that firms' accounting policies will be chosen as part of the broader problem of attaining efficient corporate governance. As an illustration of efficient corporate governance, consider the study by Mian and Smith (1990), a seminal study in this area. They examined the accounting policy choice of whether to consolidate a subsidiary company. They argue that the greater the interdependence between parent and subsidiary the more efficient it is (that is, the lower the contracting costs) to prepare consolidated financial statements. The reason is that the greater the interdependence the more desirable it is to evaluate the *joint* results of parent and subsidiary operations. Consolidated financial statements provide a basis for joint evaluation. It is more efficient to monitor manager performance by use of consolidated financial statement-based performance measures than by performance measures based on separate parent and subsidiary financial statements when interdependence is high. Thus Mian and Smith predicted that the greater the integration between parent and subsidiary the more likely the parent will prepare consolidated statements. This argument can be extended to predict that if consolidated financial statements are prepared for internal monitoring of manager performance it is less costly to also prepare consolidated statements for external reporting. Mian and Smith presented empirical evidence consistent with these predictions.

It should be noted that PAT does not go so far as to suggest that firms (and standard setters) should completely specify the accounting policies they will use. This would be too costly. It is desirable to give managers some flexibility to choose from a set of available accounting policies so that they can adapt to new or unforeseen circumstances. For example, a new accounting standard may reduce a firm's interest coverage ratio (Section 3461 of the *CICA Handbook* dealing with expensing of post-employment benefits is such a standard—see Section 7.2.6) to the point where violation of debt covenants is of concern. It would probably be less costly for management to, say, switch from the LIFO to the FIFO inventory method, or to liquidate LIFO inventory layers, or to issue preferred stock in place of debt, as a way to increase equity even after allowing for income tax effects, than to renegotiate the debt contract or suffer the expected costs of technical violation.

Usually, the set of available accounting policies can be taken as those allowed under GAAP, although there is no reason, other than cost, why the set cannot be further restricted by contract. However, giving management flexibility to choose from a set of accounting policies opens up the possibility of **opportunistic behaviour** *ex post*. That is, given the available set, managers may choose accounting policies from the set for their own purposes, thereby reducing contract efficiency.

This recognition of the possibility of opportunistic behaviour points out an important assumption. PAT assumes that **managers are rational** (like investors) and will choose accounting policies in their own best interests if able to do so. That is, managers maximize their own expected utility. Thus, PAT does *not* assume that the manager will simply act so as to maximize firm profits. Rather, the manager will only maximize profits if he/she perceives this to be in his/her own best interests. For example, managers of actively exploring oil companies whose remuneration contracts are based on reported net income may choose full-cost accounting over successful-efforts so as to smooth out income and increase the expected utility of their bonus streams, even though higher reported income under full-cost may increase firm taxes and encourage entry of additional firms into the industry. Of course, such opportunistic behaviour will be anticipated when the manager's remuneration contract is being negotiated and the firm will price-protect itself by lowering the manager's formal remuneration by the expected amount of opportunism. That is, given competition in the labour market for managers, managers will be willing to work for a lower compensation from the company if they can augment their utility by means of opportunistic behaviour. As a result, given the remuneration contract, managers have an incentive to behave opportunistically to the extent they have the ability to choose from a set of accounting policies.

The optimal set of accounting policies for the firm then represents a compromise. On the one hand, tightly prescribing accounting policies beforehand will minimize opportunistic accounting policy choice by managers, but incur costs of lack of accounting flexibility to meet changing circumstances. On the other hand, allowing the manager to choose from a broad array of accounting policies will reduce costs of accounting inflexibility but expose the firm to the costs of opportunistic manager behaviour.

PAT emphasizes the need for empirical investigation to determine how the trade-off between cost of capital and contracting costs, the flexibility for managers to choose from a set of accounting policies, and, indeed, the corporate governance structure itself, varies from firm to firm depending on its environment. Ultimately the objective of the theory is to understand and predict managerial accounting policy choice across different firms.

Thus, PAT does not attempt to tell individuals or constituencies what they *should* do. Theories that do this are called **normative**. This book draws on both positive and normative theories. The single-person decision theory and the theory of investment described in Chapter 3 can be interpreted as normative theories—if individuals wish to make a decision in the face of uncertainty so as to maximize expected utility, they should proceed as the theories recommend.

Whether normative theories have good predictive abilities depends on the extent to which individuals actually make decisions as those theories prescribe. Certainly, some normative theories have predictive ability—we do observe individuals diversifying their portfolio investments, for example. However, we can still have a good normative theory even though it may not make good predictions. One reason is that it may take time for people to figure out the theory. Individuals may not follow a normative theory because they do not understand it, because they prefer some other theory, or simply because of inertia. For example, investors may not follow a diversified investment strategy because they believe in technical analysis[9] and may concentrate their investments in firms that technical analysts recommend. But, if a normative theory is a good one, we should see it being increasingly adopted over time as people learn about it. However, unlike a positive theory, predictive ability is not the main criterion by which a normative theory should be judged. Rather, it is judged by its logical consistency with underlying assumptions of how rational individuals should behave.

Some people become engaged in the question of which theoretical approach is the correct one. See, for example, Boland and Gordon (1992) and Demski (1988). For our purposes, however, it is sufficient to recognize that both normative and positive approaches to theory development and testing are valuable. To the extent that decision-makers proceed normatively, positive and normative theories will make similar predictions. By insisting on empirical testing of these predictions, positive theory helps to keep the normative predictions on track. In effect, the two approaches complement each other.

8.6.2 The Three Hypotheses of Positive Accounting Theory

The predictions made by PAT are largely organized around three hypotheses, formulated by Watts and Zimmerman (1986). We will give these hypotheses in their opportunistic form, since according to Watts and Zimmerman (1990), this is how they have most frequently been interpreted. By opportunistic form we mean that managers choose accounting policies in their own best interests, which may not necessarily also be in the firm's best interests.

1. **The bonus plan hypothesis** All other things being equal, managers of firms with bonus plans are more likely to choose accounting procedures that shift reported earnings from future periods to the current period.

   This hypothesis seems reasonable. Firm managers, like everyone else, would like high remuneration. If their remuneration depends, at least in part, on a bonus related to reported net income, then they may be able to increase their current bonus by reporting as high a net income as possible. One way to do this is to choose accounting policies that increase current reported earnings. Of course, because of the nature of the accrual process, this will tend to lower future reported earnings and bonuses, other things equal. However, the present value of the manager's utility from his or her future bonus stream will be increased by shifting it towards the present.

   Note also that if the manager is risk-averse, he/she will prefer accounting policies that smooth reported earnings, since a less variable bonus stream has higher expected utility than a volatile one, other things equal.

2. **The debt covenant hypothesis** All other things being equal, the closer a firm is to violation of accounting-based debt covenants, the more likely the firm manager is to select accounting procedures that shift reported earnings from future periods to the current period.

   The reasoning is that increasing reported net income will reduce the probability of technical default. Most debt agreements contain covenants that the borrower must meet during the term of the agreement. For example, a borrowing firm may covenant to maintain specified levels of interest coverage, working capital, and/or shareholders' equity. If such covenants are violated, the debt agreement may impose penalties, such as constraints on dividends or additional borrowing.

   Clearly, the prospect of covenant violation constrains management's actions in running the firm. To prevent, or at least postpone, such violation, management may adopt accounting policies to raise current earnings. According to the debt covenant hypothesis, as the firm approaches default, or if it actually is in default, it is more likely to do this.

   Again, the manager may object to accounting policies that increase earnings volatility, since this increases the probability of future covenant violation.

3. **The political cost hypothesis** All other things being equal, the greater the political costs faced by a firm, the more likely the manager is to choose accounting procedures that defer reported earnings from current to future periods.

   The political cost hypothesis introduces a political dimension into accounting policy choice. For example, political costs can be imposed by high profitability, which may attract media and consumer attention. Such attention can quickly translate into political "heat" on the firm and politicians may respond with new taxes or other regulations. This has happened to oil companies, for example, during periods of restricted crude oil supply and rising gasoline prices. In the past, resulting public anger has led, in the United States, to special taxes on oil companies to take back the excess profits. As a result, oil company managers may feel that, for example, switching to LIFO would reduce the likelihood of this happening again.

Often, sheer size can lead to political costs. Very large firms may be held to higher performance standards, for example with respect to environmental responsibility, simply because they are felt to be large and powerful. If the large firms are also highly profitable, such political costs will be magnified.

Also, firms may face political costs at particular points in time. Foreign competition may lead to reduced profitability unless affected firms can influence the political process to grant import protection. One way to do this would be to adopt income-decreasing accounting policies in an attempt to convince the government that profits are suffering.

These three hypotheses form an important component of PAT. Note that they all lead to empirically testable predictions. For example, managers of firms with bonus plans are predicted to choose less conservative and less volatile accounting policies, such as full cost accounting, than managers of firms without such plans. Also, we would expect that managers of firms with bonus plans would oppose proposed accounting standards that may lower reported net income, such as the expensing of ESOs. Such standards would make it more difficult to maximize current reported earnings by choice of accounting policy. Also, managers may object to volatility-increasing accounting standards, such as those based on fair value accounting, particularly if unrealized gains and losses are included in net income.

Similarly, the debt covenant hypothesis predicts that managers of firms with high debt-to-equity ratios will choose less conservative accounting policies than managers of firms with low ratios, and will be more likely to oppose new standards that limit their ability to do this and/or that increase earnings volatility. The political cost hypothesis predicts that managers of very large firms will choose more conservative accounting policies than managers of smaller firms, and will be less likely to oppose new standards that may lower reported net income.

Theory in Practice 8.2

To illustrate how serious economic consequences can arise from the bonus plan hypothesis, consider Fannie Mae, established by the U.S. federal government in 1938, and converted to a public company in 1968. Its mandate is to facilitate home-owning by providing financing to mortgage lenders, including purchasing home mortgages from these institutions. Fannie Mae is the second-largest U.S. corporation in terms of assets. Its stability is essential to the U.S. housing market.

In 2004, the Office of Federal Housing Enterprise Oversight (OFHEO) issued a report highly critical of Fannie Mae. OFHEO is an office of the U.S. government created to oversee the operations of Fannie Mae and a related organization (Freddie Mac). One concern was about the amortization of discount and premium

continued ➜

on Fannie Mae's large mortgage portfolio, going back to 1998. In that year, falling interest rates led to a large volume of mortgage repayments, as homeowners scrambled to refinance at lower rates. This created a need for Fannie Mae to accelerate amortization of discount and premium on these mortgages. For 1998, according to OFHEO, extra amortization expense of $400 million was required. However, Fannie Mae only recorded $200 million in that year, deferring the rest to 1999. As a result, the volatility of earnings was reduced and, of particular concern to OFHEO, management bonuses would not have been paid if the 1998 net income of Fannie Mae was reduced any further.

Another concern was with Fannie Mae's accounting for hedges. Fannie Mae claimed to account for these under SFAS 133 (see Section 7.3.4) and, by the end of 2003, had about $12.2 billion of unrealized hedging losses accumulated in other comprehensive income. However, according to OFHEO, Fannie Mae did not properly designate its hedges and did not evaluate their effectiveness. Consequently, it did not qualify for the benefits of hedge accounting under SFAS 133 (recall that one of these benefits is that unrealized gains and losses on hedging instruments are included in other comprehensive income rather than in net income). As a result, Fannie Mae's net income was overstated over several years. Furthermore, transfer of this amount back against net income threatened the adequacy of Fannie Mae's regulatory capital.

OFHEO obtained an agreement from Fannie Mae's board of directors to, among other things, bring its accounting into conformity with GAAP. Subsequently, the SEC also announced that Fannie Mae should revise its earnings. In December 2004, the board dismissed its CEO and CFO, and announced a review of their bonus and severance payments. Fannie Mae's auditor was also dismissed. The company announced plans for a $5 billion preferred stock issue to help restore its required regulatory capital.

The three PAT hypotheses can also be interpreted from an efficient contracting perspective. For example, with respect to the bonus hypothesis, firms may want to exclude accounting policies that produce volatile earnings from their accounting policy set. Otherwise, the resulting earnings volatility will reduce the expected utility of future bonuses for risk-averse managers, forcing the firm to pay more to compensate. With respect to the debt covenant hypothesis, an increase in the probability of debt covenant violation (earnings volatility increases this probability) raises the firm's expected costs of financial distress. With respect to the political cost hypothesis, the firm will benefit from avoidance of political costs.

8.6.3 Empirical PAT Research

Positive accounting theory has generated a large amount of empirical research. For example, the Lev (1979) paper discussed in Section 8.4 is a PAT study. Lev makes no recommendations on how firms and investors *should* react to the SFAS 19 exposure draft. Rather, the emphasis is on how investors *did* react to the prospect of full-cost oil and gas firms being required to switch to successful efforts. Thus Lev's study helps us to understand *why* different firms may choose different accounting policies, why some managers may object to changes in these policies, and why investors may react to the potential impact of an accounting policy change on net income. Indeed, Lev includes both the bonus plan and debt covenant hypotheses as possible reasons for the market's unfavourable reaction to the prospect of full-cost firms being forced to switch to successful-efforts. To the extent that the firms' contracting becomes less efficient, and to the extent that managers would behave opportunistically to preserve their bonuses and avoid debt covenant violation, the securities market would be expected to react negatively.

Much PAT research has been devoted to testing the implications of the three hypotheses described above. For example, the bonus plan hypothesis was investigated by Healy (1985), who found evidence that managers of firms with bonus plans based on reported net income systematically adopted accrual policies so as to maximize their expected bonuses. Healy's paper and some of the research that followed from it are discussed in Section 11.3.

Dichev and Skinner (2002) (DS) examined the debt covenant hypothesis. They studied a large sample of private[10] lending agreements. They concentrated on agreements with covenants based on maintenance of a specified current ratio or on maintenance of a specified amount of net worth.

For each sample firm, DS calculate the *covenant slack*, for each quarter during which the loan is outstanding. For example, for the current ratio, covenant slack for a loan's first quarter is the difference between the firm's actual current ratio at the end of that quarter and the current ratio the firm is required to maintain under the lending agreement. This calculation is repeated for each sample firm for all quarters, for both current ratio and net worth covenants. According to the debt covenant hypothesis, managers will want to maintain zero or positive slack.

DS find that the number of quarters with zero or slightly positive slack is significantly greater than would be expected if firms were not managing their covenant ratios. Also, the number of quarters where slack is slightly negative is significantly less than expected. These results are consistent with the debt covenant hypothesis, since they suggest that managers take steps to maintain their covenant ratios so as to meet or exceed the levels required.

This tendency to maintain zero or positive slack is particularly strong for quarters leading up to and including a *first* covenant violation. That is, a firm that violates a covenant in one quarter may well violate it again in subsequent quarters. As DS point out, the costs of an initial violation are higher than for subsequent violations, since the lender will quickly take action to protect its interests, and much of the damage to the manager's and the firm's reputations occurs when a violation first occurs. Consistent with these higher costs, the evidence suggests that managers work particularly hard to manage covenant ratios so as to avoid an initial violation. This finding supports PAT's assumption that managers are rational—we would expect managers to work harder when the costs of failure are higher.

With respect to the political cost hypothesis, much empirical investigation has been based on firm size. However, this measure of political cost is complicated by the correlation of size with other firm characteristics, such as profitability and risk. Also, the bonus plan and debt covenant hypotheses work in the opposite direction to size in their accounting policy predictions, so that it is necessary to control for their effects.

These considerations suggest that empirical investigation of the political cost hypothesis should look at situations where political costs are particularly salient. One such situation occurs when firms are under pressure from foreign imports.

Jones (1991) studied the actions of firms to lower reported net income during import relief investigations. The granting of relief to firms that are affected by foreign competition is, in part, a political decision. Trade legislation allows for the granting of assistance such as tariff protection to firms in industries that are unfairly affected by foreign competition. In the United States, the International Trade Commission (ITC) is responsible for investigating whether there is injury. This investigation will consider economic factors such as sales and profits of affected firms. However, there is also a considerable political dimension to the granting of relief, since consumers will end up paying higher prices, and there may be retaliation by foreign countries. A determination of injury by the ITC goes initially to the president, who has 60 days to decide whether to grant relief. If relief is not granted, Congress may step in and override the president.

Thus, it is by no means clear that a deterioration of profitability is sufficient for relief to be granted. As a result, affected firms have an incentive to choose accounting policies to lower their reported net income even more, so as to bolster their case. Of course, this incentive will be known to the ITC, politicians, and the public. However, as Jones points out, these constituencies may not have the motivation to adjust for any downward manipulation of earnings. For example, the effect of higher prices that would follow the granting of relief to an industry may not be sufficiently great for it to be cost-effective for consumers to lobby against it. Even the ITC may not be fully motivated to adjust for manipulation of earnings if it was a priori sympathetic to the petitioning firms. These disincentives to unwind any earnings manipulation are strengthened if it is difficult to detect.

An effective way to reduce reported earnings in a hard-to-detect manner is to manipulate accounting policies relating to accruals. For example, a firm may increase amortization charges, it may record excessive liabilities for product guarantees, contingencies, and rebates, and it may record generous provisions for doubtful accounts and obsolescence of inventories. These are called **discretionary accruals**.

Jones examined whether firms used discretionary accruals to lower reported earnings. She collected a sample of 23 firms from five industries involved in six import relief investigations by the ITC over the period 1980–1985 inclusive.

It is easy to determine a firm's **total accruals** for the year. One approach, pointed out in Section 5.5, is to take the difference between operating cash flows and net income. Accruals are interpreted quite broadly here, being the net effect of all recorded operating events during the year other than cash flows. Changes in accounts receivable and payable are accruals, as are changes in inventories. Amortization expense is a negative accrual, being that portion of the cost of capital assets that is written off in the year. Jones used a conceptually equivalent approach, by taking the change in non-cash working capital for the year from the comparative balance sheets, plus amortization expense, as her measure of total accruals.

However, separating total accruals into discretionary and non-discretionary components presents a major challenge. This is because non-discretionary accruals are correlated with the level of business activity. For example, if a firm is suffering from foreign competition it may have lower receivables, it may have to delay payment of current liabilities, and it may have to write off large amounts of slow-moving inventory. These are negative accruals, but they can hardly be regarded as discretionary. How can the researcher, who does not have access to the firm's records and so must work from the financial statements, separate them out of total accruals so as to get at the discretionary component?

Jones' approach to this problem was to estimate the following regression equation for each firm j in her sample, over a period prior to the year of the ITC investigation:[11]

$$TA_{jt} = \alpha_j + \beta_{1j}\Delta REV_{jt} + \beta_{2j}PPE_{jt} + \varepsilon_{jt}$$

where:

TA_{jt} = total accruals for firm j in year t

ΔREV_{jt} = revenues for firm j in year t less revenues for year t − 1

PPE_{jt} = gross property, plant, and equipment for firm j in year t

ε_{jt} = a residual term that captures all impacts on TA_{jt} other than those from ΔREV_{jt} and PPE_{jt}

The coefficients α_j, β_{1j}, and β_{2j} are simply constants to be estimated. In particular, β_1 and β_2 have nothing to do with a stock's beta discussed in Section 3.7.1. The purpose of ΔREV_{jt} is to control for non-discretionary accruals of current assets and liabilities, on the grounds that these depend on changes in business activity as measured by revenues. Also, PPE_{jt} controls for the non-discretionary component of amortization expense, on the grounds that this depends on the firm's investment in capital assets.

With this regression model estimated for each sample firm, Jones used it to predict non-discretionary accruals during the ITC investigation years. That is:

$$U_{jp} = TA_{jp} - (\alpha_j + \beta_{1j}\Delta REV_{jp} + \beta_{2j}PPE_{jp})$$

where p is the year of investigation, TA_{jp} is firm j's total accruals for this year, and the quantity in brackets is the predicted non-discretionary accruals for the year from the regression model. The term U_{jp} is thus an estimate of discretionary accruals for year p for firm j.[12] The political cost hypothesis predicts that the U_{jp} will be negative, that is, that firms use discretionary accruals to force down reported net income.

Jones found evidence of the predicted behaviour. For almost all firms in the sample, discretionary accruals as measured above were significantly negative in the ITC investigation years. Significant negative accruals were not found in the years immediately preceding and following the investigations. These results, while perhaps not as strong as might be expected, suggest that affected firms were systematically choosing accrual policies so as to improve their case for import protection, consistent with the political cost hypothesis.

The above are just a few of numerous studies to test the predictions of PAT. More extensive discussions are contained in Watts and Zimmerman (1986, 1990). It does appear that these three hypotheses have empirical validity in explaining differential manager reaction to accounting policy choices. Estimation of discretionary accruals is an important component of much PAT research. We will return to it in our review of earnings management in Chapter 11.

While these three PAT hypotheses may explain manager reaction, the evidence is less strong that they can explain *investor* reaction to accounting policy change. In fact, the Lev study reviewed in Section 8.4 is one of the few to find a clear security market reaction to a paper policy change. However, even Lev does not clarify whether his results were due to positive theory variables or to securities market inefficiency. More generally, Bernard (1989) states that evidence that the market responds to the economic consequences of other standards than oil and gas has been hard to come by. Whether market value effects are present, but existing empirical methodology cannot uncover them, or whether the three hypotheses are not good predictors of security market reaction to economic consequences appears to be an open question.

8.6.4 Distinguishing the Opportunistic and Efficient Contracting Versions of PAT

As mentioned, the three hypotheses of PAT have been stated above in opportunistic form, that is, they assume that managers choose accounting policies to maximize their own expected utility relative to their given remuneration and debt contracts and political costs. As mentioned, these hypotheses can also be stated in efficiency form, on the assumption that compensation contracts and internal control systems and, more generally, good corporate governance, limit opportunism, and motivate managers to choose accounting policies to control contracting costs.

Frequently, these two forms of PAT make similar predictions. For example, from the bonus plan hypothesis a manager may choose straight-line amortization over declining-balance so as to opportunistically increase remuneration. However, this same policy could be chosen under the bonus hypothesis for efficiency reasons. Suppose that straight-line amortization best measures the opportunity cost to the firm of using its capital assets. Then, straight-line amortization results in a reported income that better measures manager performance. As a result, this policy would more efficiently motivate the manager (which is the purpose of the bonus in the first place) relative to other possible amortization policies.

Consequently, it can be difficult to tell whether firms' observed accounting policy choices are driven by opportunism or efficiency. Yet, without being able to distinguish these possibilities, it can hardly be said that we understand the process of accounting policy choice.

PAT research addresses this problem. We have already referred to the study of Mian and Smith in Section 8.6.1, who report evidence that firms make efficient decisions with respect to preparation of consolidated financial statements. Also, Christie and Zimmerman (1994) investigated the extent of income-increasing accounting choices in a sample of firms that had become takeover targets. Their reasoning was that if opportunistic accounting policy choice was taking place, it would be most rampant in firms that subsequently were taken over, as existing management struggled to fend off the takeover bid by maximizing reported net income and financial position. Christie and Zimmerman found that, even in such a sample, the effects of income-increasing accounting choices were relatively small. From this, they reasoned that the extent of opportunism in the population of firms at large was even less.

The research of Dechow (1994) also relates to the two versions of PAT. She argued that if accruals are largely the result of opportunistic manipulation of reported earnings, the efficient market will reject them in favour of cash flows, in which case cash flows should be more highly associated with share returns than net income. Alternatively, if accruals reflect efficient contracting, net income should be more highly associated with share returns than cash flows. Her empirical tests found net income to be more highly associated with returns than cash flows.

Dechow also argued that when accruals are relatively large (as, for example, in rapidly growing firms), net income should be even more highly associated with share returns, relative to cash flows, than when the firm is in steady state (in which case cash flows and net income will be equal). Her empirical tests found this to be the case, adding further support to efficient contracting.

The study of Dichev and Skinner (2002), outlined above, also provides evidence that the efficient contracting version of PAT is operative. They calculate the *variability* over time of each firm's covenant ratios. The more variable a ratio is, the greater the probability of covenant violation at some point over the term of the loan, other things equal. For example, the current ratio will be more variable under fair value accounting for inventories than under historical cost accounting, with the result that the probability the ratio falls below its covenant level is increased. DS find that, on average, the greater the variability of a covenant ratio, the greater the slack at the inception of the loan. This suggests efficiency because both contracting parties suffer costs from covenant violation. Since the probability of incurring these costs increases with covenant ratio variability, it is efficient to allow more slack at inception as the probability of violation goes up.

Guay (1999) studied the derivatives activities of firms in the year that they first began to use them. He argued that efficient compensation contracts will encourage managers to reduce firm-specific price risks (e.g., an oil and gas company hedges the price risk of next year's production), since this reduction in risk encourages the (risk-averse) manager to take on other firm-specific risks which are in the shareholders' interests, such as R&D, exploration, and new investment—hedging of price risks ensures an adequate future cash balance to finance these undertakings.

Some managers, however, may use derivatives to speculate. This is opportunistic behaviour, since speculation increases total firm risk, throwing out of balance the risk-return tradeoffs of diversified shareholders. Consequently, evidence that firms use derivatives primarily to hedge is consistent with efficient contracting.

In a sample of 254 U.S. firms that first began to use derivatives during the period 1991 to 1994, inclusive, Guay found that these new users experienced a significant reduction in several measures of firm risk[13] relative to a control sample of firms that did not initiate new derivatives activity, consistent with a hedging motivation. He also documented a consistency between type of risk exposure and type of hedging instrument used. For example, a majority of test firms with high interest rate risk used hedging instruments that reduced interest rate risk, such as interest rate swaps. Furthermore, the variability of daily share returns (a measure of total firm risk) of the test sample firms fell in a manner consistent with efficient contracting following initiation of derivatives use. For example, firms with high leverage experienced high risk reductions, and vice versa. This suggests that those firms with the greatest economic incentive to hedge their risk did in fact make greater use of derivatives.

Conservative accounting can also contribute to efficient contracting, as argued by Watts (2003). Consider the bonus plan hypothesis. This hypothesis implies that managers are tempted to bias upwards their estimates of future cash flows, using them to justify premature revenue recognition and asset overvaluation, both of which shift earnings from future to current periods. This temptation increases if the manager is approaching retirement or fears being replaced. Overpayments to managers can be difficult to recover.

By constraining premature revenue recognition and asset overvaluation, conservative accounting reduces the likelihood of such overpayments. For example, valuation of inventories at historical cost (rather than at fair value) forces the manager to wait until objective evidence of realization is available (e.g., sale) before recognizing revenue. This reduces the manager's ability to use premature revenue recognition to inflate current profits, and compensation. Consequently, conservative accounting promotes efficient compensation contracts.

A similar argument can be applied to the debt covenant hypothesis. Debtholders will suffer if the firm cannot meet its interest and principal payments. Consequently, they will benefit if the firm uses conservative accounting, due to a reduced likelihood that the firm will make excessive dividend payments—conservative accounting makes it more difficult for the manager to pay excessive dividends, by introducing a persistent downward bias into retained earnings. Furthermore, conservative accounting increases the protection provided by debt covenants, other things equal. For example, suppose the debt agreement includes a covenant whereby the firm must maintain a debt-to-equity ratio of not more than 2, otherwise no dividends can be paid. Since conservative accounting lowers the denominator, it increases the ratio. Thus, in real terms, the firm must retain more net assets to avoid violation, increasing the debtholders' security. This increased security enables the firm to issue its debt at a lower interest rate than otherwise.

Ahmed, Billings, Harris, and Morton (2000) (ABHM) investigate this efficient debt contracting argument. They point out that the concern of debtholders about excessive dividends increases with the riskiness of the firm's operations, with the proportion of debt in its capital structure, and with its dividend payout ratio. Consequently, ABHM predict that if debt contracts are efficient, the firm's accounting will be more conservative the higher are these three measures of concern.

ABHM's measure of conservatism is based on the firm's book to market ratio, that is, the ratio of a firm's shareholders' equity to the market value of its shares. Similar to the argument of Basu (Section 6.6), the lower this ratio the more conservative the accounting, other things equal, since the efficient market will see through the lower shareholders' equity thus generated. They predict that the higher is a firm's operating risk (measured by the standard deviation of past return on equity), debt-to-equity ratio, and dividend payout ratio, the more conservative that firm's accounting will be. For a sample of firms over 1993–1998, they find that this is indeed the case. They also find that the more conservative its accounting, the higher a firm's debt ratings, leading to lower interest costs, other things equal. These results are consistent with efficient debt contracting since they suggest that firms become more conservative when the need is greatest. If managers behaved opportunistically, they would be less concerned about interest costs and would work out from under the threat of debt covenant violation by shifting current reported earnings from future periods. These contracting-based rationales for conservatism augment the investor-oriented rationale given in Example 6.3.

8.6.5 Conclusions on Economic Consequences and Positive Accounting Theory

PAT attempts to understand and predict firms' accounting policy choices. At its most general level it asserts that accounting policy choice is part of the firm's overall need to minimize its cost of capital and other contracting costs. The accounting policies that do this are largely determined by the firm's organizational structure, which in turn is determined by its environment. Thus, accounting policy choice is part of the overall process of corporate governance.

PAT has led to a rich body of empirical literature. Three aspects of the firm's organizational structure and environment have been particularly singled out for study—its management compensation contracts, its capital structure, and its exposure to political costs.

PAT does not imply that a firm's accounting policy choice should be uniquely specified. Rather, it is usually more efficient to have a set of accounting policies, from which management may choose. This set can be taken as the set of policies allowed by GAAP or it can be further restricted by contract. Allowing management some flexibility in accounting policy choice enables a flexible response to changes in the firm's environment and to unforeseen contract outcomes. However, it also opens the door to opportunistic management behaviour in accounting policy choice.

From the perspective of PAT, it is not hard to see why accounting policies can have economic consequences. From an efficiency perspective, the set of available policies affects the firm's flexibility. From an opportunistic perspective, the ability of management to select accounting policies for its own advantage is affected. Either way, changes in the set of available policies will matter to management. Accounting standards may restrict the allowable accounting policies, as for example, in standards that propose mandatory successful-efforts accounting for the costs of oil and gas exploration. Other standards may lower reported net income, as in the accounting for OPEBs under Section 3461 of the *CICA Handbook*, or in standards to record an expense for employee stock options. Still other standards may increase earnings volatility, as in standards that require fair value accounting. Thus, we would expect management to react, and the more a new standard interferes with existing contracts and/or reduces accounting policy choice, the stronger this reaction is likely to be. Nothing in this argument necessarily conflicts with securities market efficiency.

While, as mentioned, managers' concerns about accounting policies and standards may be driven by opportunism or by efficient contracting, there is significant evidence in favour of the efficient contracting version of PAT. This suggests that firms are able to align managers' interests with those of shareholders. We now turn to consideration of how this alignment may be accomplished.

Questions and Problems

1. Explain the difference between a normative and a positive theory. Give an example of each.

2. Can a positive theory make good predictions even though it may not capture exactly the underlying decision processes by which individuals make decisions? Explain.

3. How is a firm's susceptibility to political costs often measured in positive accounting theory? Do you think this is a good measure? Explain.

4. In his article "The Impact of Accounting Regulation on the Stock Market: The Case of Oil and Gas Companies" (Section 8.4), Lev examined the daily returns on a portfolio of oil and gas company's common shares affected by SFAS 19. At the time, this standard would have required firms to use the successful-efforts method of accounting for the costs of oil and gas exploration.

Lev found that there was an average decline of 4.5% in the share prices of firms that would be affected by the new standard during a three-day period following the release of the exposure draft (July 18, 1977), which announced the FASB's intention to impose successful-efforts accounting. This illustrates the economic consequences of an accounting policy change that would have no direct impact on affected firms' cash flows.

Required
   a.   Why did Lev examine share returns around the date of the exposure draft (July 18, 1977) rather than the date SFAS 19 was issued (December 5, 1977)?
   b.   Why did Lev examine daily stock returns instead of returns over a longer period, such as a week?
   c.   Lev chronicled other events that may have affected oil company share prices around July 18, 1977, such as political developments, developments in the oil and gas market, etc. Why did he do this? (CGA-Canada)

5. In his article "The Impact of Accounting Regulation on the Stock Market: The Case of Oil and Gas Companies" (Section 8.4), Lev refers to the negative reaction to the oil and gas exposure draft by small oil and gas producers that were currently using the full-cost method. These small producers argued that successful-efforts accounting would reduce their ability to raise capital, with consequent effects on oil and gas exploration and on the level of competition in the industry.

Required
   a.   Use efficient securities market theory and positive accounting theory to explain why the stock market reacted as it did to the exposure draft of SFAS 19.
   b.   Suppose that, pursuant to the theory and evidence described in Section 6.2, securities markets are not fully efficient. What reaction to the SFAS 19 exposure draft would you then expect? Explain.

6. Lev, in his study "The Impact of Accounting Regulation on the Stock Market: The Case of Oil and Gas Companies" (Section 8.4), found a significant negative abnormal securities market return for a sample of firms that were to be required by SFAS 19 to switch from full-cost to successful-efforts accounting for the costs of oil and gas exploration.

Required
   a.   Use the bonus plan hypothesis of positive accounting theory to explain this negative securities market reaction.
   b.   Use the debt covenant hypothesis to explain this negative securities market reaction.

    c.   Explain, for a specific affected firm, how you would distinguish which of these two hypotheses was most likely to be driving that firm's negative share price reaction.

7. Use the efficient contracting form of positive accounting theory to explain why managers would prefer to have GAAP allow a *set* of generally accepted accounting policies from which to choose, rather than have GAAP set so restrictively as to completely prescribe accounting policy choice.

Use the opportunistic form of positive accounting theory to explain the same thing.

8. A new accounting standard requires a firm to accrue major new liabilities for employee pensions and benefits. As a result, its debt-to-equity ratio rises to the point where technical violation of covenants in its borrowing agreements is threatened. Management knows that renegotiation of these covenants would be difficult and costly.

Suggest some accounting policy choices that could reduce the likelihood of technical violation. Ideally, any changes in policies should not violate GAAP, not affect the firm's real operations, and not reduce cash flows. Justify your suggestions.

9. Use positive accounting theory to explain how conservative accounting can contribute to efficient contracting.

10. Before 1993 in the United States, and before 2001 in Canada, other post-employment benefits (OPEBs) were accounted for on a cash basis, allowing companies to account for these benefits as they were paid to employees. However, after December 15, 1992, FASB implemented SFAS 106, a standard that requires companies to account for post-employment benefits on an accrual basis. Section 3461 of the *CICA Handbook* contains similar provisions. (See Section 7.2.6)

According to SFAS 106 (paragraph 124), "accrual accounting will more appropriately reflect the financial effects of an employer's existing promise to provide those benefits and the events that affect that promise in financial statements, as those events occur." Furthermore, SFAS 106 (paragraph 20) states that "the expected postretirement benefit obligation for an employee is the actuarial present value as of a particular date of the post-employment benefits expected to be paid by the employer's plan to or for the employee."

This new rule has had economic consequences, whereby firms moved to reduce their postretirement benefits. For example, as reported in *The Wall Street Journal* (November 4, 1992), McDonnell Douglas Corp. cut benefits to retired employees upon realizing that it faced a $1.2-billion charge against earnings from SFAS 106.

Required

    a.   What is the after-tax impact on a firm's cash flows following adoption of SFAS 106 or Section 3461 of the *CICA Handbook*, assuming benefits are not cut?

    b.   Why would some firms move to reduce retiree benefits following adoption of SFAS 106 or Section 3461?

    c.   Give an argument how a firm's share price might rise following the reporting of a major charge for adoption of SFAS 106 or Section 3461.

11. *The Globe and Mail*, November 6, 2002, page B1, reported "New accounting rules sow confusion about oil earnings." This refers to changes, effective January, 2002, to Section 1650 of the *CICA Handbook*. These changes require firms with monetary items denominated in a foreign currency to include, and disclose, gains and losses from translating these items into Canadian dollars in the current period's income statement. Previously, such gains and losses could be deferred and amortized over the life of the monetary item.

Many Canadian oil companies have long-term debt denominated in U.S. dollars. Under the new standard, fluctuations in the value of the Canadian dollar relative to the U.S. dollar increase the volatility of the reported earnings of Canadian oil companies. For example, according to the *Globe* article, EnCana Corp. reported an after-tax loss of $145 million on its foreign currency-denominated debt for its third quarter, 2002, reducing its reported earnings by about 40%. This loss followed a foreign currency conversion gain of approximately the same amount in its second quarter. The article goes on to quote the managing director of research of a Calgary investment firm as saying that earnings are "going up and down like a toilet seat."

Required

    a.   In a follow-up article in the *Globe* on November 8, 2002 ("Accounting rule change burns big oil," page B2), Deborah Yedlin reports the president and CEO of EnCana Corp. as commenting that the new accounting rules could deter companies from being able to lock in financing at the current low interest rates. Evaluate this comment from the standpoint of efficient securities market theory.

    b.   Evaluate the comment in part **a** from the standpoint of positive accounting theory.

12. Following the 1990 Iraqi invasion of Kuwait, the price of crude oil soared, as did retail gasoline prices. This led the major U.S. oil companies to try to hold down their reported earnings.

The oil companies were anxious to avoid a repeat of an earlier episode when crude oil and gasoline prices peaked during the 1970s, and earnings soared. The public outrage was so great that the U.S. Congress imposed an excess profits tax, taxing back several billion dollars of excess profits. Warnings of similar taxes were repeated in 1990.

To limit their 1990 profits, the major oil companies did exercise some price restraint, to keep prices at the pump from rising as much as they otherwise would. They also engaged in a number of accounting practices, such as increased provisions for future environmental costs, increased maintenance, and large provisions for legal liabilities.

Required

    a.   What pricing and accounting policy behaviour is predicted by the bonus plan and debt covenant hypotheses of positive accounting theory, in response to increasing crude oil prices? Explain.

b. Use the political cost hypothesis of positive accounting theory to explain why the *major* oil companies would be the ones most concerned.

c. What inventory accounting policy would the oil companies find most effective in holding down profits? Explain.

d. Do you think the strategy of holding down reported profits by means of accounting policy choice will be effective in avoiding a backlash? Explain why or why not.

13. Many companies issue large numbers of stock options to executives and other employees. These companies frequently buy back some of their shares on the open market. For example, Microsoft Corp., which until recently was a major issuer of ESOs, bought back over $20 billion of its shares over a five year period up to 2003. In February, 2005, ConocoPhillips, a large oil company based in Houston, Texas, announced a $1 billion buyback program over the next two years. ConocoPhillips was also a major ESO issuer. Why would firms with large ESO plans buy back their stock? Explain.

14. The FASB's March 2004 exposure draft to require expensing of ESOs met considerable opposition, mostly from large technology companies. These companies formed an anti-expense lobby group, the International Employee Stock Options Coalition, to fight the proposal. As a result, several bills were introduced in the U.S. congress to override or modify the FASB proposal. Suggested modifications include expensing only ESOs for the firm's top five executives, and setting share price variability to zero in the Black/Scholes formula.

The FASB's stand was strengthened, however, because numerous companies, including General Motors Corp., Microsoft Corp., and Exxon Mobil Corp., voluntarily decided to expense their ESOs. Also many firms reduced their ESO awards. For example, the Bank of Montreal has reduced options issued as compensation by two-thirds, replacing them with increased cash bonuses and stock awards.

In October 2004, the FASB announced it was delaying implementation of its proposal for six months. It subsequently announced that implementation is required for fiscal years beginning after June 15, 2005.

Required

a. Evaluate the relevance and reliability of Black/Scholes as a measure of the fair value of ESOs.

b. Some critics of the proposed standard claim that the cost of ESOs is zero. Why? Explain to these critics why their claim is incorrect.

c. Why are some firms strongly opposed to expensing of ESOs?

d. Why would a firm voluntarily adopt expensing of ESOs?

15. On October 25, 2002, *The Globe and Mail* (page B2) reported "Former Big Bear head denies manipulation." The article describes accusations against the former CEO of Big Bear Exploration Ltd. in a hearing before the Alberta Securities Commission. The accusations are that the former CEO fed the market gloomy news about Blue Range Resources Corp., a newly acquired subsidiary of Big Bear, in order to drive down Big Bear's stock price and benefit personally from a subsequent rebound in stock price when Blue Range sprung back from some financial difficulties that were revealed shortly after it was acquired by Big Bear.

Big Bear's former CEO strenuously denied these charges, which had not been proven at the time of the article.

Required

a. Are these accusations consistent with the findings of Aboody and Kasznik (2000)? Explain why or why not.

b. If the accusations are proved, with which version of PAT (efficient contracting or opportunistic) is this episode most consistent? Explain.

c. If, as a result of a rebound at Blue Range, Big Bear's CEO's options became deep-in-the-money, would the Black/Scholes option value formula have properly measured their fair value at grant date? Explain why or why not. (CGA-Canada)

Notes

1. APB 25 distinguishes between variable and fixed ESO plans. A variable plan is one under which the number of shares the employee may acquire and/or the price to be paid are not determinable until some time after the grant date. Under a fixed plan, the number of shares and the exercise price are known at the grant date.

2. This assumes that the number of shares to be issued by means of options is not large enough to affect the market price of the firm's shares.

3. Concavity is the source of the overstatement. To see this, note first that the Black/Scholes value of an option is increasing in time to expiry, since the longer time to expiry the greater the likelihood that share price will take off. Also, recall that under APB 25, most ESOs are issued with exercise price equal to underlying share price at the grant date. When exercise price and grant date share price are equal, the Black/Scholes value may be an increasing, *concave* function of time to expiry, as argued by HMS. If so, the option value increases at a decreasing rate. The significance of concavity is that if an employee exercises his/her ESOs *before* expected time to exercise, the reduction in *ex post* cost to the firm is greater than the increase in cost if an employee exercises a similar time *after* expected time to exercise. That is, use of expected time to exercise in Black/Scholes upwardly biases ESO cost relative to *ex post* cost. When this upward bias is put together with the considerable variability of employees exercise decisions, the bias can be significant. Using a procedure suggested by HMS to approximate the effects of this concavity, Marquardt (2002) finds the tendency of Black/Scholes to bias ESO cost is reduced.

4. AK's argument assumes that investors do not know the scheduled date. If they did, they could discount the CEO's information release to adjust for manager biases. AK argue that there is considerable uncertainty that a firm will maintain its scheduled ESO grant dates, and whether or not it does is not known by the market until after the fact. Also, it would take several years before the market could identify that the firm was, in fact, adhering to a fixed schedule. AK present evidence in support of their argument.

5. AK study firms with scheduled ESO award dates to rule out the possibility that instead of manipulating information release, managers may manipulate the award date itself. This latter possibility was investigated by Yermack (1997), who reports evidence suggesting that managers pressure compensation committees to grant unscheduled ESOs shortly before good earnings news. This gives the CEO low exercise price and subsequent benefit as share price rises in response to the GN.

6. Lev refers to a FASB staff study of the impact of SFAS 19, which found 64% of firms using FC would have their reported earnings decreased by 5% or more under SFAS 19. Also, 74% of FC firms would have their shareholders' equity reduced by 5% or more.

7. In the following discussion it will be helpful to distinguish between the firm and its manager. We can think of the firm as represented by the board of directors.

8. This is the "economic Darwinism" argument of Alchian (1950).

9. Technical analysis is an approach to investing that studies past market performance for systematic patterns and attempts to predict future market performance by projecting these patterns. It is inconsistent with securities market efficiency, which predicts that share return fluctuations will be random.

10. Private lending agreements are loans that are not publicly traded, in contrast to public lending agreements where investors can buy or sell bonds and other credit instruments on the market. The private lending agreements studied by Dichev and Skinner consist of loans made by U.S. banks to large corporations. They report that such loans are the main form of private lending.

11. To standardize for firm size, Jones divides both sides of this equation by total assets.

12. This procedure, called the "Jones model," will be recognized as conceptually related to the use of the CAPM to separate security returns into expected and abnormal components, as illustrated in Figure 5.2.

13. Risk measures used by Guay include interest rate exposure, exchange rate exposure, "total" risk (based on the standard deviation of the firm's daily stock returns), firm-specific risk (based on the standard deviation of the firm's daily stock returns after using the market model to remove economy-wide effects), and beta. By and large, Guay's result that new derivatives users do so to reduce risk holds for all of these risk concepts.

Chapter 9

An Analysis of Conflict

FIGURE 9.1 ORGANIZATION OF CHAPTER 9

9.1 Overview

In this chapter, we consider the questions of manager/shareholder alignment that underlie economic consequences and positive accounting theory. To properly understand management's interests in financial reporting, it is necessary to consider some models from **game theory**. Game theory attempts to model and predict the outcome of **conflict** between rational individuals. Certainly, economic consequences are characterized by conflict. We will also consider **agency theory**. This is a version of game theory that models the process of **contracting** between two or more persons. Since each party to a contract attempts to get the best deal for him/herself, agency theory also involves conflict.

As pointed out in Chapter 8, business firms enter into many contracts. Two particularly important contracts are **employment contracts** between the firm and its managers and **lending contracts** between the firm and its lenders. Both of these types of contracts often depend on the firm's reported net income. Employment contracts frequently base managerial bonuses on net income, and lending contracts usually incorporate protection for the lenders in the form of covenants that, for example, bind the firm not to go below a stated times-interest-earned ratio, or not to pay dividends if working capital falls below a specified level.

Game theory can help us understand how managers, investors, and other affected parties can rationally deal with the economic consequences of financial reporting. Consequently, game theory and agency theory are relevant to accounting. Accounting policies can have economic consequences when important contracts are affected by those policies. Game theory helps us to see why contracts frequently depend on financial statements.

Reported net income has a different role in a contracting context than in reporting to investors. Its role is to predict the payoff from current manager activities. In so doing, it monitors and motivates manager performance. For this, net income needs to be sensitive to manager effort and precise in its measurements of the payoff from that effort. The characteristics needed to best fulfill this role are not necessarily the same as those that provide the most useful information to investors, leading to the fundamental problem of financial accounting theory outlined in Section 1.7.

Finally, the contract-based role for financial statements that emerges from game theory helps us to see how the theory of efficient securities markets is not necessarily inconsistent with economic consequences. Securities markets can be efficient and accounting policies can have economic consequences once the conflict implications for financial reporting are understood. Figure 9.1 outlines the organization of this chapter.

9.2 Understanding Game Theory

In this chapter, we will study the **economic theory of games**, or **game theory** for short. This is a large topic—we can only scratch the surface here. Nevertheless, we will see that game theory underlies many of the current issues in financial accounting theory.

Essentially, game theory models the interaction of two or more *players*. Frequently, this interaction occurs in the presence of uncertainty and information asymmetry. Each player is assumed to maximize his or her expected utility, just as the investors did in our decision theory and investment decision examples in Chapter 3. The difference is that game theory, in addition to taking into account any uncertainty arising from random realization of states of nature, requires that the players formally take the actions of the other players into account. Actions of other players can be extremely difficult to predict, because the action chosen by one player will depend on what action that player thinks the other players will take, and vice versa. Consequently, game theory tends to be more complex than decision theory and the theory of investment. However, the formal recognition of conflict between rational parties greatly expands the range of situations addressed by the theory.

Another way to view game theory is that the actual number of players lies "in between" the number in single-person decision theory and in markets. At one extreme, in decision theory, there is a *single* player, playing a game against nature—nature's play may be thought of as the realization of one of the states of nature. At the other extreme, we can think of a market as a game with a *large* number of players. If the market is perfect in the economic sense, the number of players is so large that the actions of any one player cannot influence what happens on the market—this is the notion of a *price-taker* in economics, as in our investment decisions in Examples 3.1 and 3.2, where the decision-makers took the market prices of securities as given.

However, in game theory the number of players, while greater than one, is sufficiently small that the actions of one player *do* influence the other players—hence the conflict aspect of a game where the players take the actions of the other players into account. The decision problems facing firms in cartels or in oligopolistic industries (where each of a few producers affect, but do not control, the market) can be modelled as games, for example.

There are many different types of games. One basis for classifying games is as **cooperative** or **non-cooperative**. In a cooperative game, the parties can enter into a **binding agreement**. A cartel is an example of a cooperative game. Cartels work best where it is possible to enforce binding agreements on members not to bolt the cartel in favour of high short-term profits. If such agreements are not possible, the cartel would be more like a non-cooperative game. An oligopolistic industry is an example of a non-cooperative game, at least in jurisdictions where agreements in restraint of trade are illegal. We will illustrate both types of games in our development.

9.3 A Non-cooperative Game Model of Manager-Investor Conflict

In Section 3.2, we introduced the concept of **constituencies** of financial statement users. Conflict between constituencies can be modelled as a game, since the decision needs of different constituencies may not coincide. As we explored in Chapter 3, investors will desire relevant and reliable financial statement information to assist in assessing the expected values and risks of their investments. Managers, however, may not wish to reveal all the information that investors desire. They may prefer to omit certain liabilities from the balance sheet, on the grounds that this will make it easier to raise capital by facilitating contracts with lenders. Also, they may prefer not to reveal which accounting policies are being used so as to have room to manage reported profits by discretionary accruals or changes of accounting policy. In addition, management may fear that releasing too much information will benefit their competition. These are just some of the actions that managers may take to present the firm in the best light by biasing, or otherwise managing, the financial statements for either efficient contracting or opportunistic purposes. The investor, of course, will be aware of this possibility and will take it into account when making an investment decision. Firm management, in turn, will be aware of possible investor reaction when preparing the financial statements. Game theory provides a formal framework for studying this conflict situation and for predicting the decisions the parties will make.

We will model this situation as a **non-cooperative game**, since it is difficult to envisage a binding agreement between manager and investor about what specific information is to be supplied. For one thing, such an agreement could be very costly, since similar agreements would have to be negotiated with all users. But different users may have varied decision problems and hence different information needs, so that many different sets of financial statements would be needed. Even if such binding agreements were made, they would be difficult and costly to enforce, because each user would need to conduct, or hire, an audit investigation of the firm to monitor management compliance with the agreement. In other contexts, binding agreements may be illegal, as when an oligopolistic industry enters into an agreement in restraint of trade.

To illustrate this game between the manager and the investor, consider Example 9.1.

EXAMPLE 9.1
MANAGER-INVESTOR RELATIONS AS A NON-COOPERATIVE GAME

We assume the manager has two strategies, one of which must be chosen (see Table 9.1.) We will call one of these "distort" (D), which we can think of as under-investing in the internal control system and choosing accounting policies to maximize or otherwise bias reported net income. The other strategy is to choose "honest" (H), which we can think of as maintaining a strong internal control system and preparing useful financial statements for investors. The investor also has two strategies—to buy shares in the manager's firm or to refuse to buy, denoted by B and R respectively.

TABLE 9.1 UTILITY PAYOFFS IN A NON-COOPERATIVE GAME

		Manager	
		HONEST (H)	**DISTORT (D)**
	BUY (B)	60, 40	20, 80
Investor			
	REFUSE TO BUY (R)	35, 20	35, 30

The numbers in Table 9.1 represent the utility payoffs to the investor and manager respectively for each possible strategy combination. Thus, if the manager chooses H and the investor B, the investor receives a utility of 60 and the manager receives 40, and so on for the other three pairs of numbers in the table. You should analyze the relationship between the payoffs to make sure they appear reasonable. For example, if the investor chooses B, a higher utility is attained by the investor when the manager is honest (60) than when the manager distorts the information (20). Similarly, if the investor refuses to buy, the manager would prefer to choose D (if the manager distorts the information, less money and effort is put into the internal control system and into decision-useful reporting).

It is important to emphasize the assumption here that each party has *complete information* about the other. Thus, the investor knows the strategies available to the manager and the manager's payoffs and vice versa. Game theory can be extended to relax these assumptions, but this is beyond our scope. This completeness of information does not extend to choice of strategy, however. Each player in this example chooses his or her strategy without knowing the strategy choice of the other in this game.

What **strategy pair** will be chosen? The term means simply a statement of the strategy chosen by each player. Thus, BH is a strategy pair whereby the investor buys (B) and the manager is honest (H). Review Table 9.1 and make your own prediction before reading on.

We can rule out the RH and BD strategy pairs easily. If the manager were to choose H, the investor will reason that it would be better to choose B, because it yields a utility of 60 as opposed to one of 35 from R. Thus, RH would be unlikely to happen. Similarly, if the manager were to choose D, the investor would reason that it would be better to choose R, so BD would be unlikely.

Now consider the BH pair. If the investor were to choose B, the manager would then prefer D. Thus, it seems BH must be ruled out also. The only strategy pair not subject to this problem is RD. If the manager was to choose D, the investor would prefer R. Similarly, if the investor was to choose R, the manager would prefer D. RD is the only strategy pair such that *given* the strategy choice of the other player, each player is content with his or her strategy. Such a strategy pair is called a **Nash equilibrium**. Thus, RD is the predicted outcome of the game.

However, RD is not a completely satisfactory outcome of the game in Example 9.1. Notice that *both parties would be better off* if BH were chosen rather than RD. But, as we have argued, if the investor were to choose B rather than R, he or she knows that the rational manager would then prefer D and the investor would end up with 20 rather than the 35 from choosing R. Consequently, the investor would not choose B. The Nash equilibrium outcome RD in this game is unfortunate, because it means, at least for pay-off values assumed, that the market for the firm's shares would not work very well—no one would buy them.

It is interesting to speculate what might happen next. Perhaps the parties would get together and enter into a binding agreement to choose BH, after all. However, the investor would have to be convinced the agreement was in fact binding on the manager and could be enforced. Another possibility would be to change the payoffs of the game, by introducing severe penalties for distortion. This may lower the manager's payoffs for BD and RD to, say, zero. Then it can be verified that BH would be a Nash equilibrium. This would require the intervention of some central authority, however.

Yet another approach would be to think of the game in a *long-run* perspective. If this game was repeated indefinitely, and the manager always chose H, a reputation for honesty would be established and investors would start choosing B. This would give the manager a long-run average of 40, rather than the 30 that would be obtained on a one-shot basis. Extensions of game theory to incorporate these possibilities are beyond the scope of this example. Nevertheless, game theory provides a powerful and flexible methodology for studying problems of conflict.

While this game model is a relatively simple one, it is not hard to see how it relates to recent accounting and auditing scandals, and resulting declines in stock markets in Canada and the United States in the early 2000s. In Table 9.1, if we start with the players at the cooperative solution BH, certain managers, such as those at Enron and WorldCom (see Section 1.2), moved, it is alleged, to a distort strategy D. This short-run strategy generated high payoffs for them. For example, the distortions they are alleged to have incorporated into their financial statements increased reported earnings and removed debt from the balance sheet. The resulting increase in share prices generated huge profits for them from ESOs. When the market became aware of the financial statement distortions, investors immediately moved to R, and share price fell precipitously.

Attempts by central authorities to restore investor confidence in financial reporting can be interpreted as changes in the payoffs of the game. We have already mentioned sections 1100 and 1400 of the *CICA Handbook* in Section 1.2. These standards tighten up the concept of generally accepted accounting principles, increasing the cost of distortion for the manager. In addition, the Canadian Public Accountability Board was created in 2002. This is a group of prominent persons independent of the accounting and auditing profession whose role is to enforce tougher rules on auditors. Hopefully, any Enron and WorldCom-style financial statement distortions will be deterred. In the United States, the Public Company Accounting Oversight Board with a similar function has been created under the Sarbanes-Oxley Act. To the extent these bodies succeed in their mission, the manager's payoff under strategy BD will be reduced to the point where the Nash equilibrium becomes BH. In effect, the change in payoffs increases investor confidence that the manager will not distort, with the result that the investors resume buying.

Note the essential difference between single-person decision theory and game theory approaches. In our earlier decision theory Example 3.1, Bill Cautious assessed *probabilities* of what would happen—he ended up with a 0.77 probability of the high payoff, and so on. The assumption in decision theory is that the high or low payoffs are generated by some random mechanism called **nature**. Thus, a decision theory problem is sometimes called a game against nature, because some impartial force (nature) is assumed to generate the high or low payoffs with the probabilities as given. While we gave considerable attention to how investors may assess these probabilities and revise them as new information is obtained, we made an implicit assumption throughout Example 3.1 that the particular decision chosen by the investor would not affect what these probabilities were. That is, nature does not "think."

This assumption is fine for many decision problems. Indeed, as we outlined in Chapters 3 and 4, much progress has been made in understanding the decision needs of users through study of the decision theory approach. However, the approach breaks down when the payoffs are generated by a *thinking opponent* (the manager) rather than by nature. In Example 9.1, the manager will reason that if the investor buys, his/her best act is to distort, and the investor knows this. Thus, it is not correct for the investor to assign probabilities to the manager's action choice when the manager's action is not chosen probabilistically. Similarly, it would not be correct for the manager to assign probabilities to the investor's action.[1] Such behaviour, by either or both decision-makers, would be unlikely to lead to good decisions in the conflict situation.

How can we use a game such as the one modelled in Example 9.1 in financial accounting theory? The essential point to realize here is that such models enable us to *better understand the process of accounting policy choice*. Recall that in Chapter 3 we developed a considerable body of theory to enable us to understand the information needs of investors. In that chapter we showed that major professional accounting standard-setting bodies appear to have adopted the decision usefulness approach that follows from the theory. What we did *not* consider in those chapters, however, was whether firm management would be *willing* to adopt the full disclosure policies that accounting standard setters have proposed. Indeed, the important message in Chapter 8 was that managers appear unwilling to sit idly by, and adopt whatever accounting policies are suggested by the standard setters (representing the interests of investors). The assumption of positive accounting theory that managers are rational, leading to the possibility of opportunistic behaviour, makes it clear that management has *its own* interests at stake in accounting policy choice and cannot be assumed to necessarily adopt full-disclosure or other accounting policies solely on the grounds that they will be useful to shareholders and other investors. This is shown in our Example 9.1 by the utility of the manager being lower under H than under D. In essence, the interests of the investor and manager constituencies may *conflict*.

By modeling this conflict situation as a game, we can understand the problems surrounding policy choice more clearly. In particular, we see that, depending on the payoffs of the game, it may indeed be in a manager's interests to distort the financial statements, at least in the short run. Thus, any accounting body concerned about implementing a new pronouncement must be concerned with the resulting payoffs to *both* investors and management. Only by ensuring that the payoffs to management are such that management will accept the new policy can a smooth implementation be assured.

Of course, any accountant with practical experience in choosing a firm's accounting policies will know about management's interest in and concern about these policies, without having to be convinced by a game theory example. Our point is that such interest and concern is exactly what is predicted by the game theory. Better understanding of this conflict situation by standard setters will result in more realistic accounting policy choices, which should avoid the economic consequences disputes that were documented in Chapter 8.

There are other conflict situations in financial accounting that can be studied in a game context. For example, Darrough and Stoughton (1990) (DS) analyze a game between a monopolistic firm (the incumbent) and a potential entrant to the industry (the entrant). The incumbent needs to raise equity capital for a new project. It has inside information about itself that can be either favourable or unfavourable about its future prospects. If the information is favourable, its disclosure will lower the incumbent's cost of capital for its new equity issue. However, the entrant will revise upwards its prior probability of good future prospects in the industry upon seeing the favourable disclosure. This will encourage the entrant to enter. If the information is unfavourable, its disclosure[2] will deter the entrant but raise cost of capital. What should the incumbent do—disclose or not disclose?

The answer depends on how profitable the incumbent is. If existing monopoly profits are high and the need for equity capital is moderate, the dominant consideration for the incumbent is to deter entry. Then, DS show that if the entrant has high prior probability that the incumbent's inside information is favourable and/or the costs of entry to the industry are low (i.e., the threat of entry is high), the incumbent firm will fully disclose its inside information, favourable or unfavourable. If its inside information is unfavourable, its loss of profits if the entrant enters outweighs the higher cost of capital, so the incumbent will disclose. If its inside information is favourable, the incumbent will disclose even if this attracts entry since profits will still be satisfactory, particularly in view of the lower cost of capital following the favourable disclosure.

Other outcomes are possible, however. DS show that if the entrant has low prior probability that the incumbent's inside information is favourable (low threat of entry), the incumbent will not disclose favourable or unfavourable information. Even the incumbent with favourable news will be better off not disclosing if the higher profits from discouraging entry outweigh the increased cost of capital that results.

These conclusions are of interest, because they suggest that the question of full disclosure extends into industry structure. In the DS model, the greater the competition in an industry (measured by the threat of entry), the better the disclosure. This reinforces our conclusion from positive accounting theory that full disclosure to investors is not the only consideration affecting managers' accounting policy choices.

Indeed, it also reinforces the claim of Merino and Neimark (Section 1.2) that, prior to the creation of the SEC in 1933, the primary role of full disclosure was to enable potential entrants to identify high-profit industries. Presumably, the higher an incumbent firm's monopoly profits the more incentive it had to engage in manipulative financial reporting.

Thus, the implications of the DS analysis have a deeper significance. By delineating conditions under which firms may or may not disclose voluntarily, conditions under which standard setting may or may not be needed are identified.

Since DS, other papers have refined and extended the above considerations. See, for example, Darrough (1993), Newman and Sansing (1993), Feltham and Xie (1994), and Pae (2002).

9.3.1 Summary

Non-cooperative game theory enables us to model the conflict situation that often exists between different constituencies of financial statement users. Even a very simple game-theoretic model shows that an accounting standard-setting body that fails to consider the interests of all constituencies affected by accounting policy choice is in danger of making policy recommendations that are difficult to implement. Furthermore, conflict analysis can be used to examine conditions under which standards may or may not be needed, since under some conditions firms may be motivated to release even unfavourable information voluntarily.

9.4 Some Models of Cooperative Game Theory

9.4.1 Introduction

While the non-cooperative game in Example 9.1 illustrates some of the implications of conflict between user constituencies, many other areas of accounting reflect **cooperative behaviour**. Recall that the essence of cooperation here is that the players in a game situation can enter into agreements that they perceive as binding. Such agreements are often called **contracts**. There are many such contractual agreements that have accounting implications.

In this section we will be concerned with two important types of contracts that have implications for financial accounting theory. These are **employment contracts** between the firm and its top manager and **lending contracts** between the firm manager and the bondholder. In these contracts, we can think of one of the parties as the principal, and the other the agent. For example, in an employment contract, the firm owner is the principal and the top manager is the agent hired to run the firm on the owner's behalf. This type of game theory is called **agency theory**.

> **Agency theory** is a branch of game theory that studies the design of contracts to motivate a rational agent to act on behalf of a principal when the agent's interests would otherwise conflict with those of the principal.

Actually, agency theory contracts have characteristics of both cooperative and non-cooperative games. They are non-cooperative in that both parties choose their actions non-cooperatively. The two parties do not specifically agree to take certain actions; rather, the actions are motivated by the contract itself. Nevertheless, each party must be able to commit to the contract, that is, to bind him/herself to "play by the rules." For example, it is assumed that the manager in an employment contract will not grab the total firm profits and head for a foreign jurisdiction. Such commitment may be enforced by the legal system, by use of bonding or escrow arrangements or, perhaps, by the reputations of the contracting parties. Consequently, for our discussion, we will include them under cooperative games.

9.4.2 Agency Theory: An Employment Contract Between Firm Owner and Manager

We begin with a single-period owner-manager contract example that introduces many of the concepts of agency theory and illustrates the basic moral hazard conflict between owner and manager. This section also illustrates how the owner can design an employment contract to control moral hazard.

It should be noted in our example that the use of two persons is a modelling device to keep things as simple as possible. The owner and the manager are proxies for a large number of similar investors and managers with conflicting interests. In effect, the firm exhibits a separation of ownership and control, captured by modelling the firm as two rational individuals with conflicting interests.

EXAMPLE 9.2

A FIRM OWNER-MANAGER AGENCY PROBLEM

Consider a simple firm consisting of a single owner (the principal) and a single manager (the agent). The contract is single-period. Specifically, the owner hires the manager for one year. The firm faces risk, which, as usual, we express in the form of random states of nature. Assume that there are two such states, denoted by θ_1 and θ_2. State θ_1 represents "good times" and θ_2 "bad times." If good times occur, the firm's payoff will be $x_1 = \$100$. Given bad times, the payoff will be $x_2 = \$50$.

We will think of the payoff here as the cash flows resulting from the manager's activities during the year. Many of these cash flows will be realized within the year. Activities aimed at cost control, for example, will generate cash savings with little delay. Advertising activities, if successful, will generate extra sales currently.

Other activities, such as R&D, however, may not pay off until next year, since it can take considerable time, if ever, for the results of current research to generate cash flow. In addition, current activities may generate future liabilities. Extraction of natural resources may generate environmental liabilities that may not be known for some time, for example. In effect, *the full payoff is not observable until after the current compensation contract has expired*.

It is this payoff that is the owner's ultimate interest. That is, the rational owner wishes to maximize the expected payoff, net of manager compensation.

Before proceeding with our example, we further simplify by getting rid of the need to refer specifically to the states of nature. As mentioned, each state realization leads to a specific payoff. If θ_1 occurs, net income = $x_1 = \$100$, and if θ_2 occurs, $x_2 = \$50$. Thus, we can work just as well with the probabilities of the payoffs as with the probabilities of the states of nature themselves. That is, the probability that θ_1 happens is the same as the probability that the payoff is x_1, and so on. If the probability of θ_1 is 0.6, we can say that the probability of x_1 is 0.6, rather than the more awkward "the probability of θ_1 is 0.6 and, if θ_1 occurs, $x_1 = \$100$." Consequently, we will suppress direct reference to states of nature for the remainder of the example.

Now, assume that the owner does not operate the firm. This is the responsibility of the manager. Consistent with what we observe in real employment situations, the manager will be paid at year end, despite the payoff not being observable at that time.

Assume also that, after being hired, the manager has two action choices—**work hard**, denoted by a_1, or **shirk**, denoted by a_2. These represent all of the manager's activities during the year.

The action choice of the manager will affect the probabilities of the payoffs. Let these probabilities be as follows:

- If the manager works hard:

  $P(x_1/a_1) = 0.6$
  $P(x_2/a_1) = \underline{0.4}$
  $ \underline{1.0}$

- If the manager shirks:

  $P(x_1/a_2) = 0.4$
  $P(x_2/a_2) = \underline{0.6}$
  $ \underline{1.0}$

Recall that x_1 represents the high payoff. If the manager works hard the probability of x_1 is greater (0.6) than it would be under shirking (0.4). In statistical terms, the payoff distribution conditional on a_1 stochastically dominates (in the first degree) the distribution conditional on a_2. This is a critical point to realize—the action of the agent affects the probabilities of the payoffs. In particular, the greater the effort put into the operation of the firm by the manager, the higher the probability of the high payoff and the lower the probability of the low payoff.

Of course, this is just what we would expect. Hard work by the manager increases the probability that the firm will do well, but it is still possible for the low payoff to occur. In our example, there is a 40% probability that the payoff will be low even though the manager works hard, since hard work cannot always overcome the risks faced by the firm. Similarly, if the manager shirks, it is still possible for the high payoff to occur, since the shirking manager may be "bailed out" by good economic times. In our example, there is a 40% probability of the high payoff even though the manager shirks. In general, the harder the manager works, the lower the probability of the low payoff.

Finally, note that effort is interpreted quite broadly. Effort goes beyond a literal interpretation as the number of hours worked, and includes such factors as the care the manager takes in running the firm, the diligence with which subordinates are motivated and supervised, the absence of perquisite-taking, and so on. In effect, effort is a modelling device that encompasses the whole range of activities undertaken by a manager during the year.

We summarize the example up to this point in Table 9.2. The dollar amounts in the table represent the payoffs under each of the four payoff/act combinations. The probabilities are conditional on the chosen act, that is, if a_1 is chosen by the manager the probability of x_1 is 0.6, whereas it is 0.4 if a_2 is chosen, and so on.[3]

TABLE 9.2 PAYOFFS FOR AGENCY EXAMPLE

	Manager's Effort			
	a_1 (work hard)		a_2 (shirk)	
	Payoff	**Probability**	**Payoff**	**Probability**
x_1 (high payoff)	$100	0.6	$100	0.4
x_2 (low payoff)	50	0.4	50	0.6

As mentioned, the payoff is not observable until after the expiration of the current period. Figure 9.2 shows a timeline of the agency model.

FIGURE 9.2 TIMELINE FOR AGENCY MODEL

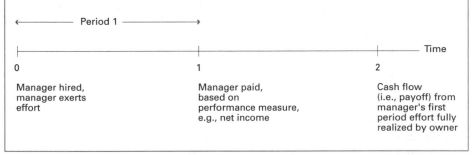

Now, consider this problem from the standpoint of the owner of the firm. The owner wishes to hire the manager to operate the firm for the year, that is, the owner will have no direct control over the act taken. Indeed, it is unlikely that the owner can even observe which act the manager takes. Nevertheless, to maximize the expected payoff, the owner would like the manager to work hard, that is, to choose a_1, because the probability of the high payoff is higher conditional on a_1 than on a_2.

To illustrate this more formally, assume that the owner is risk-neutral, and that the owner's utility from a given payoff is equal to the dollar amount of that payoff. Assume also that the manager receives a fixed salary of $25 for the period. Then, the owner's expected utility conditional on each act is:

$$\begin{aligned}
EU_o(a_1) &= 0.6(100 - 25) + 0.4(50 - 25) \\
&= 0.6 \times 75 + 0.4 \times 25 \\
&= 45 + 10 \\
&= 55
\end{aligned}$$

$$\begin{aligned}
EU_o(a_2) &= 0.4(100 - 25) + 0.6(50 - 25) \\
&= 0.4 \times 75 + 0.6 \times 25 \\
&= 30 + 15 \\
&= 45
\end{aligned}$$

where $EU_o(a_1)$ denotes the owner's expected utility given that the manager chooses a_1, and similarly for a_2. Just as in decision theory, we assume the players wish to maximize their expected utilities. Consequently, the owner wants the manager to choose a_1, because its expected utility to the owner is greater. It should be clear that this result will hold for any probabilities such that the probability of x_1 given a_1 is greater than it is given a_2.

Now consider matters from the manager's standpoint. Let the manager be risk-averse. Specifically, assume that his or her utility from remuneration equals the square root of the remuneration.

Will the manager *want* to work for the owner? Assume that there is a reasonably efficient **managerial labour market**. This market puts a value on the manager's services, where the value depends on factors including the manager's training, experience, and reputation. If the manager is to be willing to work for the owner for the current period, the compensation offered must be sufficiently large that his/her expected utility is at least equal to its opportunity cost, that is, the utility that could be attained by the manager in the next best employment opportunity. This is the concept of **reservation utility**. We assume that the manager's reservation utility is 3. If the contract does not offer at least this amount, the manager will go elsewhere. Of course, the manager would prefer to receive a utility greater than 3. However, other managers would also like to work for this firm. If the manager asks for more than 3, the owner may well hire someone else. Consequently, given reasonable competition in the labour market for managers, we expect the manager to be willing to work for a utility of 3.

Now, given that the manager is hired, will a_1 in fact be chosen, as desired by the owner? First, it is important to remind ourselves again that in game theory, and in agency theory in particular, one player will not choose an act desired by another player just because that player says so. Rather, each player chooses that act that maximizes his or her own expected utility. This observation is consistent with positive accounting theory, as discussed in Chapter 8.

Consequently, if the manager chooses a_1, it must be because the manager's expected utility is at least as great for a_1 as for a_2. Note that this assumption differs from much economic analysis, where it is simply *assumed* that firms act in a manner to maximize their profits. This expected utility-maximizing behaviour by all parties is one of the important and distinguishing characteristics of positive accounting theory and the economic theory of games.

Next, assume that the manager is **effort-averse**. This means that the manager dislikes effort and that the greater the level of effort the greater the dislike. In effect, the disutility of effort is subtracted from the utility of remuneration.

Consequently, we will assume:

Disutility of effort level $a_1 = 2$

Disutility of effort level $a_2 = 1.7$

We can now calculate the manager's expected utility, net of the disutility of effort, for each act. Recall that the manager is offered a salary of $25.

$EU_m(a_1) = \sqrt{25} - 2 \quad = 3$

$EU_m(a_2) = \sqrt{25} - 1.7 \quad = 3.3$

where $EU_m(a_1)$ denotes the expected utility of the manager, given that the manager chooses a_1, and similarly for a_2. The manager will choose a_2.[4]

This result is not very surprising. Most people, even managers, would prefer to take it easy, all other things being equal. Here, other things *are* equal, because the manager receives a salary of $25 regardless. This tendency of an agent to shirk is an example of moral hazard.

Designing a Contract to Control Moral Hazard

The question now is, what should the owner do in a situation such as that described in Example 9.2? One possibility is for the owner to refuse to hire the manager. But any other rational salaried manager would also choose a_2. Consequently, the owner could either go out of business or run the firm him/herself. These possibilities are unlikely, however. The running of an organization is a complex and specialized task for which the owner may not have the required skills, and, after all, we do witness a separation of ownership and management in all but the smallest organizations. In fact, our owner has a number of other options, which we will now consider.

Hire the manager and put up with a_2 The owner could proceed anyway, letting the manager get away with a_2 and putting up with a utility of 45 rather than 55. This also seems unlikely, however, since we will see that the owner can do better than this.

Direct monitoring If the owner could costlessly observe the manager's chosen act, this would solve the problem. Then, the contract could be amended to pay the manager a salary of $25 if a_1 was taken and, say, $12 otherwise. It is easy to verify that the manager would then choose a_1, because choosing a_2 would result in only $12 remuneration and expected utility of 1.76.

A contract where direct monitoring is possible is called **first-best**. It gives the owner the maximum attainable utility (55) and gives the agent his/her reservation utility (3). Under the assumptions of Example 9.2, no other contract can improve on this.

The first-best contract also has desirable **risk-sharing** properties. Note that under this contract the manager bears none of the firm's risk, because a fixed salary is received regardless of the payoff. Since the manager is risk-averse, this is desirable. The owner bears all the risk of the random payoff. Since the owner is risk-neutral, he or she does not mind bearing risk. Indeed, we could argue that a function of business ownership is to bear risk. If the owner was risk-averse, rather than risk-neutral, the first-best contract would involve the owner and manager sharing the risk. However, demonstration of this is beyond our scope.

Unfortunately, the first-best contract is frequently unattainable. This would seem to be the case in an owner-manager contract, because it is unlikely that the owner could monitor the agent's effort in a managerial setting. The nature of managerial effort is so complex that it would be effectively impossible for a remote owner to establish whether the manager was in fact "working hard." We thus have a case of **information asymmetry**—the manager knows the effort level, but the owner does not. As mentioned previously, this particular form of information asymmetry is called moral hazard.

Indirect monitoring Given that managerial effort is not directly observable, it may be possible under some conditions to impute the effort. To illustrate, let us change our example slightly. See Table 9.3. The only difference between this table and Table 9.2 is that the payoff for (x_2, a_2) is now $40 rather than $50. In agency theory terms, this is a case of **moving support**, that is, the set of possible payoffs is different (it moves) depending on which act is taken. Table 9.2 is a case of **fixed support**—the set of possible payoffs is fixed at (100, 50), regardless of the action choice.

TABLE 9.3 PAYOFFS FOR AGENCY EXAMPLE

	Manager's Effort			
	a_1 (work hard)		a_2 (shirk)	
	Payoff	Probability	Payoff	Probability
x_1 (high payoff)	$100	0.6	$100	0.4
x_2 (low payoff)	50	0.4	40	0.6

It is apparent from Table 9.3 that if the owner observes a payoff of $40 it will be known that the manager chose a_2 even though effort is not directly observable. Then the owner could amend the contract to offer the manager a salary of $25 unless the payoff turns out to be $40, in which case the manager would be obligated to later return $13 to the owner as a penalty, for a net salary of $12. It is easy to check that the manager would then choose a_1:

$$EU_m(a_1) = \sqrt{25} - 2 \qquad\qquad = 3$$

$$EU_m(a_2) = 0.4\sqrt{25} + 0.6\sqrt{12} - 1.7 = 2.38$$

The penalty of $13 if the $40 payoff happens is sufficient cause for the agent to choose a_1. This contract is also first-best, since the agent works hard and receives reservation utility, thereby maximizing the owner's expected payoff.

Indirect monitoring will *not* work for the fixed-support case of Table 9.2, however. The reason is that if a payoff of $50 is observed, this is consistent with either a_1 or a_2, and similarly for the $100 payoff. Thus, the owner cannot impute the act from the payoff.

It seems, then, that we cannot rely on indirect monitoring to ensure that the first-best contract will be attained. First, many contracting situations may be characterized by fixed support. For example, the payoff may be any positive or negative number. If the payoff is, say, a loss of $1 million the owner cannot be certain whether this loss resulted from low manager effort or an unfortunate realization of the firm's risk.

Second, even if moving support holds, legal and institutional factors may prevent the owner from penalizing the manager sufficiently to force a_1. For example, it may be difficult for the owner to collect $13 from the manager after the current one-year contract has expired.

Owner rents firm to the manager   At this point, the owner may well be tempted to say to the manager, "O.K., I give up—*you* take the firm and run it, taking 100% of the profits after paying me a fixed rental of $47.38." Then, the owner no longer cares what action the manager takes, since a rental of $47.38 is received regardless. This is referred to as **internalizing** the manager's decision problem.

Such arrangements do exist, or they have existed in the past, in the form of tenant farming. Tenant farming is usually regarded as inefficient, however, and it is easy to see why. The manager's expected utility would be:

$$EU_m(a_1) = 0.6\sqrt{100 - 47.38} + 0.4\sqrt{50 - 47.38} - 2$$
$$= (0.6 \times 7.25) + (0.4 \times 1.62) - 2$$
$$= 4.35 + 0.65 - 2$$
$$= 3.00$$

$$EU_m(a_2) = 0.4\sqrt{100 - 47.38} + 0.6\sqrt{50 - 47.38} - 1.7$$
$$= (0.4 \times 7.25) + (0.6 \times 1.62) - 1.7$$
$$= 2.90 + 0.97 - 1.7$$
$$= 2.17$$

Thus, the manager will choose a_1 and receive reservation utility of 3.

Note, however, that the owner receives a utility of 47.38 in this contract, compared to 55 in the first-best contract. Consequently, the owner is worse off. The reason is that this contracting arrangement has inefficient risk-sharing characteristics. The owner is risk-neutral, and hence is willing to bear risk, but there is no risk for the owner because a fixed rental is received. The risk-averse manager, who dislikes risk, is forced to bear it all. The owner must lower the rental from $55 to $47.38 to enable the manager to receive reservation utility of 3, costing the owner 7.62 in lost utility. The 7.62 is called an **agency cost** (Jensen and Meckling, 1976), and is another component of contracting costs, which the owner will want to minimize.

Give the manager a share of the profits   Finally, we come to what is often the most efficient alternative if the first-best contract is not attainable. This is to give the manager a share of firm performance. However, the owner immediately runs into a problem. The payoff is not fully observable until next period. Yet the manager must be compensated at the end of the current period.

A solution to the problem is to base compensation on a **performance measure**, that is, on some jointly observable variable that reflects the manager's performance[5] and is available at the end of the period. Net income is such a performance measure. Net income tells us *something* about what the payoff will be, since much of manager effort shows up in current earnings. Effort devoted to cost control, maintenance, employee morale, and advertising will typically affect net income with little lag, for example. Thus net income at least partly reflects current manager performance. We then say that net income is **informative** about manager effort.

Unfortunately, net income is not *fully* informative about effort. One reason is recognition lag. As mentioned above, several components of manager effort may not fully pay off during the current period. R&D is a common example. While most R&D costs are written off currently, the realization of revenues from current R&D expenditures may be delayed until after the current period. As a result, current net income may understate the ultimate payoff. Alternatively, or in addition, current manager effort may have a side-effect of creating environmental or legal liabilities that may not be known until next period, with the result that current net income may overstate the payoff. In effect, while net income tells us something about current manager performance, it by no means tells the full story.

While net income does not perfectly predict the payoff, we assume in this section that it is unbiased. That is, net income is noisy. While net income may be understated or overstated relative to the payoff, the expected value of the various understatements and overstatements is zero.[6]

In sum, in this section, we regard net income as a noisy, unbiased **message** about the payoff.

EXAMPLE 9.3
NET INCOME AS A PERFORMANCE MEASURE

To illustrate the use of net income in compensation contracts, we extend Example 9.2. Recall from Table 9.2 that if the manager works hard (a_1) the probability of the high payoff ($100) is 0.6, with 0.4 probability of the low payoff ($50). If the manager shirks (a_2), the probabilities of the high and low payoffs are 0.4 and 0.6, respectively. As explained at the time, the reason why the payoff can be low even if the manager works hard, and vice versa, is because of the various risks faced by the firm. For example, despite hard work, bad economic times may result in the low payoff. Alternatively, good times may rescue the manager who shirks. This risk continues in our example here, reflected in the 0.4 probability of low payoff given a_1 and the 0.4 probability of high payoff given a_2.

Since net income is not fully informative, the manager now faces two sources of compensation risk. As just mentioned, the payoff is risky due to the risks faced by the firm. Furthermore, net income is a noisy predictor of this payoff.

To reflect the noise in net income, assume the following:

- If the payoff is going to be $100, net income for the current period will be $125 with probability 0.5 and $75 with probability 0.5.

- If the payoff is going to be $50, net income for the current period will be $62.50 or $37.50, both with probability 0.5.

The noise in net income could result from the random effects of recognition lag, as discussed earlier.

There are thus four possible net income numbers ranging from $125 to $37.50. The manager who works hard requires a 0.326 share of net income to attain reservation utility of 3. This is verified as follows:

$$
\begin{aligned}
EU_o(a_1) &= 0.6[0.5 \sqrt{0.326 \times 125} + 0.5 \sqrt{0.326 \times 75}] \\
&\quad + 0.4[0.5 \sqrt{0.326 \times 62.50} + 0.5 \sqrt{0.326 \times 37.50}] - 2 \\
&= 0.6[0.5 \sqrt{40.75} + 0.5 \sqrt{24.45}] + 0.4[0.5 \sqrt{20.38} + 0.5 \sqrt{12.22}] - 2 \\
&= (0.6 \times 5.66) + (0.4 \times 4.00) - 2 \\
&= 3.40 + 1.60 - 2 \\
&= 3.00
\end{aligned}
$$

Recall that the manager's utility for money is given by the square root of the amount received, and that the effort disutility of working hard is 2. The expression in the first set of square brackets is the expected utility of compensation given the high payoff. That is, if the payoff is going to be $100, net income will be $125 or $75, each with probability 0.5. This is then multiplied by the probability of the high payoff (0.6). A similar interpretation applies to the second expression, given the low payoff.

If the manager shirks, expected utility is 2.96, net of effort disutility of 1.7, as follows:

$$EU(a_2) = (0.4 \times 5.66) + (0.6 \times 4.00) - 1.7$$
$$= 2.26 + 2.40 - 1.7$$
$$= 2.96$$

Consequently, the manager will work hard.[7]

As in Example 9.2, the owner is risk neutral, with utility equal to the dollar amount of the payoff, net of manager compensation. The owner's expected utility is now:

$$EU_o(a_1) = 0.6[0.5(100 - (0.326 \times 125)) + 0.5(100 - (0.326 \times 75))]$$
$$+ 0.4[0.5(50 - (0.326 \times 62.50)) + 0.5(50 - (0.326 \times 37.50))]$$
$$= 0.6[0.5(100 - 40.75) + 0.5(100 - 24.45)]$$
$$+ 0.4[0.5(50 - 20.38) + 0.5(50 - 12.22)]$$
$$= (0.6 \times 67.40) + (0.4 \times 33.70)$$
$$= 40.44 + 13.48$$
$$= 53.92$$

The first expression in square brackets is the expected payoff net of manager compensation, given the high payoff. This is multiplied by the probability of the high payoff. A similar interpretation applies to the second expression given the low payoff.

Note that the owner's utility is greater than the utility of 47.38 under the rental contract. Thus the profit-sharing contract is more efficient. However, it is less efficient than the first-best contract of Example 9.2, where the owner's utility is 55. The agency cost is now $55 - 53.92 = 1.08$.

These differences in the owner's utility can be explained in terms of the agent's compensation risk. In the first-best contract, the manager bears no risk, since a salary of $25 is expected regardless of the amount of net income (i.e., zero profit share). In the rental contract (i.e., a 100% profit share), the manager bears all of the risk. In Example 9.3, the manager bears only part of the risk (i.e., a 0.326 profit share). Given the effort level, the more risk borne by the manager the higher the profit share needed to overcome the manager's risk aversion and enable reservation utility to be attained.[8] The higher the profit share to the manager, the less there remains for the owner or, equivalently, the higher the agency cost. Thus, the agency costs are zero, 1.08, and 7.62 for the first-best, profit sharing, and rental contracts, respectively. The most efficient contract short of first-best is called **second-best**. [9]

Note that it is the *contract* that motivates the manager to work hard in this example. Given the terms of the contract, the manager *wants* to take a_1. This aspect of the contract is called **incentive-compatibility**, since the agent's incentive to take a_1 is compatible with the owner's best interests. (The first-best contract, if it is attainable, is also incentive-compatible, because the prospect of reduced remuneration following a_2 motivates the manager to take a_1.) We then say that the owner's and manager's interests are **aligned**, since they both want the firm to do well.

Agency costs are one of the costs of contracting that are part of positive accounting theory. As discussed in Section 8.6.1, the firm will want to arrange its contracts as efficiently as possible, and we pointed out there that the efficient contracts will depend on the firm's form of organization and its environment. Since the firm in Example 9.3 is organized with a separation of ownership and control, we would expect it to design and adopt profit sharing contracts with the lowest agency costs. Such contracts impose the minimum compensation risk needed to motivate the manager to work hard.

This raises the question, can accountants improve the ability of net income to predict the payoff from current manager effort? This question is an important one for accountants. A less noisy payoff prediction will reduce compensation risk, enabling a lower profit-sharing proportion for the manager and increased contracting efficiency. This enhances the role of net income as a performance measure in managerial compensation plans.

EXAMPLE 9.4
LESS NOISY NET INCOME

A possible way to improve payoff prediction is to reduce recognition lag. To illustrate, suppose that improvements in estimating environmental liabilities and the fair value of R&D enable greater precision (i.e., reduced noise) in net income compared with Example 9.3.

Assume that the lower noise in net income is as follows:

- If the payoff is going to be $100, net income for the current period will be $110 with probability 0.5 and $90 with probability 0.5.

- If the payoff is going to be $50, net income for the current period will be $55 with probability 0.5 and $45 with probability 0.5.

The only difference from Example 9.3 is that net income, while still noisy and unbiased, falls within a narrower range of the ultimate payoff. It can be verified that the manager now requires 0.322 of profits to attain reservation utility, down from 0.326 above (see problem 18). Also, the manager continues to work hard.

The owner's expected utility is now:

$$
\begin{aligned}
EU_o(a_1) &= 0.6[0.5(100 - (0.322 \times 110)) + 0.5(100 - (0.322 \times 90))] \\
&\quad + 0.4[0.5(50 - (0.322 \times 55)) + 0.5(50 - (0.322 \times 45))] \\
&= 0.6[0.5(100 - 35.42) + 0.5(100 - 28.98)] \\
&\quad + 0.4[0.5(50 - 17.71) + 0.5(50 - 14.49)] \\
&= (0.6 \times 67.80) + (0.4 \times 33.90) \\
&= 40.68 + 13.56 \\
&= 54.24
\end{aligned}
$$

The owner's expected utility is greater than that of the noisier contract of Example 9.3 (53.92), reflecting reduced agency cost of 55 − 54.24 = 0.76 in place of 1.08 in Example 9.3. The improvement in accounting precision enables a more efficient compensation contract.

9.5 Manager's Information Advantage

9.5.1 Earnings Management

In Section 9.4, we assumed that the payoff was not observable by the owner or the manager until the next period. Net income, which *is* observable currently by both parties, was viewed as a noisy, unbiased message about what the payoff will be.

Consequently, the manager had no reporting discretion in Section 9.4. Net income was viewed simply as a noisy number produced by an accounting system. The manager could not control or manage this number since the noise resulted from the characteristics of the system rather than from anything the manager does. Of course, as we showed in Example 9.4, even in the absence of earnings management, accountants can increase contracting efficiency by reducing the noise through improved measurement.

Nevertheless, as any accountant knows, managers frequently do engage in earnings management. Indeed, this is a prediction of positive accounting theory. To better understand the role of net income as a performance measure, we must allow for the possibility that the manager may bias or otherwise manipulate reported earnings.

There is a variety of forms that manager information advantage can take. One possibility is that the manager may have information about the payoff prior to signing the contract (called **pre-contract information**). For example, the manager may have information that the high payoff will occur, and, unless the owner can extract this information, may enter into the contract with the intention of shirking, taking advantage of the high payoff to generate high earnings and compensation. Alternatively, the manager may obtain payoff information after signing the contract but prior to choosing an act (**pre-decision information**). If the payoff information is sufficiently bad, the manager may resign unless this situation is allowed for in the contract. Yet another possibility is that the manager receives information after the act is chosen (**post-decision information**). For example, the manager may learn what net income is before reporting to the owner. If the owner cannot observe unmanaged net income, the manager may misreport earnings so as to maximize compensation.

Here, we will examine a case of post-decision information. Specifically, we extend Example 9.3 by adding an assumption that the owner cannot observe which of the four possible net income numbers is actually realized. Only the manager can observe this. What the owner does observe is an earnings number *reported by* the manager. This assumption seems reasonable since the manager has the ability to influence the accounting system, creating the possibility that reported net income may be biased for his/her own purposes.[10]

EXAMPLE 9.5
BIASED REPORTING

Recall from Example 9.3 that there were four possible net income numbers. If the payoff is going to be $100, unmanaged net income could be $125 or $75, with equal probability. If the payoff is going to be $50, unmanaged net income could be $62.50 or $37.50, also with equal probability. When the owner cannot observe which of these is actually realized, it is not hard to see how the manager will opportunistically exploit this information advantage in a single-period contract. Given that the manager bears no costs to manage earnings, and that the higher is reported net income the higher is compensation, he/she will shirk, and report net income of $125 regardless of what unmanaged net income is. More formally:

$$EU_m(a_1) = 0.6\sqrt{125k} + 0.4\sqrt{125k} - 2$$
$$= \sqrt{125k} - 2$$
$$EU_m(a_2) = 0.4\sqrt{125k} + 0.6\sqrt{125k} - 1.7$$
$$= \sqrt{125k} - 1.7$$

where k is the profit-sharing proportion. Obviously, the manager will choose a_2 for any k. To receive reservation utility, the manager now requires k = 0.177:

$$EU_m(a_2) = \sqrt{0.177 \times 125} - 1.7$$
$$= \sqrt{22.13} - 1.7$$
$$= 4.7 - 1.7$$
$$= 3$$

The owner's expected utility is now:

$$EU_O(a_2) = 0.4(100 - (0.177 \times 125)) + 0.6(50 - (0.177 \times 125))$$
$$= 0.4(100 - 22.13) + 0.6(50 - 22.13)$$
$$= (0.4 \times 77.87) + (0.6 \times 27.87)$$
$$= 31.15 + 16.72$$
$$= 47.87$$

This is less than the owner's utility in the contract of Example 9.3 (53.92). The reduction arises because the manager can report the maximum net income regardless of effort. Consequently, the manager will shirk, and the owner's expected utility reflects the resulting lower expected payoff. Note also that the manager bears no risk, since the same compensation is received regardless of the payoff. We know from Example 9.3 that the manager bears risk if the work-hard effort alternative is to be chosen.

While the owner's utility is lower in Example 9.5 than in Example 9.3, Example 9.5 more closely approximates the actual situation of a firm owner, since we would normally *expect* the manager to have an information advantage, possibly using it to manage earnings. Given separation of ownership and control, it is unlikely that the owner would be able to observe the detailed workings of the firm's accounting and reporting systems. Then, the question arises, can the owner do anything to control this obviously unsatisfactory situation?

* EXAMPLE 9.6
THE REVELATION PRINCIPLE

In Example 9.5, the manager does not report truthfully. Can truthful reporting be motivated? If so, this would at least eliminate earnings management, irregardless of its effect on effort. The answer is a qualified yes. To illustrate, suppose that the owner offers the following amended contract in Example 9.5:

If net income is reported as \$125, $k = 0.177$
If net income is reported as \$75, $k = 0.295$
If net income is reported as \$62.50, $k = 0.354$
If net income is reported as \$37.50, $k = 0.590$

It is easy to verify that the manager still receives compensation of \$22.13 as in Example 9.5, regardless of what net income is reported (e.g., if net income of \$37.50 is reported, compensation is $37.50 \times 0.590 = 22.13$). Consequently, since no risk is borne, he/she will continue to shirk, receiving reservation utility of 3 as before. The owner continues to receive expected utility of 47.87. *What is different is that there is now no incentive for the manager to distort reported net income, since the same compensation is received regardless of what amount is reported.*[11] This example illustrates what is called the **revelation principle**, (Myerson, 1979; see also Christensen, 1981, and Arya, Glover, and Sunder, 1998). For any contract under which the manager has an incentive to lie about his/her private information, an equivalent contract can be designed that motivates truth-telling.

The revelation principle raises an intriguing question. Why not design real compensation contracts to motivate truth-telling? Then, opportunistic earnings management would be a thing of the past. While managers would tend to shirk, the shirking would be no greater than what would take place without truth-telling, and the owner's expected utility would be the same. The benefit would be increased investor confidence that reported net income is free of manager distortion and bias.

However, the revelation principle is not a panacea. There are several conditions that must be met if it is to hold. One such condition is that the owner must be able to commit that the truth will not be used against the manager. For example, if the manager anticipates that truthfully reporting net income of \$37.50 in Example 9.6 may result in being fired by an angry owner, he/she is unlikely to report the truth. Indeed, external forces may lead to earnings management even if the owner's reaction does not. For example, the manager may anticipate that a disappointed securities market, the managerial labour market, or an audit investigation will impose costs if low earnings are reported. Then, it would take a profit share greater than the 0.590 in Example 9.6 to motivate the truth.

A second condition is that there must be no restrictions on the form of contract. For example, many compensation contracts do not provide for a bonus unless performance exceeds some specified level, such as earnings greater than 10% of shareholders' equity. In addition, the amount of bonus may be capped so that no bonus is payable on

---

*The remainder of this section, and Section 9.5.2, can be skipped with little loss of continuity.

earnings greater than, say, 25% of equity. When such restrictions exist, we cannot be sure that the contract that motivates truth-telling will meet these restrictions. Furthermore, if no bonus is paid on earnings greater than 25% of equity, it is hard to say that the owner is not using the truth against the manager.

A third condition is that there are no restrictions on the manager's ability to communicate his/her information. Suppose, for example, that a manager has a forecast of next year's earnings, but that honest reporting of the forecast is potentially very costly to the manager due to loss of reputation and possible legal liability if the forecast is not met. A contract to motivate truthful reporting of the forecast would impose so much risk on the manager that the level of compensation needed to attain reservation utility may be more than the owner is willing to pay. Honest communication is effectively blocked. Consequently, the owner may allow the manager to report a biased forecast, or no forecast at all.

The impact of these restrictions is that we cannot rely on the revelation principle to assure us that the most efficient possible compensation contract involves truth telling. Under the assumptions of Example 9.5, a profit-sharing contract of 0.177 of reported net income to the manager, with owner's utility of 47.87, *is* the most efficient one available. If the revelation principle applies, we know from Example 9.6 that an equivalent contract involving reporting the truth yields the same utility to the owner. However, if the revelation principle does not apply, motivation of truthful reporting may require an increase in manager compensation, lowering the owner's expected utility below that of a contract that allows earnings management.

To illustrate, suppose that the manager will suffer costs, with monetary equivalent of $3, from lower reputation in the managerial labour market if net income of $37.50 is reported. Then, if he/she is to report this amount truthfully, a profit share of 0.670 is needed, giving compensation of $0.670 \times 37.50 = \$25.13$. Allowing for the costs of $3, the manager's net compensation is $22.13, the same as before. However, the extra $3 of compensation lowers the owner's expected utility. The owner is better off to revert to the contract of Example 9.5, which allows earnings management, thereby saving $3 in compensation and restoring expected utility of 47.87.

In effect, it is unlikely that the revelation principle can eliminate earnings management. Yet, Example 9.5 illustrates how earnings management can lead to manager shirking. Can accountants help? An answer lies in GAAP.

While GAAP allows discretion in choosing among different accounting policies, it does limit the amount by which earnings can be managed. In Example 9.5, if unmanaged net income of, say, $37.50 is realized, could the manager really increase reported earnings to $125? Hopefully, accounting standards do not allow distortion of this magnitude, particularly when the financial statements are audited. By allowing earnings to be managed, but controlling their magnitude through GAAP, the manager's incentive to work hard can be restored and the owner made better off. To illustrate, consider the following example.

* 9.5.2 Controlling Earnings Management

A way to control earnings management is to limit it by means of GAAP, to the point where the manager's incentive to work hard is restored. Consider the following example.

---

*This section can be omitted with little loss of continuity.

EXAMPLE 9.7
LIMITING THE BIAS IN NET INCOME

Extend Example 9.5 to replace each possible net income number (i.e., $125, $75, $62.50, $37.50) with a $5 range. For example, if the payoff is going to be $100, let current period net income (before any manager bias) fall within the range of [$125 – $130] with probability 0.5, rather than simply $125 with probability 0.5. Similarly, net income of $75 is replaced with a range [$75 – $80], also with probability 0.5. If the payoff is going to be $50, let unmanaged net income fall within the ranges [$67.50 – $62.50] with probability 0.5 or [$42.50 – $37.50], also with probability 0.5.

This range assumption recognizes the flexibility allowed by GAAP as discussed in Section 2.5.1. Straight-line and declining-balance amortization of capital assets are both acceptable methods, for example. Consequently, net income will differ depending on which method is chosen. The assumption of a range for unmanaged net income is also consistent with our argument in Section 2.6 that true net income does not exist.

The payoff probabilities are assumed unchanged. For example, if the manager works hard, the probability of the high payoff is still 0.6. We assume that the owner knows the four possible earnings ranges, and knows which range has occurred. For example, if the manager reports $130, the owner knows that while the manager may have biased this number, at least GAAP net income is in the range $125 – $130. This captures the fact that GAAP does impose some discipline on reported earnings. However, the owner does not know the actual unmanaged net income within that range.

To maximize compensation in a single-period contract, the rational manager will report the upper end of the appropriate range. For example, suppose that unmanaged net income is $128, that is, it is in the [$125 – $130] range. Think of the $128 as the earnings number that results from the use of accounting policies and methods that are best suited to the firm in question. Given information advantage, however, the manager will engage in earnings management to bias reported earnings up to $130. This could be accomplished, within GAAP, in a number of ways. For example, the manager may accelerate revenue recognition, or switch from declining balance to straight-line amortization. Note however, unlike Example 9.5, that the manager cannot switch between ranges. Thus, if unmanaged net income falls in the [$75 – $80] range, net income of $130 cannot be reported, etc.

Knowing that the manager will report the upper end of the range, a compensation contract of 0.305 of reported net income enables the manager to attain reservation utility. To verify, suppose a_1 is taken. Then, the manager's expected utility is:

$$EU_m(a_1) = 0.6[0.5 \sqrt{0.305 \times 130} + 0.5 \sqrt{0.305 \times 80}]$$
$$+ 0.4[0.5 \sqrt{0.305 \times 67.50} + 0.5 \sqrt{0.305 \times 42.50}] - 2$$
$$= 0.6[(0.5 \times 6.297) + (0.5 \times 4.940)] + 0.4[(0.5 \times 4.537) + (0.5 \times 3.600)] - 2$$
$$= (0.6 \times 5.619) + (0.4 \times 4.069) - 2$$
$$= 3.371 + 1.628 - 2$$
$$= 3.00$$

The first quantity in square brackets is the manager's expected compensation if the high payoff occurs. Under the high payoff, net income is in the range [$125 –

$130] with probability 0.5 and [\$75 – \$80] with probability 0.5. As mentioned, the manager will report the upper end of the range. This expected compensation is multiplied by the probability of the high payoff (0.6). A similar interpretation applies to the second quantity.

If act a_2 is taken:

$$EU_m(a_2) = 0.4[0.5 \sqrt{0.305 \times 130} + 0.5 \sqrt{0.305 \times 80}]$$
$$+ 0.6[0.5 \sqrt{0.305 \times 67.50} + 0.5 \sqrt{0.305 \times 42.50}] - 1.7$$
$$= (0.4 \times 5.619) + (0.6 \times 4.069) - 1.7$$
$$= 2.99$$

Thus the manager will now take a_1. The restrictions imposed by GAAP and auditing on the ability to mis-report does not eliminate the manager's ability to exploit his/her information advantage, but reduces it to the point where hard work must be undertaken to attain reservation utility.

As might be expected, this limitation on the manager's ability to mis-report benefits the owner. In fact, the owner's expected utility is now:

$$EU_o(a_1) = 0.6[0.5(100 - (0.305 \times 130)) + 0.5(100 - (0.305 \times 80))]$$
$$+ 0.4[0.5(50 - (0.305 \times 67.50)) + 0.5(50 - (0.305 \times 42.50))]$$
$$= 0.6[0.5(100 - 39.65) + 0.5(100 - 24.40)]$$
$$+ 0.4[0.5(50 - 20.59) + 0.5(50 - 12.96)]$$
$$= 0.6[(0.5 \times 60.35) + (0.5 \times 75.60)] + 0.4[(0.5 \times 29.41) + (0.5 \times 37.03)]$$
$$= (0.6 \times 67.97) + (0.4 \times 33.22)$$
$$= 40.78 + 13.29$$
$$= 54.07$$

The owner is thus better off than under the contract of Example 9.5, where expected utility was 47.87. This is because the limitation imposed by GAAP on the manager's ability to misreport net income has enabled a contract that restores an incentive to work hard. Note, however, that the contract does allow for some earnings management since, unless unmanaged net income is at the upper end of its range, the manager will bias it upwards.[12] In this sense, some degree of earnings management can be "good," even in a one-period contract.[13] We will return to this point in Chapter 11.

9.6 Discussion and Summary

In this section, we have studied a single-period agency model. This model illustrates several important aspects of agency theory:

1. Observability of an agent's effort seems unlikely in an owner-manager context, because of the separation of ownership and control that characterizes firms in a developed industrial society. This is an example of information asymmetry leading to moral hazard. The rational manager will, if possible, take advantage of the lack of effort observability to shirk. Agency theory, a branch of game theory, studies the problem

of designing a contract to control moral hazard. The most efficient contract does so with the lowest possible agency cost.

2. The nature of the most efficient contract depends crucially on what can be jointly observed. Contracts can only be written in terms of performance measures that are jointly observable by both principal and agent:

- If the agent's effort can be jointly observed, directly or indirectly, a fixed salary (subject to a penalty if the contracted-for effort level is not taken) is most efficient when the principal is risk-neutral. Such a contract is called first-best. There is no agency cost. Here, *effort* is the performance measure.

- Unless the firm is of very short duration, it is unlikely that the payoff from the current period's manager effort can be observed until after the end of the current period. This is because the cash flows from certain types of manager effort, such as R&D, will not be realized until a subsequent period, that is, until after the current compensation contract has expired. Given that the manager must be paid periodically, compensation cannot be based on the payoff.

- If the agent's effort cannot be jointly observed, but net income can, the most efficient contract may give the agent a share of net income. However, net income is a risky performance measure for the manager, both because the payoff is risky and because current period net income is a noisy measure of this payoff. Since the manager shares in net income, he/she bears compensation risk from both sources. Here, *net income* is the performance measure.

- If effort, payoff, and net income are all unobservable, the optimal contract is a rental contract, whereby the principal rents the firm to the manager for a fixed rental fee, thus internalizing the agent's effort decision. Such contracts are inefficient because they impose all of the firm's risk on the agent, resulting in maximum agency cost. Here, there is *no* performance measure.

3. Since the agent is assumed risk-averse, imposing compensation risk reduces his/her expected utility of compensation. This requires the principal to increase the share of net income so as to maintain the agent's reservation utility. The second-best contract is the contract that imposes the lowest amount of risk on the manager while maintaining reservation utility and the manager's incentive to work hard. Accountants can improve the efficiency of compensation contracts by improving the ability of net income to predict the payoff.

4. When net income is the performance measure, the manager has a further information advantage over the owner. This is because the manager controls the firm's accounting system, while the owner can observe only the net income number reported by the manager. This leads to the possibility of earnings management. In theory, it may be possible to design a compensation contract to motivate the manager to report unmanaged earnings (i.e., to completely eliminate earnings management), but this is unlikely in practice since it is too costly. However, by using GAAP to limit the range over which earnings can be managed, accountants may be able to maintain the manager's incentive to work hard. This leads to a conclusion that some degree of earnings management can be "good."

9.7 Agency Theory: A Bondholder–Manager Lending Contract

We now consider another moral hazard problem, namely a contract between a lender and a firm, such as a bondholder and the firm manager. We will regard the bondholder as the principal and the manager as the agent.

EXAMPLE 9.8
A LENDER–MANAGER AGENCY PROBLEM

A risk-neutral lender faces a choice of lending $100 to a firm or investing the $100 in government bonds yielding 10%. The firm offers 12% interest, contracting to repay the loan one year later, that is, to repay $112. However, unlike for government bonds, there is credit risk, that is, a possibility that the firm will go bankrupt, in which case the lender would lose both the principal and the interest.

The firm manager can choose one of two acts. The first act, denoted by a_1, is to pay no dividends while the loan is outstanding. The second act, a_2, is to pay high dividends. If the manager chooses a_1, assume that the lender assesses the probability of bankruptcy as 0.01, so that there is a 0.99 probability of receiving repayment, including $12 interest. However, if a_2 is chosen, the lender assesses the probability of bankruptcy as 0.1, because the high dividends will reduce the firm's solvency. Thus, under a_2, the probability of repayment will be only 0.9.

Assume that the manager is paid by means of an incentive contract consisting of a salary plus a bonus based on the firm's net income. Then, since dividends are not charged against income, the manager's remuneration is unaffected by the act chosen, that is, the manager is indifferent between the two acts. Thus, there is no compelling reason to assume that the manager will or will not take a_1, the lender's preferred act. After thinking about this, the lender assesses equal probabilities for each act of the manager, that is, the probability of a_1 is 0.5 and similarly for a_2. Table 9.4 summarizes this scenario.

TABLE 9.4 PAYOFFS FOR LENDER-MANAGER CONTRACT

	Manager's Act			
	a_1 (no dividends)		a_2 (high dividends)	
	Payoff	Probability	Payoff	Probability
x_1 (interest paid)	$ 12	0.99	$ 12	0.9
x_2 (bankrupt)	−100	0.01	−100	0.1

The payoff amounts in the table exclude the $100 loaned. Thus, the lender either earns an interest income of $12 or loses the $100 investment. We could add $100 to each payoff, to express returns gross of the $100 loaned, without affecting the results.

The probabilities in the table are conditional on the manager's chosen act. Thus, if a_1 is taken, the probability of the lender receiving the interest is 0.99; hence, the probability of the lender receiving nothing is 1.00 − 0.99 = 0.01, and so on. Recall that we have also assumed that the chances are 50/50 that a_1 will be chosen.

Will the lender be willing to lend $100 to the firm? The alternative is to buy government bonds, with a return of 10%, or $10 in total. The expected profit from investing in the firm is:

$$ETR = 0.5[(12 \times 0.99) - (100 \times 0.01)] + 0.5[(12 \times 0.9) - (100 \times 0.1)]$$
$$= (0.5 \times 10.88) + (0.5 \times 0.80)$$
$$= 5.44 + 0.40$$
$$= 5.84$$

where ETR denotes expected total return.

The first term in brackets represents the lender's expected return conditional on a_1. There is a 0.5 probability that a_1 will be chosen. Similarly, the second term in brackets is the expected return conditional on a_2, also multiplied by the 0.5 probability that a_2 will be chosen.

Thus, the ETR is only $5.84 or 5.84% on the amount loaned. The reason, of course, is the probability of bankruptcy, particularly if a_2 is taken, which forces the expected return down to well below the nominal rate of 12%. Our lender, who can earn 10% elsewhere, will not make the loan.

What nominal rate would the firm have to offer in order to attract the lender? This can be calculated as follows:

$$10.00 = 0.5[(0.99R - 100) \times 0.01] + 0.5[0.9R - (100 \times 0.1)]$$

where R is the required nominal rate. The left side is the lender's required total return. Upon solving for R, we obtain:

$$R = \frac{15.50}{0.945} = 16.40$$

Thus, the firm would have to offer a nominal rate of return of over 16% in order to attract the lender.

The 16% interest rate in Example 9.8 would probably seem too high to the manager, particularly if he or she shares in net income. Consequently, the manager may try to find some more efficient contractual arrangement that would lower the interest rate. One possibility would be to *commit* to take a_1. This could be done by writing covenants into the lending agreement. An example of a covenant would be to pay no dividends if the interest coverage ratio is below a specified level. Another example would be to not undertake any additional borrowing (which would dilute the security of existing lenders) if shareholders' equity is below a specified level. Since covenants are legally binding, the lender will change the assessed probabilities of the acts. Assume the probability that the manager will take a_1 is now assessed by the lender as 1, and 0 for a_2. Thus, if the firm offers a nominal rate of 12%, the lender's ETR is:

$$ETR = 1[(12 \times 0.99) - (100 \times 0.01)] + 0[(12 \times 0.9) - (100 \times 0.1)] = 10.88$$

Since this exceeds the required $10, the lender would now make the loan.

9.7.1 Summary

The main point to realize in Example 9.8 is the existence of a moral hazard problem between lenders and firm managers—managers may act contrary to the best interests of the lenders. Rational lenders will anticipate this behaviour, however, and raise the interest rates they demand for their loans. As a result, the manager has an incentive to commit not to act in a manner that is against the lenders' interests. This can be done by inserting covenants into the lending agreement whereby the manager agrees to limit dividends or additional borrowing while the loan is outstanding. Consequently, the firm is able to borrow at lower rates.

9.8 Implications of Agency Theory for Accounting

9.8.1 Holmström's Agency Model

In a widely referenced paper, Holmström (1979) gives a rigorous development of the agency model. We now review aspects of his model from an accounting perspective.

Holmström assumes that the agent's effort is unobservable by the principal but that the payoff is jointly observable at the end of the current period. This is contrary to our Examples 9.2 to 9.7. However, Feltham and Xie (1994) show that Holmström's model carries over to the case of payoff unobservable, holding the set of possible manager acts constant. Consequently, we shall continue to assume the payoff is unobservable for purposes of this discussion.

Holmström shows formally that a contract based on a performance measure such as net income is less efficient than first-best, consistent with Example 9.3. As in that example, the source of the efficiency loss is the necessity for the risk-averse agent to bear risk in order to overcome the tendency to shirk.

This raises the question of whether the second-best contract could be made more efficient by basing it on a second performance measure in addition to net income. For example, share price is also informative about manager performance. Rather than basing manager compensation solely on net income, would basing the contract on *both* net income and share price reduce the agency costs of the second-best contract?

Holmström shows that the answer to this question is yes, provided that the second measure is also jointly observable, and conveys some information about manager effort beyond that contained in the first measure.[14] This should be the case for share price, since it is jointly observable and based on more information than just accounting information. Granted, share price reflects the information content of net income (Sections 5.3 and 5.4). However, share price on an efficient securities market also reflects other information. For example, it reflects expected future benefits of R&D, and expected future environmental and legal liabilities, sooner than the accounting system. Furthermore, share price may be less subject to manager manipulation and bias than net income. Consequently, we would expect it to reveal information about manager effort different from that in reported earnings. In effect, net income and share price together better reflect current manager effort than either variable alone.

Of course, share price tends to be quite volatile, being affected by economy-wide events. Nevertheless, Holmström's analysis shows that no matter how noisy the second variable is, it can be used to increase the efficiency of the second-best contract if it contains at least some additional effort information.[15]

The question then becomes one of the relative *proportion* of compensation based on net income, versus based on share price, in compensation contracts. Hopefully, from an accountant's standpoint, this proportion will be high. Thus, an interesting implication of the Holmström model is that, just as net income competes with other information sources for investors under efficient securities market theory, it competes with other information sources for motivating managers under agency theory.

This raises the question of what characteristics a performance measure should have if it is to contribute to efficient compensation contracts. One important characteristic is its **sensitivity**. Sensitivity is the rate at which the expected value of a performance measure increases as the manager works harder, or decreases as the manager shirks. Sensitivity contributes to efficient compensation contracts by "tightening up" the connection between manager effort and the performance measure, thereby making it easier to motivate that effort. Ideally, if the manager increases effort by, say, 10%, the expected value of the performance measure should also increase by 10%, and vice versa. This may not happen, however, to the extent that the performance measure does not currently capture all aspects of effort. For example, if an increase in effort is devoted to R&D, current net income would include little, if any, of the payoff from this effort. Note that fair value accounting for R&D can be regarded as a way to increase earnings sensitivity. By recognizing changes in fair values sooner, it captures more of the results of manager effort in current income.

Another important characteristic of a performance measure is its **precision** in predicting the payoff from current manager effort. Precision is measured as the reciprocal of the variance of the noise in the performance measure. When a performance measure is precise, there is a relatively low probability that it will differ substantially from the payoff. Precision contributes to efficient compensation contracts by reducing the manager's compensation risk. As illustrated in Example 9.4, lower compensation risk increases contract efficiency.

Note that there is a tradeoff between sensitivity and precision. Attempts to increase sensitivity of net income by adopting fair value accounting may reduce precision, since fair value estimates tend to be imprecise. For example, precision may be a serious problem if accountants were to adopt fair value accounting for R&D, due to problems of estimating its fair value.

RRA can also be viewed as an attempt to increase earnings sensitivity, since it reflects manager effort devoted to proving oil and gas reserves sooner than historical cost accounting. However, RRA suffers from low precision. We see this with a vengeance in Chieftain International's RRA income statement (Table 2.5), where adjustments of the prior period's estimates dominated the income calculation. While Chieftain's RRA earnings may be relatively sensitive to current manager exploration and development efforts, they are a relatively imprecise measure of the payoff from these efforts.

The characteristics needed by net income if it is to be a sensitive and precise performance measure are not necessarily the same as those needed if it is to be a useful input into investment decisions. RRA, for example, may provide useful information to investors (if its relevance outweighs its low reliability) while it may not contribute to efficient compensations contracts (if its lack of precision outweighs its sensitivity).

We conclude that the challenge for accountants to maintain and increase the role of net income as a manager performance measure is to produce a net income number that represents the best possible tradeoff between sensitivity and precision. This tradeoff is not necessarily the same as the best tradeoff between relevance and reliability in informing investors.

9.8.2 Rigidity of Contracts

Agency theory assumes that the courts will costlessly enforce contract provisions. While the parties to a contract could agree among themselves to amend contract provisions following an unfortunate realization of the state of nature, this can be surprisingly difficult. Contracts tend to be *rigid* once signed. The reasons for this rigidity need some discussion. Otherwise, we might ask, if economic consequences have their roots in the contracts that managers enter into, why not just *renegotiate* the contracts following a change in GAAP, or other unforeseen state realization.

Note first that it is generally impossible to anticipate all contingencies when entering into a contract. For example, unless the contract is of very short duration, it would be difficult to predict changes in GAAP that could affect the contract. In Example 9.8, the firm's ability to avoid debt covenant violation would be reduced if, say, a new accounting standard restricts the firm's ability to switch between amortization methods. Such a standard would preclude the manager from managing covenant ratios by changing amortization method. Consequently, the probability of covenant violation increases. It is unlikely that the contract anticipated the change in GAAP that caused this increase.

Contracts that do not anticipate all possible state realizations are termed **incomplete**. The contracts in Examples 9.3 to 9.8 are **complete**. Thus, in Example 9.3, the only possible state realizations are θ_1 and θ_2, leading to payoffs x_1 and x_2, respectively. While the set of possible state realizations could be expanded in the examples, in an actual contract the parties could not anticipate all possibilities.

For example, suppose that a new GAAP accounting policy lowers reported net income and increases its volatility. The manager goes to the bondholder and explains that, through no one's fault, the accounting rules have changed and requests that the coverage ratio covenant be reduced from 3:1 to 2:1. This, the manager argues, would maintain the bondholder's protection at what it was before the rule change. Why should the bondholder agree to such a request? In doing so, he or she is giving something away—namely the increased protection against excessive dividends that resulted from the new accounting policy. To be willing to do this, the bondholder may well require something in return, such as a higher interest rate. The problem for the manager is further complicated if, as is usually the case, there are many bondholders. Agreement would then be required from all of them, or, at least, a majority. The manager's compensation contract with the firm owner would be similarly difficult to amend. If the manager requests, say, a higher bonus rate, to correct for an accounting policy change that lowers reported net income and/or increases its volatility, the compensation committee of the board of directors may want something in return, or even reopen the entire contract for renegotiation.

Building a formal provision for renegotiation into the contract *beforehand* is possible, but if the renegotiation is generous towards the manager (e.g., it may let the manager "off the hook" following an unfortunate state realization), the prospect of such renegotiation reduces the manager's effort incentive, which would not be in the owner's best interests.[16]

In effect, a consequence of entering into contracts is just that—they are contracts, and hence tend towards rigidity. Thus, unforeseen state realizations impose costs on the firm and/or the manager. The manager who is unfavourably affected by a change of the accounting rules in midstream may be forced to take out his or her displeasure on the accountants who introduced the rule change rather than on the other parties to the contract. It is contract incompleteness that drives the economic consequences discussed in Chapter 8.

Theory in Practice 9.1

The severe consequences of contract incompleteness and rigidity are illustrated by Mosaic Group Inc., a large designer of marketing programs for major companies.

In its third quarter, 2002, report, Mosaic Group reported an operating loss of over $395 million, after a writedown of goodwill of $347.6 million. The company had been hit by bad economic times and the loss of several major customers, state realizations that were unanticipated when its debt contracts were signed. The large loss put the firm into violation of its debt covenants. Its lenders were unwilling to waive the covenant requirements or amend the credit agreements.

Mosaic filed for bankruptcy protection in 2003. Its shares were delisted by the Toronto Stock Exchange in April 2004.

9.9 Reconciliation of Efficient Securities Market Theory with Economic Consequences

We now see how firms are able to align manager and shareholder interests, consistent with the efficient contracting version of positive accounting theory. Agency theory demonstrates that the best attainable compensation contract usually bases manager compensation on one or more measures of performance. Then, managers have an incentive to maximize performance. Since higher performance leads to higher expected payoff, this is a goal also desired by shareholders.

This alignment explains why accounting policies have economic consequences, despite the implications of efficient securities market theory. Under efficient securities market theory, only accounting policy choices that affect expected cash flows create economic consequences. The contracting-based argument we have given for economic consequences does not depend on accounting policy choices having direct cash flow effects. This argument is the same whether direct cash flow effects are present or not.

Rather, it is the rigidities produced by the signing of binding, incomplete contracts that create managers' concerns, and that lead to their intervention in the standard-setting process. These rigidities have nothing to do with whether accounting policy changes affect cash flows.

Thus, economic consequences and efficient securities markets are not necessarily inconsistent. Rather, they can be reconciled by positive accounting theory, with normative support from agency theory that suggests *why* firms enter into employment and debt contracts that depend on accounting information. Nothing in the above arguments leading to managerial concern about accounting policies conflicts with securities market efficiency.

Similarly, nothing in the theory of efficient securities markets conflicts with managerial concern about accounting policies. Joint consideration of both theories, though, helps us to see that managers may well intervene in accounting policies, even though those policies would improve the decision usefulness of financial statements to investors. Thus, in the final analysis, the interaction between managers and investors is a game, as modelled in Sections 9.3 to 9.8.

While game theory is consistent with *managers'* concerns about accounting policies, the theory also helps us to understand Lev's finding (Section 8.4), that *investors* were also concerned about such policies. One interpretation of Lev's finding is that the securities market is inefficient. Security prices fell in response to the prospect of an accounting policy change that would tend to lower reported net income of affected firms but would not affect their cash flows.

An alternative interpretation, however, is that Lev's finding is evidence of market efficiency, rather than inefficiency. To see this, consider once again the impact of successful-efforts accounting on reported net income, namely, that it will tend to lower income and make it more volatile. Both of these effects will increase the probability of violation of covenants in borrowing agreements. Since violation of debt covenants can have serious implications, the efficient market bids down the share prices accordingly. Also, these effects reduce the expected utility of managers' future bonuses, particularly if the manager is risk-averse. Given contract rigidity, this may lead managers to change the way they operate the firm. For example, in response to the increased volatility of reported net income, managers of firms affected by the switch to successful-efforts may adopt safer exploration policies to reduce their compensation risk. Since these policies may offer significantly lower expected returns than the policies they replace, diversified investors may bid down share prices in response. Thus, when contracting effects are recognized, securities market reaction to a paper change in accounting policy may support the theory of market efficiency rather than inefficiency.

9.10 Conclusions on the Analysis of Conflict

The various conflict-based theories described in this chapter have important implications for financial accounting theory. These can be summarized as follows:

1. Conflict theories enable a reconciliation of efficient securities markets and economic consequences. Early applications of efficient market theory to financial accounting (as, for example, in Beaver's early article, discussed in Section 4.3) suggested that accountants concentrate on full disclosure of information useful for investors' decision needs. The form of disclosure and the particular accounting policies used did not matter, as the market would see through these to their ultimate cash flow implications.

   Certainly, accountants have adopted the decision usefulness approach and its full-disclosure implications, and there is extensive empirical evidence that markets do respond to accounting information much as the theory predicts. Frequently, however, as noted in Chapter 8, management intervened in the standard-setting process. This was not predicted by efficient securities market theory, since under that theory the market value of a firm's securities should be independent of its accounting policies, unless cash flows were affected. Why would management care about accounting policies if these do not affect its cost of capital? An answer is that changes in account-ing policies can affect provisions in contracts that firm managers have entered into, thereby affecting their expected utility and the welfare of the firm.

The reason why accounting policies can affect manager and firm welfare should be carefully considered. The basic problem is one of information asymmetry. In an owner–manager context, the manager knows his or her own effort in running the firm on the owner's behalf, but typically the owner cannot observe this effort. Knowing this, the manager faces a temptation to shirk. Thus, there is a moral hazard problem between owner and manager. To control moral hazard, the owner can offer the manager a share of reported net income. This profit sharing motivates the manager to work harder. However, it also means that the manager has a personal interest in how net income is measured. The firm will want to induce the desired effort as efficiently as possible.

When managers enter into borrowing contracts with lenders, similar implications for manager and firm welfare occur. Borrowing contracts typically contain covenants that restrict the payment of dividends depending on the values of certain financial-statement-based ratios, such as interest coverage. Since covenant violations can be cost-ly to the firm, both the manager and the firm will have a personal interest in accounting policy changes that affect the probability of covenant violation, particu-larly if they share in firm profits.

Thus, economic consequences can be seen as a rational result of the rigidities introduced by entering into binding, incomplete contracts. The conflict situation between managers, who may object to accounting policies that have adverse eco-nomic consequences for them and their firms, and investors, who desire full disclo-sure, can be modelled as non-cooperative or cooperative games.

2. An implication of agency theory is that net income has a role to play in motivating and monitoring manager performance. Arguably, this role is equally as important in society as facilitating the proper operation of capital markets by providing useful information to investors. The characteristics needed for net income to fulfil an impor-tant role in efficient contracting differ from those needed to provide useful infor-mation to investors. The ability of net income to fulfil a manager performance-enhancing role depends on its sensitivity and precision as a measure of the payoff from current manager effort while usefulness for investors depends on its ability to reliably provide relevant information about future firm performance.

3. Net income competes with other performance measures, such as share price. Unless accountants maintain and improve the precision and sensitivity needed for a good per-formance measure, they may expect to see a decline in the role of net income in manager compensation plans.

4. If carried to the extreme, earnings management allows manager shirking, with result-ing low payoffs to owners. Complete elimination of earnings management is not cost-effective. However, by controlling earnings management through GAAP, accountants can restore the manager's incentive to work hard, thereby increasing payoffs to owners.

For these various reasons, game theory is an important component of financial accounting theory. In addition to enabling a better understanding of the conflicting interests of various constituencies affected by financial reporting, it has encouraged research into executive compensation and earnings management. Chapters 10 and 11 will review some of this research.

Questions and Problems

1. Why is manager effort usually unobservable to the firm's owners? What problem of information asymmetry results? If the manager receives a straight salary, what is the effect of this information asymmetry on the rational manager's effort in a single-period contract?

2. Give some reasons why the payoff from the manager's current-period effort is typically not fully observable until a subsequent period.

3. If net income is an unbiased (i.e., noisy) measure of manager performance, lower noise enables a more efficient compensation contract. Explain why. Suggest ways that accountants can reduce noise in net income.

4. Why do debt contracts typically impose covenants based on accounting information such as working capital, times interest earned, and debt-to-equity, etc.?

5. Why is net income not fully informative about manager effort?

6. Define the concepts of sensitivity and precision of a performance measure. How can accountants increase sensitivity? Precision? Why do these two desirable qualities have to be traded off?

7. Suppose in Example 9.3 that net income turns out to be $25, despite the assumption that net income can only be one of $125, $75, $62.50, and $37.50. How could this happen, and what does it say about the completeness of the compensation contract in the example? How might the manager react to this lower net income number?

8. U-Haul, a "do-it-yourself" moving company, is doing a booming business these days. The reason is that some companies relocating employees are changing the way they reimburse moving expenses. Before the change, moves were very expensive, because the companies paid for everything. Now, the companies pay a fixed amount to the employee, who can keep the savings, if there are any. Explain this change using agency theory concepts. Also, U-Haul offers to reimburse customers for the cost of oil used during the move, while customers have to pay for their own gasoline. Why? (CGA-Canada)

9. The controversy over expensing of ESOs in the United States can be analyzed as a non-cooperative game. Let the two players be the large, powerful corporations who wish to prevent expensing, and the FASB. Each player faces two strategies. The "cooperate" strategy happens when a player accedes to the demands of the other, or, at least, expresses a willingness to compromise. One compromise, for example, could be to expense only ESOs granted to senior officers, with those granted to all other employees reported only as supplementary information. Another could be to delay an expensing decision to give time to work out a compromise. The "strong" strategy

involves a player sticking to its own preferred policy and attempting to win support in the Congress.

Hypothetical, but reasonable, payoffs for each player are summarized in the following table.

		FASB	
		Cooperate	**Strong**
	Cooperate	30, 30	8, 40
Corporations			
	Strong	20, 10	12, 15

In each box, the first number represents the corporations' payoff and the second number the FASB's payoff. Consider the lower left payoffs. Here, the corporations play strong, that is, they vigorously oppose expensing and proceed to gather support for their position from the Congress. The FASB backs down, as it did in 1994, and allows all ESO expense to continue to be reported in the financial statement notes. The corporations' payoff is 20 in this case, because it is seen as the dominant player. However, because this strategy erodes their relationship with the FASB, generates political controversy, and alienates other constituencies who feel that standard setting should be done in the private sector, its payoff is less than the 30 it would receive if both players had cooperated to reach a compromise solution. The FASB receives a very low payoff of 10, because it is perceived as capitulating to the corporations' demands. If the corporations cooperate, however, and formulate a compromise, with payoffs of 30 each, the FASB may seize on this as an expression of weakness and force through its preferred expensing option. Then, the FASB's payoff is 40, since it is seen as the dominant player, and the corporations suffer an embarrassing defeat with payoff of only 8. If both parties play strong, no agreement is possible and the question of ESO expensing has to be settled in the Congress. Here, both parties lose, with low payoffs as shown in the lower right of the table.

Required
a. Given the payoffs as shown, which strategy pair do you predict the players will choose?
b. Is this strategy pair a Nash equilibrium? Explain.
c. Both parties would be better off if they cooperated. Explain why this strategy pair is unlikely to be chosen.

10. The shareholders of X Ltd. will vote at the forthcoming annual meeting on a proposal to establish a bonus plan, based on firm performance, for X Ltd. management. Proponents of the plan argue that management will work harder under a bonus plan and that expected cash flows will thereby increase. However, a dissident shareholder group argues that there is little point in granting a bonus plan, because management will bias or otherwise manage earnings to increase their bonus, rather than working harder.

Upon investigation, you estimate that if the bonus plan is granted, expected operating cash flows will be $150 if management does not manage earnings, and $140 if it does, *before* management remuneration in each case (cash flows are lower in the latter case because management uses earnings management to disguise shirking). Management remuneration, including the bonus, would be $50 if it does not manage earnings and $60 if it does. Assume that cash flows not paid as management remuneration will go to the shareholders. If the bonus plan is not granted, expected cash flows will be $140 before management remuneration if management does not manage earnings and $100 if it does. Management remuneration would be $30 in either case, with the balance of cash flows going to the shareholders.

Required
a. Prepare a payoff table for the above game between shareholders and management.
b. Which strategy pair will be chosen? That is, identify a Nash equilibrium for the game. Assume both players are risk-neutral.
c. What is the main advantage of a game theory approach to modelling the management's decision whether to manage earnings, rather than modelling it as a single-person decision theory problem of the manager?

11. The following table depicts a non-cooperative game between an investor in a firm's shares and the firm's auditor.

		Auditor	
		Work for Investor	**Work for Manager**
	Invest	5, 4	2, 6
Investor			
	Do not Invest	3, 1	3, 3

The investor has two strategies—invest or not invest. The auditor can choose to work for the investor by ensuring that the firm's financial statements are free of opportunistic earnings management, or to work for the manager by allowing opportunistic earnings management which may mislead the investor but benefit the manager.

The number pairs in the table represent the utility payoff to the investor and manager, respectively, for each strategy combination. The rationale for these payoffs is as follows:

Invest, Work for investor: The investor receives high-quality information, but the auditor incurs high audit costs due to time spent arguing with the manager and possible loss of audit engagement.

Invest, Work for manager: The investor receives low-quality information, but the auditor's costs are lower.

Do not invest, Work for investor:	The investor buys lower-yielding securities. The firm's cost of capital rises due to lower demand for its shares. As a result, its earnings fall. Auditor incurs high audit costs and manager demands lower audit fee due to lower firm earnings.
Do not invest, Work for manager:	The investor buys lower-yielding securities. The auditor's audit costs are lower due to less arguing with manager but audit fee is still low due to lower firm earnings.

Required

a. Identify the Nash equilibrium of this game and explain why this is the predicted outcome of the game.

b. Identify the cooperative solution. Explain why it is unlikely to be attained in a single-play of this game.

c. Outline three possible ways that the cooperative solution may be attained.

12. Pierre's small business has grown to the point where he plans to hire a full-time manager. Pierre, an architect, has little inclination and ability to manage a medium-sized, fast-growing business himself. He plans to semi-retire, devoting his working hours to consulting on issues of design and project management. Pierre's accounting system is quite simple. There is no R&D or other recognition lags. Consequently, the firm's payoff and its net income for the year are equal.

Pierre is negotiating with Yvonne as a possible manager. He wants the manager to work hard, since his past experience is that hard work generates a net income (before any manager compensation) of $2,000 90% of the time, and $900 10% of the time. Pierre's recent experience, when he has not worked hard, is that the $2,000 net income is generated only 10% of the time, otherwise net income is $900.

During the negotiations, Pierre ascertains that Yvonne is both risk- and effort-averse. Her utility for money is equal to the square root of the amount of money received. Her disutility for effort is 4 if she works hard and 1.1 if she shirks. Her reservation utility is 11.

Pierre decides that Yvonne is ideal for the job. He quickly offers her annual cash compensation of a $100 salary plus 10% of net income before manager compensation. Yvonne immediately accepts.

Required

a. Show calculations to demonstrate why Yvonne accepts the position.

b. After two years, Pierre is worried because net income has been $900 each year. He decides to change Yvonne's compensation contract. After consulting a compensation specialist, he offers her a salary of $52.30 plus a profit share of 9.21% of net income before manager compensation. Yvonne hesitates, but decides to accept. Show calculations to demonstrate why she hesitates but accepts.

c. Pierre is risk neutral, with utility equal to the amount of profit received after manager compensation. Is Pierre's expected utility higher or lower under the new contract in **b**, compared to the original contract in **a**? Show calculations and explain why there is a difference.

Note: Take calculations to two decimal places.

13. Growth Ltd. is a high-tech firm whose owner does not have the required management expertise to run the firm. The owner wants to hire a manager with the required expertise. The continued success of Growth Ltd. depends crucially on how hard the new manager works.

If the manager works hard (a_1), firm net income will be $500 with probability 0.7 and $200 with probability 0.3. If the manager shirks (a_2), net income will be $500 with probability 0.2 and $200 with probability 0.8. In both cases, profits are before manager compensation.

The owner is interviewing a prospective manager, and finds out that she is risk-averse, with utility for compensation equal to the square root of the dollar compensation received. Like most people, however, she is also effort-averse. If she works hard, she suffers a disutility of effort of 2 units of utility. If she shirks, her effort disutility is zero.

Required

a. Growth Ltd. offers the manager a one-period contract with a salary of $41 per period plus 20% of net income before manager compensation. Will the manager take a_1 or a_2? Show your calculations.
b. Instead, Growth offers the manager zero salary plus 30% of net income before manager compensation. Assuming the manager accepts, will she take a_1 or a_2? Show your calculations.
c. Does the manager's effort decision change between parts **a** and **b** above? Explain why or why not.
d. Many executive compensation contracts base the manager's compensation on *both* net income and share price performance. Explain an advantage of using two performance measures rather than one in compensation contracts.

14. Tom operates a small, fast-growing electronics business. His workload has expanded to the point where he decides to hire a full-time manager, so that he can concentrate on the technical aspects of the business.

Tom is negotiating with Lily for the manager job. He ascertains that Lily is risk averse, with utility for money equal to the square root of the dollar compensation received.

Lily advises Tom that she already has a job offer, which yields her an expected utility of 6. She is not willing to work for less than this, but would accept an expected utility of 6 from Tom. Lily also advises that she is effort-averse, with disutility of effort of 2 if she works hard, and 1 if she does not work hard.

Tom's business has, in previous years, earned net income (before manager compensation) of $725 75% of the time, and income of $0 25% of the time. Tom has always worked hard (a_1), and reckons that if he did not work hard net income would have been $725 only 20% of the time and zero for 80% of the time. He expects this earnings pattern to continue into the future with a new manager. Tom realizes that he must motivate Lily to work hard, and offers her compensation based on a proportion of reported net income before manager compensation.

Required

a. What proportion of net income must Tom offer Lily so that she will accept the position and work hard? Show calculations.

b. Assuming that Lily accepts Tom's offer, verify that she will in fact work hard.

c. Having accepted the position, Lily soon realizes that she can opportunistically manage earnings so as to *ensure* that net income of $725 is reported, even if she does not work hard. Calculate whether or not, in a one-year contract, Lily is better off to work hard and not manage earnings or to not work hard and manage earnings.

d. State and explain two reasons why a manager who may be tempted to *not* work hard and cover up by opportunistic earnings management would not do so.

15. Henri owns and operates a small successful sporting goods store. He has not had a holiday for three years. He decides to take an extensive one-year trip around the world, and is negotiating with Marie to operate the store while he is away. The store's earnings are highly dependent on how hard the manager works, as per the following table:

	a_1: Work Hard		a_2: Shirk	
	Net Income	Prob.	Net Income	Prob.
x_1: High Earnings	$300	0.7	$300	0.2
x_2: Low Earnings	$80	0.3	$80	0.8

Marie, like most people, is risk-averse and effort-averse. Her utility for money is equal to the square root of the amount of money received. If she works hard, her effort disutility is 2. If she shirks, her effort disutility is 1.6.

Marie informs Henri that she is willing to accept the manager position but that she must receive at least an expected utility of 3.41, or she would be better off to work somewhere else. Henri, who is not an agency theory expert, offers Marie a salary of $20 plus 5% of the store earnings (after deducting $20 salary from the earnings in the table). Marie immediately accepts.

Required

a. If Henri hires her, which act will Marie take? Why did she immediately accept? Show calculations.

b. Henri's bank manager, to whom he has turned for advice, suggests that if he hires an agent, the store's annual earnings should be audited by a professional accountant. Explain why.

c.   Assume that Henri hires Marie under the contract proposed, that is, $20 salary plus 5% of profits after salary. Shortly after he leaves, a new accounting standard requires that estimated customer liability be accrued. This lowers the high earnings to $286 and the low earnings to $40 in the table above. The payoff probabilities are unaffected. Which act will Marie now take? Show calculations. Will Marie be concerned about the new standard? Explain why or why not.

16. Mr. K, a risk-neutral investor, is contemplating a one-year 8% loan of $500 to firm J. Mr. K demands at least a 6% expected return per annum on loans like this. K is concerned that the firm may not be able to pay the interest and/or principal at the end of the year. A further concern is that if he makes the loan, firm J may engage in additional borrowing. If so, K's security would be diluted and the firm would become more risky. Since firm J is growing rapidly, K is sure that the firm would engage in additional borrowing if he makes the loan.

K examines firm J's most recent annual report and calculates an interest coverage ratio (ratio of net income before interest and taxes to interest expense) of 4, including the contemplated $500 loan.

Upon considering all of these matters, K assesses the following probabilities:

Payoff	Probability
θ_1: Interest and principal repaid	0.80
θ_2: Reorganization, principal repaid but not interest	0.18
θ_3: Bankruptcy, nothing repaid	0.02
	1.00

Required

a.   Should Mr. K make the loan? Show calculations.

b.   Firm J offers to add a covenant to its lending agreement with Mr. K, undertaking not to engage in any additional borrowing if its interest coverage ratio falls below 4 before the next year-end. Mr. K estimates that there is a 60% probability that the interest coverage ratio will fall below 4. If it does, there would be no dilution of his equity by additional borrowing, and he feels the lower coverage ratio would still be adequate. He assesses that his payoff probabilities would then be:

Payoff	Probability
θ_1	0.95
θ_2	0.04
θ_3	0.01

If the coverage ratio does not fall below 4, the resulting additional borrowing and dilution of security would cause him to assess payoff probabilities as:

Payoff	Probability
θ_1	0.85
θ_2	0.14
θ_3	0.01

Should Mr. K now make the loan? Show calculations. (CGA-Canada)

17. Toni Difelice is contemplating lending $10,000 to Tech Enterprises Ltd. Tech offers her 8% interest with the principal to be repaid at the end of the year. Toni carefully examines the financial statements of Tech Enterprises and is concerned about its interest coverage ratio, which is currently at 1.8:1. She feels that there is a 5% chance that Tech will go bankrupt, in which case she would only recover $2,000 of her principal and no interest. She suggests a debt covenant in the lending contract, whereby Tech promises not to issue any more debt beyond what Toni invests if its interest coverage ratio falls below 1.6:1. With such covenant protection, Toni assesses only a 1% probability of bankruptcy and subsequent recovery of only $2,000.

The manager of Tech Enterprises agrees to this request, providing that Toni reduce her interest rate to 5%.

Toni is risk-averse, with a mean-variance utility function:

$$U(a) = 2x_a - \sigma_a^2$$

where a is her investment act, x_a is the expected return on a, and σ_a^2 is the variance of the return of a.

Required

a. Which act should Toni take?

a_1 : 8% interest, no debt covenant

a_2 : 5% interest, debt covenant

b. Explain why the manager of Tech Enterprises would be concerned about new accounting standards that may come into effect after the lending contract with Toni is concluded. Consider both standards that will tend to lower reported net income and standards that will increase its volatility.

18. Refer to Example 9.4. Show calculations to verify the statement in the example that with a profit share of 0.322 the manager will work hard and receive reservation utility.

Explain why the contract of Example 9.4 is more efficient than the contract of Example 9.3. How can accountants contribute to this greater efficiency?

19. A problem with many games is that they can have multiple Nash equilibria. This makes it difficult to predict the outcome of the game.

As an illustration of a non-cooperative game with multiple equilibria, consider the following payoff table:

		Country 1	
		Keep	**Violate**
Country 2	**Keep**	100, 100	50, 200
	Violate	200, 50	50, 50

Required

a. Identify three Nash equilibria of this game.

b. Suppose that this game will be repeated a known, finite number of times. Suppose that the current equilibrium is in the lower left portion of the table. Describe an action by country 1 that would cause a shift to a new equilibrium.

c. Suppose that the game will be repeated an indefinite (i.e., infinite) number of times. What equilibrium would you then predict? Explain.

Notes

1. The discussion here assumes only pure strategies, that is, strategies where one act is chosen with probability 1. It is possible to have mixed-strategy solutions, where players randomize between acts over which they are indifferent. Then, this statement would need modification.

2. Darrough and Stoughton assume that if disclosure is made, it is honest. This assumption can be motivated by an audit and/or by severe penalties for fraudulent disclosure.

3. There is an implicit assumption throughout Section 9.4 that principal and agent have the same state and payoff probabilities when the contract is being negotiated. This assumption is made in most agency models. See also Note 7.

4. For simplicity, we ignore here what might happen next. Given a reasonably efficient managerial labour market, other similar managers would also like to work for this firm. Once they see that the job promises more than reservation utility, they will offer to work for less. The resulting bidding process will drive the salary down to $22.10, so that the shirking manager earns only reservation utility, as follows:

$$EU_m(a_1) = \sqrt{22.10} - 2 = 2.7$$
$$EU_m(a_2) = \sqrt{22.10} - 1.7 = 3$$

Whether or not the owner opens the job up for bids, the important point is that the manager will prefer to choose a_2, contrary to the best interests of the owner.

5. If the payoff was observable at period end, it would also be a performance measure.

6. This unbiased assumption omits the possibility of earnings management. For example, if compensation is based on reported net income, the manager may bias it upward to increase compensation, as predicted by the bonus plan hypothesis of positive accounting theory. We will extend agency theory to include earnings management in the next section.

7. Note that the owner *knows* which act the manager will take (i.e., it is the owner that designs the compensation contract to motivate the manager to work hard.) This points out additional agency theory assumptions: the principal knows the agent's utility function, the principal and agent agree on the payoffs that will result from the agent's effort, and they have the same probabilities over these payoffs (called **homogeneous probabilities**). Without knowing the agent's utility for compensation, the payoffs, and the agent's payoff probabilities, the principal could not calculate the agent's act. Since the principal knows which act will be taken, the payoff reveals no information about the agent's ability. This justifies taking the agent's reservation utility as a fixed constant, as discussed earlier in this section. In a more complex agency model, the agent would take into account the effect of his/her action on reservation utility.

8. It is easy to verify that the manager's expected compensation is now:

$$
\begin{aligned}
\text{Expected comp.} \ &= 0.6[0.5(0.326 \times 125) + 0.5(0.326 \times 75)] \\
&\quad + 0.4[0.5(0.326 \times 62.50) + 0.5(0.326 \times 37.50)] \\
&= 0.6[(0.5 \times 40.75) + (0.5 \times 24.45)] + 0.4[(0.5 \times 20.38) + (0.5 \times 12.22)] \\
&= (0.6 \times 32.60) + (0.4 \times 16.30) \\
&= 19.56 + 6.52 \\
&= 26.08
\end{aligned}
$$

The manager's expected compensation has to be raised from $25 under the first-best contract to $26.08 under profit sharing to offset the compensation risk that the manager now bears, and enable reservation utility to be attained. This increase in expected compensation accounts for the agency cost of 1.08 now borne by the owner.

9. Agency theory seeks to find the contract with the lowest possible agency cost (i.e., the most efficient form of contract). We do not claim that the contract of Example 9.3, based on 32.6% of net income, is necessarily the most efficient. In fact, it can be verified that a contract paying the manager a salary of $2.30 plus 0.296 of net income (or, equivalently, 0.319 of net income if net income is $125 or $75, and 0.342 of net income if net income is $62.50 or $37.50) is slightly more efficient. This contract makes the manager indifferent between a_1 and a_2 (in which case it is assumed the agent will take a_1), and yields the owner expected utility of 54.02, up from 53.92 in our contract. The reason for the greater efficiency is that this contract places less risk on the manager, due both to the salary and the smaller profit share. This enables a lower risk premium for the agent to attain reservation utility. We use a straight profit share in the body of the text primarily for simplicity.

Note that both of the contracts here are linear in the performance measure. When there are more than two states of nature, it is possible that a non-linear contract would be more efficient. This is beyond our scope here.

10. This assumption may seem to violate our statement in Section 9.4.2 that contracts are based on variables that are jointly observable. However, this is really not the case. Reported net income (as opposed to unmanaged net income) *is* jointly observable. The question then is, does reported net income have sufficient credibility that parties are willing to contract on it? If not, other performance measures, such as share price, may take over. However, GAAP and auditing help to give the owner confidence in reported net income as a performance measure. Furthermore, as we will see in Chapter 10, actual compensation contracts are based, at least in part, on reported net income.

11. There is no incentive to report truthfully, either, since the manager receives the same utility regardless. The theory assumes that, if indifferent, the manager will report truthfully.

12. The revelation principle could in turn be applied to this contract. The owner could simply agree to pay 0.305 times the upper limit of the range that occurs, regardless of the amount of unmanaged net income reported within that range. The manager then has no incentive to manage earnings upward. However, paying the manager on the basis of a higher net income than reported may impose costs on the manager, since such compensation may be regarded as excessive in the media and by regulators. In view of the restrictions on the revelation principle discussed in Section 9.5.1, we do not pursue this here.

13. Another way to eliminate the manager's incentive to manage earnings is to pay a constant wage. However, with a constant wage, the manager will shirk, and the owner would be back in the situation of Example 9.6.

14. More precisely, for the second performance measure to reduce agency costs it must be false that the first measure is a sufficient statistic for the pair of variables (first performance measure, second performance measure) with respect to effort.

15. Holmström points out that if the contract with the manager is confined to a limited class, such as the linear contract with a straight profit share assumed in Example 9.3, this result may not hold.

16. Christensen, Demski, and Frimor (2002) present a two-period agency model that allows contract renegotiation at the end of the first period, but also allows the manager to underreport first period output (i.e., conservative accounting). Since accruals reverse, any underreporting of first period output must be added to second period reported output, however. This restores some of the agent's incentive to work hard since working hard in the first period leads to extra expected compensation in the second. This provides another argument that some degree of earnings management can be good. Further pursuit of contract renegotiation is beyond our scope.

Chapter 10

Executive Compensation

FIGURE 10.1 ORGANIZATION OF CHAPTER 10

10.1 Overview

In this chapter we consider **executive compensation plans**. We will see that real incentive plans follow from the agency theory developed in Chapter 9, but are more complex and detailed. They involve a delicate mix of incentive, risk, and decision horizon considerations.

> An **executive compensation plan** is an agency contract between the firm and its manager that attempts to align the interests of owners and manager by basing the manager's compensation on one or more measures of the manager's performance in operating the firm.

Many compensation plans are based on two performance measures —net income and share price. That is, the amounts of bonus, shares, options, and other components of executive pay that are awarded in a particular year depend on both net income and share price performance. The analyses of Holmström (1979) and Feltham and Xie (1994) outlined in Section 9.8.1 suggest that multiple performance measures increase contracting efficiency.

The role of net income in reporting on manager performance is equally as important as its role in informing investors. This is because the motivation of responsible manager performance and the enhancing of proper operation of managerial labour markets are desirable social goals. They are equally as important as the enabling of good investment decisions and proper securities market operation. Consequently, an understanding of the properties that net income needs in order to measure manager performance is important for accountants. Unless net income has desirable qualities of sensitivity and precision, it will not be informative about manager effort. That is, it will not measure performance efficiently and will not enable the market to properly value the manager's worth. It will also be "squeezed out" of efficient compensation plans. Figure 10.1 outlines the organization of this chapter.

10.2 Are Incentive Contracts Necessary?

Fama (1980) makes the case that incentive contracts of the type studied in Section 9.4.2 are not necessary because the managerial labour market controls moral hazard. If a manager can establish a **reputation** for creating high payoffs for owners, that manager's market value (i.e., the compensation he or she can command) will increase. Conversely, a manager who shirks, thus reporting lower payoffs on average, will suffer a decline in market value. As a manager who is tempted to shirk looks ahead to future periods, the present value of reduced future compensation, Fama argues, will be equal to or greater than the immediate benefits of shirking. Thus, the manager will not shirk. This argument, of course, assumes an efficient managerial labour market that properly values the manager's reputation. Analogous to the case of a capital market, the proper operation of a managerial labour market is enhanced by full disclosure of the manager's performance.

Fama also argues that for lower-level managers, any shirking will be detected and reported by managers below them, who want to get ahead. That is, a process of "internal monitoring" operates to discipline managers who may be less subject to the discipline of the managerial labour market itself.

Since the owner knows which action the manager will take in the single-period models of Chapter 9, [1] these models do not reveal any information about manager ability. Thus they cannot deal directly with the multi-period horizon that is needed for reputation formation and internal monitoring. Recall that in the single-period model, the manager's market value enters only through the reservation utility constraint—the utility of the compensation of the next-best available position. In a one-period model, this utility is taken as a constant. Fama's argument is that if the manager contemplates the downwards effect of current shirking on the reservation utility of future employment contracts, shirking will be deterred.

The agency model can be extended to deal with these considerations. With respect to internal monitoring, we outline the study of Arya, Fellingham, and Glover (1997) (AFG). They design a two-period model with one owner and two risk-averse managers. The managers' efforts produce a joint, observable payoff in each period. The owner cannot observe either manager's effort but each manager knows the effort of the other. One way for the owner to motivate the managers to work hard is to offer each of them an incentive contract similar to the ones in Section 9.4.2, in each period. However, AFG show that the owner can offer a more efficient contract by exploiting the ability of each manager to observe the other's effort. Since the payoff is a joint effort, shirking by either manager will reduce the payoff for *both*. Then, in the AFG contract, each manager threatens the other that he/she will shirk in the second period if the other shirks in the first. If the contract is designed properly, the threat is credible and each manager works hard in both periods. The resulting two-period contract is more efficient because it imposes less risk than a sequence of two single-period contracts. As a result, managers can attain their reservation utility with lower expected compensation.

The important point for our purposes is that the contract continues to base manager compensation on some measure of the payoff. In effect, while exploitation of the ability of managers to monitor each other can *reduce* agency costs of moral hazard, it does not eliminate them. Thus, AFG's model suggests that an incentive contract for lower-level managers is still necessary.

With respect to the ability of manager reputation to control moral hazard, Fama's argument does not consider that the manager may be able to disguise the effects of shirking, at least in the short run, by managing the release of information. That is, the manager may try to "fool" the managerial labour market by opportunistically managing earnings to cover up shirking. Since persons with a tendency to do this will be attracted to the opportunity, the managerial labour market is subject to adverse selection as well as moral hazard.

Of course, GAAP limits, to some extent, the manager's ability to cover up shirking. Also, since accruals reverse, such behaviour will eventually be discovered, in which case the manager's reputation will be destroyed. The question then is, are the expected costs of lost reputation strong enough to supply the missing effort motivation? If they are, then an incentive contract would not be necessary, as Fama argues. The manager could be paid a straight salary, and the manager's reputation on the managerial labour market would prevent shirking.

In this regard, some empirical evidence on the market's ability to control the manager's incentive to shirk is presented by Wolfson (1985). He examined contracts of oil and gas limited partnerships in the United States. These are tax-advantaged contracts between a general partner (agent) and limited partners (principal) to drill for oil and gas. The general partner provides the expertise and pays some of the costs. The bulk of the capital is provided by the limited partners.

Such contracts are particularly subject to moral hazard and adverse selection problems, due to the highly technical nature of oil and gas exploration. For example, the general partner privately learns the results of the drilling. This leads to the "noncompletion incentive problem." Once drilled, a well should be completed if its expected revenues—call them R—exceed the costs of completion. However, for tax reasons, completion costs are paid by the general partner. If the general partner receives, say, 40% of the revenues, then, from his/her perspective, it is worthwhile to complete only if 0.40R is greater than the completion costs. Given that only the general partner knows R, a well may not be completed (i.e., the manager covers up shirking by withholding information about R) unless R is very high.

Wolfson studied two types of well-drilling: exploratory wells and development wells. The noncompletion problem is not as great for exploratory wells since, if an exploratory well does come in, the chances are that R will be high indeed.

Investors will be aware of this noncompletion problem, of course, and will bid down the price they are willing to pay to buy in, possibly to the point where the general partner cannot attract limited partners at all. The question then is, can a general partner ease investor concerns by establishing a reputation, thereby increasing his/her market value and the amounts that investors are willing to pay?

To measure reputation, Wolfson collected information on the past performance of a sample of general partners over 1977–1980. The higher a general partner's past success in generating a return for limited partners, the higher that partner's reputation was taken to be. Wolfson found that the higher the reputation of a general partner, the more he/she received from limited partners to buy in, suggesting that investors were responding to the manager's reputation.

However, Wolfson also found that investors paid significantly less to buy into development wells than into exploratory wells. As mentioned, the undercompletion problem is greater for development wells.

Combination of these two findings suggests that while market forces can *reduce* the managers' moral hazard problem, *they do not eliminate it*. If reputation-building completely eliminated the undercompletion problem, we would not see investors paying less when the problem is greater.

While Wolfson's results apply only to a small sample of oil and gas contracts, they are of more general interest because of their implication that the managerial labour market is not completely effective in controlling moral hazard, contrary to Fama's argument. An agent's past success in generating payoffs for investors does not perfectly predict that he/she always "works hard."

We conclude that while internal and market forces may complement GAAP by helping to control managers' tendencies to shirk, they do not eliminate them. Thus, effort incentives based on some measure of the payoff are still necessary. We now turn to an examination of an actual managerial compensation contract of a large corporation. As we will see, incentives loom large.

10.3 A Managerial Compensation Plan

In this section, we present an example of a managerial compensation plan. The following exhibit describes the plan of BCE Inc., a large Canadian corporation with shares traded on the Toronto, New York, and Zurich stock exchanges. Exhibit 10.1 presents excerpts from BCE's 2004 Management Proxy Circular.

Several aspects of this compensation plan should be noted. First, officers are required to hold a significant amount of BCE shares, ranging from 2 to 5 times base salary. Second, there are three main compensation components: salary; annual short-term incentive awards, consisting of cash bonuses or, for senior officers, deferred share units (DSUs); and stock options. DSUs are BCE shares that cannot be sold while the holder remains with the company.

Observe that the short-term incentive awards depend on both corporate performance and individual creativity and initiative. Corporate performance includes the attainment of financial targets such as earnings per common share (a net income-based measure of performance) and achievement of strategic business objectives such as market share and customer satisfaction. The more senior the manager, the more his/her compensation depends on performance. For example, the target award of the president and CEO is set at 125% of base salary, whereas awards for other senior executives are as low as 30%.

Stock options are awarded under the long-term component of the plan. Since the value of the stock options depends on BCE's share price, these provide an incentive to increase share price.

Third, many compensation plans require that a certain level of earnings, or other performance measure, be reached before incentive compensation becomes payable. The

Exhibit 10.1 Executive Officers' Compensation, BCE Inc.

Executive officers' compensation

The executive compensation policy is designed to attract, motivate and retain the executive officers needed to achieve and surpass BCE'S corporate objectives and to build an industry-leading company in terms of operational performance and creation of value for the shareholders.

BCE's compensation philosophy is to offer total compensation which is competitive in the marketplace. To complement this market positioning, BCE also ensures (for internal equity) that the compensation of each position fairly reflects the responsibilities of that position relative to other positions at BCE.

A substantial portion of each executive officer's cash compensation each year depends on meeting annual corporate performance objectives. In addition, BCE has in place long-term incentive programs. These are mainly stock options that are designed to:

- compensate and retain executive officers
- link the executive officers' interests to those of the shareholders
- encourage executive officers to pursue value-creating opportunities for BCE by allowing them to participate in the appreciation in share value.

The MRCC periodically reviews BCE'S executive compensation policy to make sure that it continues to meet its objectives. This review also includes a specific review of the compensation of the President and Chief Executive Officer and of the executive officers. In this document, executive officers whose compensation is disclosed in the *Summary compensation table* are referred to as the "named executive officers".

In 2003, in light of the evolving internal and external environments, the MRCC conducted a comprehensive review of BCE's executive compensation policy. Following this review, changes to the compensation policy were recommended by the MRCC and approved by the board in November 2003. The changes to the compensation policy are discussed in more detail under *Change in compensation strategy for 2004 and in the future*.

Total compensation
In 2003, total compensation consisted of:

- base salary
- annual short-term incentive awards
- long-term incentives
- benefits and perquisites including pension benefits, described under *Other compensation information*.

continued →

For 2003 and consistent with past practices, total compensation was positioned at the median of what is paid by the group of companies with which BCE compares itself (comparator group). Paying at the median of the comparator group means that 50% of the companies in the comparator group pay more than BCE and 50% pay less for similar positions.

In 2003, as part of its periodic reviews of the comparator group, the MRCC decided to expand the group from 22 to 43 publicly traded Canadian and U.S. companies. The 2003 comparator group includes 23 Canadian companies and 20 U.S. companies. The Canadian and the U.S. companies were selected based on one or more of the following criteria: telecommunications/high technology, strategic use of technology, most admired companies and revenues. This larger group of companies is more representative of BCE's current environment and will therefore provide a better basis for comparisons to the market.

Total compensation that the executive officers received was between the median and the 75th percentile of what the comparator group offered for similar positions, based on each individual's contribution to BCE's performance and how successful BCE was in achieving its strategic business objectives and financial targets. Consistent with past practices, the 75th percentile was reserved for those few individuals who contributed in an outstanding fashion. The 75th percentile means that 25% of the comparator group pay more than BCE and 75% of the comparator group pay less. The MRCC did not assign weightings to any elements of the total compensation.

Please see *Other compensation information — Executive compensation table* for total compensation paid to the named executive officers over the past three years.

Base salary

The MRCC determines the base salary of each executive officer within a salary range to reflect individual performance and responsibilities related to the position. The midpoint of the salary range corresponds to the median of the comparator group for similar positions. The minimum for the salary range is 20% below the mid-point and the maximum is 20% above.

Annual short-term incentive awards

The short-term incentive program is designed to support the achievement of corporate objectives and reward executives officers based on BCE's success. Financial targets account for 70% of the corporate performance factor while the remaining portion is based on the achievement of strategic business objectives. The board sets these objectives in the corporate mandate at the beginning of each year. Please see *Statement of corporate governance practices — How we are meeting the TSX guidelines — guidelines 1(a) and 1(c)* for more information. The MRCC determines the annual short-term incentive awards by considering both the corporate performance and the executive officer's contributions.

continued ➜

For the year 2003, BCE's financial targets were set with respect to net earnings applicable to common shares (EPS), revenue growth, EBITDA[1] growth, capital intensity (% of revenues), free cash flow[2] and ROIC[3]. Each of these components has a weight of 10% except the EPS which is at 20%. Strategic business objectives which account for the remaining 30% of the corporate performance factor might include, for example, a specific corporate objective with respect to a particular subsidiary, the development of new businesses, higher penetration of products and services, the improvement of management development or the strengthening of certain relationships. Further to the implementation of a new structure at Bell Canada in June 2003 and in recognition of the increased focus of BCE's executive officers on Bell Canada, BCE's core asset, the MRCC and the board decided to adjust BCE's corporate performance factor based on Bell Canada results. In 2003, Bell Canada's performance was evaluated based on NIAC[4] (45%), revenue (25%) and customer satisfaction (30%), which resulted in a Bell Canada corporate performance factor of 50%. Consequently, a corporate performance factor of 50% instead of 65% was used to determine the annual short-term incentive awards of BCE's executive officers.

The individual's contribution is evaluated based on criteria that affect corporate performance such as creativity and initiative in addressing business issues, succession planning and management development. The individual performance factor may vary between 0 and 200%.

Each year, the MRCC sets target values for the awards. In 2003 the target awards ranged from 30% of base salary for the lowest eligible officer's position to 125% of base salary for the President and Chief Executive Officer. The minimum target for the named executive officers was 75% of base salary.

---

1 The term EBITDA (earnings before interest, taxes, depreciation and amortization) does not have any standardized meaning prescribed by Canadian generally accepted accounting principles (GAAP) and is therefore unlikely to be comparable to similar measures presented by other issuers. We define it as operating revenues less operating expenses, which means it represents operating income before amortization expense, net benefit plans credit (cost) and restructuring and other charges. EBITDA should not be confused with net cash flows from operating activities. The most comparable Canadian GAAP earnings measure is operating income.

2 The term free cash flow does not have any standardized meaning prescribed by Canadian GAAP and is therefore unlikely to be comparable to similar measures presented by other issuers. Free cash flow is calculated as cash from operating activities after total dividends, capital expenditures and other investing activities. The most comparable Canadian GAAP financial measure is cash from operating activities.

3 The return on invested capital (ROIC) is defined as the latest twelve month's net earnings divided by the most recent quarter invested capital (long-term debt plus common and preferred stock equity).

4 NIAC (Net Income Applicabie to Common Shares) is based on net revenues earned, minus the cost of conducting business. NIAC represents a good estimate of funds generated from operations available to holders of common shares. Such funds can either be distributed as dividends, or kept for reinvestment in the company.

continued ➡

On the basis of the above factors, the MRCC determines the size of the annual short-term incentive awards. More specifically, awards are computed based on the product of the target award, the corporate performance factor and the individual performance factor. The maximum payout is two times the target award.

In most cases, awards granted for a year are paid at the beginning of the following year.

Executive officers who are eligible to participate in the *BCE share unit plan for senior executives and other key employees (1997)* (deferred share unit plan) and in the *Employees' profit sharing plan* can elect to have up to 100% of their annual short-term incentive award paid in deferred share units (DSUs) or contributed to the *Employees' profit sharing plan.* They must decide how they wish to receive their award by the end of the year in which the award is earned. Please see *Deferred share unit plan* for more information. Contribution to the *Employees' profit sharing plan* permits tax on the incentive award to be paid by the time of the required filing date of the income tax return for the year of contribution.

Election to receive the award in the form of DSUs can be used as a means to achieve mandatory share ownership levels as described under *Share ownership requirements.*

Long-term incentives

In light of BCE's internal and external environments and to create an even stronger link between executive compensation and BCE's mid-term and long-term operational and financial success, the board has approved, for 2004 and onward, a significant shift in BCE's long-term compensation strategy which includes the introduction of a mid-term incentive and a reduction in the use of stock options. These are discussed under *Change in compensation strategy for 2004 and in the future.*

Stock Options

The MRCC may grant BCE's executive officers and other key employees, and those of certain of BCE's subsidiaries, options to buy BCE common shares under the stock option plans. The number of outstanding options is not taken into account when determining if and how many options will be awarded.

Multiples of the base salary are used as a basis to grant stock options. The multiples vary depending on the position and are designed to bring total compensation, depending on individual performance, to between the 50th and 75th percentile of what is paid by the comparator group for similar positions. The 75th percentile is reserved for those few individuals who have contributed in an outstanding fashion. The option multiples used in 2003 were reduced by an average of 20% from the 2002 levels in order to reflect the downward trend in the size of stock option grants.

The number of options granted is calculated by dividing the value of the grant by the subscription price i.e., the market value of BCE common shares on the day before the grant is effective. The MRCC may approve special grants of stock options to recognize singular achievements or, exceptionally, to retain or motivate executive officers and key employees.

continued →

The price at which a common share may be purchased when the option is being exercised is called the exercise price. The exercise price is at least equal to the subscription price, except under certain circumstances. For example, the MRCC may set a higher exercise price when it grants the option. Or it may set a lower exercise price to maintain the economic position of the option holder. This may take place when an option to acquire shares of one of BCE's subsidiaries or of a company that BCE is acquiring is converted into an option to acquire BCE common shares. The lower price would be subject to any required approval of the stock exchanges on which BCE common shares are listed.

The term of an option is normally 10 years from the day it is granted, unless the option holder retires, leaves the BCE group of companies, dies, or the company he or she works for is no longer part of the BCE group of companies. In these cases, the term may be reduced in accordance with the stock option plan under which it was granted or in accordance with decisions made by the MRCC.

The right to exercise an option normally accrues or "vests" by 25% a year for four years from the day of grant, unless there is a change of control of BCE or of a designated subsidiary or the MRCC sets different terms. Please see *Change of control* for details.

Option holders will lose all of their unexercised options granted after 2001 if they engage in prohibited behavior after they leave the BCE group of companies. These include using BCE's confidential information for the benefit of another employer. In addition, the option holder must reimburse BCE the after-tax profit realized on exercising any options during the twelve-month period preceding the date on which the unfair employment practice began.

Prior to November 1999, some options were granted with related rights to special compensation payments (SCPs). SCPs are cash payments representing the excess of the market value of the shares on the day of exercise of the related options over the subscription price of the options. SCPs, if any, are attached to options and are triggered when the options are exercised.

Effective January 1, 2003, BCE adopted the fair value method of accounting for stock option compensation on a prospective basis.

Stock options for executive officers of BCE subsidiaries

The number of options granted to Bell Canada's executive officers in 2003 was based on the economic profit target of 2002. As the 2002 target was exceeded, their stock option grant was increased by 10% which means that they received 110% of their normal grant in February 2003. If 90% to 100% of the target had been achieved, 100% of the grant would have been awarded. If less than 90% of the target had been achieved, executive officers would have received only 50% of their grant.

In 2003, the economic profit target was replaced by the return on equity (ROE)[1] target and therefore 100% of the grant was taken into consideration when establish-

---

[1] ROE (return on common shareholders' equity) is calculated as net earnings applicable to common shares as a percentage of average common shareholders' equity.

continued →

ing the 2004 grants under the new executive compensation policy. Please see *Change in compensation strategy for 2004 and in the future* for details.

The share option plan of BCE Emergis is almost the same as BCE's stock option plans, except that the term of the options is six years and options vest by 25% after two years, 75% after three years and 100% after four years. As Chief Executive Officer of BCE Emergis until May 13, 2003, Mr. Blouin participated in the BCE Emergis share option plan.

You will find more information about options granted and exercised under these programs in the tables under *Other compensation information — Stock options.*

Deferred share unit plan

The deferred share unit plan is designed to more closely link the interests of the executive officers to those of the shareholders. DSUs may be awarded to certain executive officers and other key employees and those of certain subsidiaries.

DSUs have the same value as BCE common shares. The number and terms of outstanding DSUs are not taken into account when determining if and how many DSUs will be awarded. There is no vesting period for DSUs.

DSUs receive payments that are equivalent to the dividends on BCE common shares. Additional DSUs are credited on each dividend payment date and are equivalent in value to the dividend paid.

Eligible executive officers can choose to have up to 100% of their annual short-term incentive award and capital efficiency incentive award paid in DSUs instead of cash. The award is converted into DSUs based on the market value of a BCE common share on the day before the award is approved by the board. These DSUs count towards the minimum share ownership requirements, which are described under *Share ownership requirements.*

The MRCC may also grant special awards of DSUs to recognize outstanding achievements or for attaining certain corporate objectives.

Holders of DSUs may not sell their units while they are employed by a company of the BCE group. Once they leave the BCE group, BCE will buy the same number of BCE common shares on the open market as the number of DSUs a participant holds in the plan, after deductions for applicable taxes. These shares are then delivered to the former employee.

Share ownership requirements

BCE believes in substantial share ownership and is providing compensation programs designed to encourage executive officers to own shares of BCE through common shares or DSUs. A minimum share ownership level has been set for each position, based on a percentage of annual base salary:

- President and Chief Executive Officer — 500%
- Group Presidents and heads of major lines of business — 300%
- other officers — 200%.

continued →

These officers must meet their target within five years with the objective that 50% of their target will be reached within 3 years. The 5-year target must be reached by April 2006, or within 5 years from their date of hire or promotion, if such event occurred after April 1, 2001.

Share ownership requirements also apply to all Vice-Presidents with a target of 100% of annual base salary.

Shares or DSUs received through the following programs can be used to reach the minimum share ownership level:

- deferred share unit plan, which is described under *Deferred share unit plan*
- employees' savings plan, which is described in *Other compensation information — Executive compensation table*, footnote (6)
- shares acquired and held by exercising stock options granted under BCE's stock option plans which are described under *Long-term incentives*.

As part of the new compensation policy for 2004 and beyond, concrete measures will be taken to ensure that share ownership requirements are met.

Compensation policy of subsidiaries

Bell Canada's and BCE Emergis' compensation policies are similar to BCE's. Payments under their short-term incentive plans depend on achieving their respective corporate objectives, which are set out at the beginning of each year.

The board approved the recommendations of Bell Canada for grants of BCE options to Mr. Blouin, Mr. Wetmore, Mr. Roman and Mr. Sheridan in 2003. Grants of options to Mr. Blouin while he was employed by BCE Emergis were made under the BCE Emergis share option plan, according to BCE Emergis' compensation policy.

Change in compensation strategy for 2004 and in the future

BCE and its core asset, Bell Canada, are dealing proactively to the changing competitive landscape and customer needs. During the last year, the structure and business strategy have been realigned to deliver on these business realities. BCE and Bell Canada have worked to simplify both the customer experience and the internal operations. As well, the type of leadership considered essential for success now and into the future was redefined.

In light of these important changes, starting in 2004, the executive compensation policy has been redesigned to ensure close alignment and support with the company's new direction and strategic objectives. The committee has been closely involved in developing the overall design. The design delivers clear direction as to what is important to BCE executives and Bell Canada executives and what behaviors and types of results will be rewarded. Fundamentally, the new executive compensation policy is designed to drive a shift in culture toward greater individual accountability and higher levels of performance.

The underlying philosophy is to remain conservative with regards to fixed compensation (such as base salary) while placing more emphasis on variable (at risk)

continued →

compensation, through the use of three different compensation vehicles, short-term, mid-term and long-term incentive plans. Each of these variable compensation vehicles contains specific performance targets which must be met in order to trigger any payments. These targets are not achievable by incremental change alone, in some cases they will require a complete process redesign.

The key components of this policy are:

- increase total compensation from the median (50th percentile), where it is today, to the 60th percentile of a specific comparator group of companies. This will provide BCE and Bell Canada with the ability to attract and retain the type of executives needed to deliver at required performance levels.

- elements within the total compensation policy at the 60th percentile

  - maintain base salaries at the median (50th percentile), their current level

  - increase the short-term annual incentive target awards from the median to the 75th percentile of the comparator group for similar positions. This will further reinforce the importance of meeting the annual financial drivers and the fashion in which they are delivered.

  - transfer approximately 50% of the value of the long-term incentive plan, where stock options are granted, into a new mid-term plan under which Restricted Share Units (RSU) are used as the vehicle:

    - dependent on their level, each executive is granted a specific number of RSUs for a two-year period. The RSUs will either vest or be forfeited two years from the grant date.

    - vesting is conditional on achieving specific operational targets by the end of a two-year performance period. These targets are directly aligned to achieving the company's strategic goals for each of the core business units of Bell Canada.

    - at the end of the performance period, subject to compliance with individual share ownership requirements, vested RSUs will be paid in BCE common shares or in cash.

  - reduce the value of stock options granted in the long-term incentive plan by approximately 50% and changing the key design features:

    - vesting is subject to a combination of time and performance. The performance metric is based on meeting or exceeding the median total shareholder return of a group of North American telecommunications companies. 50% of the stock options will vest after two years and 100% after three years, subject to achieving the performance metric.

    - option period reduced from ten to six years

    - number of stock options granted cover a three-year period (front-loaded).

Conclusion

In the MRCC's view, the total compensation of the named executive officers for 2003 was appropriate and competitive in the marketplace. The MRCC believes that it was also

continued →

consistent with the compensation policy of linking a large part of executive officers' compensation to the achievement of corporate performance objectives and the creation of shareholder value.

The MRCC believes that the compensation must reflect corporate performance. As such, the annual short-term incentive award of the named executive officers was based on a corporate performance factor of 50% as the corporate objectives were not fully achieved.

Overall, the MRCC is confident that this approach to compensation has allowed BCE to attract, motivate and retain executive officers, while aligning their interests with those of its shareholders. The new compensation strategy implemented in 2004 will help further support the company's goal to become the best telecommunications company in North America.

Report presented March 10, 2004 by:

P.M. Tellier, Chairman
R.A. Brenneman
A.S. Fell
B.M. Levitt
J.H. McArthur
V.L. Young

Reproduced with permission from BCE Inc.

---

threshold level of performance is called the **bogey**. Also, many plans contain an upper limit to compensation, called the **cap**.

In BCE's case, no formal bogey or cap is stated. However, these seem implicit. We are told that total compensation is positioned between the 50th and 75th percentiles of that of a group of comparable companies, thereby placing an upper limit on compensation. Also, the amounts of short-term incentive awards are geared to targets set at the beginning of the year. If these bogeys are not met, the awards are, presumably, zero, or at least reduced. Also, the short-term awards are capped at two times the amount based on the target.

It should be noted that the compensation committee of BCE's board of directors (MRCC) has the ultimate say in the amounts of salary, bonus, and option awards, within the above guidelines. The compensation committee is a corporate governance device, to deal with the fact that the BCE plan, like all real compensation contracts, is *incomplete* (see the discussion of complete and incomplete contracts in Section 9.8.2). While contracts tend to be rigid, the compensation committee may have some discretion to deal with the effects on compensation of an unanticipated outcome. For example, we are told that short-term incentive awards were reduced by 50% of target since corporate objectives for 2003 were not fully achieved. One might expect that if targets are not achieved, no bonus is payable. However, the MRCC must have felt that sufficient progress was made that some bonus is justified.

Fourth, the incentive effects of BCE's compensation plan should be apparent. For highest-ranking officers, annual incentive awards are based primarily on attainment of financial targets, such as earnings per share, and are paid either in cash or DSUs. Since the short-term incentive awards depend largely on current year's performance, this creates an incentive to maximize the current year's levels of the performance measures. Note, however, that maximizing current reported performance, such as earnings per share, may be at the expense of the firm's longer-run interests, leading to dysfunctional tactics such as deferral of maintenance, underinvestment in R&D, premature disposal of facilities in order to realize a gain, and other opportunistic earnings management techniques. However, the requirement of substantial share ownership gives officers a longer-term interest in the success of the firm. Presumably, this reduces the temptation to engage in dysfunctional practices such as those mentioned.

To reinforce these longer-term considerations, all executives and other key employees participate in the stock option-based long-term incentive plan. Here, recipients will benefit to the extent that BCE's common share price when an option is exercised exceeds the price when the option is granted. Note that the exercise price of the option is generally equal to the market value of a BCE share on the day prior to the effective date of the grant (the subscription price). In terms of our discussion of ESOs in Section 8.3, the option's intrinsic value is zero. As a result, no expense has been recognized by BCE for options granted. This will change, however, beginning in 2004, since Canadian accounting standards now require that an expense be recognized based on the ESOs' fair value—see our discussion in Section 8.3. Note that BCE has anticipated this requirement by voluntarily expensing its ESOs from January 1, 2003.

The options have a 10-year term, and, normally, the right to exercise early is not fully available until four years after the grant date.

Fifth, the *mix* of short- and long-term incentive components in a compensation plan is important. As mentioned above, a high proportion of long-term incentive components should produce a longer manager decision horizon, and vice versa. The MRCC can influence the mix, since it determines the size of the annual short-term incentive awards. That is, since options are awarded to bring an executive's total compensation up to the 50th to 75th percentile of that of comparable corporations, the greater the size of the short-term award the smaller the options award and vice versa, other things equal. We will outline in Section 10.4.2 why some flexibility in the short-term/long-term incentives mix is desirable.

Finally, consider the risk aspects of BCE's plan. Certainly, compensation is risky for BCE managers since economy and industry-wide events, which may not be controllable or informative about the manager's effort, will affect both earnings per share and share price. However, aspects of the BCE plan operate to limit compensation risk. Base salary, of course, is relatively risk-free. Also, the lower limit on both short-term incentive awards and stock option value is zero. This reduces downside risk since, if the bogey is not attained or if share value falls below the exercise price, the manager does not have to pay the firm. In addition, as mentioned, total compensation is adjusted to the 50th to 75th percentile of that of the comparison group. By setting total compensation in this way, an averaging effect is introduced, which would tend to make a BCE executive's total compensation less subject to variations in the performance of BCE itself.

In sum, the BCE compensation structure appears to be quite sophisticated in terms of its incentives, decision horizon, and risk properties. For our purposes, the most important point to note is that there are two main incentive components: short-term incentive awards based on earnings and individual achievement, and longer-term stock options whose value depends on share price performance. Thus, both accounting and market-based performance incentives are embedded in the plan. These give management a vital interest in how net income is determined, both because earnings per share is a direct input into compensation and because, as we saw in Chapter 5, net income affects share price.

Of particular interest are the changes in compensation strategy for 2004. Two aspects of the new strategy should be particularly noted:

- An increase in total compensation (to help retain executive talent) combined with a greater proportion of total compensation depending on performance.
- A shortening of the decision horizon, by increasing the weight of the short-term incentive awards, creation of a new mid-term compensation component, and reductions in the value and vesting period of stock options.

The reduced role of stock options consists of a 50% reduction in the value granted plus a reduction of term to expiry from 10 to 6 years. These reductions are due, presumably, to the "pump and dump" abuses of ESOs in recent years whereby it seems that many CEOs artificially inflated share price so as to increase the value of their vested options (see Section 8.3). In effect, ESOs seem to have motivated very short-run decision horizons—the opposite of the longer-run horizons that were intended. BCE Inc. is one of several large companies that have reduced their usage of ESOs as a way to increase public confidence that management will not abuse them.

The shortening of decision horizon is of particular interest. As mentioned earlier, BCE did not achieve all of its short-term corporate objectives in 2003. It seems that the company wants to increase incentives to attain these objectives in future. However, this raises the possibility of dysfunctional behaviour to increase reported performance in the short run, as described above. Consequently, the company has created a mid-term compensation plan. This plan introduces a two-year performance period, and pays compensation in the form of **restricted share units**. These are units of company stock that will only be awarded if one or more targets are met, such as attainment of a specified return on assets and/or a specified share price. In the case of BCE, the restricted stock vests only if some specific two-year operational objectives are attained. Presumably, the combination of a two-year performance period, and the reduction in ESOs, will control tendencies for dysfunctional short-run behaviour.

We now turn to a more general consideration of the compensation issues raised above.

10.4 The Theory of Executive Compensation

10.4.1 Review of Agency Theory Implications

The theory of executive compensation is largely based on the agency models developed in Chapter 9. For our purposes, the role of accounting information in this theory derives from Holmström (see Section 9.8.1). Recall that he predicts that the efficiency of a compensation contract is increased if it is based on two or more performance measures, providing that the additional performance measures contain information about effort beyond that contained in the first performance measure. This implies that net income competes with other performance measures for importance in compensation contracting.

10.4.2 The Relative Proportions of Net Income and Share Price in Evaluating Manager Performance

Given that compensation depends on both net income and share price, and that these two performance measures compete for importance, what determines their relative weights (i.e., the mix) in evaluating the manager's overall performance?

This question was studied by Banker and Datar (1989). Banker and Datar demonstrated conditions under which the linear mix of performance measures depends on the product of the sensitivity and precision of those measures. These concepts were introduced in Section 9.8.1, where sensitivity was defined as the rate at which the expected value of the measure responds to manager effort, and precision as the reciprocal of the variance of the noise in the measure.[2] Banker and Datar showed that the lower the noise in net income and the greater its sensitivity to manager effort, the greater should be the proportion of net income to share price in determining the manager's overall performance.

There are a number of ways that accountants can increase the sensitivity of net income. One possibility, raised in Section 9.8.1, is to reduce recognition lag by moving to fair value accounting. Reduced recognition lag increases sensitivity since more of the payoffs from manager effort show up in current net income.

However, fair value accounting is a double-edged sword in this regard, since it also tends to reduce precision. As mentioned above, Banker and Datar show that lower precision reduces the optimal proportion of a performance measure in the contract. It is thus unclear whether adoption of fair value accounting would result in a net gain in importance for net income. Indeed, if the negative precision effect of fair value accounting outweighs its positive sensitivity effect, a bit of conservatism, such as in historical cost accounting, is preferable to fair value for compensation contracting.[3]

Another approach to increasing sensitivity is through full disclosure, particularly of unusual and non-recurring items. Full disclosure increases sensitivity by enabling the compensation committee to better evaluate earnings persistence. Persistent earnings are a more sensitive measure of current manager effort than transitory or price-irrelevant earnings, which often arise independently of effort. A related approach is to use GAAP to reduce the scope for opportunistic earnings management, as illustrated in Example 9.7. Reduced earnings management increases sensitivity by reducing the manager's ability to disguise shirking.

With respect to share price, a major reason for its relatively low precision derives from the effects of economy-wide factors. For example, if interest rates increase, the expected effects on future firm performance will quickly show up in share price. These effects may say little about current manager effort, however. As a result, they simply add volatility to share price. Nevertheless, as we pointed out in Section 9.8.1, Holmström's analysis shows that share price could never be completely replaced as a performance measure as long as it contains some additional effort information. The sensitivity of share price is sufficiently great that it will always reveal additional payoff information beyond that contained in net income. Thus, we may expect both measures to coexist.

This coexistence, however, creates an opportunity for the owner to control the length of the manager's decision horizon. To explain, assume two types of manager effort—short-run and long-run. The owner can adjust the relative proportions of net income-based and share price-based compensation to exploit the fact that current net income aggregates the payoffs from only some manager activities in the current period. For example, to encourage more R&D (i.e., long-run effort), the owner can reduce the proportion of the manager's compensation based on net income and increase the proportion based on share price. His/her compensation will now rise more strongly due to securities market response to an increase in R&D, and there will be less compensation penalty from writing R&D costs off currently. Consequently, it will be in the manager's interest to increase R&D. More generally, firms with substantial investment opportunities will want to increase the proportion of share price-based compensation.[4]

Alternatively, suppose that the firm has to cut costs in the short run. Net income will aggregate the favourable cash flow effects of cost cutting quickly and accurately, perhaps even more so than share price, particularly if the cost-cutting measures are complex or constitute inside information, or if the market is concerned about the longer-run effects of short-run cost cutting. Also share price may not perfectly aggregate the cost-cutting information in the presence of noise trading or market inefficiencies. Then, the firm may wish to increase the weight of net income relative to share price in the manager's compensation.

In effect, when share price and net income differentially reflect the short- and long-run payoffs of current manager actions, the length of the manager's decision horizon can be influenced by the mix of share price-based and net income-based compensation—more share-based compensation produces a longer decision horizon and vice versa. This was demonstrated theoretically by Bushman and Indjejikian (1993). As we pointed out in Section 10.3, the BCE compensation plan allows the Compensation Committee some flexibility with respect to the mix of short- and long-term compensation. Furthermore, the 2004 revisions to BCE's compensation plan seem to shorten the decision horizon.

The mix of performance measures was further studied by Datar, Kulp, and Lambert (2001). Their analysis suggests that decision horizon must be traded off with the sensitivity and precision of performance measures. For example, the owner will increase the weight on a performance measure, even if this results in a manager decision horizon that is not exactly what the owner wants, if that performance measure is sensitive and precise. The reason is that such a performance measure "tells more" about effort, hence enables a more efficient contract. This greater efficiency is traded off against the benefits of controlling the manager's decision horizon. Consequently, sensitivity and precision remain as important characteristics in the presence of more than one type of managerial effort.

* 10.4.3 Short-Run and Long-Run Effort

Our discussion of agency theory in Chapter 9 assumed that manager effort is single-dimensional—a modelling device to encompass the whole range of managerial activities. Thus, we were interested in the *intensity* of effort, and envisaged two levels of intensity—"working hard" or "shirking." To enable us to better understand executive compensation, we now extend the agency model to regard effort as multi-dimensional. Specifically, we pursue the assumption in the previous section that effort consists of **short-run effort** (SR) and **long-run effort** (LR). SR is effort devoted to activities such as cost control, maintenance, employee morale, advertising, and other day-to-day

*This section can be omitted with little loss of continuity.

activities that generate net income mainly in the current period. LR is effort devoted to activities such as long-range planning, R&D, and acquisitions. While LR effort may generate some net income in the current period, most of the payoffs from these activities extend into future periods. Our development here is based on Feltham and Xie (1994).

The manager can either work hard or shirk along either or both effort dimensions. Then, we can regard current period net income (NI) as being generated by the following equation:

$$NI = \mu_1 SR + \mu_2 LR \pm \text{random factors with expected value zero,} \qquad (10.1)$$

where SR and LR are the quantities of short-run and long-run effort, respectively. There are now two sensitivities of net income rather than one. Thus μ_1 is the sensitivity of earnings to SR effort and μ_2 is sensitivity to LR effort. The assumption that the random factors affecting net income have expected value of zero implies that net income is not subject to manager manipulation and bias, consistent with our assumption in Section 9.4.2.

The firm's payoff x is also affected by these SR and LR activities. Thus, we can write the payoff as:

$$x = b_1 SR + b_2 LR \pm \text{random factors with expected value zero,} \qquad (10.2)$$

where b_1 and b_2 are sensitivities of the payoff to SR and LR effort, respectively. We assume here that the manager exerts effort only in the first period, and that net income is reported at the end of this period. However, consistent with our assumption in Chapter 9, the payoff is not fully observable until the next period. That is, the full payoff from the manager's first period effort is not realized until that time. Net income is a message that predicts what this payoff will be. The manager is compensated based on first period net income. Any additional payoff in the next period goes wholly to the owner.

Recognition of effort as a set of activities introduces a new concept—the **congruency** of a performance measure. To illustrate congruency, consider the following example.

EXAMPLE 10.1
A CONGRUENT PERFORMANCE MEASURE

Assume that the manager can work hard or shirk on both SR and LR effort, and that the net incomes and payoffs are as given in Table 10.1:

TABLE 10.1 EXPECTED NET INCOMES AND PAYOFFS FOR CONGRUENT PERFORMANCE MEASURE

	Manager's Effort			
	Short-run Effort (SR)		**Long-run Effort (LR)**	
	Work Hard	Shirk	Work Hard	Shirk
Expected Net Income E(NI)	$4	$1	$3	$2
Expected Payoff E(x)	$6	$1.5	$4.5	$3

If the manager allocates all effort to SR, and works hard, expected net income is $4. However, some of this effort, such as cost control, may remain to benefit next period, assuming that at least some of the lower costs will persist. Let these future benefits amount to $2. Then the expected *payoff* from SR effort totals $6. If the manager works hard at LR effort, say by devoting time to R&D, this generates expected net income of $3 currently but is expected to create additional payoff of $1.5 next period, for a total of $4.5. Similar comments apply if the manager shirks.

From Table 10.1, the *increases* in expected payoffs if the manager works hard, compared to shirking, are given in Table 10.2:

TABLE 10.2 INCREASES IN NET INCOMES AND PAYOFFS FROM WORKING HARD

	Manager's Effort	
	Short-run Effort (SR)	**Long-run Effort (LR)**
Expected Net Income E(NI)	$\mu_1 = \$3$	$\mu_2 = \$1$
Expected Payoff E(x)	$b_1 = \$4.5$	$b_2 = \$1.5$

The μ_1 and μ_2 in Table 10.2 are the sensitivities of net income to SR and LR effort, respectively—see Equation 10.1. Similarly, b_1 and b_2 are the sensitivities of the payoff to effort—see Equation 10.2. Note that b_1 is in the *same proportion* to μ_1 (4.5:3 = 3:2) as b_2 is to μ_2 (1.5:1 = 3:2). Then, net income is said to be **congruent** to the payoff. That is, an increase of expected net income by, say, $1 will increase the expected payoff by $1.5 regardless of whether the increase in expected net income comes from LR or SR effort or any combination of the two.

This being the case, the owner can design a contract that compensates the manager on the basis of reported net income for the first period without worrying about how the manager allocates effort between short-run and long-run activities. Given the contract, the manager will choose an effort intensity and allocation to maximize his/her expected utility of compensation, net of effort disutility. This was illustrated in Examples 9.3 – 9.7.

In sum, if there is more than one dimension to manager effort, and if net income is congruent to the payoff, the owner need not be concerned how the manager allocates effort across the dimensions. Each type of effort is equally effective in generating payoff.

Unfortunately, congruent net income is unlikely to be the case. Again, the reason derives from recognition lag. Consider Table 10.1 once more. While SR effort, such as cost control, may be an effective way to generate current net income, this is unlikely to be as effective in generating payoff in the next period, contrary to our assumption above. While some of the lower costs may persist, the cost-cutting nature of SR effort is likely to reduce employee morale and organization effectiveness in the next period, and this effect is not recognized in current net income. A more likely payoff from SR effort is, say, $2 if the manager works hard (i.e., the net income of $4 in the current period is reduced by $2 in the next, giving a net payoff of $2) and, say, $1.5 if he/she shirks. LR effort, however, is likely to have an opposite effect. Effort devoted to R&D, for example, will likely generate a high longer-run payoff, say $9 if the manager works hard and $4 if he/she shirks. Tables 10.3 and 10.4 summarize these assumptions:

TABLE 10.3 EXPECTED NET INCOMES AND PAYOFFS FOR NONCONGRUENT PERFORMANCE MEASURE

| | Manager's Effort | | | |
| | Short-run Effort (SR) | | Long-run Effort (LR) | |
	Work Hard	Shirk	Work Hard	Shirk
Expected Net Income E(NI)	$4	$1	$3	$2
Expected Payoff E(x)	$2	$1.5	$9	$4

TABLE 10.4 INCREASES IN NET INCOMES AND PAYOFFS FROM WORKING HARD

| | Manager's Effort | |
	Short-run Effort (SR)	Long-run Effort (LR)
Expected Net Income E(NI)	$\mu_1 = \$3$	$\mu_2 = \$1$
Expected Payoff E(x)	$b_1 = \$0.5$	$b_2 = \$5$

Now, for SR effort, the proportion of b_1 to μ_1 is 0.5:3 = 1/6. For LR effort, the proportion is 5:1 = 5. Thus net income is **noncongruent** to the payoff—it *does* matter to the owner which type of effort generates net income. An increase of $1 in net income from SR effort will increase expected payoff by $1/6 whereas an increase in net income of $1 from LR effort will increase it by $5.

In our example, the owner will want high R&D, because of its high ultimate payoff (i.e., b_2 is greater than b_1 in Table 10.4). But the manager, whose compensation is based on first period net income, will tend towards a short-run decision horizon since effort allocated to SR activities generates greater expected net income and compensation (i.e., μ_1 is greater than μ_2 in Table 10.4). The compensation contract must now consider not only the intensity of manager effort but also the *allocation* of effort across activities. Raising the manager's profit share will not serve to lengthen the manager's decision horizon—it will simply encourage more SR effort. As a result, the owner settles for less LR effort than he/she would like.

The question then is, what might the owner do about this? One possibility is to use a more congruent performance measure, such as share price. It is not hard to see that share price is more congruent with payoff than net income, since it is less subject to recognition lag. Then, favourable share price sensitivity to R&D will motivate the manager to increase LR effort. However, share price is less precise than net income. Consequently, it is not clear that share price-based compensation would increase contracting efficiency.

A second possibility is to add another performance measure. As noted in Section 9.8.1, Feltham and Xie show conditions under which Holmström's (1979) result continues to apply when effort is multi-dimensional. Then, theory predicts that compensation will depend on both net income and share price, consistent with what we observe in real compensation contracts.

10.4.4 The Role of Risk in Executive Compensation

Forcing managers to bear compensation risk is consistent with agency theory, which, from Chapter 9, tells us that in the presence of moral hazard the manager must bear some compensation risk if effort is to be motivated. Since managers, like other rational, risk-averse individuals, trade off risk and return, the more risk managers bear the higher must be their *expected* compensation if reservation utility is to be attained. Thus, to motivate the manager at the lowest cost, designers of efficient incentive compensation plans try to get the most motivation for a given amount of risk imposed or, equivalently, the least risk for a given level of motivation.

There are several ways to control compensation risk. Perhaps the most important of these from a theoretical perspective is **relative performance evaluation** (RPE). Here, instead of measuring performance by net income and/or share price, performance is measured by the *difference* between the firm's net income and/or share price performance and the average performance of a group of similar firms, such as other firms in the same industry. The theory of RPE was developed by Holmström (1982). By measuring the manager's performance relative to the average performance of similar firms, the systematic or common risks that the industry faces will be filtered out of the incentive plan, especially if the number of firms in the industry is large. To see this, note that when there are noisy performance measures in the contract, there will be some risks that are common to all firms in the industry.[5] For example, at least some of the effects on share price and earnings of a downturn in the economy, such as a reduction in sales, will also affect other firms in the industry. RPE deducts the average earnings and share price performance of other firms in the industry from the manager's performance measures, leaving a net performance that more precisely reflects the manager's efforts in running the firm in question. Thus, under RPE, it is possible for a manager to do well even if the firm reports a loss and/or share price is down, providing the losses are lower than those of the average firm in the industry.

If the RPE theory is valid, we would expect to observe total manager compensation negatively related to average industry performance. For example, when industry performance is low, high earnings and/or share price performance for the firm in question is even more impressive since it overcomes negative factors affecting the whole industry. Consequently, the compensation committee will award higher bonuses. When industry performance is high, high earnings and/or share price for the firm in question is less impressive, so that lower bonuses are awarded.

However, despite RPE's theoretical appeal, strong statistical evidence that managers are compensated this way has been hard to come by. Antle and Smith (1986) found weak evidence for RPE, and, according to Pavlik, Scott, and Tiessen (1993), a survey of RPE articles shows that the ability of RPE to predict manager compensation is modest. A possible reason for the weak empirical support is given by Sloan (1993), who argues that net income is less affected in the current period by economy-wide risks than share price. Inclusion of net income as a performance measure in addition to share price shields manager compensation from these economy-wide effects. As a result, Sloan concludes, RPE is not needed since basing compensation on both share price and net income accomplishes a similar result.

Nevertheless, while the theory underlying RPE seems valid, it is possible that strategic factors work against finding empirical evidence in its favour. For example, Aggarwal and Samwick (1999) (AS) present a model of firms in an oligopolistic industry, where the demand for a firm's product depends not only on its own product price but also on the prices of its competitors' products.[6] That is, the lower are competitors' prices the lower is the demand for the product of the firm in question, and vice versa. This creates an incentive for managers to engage in cooperative pricing behaviour to "soften" competition, as AS put it. This raises profits for all firms in the industry. To encourage this cooperative behaviour, compensation plans put positive, not negative, weight on other firms' performance. Furthermore, the magnitude of this positive weight should be stronger the greater the degree of competition in the industry. AS report empirical evidence consistent with this prediction. The BCE plan has a similar characteristic, since total compensation is positioned at the median of that paid by a group of comparable companies. To the extent that profits, and thus compensation, of BCE's competitors are high, BCE's compensation will also rise. The difficulty of finding empirical support for RPE could be due to countervailing effects such as these.

Another way to control risk is through the bogey of the compensation plan. Consider the manager in Example 9.3 who receives compensation of 32.6% of earnings. Suppose the firm loses $50 million. That is, earnings are negative, and so would be the manager's compensation. Instead of receiving compensation, the manager would have to pay the firm over $16 million! Under such a risky contract, the average level of compensation needed for the manager to attain reservation utility would be prohibitive. In other words, fear of personal bankruptcy is probably not the most efficient way to motivate a manager to work hard. For this reason, compensation plans usually impose a bogey. That is, incentive compensation does not kick in until some level of financial performance—10% return on equity, for example—is reached. The effect is that if the bogey is not attained, the contract does not award any incentive compensation. However, an ancillary effect is that the manager does not have to pay the firm if there is a loss.[7]

If downside risk is limited, it seems reasonable for upside risk to be limited too; otherwise the manager would have everything to gain and little to lose. As a result, many plans impose a cap, whereby incentive compensation ceases beyond a certain level. For example, no bonus may be awarded for return on equity exceeding 25%. Note that the BCE plan imposes a cap on short-term incentive awards of two times the award based on the target.

Another approach to controlling risk is through the compensation committee. As we saw in the BCE plan, this committee has the ultimate responsibility to determine the amounts of cash and stock compensation, and it has the flexibility to take special circumstances into account. For example, if the firm reports a loss, or earnings below the bogey, it may award a bonus anyway, particularly if it feels that the loss is due to some low-persistence item such as an unusual, non-recurring, or extraordinary event. However, the committee must exercise some restraint in this regard. If it is overly generous in not penalizing the manager for state realizations that are not his/her "fault," this will destroy contract rigidity and reduce effort incentive.

It is important to realize that risk affects how the manager operates the firm. If not enough risk is imposed, the firm suffers from low manager effort. If too much risk is imposed, the manager may underinvest in risky projects even though such projects would benefit diversified shareholders. There are a number of ways that managers can be encouraged to invest in risky projects. For example, awarding ESOs will encourage the manager to do so. If the projects do not succeed, the lowest the ESOs can be worth is zero. However, if the projects succeed, the ESOs can become very valuable.

Given the amount of risk imposed on the manager by the compensation committee, it is important that the manager not be able to work out from under this risk. The manager can shed compensation risk by, for example, selling shares and options acquired and investing the proceeds in a risk-free asset and/or a diversified portfolio. However, compensation plans typically reduce this possibility by restricting the manager's ability to dispose of shares and options. Thus the BCE plan requires officers to hold from 2 to 5 times annual base salary in BCE shares. Also, stock options will not be fully exercisable until three years after the grant date.

The manager can also shed risk by excessive hedging. Not only is hedging costly, effort incentive will suffer if the manager works out from under risk this way. Consequently, the firm may limit the manager's hedging behaviour.

Theory in Practice 10.1

Suncor Energy Inc., in its 2003 annual report MD&A (page 28), describes how it controls possible excess hedging in its oil and gas cash flow hedging program. Suncor's board and Audit Committee meet regularly with management to assess the extent of hedging. The board has restricted cash flow hedging to a maximum of 35% of crude oil volume for 2004, and 30% for 2005 to 2007.

Managers may also be motivated to increase risk, rather than reduce it. In the process, they impose excess risk on the firm as well. Excessive ESO awards can be a major contributor to such risk taking. Their large rewards if the risks pay off, but little penalty if they do not, create a situation where even risk-averse managers may take on excessive firm risk. Indeed, ESOs seem to have been a driving force behind horror stories such as Enron and WorldCom, as described in Section 1.2. It seems that manager effort was diverted away from value-increasing activities into opportunistic actions to increase share price, hence ESO value. The resulting risky and deceptive practices eventually led to the firms', and the managers' downfall. In this regard, it is interesting to recall BCE's changes to compensation for 2004, in Exhibit 10.1. These include a 50% reduction in ESO awards.

Thus, it seems that an efficient compensation plan must engage in a careful tradeoff between imposing too much risk and too little, and control any manager tendency to opportunistically decrease or increase risk. Evidence that, despite Enron and WorldCom, at least some compensation plans do this is provided by Rajgopal and Shevlin (2002). In a sample of oil and gas firms over 1992–1997, they found that ESOs did motivate managers to increase firm risk. This increased risk showed up both in increased exploration risk and reduced hedging activity. Rajgopal and Shevlin also found, however, that the effect of ESOs in their sample firms was to encourage risk-averse managers to undertake risky projects when these projects were economically desirable, not to encourage excessive risk taking. In effect, as in the results of Guay (1999) outlined in Section 8.6.4, their findings are consistent with efficient contracting.

10.5 Empirical Compensation Research

The research of Rajgopal and Shevlin provides some evidence that real compensation plans are designed as the theory suggests. In this section, we review other empirical studies bearing on the relation between compensation theory and practice, concentrating on studies that examine the role of accounting information.

An early study in this area was conducted by Lambert and Larcker (1987) (LL). Using a sample of 370 U.S. firms over 1970–1984 inclusive, LL investigated the relative ability of return on shares and return on equity to explain managers' cash compensation (salary plus bonus). If, for example, compensation plans and compensation committees primarily use share return as a manager performance measure, then share return should be significantly related to cash compensation. Alternatively, if they primarily use net income as a performance measure, return on equity (a ratio based on net income) should be significantly related to cash compensation.

Note that LL examined only cash compensation. Empirically, accounting variables do not seem to explain the options component of manager compensation. Indeed, this can be seen in the BCE plan. While short-term incentive awards are based on individual achievement and net income, stock option awards are not. Rather, they are made to bring total compensation up to the 50th to 75th percentiles of that paid by the group of comparison companies. Consequently, many studies of the role of net income in compensation concentrate on cash awards.

LL found that return on equity was more highly related to cash compensation than was return on shares. Indeed, several other studies have found the same results. This supports the decision horizon-controlling and risk-controlling roles for net income in compensation plans that were suggested in Sections 10.4.2 and 10.4.4.

LL also found that the relationship of these two payoff measures to cash compensation varied in systematic ways. For example, they found some evidence that the relationship between return on equity and cash compensation strengthened when net income was less noisy relative to return on shares. They measured the relative noisiness of net income by the ratio of the variability of return on equity over 1970–84 to the variability of return on shares over the same period. The lower the noise in net income, the better it predicts the payoff, as illustrated in Example 9.4. This finding is also consistent with Banker and Datar's analysis.

Moreover, managerial compensation for growth firms' executives tended to have a lower relationship with return on equity than average. This too is consistent with Banker and Datar, since, for growth firms, net income is relatively less sensitive to manager effort than it is for the average firm. Historical cost-based net income tends particularly to lag behind the real economic performance of a growth firm, because this basis of accounting does not recognize value increases until they are realized. The efficient market, however, will look through to real economic performance and value the shares accordingly. Thus, return on equity should be related less to compensation than share return for such firms, consistent with what LL found.

Perhaps the most interesting finding of LL, however, was that for firms where the correlation between share return and return on equity was low, there tended to be a higher weight on return on equity in the compensation plan, and vice versa. In other words, when net income is relatively uninformative to investors (low correlation between share return and return on equity) that same net income is relatively informative about manager effort (higher weight on return on equity in the compensation plan). This provides empirical evidence on the impact of the fundamental problem of financial accounting theory—the investor-informing and the manager-performance-motivating dimensions of usefulness must be traded off.

Also in an empirical study, Bushman, Indjejikian and Smith (1996) found that CEOs of growth firms, and of firms with long product development and life cycles, derived a greater proportion of their compensation from *individual* performance measures relative to net-income- and stock-price-based measures. Recall that BCE's compensation plan bases short-term incentive awards on individual creativity and initiative in addition to earnings.

In Section 10.4.2, we suggested that accountants could improve the sensitivity of net income to manager effort by enabling identification of persistent earnings by the compensation committee. Evidence that suggests compensation committees do indeed value persistent earnings more highly for compensation purposes than transitory or price-irrelevant earnings is provided by Baber, Kang, and Kumar (1999). In a sample of 712 firms over the years 1992 and 1993, their results include a finding that the effect of earnings changes on compensation increases with the persistence of those earnings changes.

In Section 9.4.2 (Example 9.4) we showed that lower noise in net income benefits the owner by enabling a more efficient compensation contract. Consequently, we expect that accounting-based incentive compensation will be greater relative to other forms of compensation the lower the noise in earnings. Some evidence in this regard is provided by Indjejikian and Nanda (2002). In a sample of 2,981 senior executives over 1988–1995, they found that, on average, the lower the riskiness of earnings (measured as the variance of ROE) the higher the target bonus[8] relative to base salary. This suggests that firms substitute out of salary (riskless, but little incentive effect) into bonus (risky, but greater incentive) as firm risk is less. This is consistent with agency theory and efficient contracting since, when firm risk is relatively low, the incentive benefits of a bonus can be attained with relatively low compensation risk loaded onto the manager.

It should be noted that Indjejikian and Nanda also found that target bonuses, especially for the CEOs in their sample, tended to increase, relative to base salary, with the volatility of return on shares. One interpretation is that firms in high-risk environments (hence, more volatile share prices) rely more on accounting-based performance measures relative to those based on stock price performance. Again, this is consistent with theory.

In sum, the above empirical results suggest that, like investors, compensation committees are on average quite sophisticated in their use of accounting information. Just as full disclosure of reliable, value relevant information will increase investors' use of this information, full disclosure of precise, "effort informative" (i.e., sensitive) information will increase its usage by compensation committees, thereby maintaining and increasing the role of net income in motivating responsible manager performance.

10.6 The Politics of Executive Compensation

The question of manager compensation has been a longstanding one in the United States and Canada. Many have argued that top managers are overpaid, especially in comparison to those in other countries, such as Japan.

In 1990, Jensen and Murphy (JM) published a controversial article about top manager compensation. They argued that CEOs were not overpaid, but that their compensation was far too unrelated to performance, where performance was measured as the change in the firm's market value (that is, the change in shareholder wealth). They examined the salary plus bonus of the CEOs of the 250 largest U.S. corporations over the 15 years from 1974 to 1988. For each year, they added the current year's and next year's salary and bonus and found that on average the CEOs received an extra 6.7 cents compensation over the two years for every $1,000 increase in shareholder wealth. When they added in other compensation components, including stock options and direct share holdings, the CEOs still received only $2.59 per $1,000 increase in shareholder wealth.

Other aspects of JM's investigation were consistent with these findings. For example, the variability (as measured by the standard deviation) over time of CEOs' and regular workers' compensations were almost the same. JM concluded that CEOs did not bear enough risk to motivate good performance, and consequently recommended larger stock holdings by managers. With respect to the BCE plan, note again that there are guidelines that require substantial stock holdings by officers.

However, some counterarguments can be made to JM.[9] First, we would *expect* the relationship between pay and performance to be low for large firms, simply because of a size effect. Suppose that a large corporation increased in value by billions of dollars last year (for example, BCE Inc's 2003 net income was $1.815 billion). An increase of even a small proportion of this amount in the CEO's remuneration would likely attract media attention.

Second, for large corporations at least, it is difficult to put much downside risk on an executive, as we argued in Section 10.4.4. An executive whose pay is highly related to performance would have so much to lose from even a small decline in firm value that this would probably lead to excessive avoidance of risky projects. As a result, the compensation committee may, for example, exclude extraordinary losses when deciding on bonus awards, particularly if the extraordinary loss is not informative about manager effort. Extraordinary losses do, however, lower company value and net income. Consequently, such exclusions lower the pay-performance relationship. If, in addition, upside risk is limited, the relationship is further lowered. While excluding extraordinary items from compensation does lower the CEOs risk, it may be that this risk reduction is consistent with efficient contracting since, as mentioned, extraordinary items may not be informative about manager effort.

Theory in Practice 10.2

To illustrate the treatment of extraordinary items in compensation, it is worthwhile to consider BCE Inc.'s accounting for the results of telecommunications deregulation in Canada during the 1990s. In 1997, BCE Inc. reported a net loss of $1.536 billion, compared to net earnings of $1.152 billion for 1996. Nevertheless, 60,881 share units were awarded to six senior officers for 1997 under the short-term compensation plan in effect at that time, compared to 55,299 share units in 1996. Salaries were also up for 1997, as were stock options awarded under the long-term incentive plan.

continued →

BCE's 1997 net loss resulted from an extraordinary item of $2.950 billion for "stranded costs." That is, increasing competition as a result of telecommunications deregulation resulted in BCE's inability to recover the full costs of certain assets from revenues. The extraordinary charge represented a writedown of these assets to estimated future cash flows, consistent with the ceiling test of Section 3063 of the *CICA Handbook*, discussed in Section 7.2.5. BCE's 1997 earnings before this extraordinary item were $1.414 billion.

One could argue that deregulation of the telecommunications industry has little to do with manager effort, consistent with BCE's treatment of the writedown as an extraordinary item under Section 3480 of the *CICA Handbook* (see Section 5.5). In effect, the item is transitory, hence of low persistence. Low persistence supports a low weighting in determining compensation. Nevertheless, exclusion of the writedown for bonus purposes also supports an argument that a low pay-performance relationship is to be expected.

BCE's exclusion of an extraordinary loss, as just described, is consistent with the results of Gaver and Gaver (1998). For a sample of 376 large U.S. firms over the years 1970–1996, these authors found that while extraordinary gains tended to be reflected in CEO cash compensation, extraordinary losses were not. This result suggests that compensation committees feel that reducing manager compensation for extraordinary losses imposes excessive downside risk on the manager, since the extraordinary loss may be the result of a market downturn rather than manager shirking. Of course, to the extent that extraordinary losses *are* informative about manager effort, their exclusion from bonus calculations is questionable, since their anticipation reduces the manager's effort incentive.

Despite these counterarguments to JM, compensation concerns continue to appear. For example, political attention has grown in the 1990s and early 2000s with respect to ESOs. For CEOs of large U.S. corporations, the market value of these awards often ran into the hundreds of millions of dollars. This attention intensified as the proportion of compensation based on ESOs steadily increased during the 1990s. For example, according to Hall and Murphy (2002), options grants to CEOs of the S&P 500 industrial firms increased from 22% of median total compensation in 1992 to 56% in 1999. Furthermore, option grants continued to rise in the early 2000s, despite a severe decline in the stock market.

Another focus of political attention involves "golden parachutes." These components of compensation contracts often oblige a company to pay multi-million dollar settlements to executives who leave, for whatever reason. For example, *The Economist* (October 9, 2003) reports the objections of the shareholders of GlaxoSmithKline, a large pharmaceutical company, to severance pay included in the compensation contract with its CEO, of $37.5 million U.S. This would be paid even if he was dismissed for poor performance. Angry shareholders voted down the contract at the firm's 2003 annual meeting. However, the vote was advisory only, and the company went ahead despite the vote. GlaxoSmithKline's chairman announced that the company was reviewing its remuneration policy.

Since ESOs bear little downside risk, and golden parachutes reward even poor performance, some support is provided for JM's claim that executives do not bear enough risk. In this regard, many companies, such as BCE Inc., have recently moved to award stock instead of ESOs. Since the ability to sell such stock is restricted while the employee remains with the company, it is less subject to the pump and dump strategy documented for ESOs. In other words, the employee cannot work out from under the risk imposed by owning restricted shares by disposing of them.

To fully understand the politics of executive compensation, however, it is important to realize that the value of a given amount of risky compensation to a manager is lower than it might appear at first glance. For example, the cost of ESOs to the firm is usually based on the Black/Scholes formula. This provides a reasonable measure of the *firm's* ESO cost, since this is the opportunity cost of issuing ESOs to managers (see Section 8.3). However, Black/Scholes assumes that options can be freely traded, whereas compensation plans usually limit the manager's ability to exercise ESOs. For example, under the revised BCE plan, vesting takes place over a three-year period, and a manager's ability to pump and dump does not come into effect until the ESOs vest. To the extent that managers are risk-averse, and forced to hold ESOs (i.e., managers cannot diversify their risk), these restrictions reduce their value to the manager. The more risk-averse the manager, the greater the reduction.

This effect was studied by Hall and Murphy (2002) (HM), building on an earlier analysis by Lambert, Larcker, and Verrecchia (1991). HM report, for example, that the median 1999 total compensation of CEOs of S&P 500 industrial firms was $5.695 million U.S., of which 74% was in the form of ESOs and company stock (ESOs valued on a Black/Scholes basis). For a moderately risk-averse and diversified CEO, however, the cash-equivalent value of this compensation was $3.420 million, a reduction of almost 40%. For a more risk-averse CEO, the reduction was almost 55%. By ignoring the risk factor, media and politicians substantially overstate CEO compensation.

HM's analysis also supports the increasing use of **restricted stock** in place of ESOs. Restricted stock is stock for which sale is restricted for a given period of time. If an increase of such stock-based compensation is accompanied by a reduction in CEO cash compensation, as opposed to simply being added on to existing compensation (this seems reasonable at a time when CEO compensation is under considerable political scrutiny),[10] the firm is better off to use restricted stock rather than ESOs with a positive strike price.[11] The reason, according to HM, derives from the fact that, other things equal, a share of restricted stock is preferred by the CEO to an ESO (since the ESO requires payment of the strike price while no payment is required for a share). Consequently the CEO is willing to give up more cash compensation for restricted stock than for ESOs. Then, for a given reduction in cash compensation, the firm can issue more shares via restricted stock than via ESOs, increasing the CEO's incentive to work hard.

Of course, if labour markets are to work well, politicians, media, and shareholders must know how much compensation the manager is receiving. Indeed, the concerns and analyses of executive compensation outlined above would not be possible without adequate information. In this regard, it is interesting to recall that in 1993 the Ontario Securities Commission adopted regulations to require firms to give more disclosure of their executive compensation. These regulations are similar to those of the SEC (1992) in the United States. For example, a detailed explanation of the compensation of firms' five highest-paid executives is required, as is a report from the compensation committee justifying the pay levels. The BCE Inc. compensation information in Exhibit 10.1 is pursuant to these regulations, for example. Presumably, the securities commissions feel that if shareholders and others have enough information to intelligently evaluate manager compensation levels and components, they will take appropriate action if these appear out of line.

Some evidence that the 1992 SEC regulations did have the desired effect is presented by Lo (2003). Lo studied the subsequent operating performance (measured by ROE and ROA) and share price performance of firms that had lobbied against the SEC regulations, relative to a control sample of similar firms that did not lobby. Note that if a firm's compensation contract is not very efficient (i.e., if it is tilted in the manager's favour, so that the manager receives excess compensation), that firm's manager has an incentive to lobby against fuller disclosure of compensation plan details. Lo found that on average both the operating and share returns of the lobbying firms improved relative to the control firms subsequent to the new regulations. This improved performance is consistent with more efficient compensation contracts, imposed on the lobbying managers as more compensation information became available.

Whether measures to increase available compensation information, and better understanding by politicians, media, and shareholders of the value of share-based compensation to the manager, will suffice to stem the concern about executive compensation is unclear at the present time. Possibly, stronger action will be needed. One such action is to require expensing of ESOs, as has been done in North America and internationally. Another is to limit the amount of manager compensation deductible for tax purposes, as has been done in the United States.

10.7 Conclusions on Executive Compensation

Managerial labour markets undoubtedly reduce the severity of moral hazard. However, past manager performance is not an iron-clad indicator of future performance. Also, labour markets are subject to moral hazard and adverse selection problems, since managers may withhold or bias information to disguise shirking. Consequently, incentive contracts arc still necessary.

Executive compensation contracts involve a delicate balancing of incentives, risk, and decision horizon. To properly align the interests of managers and shareholders, an efficient contract needs to achieve a high level of motivation while avoiding the imposition of too much risk on the manager. Too much risk can have dysfunctional consequences such as shortening a manager's decision horizon, adoption of earnings-increasing tactics that are against the firm's longer-run interests, and avoidance of risky projects. Managers are particularly sensitive to risk, because they cannot diversify it away as can shareholders.

To attain proper alignment, incentive plans usually feature a combination of salary, bonus, and various types of stock plans including restricted stock and options. These components of compensation are usually based on two performance measures—net income and share price. We can think of these as two noisy measures of the unobservable payoff from current-period manager effort. Theory predicts that the relative proportion of each in the compensation plan depends on both their relative precision and sensitivity, and the length of manager decision horizon that the firm wants to motivate. Empirically, it appears that executive compensation is related to performance but that the strength of the relationship is low. However, for large firms at least, this low relationship is to be expected. Also, the relative proportion of net income-based and share price-based compensation components seems to vary as the theory predicts.

Executive compensation is surrounded by political controversy. Regulators have responded by expanding the information available to shareholders and others, on the assumption that they will take action to eliminate inefficient plans, or the managers and firms that have them. There is some evidence that expanded information is having the desired effect. However, politicians, media, and shareholders should realize that the value of risky compensation to managers is less than it may seem at first glance.

We may conclude that financial reporting has an important role in motivating executive performance. This role extends to improving the working of managerial labour markets by reducing the extent to which manager reputation may be based on incomplete or biased information, and to serving as a payoff measure in compensation contracts. This role is equally important as its role in promoting good investment decisions and improving the operation of securities markets.

Questions and Problems

1. Below is a portion of a 2005 proxy form sent to shareholders of Miracle-J Corporation. It reveals that Miracle-J has a bonus plan for its three senior executives that allocates them 10% of before-tax profits. Also, under the Employee Stock Option Plan, share options up to 12% of capitalization may be granted to directors or employees.

Miracle-J Corp.

Executive and Management Compensation
The Corporation's five executive officers were remunerated, in total, $440,000 by way of fees, salaries, and bonuses for the fiscal year ended May 31, 2005.

Included in the aforesaid sum was $280,000 paid to the three senior executive officers as full-time employees of the Corporation, pursuant to individual four-year Management Agreements made between the Corporation and those senior executive officers, effective June 1, 2003. Under the terms of the Agreements, the three senior executives are entitled to receive an aggregate bonus of 10% of before-tax profits earned by the company and their base salaries are to be increased 10% per year. For the 2005 fiscal year, the three senior executive officers waived their bonus entitlements to the extent that each received dividends on shares of the Corporation held by them which dividend was declared and paid for the fiscal year ended May 31, 2005.

It is to be noted that the Directors have adopted a form of Employee Stock Option Plan under which share options of up to 12% of the capitalization of the Corporation may be granted to Directors or employees. There are presently reserved, to that end, 930,000 common shares of the Corporation; but the Corporation has not granted any option to any Director or employees as of the date of this Information Circular.

Required
a. Explain the reason for the 10% bonus plan for senior executives. Are there any possible dysfunctional consequences of the bonus plan resulting from the appar-

ent lack of a cap? Why is the bonus based on before-tax profits, rather than after-tax?

b. Explain why there is also an Employee Stock Option Plan.

c. To what extent would the bonus plan cause management to be concerned about accounting policies and changes in GAAP?

2. Agency theory suggests that a way to motivate managers to act in the best interests of the owners/shareholders is to link managerial compensation to performance measures, such as net income or share price. However, such a linkage imposes risk on the manager.

Required

a. Why is it important to control or reduce some of the risk thus imposed on managers? Explain.

b. Explain *two* methods by which risk imposed on the managers could be reduced. What happens if too much compensation risk is eliminated?

c. Many managerial compensation packages impose restrictions on *when* managers can sell stock granted to them as a part of their compensation. For example, some compensation packages indicate that restricted stock awards may be forfeited unless the manager continues to work for the firm for a certain number of years after the granting of the award. Discuss the justification behind such restrictions.

d. Inclusion of shares and options in managerial compensation packages has been attributed to the desire of the owners/shareholders to provide managers an incentive to undertake policies that benefit the firm's long-term rather than short-term interests. If this is true, why not compensate the manager only on the basis of share return (for example, only by stock options)? In other words, under these circumstances, what is the justification for having a cash or bonus element in the compensation package?

3. A proponent of ESOs argues that no expense should be recorded for ESOs issued to managers and other employees, since they do not cost the employer anything. On the contrary, the employer *receives* cash equal to the ESOs' exercise price.

Do you agree that no expense should be recorded? Explain why or why not.

4. Explain why the value of ESOs and restricted stock to a manager is generally less than their Black/Scholes value (for ESOs) or stock market value (for restricted stock).

5. Explain why, for large corporations, a low pay/performance relationship is to be expected.

6. Firms A and B are roughly the same size, but operate in different industries. Firm A bases a high proportion of its executive compensation on net income and a relatively low proportion on share price performance. For firm B, these proportions are reversed. Yet, both firms appear to be well managed, consistently profitable, and growing. Use the concepts of sensitivity and precision of a performance measure to explain why both firms' compensation plans are efficient, despite the differing proportions.

7. In 2002, the Toronto-Dominion Bank (TD) announced that it would voluntarily expense ESOs, starting with its 2003 fiscal year beginning November 1, 2002. In the MD&A section of its 2003 *Annual Report*, TD stated that it had charged to expense for 2003 an amount of $9 million for ESOs, using the fair value method. Canadian GAAP at the time did not require that ESOs be expensed.

TD's reported net income for 2003 was $1.076 billion, compared to a net loss of $67 million for 2002.

Suggest reasons why TD would voluntarily expense its ESOs.

8. Microsoft Corp. announced in 2002 that it was discontinuing its employees' stock option plan in favour of restricted stock, vesting over a five-year period. At that time, many of its already-granted ESOs were under water (i.e., exercise price greater than share market value).

In 2003, no expense needed to be recorded for ESOs if they were granted with an intrinsic value of zero. However, generally speaking, the fair value of restricted stock issued to employees *is* charged to expense. For 2003, Microsoft reported earnings per share of 14 cents, after stock-based compensation expense of $2.17 billion U.S. Its 2003 earnings were 17 cents per share. Microsoft reported that before stock-related expenses its 2002 earnings would have been 34 cents per share, compared with analysts' consensus estimate of 30 cents.

Required

a. Give a reason why Microsoft's share price would be unaffected by the news of its reduction in reported earnings due to the 2003 stock-based compensation expense. Give two reasons why stock price may fall.

b. Give two reasons why Microsoft's share price might rise as a result of this news.

c. Why might Microsoft, and numerous other large corporations, such as BCE Inc. (Section 10.3), have eliminated or reduced the usage of ESOs in their compensation plans?

9. In its 2004 proxy statement to shareholders, the compensation committee of General Electric Company (GE) reported that in 2003 it had discontinued ESOs for its CEO, Jeffrey Immelt. In their place, GE awarded 250,000 restricted share units. One-half of these units entitle Mr. Immelt to one share each in 2008 if operating cash flow growth, adjusted for the effect of unusual events, increases at an average rate of 10% or more during 2003–2007. Otherwise, the share units will be cancelled. The other 125,000 units entitle him to one share each in 2008 if the total return on GE shares over 2003–2007 meets or exceeds the return on the S&P 500 Index for the same period. Otherwise, the share units will be cancelled. GE's shares were trading for about $30 U.S. at the time of this announcement.

For 2003, Mr. Immelt's compensation also included a base salary of $3 million plus a cash bonus of $4.325 million. The amounts of cash bonuses are determined by GE's compensation committee upon evaluation of an individual's performance for the year, including contribution to financial performance. According to the compensation committee, after taking into account cash bonus and restricted share units, more than 75% of Mr. Immelt's potential compensation for 2003 is at risk. GE also requires that its CEO own six times salary in company shares.

Required

a. What balance between short-run and long-run CEO effort is the GE compensation plan likely to induce? Explain.

b. What are some of the dysfunctional effects for the firm of too much risk imposed on a risk-averse manager?

c. One-half of the restricted share units awarded to Mr. Immelt are based on meeting an operating cash flow target. Evaluate the relative precision and sensitivity of operating cash flow and net income as performance measures. Also, evaluate the effects on manager motivation of eliminating "unusual events" from the performance measure.

d. To what extent are the restricted share units awarded to Mr. Immelt based on shareholder return subject to the "pump and dump" behaviour that some managers seem to adopt when their compensation is based on ESOs?

10. In 1993, the OSC implemented new executive compensation disclosure rules (OSC, Form 40, Securities Act, Regulation 638/93). Similar requirements are in place in the United States. These specify that shareholder proxy statements contain tables spelling out compensation for the five highest-paid executives, plus a report from the board's compensation committee explaining the firm's compensation practices. (The BCE Compensation Committee report in Exhibit 10.1 is an example of reporting under these rules.)

Required

a. To what extent do you think that such disclosure requirements will assist an efficient managerial labour market to work well? Explain. Include a definition of an efficient managerial labour market in your answer.

b. If the managerial labour market is fully efficient (that is, analogous to an efficient securities market), would manager incentive plans based on risky performance measures such as share price and reported net income be needed? Explain why or why not.

11. On November 18, 2002, *The Globe and Mail* (page B4) reported "CEO assails pay disclosure rules." This referred to a speech by Claude Lamoureux, CEO of Ontario Teachers Pension Plan Board. The board is a major owner of and shareholder in numerous companies, hence vitally interested in questions of executive motivation and compensation. Mr. Lamoureux's concern is with the OSC rules requiring firms to disclose and explain the compensation of their five most highly paid employees. He argues that the effect of these rules is simply to put upward pressure on pay levels, as executives demand raises to meet or exceed that of their peers in other companies.

In this regard, the BCE Compensation Committee states (Exhibit 10.1) that an executive's total compensation is positioned at the median of what is paid by a group of similar companies. In the changes to the BCE plan for 2004, the committee advises that total compensation will be increased to the 60th percentile of that paid by the comparable companies.

Required

a. Explain the argument in favour of companies disclosing compensation information of their senior executives. Why do you think that Mr. Lamoureux, CEO of a very large and powerful institutional investor, rejects this argument?

b. How do you think the policy of BCE Inc. of fixing its total executive compensation at the 60th percentile of that paid by the comparable companies will affect the level of executive compensation in the telecommunications industry?

12. Refer to the Theory in Practice 10.2 in Section 10.6. Reproduced below are the 1997 consolidated statement of operations and Note 2 to the financial statements of BCE Inc. The statement of operations shows an extraordinary charge of $2.950 billion for stranded costs. After this extraordinary charge, operations showed a net loss for the year of $1.536 billion.

Required

a. Does the charge for stranded costs meet the definition of an extraordinary item under Section 3480 of the *CICA Handbook* (see Section 5.5)? Discuss.

b. Regardless of whether or not the $2.950 billion is an extraordinary item, as a member of BCE's compensation committee would you support exclusion of the charge from earnings for the purpose of managers' short-term incentive awards? Discuss.

c. What is the persistence of the $2.950 billion component of 1997 earnings? Your answer should be in the range [0–1]. Explain your answer.

d. On April 23, 1998, *The Globe and Mail* reported "Earnings results fuel BCE shares to 52-week high." This headline refers to BCE's record reported earnings for its first quarter, 1998, of 48 cents per share excluding "onetime items." This is a 46% increase over 33 cents per share for the same quarter of 1997. The article quoted the CEO of BCE as saying, "We continue to see solid growth in all areas of our operations." According to the article, these first-quarter results suggest a good performance by BCE in 1998, after a $1.5 billion loss in 1997 due to a record $2.9 billion charge at its telephone company subsidiary.

Give another reason, in addition to "solid growth" that may explain the record first-quarter results. As a member of the BCE compensation committee contemplating the 1998 annual short-term incentive awards, would you support basing these awards on the record first-quarter earnings? Explain your position.

CONSOLIDATED FINANCIAL STATEMENTS—BCE INC.
CONSOLIDATED STATEMENT OF OPERATIONS

	($ million, except per share amounts)		
For the years ended December 31	1997	1996	1995
Revenues	33,191	28,167	24,624
Operating expenses	25,795	22,011	19,434
Research and development expense	2,911	2,471	2,134
Operating profit	4,485	3,685	3,056
Other income	365	393	238
Operating earnings	4,850	4,078	3,294
Interest expense – long-term debt	1,111	1,160	1,154
– other debt	121	141	172
Total interest expense	1,232	1,301	1,326
Earnings before taxes, non-controlling interest and extraordinary item	3,618	2,777	1,968
Income taxes	(1,522)	(1,118)	(819)
Non-controlling interest	(682)	(507)	(367)
Net earnings before extraordinary item	1,414	1,152	782
Extraordinary item	(2,950)	—	—
Net earnings (loss)	(1,536)	1,152	782
Dividends on preferred shares	(74)	(76)	(87)
Net earnings (loss) applicable to common shares	(1,610)	1,076	695
Earnings (loss) per common share[1]			
Net earnings before extraordinary item	2.11	1.70	1.12
Extraordinary item	(4.64)	—	—
Net earnings (loss)	(2.53)	1.70	1.12
Dividends per common share[1]	1.36	1.36	1.36
Average number of common shares outstanding (millions)[1]	636.0	632.7	622.9

1 Reflects the subdivision of common shares on a two-for-one basis on May 14, 1997.

Extraordinary Item

As at December 31, 1997, BCE determined that most of its telecommunications subsidiary and associated companies no longer met the criteria necessary for the continued application of regulatory accounting provisions. As a result, BCE recorded an extraordinary non-cash charge of $2,950 million, net of an income tax benefit of $1,892 million and a non-controlling interest of $38 million. Also included in the extraordinary item is an after-tax charge of

$97 million representing BCE's share of the related extraordinary item of its associated companies.

The operations of most of BCE's telecommunications subsidiary and associated companies no longer met the criteria for application of regulatory accounting provisions due to significant changes in regulation including the implementation of price cap regulation which replaced rate-of-return regulation effective January 1, 1998 and the concurrent introduction of competition in the local exchange market. Accordingly, BCE adjusted the net carrying values of assets and liabilities as at December 31, 1997 to reflect values appropriate under GAAP for enterprises no longer subject to rate-of-return regulation.

The determination by BCE that most of its telecommunications subsidiary and associated companies no longer met the criteria for the continuing application of regulatory accounting provisions is the result of a review, which began in 1997, to assess the impact of the introduction of price cap regulation coupled with the introduction of competition in the local exchange market. Before the advent of these two factors, accounting practices were based on a regulatory regime which provided reasonable assurance of the recovery of costs through rates set by the regulator and charged to customers. These regulatory accounting provisions resulted in the recognition of certain assets and liabilities along with capital asset lives which were substantially different from enterprises not subject to rate-of-return regulation.

The extraordinary charge consists of a pre-tax charge of $3,602 million related to capital assets and a pre-tax charge of $1,181 million to adjust the carrying values of other assets and liabilities to arrive at carrying values appropriate for enterprises not subject to rate-of-return regulation. The amount of the charge related to capital assets was determined based upon an estimate of the underlying cash flows using management's best estimate assumptions concerning the most likely course of action and other factors relating to competition, technological changes and the evolution of products and services. The net carrying values of capital assets were adjusted primarily through an increase in accumulated depreciation. The primary component of the $1,181 million charge relates to the write-off of deferred business transformation and workforce reduction costs.

SOURCE: BCE Inc., *1997 Annual Report*. Reprinted by permission.

13. Many firms "reprice" ESOs following major declines in their share price, by lowering the exercise price. This is because ESOs issued before the decline are deep out of the money, hence unlikely to be of any value. Such moves usually outrage shareholders, who have seen the value of their shares also fall but who receive no comparable benefits, and are prominently reported in the media.

Saly (1994) was an original analytical study of the repricing of ESOs. Her analysis applies to repricing after a market downturn, such as the downturn experienced in the early 2000s, and not to a firm-specific fall in share price that may be due to manager shirking.

As Saly points out, compensation contracts are incomplete. That is, it is unlikely that provisions for adjustments to compensation following a market downturn are anticipated and written into the compensation plan. The question then is, should the contract be "renegotiated" following a market downturn, by repricing ESOs? If so, this would violate the general rule that, once signed, contracts tend to be rigid.

In Saly's model, the answer is yes. Renegotiation of the ESOs' strike price increases the correlation between manager effort and the performance measure (share price), since a market downturn is not a result of low manager effort. Without the possibility of renegotiation, the risk-averse manager would have to be compensated for the risk inherent in the possibility of a market downturn, to attain reservation utility. If a downturn occurs and there is no repricing, the manager's expected utility will fall, since the expected proceeds from ESOs are effectively zero. This will cause him/her to either shirk or leave the company.

In June 2001, Nortel Networks Corp. announced that it was cancelling its existing ESOs and replacing them with new ESOs with a lower strike price. Nortel's share price, which had been in excess of $100 when many of the ESO's were issued, suffered following the market collapse of share prices of hi-tech firms, and was trading in the $20 range at the time of the announcement. Nortel's move was widely reported in the financial media and drew significant negative comment. For example, *The Globe and Mail* (June 5, 2001) quoted Carol Bowie of the Investor Responsibility Research Center as saying " . . . you can't make the 50-yard kick. So we'll cut it down to 35." It also quoted J. Richard Finlay, head of the Center for Corporate and Public Governance as saying "We'd all like to be told our high school physics test where we got 35 out of 100 is now 35 out of 50, but shareholders don't have that luxury."

Nortel defended its move by claiming it was necessary to retain key employees, pointing out that top manager ESOs were not being repriced (this would require shareholder approval) but only those of lower level employees. In the same issue of the *Globe*, Brian Milner pointed out that the cost to Nortel of repricing the ESOs is zero, and that no further dilution of shareholders' equity will result since the old ESOs are being cancelled. Nevertheless, Milner comments that in the public eye the repricing is still "a reward for crummy performance."

Required
a. In the light of Saly's model, do you agree with Nortel's ESO repricing? Explain why or why not.
b. Nortel planned to cancel existing ESOs and replace them with new ones, rather than simply repricing the existing options to a lower exercise price. Recall that in 2001, GAAP did not require expensing of ESOs. Rather, most firms, including Nortel, followed APB 25 (See Section 8.3) in the financial statements proper, reporting the fair value of ESO expense in a note to the financial statements. Why do you think Nortel replaced the old ESOs with new ones, rather than simply repricing the existing ones?
c. In its 2003 proxy statement, the Compensation Committee of General Electric Company reported that the company has a policy of not repricing ESOs. Why would a company have such a policy?

14. Following major declines in their share prices, firms frequently "reprice" outstanding stock options issued to executives and employees as part of their incentive compensation. Reproduced here is an article from the *Financial Post* (April 3, 1997), describing such a repricing by Rogers Communications Inc. According to the article, Rogers' stock options with exercise prices ranging from $12.64 to $19.38 were lowered to an exercise price of $8.31.

Required

a. Give reasons why firms frequently issue stock options to executives and senior employees as part of their incentive compensation.

b. If options are always repriced when share prices fall, what effects may there be on the incentives to work hard of officers and employees involved?

c. If you were a shareholder of Rogers Communications, how would you react to the repricing?

d. It has been argued that options held by the CEO should not be repriced, even if repricing is extended to less senior executives and employees. Note that the article reports that options held by Ted Rogers, president and CEO of Rogers Communications, are not being repriced. Why?

Rogers Reprices Compensation Options

Rogers Communications Inc. repriced all the options its executives and other employees have received as part of their compensation packages in 1994 and 1995 because the company's share price has fallen so far, Rogers' annual shareholder circular says.

The options' new exercise price is $8.31, significantly lower than the earlier prices, said Rogers spokeswoman Jan Innes.

Previously, exercise prices ranged from $12.64 to $19.38. Also, the exercise period was extended to 2006.

"If you've got options and they're well above what the stock is trading at, they're certainly not very interesting," explained Jan Innes.

Rogers' circular says the company awards options to "focus executives' attention on the long-term interests of the corporation and its shareholders."

Analysts were surprised by the move.

"I can imagine that shareholders will be a bit perturbed," said one. "After all, their shares didn't get repriced. But I suppose it will help keep people motivated."

Rogers shares have fallen drastically since 1993, when they hit a $21.88 high. The shares (RCIb/TSE) closed yesterday at $8, down 55¢.

Ted Rogers' options, along with other non-management directors' options, will not be repriced.

Rogers' class A shareholders, the only ones entitled to vote, will vote on the arrangement at the company's annual meeting May 2. Ted Rogers controls over 90% of the A shares, so the vote should pass.

Meanwhile, working two jobs is paying off for Ted Rogers, president and chief executive of Rogers Communications and acting president of Rogers Cable-systems Ltd.

continued →

> Rogers got a 21% salary increase to $600,000 for 1996, plus a 160% rise in his bonus, to $260,110, for a total of $860,110. In addition, he was given 300,000 new options.
>
> But he was not the highest paid executive at the cable and telecommunications company he founded.
>
> That distinction went to Stan Kabala, chief operating officer of telecommunications and chief executive of Rogers Cantel Mobile Communications Inc.
>
> Kabala, who joined Rogers Jan. 1, 1996, got a salary of $600,000, plus a bonus of $925,000, for a total of $1,525,000. He was also awarded 119,000 stock options.
>
> Kabala's big bonus was related to a deal completed in November 1996 with U.S. phone giant AT&T Corp., as well as for Cantel's performance.
>
> The last time Rogers paid bonuses of such magnitude was in 1994 after it completed its takeover of Maclean Hunter Ltd.
>
> ───────
>
> Source: *The National Post*, April 3, 1997. Reprinted by permission.

15. Ittner, Larcker, and Rajan (1997) studied the relative weights placed on financial and non-financial performance measures in CEO bonus contracts for a sample of 317 U.S. firms across 48 industries for 1993–1994. Recall that BCE Inc. (Section 10.3) has both types of performance measures in its short-term incentive awards. Non-financial performance measures in the BCE plan include creativity and initiative, succession planning, and management development. Financial performance measures include earnings per share, revenue growth, cash flow, and return on invested capital.

    Ittner, Larcker, and Rajan find empirical support for the following hypotheses about the relative weights on financial and non-financial performance measures in compensation plans:

    i. *Noise.* The higher the correlation between manager effort and net income (measured by the correlation between stock market and accounting-based returns), the greater the relative weight on financial performance measures.
    ii. *Firm strategy.* "Prospector firms" (growth and innovation oriented, identify and adapt quickly to new product/service opportunities) will have greater relative weight on non-financial performance measures than "defender" firms (stable set of products/services, emphasis on increasing efficiency to reduce operating costs).
    iii. *Product quality.* The greater the firm commitment to quality, the greater the relative weight on non-financial performance measures.
    iv. *Regulation.* Regulated firms will have greater relative weight on non-financial performance measures than non-regulated firms.

    Required
    a. Give intuitive arguments to explain these four hypotheses.
    b. Which of these four hypotheses might explain the inclusion by BCE Inc. of non-financial performance measures in its short-term incentive awards?

Notes

1. See Note 7, Chapter 9.

2. When there is more than one performance measure in the contract, the sensitivity concept becomes more complex. An increase, say, in effort increases the expected value of *all* of the performance measures. In our context, an effort increase has a direct effect of increasing the expected value of net income. However, the expected value of share price also increases. To the extent that there is positive covariance between net income and share price, the increase in expected share price dilutes the ability of net income to convey information about effort, reducing its sensitivity and hence its weight in the mix of performance measures. A similar phenomenon reduces the sensitivity of share price.

   This argument can also be interpreted from a risk standpoint. Covariance between net income and share price measures the extent to which random factors affecting net income also affect share price, that is, the *common noise*. To avoid impacting the manager's compensation twice for the same noise, the weights on the performance measures are reduced by an amount that depends on the covariance between them.

3. A compromise, as in SFAS 130 introduced in Section 7.3.2, is to record unrealized gains and losses from fair valuing assets and liabilities in other comprehensive income. Then, net income omits the sensitivity and precision effects of fair value accounting.

4. For a methodology to estimate a firm's investment opportunities, and evidence that the proportion of share price-based compensation in firms' compensation contracts increases with investment opportunities, see Baber, Janakiraman, and Kang (1996).

5. In statistical terms, the performance measures covary.

6. In economics, a situation where an oligopolist chooses product price is known as Bertrand competition. This is contrasted with Cournot competition, where the firm chooses the amount of production.

7. In technical terms, compensation from plans that limit downside risk but not upside risk is a convex function of performance. Thus plans with a bogey but no cap are convex, as are ESO plans.

8. A target bonus is the bonus a firm pays if the executive's performance reaches a predetermined level. If performance is greater than target, a larger bonus is paid, and vice versa. The BCE plan contains a target bonus, and this bonus increases with corporate performance (the corporate performance factor).

9. These arguments are based on R.A. Lambert and D.F. Larcker, "Firm Performance and the Compensation of Chief Executive Officers," working paper, January 1993.

10. Note that in the revised BCE compensation plan, issuance of restricted stock is accompanied by a reduction in ESO compensation, not cash compensation. The reason, presumably, is that BCE is moving to shorten managers' decision horizons at the same time.

11. Restricted stock is equivalent to an ESO with a zero strike price.

Chapter 11

Earnings Management

FIGURE 11.1 ORGANIZATION OF CHAPTER 11

11.1 Overview

Earnings management can be viewed from both a financial reporting and a contracting perspective. From a financial reporting perspective, managers may use earnings management to meet analysts' earnings forecasts, thereby avoiding the strong negative share price reaction that quickly follows a failure to meet investor expectations. Also, they may record excessive write-offs, or emphasize earnings constructs other than net income, such as "pro forma" earnings. Some of these tactics suggest that managers do not fully accept securities market efficiency.

There is another view of earnings management, however. Management may use it to create a stream of smooth and growing earnings over time. Given securities market efficiency, this requires management to draw on its inside information. Thus, earnings management can be a vehicle for the communication of management's inside information to investors. Interpreted this way, income smoothing leads to the interesting, and perhaps surprising, conclusion that some earnings management can be useful from a financial reporting perspective.

From a contracting perspective, earnings management can be used as a way to protect the firm from the consequences of unforeseen events when contracts are rigid and incomplete. Also, as we saw in Chapter 9, managerial compensation contracts that allow some earnings management can be more efficient than ones that do not, due to the high costs of eliminating earnings management completely.

Too much earnings management, however, reduces the ability of investors to interpret current net income, particularly if the earnings management is buried in core earnings or otherwise not fully disclosed. As we saw in Chapter 5, reported net income is useful to investors in evaluating future firm performance. Excessive earnings management may reduce this usefulness. Also, earnings management affects the manager's motivation to exert effort, because managers can use earnings management opportunistically to smooth their compensation over time, thereby reducing compensation risk. But, we have seen that managers need to bear some risk if they are to work hard.

For whatever reason, it should be apparent that managers have a strong interest in the bottom line. Given that managers can choose accounting policies from a set of policies (for example, GAAP), it is natural to expect that they will choose policies so as to help achieve their objectives. As mentioned, these choices can be motivated either by efficient markets and contracts, or by opportunism and rejection of market efficiency. Whatever the reason, this is called **earnings management**.

An understanding of earnings management is important to accountants, because it enables an improved understanding of the usefulness of net income, both for reporting to investors and for contracting. It may also assist accountants to avoid some of the serious legal and reputation consequences that arise when firms become financially distressed. Such distress is often preceded by serious abuse of earnings management.

> **Earnings management** is the choice by a manager of accounting policies so as to achieve some specific objective.

It should be mentioned that choice of accounting policies is interpreted quite broadly. While the dividing line is not clear-cut, it is convenient to divide accounting policy choice into two categories. One is the choice of accounting policies per se, such as straight-line versus declining-balance amortization, or policies for revenue recognition. The other category is discretionary accruals, such as provisions for credit losses, warranty costs, inventory values, and timing and amounts of non-recurring and extraordinary items such as write-offs and provisions for reorganization.

Regardless of its rationale, it is important to realize that there is an "iron law" surrounding earnings management, which will be familiar from introductory accounting. This is that *accruals reverse*. Thus, a manager who manages earnings upwards to an amount greater than can be sustained will find that the reversal of these accruals in subsequent periods will force future earnings downwards just as surely as current earnings were raised.[1] Then, even more earnings management is needed if reporting of losses is to be further postponed. In effect, if a firm is performing poorly, earnings management cannot indefinitely postpone the day of reckoning. Thus, the possibility that earnings management can be good should not be used to rationalize misleading or fraudulent reporting. The accountant treads a fine line between earnings management and earnings mismanagement. Ultimately, the location of this line must be determined by effective corporate governance, reinforced by securities and managerial labour markets, standard setters, securities commissions, and the courts.

The iron law of accruals reversal leads to an important aspect of earnings management. All of the models of earnings management in Chapter 9 were single-period. Even then, we showed that earnings management could, in theory, be beneficial. However, to better understand earnings management, we need to think in terms of multiple periods. Then, further earnings management potential, such as income smoothing and "big bath," is revealed. Indeed, the three hypotheses of positive accounting theory (Section 8.6.2) implicitly assume a multi-period horizon.

Yet, multi-period horizons also operate to inhibit earnings management. For example, to what extent is a manager's propensity to over or understate reported net income reduced by the knowledge that such mis-statements will inevitably reverse? To what extent do markets, such as the securities market and the manager's reputation on the managerial labour market, help to control opportunistic earnings management? We saw some evidence in Wolfson's (1985) study of oil and gas limited partnerships in Section 10.2 that reputation effects reduce but do not eliminate the moral hazard problem. While a multi-period horizon increases the potential for earnings management, it also operates to constrain the practice.

Finally, it should be noted that we define earnings management in terms of accounting policy choice. Another way to manage earnings is by means of *real* variables, such as R&D, maintenance, timing of disposals of capital assets, etc. Presumably, these devices are more costly than managing accounting policies, since they directly affect the firm's longer-run interests. Nevertheless, managers may use them since the costs of managing earnings using accounting variables has increased of late, due to reporting failures such as Enron and WorldCom and resulting legislation, notably Sarbanes-Oxley (see Section 1.2). Nevertheless, we concentrate primarily on management of accounting variables rather than real variables due to both their historical importance and their relevance to accounting. Figure 11.1 outlines the organization of this chapter.

11.2 Patterns of Earnings Management

Managers may engage in a variety of earnings management patterns. Here, we collect and briefly summarize these patterns.

1. **Taking a bath** This can take place during periods of organizational stress or reorganization. If a firm must report a loss, management may feel it might as well report a large one—it has little to lose at this point. Consequently, it will write off assets, provide for expected future costs, and generally "clear the decks." Because of accrual reversal, this enhances the probability of future reported profits. In effect, the recording of large write-offs puts future earnings "in the bank."

2. **Income minimization** This is similar to taking a bath, but less extreme. Such a pattern may be chosen by a politically visible firm during periods of high profitability. Policies that suggest income minimization include rapid write-offs of capital assets and intangibles, expensing of advertising and R&D expenditures, successful-efforts accounting for oil and gas exploration costs, and so on. Income tax considerations, such as for LIFO inventory in the United States, provide another set of motivations for this pattern, as does enhancement of arguments for relief from foreign competition.

3. **Income maximization** From positive accounting theory, managers may engage in a pattern of maximization of reported net income for bonus purposes, providing this does not put them above the cap. Firms that are close to debt covenant violations may also maximize income.

4. **Income smoothing** This is perhaps the most interesting earnings management pattern. From a contracting perspective, risk-averse managers prefer a less variable bonus stream, other things equal. Consequently, managers may smooth reported earnings over time so as to receive relatively constant compensation. Efficient compensation contracting may exploit this effect, and condone some income smoothing as a low cost way to attain the manager's reservation utility.

   We considered covenants in long-term lending agreements in Section 9.7. The more volatile the stream of reported net income, the higher the probability that covenant violation will occur. This provides another smoothing incentive—to reduce volatility of reported net income so as to smooth covenant ratios over time.

   Managers may feel, with some justification, that they may be fired when reported earnings are low. Income smoothing reduces the likelihood of reporting low earnings.

   Finally, firms may smooth reported net income for external reporting purposes. As we have suggested, smoothing can convey inside information to the market by enabling the firm to communicate its expected persistent earning power.

It should be apparent that these various earnings management patterns can be in conflict. Over time, the pattern chosen by a firm may vary due to changes in contracts, changes in levels of profitability, and changes in political visibility. Even at a given point in time, the firm may face conflicting needs to, say, reduce reported net income for political reasons, increase it to meet analysts' forecasts, or smooth it for borrowing purposes.

11.3 Evidence of Earnings Management for Bonus Purposes

A paper by Healy (1985), entitled "The Effect of Bonus Schemes on Accounting Decisions," is a seminal investigation of a contractual motivation for earnings management. Healy observes that managers have inside information on the firm's net income before earnings management.[2] Since outside parties, including the board itself, may be unable to learn what this number is, he predicted that managers would manage net income so as to maximize their bonuses under their firms' compensation plans. Here, we will review Healy's methods and findings.

Healy's paper is based on positive accounting theory (Section 8.6). It attempts to explain and predict managers' choices of accounting policies. More specifically, it is an extension of the bonus plan hypothesis, which states that managers of firms with bonus plans will maximize current earnings. By looking more closely at the structure of bonus plans, Healy comes up with specific predictions of how and under what circumstances managers will engage in this type of earnings management.

Healy's study was confined to firms whose compensation plans are based on current reported net income only. These will be called **bonus schemes** for the rest of this section. As we saw for BCE Inc. in Section 10.3, net income-based financial targets are a major input into short-term incentive awards. We also pointed out, in Section 10.4.4, reasons why bonus schemes may have bogeys and caps. In Healy's sample, not all schemes have caps, although they all have bogeys. Figure 11.2 illustrates a typical bonus scheme.

FIGURE 11.2 TYPICAL BONUS SCHEME

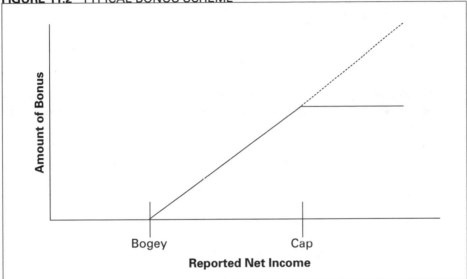

In the figure the bonus increases linearly (for example, 10% of net income) between the bogey and the cap. Below the bogey, bonus is zero. If there is no cap, the bonus would increase along the dotted line. Otherwise, the bonus becomes a constant for net income greater than the cap. Such a bonus plan is called **piecewise linear.** A piecewise linear bonus scheme is simpler than that of BCE's short-term incentive plan, where the bogey and cap are implicit. Nevertheless, the basic idea of compensation increasing in earnings performance carries over. The question then is, do managers manage earnings as predicted by the bonus hypothesis?

To explore this question, consider the incentives to manage reported net income faced by a manager subject to such a scheme. If net income is low (that is, below the bogey), the manager has an incentive to lower it even further, that is, to take a bath. If no bonus is to be received anyway, the manager might as well adopt accounting policies to further reduce reported net income.[3] In so doing, the probability of receiving a bonus the following year is increased since current write-offs will reduce future amortization charges. Similarly, if net income is high (above the cap), there is motivation to adopt income minimization policies, because bonus is permanently lost on reported net income greater than the cap.

Only if net income is between the bogey and cap (except for the case in note 3) is the manager motivated to adopt accounting policies to increase reported net income. Thus, Healy refines the bonus plan hypothesis—it really only applies when net income is between the bogey and the cap.

How does a manager manage net income? Healy assumes that managers use accruals. To illustrate how accruals may be used to manage earnings, we begin by repeating again the formula given in Sections 5.4.1 and 6.2.6:

Net income = cash flow from operations ± net accruals

This can be broken down into:

Net income = cash flow from operations ± net non-discretionary accruals
             ± net discretionary accruals.

The concept of discretionary accruals was introduced in Section 8.6.3. These are accruals over which the manager can exercise some control. As pointed out there, the estimation of discretionary accruals by researchers poses a major challenge. Estimates based on the Jones (1991) model are the currently accepted estimation methodology. However, other approaches are possible. One of these is an item-by-item procedure, which considers the change in each accrual and classifies it as primarily discretionary or primarily non-discretionary. Usually, these amounts can be obtained from the statement of cash flows.[4]

To illustrate, consider the hypothetical example in Table 11.1.

TABLE 11.1 DISCRETIONARY AND NON-DISCRETIONARY ACCRUALS

Cash flow, as per cash flow statement		$1,000
Less: Amortization expense	− 50	
Add: Increase in (net) accounts receivable during the year	+ 40	
Add: Increase in inventory during the year	+100	
Add: Decrease in accounts payable and accrued liabilities during the year	+ 30	120
Net income, as per income statement		$1,120

In the table, a positive sign for an accrual means that, for given cash flow, it increases net income, and vice versa. For simplicity, we have assumed that there are no extraordinary income statement items and no income tax expense. Assume that explanations for the four accrual items are as follows:

- **Amortization expense** Annual amortization expense is laid down by the firm's amortization policy and its estimates of assets' useful lives. Given this policy, amortization expense is a non-discretionary accrual.

- **Increase in net accounts receivable** Assume that this derives from a decrease in the allowance for doubtful accounts, resulting from a less conservative estimate than in previous years. This accrual is discretionary, because management has some flexibility to control the amount. Other reasons for the increase could include a more generous credit policy, keeping the books open beyond the year-end, or simply an increase in volume of business. The first two of these accruals are discretionary, the third is non-discretionary.

Thus, we see that there can be several reasons for an increase in receivables. A researcher with access only to the comparative financial statements would be unlikely to know what particular reason or reasons accounted for the increase or whether the increase was discretionary or non-discretionary or both. Nevertheless, it is clear that the manager who wishes to increase reported net income through accounts receivable accruals has several means available.

- **Increase in inventory** Assume that this derives from the firm manufacturing for stock during a period of excess manufacturing capacity. The result is to include fixed overhead costs in inventory rather than charging them off to expense as unfavourable volume variances.

  While other reasons for the increase are possible, just as in the case of accounts receivable, this illustrates that discretionary, income-increasing accruals are available for inventory as well.

- **Decrease in accounts payable and accrual liabilities** Assume that this derives from the firm being more optimistic about warranty claims on its products than it has been in previous years. Alternatively, or in addition, the decrease could be due to regarding certain borderline items as contingencies rather than accruals. Again, we see that there can be ample room for discretionary accruals in accounts payable.

The main point to note is that the manager has considerable discretion to manage reported net income within the rules of GAAP. Notice also that, for many of these discretionary accruals, it would be difficult for the firm's auditors to discover the earnings management or, if they did discover it, to object, since all of the techniques mentioned, with the exception of holding the books open past the year-end, are within GAAP. It is also clear that a similar set of discretionary accruals to decrease reported net income is available to the manager, simply by reversing those described above.

Healy did not have access to the books and records of his sample firms. Consequently, he was unable to determine the specific discretionary accruals made by those firms' managers. As a result, he used another approach, namely to take total accruals as a proxy for discretionary accruals (his study preceded the Jones model). Thus, in our example, he would estimate discretionary accruals as +$120, instead of the +$170 that would be used if he had full information. The +$170 of discretionary accruals will raise total accruals by $170, regardless of what other non-discretionary accruals may be present; that is, higher total accruals contain higher discretionary accruals, and vice versa. However, using total accruals as a proxy for discretionary accruals may get the researcher into trouble if non-discretionary accruals are large relative to discretionary. Then, finding evidence of earnings management is like finding a needle in a haystack.

Healy obtained a sample of 94 of the largest U.S. industrial companies. He followed each company over the period 1930–1980 and obtained a total of 1,527 usable observations, that is, 1,527 firm years where the bogey and (if applicable) cap for a firm's bonus scheme could be calculated. Of these, 447 observations included both a bogey and a cap.

Each observation was then classified into one of three categories, or "portfolios" as Healy calls them. Portfolio UPP consisted of observations where earnings were above the cap, portfolio LOW of observations where earnings were below the bogey, and portfolio MID where they were between the bogey and cap. The theory underlying Table 11.1 predicts that total accruals should be greater for the MID portfolio than for UPP and LOW—recall that income-increasing accruals have a positive sign in Table 11.1.

For the 447 observations that had both a bogey and a cap, the results are summarized in Table 11.2. We see that 46% of the 281 observations in the MID portfolio had total accruals that were positive, that is, income-increasing. This is consistent with our firm in Table 11.1, where total accruals were +$120. The average accrual of these 281 observations was +0.0021 of total assets (accruals were deflated by total assets so that they could be compared across firms of different sizes). For the observations in the LOW and UPP portfolios, the proportions with positive total accruals were much lower—only 9% and 10% respectively. In fact, the average accruals for these observations were negative (income-decreasing). These results are consistent with Healy's arguments (see Figure 11.2), that firm managers whose net incomes are below the bogey and above the cap will tend to adopt income-decreasing accruals and only managers with net income between the two will tend to adopt income-increasing accruals. Thus, Healy's predictions of earnings management by managers subject to bonus schemes were supported by the empirical results.

TABLE 11.2 OBSERVATIONS WITH BOTH A BOGEY AND A CAP

	Proportion of Accruals with Given Sign		Number of Observations	Average Accruals
	Positive	**Negative**		
LOW	0.09	0.91	22	−0.0671
MID	0.46	0.54	281	+0.0021
UPP	0.10	0.90	<u>144</u>	−0.0536
			<u>447</u>	

Source: P. M. Healy, "The Effect of Bonus Schemes on Accounting Decisions," Journal of Accounting and Economics (April 1985), p. 96, Table 2. Reprinted by permission.

Results for observations where the bonus scheme had only a bogey are summarized in Table 11.3. Here, there is no UPP portfolio. The proportions of positive and negative accruals are about the same for each portfolio. However, the average accrual is significantly greater for MID, being −0.0155 of total assets compared to −0.0367 for LOW. Thus, we can conclude that while the MID observations did not engage in a higher proportion of positive accruals, the accruals they did make were significantly larger (that is, less negative) on average. These results, while perhaps not as dramatic as those of Table 11.2, also are significantly consistent with Healy's arguments for earnings management by managers subject to bonus schemes.

TABLE 11.3 OBSERVATIONS WITH BOGEY ONLY

	Proportion of Accruals with Given Sign		Number of Observations	Average Accruals
	Positive	**Negative**		
LOW	0.38	0.62	74	−0.0367
MID	0.36	0.64	1,006	−0.0155
			1,080	

Source: P. M. Healy, "The Effect of Bonus Schemes on Accounting Decisions," Journal of Accounting and Economics *(April 1985), p. 96, Table 2. Reprinted by permission.*

It should be emphasized that empirical earnings management studies face severe methodological problems. As mentioned earlier, a major difficulty is that discretionary accruals cannot be directly observed. Consequently, some proxy must be used. Using total accruals, as Healy did, introduces measurement error into the discretionary accruals variable, which makes it more difficult to detect earnings management should it exist. Another problem arises if the amount of non-discretionary accruals is correlated with net income. For example, as Kaplan (1985) pointed out, a firm with reported net income above the cap of its bonus plan may have low non-discretionary accruals if its high income is due to an unexpected increase in demand that runs down inventory. Then, the low total accruals that are used to infer earnings management are really due to the level of the firm's real economic activity and not to low discretionary accruals. Healy was aware of these problems and conducted additional tests to control for them, which he interpreted as confirming his findings. As mentioned above, the methodology used by Jones (1991) provides a more refined way to estimate non-discretionary accruals. For further discussion of methodological issues in this area see McNichols and Wilson (1988), Schipper (1989), Dechow, Sloan, and Sweeney (1995), and Bernard and Skinner (1996).

McNichols and Wilson (1988) also studied the behaviour of accruals in a bonus context. They confined their investigation to the provision for bad debts, on the grounds that a precise estimate of what the bad debts allowance should be (that is, the non-discretionary portion of the bad debts accrual), can be made. Then, discretionary accruals can be taken as the difference between this estimate and the actual bad debts provision. A precise estimate of non-discretionary accruals will reduce the problem of measurement error in the discretionary accruals variable. This approach also reduces the problem of correlation between net income and non-discretionary accruals, since the impact on the bad debts provision of the firm's level of economic activity is captured by their estimate of what the bad debts allowance should be. They found that, over the period 1969–1985, discretionary bad debt accruals were significantly income-reducing both for firm years that were very unprofitable and those that were very profitable (and thus likely to be below and above the bogeys and caps, respectively, of the bonus agreements). For firm years that were between these profitability extremes, discretionary accruals were much lower, and usually income-increasing. These results are consistent with those of Healy.

Subsequently, Holthausen, Larcker, and Sloan (1995) (HLS) studied managers' accruals behaviour for bonus purposes. They were able to obtain data on whether managers' annual earnings-based bonuses were in fact zero, greater than zero but less than the maximum bonus, or at the maximum. These are substantially better data than Healy, who had to estimate whether earnings before discretionary accruals were below bogey, between bogey and cap, or above cap on the basis of available descriptions of bonus contracts, and *assume* that if earnings were below the bogey the manager would not receive a bonus, etc.

Using a version of the Jones (1991) model to estimate non-discretionary accruals for a sample of 443 firm-year observations over 1982–1990, HLS found that managers who were at their bonus maxima managed accruals so as to lower reported earnings. This is consistent with Healy's results—see row 3 of Table 11.2. However, HLS did not find that managers who received zero bonus also used accruals to manage earnings downward, which differed from Healy's findings (row 1, Table 11.2). HLS concluded that methodological problems arising from Healy's procedures for estimating discretionary accruals explained why he appeared to find negative accruals for his low portfolio.[5]

We may conclude that, despite methodological challenges, there is significant evidence that, on average, managers use accruals to manage earnings so as to maximize their bonuses, particularly when earnings are high. This evidence is consistent with the bonus plan hypothesis of positive accounting theory.

However, we can think about consistency with the bonus plan hypothesis in two ways. Perhaps the most natural way is to view it as opportunistic behaviour by managers to maximize their utility at the expense of the firm's shareholders and other investors.

This raises a question, however. Why can't boards of directors, lenders, and other interested parties "unravel" the opportunistic earnings management, so that there is no point in engaging in it?

One reason, as pointed out by Schipper (1989), is that it is prohibitively costly for others to find out managers' inside information. For example, amounts of discretionary accruals would be very difficult to discover, even by boards of directors. Even more visible earnings management techniques, such as accounting policy changes, timing of capital gains and losses, and provisions for restructuring can be difficult to interpret. For example, is a firm's sale of one of its divisions driven by necessity or by timing considerations, or is a provision for restructuring excessive? Answers to questions such as these are typically private, inside information of the manager.

A second way to think about earnings management, however, is from an efficient contracting perspective. When setting compensation contracts, firms will rationally anticipate managers' incentives to manage earnings and will allow for this in the amount of compensation they offer. This was illustrated in Example 9.7, where a contract that allowed for earnings management was less costly than eliminating it completely. Consequently, boards of directors may not be motivated to unravel earnings management.

Nevertheless, whether we view them from an opportunistic or efficient contracting perspective, compensation contracts do create earnings management incentives.

11.4 Other Motivations for Earnings Management

Healy's study applies to bonus contracts. However, managers may engage in earnings management for a variety of other reasons. Now, we will briefly look at some of these.

11.4.1 To Meet Investors' Earnings Expectations

Investors' earnings expectations can be formed in a variety of ways. For example, they may be based on earnings for the same period last year, or on recent analysts' forecasts.

Firms that report earnings greater than expected typically enjoy a significant share price increase, as investors revise upwards their probabilities of good future performance. Conversely, firms that fail to meet expectations suffer a significant share price decrease. For example, Bartov, Givoly, and Hayn (2002), in a study over the years 1983–1997, documented significantly greater abnormal share returns for firms that exceeded their most recent analysts' earnings forecasts, relative to firms that failed to meet their forecasts. Skinner and Sloan (2002), in a study over 1984–1996, documented negative share returns for firms that failed to meet earnings expectations. These were significantly greater in magnitude than the positive returns for firms that exceeded expectations. This suggests that the market penalizes firms that fall short of expectations by more than it rewards firms that exceed them.[6]

As a result, managers have a strong incentive to ensure that earnings expectations are met, particularly if they hold ESOs or other share-related compensation. One way to do this is to manage earnings upwards.[7] Rational investors will be aware of this incentive, of course. This makes meeting expectations all the more important for managers. If these are not met, the market will reason that if the manager could not find enough earnings management to avoid the shortfall, the firm's earnings outlook must be bleak indeed, and/or the firm is not well managed since it cannot predict its own future. Consequently, the manager's reputation suffers as well as share price.

We conclude that meeting investors' earnings expectations is a powerful earnings management incentive.

11.4.2 Debt Contract Motivations

Debt contracts typically depend on accounting variables, arising from the moral hazard problem between manager and lender analyzed in Section 9.7. To control this problem, long-term lending contracts typically contain covenants to protect against actions by managers that are against the lenders' best interests, such as excessive dividends, additional borrowing, or letting working capital or shareholders' equity fall below specified levels, all of which dilute the security of existing lenders.

Earnings management for covenant purposes is predicted by the debt covenant hypothesis of positive accounting theory. Given that covenant violation can impose heavy costs, firm managers will be expected to avoid them. Indeed, they will even try to avoid being close to violation, because this will constrain their freedom of action in operating the firm. Thus, earnings management can arise as a device to reduce the probability of covenant violation in debt contracts.

Earnings management in a debt covenant context was investigated by Sweeney (1994). For a sample of firms that had defaulted on debt contracts, Sweeney found significantly greater use of income-increasing accounting changes relative to a control sample, and also found that defaulting firms tended to undertake early adoption of new accounting standards when these increased reported net income, and vice versa.

DeFond and Jiambalvo (1994) also examined earnings management by firms disclosing a debt covenant violation during 1985–1988. They found evidence of the use of discretionary accruals to increase reported income in the year prior to and, to a lesser extent in the year of, the covenant violation.

Somewhat different results are reported by DeAngelo, DeAngelo, and Skinner (1994), however. They studied a sample of 76 large, troubled firms. These were firms that had three or more consecutive loss years during 1980–1985 and that had reduced dividends during the loss period. For 29 of these firms, the cut in dividends was forced by binding debt covenant constraints.

After controlling for the influence of declining sales and cash flows on accruals, DeAngelo et al. failed to find evidence that these 29 firms used accruals to manage earnings upward in years prior to the cut in dividends, relative to the remaining sample firms that did not face debt covenant constraints. Rather, all the 29 firms exhibited large negative (that is, earnings-reducing) accruals extending for at least three years beyond the year of the dividend cut. DeAngelo et al. attribute this behaviour as due in part to large, discretionary non-cash writeoffs. Apparently, these were to signal to lenders, shareholders, unions, and others that the firm was facing up to its troubles, and to prepare the ground for subsequent contract renegotiations that frequently took place.

It thus seems that when its troubles are profound, the firm's behaviour transcends that which is predicted by the debt covenant hypothesis and, instead, earnings management becomes part of the firm's (and its manager's) overall strategy for survival.

Earnings management incentives also derive from **implicit contracts**, also called relational contracts. These are not formal contracts, such as the compensation and debt contracts just considered. Rather, they arise from continuing relationships between the firm and its stakeholders (e.g., employees, suppliers, lenders, customers) and represent expected behaviour based on past business dealings. For example, if the firm and its manager develop a reputation for always meeting formal contract commitments they will receive better terms from suppliers, lower interest rates from lenders, etc. In effect, the parties act *as if* such favourable contracts exist. In terms of our game theory Example 9.1, the manager and the firm's stakeholders trust each other sufficiently that they play the cooperative solution rather than the Nash equilibrium.

Earnings management for implicit contracting purposes was investigated by Bowen, DuCharme, and Shores (1995) (BDS). They argued that the manager's implicit contracting reputation can be bolstered by high reported profits, which increase stakeholders' confidence that the manager will continue to meet contractual obligations.[8] For example, they predicted that firms with relatively high cost of goods sold and notes payable (used as proxies for high continuing involvement with suppliers and short-term creditors, respectively) would be more likely to choose FIFO inventory and straight-line amortization accounting policies than LIFO and accelerated amortization policies. FIFO and straight-line amortization are regarded as income-increasing since they tend to produce higher reported earnings over time than their LIFO and accelerated amortization counterparts.

Based on a large sample over 1981–1993, BDS found that firms with a high level of continuing involvement with stakeholders were more likely to choose FIFO and straight-line amortization policies than firms with lower levels of continuing involvement, consistent with their prediction. Furthermore, this tendency was still evident even after they controlled for other earnings management motivations, such as those arising from the compensation and debt contracts discussed above.

11.4.3 Initial Public Offerings

By definition, firms making initial public offerings (IPOs) do not have an established market price. This raises the question of how to value the shares of such firms. Presumably, financial accounting information included in the prospectus is a useful information source. For example, Hughes (1986) showed analytically that information such as net income can be useful in helping to signal firm value to investors, and Clarkson, Dontoh, Richardson, and Sefcik (1992) found empirical evidence that the market responds positively to earnings forecasts as a signal of firm value. This raises the possibility that managers of firms going public may manage the earnings reported in their prospectuses in the hope of receiving a higher price for their shares.

Friedlan (1994) investigated this issue. For a sample of 155 U.S. IPOs during 1981–1984 he examined whether the firms managed earnings upward in the latest accounting period prior to the IPO by means of discretionary accruals. Since IPO firms are usually growing rapidly, it is particularly difficult to estimate their discretionary accruals, because growth itself drives an increase in accruals, such as accounts receivable, inventories, etc. After extensive tests to control for this problem, Friedlan concluded that IPO firms did indeed make income-increasing discretionary accruals in the latest period prior to the IPO, relative to accruals in a comparable previous period. Furthermore, accruals management seemed to be concentrated in the poorer-performing sample firms as measured by operating cash flows (such firms presumably have greater motivation to increase reported income) and in the smaller sample firms (about which less may be known).

11.5 The Good Side of Earnings Management

We suggested above that earnings management can be good. Here, we review these arguments, and outline theoretical and empirical evidence in their favour.

An argument in favour of good earnings management is based on the **blocked communication** concept of Demski and Sappington (1987) (DS). Frequently, agents obtain specialized information as part of their expertise, and this information can be prohibitively costly to communicate to the principal, that is, its communication is blocked. For example, it may be difficult for a physician to communicate to the patient exact details of an examination and diagnosis. Then, the physician's act (e.g., operating on the patient) must stand in not only for the physician's surgical skills but also for the information acquired during the diagnosis. DS show that the presence of blocked communication can reduce the efficiency of agency contracts, since the agent may shirk on information acquisition and compensate by taking an act that, from the principal's standpoint, is sub-optimal— the physician may simply sew up a badly cut hand on the basis of a cursory examination that fails to check for possible tendon or nerve damage, for example. If so, the principal has an incentive to try to eliminate or reduce the blocked communication.

In a financial reporting context, earnings management can be a device to do this. To illustrate, suppose that the manager desires to communicate the firm's expected long-run, persistent earnings potential. Assume that this amount is $1 million per annum. This earnings potential is complex inside information of the manager. If the manager simply announced it, the announcement would not likely be credible, since the market would find it prohibitively costly to verify. In effect, communication of this information is blocked. Suppose, however, that the firm has just realized a profit of $200,000 from the sale of a division. Suppose also that this item increases current reported net income to $1,180,000, well above its sustainable level of $1 million. Rather than report a net income substantially higher than what is expected to persist in the long run, the manager decides to record a provision for restructuring of $180,000, thereby reducing current earnings to the $1 million the manager feels will persist.

This "unblocking" of the manager's inside information by means of large discretionary accruals to produce a desired result has some credibility, since it involves the financial statements, which are prepared in accordance with GAAP and for which the manager has formal responsibility. Notice that the market cannot unravel this earnings management, since it is based on inside information about sustainable earning power. However the market can use the earnings management to infer what this inside information is.

Arguments for good earnings management are strengthened by a further paper by Demski and Sappington (1990) (DS), who show conditions under which management's inside information can always be conveyed by means of earnings management, should management wish to do so.

DS point out that operating cash flows, or some other relatively unmanaged performance measure such as core earnings (see Section 5.5), convey *some* information about future firm performance. However, management typically has additional information about future performance, such as new firm strategies or changes in market conditions. While quite relevant, this information is likely to be sufficiently complex that its direct communication is blocked. Then, DS show that judicious choice and disclosure of discretionary accruals can reveal this information to investors.[9]

More recently, Stocken and Verrecchia (2004) argue that while earnings management can be used to reveal inside information as just described, it also imposes a cost since, if it is buried in operations, the ability of investors to make good investment decisions is reduced. That is, the ability of current net income to predict future performance is "jammed." For example, the inside information may be unreliable since, by definition, it has not yet been recognized by the firm's accounting system (if it was, it would no longer be inside). We saw in Chapter 5 that investors find current net income useful. We also know, however, that low reliability reduces this usefulness. To the extent investors' decisions are jammed, the firm faces higher cost of capital and reduced profits. This cost affects both shareholders and, through lower compensation, the manager.

The manager also faces another cost of earnings management. He/she may be held liable for excessive earnings management, as illustrated by the Qwest Communications vignette in Section 1.2. Here, early revenue recognition, which Qwest's managers may, at the time, have felt revealed relevant inside information about future earnings, was proven unreliable by later events.

Stocken and Verrecchia go on to show conditions under which earnings management can be good, that is, under which the benefits of revealing inside information outweigh the costs just mentioned. Essentially, these are that the firm faces high uncertainty (so that there is lots of potential for inside information to be useful) and the amount of inside information is high. Then, earnings management benefits both investors and the manager.

The good side of earnings management is also supported by efficient contracting theory. Some support was provided in Chapter 9 in a single-period context. However, as argued above, a multi-period horizon increases both the potential for and the constraints on earnings management. In this regard, Evans and Sridhar (1996) (ES) present a two-period contract where the manager has an information advantage. Specifically, the manager knows the firm's unmanaged earnings but the owner can only observe the net income reported by the manager.

The potential for earnings management in the ES analysis is determined by GAAP, which they view as changing over time. The probability that GAAP completely specifies the firm's accounting and accrual policies next period is termed the *flexibility* of its accounting system. If this probability is high, leaving little likelihood of earnings management, the system has low flexibility, and vice versa. Nevertheless, for given GAAP, there will typically be *some* flexibility. The amount of this earnings management discretion will be determined by the firm's detailed accounting and accrual policies. These policies are assumed to be inside information of the manager. Furthermore, they are sufficiently complex and technical that their communication to the owner is blocked. This creates the potential for low manager effort to be concealed by earnings management.

As mentioned, the ES model spans two periods. Thus, in accordance with the iron law, any earnings overstatement in the first period will reverse in the second, and vice versa. The question then is, will the manager still manage earnings? ES show that the answer is yes, under two conditions. First, the probability of earnings management being caught and/or the penalty if caught must be sufficiently low that the manager can attain reservation utility. Second, the accounting system must have low flexibility (i.e., strong GAAP).

This latter condition stems from the fact that to motivate effort in the presence of moral hazard, the compensation contract must impose risk on the manager. In a two-period contract, a source of risk is the possibility that first-period earnings might be, say, low due to random state realization. Then, if the manager reports earnings truthfully, compensation will be low. This creates an incentive for earnings management. That is, even though accruals reverse, the manager faces less risk in the ES model if some earnings can be "borrowed" from the expected earnings of the second period, thereby smoothing compensation across periods. If unmanaged first-period earnings are high, the manager can accomplish the same thing by deferring earnings from the current period to the next.

This risk reduction through earnings management enables the manager to attain reservation utility with a lower profit share than if earnings management was not possible. In effect, in the ES model, a contract that allows for earnings management can be more efficient than one that does not.

The reason why this result only works when the accounting system has low flexibility (i.e., strong GAAP) is that if GAAP is weak the manager can shed too much risk through earnings management. Then, the incentive to exert effort falls. In effect, the manager "overdoses" on earnings management, resulting in an inefficient contract. We saw a similar effect in Chapter 9. There, the limitation on earnings management created by GAAP enabled a contract whereby the manager worked hard (Example 9.7). When GAAP is weak or non-existent (Example 9.5), the manager shirked. As a result, the owner was better off under strong GAAP.

The Demski and Sappington models consider earnings management from a financial reporting perspective, while Evans and Sridhar consider it from the perspective of contracting. Dye (1988) investigated the possibility of earnings management when both motivations are considered. In a multi-period analysis that allows for accruals reversal, he showed conditions under which current shareholders will prefer a compensation contract that motivates the manager to smooth reported income. This contract benefits current shareholders not only by efficiently implementing a desired level of manager effort, as in the Evans and Sridhar analysis, but also by maximizing the proceeds received by current shareholders when they sell their shares to new investors.

It may seem that maximizing the proceeds received by current shareholders benefits one class of investors relative to another. However, this is not necessarily so. If the efficient securities market correctly anticipates the earnings management incentives (i.e., if it has rational expectations), it will adjust for any overstatement or understatement of earnings in setting the firm's share price. Thus, when current shareholders sell their shares, they receive what the shares are really worth, not some lower amount.

When markets have rational expectations, the manager may as well go ahead and manage earnings since the market anticipates it. For example, if the manager in Dye's model does not smooth earnings as expected, the proceeds received by current shareholders will not be maximized, adversely affecting the manager's compensation as well as the current shareholders' welfare.

We conclude on the basis of the models described in this section that, even in the presence of the iron law of accruals reversal, the possibility of good earnings management for both contracting and financial reporting purposes is predicted by theory.

However, given the variety of motivations for earnings management, and the difficulty of discovering and interpreting discretionary accruals including extraordinary items, it is a complex task to establish empirically whether the stock market reacts to earnings management as the theory predicts. In particular, does the market react to earnings management as if it is good? The answer to this question is important to accountants since they are prominently involved in the techniques and implementation of earnings management, and will get drawn into the negative publicity and lawsuits that inevitably follow the revelation of bad earnings management practices. Also, to the extent that earnings management is good, excessive standard setting, which overly limits accounting choice, may not be cost-effective.

Subramanyam (1996) provides some evidence on this issue. He separated accruals into discretionary and non-discretionary components, using the Jones model (Section 8.6.3), for a sample of 2,808 firms over the years 1973–1993, for a total of 21,135 firm-year observations. Subramanyam found, after controlling for the effects of operating cash flows and non-discretionary accruals on share returns, that the stock market responded positively to discretionary accruals, consistent with managers, on average, using earnings management responsibly to reveal inside information about future earning power.

As Subramanyam points out, however, this finding is subject to different interpretations. For example, the market may be responding naively to the higher/ lower reported earnings that result from high/low discretionary accruals. If so, a securities market anomaly similar to that of Sloan (Section 6.2.6) may be operating.

Subramanyam conducts extensive tests, though, that tend to support that the market responds efficiently to the discretionary accruals. We will return to Subramanyam's study in the next section.

Subramanyam also points out that his findings depend on the ability of the Jones model to separate accruals into discretionary and non-discretionary components in a manner consistent with how the market interprets them. This suggests that alternate approaches to studying the market's reaction to earnings management are desirable. For example, Liu, Ryan, and Wahlen (1997) examined the quarterly loan loss accruals (a vehicle for earnings management) of a sample of 104 U.S. banks over 1984–1991. After separating these accruals into expected and unexpected components, they found a significantly positive share price reaction to unexpected increases in loan loss provisions for "at-risk" banks (banks with regulatory capital close to legal minimums), but only in the fourth quarter. For banks not at risk, share price reaction to unexpected loan loss provisions was negative. These results suggest that at-risk banks, by managing their earnings downwards, credibly convey to the market that they are taking steps to resolve their problems, which should improve their future performance. This good news was strong enough to outweigh the bad news of the fact of the loan writedowns per se, particularly since the market may have already reacted to the banks being at risk. For banks not at risk, there is less need to take steps to resolve problems, with the result that the bad news component dominated the market's reaction. The reason why the at-risk banks' share prices rose only in the fourth quarter appears to be due to auditor involvement in that quarter. Presumably, management takes loan loss provisions much more seriously when auditors are involved.

In addition to providing further evidence of how earnings management can convey inside information, Liu, Ryan, and Whalen's results suggest considerable sophistication in the securities market's response, supporting Subramanyam's efficient market interpretation of his findings.

Additional evidence consistent with responsible earnings management is provided by Barth, Elliott, and Finn (1999). From a large sample of U.S. corporations over the years 1982–1992, they report evidence that firms with patterns of steadily increasing earnings for five years and longer enjoy higher price/earnings multiples than firms with equivalent levels and variability of earnings growth but absent the steadily increasing pattern. To the extent the steadily increasing earnings patterns are created by earnings management, the market appears to reward earnings management that does not overstate future earning power.

It should be noted that in deriving their result, Barth, Elliott, and Finn control for earnings persistence. Thus, the increased market valuation of their subject firms derives from factors beyond the use of earnings management to reveal persistent earning power. The most likely explanation, they suggest, is that the increasing earnings patterns reveal inside information about growth opportunities. For a specific example of a firm that reports steadily increasing earnings, see problem 9.

Callen and Segal (2004) also study the market response to accruals. They point out that increases in expected future share returns drive down current share returns, much like increases in expected future interest rates drive down current bond prices. After allowing for this effect in a large sample of firms over 1962–2000, they report that both accrual information and operating cash flow information have a positive effect on current share returns, with some evidence that the accrual effect is the stronger of the two.

While Callen and Segal do not break accruals into discretionary and non-discretionary components, their findings of a positive relationship between accruals and current share returns suggest that, on balance, accruals have information content for investors. If opportunistic earnings management overwhelmed the information content of accruals, an efficient market would not react positively to them.

11.6 The Bad Side of Earnings Management

11.6.1 Opportunistic Earnings Management

Despite theory and evidence of responsible use of earnings management, there is also evidence of bad earnings management. From a contracting perspective, this can result from opportunistic manager behaviour. The tendency of managers to use earnings management to maximize their bonuses, as documented by Healy, can be interpreted this way, for example.

Further evidence is supplied by Dechow, Sloan, and Sweeney (1996), who examined the earnings management practices of a test sample of 92 firms charged in the United States by the SEC with alleged violation of GAAP (i.e., bad earnings management), compared to a control sample of firms of similar size and industry. Their investigation revealed a number of motivations for such earnings management. A common one was closeness to debt covenant constraints. The firms in their test sample had, on average, significantly greater leverage and significantly more debt covenant violations than the control sample.

As mentioned earlier, another motive for bad earnings management arises when a manager intends to raise new share capital and wants to maximize the proceeds from the new issue. A variety of discretionary accruals can be used to increase reported net income in the short run, such as speeding up revenue recognition, lengthening the useful life of capital assets, underprovision for environmental and restoration costs, etc. The iron law of accruals reversal is of less concern due to the short decision horizon. To the extent that earnings management to raise the issue price is unanticipated, the current shareholders benefit at the expense of new ones. Dechow, Sloan, and Sweeney (1996), mentioned above, also studied the financing decisions of their sample firms. They found that their charged firms (which, by definition, were heavy users of earnings management) issued, on average, significantly more securities during the period of earnings manipulation than the control sample.

Hanna (1999) discusses another type of earnings management. This is the frequent recording of excessive charges for non-recurring items such as writedowns under ceiling test standards, and provisions for reorganization. Hanna asserts that manager bonuses are typically based on core earnings. Furthermore, analysts' forecasts are typically of core earnings. Thus non-recurring charges do not affect manager bonuses and do not take away from the ability to meet earnings forecasts. But, excessive non-recurring charges increase *future core earnings*, by putting them in the bank through reduced future amortization charges and absorption of future costs that would otherwise be charged to expense when incurred. Then, the manager benefits both ways. Major costs that may have been accumulating for several years (i.e., the non-recurring charges) do not affect bonuses or ability to meet earnings forecasts, and the future expense reductions increase future core earnings, on which the manager *is* evaluated.

Furthermore, the upwards effect on future core earnings is very difficult to detect, since reduced future amortization charges and other expense reductions are buried in larger totals. In effect, poor disclosure of the effects of past non-recurring charges enables managers to engage in this type of earning management. Nevertheless, the market does appear to react to earnings management of this nature. As mentioned in Section 5.5, Elliott and Hanna (1996) found that the ERC for a dollar of quarterly core earnings is lower for firms that have frequently recorded large unusual and non-recurring charges than for firms that have not recorded such charges. This is consistent with the market using the frequency of non-recurring charges as a proxy for the extent to which core earnings may be overstated. Of course, if accountants would disclose the effect on core earnings of past non-recurring writeoffs, a proxy such as this would not be needed.

Theory in Practice 11.1

In April 2004, Nortel Networks Corp. announced that it had fired its CEO, Chief Financial Officer, and Controller. Its share price, over $11 prior to the announcement, fell to $5.26. The company later announced that several more senior managers were also fired. It appears that Nortel's 2003 reported net income of $734 million U.S. was substantially overstated.

The overstatement arose out of the collapse of the technology boom in the early 2000s. This left many of Nortel's customers and subsidiary companies in financial distress. Accruals were recorded by Nortel in 2001 and 2002 to provide for costs of contract cancellations, bad debts, layoffs, and plant closures. By mid-2002, about $5 billion of such accruals were on Nortel's balance sheet.

It appears, however, that many of these accruals were excessive, and in 2003 the company reversed them. The reversals, which were not disclosed to investors, were credited to operating expense. In retrospect, Nortel's 2001 and 2002 losses were overstated and its 2003 profit was overstated.

The significance of the 2003 profit overstatement was that Nortel's compensation plan provided for bonuses if the company returned to profitability, where profits were defined as quarterly pro-forma income (see Section 7.4.2). The company reported pro-forma income of $40 million U.S. in the first quarter of 2003 and $34 million U.S. in the second. Consequently, most employees received cash bonuses, including the CEO, who received $3.6 million U.S. However, after the effects of excessive accrual reversals are taken into account, it appears that the first two quarters of 2003 may have been loss quarters.

The company announced that it would restate its 2001–2003 results, and demand bonus repayments if warranted. In January 2005, it reported first and second quarter, 2003 net losses of U.S. $146 and $128 million respectively, compared with an originally-stated first quarter loss of $16 million and a second quarter profit of $40 million. In February 2005, the company announced that it was suing three former executives to recover $13 million in bonuses.

11.6.2 Do Managers Accept Securities Market Efficiency?

The earnings management techniques just outlined, including those of Nortel, are not necessarily inconsistent with securities market efficiency. They rely on poor disclosure to keep the extent of earnings management as inside information. Yet, other results question management's acceptance of efficiency itself. In Section 11.5, we discussed Subramanyam's (1996) study, which he interpreted as providing evidence for good earnings management. However, a study by Xie (2001) casts doubt on this interpretation. For a large sample of firms over the period 1971–1992, Xie used the Jones model to estimate discretionary and non-discretionary accruals for each firm-year observation. He then estimated the persistence of these two accruals components. As we would expect, he found the persistence of discretionary accruals to be less than that of non-discretionary accruals. As a result, the efficient market should assign a lower ERC to a dollar of discretionary accruals than to a dollar of non-discretionary. However, Xie found that the ERCs for discretionary accruals in his sample were significantly higher than their low persistence would suggest. In other words, the market appears to overvalue discretionary accruals.

Thus, Subramanyam's efficient markets interpretation of his results is questioned. It may be that the favourable market reaction to discretionary accruals in Subramanyam's study is driven simply by market overreaction to them rather than by their information content. That is, managers may be exploiting another efficient securities market anomaly.

In a similar vein, we reported in Section 11.5 on the finding of Barth, Elliott, and Finn (1999) that the market favours firms with steadily increasing earnings patterns. Their interpretation is that the efficient market responds to the persistence and growth information implicit in the increasing earnings. However, Barth, Elliott, and Finn do not rule out an alternative, inefficient market interpretation, which is that momentum trading (see Section 6.2.1) in response to the increasing earnings pattern drives the favourable market reaction.

Schrand and Walther (2000) report yet another form of earnings management. They analyze a sample of firms that reported a material, non-recurring gain or loss on disposal of property, plant, and equipment in the *prior* quarter but no such gain or loss in the *current* quarter. In news releases that typically accompany earnings announcements, managers compare the current quarter's performance with a prior quarter. The question then is, in these news releases, do managers remind investors of the non-recurring gain or loss in the prior quarter? Schrand and Walther found that the likelihood of such a reminder was significantly greater if the prior quarter's non-recurring item was a gain rather than a loss. In this way, the lowest possible prior period benchmark was emphasized (i.e., managed), thereby showing the change in earnings from the prior quarter in the most favourable light.

Pro-forma earnings (see section 7.4.2) represent another form of earnings management that questions managers' acceptance of market efficiency. Managers who emphasize pro-forma earnings claim that this measure better portrays the firm's (and their own) performance than GAAP net income. However, since there are no standards to determine pro-forma earnings, managers may be tempted to leave out expense items that do contain relevant, persistent information, in order to meet earnings targets, maximize compensation, and/or improve reputation. Since the GAAP-based income statement is also available, an efficient market would quickly adjust for the omitted items. Consequently, managers' emphasis on pro-forma earnings suggests they do not accept efficiency.

Investor reaction to pro-forma earnings was studied by Doyle, Lundholm, and Soliman (2003) (DLS). They obtained a large sample of firms that reported pro-forma quarterly earnings over 1988–1999 and, for each firm and quarter, calculated the difference from GAAP net income. They found, contrary to management's claim, that many expenses excluded from GAAP net income (for example, provisions for reorganization) did have significant future effects on operating cash flows, persisting for up to three years from the dates of the quarterly announcements. Consequently, investors who look only at pro-forma earnings ignore useful information.

DLS also examined abnormal share returns of their sample firms over a three-day window surrounding the date of their quarterly earnings announcements. After controlling for other factors that affect share returns, they found that the greater the difference between pro-forma and GAAP earnings (recall that since there are no rules surrounding pro-forma earnings, some managers may leave out more expenses than others) the lower the abnormal share return over the three days. This suggests that the market does not ignore the excluded items—if it did, the abnormal returns would not be affected by the amounts of omitted expenses.

However, the market's reaction was not complete. DLS report that the lower share returns for firms with greater pro-forma-GAAP discrepancies continued for up to three years. If the market was fully efficient, all of the negative reaction would have taken place within the three-day window.

The important point from the Schrand and Walters and DLS studies is that these earnings management policies make little sense if securities markets are efficient. Consequently, managers who engage in them must not fully accept efficiency. Furthermore, despite our suggestion in Section 9.9, rejection of efficiency implies that contracting variables do not completely reconcile economic consequences and market efficiency. That is, accounting policies without cash flow effects can matter to managers simply because they believe that the market will not see through them.

11.6.3 Implications for Accountants

The implication for accountants of bad earnings management, however, is not to reject market efficiency, but to *improve disclosure*. As argued in Section 6.2.7, full disclosure helps investors to evaluate the financial statements, thereby reducing their susceptibility to behavioural biases and reducing managers' ability to exploit market inefficiencies. For example, clear reporting of revenue recognition policies, and detailed descriptions of major discretionary accruals such as writedowns and provisions for reorganization, will bring bad earnings management into the open, reducing managers' ability to manipulate and bias the financial statements for their own advantage. Other ways to improve disclosure include reporting the effects on core earnings of previous writeoffs and, in general, assisting investors to diagnose low-persistence items. Managers would then bear the full consequences of their actions and bad earnings management would decrease.

11.7 Conclusions on Earnings Management

Earnings management is made possible by the fact that GAAP do not completely constrain managers' choices of accounting policies and procedures. Such choices are much more complex and challenging than simply selecting those policies and procedures that best inform investors. Rather, managers' accounting policy choices are often motivated by strategic considerations, such as meeting earnings expectations, contracts that depend on financial accounting variables, taxation, new share issues, takeover bids, discouraging of potential competition, and unblocking of inside information. In effect, accounting policy choice has characteristics of a game. Economic consequences are created when changes in GAAP adversely affect managers' abilities to play the game. That is, managers will react against rule changes that reduce their flexibility of accounting choice. As a result, accountants need to be aware of the legitimate needs of management, as well as of investors. Actual financial reporting represents a compromise between the needs of these two major constituencies.

Despite the reduction of reliability that accompanies earnings management, a strong case can be made that it is useful if kept within bounds. First, it gives managers flexibility to react to unanticipated state realizations when contracts are rigid and incomplete.

Second, earnings management can serve as a vehicle for the credible communication of inside information to investors and for efficient compensation contracts. Both of these arguments are consistent with efficient securities markets and the efficiency version of positive accounting theory.

Nevertheless, some managers may abuse the communications potential of GAAP by pushing earnings management too far, with the result that persistent earning power is overstated, at least temporarily. This behaviour can result from a failure to accept securities market efficiency or from an ability to hide bad earnings management behind poor disclosure, or both. To the extent managers do not accept securities market efficiency, believing instead that they can fool the market by their disclosure decisions, positive accounting theory does not fully reconcile market efficiency and economic consequences.

Thus, whether earnings management is good or bad depends on how it is used. Accountants can reduce the extent of bad earnings management by bringing it out into the open. This can be accomplished by improved disclosure of low-persistence items and reporting the effect of previous writeoffs on core earnings.

Questions and Problems

1. Explain why a firm's manager might both believe in securities market efficiency and engage in earnings management.

2. For an income management strategy of taking a bath, the probability of the manager receiving a bonus in a future year rises. Explain why. (CGA-Canada)

3. A manager increases reported earnings by $1,300 this year. This was done by reducing the allowance for credit losses by $500 below the expected amount, and reducing the accrual for warranty costs expense to $800 below the expected amount. Explain why, other things equal, this will lower next year's earnings by $1,300.

4. You are a CEO operating under a bonus plan similar to the one assumed by Healy (Section 11.3). Explain whether you would react favourably or negatively to an exposure draft of a proposed change in GAAP that has the following effects on your financial statements. Treat each effect as independent of the others.
   a. The effect will be to increase liabilities. Examples of such GAAP changes include capitalization of long-term leases (Section 7.2.2), and recording of pension plan obligations and other postretirement benefits (Section 7.2.6).
   b. The effect will be to increase the volatility of reported net income. An example would be a standard that required unrealized gains and losses on available-for-sale securities to be included in net income, rather than in other comprehensive income under SFAS 115 (Section 7.3.2)

c. The effect will be to exert downward pressure on reported net income. An example is the expensing of employee stock options (Section 8.3) and the ceiling tests for property, plant and equipment (Section 7.2.5), and purchased goodwill (Section 7.4.2).

d. The effect will be to eliminate alternative ways of accounting for the same thing. For example, forthcoming changes to Canadian accounting standards will move accounting for derivatives into harmony with SFAS 133 (Section 7.3.3).

5. The firms in Healy's study of earnings management (Section 11.3) would have been using the historical cost basis of accounting. Given that firms are moving to greater use of fair value accounting for financial instruments, as described in Section 7.3.2, would this increase or decrease the potential for opportunistic earnings management for bonus purposes? Explain.

6. The comparative balance sheet of JSA Ltd. as at June 30, 2005 is as follows:

	June 30, 2005	June 30, 2004
	Assets	
Current assets:		
Accounts receivable (net)	$ 76	$ 60
Inventories	35	53
Prepaid expenses	2	1
	113	114
Capital assets (net)	37	39
Long-term investments	2	2
Deferred development costs	40	39
	$192	$194
	Liabilities and Shareholders' Equity	
Current liabilities:		
Bank indebtedness	$ 18	$ 4
Accounts payable	64	71
Customer advances	13	8
Current portion of long-term debt	1	2
Current portion of future income taxes	2	1
	98	86
Long-term debt	5	3
Liability for future income taxes	0	6
Share capital	73	71
Retained earnings	16	28
	$192	$194

JSA Ltd.'s 2005 income statement is as follows:

Sales		$233
Expenses:		
Cost of sales	184	
Administrative and selling	35	
Research and development	4	
Depreciation and amortization	14	
Interest	3	240
Loss before undernoted items		(7)
Income tax recovery		7
Provision for reorganization		(12)
Net loss for the year		$(12)

Cash flow from operations for 2005 was $7.

Required

a. Calculate the various accruals on an item-by-item basis. For each accrual indicate the extent to which that accrual may contain a discretionary component and briefly explain why.

b. Briefly describe two other ways that researchers have used to estimate the discretionary component of total accruals.

c. A manager, whose bonus is related to reported net income, finds that net income for the year (before bonus) is below the bogey of the incentive plan. What type of earnings management might the manager then engage in? Which of the accruals in **a** would be most suitable for this purpose? Explain.

7. A common tactic to manage earnings is to "stuff the channels," that is, to ship product prematurely to dealers and customers, thereby inflating sales for the period. A case in point is Bristol-Myers Squib Co. (BMS), a multinational pharmaceutical and baby food company headquartered in New York. In August 2004, the SEC announced a $150 million penalty levied against BMS. This was part of an agreement to settle charges by the SEC that the company had engaged in a fraudulent scheme to inflate sales and earnings, in order to meet analysts' earnings forecasts.

The scheme involved recognition of revenue on pharmaceutical products shipped to its wholesalers in excess of the amounts demanded by them. These shipments amounted to $1.5 billion U.S. during 2001–2002. To persuade its wholesalers to accept this excess inventory, BMS agreed to cover their carrying costs, amounting to millions of dollars per quarter. In addition, BMS understated its accruals for rebates and discounts allowed to its large customers.

According to the SEC, the company also engaged in "cookie jar" accounting. That is, it created phoney reserves for disposals of unneeded plants and divisions during high-profit quarters. These would be transferred to reduce operating expenses in low-profit quarters when BMS' earnings still fell short of amounts needed to meet forecasts.

Required

a. Give reasons why managers would resort to extreme earnings management tactics such as these.

b. Evaluate the effectiveness of stuffing the channels as an earnings management device. Consider both from the standpoint of a single year and over a series of years.

c. Evaluate the effectiveness of cookie jar accounting as an earnings management device. What earnings management pattern did BMS appear to be following by means of this tactic?

8. The potentially serious consequences of bad earnings management are illustrated by the case of Atlas Cold Storage Income Trust, which operates a system of refrigerated warehouses across Canada and the United States. During June 2004, the Ontario Securities Commission (OSC) filed quasi-criminal charges under the Ontario Securities Act against four senior officials of the company, including its CEO. The company itself was not charged because it cooperated with the investigation and took steps to remedy the problems.

The OSC charged that during 2001–2003, Atlas had engaged in several types of financial statement manipulations. One tactic was to capitalize certain costs that, according to GAAP, should have been charged to expense. Another involved deferring recognition of a large customer claim for damaged goods from 2001, where it belonged, to 2002. A third tactic was to disguise breaches of debt covenants by a subsidiary company by advancing money to the subsidiary at financial statement dates. These advances were repaid shortly thereafter. According to revised financial statements filed by the company, net income was originally reported too high by $5.2 million for 2001 and $32.4 million for 2002. The company also faced a class action lawsuit by investors.

Required

a. Evaluate the short-run (i.e., one year) and long-run effectiveness of capitalizing expenses as an earnings management device.

b. The motivation for some of the claimed manipulations was apparently to meet earnings targets. Why is it important to managers to meet earnings targets? Use concepts of market efficiency and investor rationality in your answer.

c. With respect to earnings targets, Coca-Cola Co. announced in December 2002 that it was discontinuing the provision of quarterly and annual earnings forecasts to analysts. Some other large public companies, including BCE Inc., have taken similar action. Why would they do this?

9. The article by Randall Smith, Steven Lipin, and Amal Kumar Naj, here reproduced from *The Wall Street Journal* (November 3, 1994), "Managing Profits" describes some of the earnings management devices used by General Electric to report strong, consistent earnings growth over the last decade.

Managing Profits

How General Electric Damps Fluctuations in Its Annual Earnings

The debacle at Kidder, Peabody & Co. might ruin the year for most companies.

But the roughly $750 million in losses and after-tax charges that General Electric Co. will incur this year before finally unloading Kidder will barely dent GE's smooth, consistent earnings growth. Despite those losses, some analysts believe, GE may be able to match or top last year's profit of $5.15 billion before accounting charges.

In the past decade, GE's earnings have risen every year, although net income fell in 1991 and 1993 because of accounting changes related to post-retirement benefits. The gains, ranging between 1.7% and 17%, have been fairly steady—especially for a company in a lot of cyclical businesses. As a result, GE almost seems able to override the business cycle.

How does GE do it? One undeniable explanation is the fundamental growth of its eight industrial businesses and 24 financial-services units. "We're the best company in the world," declares Dennis Dammerman, GE's chief financial officer.

But another way is "earnings management," the orchestrated timing of gains and losses to smooth out bumps and, especially, avoid a decline. Among big companies, GE is "certainly a relatively aggressive practitioner of earnings management," says Martin Sankey, a CS First Boston Inc. analyst.

To smooth out fluctuations, GE frequently offsets one-time gains from big asset sales with restructuring charges; that keeps earnings from rising so high that they can't be topped the following year. GE also times sales of some equity stakes and even acquisitions to produce profit gains when needed.

Asked several times about earnings management, Mr. Dammerman declines to discuss directly whether GE engages in the practice. Asked whether offsetting one-time gains with one-time charges could be considered earnings management, he says, "I've never looked at it in that manner." He also declines to say whether other companies use such tactics.

Most U.S. companies do try to smooth profit growth. Walt Disney Co., for example, can decide when it wants profits from a videocassette re-release of Snow White. Banks and insurance companies do a lot of smoothing by adjusting the level of their reserves, and many companies time write-offs carefully.

A look at GE illustrates how analysts say one giant corporation manages earnings. They add that few companies have maneuvered so successfully for so long on so large a scale. GE's size and diversity give it an unusual array of opportunities, of course. Moreover, Chairman Jack Welch relentlessly monitors GE's profit growth.

A Dismayed Mr. Welch

Last April, when announcing that a bond-trading scheme at Kidder had generated false 1993 profits and triggered a $210 million first-quarter charge, Mr. Welch said investors prize GE's ability "to deliver strong, consistent earnings growth in a myriad of global economic conditions. Having this reprehensible scheme... break our more-than-decade-long string of 'no surprises' has all of us damn mad."

continued ➡

His dislike of surprises extends beyond what GE's operating executives tell him to what GE tells Wall Street. Russell Leavitt, a Salomon Brothers analyst, says GE executives "give you some guidance" on what other analysts' estimates are and how reasonable they are. The result, says Ben Zacks of Zacks Investment Research, is that analysts' GE estimates fall in a "very, very tight range."

GE especially prizes consistent growth because it has so many different businesses that most analysts can't track them all. For example, GE is followed by electrical-equipment analysts, most of whom have a loose grasp of financial services.

Narrowing the Discount

GE's two major parts are an industrial conglomerate and a financial-services conglomerate, and both segments outdo their market peers. According to an analysis of data from Morgan Stanley & Co., industrial conglomerates sold at an average 20% discount to the market as of Sept. 30, based on their multiple of price to next year's anticipated earnings, while financial-services companies—banks, finance and insurance—were at a 35% discount. But partly because of its consistent earnings growth, GE sold at a discount of only 11%.

One financial calculation that helped smooth earnings at GE a few years ago was an increase in the assumed rate of future investment returns on pension funds. In 1991, a weak year at many companies, GE raised its return-rate assumption a full percentage point, to 9.5% from the 8.5% in effect for five years.

That change, by reducing GE's pension costs, helped lift what it terms the profits on its pension fund to $696 million in 1991 from $380 million in 1990, a pretax swing of $316 million. For companies like GE with overfunded pension plans, accounting rules require such changes to be reflected in corporate profits.

How much did GE's overall profit rise in 1991? Just $132 million after tax.

HOW GE OFFSETS GAINS FROM ASSET SALES

Year	Pretax Gain (millions)	Source of the Gain	Pretax Restructuring Charges (millions)
1993	$1,430	Sale of aerospace unit to Martin Marietta	$1,011
1987	858	Change in accounting for taxes and inventory	1,027
1986	50	Sale of foreign affiliate	311
1985	518	Sale of three coal properties and 37% cable stake	447
1984	617	Sales of Utal Int'l, small appliance unit, cable company	636
1983	117	Sale of radio/TV stations and Gearhart Industrial stake	147

Source: General Electric Co.

continued →

However, GE says the increase in its assumed return on pension assets reflected the lofty investment returns in the 1980s and wasn't any higher than rates assumed by other big companies. It says the change wasn't designed to raise reported 1991 profits.

The clearest way GE manages earnings is through restructuring charges. When GE sells a business at a profit or takes an unusual gain, it generally takes an offsetting restructuring charge of roughly equal size. In six of the years since 1983, GE has taken charges totalling $3.95 billion in this way.

Last year, when GE booked a $1.43 billion pretax gain on the sale of its aerospace business, for example, it took a $1.01 billion charge to cover costs of "closing and downsizing and streamlining of certain production, service and administrative facilities world-wide." After tax, the gain and the charge matched up exactly at $678 million.

And that 1993 charge, by anticipating some specific 1994 expenses such as "asset write-offs, lease terminations and severance benefits," is helping GE report better profit this year. Without the 1993 charge, some of those expenses could have reduced this year's net income. Because some of the expenses eventually would have to be paid anyway, First Boston's Mr. Sankey says, this reporting strategy allows GE to "transmute" one-time gains into future operating income.

One rationale for using this tactic: GE executives believe that many investors ignore one-time gains from asset sales in valuing companies. But clearly, taking an offsetting charge against a big gain prevents GE's earnings from getting too high in any one year; by spreading the gain into future years, the company can more easily report the steady growth that investors prefer.

Mr. Dammerman, the finance chief, says that whenever GE anticipates a gain on an asset sale or a tax or accounting change, its executives "sit down with our businesses and say, 'What are some strategic decisions that you would make to make the business better going forward?' " He says GE's use of such charges is one way it pursues both short-term and long-term goals; without such gains, he adds, some of the spending wouldn't have been planned or would have been timed differently.

Practice Under Scrutiny

Richard Leftwich, an expert in financial-statement analysis at the University of Chicago business school, says analysts and regulators are questioning U.S. corporations' widespread use of restructuring charges. He wonders how companies distinguish between everyday expenses needed to remain competitive and truly extraordinary events. Such use of restructuring charges "raises real issues for how to think about what the future profits mean," he adds, "because the costs are being written off now, but the profits are being reported in the future."

Later this month, accounting rule-makers, under prodding by the Securities and Exchange Commission, are expected to sharply limit such big one-time write-offs. The new rules would force companies to spread such charges over future years or take them when the relevant expenses are actually paid rather than when planned.

While conceding the SEC "hates" such charges, Mr. Dammerman adds: "It's not like we're creating some big cookie jar" from which GE takes profits at will.

continued ➡

Another way GE manages its earnings is by literally buying them—by acquiring companies or assets that are immediately profitable because they throw off more income than GE's cost of financing. Much of the growth in GE Capital's earnings in the past few years has been generated by a spate of acquisitions.

"Of course we're buying earnings when we do an acquisition," says James Parke, GE Capital's chief financial officer. The financial-services subsidiary acquired assets totalling $16.9 billion in 1993 alone.

Daniel Porter, GE Capital's North American chief of retailer financial services, says he and his colleagues may hunt for acquisitions if his division might miss its annual earnings target. He says they ask: "Gee, does somebody else have some income? Is there some other deals we can make?"

Risk in Hasty Action

The danger, of course, is that a headlong rush into acquisitions to book earnings could lead to unwise decisions. Management's ambitious growth targets create GE Capital's biggest business risk, according to Sanjay Sharma, a Moody's Investors Service analyst.

"As growth in the commercial finance sector has become difficult to achieve because of growing bank and nonbank competition, an aggressive strategy in this sector can only be accomplished by paying higher premiums for portfolio acquisitions—in effect, by taking greater risks," Mr. Sharma says. Already, he notes, the returns on GE Capital's mushrooming trove of assets are slipping, to 1.4% in 1993 from 1.61% in 1989. To keep growing so fast without major gains from operations, GE would have to make more and more acquisitions, possibly compounding the risk.

Isn't it unsound to have earnings-report considerations drive the timing of acquisitions? Mr. Dammerman says that as long as executives keep both long-term and short-term goals in mind, "I see nothing wrong with someone saying, 'Look, I have an earnings objective for the year, and to achieve that earnings objective maybe I need to go make an acquisition.' That's fine if the individual can come up with a good acquisition."

Two former GE Capital executives say GE's financial business contains a wealth of hidden value—which they call reserves—that can be tapped to get income as needed. "Are there hidden values there? Absolutely," Mr. Parke says, though they are "impossible to measure."

One way GE stores profits for future use is, ironically, by following fairly conservative accounting practices. In fact, John W. Stanger, GE Capital's president from 1975 to 1984, says those practices would occasionally annoy managers who believed the company was "trying to bury profits" that they had racked up in a stellar year.

Handling Used Aircraft

GE Capital also has considerable discretion over the timing of sales of warrants or equity kickers obtained in the course of lending and in deciding whether to sell or re-lease aircraft coming off lease. GE Capital has "significant ability to come up with earnings on demand," First Boston's Mr. Sankey says, because of its "diversified portfolio" and "very large amount of flexibility in how you report earnings."

continued →

Take the hypothetical example of an aircraft nearing the end of a 15-year lease. GE may have already written off most of the plane's cost, leaving its book value low. GE can potentially book a gain if it then sells the plane, Mr. Sankey says, but not if the jet is re-leased to another airline.

Mr. Parke denies that GE Capital fattens its earnings by selling aircraft. It has some discretion, he says, but this is limited because "you have to have a buyer, and you have to have the right market conditions in order to maximize the value."

The timing of sales of equity interests obtained throughout warrants—the equity operations that GE often gets for lending on especially risky buyouts—also is "very discretionary," Mr. Sankey says. But GE executives say they have only a little discretion because such sales usually depend on when a company goes public. Now holding a potentially valuable 50% stake in Montgomery Ward, however, GE Capital would have considerable say over when the retailer went public.

Such maneuvers are particularly difficult to monitor at GE Capital because the amount of information it discloses is relatively scant compared with the wealth of information about its parent company. GE Capital, for example, doesn't differentiate its income from asset sales.

"You look at their financial reports—they are pretty skinny. A lot of analysts feel frustrated because it's such a complex organization," says Richard Schmidt of Standard & Poor's Corp., the credit-rating agency. He concedes that many commercial finance companies keep their numbers close to the vest, too.

As an unregulated financial-services company, GE Capital also has more flexibility to defer write-offs than do highly regulated U.S. banks. During the 1990–1991 recession, regulators required banks to take write-downs, add reserves and sell assets. But GE Capital contends that it writes off bad assets faster than banks do and that rating agencies and the markets are tougher than bank regulators.

The RCA Acquisition

One of GE's most intriguing moves to boost its net income was in its accounting for its $6.4 billion acquisition of RCA Corp. in 1986. Anytime an acquisition is made for a price exceeding the book value of the business, the premium over book value must be recorded on the buyer's books.

In the case of RCA, one former GE executive recalls that GE allocated a disproportionate amount of this so-called goodwill to NBC, increasing the TV network's book value while reducing that of other RCA assets. GE's own annual reports appear to substantiate his recollection. In 1987, the year after the acquisition, GE raised NBC's book value to $3.8 billion from $3.4 billion. The higher book value for NBC and the resulting lower value for other RCA assets raised GE's profits on sales of some of RCA's non-NBC assets.

Among the RCA units sold, GE recorded a $110 million gain on the disposition in 1991 of NBC's interest in an RCA-Columbia home-video joint venture. And the aerospace business was sold in 1993 at a pretax profit of $1.43 billion. That leaves NBC as the last major piece of RCA still on GE's books.

continued ➔

Mr. Dammerman says that boosting gains from future non-NBC asset sales didn't enter into how NBC was valued and that GE didn't know at the time which businesses would be sold. He adds that GE couldn't record profits from some RCA assets sold soon after the acquisition.

However, one consequence of assigning a higher book value to NBC eventually became apparent when GE began considering the sale of the network in the early 1990s. The higher book value raised the price GE would have had to obtain to avoid booking a loss. When GE held talks about selling NBC to Paramount Communications Inc. (now owned by Viacom Inc.), Paramount proposed to structure the sale financing in a way that would help GE avoid an immediate write-down, according to two people familiar with the negotiations. Mr. Dammerman says that although GE wanted to avoid a loss, the proposed transaction wasn't structured with that aim.

Despite some experts' doubts about earnings management, some accountants say it can be helpful as long as corporate executives try to convey a fair picture. "Some people would say maybe smoothing makes sense because it gives the best indication of the future and the long-term trend," says Peter Wilson, who specializes in financial-statement analysis at the Sloan School of Management at Massachusetts Institute of Technology.

But Howard Schilit, an accounting professor at American University in Washington, comments: "Earnings management can be very dangerous for the investor because you are creating something artificial. The numbers should reflect how the company is actually doing."

GE executives differ in how much smoothing they acknowledge. In an initial interview, GE Capital Chairman Gary Wendt said, "We do a little, not a lot." His financial chief, Mr. Parke, said, "We have a lot of assets in this business.... Obviously, there are timing issues associated with when those assets are sold."

Source: Reprinted by permission of *The Wall Street Journal*, © 1994 Dow Jones & Company, Inc. All rights reserved worldwide.

Required

a. Evaluate the effectiveness of restructuring charges as an earnings management device. Do you agree with Professor Leftwich's reservations about such charges and with the SEC's expected limitations on such provisions? Explain.

b. Explain whether you agree with Peter Wilson, who says "maybe smoothing makes sense" or with Howard Schilit, who says "earnings management can be very dangerous."

c. One of the most interesting aspects of the article is its implications for securities market efficiency. If large, complex firms such as GE have "so many different businesses that most analysts can't track them all," how can the market price of GE's shares properly reflect all that is known about the firm? To what extent do you think earnings management is a substitute for analysts in informing the market about the firm's value and prospects?

10. The article "Dangerous Games," by Jonathan Laing is here reproduced from *Barron's* (June 8, 1998). The article describes apparent earnings management devices used

by Sunbeam Corp., with "Chainsaw Al" Dunlap as CEO, to "largely manufacture" its 1997 reported earnings of $109.4 million.

Dangerous Games

Did "Chainsaw Al" Dunlap manufacture Sunbeam's earnings last year?

Albert Dunlap likes to tell how confidants warned him in 1996 that taking the top job at the small-appliance maker Sunbeam Corp. would likely be his Vietnam. For a time, the 60-year-old West Point graduate seemingly proved the Cassandras wrong. As the poster boy of 'Nineties-style corporate cost-cutting, he delivered exactly the huge body counts and punishing airstrikes that Wall Street loved. He dumped half of Sunbeam's 12,000 employees by either laying them off or selling the operations where they worked. In all, he shuttered or sold about 80 of Sunbeam's 114 plants, offices and warehouses.

Sunbeam's sales and earnings responded, and so did its stock price, rising from $12.50 a share the day Dunlap took over in July 1996 to a high of $53 in early March of this year.

But last month Sunbeam suffered a reversal of fortune that was as sudden and traumatic for Dunlap as the Viet Cong's Tet offensive was to U.S. forces in 1968. After several mild warnings of a possible revenue disappointment, Sunbeam shocked Wall Street by reporting a loss of $44.6 million for the first quarter on a sales decline of 3.6%. In a trice, the Sunbeam cost-cutting story was dead, along with "Chainsaw Al" Dunlap's image as the supreme maximizer of shareholder value. Now Sunbeam stock has fallen more than 50% from its peak, to a recent $22.

And just as suddenly, what was supposed to be an easy sprint, Dunlap's last hurrah as a corporate turnaround artist, has turned into a grinding marathon. Lying in tatters is his growth scenario for Sunbeam, based on supposedly sexy new offerings such as soft-ice cream makers, fancy grills, home water purifiers and air-filter appliances. Many of the new products have bombed in the marketplace or run into serious quality problems. Moreover, Sunbeam has run into all manner of production, quality and delivery problems. It recently announced the closing of two Mexican manufacturing facilities with some 2,800 workers, citing the facilities' lamentable performance. Dozens of key executives, members of what Dunlap just months ago called his Dream Team, are bailing out. And now he faces another year or more of the wrenching restructuring that's needed to meld Sunbeam with its recently announced acquisitions, including the camping-equipment maker Coleman Co., the smoke detector producer First Alert and Signature Brands USA, best known for its Mr. Coffee line of appliances. These acquisitions will double the size of a company whose wheels are coming off. This may not be Vietnam, but it sure ain't Kansas, Toto.

Sunbeam declined to discuss the company's problems with *Barron's*. In some ways, Dunlap seems to have morphed into a latter-day Colonel Kurtz of the movie *Apocalypse Now*, increasingly out of touch with the grim realities of Sunbeam's situation and suspicious of friend and foe alike. For example, Wall Street is still buzzing over a con-

continued ➜

frontation that Dunlap had with PaineWebber analyst Andrew Shore at a Sunbeam meeting with the financial community in New York three weeks ago. Shore had the temerity to ask several questions that Dunlap deemed impertinent, and Dunlap snarled, "You son of a bitch. If you want to come after me, I'll come after you twice as hard."

Shore, the first major analyst to downgrade Sunbeam's stock in April when word began to circulate of a possible first-quarter earnings debacle, is still upset over the incident. "As far as I'm concerned, Al is the most overrated CEO in America," he grouses. "He's nothing but a bully who speaks in sound bites and completely lacks substance."

Despite Sunbeam's latest reversal of fortune, don't expect Al Dunlap to be headed for the poorhouse any time soon. Though the swoon in Sunbeam shares has vaporized the value of the options held by most of the company's executives and managers, Dunlap's large option and stock grants are still worth about $70 million, down from a peak value of over $300 million when the stock was at its high. Moreover, in February Dunlap negotiated a new contract, doubling his annual base salary of $2 million. Under a rich benefits package, Sunbeam even foots the bill for Dunlap and his wife's first-class air fare from Florida, where Sunbeam is headquartered, to Philadelphia so that Dunlap can visit his personal dentist to keep his latest bridge comfy and pearly white. Limo charges and overnights at the Four Seasons hotel are included as well. All this from the self-styled champion of shareholder value.

We can't say we are surprised by Sunbeam's current woes. In a cover story last year entitled "Careful, Al" (June 16), we cast a skeptical eye on Dunlap's growth objectives in the low-margin, cutthroat small-appliance industry. We also pointed out the yawning gap between Sunbeam's performance claims and reality. We took special note of Sunbeam's accounting gimmickry, which appeared to have transmogrified through accounting wizardry the company's monster 1996 restructuring charge ($337 million before taxes) into 1997's eye-popping sales and earnings rebound. But to no avail. Wall Street remained impressed by Sunbeam's earnings, and the stock continued to rise from a price of $37 at the time of the story.

Sunbeam's financials under Dunlap look like an exercise in high-energy physics, in which time and space seem to fuse and bend. They are a veritable cloud chamber. Income and costs move almost imperceptibly back and forth between the income statement and balance sheet like charged ions, whose vapor trail has long since dissipated by the end of any quarter, when results are reported. There are also some signs of other accounting shenanigans and puffery, including sales and related profits booked in periods before the goods were actually shipped or payment received. Booking sales and earnings in advance can comply with accounting regulations under certain strict circumstances.

"We had an amazing year," Dunlap crowed in Sunbeam's recently released 1997 annual report, taking an impromptu victory lap for the profit of $109.4 million, or $1.41 a share, on sales of $1.2 billion. Sunbeam had every incentive to try to shoot the lights out in 1997. Dunlap and crew were convinced they would be able to attract a buyer for the company just as they had done in the second year of their restructuring of Scott Paper in 1995, when Dunlap managed to fob Scott off on Kimberly Clark for

continued ➜

$9 billion. They openly shopped Sunbeam around in the second half of last year, but the offer never came. The rising stock price made the company too expensive, and would-be buyers were also deterred by the nightmares Kimberly Clark experienced after buying Scott.

Yet, sad to say, the earnings from Sunbeam's supposed breakthrough year appear to be largely manufactured. That, at least, is our conclusion after close perusal of the company's recently released 10-K, with a little help from some people close to the company.

Start with the fact that in the 1996 restructuring, Sunbeam chose to write down to zero some $90 million of its inventory for product lines being discontinued and other perfectly good items. Even if Sunbeam realized just 50 cents on the dollar by selling these goods in 1997 (in some cases, they reportedly did even better), that would account for about a third of last year's net income of $109.4 million.

One has to go to the 1997 year-end balance sheet to detect more of mother's little helpers. One notes a striking $23.2 million drop, from $40.4 million in 1996 to $17.2 million in 1997, in pre-paid expenses and other current assets. There's no mystery here, according to a former Sunbeam financial type. The huge restructuring charge in 1996 made it a lost year anyway, so Sunbeam prepaid everything it could, ranging from advertising and packaging costs to insurance premiums and various inventory expenses. The result: Costs expensed for 1997 were reduced markedly, if unnaturally. This artifice alone probably yielded an additional $15 million or so in 1997 after-tax income.

Why did Sunbeam's "Other Current Liabilities" mysteriously drop by $18.1 million and "Other Long-Term Liabilities" fall by $19 million in 1997? The answer is simple, according to folks close to the company. Various reserves for product warranties and other items that were set aside during Sunbeam's giant 1996 restructuring were drained down in 1997, creating perhaps an additional $25 million or so in additional net income for the year.

On top of all that, as part of the 1996 restructuring charge, Sunbeam reduced the value of its property, plant, equipment and trademarks by $92 million. Though some of these charges applied to assets Sunbeam was selling off, the bulk of the charge related to ongoing operations. This allowed Sunbeam to lower its depreciation and amortization expense on the 1997 income statement by nearly $9 million. That would create about $6 million of additional after-tax income.

Oddly enough, the figure for net property, plant and equipment on Sunbeam's balance sheet still rose during 1997, to $241 million from $220 million the year before. This is likely an indication that such costs as product development, new packaging and some advertising and marketing initiatives were capitalized or put straight on the balance sheet instead of being expensed in the year they were incurred, as was the previous practice. In this manner, expense could have been shifted from 1997 into future years, when they can be burned off at a slower, more decorous pace afforded by multi-year depreciation schedules. Why else would Sunbeam's advertising and promotion expense drop by some $15 million, from $71.5 million in 1996 to $56.4 million last year? Particularly when Sunbeam trotted out a splashy national television ad campaign in 1997 to boost consumer demand

continued ➜

for its new products. This advertising shortfall alone contributed another $10 million to Sunbeam's 1997 profits.

The company also got a nice boost from a 61% drop in its allowance for doubtful accounts and cash discounts, from $23.4 million in 1996 to $8.4 million in 1997. And this decline occurred despite a 19% rise in Sunbeam's sales last year. The milking of this bad debt reserve in 1997 likely puffed net income by an additional $10 million or so.

Then there's the mystery of why Sunbeam's inventories exploded by some 40%, or $93 million, during 1997. Quite possibly, Sunbeam was playing games with its inventories to help the income statement. By running plants flat out and building inventories, a company can shift fixed overhead costs from the income statement to the balance sheet where they remain ensconced as part of the value of the inventory until such time as the inventory is sold. To be conservative, let's assume this inventory buildup might have helped Sunbeam's profits to the tune of, say, $10 million.

Lastly, there are more than superficial indications that Sunbeam jammed as many sales as it could in 1997 to pump both the top and bottom lines. The revenue games began innocently enough early last year. Sales were apparently delayed in late 1996, a lost year anyway, and rammed into 1997. Likewise, *The Wall Street Journal* reported several instances of "inventory stuffing" during 1997, in which Sunbeam either sent more goods than had been ordered by customers or shipped goods even after an order had been cancelled. But these are comparatively venial sins that companies engage in all the time to make a quarter's results look better. Besides, Sunbeam gave the plausible excuse at the time that glitches in a computer system consolidation in the first quarter had them flying blind for a time.

But as 1997 dragged on and the pressure to perform for Wall Street intensified, Sunbeam began to take greater and greater liberties with sales terms to puff current results. The latest 10-K, for example, discloses that in the fourth quarter of last year Sunbeam recorded some $50 million in sales of cooking grills under an "early buy" program that allowed retailers to delay payment for the items as long as six months. Moreover, some $35 million of these "early buys" were categorized "bill and hold" sales and never even left Sunbeam's warehouses.

Sunbeam engaged in bill-and-hold transactions in other product lines, too, according to a number of people in the appliance industry. In the second quarter, for example, Sunbeam booked a sale and "shipped" some $10 million of blankets to a warehouse it had rented in Mississippi near its Hattiesburg distribution center. They were held there for some weeks for Wal-Mart. The company also pumped millions of dollars of goods into several national small-appliance distributors on such easy payment terms as to call into question whether a sale ever took place. Some with knowledge of Sunbeam's business practices say the appliance maker in some instances transferred title for the goods to distributors but then agreed to not only delay payment but actually pay the distributors what amounted to a storage charge for taking the goods. These sources also said that in some cases distributors also had the right to return the items to Sunbeam without suffering any loss.

How much did various types of questionable sales add to 1997's net income? No outsider can know for sure. But we can make an educated guess based on the fact that

continued ➔

Sunbeam's receivables, or unpaid customer accounts, jumped by 38%, or $82 million, in 1997. Taking into account Sunbeam's profit margins, it seems that questionable sales could have boosted 1997 net income by as much as $8 million.

We by no means are privy to all Sunbeam's techniques for harvesting current earnings from past restructuring charges and future sales. Deconstructing Al Dunlap is a daunting task. But to save our gentle readers the effort, our total estimate of artificial profit boosters in 1997 came to around $120 million compared with the $109.4 million profit the company actually reported. Thus, one is left to wonder whether Sunbeam made anything at all from its actual operations, despite Dunlap's claim to have realized some $225 million in cost savings as a result of his restructuring prowess.

Our dour view of Sunbeam's current financial health is only confirmed by the company's consolidated statement of cash flow in the latest 10-K. These numbers, of course, are harder to finesse because they track the actual cash that flowed in and out of the company during 1997. And the statement doesn't paint a pretty picture. Despite 1997's eye-catching $109.4 million net profit, Sunbeam still suffered negative cash flow from operations of $8.2 million, after taking into account the explosion in Sunbeam's inventory and accounts receivable during the year. And that operating cash flow deficit would have been an even larger $67.2 million if not for the sale of $59 million in receivables in the last week of 1997. After capital expenditures of $58.3 million is thrown into the equation, Sunbeam's free cash flow deficit amounts to more than $125 million.

Sunbeam's first-quarter earnings debacle is yet another sign of a company that's in anything but the pink of health. Despite management assertions into April that Sunbeam's first-quarter sales would finish comfortably ahead of those for the first quarter of 1997, they ended up declining 4%. Even more shocking to Dunlap's fans was the $44.6 million loss in the March quarter compared with a profit in the year earlier period of $6.9 million. Sure, $36.8 million of that first-quarter loss was the result of nonrecurring charges, mostly a handsome new pay package Dunlap managed to negotiate in February. But the operating loss Sunbeam suffered of $7.8 million was a clear sign of its true earnings power once the tank from the 1996 restructuring charge had run dry.

Dunlap trotted out a whole raft of excuses for the company's lamentable first-quarter performance. He cited dumb deals his former No. 3 executive had made with major retailers before Chainsaw fired him in April, the effect of bad weather on grill sales caused by El Nino, and so forth.

Whatever the case, the first-quarter disaster wasn't the result of any lack of effort on Sunbeam's part to pump up the results. The company recorded $29 million of additional "buy now, pay later" grill sales. In fact, the company is now holding so many grills, in various warehouses around its Neosho, Missouri, grill plant that it has had to lease warehouse space in nearby Oklahoma. Who knows how many of these grills will ever make it to the selling floor?

Sunbeam also extended its quarter by three days, from March 28 to March 31. This allowed the company to book an extra $20 million in sales both from ongoing Sunbeam operations and two days of sales from Coleman (its acquisition closed on March 30). But to no avail. Sunbeam still fell $9 million short of last year's sales of $253.5 million.

continued →

Reports are rife that Sunbeam tried to strong-arm suppliers into "recutting" their invoices for various goods and services so that Sunbeam would officially owe less money. The proviso was that the suppliers would be allowed to add back the amount forgone, plus interest, in invoices submitted after the first quarter had ended. A Sunbeam financial official denies the "recutting" charge and characterizes the activity by the company's procurement department as the normal give-and-take that goes on between suppliers and companies seeking rebates.

But that's not the understanding held by an official at one China-based supplier. When contacted by Barron's, this official readily acknowledged that he had sent Sunbeam a check for $500,000, or 5% of the business he does annually with the company, in late March. "The only reason I sent them a check rather than a new invoice is that we had no invoices outstanding at the time we received the call," he explained. "We figure our contribution dropped right down to the bottom line if Sunbeam actually booked it. I don't know what happened, though."

For the next few quarters, expect the recent acquisition of Coleman, First Alert and Mr. Coffee to restore a measure of calm to Sunbeam's financial performance. The giant restructuring charges that Sunbeam is taking to integrate the new units, at $390 million before taxes, will give the company plenty of fodder with which to play earnings games. The company is even forecasting earnings of $1 a share this year and $2 next year—before extraordinary items, naturally.

But Dunlap's days at Sunbeam may be numbered. The already-ailing company now has to struggle under $2 billion of additional debt and a negative tangible net worth of $800 million. And his enemies, including disenchanted shareholders, angry securities analysts, and bitter former employees, are growing in number and circling ever closer to the company's headquarters in Delray Beach. Of course, Dunlap could always escape by using the building's flat roof to chopper out, should it come to that. One can only hope he'll remember to take the American flag with him.

Required

a. Jonathan Laing notes that Sunbeam's prepaid expenses declined from $40.4 million at December 31, 1996 to $17.2 at December 31, 1997, a reduction of $23.2 million. He points out that 1996 was a "lost year anyway" (because of a 1996 restructuring charge of $337 million), so Sunbeam "prepaid everything it could." Laing then states that this "artifice alone probably yielded" $15 million in 1997 after-tax income.

   Do you agree with Laing's analysis of the effect of the decline in prepaid expenses during 1997 on 1997 net income? Explain why or why not.

b. Laing reports that 1997 operating cash flow was −$8.2 million. Since net income was reported as $109.4 million, net income-increasing accruals must have totalled $117.6 million. Use the information in the article to itemize the impacts on net income of the various earnings management devices described. How close does your itemized list come to $117.6 million? In arriving at your itemized total, take your answer to part **a** into account.

Do you agree with Laing's statement that 1997 earnings "appear to be largely manufactured"? Explain why or why not.

c. On the last page, the article refers to Sunbeam's acquisition of Coleman, First Alert, and Mr. Coffee, indicating that Sunbeam is taking restructuring charges of $390 million to integrate these firms into its operations. Explain how this will "give the company plenty of fodder with which to play earnings games."

d. Use the "iron law" of accruals reversal to help explain why there was a substantial first quarter 1998 loss.

11. Barton (2001) studied managers' use of derivatives and discretionary accruals to smooth reported earnings. As Barton points out, both of these devices have smoothing potential—since earnings can be expressed as the sum of operating cash flows and total accruals, smoothing can be accomplished through operating cash flows (which can be hedged by derivatives) and/or through accruals (by means of the discretionary portion).

From a sample of large U.S. firms during 1994–1996, incl., Barton found that managers trade off the use of derivatives and discretionary accruals in order to maintain (i.e., smooth) earnings volatility at a desired level. Specifically, firms that were heavy derivatives users tended to be low users of discretionary accruals, and vice versa. Other things equal, this suggests that managers are sensitive to the costs of smoothing earnings. That is, firms appear to use the combination of smoothing devices that are, for them, the least costly.

Required

a. Give reasons why managers may want to smooth earnings.

b. What are some of the costs of smoothing earnings? Why would managers trade off these two earnings smoothing devices, rather than using only one or the other?

c. When the Accounting Standards Board of Canada implements a new standard on accounting for derivative financial instruments similar to SFAS 133 of the FASB, will this be likely to increase or decrease, or have little effect on, the use of derivatives for smoothing purposes in Canada? Explain.

d. Are Barton's results more consistent with the opportunistic or efficient contracting version of positive accounting theory? Why?

12. Refer to the Theory in Practice 11.1 in Section 11.6.

Required

a. Which earnings management policy did Nortel appear to be using in 2001 and 2002? Why? Which policy did it appear to be using in 2003? Why?

b. Discuss the possible impacts on manager effort of the Nortel compensation plan's tying of bonuses to a return to profitability.

c. Use the concept of conservatism to justify Nortel's apparent over-provision of accruals in 2001 and 2002 (see Section 8.6.4).

d. Assuming that the accruals recorded by Nortel in 2001 and 2002 were justified by pessimistic economic conditions at the time, and conservatism, where did Nortel management go wrong? Explain.

Notes

1. This assumes that the manager stays with the firm throughout the period required for the accruals to reverse. Should this not be the case, the manager may escape some of the accrual reversal consequences.

2. This is a case of post-decision information. See Section 9.5.1.

3. Healy points out that if net income is just below the bogey, the manager might instead adopt policies to increase net income, so that at least some bonus would be received.

4. An alternative is to take changes in working capital items from the comparative balance sheets. However, Hribar and Collins (2002) caution that this may bias the accruals estimates. The reason is that many firms engage in acquisitions and divestitures. Then, working capital items are increased or decreased on the consolidated balance sheet but these changes do not affect net income, and thus are not subject to earnings management. Changes in working capital items on the statement of cash flows do not include these non-earnings-related changes.

5. Evidence for an alternative explanation is provided by Abarbanell and Lehavy (2003). They argue that if managers are also compensated based on share price performance (recall that Healy studied only bonus plans, which are typically based on earnings), they will want to avoid the negative share price reaction that follows bad earnings news.

6. Skinner and Sloan studied growth firms (firms with a high ratio of market value to book value). They argue that investors overestimate the future performance of growth firms, due to behavioural factors such as self-attribution bias discussed in Section 6.2. Failure to meet earnings expectations brings investors "back to earth," resulting in a major share price decline.

7. Another way is to lower investors' expectations by "talking down" analysts, to the point where reported earnings meet or exceed the analysts' revised, lower forecasts. This was studied by Matsumoto (2002), who found that firms in her sample used both approaches. As Matsumoto points out, however, her study preceded regulation FD (an SEC regulation introduced in 2000 to prohibit firms from releasing material information only to analysts). Subsequent to 2000, the incidence of talking down analysts should decrease.

8. This assumes that stakeholders do not unwind the earnings management. Consistent with our argument in Section 11.3, BDS argue that it is not cost-effective for them to do so since it is difficult to isolate effects on reported income of continuing use of FIFO or accelerated amortization, particularly since many stakeholders have limited ability to process information and may not have enough at stake to warrant careful evaluation of reported earnings.

9. As DS point out, the information conveyed by the financial statements in their model does not purport to fully convey the value of the firm. All that is claimed is that *some* value-relevant information is conveyed by net income. That is, their model does not get around our general observation that net income is only well defined under ideal conditions.

Chapter 12

Standard Setting: Economic Issues

FIGURE 12.1 ORGANIZATION OF CHAPTER 12

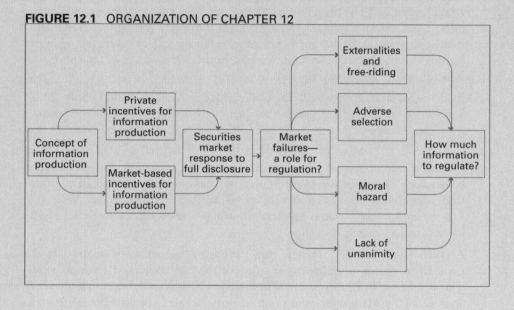

12.1 Overview

We now return to the role of standard setting that was introduced in Chapter 1. Recall that we view the standard setter as a mediator between the conflicting interests of investors and managers. The fundamental problem of financial accounting theory is how to conduct this mediation, that is, how to reconcile the financial reporting and efficient contracting roles of accounting information or, equivalently, how to determine the socially "right" amount of information. We define the right amount as that amount that equates the marginal social benefits of information to the marginal social costs.[1]

Of course, we should not take for granted that regulation is necessary for this reconciliation. Much of the required mediation can be accomplished by market forces. Nevertheless, substantial arguments can be made that market forces alone are unable to drive the right amount of information production. Our purpose in this chapter is to review and evaluate these arguments.

The extent of standard setting is a challenging one for accountants. Many aspects of firms' information production are regulated, and many of these regulations are laid down by accounting standard-setting bodies themselves, in the form of GAAP. Furthermore, the extent of regulation is increasing all the time, as more and more accounting standards are promulgated.

As you are aware, many industries in recent years have been deregulated. Airlines, trucking, financial services, telecommunications, and electric power generation are examples of industries that have seen substantial deregulation. What would happen if the information industry was deregulated? Would this produce a flood of competition and innovation, or would information production collapse into chaos? At present, the answers to these questions are not known. However, discussion of the pros and cons of standard setting helps us to see the tradeoffs that are involved and to appreciate the crucial role of information in society. Figure 12.1 outlines the organization of this chapter.

12.2 Regulation of Economic Activity

There are numerous instances of regulation of economic activity in our economy. Firms that have a monopoly, such as electricity distribution, local telephone companies, and transportation companies are common examples. Here, regulation typically takes the form of regulation of rates, regulation of the rate of return on invested capital, or both. Public safety is an area subject to frequent regulation as, for example, in elevator inspection laws, standards for automobile tire construction, and fire protection regulations. Communications is another area that, in many countries, is deemed sufficiently sensitive to attract regulation.

Other sets of regulations affect financial institutions and securities markets. The primary reason for such regulation is to protect individuals who are at an information disadvantage. This points up the fact that information asymmetry underlies the regulation of information production. If there was no information asymmetry, so that managerial actions and inside information were freely observable by all, there would be no need to protect individuals from the consequences of information disadvantage.

Information asymmetry is thus frequently used to justify regulations to protect the information-disadvantaged. Insider trading rules, executive compensation disclosures in management proxy circulars, public access to corporate conference calls with analysts, and regulations of full disclosure in prospectuses are examples. In addition to protecting ordinary investors, such regulations are also intended to improve the operation of capital markets by enhancing public confidence in their fairness.

Accounting practice is also strongly affected by regulations designed to protect against information asymmetry. An important role of accounting and auditing is to report relevant and reliable information, thereby reducing information asymmetry between firm insiders, the investing public, and other users. However, this role requires that accountants and auditors be credible and competent. Thus, there are laws to regulate the accounting professions that control entry and maintain high standards. Many other regulations also affect accountants. Minimum disclosure requirements for annual reports are required by corporations acts. Government statistical agencies and taxation authorities require financial information. Quasi-governmental bodies such as the OSC and the SEC require a variety of information disclosures for firms whose shares are publicly traded. Private bodies such as stock exchanges require periodic disclosures from firms whose securities are traded on the exchange. Finally, other private bodies, such as the AcSB and the FASB, set accounting and auditing standards.

Thus, we see that accounting is a highly regulated area of economic activity. Governments are directly involved in this regulation through laws to control the creation of professional accounting bodies and their rights to public practice, and also through minimum disclosure requirements for annual reports and prospectuses. Indirect government involvement comes, for example, through securities commissions' standards, such as MD&A and management proxy circulars. Furthermore, the professions themselves do much of their own regulating by formulating and monitoring accounting and auditing standards. Henceforth, we will use the term **central authority** to refer to any of these regulatory bodies.

In this chapter our primary concerns are the regulation of minimum disclosure requirements, generally accepted accounting and auditing standards, and the requirement that public companies have audits. We will use the term **standard setting** to denote the establishment of these various rules and regulations. Note that standard setting involves the regulation of firms' external information production decisions. For our purposes, it does not matter whether these standards are set by direct or indirect regulation. In the case of indirect regulation, such as AcSB and FASB standards, authority to set standards is allowed by the government. The main point is that firms are not completely free to control the amount and timing of the information they produce about themselves. Rather, they must do so under a host of regulations that we will call standards, laid down by some central authority.

> **Standard setting** *is the regulation of firms' external information production decisions by some central authority.*

In considering issues of information production, it is helpful to distinguish between two types of information that a manager may possess. The first type is called **proprietary information**. This is information that, if released, would directly affect future cash flows of the firm.[2] Examples are technical information about valuable patents, and plans for strategic initiatives such as takeover bids or mergers. The costs to the manager and firm of releasing proprietary information can be quite high.

The second type is called **non-proprietary information**. This is information that does not directly affect firm cash flows. It includes financial statement information, earnings forecasts, details of new financing, and so on. The audit is also included in non-proprietary information.

12.3 Private Incentives for Information Production

12.3.1 Ways to Characterize Information Production

While the term "production" of information may take some getting used to, we use it for two reasons. First, we want to think of information as a commodity that can be produced and sold. Then, it is natural to consider separately the costs and benefits of information production.

Second, we want a unified way of thinking about the various ways information production can be accomplished. Information is a complex commodity. Just what do we mean when we speak of the quantity of information produced? There are several ways to answer this question.

First, we can think of **finer information**. For example, a thermometer that tells you the temperature in degrees is a finer information system than one that only tells you if the temperature is above or below freezing—the first thermometer tells you everything that the second one does, and more. It enables a finer reading of the temperature. In an accounting context, a finer reporting system adds more detail to the existing historical cost-based statements. Examples of finer reporting include expanded note disclosure, additional line items on the financial statements, segment reporting, and so on. In terms of our decision theory discussion of Chapter 3, finer information production means a better ability to discriminate between realizations of the states of nature. For example, in a decision problem where the relevant set of states of nature is the temperature, a thermometer that tells you degrees enables better discrimination between different temperature states than one that only tells you if the temperature is above or below freezing. We can also think of the information perspective on decision usefulness, discussed in Chapter 5, as implying finer information production, since the information perspective encourages elaboration of the financial statements proper by means of MD&A and notes.

Second, we can think of **additional information**. For example, we might add a barometer to our thermometer. In an accounting context, additional information means the introduction of new information systems to report on matters not covered by the historical cost system. Examples would include fair value accounting, which introduces the effects of changing values into financial reporting, and future-oriented financial information included in MD&A, which expands reporting to include expected future operations. In decision theory terms, additional information means an expansion of the set of relevant states of nature upon which the firm's performance depends. Thus a thermometer-barometer reports on atmospheric pressure as well as temperature. In effect, additional information can produce greater relevance in reporting. We can think of the measurement perspective on decision usefulness discussed in Chapter 6 as a move towards producing additional value-relevant information.

A third way to think about information production is in terms of its **credibility**. The essence of credibility is that the receiver knows that the supplier of information has an incentive to disclose truthfully. In our thermometer example, the purchaser knows that the manufacturer must produce an accurate product in order to stay in business. Thus, the purchaser accepts the thermometer as a credible representation of the temperature. In an accounting context, it is often suggested that a "Big Four" audit is more credible than a "non-Big Four" audit because a large audit firm has more to lose,[3] both in terms of reputation and "deep pockets;" hence, it will maintain high audit standards. Also, the greater the penalties for managers who divulge false information, the more credibility investors attach to managers' disclosures.

In this chapter we will not need to distinguish these different ways to produce information and will refer to them all, rather loosely, as **information production**. Note that however we think of its production, more information will require higher costs, some of which may be proprietary.

12.3.2 Contractual Incentives for Information Production

Incentives for private information production arise from the contracts that firms enter into. As we saw in Chapter 9, information is necessary to monitor compliance with contracts. For example, if managerial effort is unobservable, this leads to an incentive contract based on the results of the firm's operations. Then, information about profitability is needed to provide a measure of performance. Also, an audit adds credibility to reported net income, so that both the owner and the manager of the firm are willing to accept reported net income as a precise measure of current managerial performance.

Similarly, when a firm issues debt, it typically includes covenants in the contract. Information is needed about the various ratios on which the covenants are based, so that the firm's adherence to its covenants can be monitored over the life of the debt issue. Again, an audit adds credibility to the covenant information.

Another contractual reason for private information production arises when a privately owned firm goes public. This was modelled by Jensen and Meckling (1976). The owner–manager of a firm going public, after selling all or part interest, has a motivation to increase shirking. Note that prior to the IPO the shirking problem was internalized—the owner–manager bore all the costs. The costs of shirking are the reduced profits that result. Subsequent to the new issue, the owner–manager does not bear all the costs—the new owners will bear their proportionate share. Thus, shirking costs the owner–manager less after going public, so he or she will engage in more of it. This is an agency cost to the new owners of the firm.

Investors will be aware of this motivation, however, and will bid down the amount they are willing to pay for the new issue by the expected amount of agency costs. In effect, the firm's cost of capital rises. Consequently, the owner–manager has an incentive to contract to limit his or her shirking and thereby raise the issue price. For example, the contract between the owner–manager and the new investors in the firm may include a forecast, which the owner–manager will be motivated to meet (this will be recognized as the production of additional information). Alternatively, the contract may provide for a lot of detail in the financial statements (finer information), to make it more difficult for the owner–manager to hide or bury costs of perquisites. Also, the contract may provide for an audit to increase the credibility of the information production. In all of these cases, the owner–manager commits by contract to produce information that will convince investors that he or she will in fact continue to manage diligently. Investors, realizing this, will be willing to pay more for an interest in the firm than they would otherwise.

The key point here is that the firm has a private incentive to produce information in all of these contracting scenarios—no central authority is needed to force information production. Furthermore, since the types and amounts of information to be produced under the contract are negotiated and agreed to by all contracting parties, the right amount of information is produced, by definition. That is, the information production decision is internalized between the contracting parties. Then, the question of whether too much or too little information is produced does not arise. Failure to provide for information production in the contract will make it more incomplete, hence more difficult or impossible to enforce.

In principle, the contractual motivation for information production can be extended to any group of contracting parties. Consider, for example, the relationship between the firm manager and investors. The investor's decision problem was reviewed in Chapter 3, where we concluded that rational investors want information about the expected return and risk of their investments. The firm manager and each investor could contract for the desired amount of information about the firm's future cash flows, financial position, and so on. The contract could provide that the investor pay for this information or, perhaps, the manager would offer it free to raise the demand for the firm's shares. Note that different investors would, in general, want different amounts of information about the firm. One investor, adept at financial analysis, might demand a very fine projection of future operations, from which to prepare an estimate of future cash flows and returns on investment. Another investor may simply want information about the firm's dividend policy. A very risk-averse investor might demand a very credible audit, at a correspondingly high cost, while another investor would prefer the least costly audit available. Other investors may not demand any information at all, particularly if their investment portfolios are well diversified. Instead, they might rely on market efficiency to price-protect them.

Unfortunately, while direct contracting for information production may be fine in principle, it will not always work in practice. The reason should be apparent from the previous paragraph. In many cases there are simply too many parties for contracts to be feasible. If the firm manager was to attempt to negotiate a contract for information production with every potential investor, the negotiation costs alone would be prohibitive. In addition, to the extent that different investors want different information, the firm's costs of information production would also be prohibitive. If, as an alternative, the manager attempted to negotiate a single contract with all investors, these investors would have to agree on what information they wanted. Again, given the disparate information needs of different investors, this process would be extremely time-consuming and costly if, indeed, it was possible at all. Hence, the contracting approach only seems feasible when there are a few parties involved. The owner–manager incentive contracts studied in Section 9.4.2 involved only two persons. Our long-term lending contract example in Section 9.7 involved a manager and a lender.

Even if contracting parties do reach an information production agreement, another problem arises. Unless the agreement can be enforced (as in a cooperative game), parties to the agreement may be tempted to violate it for their own short-run benefit. For example, suppose that a managerial compensation contract provides for a year-end audit. Knowing this, the manager works hard during the year. Then, since the manager's effort has already been exerted, the principal would benefit from cancelling the audit, thereby saving the audit costs. But, cancelling the audit this year will reduce the incentive for the manager to work hard next year.

It seems that while contracts are an important source of private information production, we cannot rely on them completely for the information needs of society. Accordingly, we now turn to a second set of private incentives for firms' information production. We will call these **market-based incentives**.

12.3.3 Market-Based Incentives for Information Production

Private incentives for managers to produce information about their firms also derive from market forces. Several markets are involved.

The *managerial labour market* constantly evaluates manager performance. As a result, managers who release false, incomplete, or biased information will suffer damage to their reputations. While reputation considerations do not completely remove the need for incentive contracts, as discussed in Section 10.2, they do reduce the amount of incentives needed. In terms of Example 9.3, where the manager received a 32.6% profit share, a profit share of, say, 20% may be sufficient when reputation considerations are taken into account.[4] Consequently, less risk is imposed on the (risk-averse) manager, thereby making him/her less reluctant to release information that affects firm value. Thus, the managerial labour market provides important incentives for information production.

Similar incentives are provided by *capital markets*. Managers are motivated by reputation and contracting considerations to increase firm value. This creates an incentive to release information to the market. The reason is that more information, by reducing concerns about adverse selection and estimation risk (see Sections 4.5 and 6.2.3), increases investor confidence in the firm, with the result that the market prices of its securities will rise or, equivalently, its cost of capital will fall, other things being equal. This will show up in enhanced firm profitability and value, hence enhanced market value for the manager.

Another market that disciplines managers is the *takeover market*, also called the market for corporate control. If the manager does not increase firm value, the firm may be subject to a takeover bid, which, if successful, frequently results in replacement of the manager. The more disgruntled the shareholders are, the more likely that such a takeover bid will be successful. Consequently, the takeover market also motivates managers to increase firm value, with implications for information production similar to those of the managerial labour and capital markets.

Formal models that relate information release to the firm's market value are presented by, for example, Merton (1987) and Diamond and Verrecchia (1991). In the Merton model, information asymmetry is modelled as only a subset of investors knowing about each firm. As a result, investors cannot fully diversify. Then, the firm's cost of capital is greater than that given by the CAPM (Section 4.5), since its risk is spread over relatively few investors. If the firm can increase the size of its subset of investors, say by the voluntary release of information, its cost of capital will fall and its market value rise, other things equal. In the Diamond and Verrecchia model, voluntary disclosure reduces information asymmetry between the firm and the market, which facilitates trading in its shares. The resulting increase in **market liquidity**[5] attracts large institutional investors who, if they have to do so in future, can then sell large blocks of shares without lowering the price they receive. The firm's share price increases as a result of this greater demand.[6]

More recently, Easley and O'Hara (2004) present a model with two kinds of information—inside and outside. Easley and O'Hara show that investors demand a higher expected return (i.e., higher than the CAPM) the greater the ratio of inside information to outside. The reason is that insiders can make better investment decisions than outsiders due to their information advantage. Outside investors know this but, due to noise trading, are unable to fully infer from share price what this inside information is—it could be good or bad. Thus, outsiders face additional estimation risk, which cannot be diversified away because buying more stocks simply compounds their information disadvantage. Consequently, they demand a higher expected return to compensate. The more inside information there is relative to outside, the stronger this effect is. It follows that firms can reduce their costs of capital and increase market value by credible release of inside information.

Thus, labour markets and the market for corporate control, along with efficient securities markets, are important noncontractual sources of private information production. In all cases, it is market prices that provide the motivation—security prices and managers' market values on the labour market are affected by the quality of firms' information production decisions.

12.3.4 Securities Market Response to Full Disclosure

The theoretical arguments in Section 12.3.3 predict that the securities market will respond positively to increased disclosure. In this section, we review some empirical studies of this prediction. The Merton model was tested by Lang and Lundholm (1996). They used financial analysts' ratings of disclosure quality, based on evaluations of firms' quarterly and annual reports and investor relations, for a large sample of firms over the years 1985–1989. The authors found that, other things equal, the higher the disclosure quality as judged by the analysts, the greater the number of analysts following the firm. This result is not obvious, a priori, because one could argue that better information production by a firm reduces the need for analysts to interpret it for investors. The finding that analyst following increased suggests that analysts can do a better job when they have more information to work with; that is, increased analyst following leads to increased investor interest. Merton's model then predicts increased demand for the firm's shares, or, equivalently, lower cost of capital.

Healy, Hutton, and Palepu (1999) tested implications of the Diamond and Verrecchia model. Using the same analysts' disclosure quality ratings as Lang and Lundholm, they found that firms with improved disclosure ratings were associated with a significantly improved share price performance in the year following the rating increase, compared to other firms in their same industry. They also found a significant increase in institutional ownership. Both of these results are predicted by Diamond and Verrecchia.

Welker (1995) investigated the effect of disclosure quality on the bid-ask spread component of market liquidity (see Note 5). He predicted that shares of firms with better disclosure policies would have lower spreads, the reason being that better disclosure policy implied less investor concern about insider trading and other adverse selection problems. After controlling for other factors that also affect spread, such as trading volume,[7] Welker found a significant negative relationship between disclosure quality (as measured by analysts' disclosure quality ratings) and bid-ask spread. Again, this result is consistent with the Diamond and Verrecchia model.

Botosan and Plumlee (2002) reported the results of a direct test of disclosure quality and cost of capital. For a large sample of U.S. firms across many different industries over 1985–1996, these researchers found that superior annual report disclosure reduced cost of capital of their sample firms by an average of 0.7%, other things equal.[8] Botosan and Plumlee's estimates of disclosure quality were based on firms' disclosure ratings published by the Association for Investment Management and Research, a large international non-profit organization of investment professionals and educators.

Sengupta (1998) investigated the impact of disclosure quality on the cost of debt. He found that, on average, his sample firms enjoyed a 0.02% reduction in interest cost for every 1% increase in their disclosure quality as rated by financial analysts over 1987–1991. He also found that this result strengthened for riskier firms, where a firm's riskiness was measured by the standard deviation of the return on its shares. The reason for this favourable impact, according to Sengupta, was that lenders assigned lower credit risk to firms with superior disclosure policies.

The market response to *lack of* full disclosure is also worth noting. When investors lose faith in a firm's financial reporting, the consequences can be severe indeed. In their study of firms under investigation by the SEC for violations of GAAP, Dechow, Sloan, and Sweeney (1996) report an average drop of 9% in share price on the day the investigation is announced. The collapse of Enron Corp. and WorldCom Inc., outlined in Section 1.2, provides a dramatic example of the consequence of poor disclosure. The loss of investor confidence was so severe that these firms' costs of capital effectively became infinite.

Collectively, these results suggest that firms with high-quality disclosure enjoy lower costs of debt and equity capital, and vice versa. They support our theoretical arguments that market forces encourage information production.

12.3.5 Other Information Production Incentives

The Disclosure Principle   A simple argument can be made that suggests that a manager will release all information, good or bad. This is known as the **disclosure principle**.[9] If investors know that the manager has the information, but do not know what it is, they will assume that if it was favourable the manager would release it. Thus, if investors do not observe the manager releasing it, they will assume the worst and bid down the market value of the firm's shares accordingly. For example, suppose that investors know that a manager possesses a forecast of next year's earnings, but they do not know what the forecast is. The manager may as well release it, as failure to do so would be interpreted by the market as the lowest possible forecast.

This argument is reinforced by the manager's incentive to keep the firm's share price from falling. A fall in share price will harm the manager through lower remuneration, and/or through lower value on the labour market for managers. Since the market will assume the worst if the information is not released, any release of credible information will prevent share price and market value from falling as low as it would otherwise.

Undoubtedly, the disclosure principle operates in many situations. However, as Dye (1985) discusses, it does not always work. Note that it requires that investors know that the manager has the information. If they do not know this, the argument breaks down. For example, the firm may not have prepared earnings forecasts in the past and the market may not be sure whether one has been prepared this year.

A second reason for failure of the disclosure principle derives from costs of disclosure. This was examined by Verrecchia (1983), who sought to reconcile the disclosure principle with the empirical observation that managers do not always fully disclose. For example, they may delay the release of bad news. Verrecchia assumed that, if disclosure is made, it is truthful. He also assumed that there is a cost of disclosure. The cost is constant, independent of the nature of the news. For example, there may be a proprietary cost of releasing valuable patent information. Investors know that the manager has the news, and know its cost of disclosure, but do not know what the news is. Then, if the information is withheld, investors do not know whether it is withheld because it is bad news or because it is good news but not sufficiently good to overcome the disclosure cost, and the disclosure principle fails.

If we rank the nature of the news on a continuum from bad to good, Verrecchia showed that for a given disclosure cost there is a threshold level of disclosure. The lower the disclosure cost, the lower the threshold, and if disclosure cost is zero, as it would be for non-proprietary information, the disclosure principle is reinstated.

However, consistent with the disclosure principle, Verrecchia assumed that the market knows that the manager has the information. But, the market may be unsure about this. For example, as mentioned above, the firm may or may not have prepared a forecast. Then, failure to disclose cannot be interpreted by investors as the lowest possible forecast. This assumption limits the generality of a conclusion that the disclosure principle is reinstated for non-proprietary information.

These considerations were modelled by Penno (1997). He assumed that the manager's nonproprietary information is noisy, with the quality of the information measured by the noise term's variance. He also assumed that the market has only a probability (as opposed to knowing for sure) that the manager has the information and that this probability is decreasing in information quality (i.e., higher-quality information is more difficult to obtain). Penno shows that, similar to Verrecchia, there is a threshold level of forecasted profits below which the manager would not disclose. In Penno's model, the likelihood of disclosure decreases as the manager's information quality increases.

Theory in Practice 12.1

This effect can be seen in the case of Mark's Work Wearhouse, Ltd., a large Canadian clothing retailer. For many years, Mark's included a high-quality forecast of next year's earnings in its MD&A. Such a forecast can be regarded as non-proprietary information since it is unlikely to directly affect future cash flows. However, Mark's did not release a forecast for 1992, a year in which it was expecting a loss. The reason, presumably, was that if Mark's released the bad news forecast, its high quality would greatly affect investors' perceptions of the firm's future prospects. In effect, the likelihood of disclosure decreases with information quality—why should a firm release a high-quality forecast of trouble ahead? Consequently, high-quality disclosures will tend to be for good news.

We may conclude that, even for non-proprietary information, the disclosure principle is prone to failure.

Information released under the disclosure principle must be credible. That is, the market must know that the manager has an incentive to reveal it truthfully. Obviously, if a manager lies about next year's forecast of net income it can hardly be said that information is being disclosed. Information that is subject to verification after the event, such as a forecast, will be credible to the extent that penalties can be applied for deliberate misstatement. Another way to secure credibility is to have released information attested to by a third party, such as an auditor. However, because much inside information is not verifiable even after the fact, or subject to audit, truthful disclosure cannot always be attained.

The need for truthful disclosure has been relaxed somewhat by Newman and Sansing (1993) (NS). They analyzed a two-period model consisting of an incumbent firm, a representative shareholder, and a potential entrant to the industry. The firm manager, who is assumed to act in the shareholder's best interests, knows firm value exactly. If it were not for the potential entrant, the shareholder's best interests would be served by publicly disclosing this value, since the shareholder could then optimally plan consumption and investment over the two periods. However, this may trigger entry, in which case the incumbent firm will suffer a loss of profits and value. How should the firm report?

The answer depends on the costs to the entrant should it decide to enter the industry, and the resulting loss of profits to the incumbent. For example, if entry costs are high and there is substantial loss of profits upon entry, the incumbent firm may disclose imprecise information about its value. That is, instead of an exact disclosure, it will disclose an interval within which its value lies. If it reported its value exactly, its disclosures would not be credible, since everyone knows it has an incentive to deter entry.[10]

Disclosure in the NS model is truthful in the sense that the firm credibly reveals an interval within which its value lies, that is, a range estimate. Nevertheless, the disclosure principle fails in the sense that the firm does not report its value exactly.

Finally, as shown by Dye (1985), the disclosure principle can break down due to a conflict between information desired by investors and information needed for contracting purposes. Recall from our discussion in Chapter 10 that manager compensation is based, at least in part, on share price performance. Suppose, however, that the manager has a forecast of net income. The market knows the forecast exists but does not know the amount. If reported, the forecast will affect share price. This reduces the ability of share price to reflect manager effort, since this ability is swamped by the impact of the forecast on price. In effect, release of the forecast incurs an agency cost that reduces the efficiency of the manager's compensation contract. Thus, it may be desirable to discourage the reporting of forecasts even though a forecast provides useful information to investors. The best information for contracting may not be the best information for investor decision-making, and the investor information may not be reported for contracting reasons. Then, the disclosure principle breaks down. Dye's model provides a supplement to legal liability as a reason why reporting of forecasts is rare. A similar tradeoff between cost of capital and the costs of motivating the manager is demonstrated by Baiman and Verrecchia (1996).

In sum, the disclosure principle is a simple and compelling argument for release of inside information. However, it breaks down in numerous instances, and hence cannot be relied upon to ensure that firms always release full information.

Signalling

It frequently happens that firms differ in quality. For example, a firm may have better investment opportunities than other firms. Alternatively, a firm may conduct superior R&D, leading to potentially valuable patents. Such information would be of considerable usefulness to investors. Yet, disclosure of the details of high-quality projects and technology may reveal valuable proprietary information. Furthermore, even if the manager did disclose the details, he or she may not be believed by a skeptical marketplace. How can the manager credibly reveal the firm's **type**, as these underlying quality differences are called, without incurring the excessive costs?

This problem of separating firms of different types has been extensively considered by means of signalling models.

*A **signal** is an action taken by a high-type manager that would not be rational if that manager was low-type.*

A crucial requirement for a signal is that it be less costly for a high-type manager than for a low-type. This is what gives a signal its credibility, since it is then irrational for a low-type to mimic a high-type, and the market knows this.

Spence (1973) was the first to formally model signalling equilibria. He did so in the context of a job market. Given that it is less costly to a high-type job applicant to obtain a specified level of education than to a low-type, Spence showed that equilibria exist where employers can rely on the applicant's chosen level of education as a credible signal of that person's underlying competence.

A number of signals have been suggested that are relevant to accounting. One such signal is **direct disclosure**. Hughes (1986) showed how such disclosure can be a credible signal. In her model, a manager wants to reveal his or her expectation of firm value, by making a direct disclosure at the beginning of the period. Investors observe the firm's cash flows at the end of the period. They then infer the probability of the realized cash flow contingent on the manager's disclosure. For example, if the manager disclosed a high firm value but cash flow is very low, investors will assess a high probability that the disclosure was untrue, and penalties will be applied. To avoid this cost, the manager is motivated to report truthfully, so that in equilibrium investors can correctly infer his or her expectation of firm value.

While Hughes' model does not apply to the moral hazard problem (the manager's expectation of firm value is independent of his or her effort), it does demonstrate how direct disclosure can operate to reduce adverse selection. Firms of different types can separate themselves, so that the market value of their securities better reflects fundamental firm value.

A variety of **indirect signals** has been studied to further understand disclosure issues. As Leland and Pyle (1977) show for an entrepreneur going public, the proportion of equity retained is a signal, because it would not be rational for a bad-news manager to retain a high equity position—this would be too costly. Also, audit quality can be a signal of the value of a new securities issue. A rational manager would be unlikely to retain a high quality (and high-cost) auditor when the firm is a low-type—why pay more to credibly reveal poor prospects? Similar arguments relate to the choice of underwriter for a new stock issue. Titman and Trueman (1986) and Datar, Feltham, and Hughes (1991) developed models where audit quality is a signal.

A forecast can be a signal. For example, it is less costly for a high-type firm to release a high-quality, good news forecast—a low type firm would be unlikely to meet a good news forecast and its high quality would only increase investor backlash. In MD&A (Section 4.8), information about future firm prospects (i.e., a forecast) is required. However, there is sufficient latitude in the requirements that firms can signal by means of their forecast quality. For example, we concluded in Section 4.8.2 that Canadian Tire's forecast disclosure went beyond minimal requirements. As a result, its disclosure has a signalling component, since in addition to the information in the disclosure itself, the firm's willingness to choose a high-quality forecast credibly reveals inside information that management has a confident and well-planned view of its future.

A firm's capital structure has signalling properties. There is evidence, for example, that the market value of existing common shares falls when the firm issues new shares. While dilution of existing shareholders' equity is one possibility, another explanation is the market's concern that the new shares may be issued by a low-type firm—a high-type firm would be more likely to issue bonds or finance internally. One reason is that the high value increments would then accrue to existing shareholders. Another reason is that a high-type firm would assess its probability of bankruptcy as low (thus, the probability that the bondholders would take over the firm is low).

Dividend policy can also be a signal. A high payout ratio may signal a firm as having a confident future. However, a high payout ratio could also mean that the firm sees little prospect for profitable internal financing from retained earnings. Thus, dividend policy may not be as effective a signal as others.

Accounting policy choice also has signalling properties. For example, a firm may adopt a number of conservative accounting policies. A high-type firm can do this and still report profits, while a low-type firm would report losses. Thus, conservative accounting policies can also signal a manager's confident view of the firm's future.

Note that for signals to be applicable, the manager must have a *choice*. Indeed, Spence (1973) shows that for a viable signalling equilibrium to exist there must be a sufficient number of signals available to the manager. For example, if some central authority imposed a uniform standard of audit quality on all firms, audit quality would not be available as a signal. Furthermore, reducing the latitude to choose forecasting quality in MD&A would reduce its signalling content.

This argument, that standards to enforce uniform accounting destroy managers' abilities to signal, is important for standard setting. In Section 2.5.1 we suggested that the major problem with historical cost accounting is that there is no unique way to match costs with revenues. We also suggested that standard-setting bodies may then have to step in to impose uniformity. The clear implication was that diversity in reporting practices was "bad." This implication is correct, as far as it goes. Diversity in reporting practices imposes costs on investors who want to compare the performance of different entities, because it is necessary to restate their financial statements to a common basis before valid comparisons can be made.

However, if we reconsider this implication in the light of signalling theory, we see that diversity may not be as bad as first suggested. To the extent that firms' choices of accounting policies signal credible information about those firms, diversity of reporting practices is desirable. This argument is reinforced by our discussion of earnings management in Chapter 11. We argued there that some earnings management can be good since it can serve as a vehicle for the release of inside information. Earnings management to reveal persistent earning power can be interpreted as a signal since it can be very costly for a low-type manager to report higher earnings than can be maintained (since accruals reverse). Obviously, earnings management by means of accounting policy choice is only possible if there is a sufficiently rich set of accounting policies, such as GAAP, from which to choose. Signalling theory serves as a counterargument to the continual refinement of GAAP so as to eliminate accounting policy choice.

Financial Policy as a Signal

In this section we review a paper by Healy and Palepu (1993) (HP). HP address the question of what managers might do to signal their inside information to the efficient market. We have already discussed how market forces motivate managers to communicate information so as to increase their firm's market value. But since, as we shall see, these forces are subject to various degrees of market failure, and also since noise trading can distort a firm's share price, managers of some firms may find their firms undervalued by the capital market relative to their inside information. The question then is, how can they best signal the real value of the firm?

HP provide an illustration of the above problem. Patten Corp.[11] acquires large undeveloped tracts of land, subdivides them into lots, and sells them, with up to 90% of the financing supplied by Patten. Revenue is recognized upon sale, that is, when at least 10% of the purchase price has been received and collection of the balance is reasonably assured. This creates a potential problem of bad debt losses. However, in its 1986 financial statements Patten provided a bad debt allowance of only $10,000 on accounts receivable of $29.4 million. The firm claimed that this low amount was justified by past experience and a low current delinquency rate.

In 1987, concern appeared in the financial media that Patten's bad debt allowance was too low. Specifically, the fear was expressed that past delinquency rates may not be representative of future delinquency. Patten's share price plunged following the publication of these concerns, as investors quickly revised their beliefs about Patten's future performance.

HP suggest several possible manager responses to convince the market of their inside information that the value of the accounts receivable is substantially as shown in the financial statements. One response is direct disclosure of credit granting and collection procedures, so as to inform the market of their integrity. Direct disclosure should be a credible signal here, since management would be foolish to overly expose itself to penalties such as loss of reputation and legal liability by disclosing incorrect information at such a critical time.

However, details of the firm's credit and collection policies are likely to be proprietary information, which could harm its competitive position—recall our discussion of the Darrough and Stoughton model in Section 9.3 and of Newman and Sansing in this section. Consequently, HP suggest several financial policies that could serve as indirect signals of management's information.

One such policy would be to raise private financing and/or to sell accounts receivable without recourse to a financial institution. Our discussion of contractual incentives for information production in Section 12.3.2 suggests that when there are only a few parties involved in a contract they can agree among themselves what information to provide. Here, it may be less costly for Patten to provide a private lender with information about the real value of its receivables than to provide it to the market, since, as mentioned, providing it to the market would require public release of proprietary information. The market, upon becoming aware of the private financing, would realize that this is an indirect signal and would raise its evaluation of Patten.

Another possibility would be for Patten to engage in a hedging strategy. Then, credit losses on accounts receivable would be offset by gains on the hedging instrument. Such a policy would be prohibitively expensive if large credit losses were anticipated. Consequently, it should be a credible signal.

Yet another signalling strategy would be for management to increase its holdings of Patten shares. This would load additional risk on to management, thereby increasing their incentive to work hard as well as giving them a longer-run perspective in operating the firm.

Note the common theme in all of these signalling strategies. Management would be foolish to undertake any of them unless it really believed its inside information about asset values. This is what gives signals their credibility. The market will realize this, with the result that the fall of Patten's share price should be reversed. HP's article insightfully demonstrates the rich variety of signals available for credible communication of inside information to an efficient market.

Private Information Search

To this point, our investigation of private incentives for release of inside information has centred on the manager. The argument has been that a high level of information release will improve the manager's reputation, lower estimation risk, and reduce the firm's cost of capital, to the manager's benefit. Thus, the onus is on the manager to release information.

Implicit in this line of reasoning is that investors are passive. They merely react to whatever information the manager releases in deciding on their demand for the firm's securities. In effect, they are price-protected by the market. It may be, however, that many investors will be active in seeking out information, particularly in the presence of noise traders or securities market inefficiencies. For example, they may conduct their own investigations and analyses of fundamental firm value, or hire financial analysts, mutual fund managers, and other experts to assist them. They may watch closely persons that they suspect have inside information and mimic their actions.

Thus, there is a variety of ways that investors or their representatives can conduct a **private information search**. Bill Cautious, in Example 3.1, did so by analysis of the annual report, using Bayes' theorem to process the resulting information. To the extent that such activities are successful, inside information is very quickly transferred to the public domain. By limiting the ability of insiders to capitalize on inside information, the severity of the adverse selection problem is reduced.

Unfortunately, private information search can be quite costly, from society's perspective, since more than one investor incurs costs to discover the same information. It would be cheaper, in terms of total resources used to generate information, if the firm produced and publicized the information only once, so that each investor would not have to rediscover it.

Hirschleifer's (1971) analysis is a classic in the area of private information search. Hirschleifer considered an exchange economy, that is, an economy without production, so that there is no scope for information search to affect the manager's effort. Then, Hirschleifer showed that the social value of information search is negative, even though individual investors may perceive it as valuable. The reason is that, without production, the amount of goods and services in the economy is fixed, so that private information search just redistributes wealth, it does not create wealth. Then, since information search has a cost, the net social effect is negative.

If we consider a production economy, private information search may improve the operation of markets, with resulting impacts on firms' costs of capital and manager effort. However, to the extent that a redistributive component to private information search remains, this will still constitute a cost to society.

One such cost is unequal distribution of information across investors, as discussed by Beaver (1989). For example, the "big guys" may have more resources to find and analyze information, leaving the small investor at a disadvantage. This leads to suggestions, such as by Lev (1988), for regulation to require firms to release information to everyone, thereby enhancing public confidence in a fair marketplace and contributing to market liquidity. Interestingly, the SEC has done just this. Regulation FD, adopted in 2000, prohibits companies from selectively disclosing information. In Canada, the Ontario Securities Act prohibits companies from releasing information to selected individuals before releasing it to the general public.

The effectiveness of regulation FD was investigated by Gintschel and Markov (2004). They examined a sample of firms over October 23, 1999 to October 23, 2001 (one year on each side of the date of regulation FD). They report evidence that over this period the volatility of share returns (a measure of information content, since new information causes a rapid change in share prices) increased sharply during the five days leading up to analyst announcements. This is consistent with firm managers feeding private information to analysts, who, with their clients, buy or sell the firm's shares on the basis of this information before it is publicly released in the analyst announcement. Gintschel and Markov also report a significant decline in this volatility in the year following October 23, 2000, suggesting that the regulation has reduced this advance information flow.

12.3.6 Summary

There are many private vehicles and incentives for managers to produce information. Furthermore, empirical research suggests that firms and managers are rewarded for superior disclosure decisions, and punished when misleading information release is discovered. However, it should be emphasized that market forces will not motivate the release of all inside information, since there are costs to the firm of information release. In addition to proprietary costs, agency costs arise because information production for investors, which lowers cost of capital, may render compensation contracts less efficient, and vice versa.[12]

Assuming that firms choose the lowest cost point of this tradeoff, it might seem that market forces can drive the right amount of information production from society's perspective. However, we now review some counterarguments, called **market failures**, which suggest that regulation may still be needed.

12.4   Sources of Market Failure

12.4.1 Externalities and Free-Riding

Frequently, information released by one firm will convey information about other firms. For example, if a firm reveals a sharp increase in sales and profits, this may affect the market's expectations for other firms in the industry. Also, if a firm releases proprietary information (for example, details about a valuable patent) this could affect the market's expectations of future earnings of competing firms. Interactive effects such as these are called **externalities**.

The effect of externalities is to cause the private and social values of information to diverge. The Darrough and Stoughton (1990) model, reviewed in Section 9.3, of a game between a monopolist incumbent and a potential entrant to the industry also illustrates the effect of externalities. Under some conditions, the monopoly firm does not release information, so as to deter entry. While this may benefit the monopolist, it does reduce the flow of information to the market, thereby imposing a cost on society.

In Section 5.6, we noted that accounting information has characteristics of a public good. We pointed out that this makes it difficult for the firm to charge for producing this information. In effect, when the use of information by one individual does not destroy it for use by another, other investors can "free-ride" on this information. Since all investors will realize this, no one has an incentive to pay. Then, if the firm cannot recover the costs of information production it will produce less than it would otherwise.

*An **externality** is an action taken by a firm or individual that imposes costs or benefits on other firms or individuals for which the entity creating the externality is not charged or does not receive revenue. **Free-riding** is the receipt by a firm or individual of a benefit from an externality.*

The crucial aspect of both externalities and free-riding is that the costs and benefits of information production as perceived by the firm differ from the costs and benefits to society. For example, if accounting information produced by one firm informs investors about other firms, this is a benefit to society for which the producing firm receives no benefit. Hence, the firm will underproduce relative to the first-best amount for society. A similar phenomenon operates for the free-rider problem.

Externalities and free-riding are well-known reasons used to justify regulation. The regulator steps in to try to restore the socially right amount of production because market forces alone fall short.

12.4.2 The Adverse Selection Problem

Given our conclusion in Section 12.3.6 that market forces do not motivate full information release, some inside information remains. Then, the adverse selection problem arises. Persons with access to this inside information may well exploit their advantage at the expense of outside investors.

In our context, there are two versions of the adverse selection problem. First, we have the problem of insider trading, which was introduced in Chapter 4. If opportunities exist for insiders, including managers, to generate excessive profits by trading on the basis of their insider information, persons willing to do this will be attracted to the opportunity. Then, outside investors will not perceive the securities market as a level playing field and may withdraw. This will reduce market liquidity. For the market to operate properly, it is necessary that there be enough traders that the buy or sell decisions of any one of them does not affect the market price of a security. This will not happen unless the market is sufficiently liquid. Thus, the ability of insiders to earn excessive trading profits constitutes a securities market failure.

A second version of adverse selection arises when managers who are privy to bad news about the firm's future do not release that information, thereby avoiding, or at least postponing, the negative firm consequences. This has two adverse effects. First, investors are less able to distinguish between securities of different qualities. Then managers with low-quality, bad-news securities will be encouraged to bring them to market and managers with good-news securities may not bring them to market (if the market cannot distinguish between securities of different qualities then the market price will reflect the average quality—this is called **pooling**). Second, since owners do not know that the bad news firm is doing badly, the ability of the takeover market to purge poor managers is reduced, so that the average quality of managers is lowered.

Both of these effects of failure to release bad news mean that investors have a continuing concern about adverse selection.

12.4.3 The Moral Hazard Problem

We suggested in Section 12.3.3 that reputation formation on the managerial labour market, in conjunction with incentive-based compensation contracts, operates to encourage managers' information production. However, these forces may not be completely effective. The reason is that managers may be able to disguise shirking, and resulting low profitability, by opportunistic earnings management. Thus, despite managerial labour markets and incentive contracts, investors will also be concerned about moral hazard and (bad) earnings management.

12.4.4 Unanimity

A characteristic of economies with markets that do not work well is a lack of unanimity, which derives from the effects of adverse selection and moral hazard just described. If markets work well, shareholders will be unanimously in favour of the manager maximizing the market value of the firm. When markets do not work well because of adverse selection and moral hazard, this need not be the case. Eckern and Wilson (1974) studied this problem with respect to the physical production of the firm—that is, the types and quantities of products to be produced—and showed that the manager's choice of production plan to maximize the market value of the firm would not in general be approved by all shareholders under certain market conditions.

A similar result applies to firms' production of information. Blazenko and Scott (1986) demonstrated that in an economy where the information market does not work well, due to adverse selection, the firm manager was motivated to choose that audit quality that would maximize firm market value (recall that an audit is a form of information production). All shareholders, however, would prefer a higher-quality audit. The reason is that from the shareholders' perspective, there are two valuable functions of the audit. One is to add credibility to the firm's financial statements, as we have mentioned. The other is that, if the audit catches the manager in fraud or shirking, the shareholders may recover damages. Since only the first function has value to the manager, the audit is of greater value to the shareholders. Consequently, they will demand more of it than the manager wishes to supply.

To put this argument another way, an effect of investor concerns about adverse selection and moral hazard is to lower share prices below their fundamental values. Even if a manager does engage in information release to maximize firm value, this maximization is with respect to a share price that is "too low." Thus, shareholders and society would benefit if the manager was to release more information than the manager feels is optimal.

12.4.5 Summary

Markets for information are characterized by externalities and free-riding. These problems, if sufficiently serious, can justify central authority intervention. Furthermore, since market forces do not motivate full information release, securities and managerial labour markets do not fully protect investors from the consequences of insider trading and earnings management. As a result, shareholders will not be unanimous in their support of manager policies, even policies that involve firm value maximization.

12.5 How Much Information Is Enough?

Starting from the standard economic prescription that firms should produce information to the point where its marginal social benefit equals its marginal social cost, we see that private market forces are unlikely to produce this result. One reason is externalities and free-riding—market forces are unable to give firms the full social benefits of their information production decisions and are unable to fully internalize the costs of these decisions. Even if they could, the forces of moral hazard and adverse selection lead to a fundamental lack of unanimity between managers' decisions and investors' interests, motivating investors to demand regulation to protect their interests.

Nevertheless, we must not assume that ever-increasing regulation is necessarily socially desirable. This is because regulation carries with it substantial costs. These include direct costs of the bureaucracy needed to establish and administer the regulations, and compliance costs imposed on firms. Of possibly greater magnitude are indirect costs. One such indirect cost arises from the fact that when standards are set to enforce uniform accounting and reporting, managers' opportunity to signal is reduced. Uniform audit standards for all firms and stricter forecasting requirements are examples of standards that would reduce signalling potential.

A second indirect cost arises because the regulator may not, and in general will not, be able to calculate the socially optimal amount of information to require.[13] This is because information is such a complex commodity, because there are conflicts between decision usefulness and contracting needs for information, and because different investors have different decision needs.[14] Since information regulations affect firms' financing, investment, and production decisions, the indirect costs of any "wrong" amount of information production can be large indeed.

Given these complex cost-benefit considerations, we simply do not know how much regulation is enough. However, it is safe to say that complete deregulation would not be socially desirable. The uncontrolled impacts of externalities, adverse selection, and moral hazard would be sufficiently serious that markets would probably cease to function. Nor is complete regulation desirable, since the costs to completely eliminate accounting policy choice would be astronomic. However, this leaves a considerable range over which to debate the extent of regulation. Much more knowledge of the benefits and costs of financial reporting will be needed before the question of extent of regulation can be answered.

In this regard, the usefulness of regulation has been studied empirically. Indeed, we have already seen some evidence in our discussion of the value relevance of earnings in Section 6.4. While the results outlined there are somewhat controversial, recall that some authors have documented a low and declining ability of net income to explain share returns (measured by R^2 and ERC), suggesting a decrease in the value relevance of earnings over time. However, the number of accounting standards has been increasing over time. If this greater extent of regulation was socially useful, we would expect to see value relevance increase, not decrease, as investors and markets responded to higher earnings quality.

A more formal test of the extent of regulation was conducted by Ely and Waymire (1999). They studied the period 1927–1993. For each year in this period they estimated the share price response to net income for a sample of 100 firms, similar to the procedure used by Lev (1989) outlined in Section 6.4. Ely and Waymire found an average R^2 of 0.185 over this period, suggesting a "market share" of slightly over 18% for net income during this time.

The researchers then examined separately four sub-periods. The first was 1927–1939. This was prior to the creation of the Committee on Accounting Procedure (CAP) of the AICPA. CAP was the first professional accounting standard-setting body in the United States. Subsequent periods examined coincided with major reorganizations of U.S. standard-setting bodies. For example, the fourth period began in 1973 with the creation of the FASB. In sum, in the 1927–1939 period there were no accounting standards. In the three subsequent periods, the number of standards increased steadily, with the FASB being the latest and most active.

If these new accounting standards were socially desirable, Ely and Waymire argued, the value relevance of net income should increase in the later periods, relative to the 1927–1939 period, and there should be further increases in each successive standard-setting regime. However, using a variety of tests, no significant increases were found. A failure to find increased value relevance of earnings as the number of accounting standards increases raises questions about the benefits of increased regulation.

Theory in Practice 12.2

Jamal, Maier, and Sunder (2003) (JMS) examined the privacy policies and practices of the web site industry. In the United States, this industry is unregulated. Consequently, there is an adverse selection problem that web sites will abuse the privacy of visitors to the site, such as bombarding them with unsolicited e-mails, including from third parties to whom the site may have sold private information.

As JMS suggest, market forces constrain such acts—web sites may feel that it is in their long-run interests to protect the privacy of their customers. They can do so, for example, by establishing and following privacy policies that enable site visitors to opt out of receiving subsequent advertising messages. These policies can be reinforced by voluntarily hiring an assurance service. Several such services exist, including WebTrust offered by the AICPA and CICA which includes a full audit of clients' privacy policies.

With these considerations in mind, JMS evaluated 100 high-traffic web sites. Of these, 34 had some form of assurance service and all 34 posted an easily accessible privacy policy on their sites. However, of the 66 sites without an assurance service, 63 also posted a privacy policy. This suggests that most web sites were at least aware of the benefits of protecting users' privacy.

To evaluate whether the sites actually followed their posted policy, JMS registered at each site twice, under separate identities. In one identity, they opted to allow their identity information to be shared with others. In the other, they did not. They then kept track of subsequent e-mails received by each identity for

continued →

26 weeks. For those registrations for which they had opted to allow identity sharing, 15,143 e-mails were received. Most of these were generated by five sites, none of which used an assurance service. For those registrations for which they opted out, only 501 messages were received. It seems that even without regulation, almost all web sites respect the privacy wishes of registrants.

JMS concluded that market forces can drive substantial voluntary use of assurance services to signal integrity, and can drive substantial respect for the interests of consumers. However, they caution that the web site industry and the accounting industry differ. For example, they are at different stages of development. Nevertheless, their findings question whether constantly increasing regulation of accounting —also intended to secure integrity and protect customers (investors)—should be taken for granted.

Despite questions about the extent of regulation, we can still ask if the efficiency of regulation can be improved. That is, how might standards generate more information at less cost? In the next section, we consider a suggestion in this regard.

12.6 Decentralized Regulation

Information about firm segments—where segmentation may be on the basis of product lines, subsidiary companies, geography—has been required disclosure in firms' annual reports for some time. Segment information should be useful to investors, since, in evaluating the expected performance and risk of large and complex firms, relevant information, such as differing opportunities for growth, may be buried in consolidated totals. Also, with segment disclosure it is more difficult to disguise poor performance in one segment by means of good performance in another.

In 1997, Section 1701 of the *CICA Handbook* was issued by the AcSB in conjunction with a similar standard (SFAS 131) by the FASB. Of interest is the basis of segmentation in these revised standards. They require that the firm report segment information on the same basis as it organizes its segments internally for top management decision-making and performance evaluation. For our purposes, two aspects of this requirement are of interest. First, of the various bases of segmentation that are possible, reporting on a basis consistent with the internal organization should be of greatest usefulness to investors, since it is management that knows best how to organize the business. Thus, reporting externally on the same basis will give investors the best insights into the firm's operations. Second, the costs to the firm of complying with the new standard should be low since the firm is already preparing the required information internally. Evidence supportive of the usefulness of these segment disclosures is provided by Berger and Hann (2003), who report that disclosures under SFAS 131 has revealed additional information to the market.[15]

Another example of this approach is the SEC's (1997) requirement for risk disclosure, discussed in Section 7.5.3. This standard also allows management a choice of how best to report on the riskiness of its operations. Presumably, the best way to report on risk is in a manner consistent with the firm's internal risk management procedures.

We call this approach "decentralized regulation." While there is regulation involved, compliance is decentralized to the internal decisions of management.[16] This improves relevance of reporting and at the same time is less costly. Note that, unlike most standards, management retains the ability to signal through its choice of reporting methods.

12.7 Conclusions on Standard Setting Related to Economic Issues

The question of the extent to which standards for information production should be imposed is a complex and important one for a market economy. At present, we witness substantial regulation of firms' information production decisions. These regulations include insider trading laws and laws to regulate full disclosure. They also include laws to establish accounting and auditing professions. These professions, in turn, may form bodies empowered to establish GAAP, such as the AcSB and the FASB. However, it can be argued, by analogy with other industries where regulation has been eased, that deregulation of the information industry would result in a flood of innovation and competition, to society's advantage.

Indeed, theory suggests a number of reasons why firms would produce information in the absence of standards. These derive from the information needs of contracts and from market forces. Parties to contracts will want information to motivate effort and to reward accomplishment. Managerial labour markets and takeover markets interact with securities markets to motivate managers to release information so as to increase market value. Signalling is an important vehicle for credible information release.

Such private forces undoubtedly result in much information production. Theory also suggests, however, that even if we ignore externalities and free-riding, the amount produced by private forces alone may fall short of society's demands. The reason can be seen by means of a two-stage argument. First, contracts for information production break down when a large number of persons are involved. Consequently, we cannot rely on contracts for all of society's information needs.

Second, when contracts break down, market prices (for managerial services and for securities) must take over as motivators of information production. However, market forces do not motivate full information release, since there are costs of releasing information and firms will trade off the costs with the benefits. As a result, some inside information remains, creating a fundamental lack of unanimity between managers' information production decisions and information demanded by investors. Investors may then turn to regulation to remedy the perceived deficiency.

However, it is important to realize that private forces need not completely eliminate market failures to preclude regulation. This is because regulation also has costs. These include direct costs, such as a bureaucracy to set and enforce the standards, and compliance costs imposed on firms. More importantly, however, they include indirect costs imposed on society if the central authority mandates the wrong amount of information. Since information is such a complex commodity, this is quite likely to happen. Given the impact of information on firms' production, financing, and investment decisions, the costs to society here can be significant.

The question of standard setting then boils down to a cost-benefit tradeoff. The costs of regulation include not only the enforcement costs, but also the costs of any wrong decisions made by the regulator. The benefits lie in reduced market failures that persist after private market forces have done their best. At present, the extent to which the benefits of regulation exceed the costs is not known, although giving firms some flexibility in how they meet reporting standards may be worthwhile.

Finally, it should be noted that lack of unanimity leads directly to questions about the fairness of the distribution of information. That is, standard setting may need to draw on political theory as well as economics. We will explore this suggestion in Chapter 13.

Questions and Problems

1. Information has both costs and benefits to a firm. What are the costs and benefits of information production to a firm? How much information should the firm produce? (CGA-Canada)

2. Explain why a voluntary forecast can be an indirect signal but a mandated forecast cannot. (CGA-Canada)

3. "Contracting internalizes the problem of information production." Explain what this statement means. (CGA-Canada)

4. Describe the difference between a direct and an indirect signal, using the quality of a forecast in MD&A (see Section 4.8.2) as an example.

5. To what extent do (i) security market forces and (ii) managerial labour market forces operate to motivate managers to operate their firms in the best interests of the shareholders? In your answer, identify how financial accounting information enables the market forces to operate.

6. The notion of a market for information, unlike markets for agricultural commodities, transportation services, and so on, may be unfamiliar to most people. A main reason for this is that information is a very complex commodity.

   List three ways that we can think about the quantity of information and explain each briefly.

7. An adverse selection problem can arise from information asymmetry between issuer and buyer of securities.

   Required
   a. Explain what the adverse selection problem is in this context.
   b. How can financial accounting information reduce the adverse selection problem?
   c. Can financial accounting information eliminate the problem completely? Explain.
   d. What other ways are used to reduce the problem of inside information?

8. The failure of managers to release bad news is a version of the adverse selection problem. Such failure indicates that the securities market is not working properly.

   Required
   a. Why might a manager withhold bad news?
   b. To what extent does the disclosure principle operate to reduce the incentive of a manager to withhold bad news? Explain. (CGA-Canada)

9. On September 15, 2004, the Dow Jones Industrial Index suffered its largest fall in a month, dropping by 0.8% or 86.8 points. The Standard & Poor's 100, 400, and 500 indices also dropped by similar amounts.

According to media reports, the market declines were triggered by Coca-Cola Co. and Xilinx Inc. (a large producer of computer logic chips and related products). These companies announced that sales and profits for the third quarter 2004 would be less than analysts' estimates.

Required
a. Why did the whole market decline?
b. What market failure does this episode illustrate? Explain why this is a failure.

10. In February 1998, Newbridge Networks Corp., a telecommunications equipment maker based in Kanata, Ontario, announced that its revenues and profits for the quarter ending on February 1, 1998 would be substantially below analysts' estimates. Its share price immediately fell by 23% on the Toronto and New York stock exchanges.

The sale, in December 1997, of over $5 million of the company's shares by an inside director of Newbridge was widely reported in the financial media during February 1998. Details of sales by other Newbridge insiders, including its CEO, during previous months were also reported. The implication of these media reports was that these persons had taken advantage of inside information about disappointing sales of a new product line.

Required
a. Which source of market failure is implied by these media reports?
b. What effects on investors, and on liquidity of trading in Newbridge shares, would media reports of such insider sales be expected to create?
c. Suppose that Newbridge's management felt that its share price was undervalued by the market after the February earnings announcement. Describe some signals that management and directors could engage in to counter the public impression of lower-than-expected profitability.

11. On March 15, 2004, Canadian Superior Energy Inc. held a conference call concerning the recent abandonment of its Mariner E-85 exploration well off the coast of Nova Scotia. The company's CEO explained that the well was a success but that its partner, El Paso Corp., had decided not to invest more money into it. The CEO indicated his optimism that a new partner could be lined up, but refused to answer any questions from the audience.

Previously, in January 2004, Canadian Superior had issued favourable press releases about the Mariner well. However, its CEO had sold $4.3 million of his holdings of company stock in the same month. Following the news of well abandonment in March, class action lawsuits were initiated on behalf of U.S. investors (Canadian Superior shares were traded in the United States as well as in Canada), claiming that investors had been misled.

The company's shares lost half their value in the few days following the March abandonment announcement, closing at $1.72 on the Toronto Stock Exchange on March 18, 2004.

Required

a. Obviously, the news of well abandonment was a major factor contributing to Canadian Superior's share price decline in March. However, other reasons can also be suggested. Give two other reasons.

b. What well-known problem of information asymmetry is suggested by the CEO's sale of stock in January 2004? Explain.

c. Assuming that the market's concerns about the information asymmetry problem you identified in **b** are well-founded, what is the likely effect of these concerns on the share prices of all Canadian oil and gas companies? Why?

d. Suppose that given the CEO's optimism about the ultimate success of the well, the company believes that its share price is undervalued by the market. Suggest three credible signals that the company and/or its CEO could give to increase its share price. Explain why the signals you suggest are credible.

12. Imax Corp. is a large entertainment technology company, with headquarters in New York and Toronto. Currently, it has over 235 theatres in 34 countries. Its share price, which was as high as $13.89 on the Toronto Stock Exchange in 2003, had fallen to a low of $5.50 following its reporting of a loss, in accordance with U.S. GAAP, of $896,000 U.S. for the first quarter of 2004. This compared with a profit of over $2.4 million for the same quarter of 2003.

On May 14, 2004 (i.e., after reporting the first quarter loss), *The Globe and Mail* reported that a group of senior Imax executives had bought about $1 million U.S. of Imax shares on the open market. The company's share price immediately rose by $1.17 to $7.20. Imax later reported earnings for the second quarter of 2004 of $1.552 million.

Required

a. What new information is conveyed to the market by the executive share purchase?

b. Does the share repurchase constitute a credible signal? Explain why or why not.

13. On May 16, 2002, The Toronto-Dominion Bank (TD) announced that it would voluntarily begin expensing its executive stock options, effective for its fiscal year beginning November 1, 2002. This announcement coincided with the release of its earnings for the quarter ended April 30, 2002. Net income was $132 million, down substantially from earnings of $359 million for the same quarter of 2001. While profits in TD's retail banking division were down somewhat, the main component of the earnings decrease came from writeoffs of problem loans and massive provisions for further loan losses.

Required

a. Given its sharply reduced earnings, why would the bank make matters worse by expensing its ESOs?

b. As noted in Section 8.3, Canadian accounting standards require expensing of ESOs beginning in 2004 and the FASB has followed with a similar standard effective in 2005. Previously, ESO fair value was reported in the financial statement notes. TD was one of numerous firms that voluntarily decided to expense their ESOs prior to these standards coming into effect. Given this voluntary expensing, the question arises as to whether a standard is needed. Explain some of the costs and benefits of a standard requiring ESOs to be expensed.

14. XYZ Ltd. is an owner-managed retail hardware store that went public on January 1, 2005. Afterwards, Tom Harris, the fun-loving owner–manager, held 40% of the common stock and remained the chief executive of the company.

    Required
    a. Why is it likely that Tom Harris will shirk more after going public relative to the time he was the owner–manager of the company prior to January 1, 2005?
    b. How might potential investors protect themselves from the adverse effects of likely excessive shirking by the CEO/major shareholder, Tom Harris, after the issuance of shares?
    c. Prior to going public, does Tom Harris have an incentive to convince potential shareholders that he will not engage in excessive shirking? Discuss.
    d. What steps can Tom Harris take to convince potential shareholders that he will not engage in excessive shirking? (CGA-Canada)

15. Regulation FD of the SEC came into effect in 2000. This standard requires firms that release material information that may affect their share price to release it to all investors simultaneously. The purpose is to stop "selective disclosure," whereby managers release information, such as changes in earnings forecasts, to a select group of analysts and institutional investors, relying on these persons to convey the information to the market.

    Required
    a. Explain the market failure that has led to this new standard.
    b. Describe the effects on market liquidity of selective disclosure.
    c. In an article in *The Globe and Mail*, November 8, 2000, Paul Hill noted that an effect of Regulation FD has been to cause firms to reduce the amount of information they release. This suggests that the regulation has increased the costs of information production. Describe and explain two sources of increased cost resulting from this regulation.
    d. Do you feel that Regulation FD will improve the operation of securities markets? Explain why or why not.

16. On October 7, 2000, *The Globe and Mail* reported that Air Canada had slashed its third and fourth quarter 2000 earnings forecasts. The company had revealed this information by phone calls to a select group of analysts. Air Canada's share price dropped by 12% on the day it revealed this information, and by another 3% on the next trading day.

    The selective disclosure to certain analysts immediately produced strong negative reactions by angry investors and media, and led to calls for investigation by the Ontario Securities Commission and the Toronto Stock Exchange.

This episode was particularly embarrassing to Canadian securities regulators since, a few weeks previously, the SEC had passed Regulation FD in the United States. This is a fair disclosure regulation that prohibits material information from being revealed only to investment analysts. Canadian regulators said at the time that a similar regulation was not needed in Canada because Canadian laws already prohibited such selective disclosure.

Air Canada defended its disclosure policy by claiming that the information underlying the lower earnings forecasts (e.g., higher fuel prices and increased payments to pilots) was already in the public domain. It was attempting to remind analysts that they had not properly incorporated this information into their earnings forecasts.

Subsequently, Air Canada agreed to pay a fine of $1,080,000 in settlement of the charges.

Required

a. Why would Air Canada want to disclose information about lower-than-expected earnings prior to the actual release of its quarterly income statements?

b. Give two reasons why share price fell in the days following the selective disclosure.

c. Explain the impact of selective disclosure practices on the proper operation of the securities market.

d. *The Globe and Mail* also reported that a huge block of Air Canada shares had traded on the day prior to the selective disclosure. What problem of information asymmetry is suggested by this trade? Explain.

e. Canadian securities legislation prohibits use for personal gain of such material information by the analysts to whom it is given. Assuming that the analysts did not use the information for personal gain, do you think that Air Canada should have been charged? Explain why or why not.

17. In *The Wall Street Journal*, June 30, 1997, Suzanne McGee describes how institutional investors, such as mutual fund managers, are searching for highly liquid stocks to invest in. If the market for a stock is not liquid, these large investors will have to pay a higher price to buy in, and receive a lower price if they sell out, simply because the quantities they deal in are large enough to affect share price. These concerns are heightened, according to McGee, because many large investors adopt a strategy of selling out at the first sign of trouble and buying back in at the first sign of recovery.

McGee points out that liquidity has a favourable effect on share price. For example, highly liquid stocks such as Coca-Cola are selling at 46 times earnings, whereas the Standard & Poor's 500-stock index trades at 22 times earnings. In effect, McGee argues, the market pays a premium for liquidity.

Required

a. Given its size and number of shares outstanding, how can a firm increase the liquidity of its shares? Consider both depth and bid-ask spread in your answer.

b. What are some of the costs to a firm of increased disclosure?

Note: See Notes 5, 6, and 9.

18. The following article by John Partridge appeared in *The Globe and Mail*, August 23, 2001. It discusses the decision by Canadian Imperial Bank of Commerce (CIBC) to discontinue separate disclosure of gains on sales of portions of its "bonanza" investment in Global Crossing Ltd.

Silence on Global Gains Seen Helping CIBC

When Canadian Imperial Bank of Commerce reported its third-quarter results on Monday, it kept its mouth firmly shut about its bonanza investment in Global Crossing Ltd. for the first time since 1999.

Analysts say that CIBC's sudden reticence about the rich gains it has been making on its original $30-million (U.S.) stake in the Bermuda-based telecommunications company could help start a recovery in the bank's lagging stock market valuation—although some of them contend that the change in disclosure is a step backwards.

"We debated whether we should continue to disclose the [gains on] Global Crossing and other large merchant banking investment, and we concluded that we wouldn't be going forward," Tom Woods, CIBC's chief financial officer, told analysts during the quarterly conference call.

Despite the new vow of silence, Global Crossing has given CIBC a lot to crow about.

Back in 1999, the value of the bank's initial investment in Global Crossing soared to more than $4.3-billion as the Bermuda company caught the updraft of the telecom and high-tech boom. Its shares skyrocketed to a high of $54.

CIBC made a pretax gain of $583-million (Canadian) by selling some of its Global Crossing stock that year, and another $697-million in 2000. This second sale translated to $397-million after tax, equal to nearly 20 percent of the bank's $2.06-billion profit last year.

And in this year's second quarter, when CIBC put a total of $426-million on the bottom line, Global Crossing gains brought it another tidy $314-million before taxes.

The Bermuda company's shares have plummeted to less than $5 (U.S.) apiece in the telecom and tech meltdown, but CIBC had already hedged much of its remaining stake in the company through forward sales contracts. According to its annual report for 2000, the hedges mature between this year and 2003, and are at prices ranging from a "floor" or low of $20 to $28 a share to a "ceiling" of $46 to $64.

Analysts figure CIBC still has about $1.5-billion (Canadian) in unrealized but locked-in gains on its big score. "It's a huge number," one said.

During Monday's conference call, Mr. Woods didn't explain why the bank has decided to stop breaking out these gains.

But analysts are pretty sure they know the reason. CIBC, they say, figures it has been penalized for disclosing them, and is betting that silence on the topic may be golden for its share price.

That price could unquestionably do with a bit of help. Despite rallying this week, CIBC's stock currently carries the worst "beta" or volatility rating among the five biggest domestic banks, and the lowest price-earnings multiple.

continued →

"Everybody would strip out the Global Crossing gains from the numbers," one analyst said, explaining how he and his colleagues have used the information until now.

"They're saying 'Well, how is it that when we do well you take it out, but when we do badly you analysts leave it in? We're not getting any credit for it, so we're going to bury it in our earnings, and you guys can do whatever you want to do.'"

CIBC's new approach will instead allow it to use the Global Crossing gains to discreetly smooth and manage—and make more predictable—its overall financial results, without observers being able to divine precisely how this was done. This is a practice already widely followed by other banks in similar situations, and as another analyst put it, CIBC was simply "trying to be too honourable."

Some observers are unhappy that the bank has decided to go quiet on Global Crossing. For instance, in a report issued Tuesday, analyst James Bantis of Credit Suisse First Boston called the move "a step back" after two years in which the bank has "made great strides towards improving the level of financial disclosure and source of earnings."

Mr. Bantis complained that no longer disclosing the Global Crossing gains—which he considers non-recurring—"reduces the quality and transparency of CIBC's earnings over the medium term."

Still, the view is that over time, CIBC's market valuation will benefit because there are few things investors like banks to have more than "earnings visibility," that is, predictable results.

"Historically, CIBC has not been prepared to smooth their earnings, but that changed in this quarter," one of the analysts said. "What it means is that there's going to be much better earnings visibility out of the Commerce, because they've got $1.5-billion in gains left and total flexibility about bringing it in whenever they want . . . Intuitively, they're going to book them when they most need them."

Another analyst concurred, saying that the new approach will likely be a positive influence on Bay Street's profit forecasts for the bank, and that this, in turn, "will be positive for their valuation."

Source: Used by permission of *The Globe and Mail*

Required

a. Will this reduction of disclosure affect the market's ability to evaluate the persistence of CIBC's earnings? Explain.

b. Section 1520.03(o) of the *CICA Handbook* requires separate income statement disclosure of gains and losses that do not have all of the characteristics of extraordinary items but which are not expected to occur frequently over several years or do not typify normal business activities. Do you feel that CIBC's reduction of disclosure violates this requirement? Explain why or why not.

c. How do you think the securities market will react to this reduction of disclosure? Explain.

d. In this case, it seems that private market forces to motivate information production have failed. Should new regulations be put into place to require separate disclosure of gains and losses on sales of this nature? Explain why or why not.

Notes

1. This is a purely economic definition. Note that it is in terms of *total* information production. The benefits and costs of information production are aggregated across all members of society. The reason why economists define the socially right amount of information this way derives from a desire to attain the largest possible information "pie" in the economy (equating marginal total benefits with marginal total costs does this). Also of concern, however is the *distribution* of total information across investors. Economists may not feel that they have a comparative advantage in advising how the pie should be carved up. To illustrate, hold total information production constant at a level that satisfies the definition and consider two scenarios. In the first, 80% of the benefits of information production go to the wealthiest 10% of investors. In the second, the benefits are distributed equally across all investors. Most people would not feel that the two scenarios were equivalent. Thus, issues of distribution quickly get caught up in ethical and political debate—they are no longer strictly economic.

   In this chapter, we are primarily concerned about aggregate information production. In Chapter 13, we examine the role of accounting standard-setting bodies in promoting distribution of information in a manner that is fair to managers and investors.

2. The dividing line between proprietary and non-proprietary information is somewhat ambiguous. For example, as we saw in our review of Darrough and Stoughton (Section 9.3), the release of information that may seem non-proprietary (such as a financial forecast) could affect future cash flows if it attracts entry to the industry. Nevertheless, the distinction is a useful one. For further discussion of the interrelationships between proprietary and non-proprietary information, see Dye (1986).

3. See, for example, L. DeAngelo (1981).

4. It would be necessary to top up the manager's contract with, say, a fixed salary to meet the manager's reservation utility.

5. By market liquidity we mean the ability of investors to quickly buy and sell large quantities of securities at the market price with reasonable transactions costs. Liquidity is a composite of market **depth**—the number of shares that investors are willing to buy or sell at any given price—and the **bid-ask spread**—the contemporaneous difference between buying price and selling price of a share. Information asymmetry is one of the factors affecting the spread. The more investors are wary of buying a lemon, the greater the asymmetry—the market protects itself from asymmetry by increasing the spread. Information asymmetry also reduces depth, by causing investors to leave the market.

6. For these effects on cost of capital to operate, the market must perceive the information released to be credible. Devices to attain credibility include lawsuits, audits, and stock exchange or country of listing. Hiring a higher-quality auditor implies a commitment to greater information release. Alternatively, or in addition, a manager

could commit to a higher level of information production by moving the firm to an exchange, possibly in a different country, with higher information standards. For example, Lang, Lins and Miller (2003) report lower cost of capital for a sample of non-U.S. firms that cross-list their shares in the United States. Such cross-listing commits the firm to increased disclosure

7. Lee, Mucklow, and Ready (1993) find that a share's spread increases when its trading volume is unusually high. They suggest that the market interprets the high volume as due to insiders or other traders with superior information trading on the basis of this information. Without knowing what this information is, the market becomes more uncertain about the share's future return prospects, and increases the spread to protect itself.

8. Botosan and Plumlee also found a *positive* relationship between cost of capital and the quality of more timely disclosures (i.e., more timely than the annual report) such as quarterly reports. It seems that superior disclosure of more timely information increases cost of capital in their sample, contrary to expectation. Their suggested explanation is that superior timely information attracts short-term, transient investors whose actions increase share price volatility. Increased volatility can increase a stock's beta, thereby increasing cost of capital according to the CAPM.

9. The disclosure principle is attributed to Grossman (1981) and Milgrom (1981).

10. This type of game is called a **cheap talk game**, since, unlike the signalling models to be discussed next, there is no *direct* cost of disclosure to the manager. However, there is an indirect disclosure cost. This is because the reporting of imprecise interval information to deter entry reduces the ability of the shareholder to optimally plan consumption. It is this tension between deterring entry and reporting accurately to the shareholder that drives the reporting of imprecise information. Such games were first modelled by Crawford and Sobel (1982).

11. For further discussion see Healy and Palepu (1993). Data on Patten Corp. are from Harvard Business School case #9-188-027.

12. Another cost arises if we recognize more than one type of investor. Large institutional investors will have greater ability and resources to analyze information than ordinary investors. Ordinary investors may feel that this disadvantage will increase as more firm information is released, and they may reduce their demand for the firm's shares at the same time that demand from institutional investors is increasing. (As an example, consider the practice of many firms of giving "guidance" to analysts, or releasing information in conference calls with a select group of analysts and large institutions. The SEC has prohibited this practice, on the grounds that it puts ordinary investors at a disadvantage—see problem 15.) If ordinary investors leave the market, this puts a brake on the increase in market liquidity, which will cause the firm to stop short of full information release.

13. The impossibility of accounting standards that are "right" from society's perspective follows from the Possibility Theorem of Arrow (1963). Demski (1973) demonstrates that, even for a single individual, such standards do not in general exist

independently of the decision problem and utility function of that individual. Scott (1977) shows, however, that socially right standards are possible for a special case of decision problem (the "single-peakedness" condition), and argues that this condition is quite common.

14. Indeed, this complexity is recognized by standard setters. Thus SFAC 1.23 of the FASB (see Section 3.8) states " . . . the benefits from financial information are usually difficult or impossible to measure objectively, and the costs often are; different persons will honestly disagree about whether the benefits of information justify its costs."

15. This "low-cost" argument assumes that the external reporting of internal information does not incur substantial proprietary costs, or reveal information that the firm is having trouble coordinating and controlling its various divisions. However, Berger and Hann also report that firms that were forced to reveal previously hidden information suffered a decline in market value, and that they may have tightened up their monitoring of divisions as a result. This suggests that SFAS 131 has economic consequences, as some firms change their internal organization to reduce proprietary costs.

16. Section 1701 of the *CICA Handbook* calls this the "management approach."

Chapter 13

Standard Setting: Political Issues

FIGURE 13.1   ORGANIZATION OF CHAPTER 13

13.1 Overview

In Chapter 12 we saw that, from the perspective of economic theory, the question of the extent of regulation of accounting and reporting standards is unsettled. While we can suggest a number of contractual and market-based incentives for private information production, we simply do not know whether increased market failures that would follow from deregulation of firms' information production decisions would be more or less costly to society than the various costs of the standard-setting process. It does appear, however, that the problem of market failure is quite fundamental. Information asymmetry (and the resulting problems of moral hazard and adverse selection), which creates the demand for information production by firms, also creates a demand for regulation of that information production. This is because of the problem of unanimity—the amount of information that firms would privately produce need not, and in general will not, equal the amount that investors want. As a result, investors may push for regulation to remedy the perceived deficiency.

This suggests that standard setting is fundamentally as much a political process as an economic one. Such a viewpoint is consistent with the concept of constituencies of accounting, with the political cost hypothesis of positive accounting theory in Section 8.6.2, and with the game theoretic and agency theoretic views of constituency conflict in Chapter 9. It seems natural to expect that the various accounting constituencies would appeal to the political process when their conflicting interests cannot be resolved by contractual or market forces.

Our first objective in this chapter is to review two theories of regulation. The first, the **public interest theory**, takes the view that regulation should maximize social welfare. This was the viewpoint of Chapter 12. The second, the **interest group theory** of regulation, suggests that individuals form coalitions, or constituencies, to protect and promote their interests by lobbying the government. These coalitions are viewed as in conflict with each other to obtain their share of benefits from regulation.

Our second objective is to examine the *processes* of standard setting. Besides being of interest in their own right, we will see that these processes are largely consistent with the interest group theory of regulation.

Our third objective is to consider the criteria that standard setters need to consider if their standards are to be acceptable. While decision usefulness and reduction of information asymmetry are necessary for any standard, we shall see that much more is needed. Specifically, the standard must be acceptable to its various constituencies. This requires a careful attention to due process by the standard setter. Figure 13.1 outlines the organization of this chapter.

13.2   Two Theories of Regulation

13.2.1   The Public Interest Theory

The public interest theory of regulation was implicit in our examination of standard setting in Chapter 12. This theory suggests that regulation is the result of a public demand for correction of market failures. In this theory, the central authority, also called the regulatory body or the regulator, is assumed to have the best interests of society at heart. It does its best to regulate so as to maximize social welfare. Consequently, regulation is thought of as a tradeoff between the costs of regulation and its social benefits in the form of improved operation of markets. Chapter 12 addressed these various costs and benefits.

While this view represents an ideal of how regulation should be carried out, there are problems with its implementation. It can be argued, from the standpoint of how regulation works in practice, that the theory is superficial and perhaps naïve. Our discussion here is based on Stigler (1971), Posner (1974), and Peltzman (1976).

One problem with the public interest theory is the very complex task of deciding on the right amount of regulation. This is particularly true for a complex commodity like information where, as Chapter 12 makes clear, it is effectively impossible to please everyone. Then, the door is left open for other theories of how the amount of regulation is determined.

An even more serious problem, however, lies in the motivation of the regulatory body. Given the complex nature of its task, it is difficult for a legislature to monitor the operations of the regulator. In effect, the ability of the legislature to force the regulatory body to act in the public interest is weak, because of the complex nature of regulation and the fact that costly and lengthy hearings would be needed for the legislature to know whether the regulator is doing a good job. This creates a moral hazard problem—the possibility that the regulatory agency will operate on its own behalf rather than on behalf of the public. The situation here is reminiscent of the manager in our agency theory discussion of Example 9.2, who was motivated to shirk because his or her action was unobservable to the owner. Thus, the public interest theory represents a sort of first-best approach to regulation. In practice, the first-best solution may not be attainable, because of problems of implementation. This leads directly to another theory.

13.2.2 The Interest Group Theory

The interest group theory of regulation takes the view that an industry operates in the presence of a number of interest groups (or constituencies, as we have used the term in earlier chapters). Consider any manufacturing industry as an example. The firms in the industry comprise an obvious interest group, as do the firms' customers. Another interest group would be environmentalists, who would be concerned about the industry's social responsibility. These various interest groups will lobby the legislature for various amounts and types of regulation. For example, the industry itself may demand regulation to protect it against foreign price competition or against encroachments on its operations by related industries. Customers may form groups to lobby for quality standards or price controls. Environmentalists may lobby for emission control regulations and greater disclosure of environmental performance. These various constituencies can be thought of as demanders of regulation. Note that the nature and extent of the regulation they demand will differ across constituencies.

The political authority, or legislature, can also be thought of as an interest group, which has the power to supply regulation. The interests of the political authority lie in retaining power. Consequently, it will supply regulation to those constituencies that it believes will be most effective and useful in helping it retain power. The regulatory body is then in the middle. It is the vehicle whereby regulation is supplied. It attempts to maximize its own welfare while at the same time balancing the demands of the various constituencies, including the political authority.

In effect, the interest group theory regards regulation as a commodity for which there is a demand and a supply. The commodity will be allocated to those constituencies that are most politically effective in convincing the legislature to grant them regulatory favours.

While it may seem rather cynical, the interest group theory may well be a better predictor of how regulation really works than the public interest theory. Before considering the extent to which the theory fits the regulation of the information industry, we will examine the standard setting process.

13.3 Standard Setting in Canada and the United States

13.3.1 The Canadian Institute of Chartered Accountants (CICA)

Accounting Standards Committee The *CICA Handbook* contains standards for financial accounting and for auditing, as laid down by the Accounting Standards Board (AcSB) and the Auditing and Assurance Standards Board (AASB) respectively of the Canadian Institute of Chartered Accountants. The *CICA Handbook* is the major source of accounting and auditing standards in Canada. Its authority is enhanced because it has a special legal status. For example, the Canada Business Corporations Act, Regulation 70, states:

> *The financial statements referred to in paragraph 155(1)(a) of the Act shall, except as otherwise provided by this Part, be prepared in accordance with generally accepted accounting principles as set out in the Handbook of the Canadian Institute of Chartered Accountants.*

The AcSB and AASB are authorized by the Board of Governors of the Canadian Institute of Chartered Accountants to publish reports on their own responsibility. There is also a third CICA standard-setting body, the Public Sector Accounting Board (PSAB). Our coverage here is of the AcSB.

Process of Standard Setting The following points should be noted about the process of setting standards for the *CICA Handbook*:

- The AcSB is advised on its priorities and agenda by an oversight body, the Accounting Standards Oversight Council (AcSOC). This is a body with widely based membership. It appoints the members of the AcSB, and provides an outside perspective on priorities for possible new standards.

- In addition to perspectives from AcSOC, there are other ways for a possible new standard to be placed on the agenda of the AcSB. For example, board members and full-time institute staff are close enough to public practice to know what topics require attention. Suggestions may also come from the Emerging Issues Committee (discussed below).

- There is a maximum of nine members of the AcSB, chosen to represent diverse constituencies. Membership is voluntary. That is, with the exception of the chairperson, these are not full-time, salaried positions. In effect, the organizations that employ the board members bear the costs. Whether this is a desirable state of affairs is difficult to say. An alternative scenario might be one in which board members were full-time, paid employees (like FASB members in the United States). Of course, this would require that considerably more money be raised to support the board's activities. To the extent that this was raised from a variety of different constituencies, this would broaden the base of financial support for the standard-setting process. For example, in the United States, funding for the FASB is provided by an assessment on firms that report to the SEC. However, we saw in Chapter 12 that the direct costs of setting and administering standards were only a part, and probably a small part, of the overall costs of standard setting. Nevertheless, such an alternative funding scenario might reduce any possibility that organizations that employ the board members may "call the tune." Yet another possibility would be to discontinue the AcSB, and adopt GAAP as laid down by the FASB (Section 13.3.3) and/or the International Accounting Standards Board (Section 13.4).

- As mentioned, the AcSB publishes accounting standards "on its own responsibility." Presumably, this is to give it a measure of independence from the CICA itself and reduce the possibility of interference in its deliberations.

- New standards require the approval of at least two-thirds of the members of the board. This is an example of **super-majority voting**, which decreases the possibility of approval of a standard that is only marginally acceptable to the board. This will also tend to produce a process of compromise in the creation of a new standard. Dissenting members will be in a stronger position than they would be if only a simple majority was required and thus would be less likely to feel that their views and concerns had been ignored.

- The AcSB follows **due process** to formulate new standards. First, an exposure draft is prepared and widely distributed, to enable interested parties to react before the standard is finalized. Meetings with concerned constituencies may take place. Comments are analyzed and a revised version prepared. A statement of Background Information and Basis for Conclusions may be also issued to explain the standard to users. Super-majority voting also contributes to due process.

- The AcSB recognizes that due process in establishing a new standard carries a time penalty. This slows the ability of the board to respond to new issues. In effect, the board may be able to react to problems only after they have arisen.

  However, the board can also issue **Accounting Guidelines**. These are interpretations of existing *CICA Handbook* recommendations or opinions on other matters for which a *CICA Handbook* provision does not exist. While Guidelines do not have the authority of *CICA Handbook* recommendations, they do have the potential to enable a relatively quick reaction when a need arises.

- Also, the **Emerging Issues Committee (EIC)** was established in 1988 to provide a forum for timely review of emerging accounting issues that are likely to receive divergent or unsatisfactory treatment in practice in the absence of some guidance. Its pronouncements require a consensus, defined as the existence of no more than two dissenting members of those present at the meeting. While these pronouncements do not amend or override the *CICA Handbook*, they represent a major step towards improving the timeliness of the standard-setting process.

Our main observation from this discussion is that the various steps to create a new standard suggest that the process is quite "political," with emphasis on due process. In other words, many of the various constituencies of accounting are invited to take part, either as part of the process leading to insertion of an item into the board agenda, as members of the board itself, or as respondents to exposure drafts. If the process was strictly economic, as was implicit in our discussion in Chapter 12, such broad-based representation would not be necessary since correct standards could simply be deduced from theory.

13.3.2 The Ontario Securities Commission (OSC)

In Canada, securities regulation is under provincial jurisdiction. Canada does not at present have a national securities administrator similar to the SEC in the United States. Here, we examine the securities commission of Ontario. The Ontario Securities Commission (OSC) administers securities legislation in Ontario, including regulation of the largest stock exchange in the country (the TSX) and is one of the most active securities commissions. It should be noted, however, that the OSC is a member of the

Canadian Securities Administrators (CSA), a forum of the 13 provincial and territorial securities regulators in Canada. The mission of the CSA is to coordinate and harmonize the regulation of Canadian capital markets. Consequently, many of the policies of the OSC also apply to other Canadian jurisdictions.

Role and Authority of the OSC The OSC is composed of from 9 to 14 members, appointed by the Ontario Lieutenant Governor in Council for terms not exceeding five years. Its authority derives from the Securities Act of Ontario. According to this act, the OSC shall lay down:

- requirements for the timely, accurate, and efficient disclosure of information;
- restrictions on fraudulent and unfair market practices and procedures; and
- requirements for the maintenance of high standards of fitness and business conduct to ensure honest and responsible conduct by market participants.

Thus, the role of the OSC is to regulate securities trading in Ontario, including both the issuers of the securities themselves and the exchanges on which they are traded, and to maintain public confidence in capital markets.

OSC's Relation to the *CICA Handbook* According to the Ontario Securities Act, issuers of securities under the OSC's jurisdiction must file financial statements in accordance with GAAP. As mentioned above, the OSC has the power to lay down requirements for timely, accurate, and efficient disclosure. To date, the OSC has accepted GAAP as laid down in the *CICA Handbook* as fulfilling these requirements.

Thus, the OSC effectively delegates financial statement accounting standards to the AcSB. However, the OSC issues standards itself where these do not directly affect the financial statements. For example, MD&A (Section 4.8.2) and requirements for disclosure of executive compensation (Section 10.6) are OSC standards.

13.3.3 The Financial Accounting Standards Board (FASB)

Establishment and Purpose of the FASB The Financial Accounting Standards Board (FASB) in the United States was established in 1973. Its purpose is to establish and improve standards of financial accounting and reporting for the guidance and education of the public. To accomplish this, the FASB attempts to improve the usefulness of financial reporting by focusing on relevance and reliability, by updating standards (if necessary) for changes in the business and economic environment, improving the public understanding of the nature and purpose of information contained in financial reports, and promoting international convergence of quality accounting standards.

In conducting its activities, the FASB is guided by certain perceptions. These include: objectivity in decision-making, consideration of the views of its constituents, promulgation of standards only when the expected benefits exceed the expected costs, implementation of changes in a manner that minimizes disruption to existing practice, and review and possible amendment of past decisions. It should be noted that, unlike the structure in Canada, the FASB is a body distinct from the American Institute of Certified Public Accountants (AICPA). While the AICPA is one of the sponsoring bodies and endorses FASB standards, many other bodies are also involved in sponsoring the FASB.

Structure of the FASB   The FASB is the operational arm of a three-part organizational structure for financial accounting standard setting; the other two parts are the Financial Accounting Foundation (FAF) and the Financial Accounting Standards Advisory Council (FASAC).

The FAF consists of 16 trustees, of which 11 are elected from sponsoring organizations, including professional accountants, academe, management, and the securities industry. The remaining trustees are elected by the above trustees. Following from the accounting scandals of the early 2000s and the Sarbanes-Oxley Act (see Section 1.2), a majority of trustees must not have been recently associated with a professional accounting firm.

The FAF appoints FASB board members, reviews FASB performance, and appoints FASAC members.

The FASAC consists of 33 members appointed by the FAF and drawn from various business and professional constituencies, including accountants, managers, analysts, and academe. FASAC acts as the liaison between FASB and the business and economic communities. It advises on project priorities and on the suitability of the FASB's preliminary positions on issues.

The FASB consists of seven board members, appointed by the FAF for a maximum of two five-year terms. Although background is taken into account when selecting board members, it is considered secondary to such qualifications as accounting knowledge, integrity, discipline, and judicial temperament. A majority of five of the seven members in favour is required to pass a new standard.

FASB board members are expected to be independent. They must sever all ties with previous employers, declare conflict of interest if necessary, and not accept fees or honoraria from any institution other than the FASB.

In 2002, the FASB established a **User Advisory Council.** This is a group of over 40 investment professionals who assist the FASB in raising awareness of how investors, analysts, and rating agencies use financial information and how to better design accounting standards to meet their needs.

In setting and updating accounting and reporting standards, the FASB, like the AcSB, places heavy emphasis on due process. Procedures for initiating and adopting new standards are broadly similar to those of the AcSB outlined above.

13.3.4   The Securities and Exchange Commission (SEC)

The SEC was founded in the United States in 1934 to regulate trading in the securities of firms whose securities are traded in more than one state and that meet certain size tests. As part of its mandate, the SEC has the responsibility to ensure that investors are supplied with adequate information. Consequently, like the OSC, it has the authority to issue accounting standards for firms under its jurisdiction. However, in ASR 150, the SEC delegated this responsibility to the FASB. This delegation was reaffirmed by the SEC in April 2003, following passage of the Sarbanes-Oxley Act.

This is not to say that the SEC does not intervene in standard setting from time to time. For example, the SEC overrode SFAS 19, which required oil and gas companies to use successful-efforts accounting for exploration costs (recall our discussion in Section 8.4). This was done by means of ASR 253 (1978), which allowed use of either full-cost or successful-efforts accounting, and also proposed RRA, initially as supplementary information. As a result of this intervention, the FASB issued SFAS 25 in 1978, which amended SFAS 19 to allow both cost methods.

Nevertheless, it can be argued that instances such as these are "the exceptions that prove the rule," and that it is correct to say the SEC effectively delegates standard setting authority to the FASB.

13.4 The International Accounting Standards Board (IASB)

13.4.1 Establishment and Objectives of the IASB

The International Accounting Standards Committee, (IASC) the parent body of the **International Accounting Standards Board (IASB)**, was established in 1973 by agreement between accountancy bodies in Australia, Canada, France, Germany, Japan, Mexico, the Netherlands, the United Kingdom and Ireland, and the United States.

In 2001, the IASC reorganized, adopting a structure somewhat similar to that of the FASB in the United States. The objectives of the reorganized IASC (now called the IASC Foundation) are:

- to develop, in the public interest, a single set of high-quality, understandable, and enforceable global accounting standards that require high-quality, transparent, and comparable information in financial statements and other reporting to help participants in the world's capital markets and other users to make economic decisions;

- to promote the use and rigorous application of those standards; and

- to bring about convergence of national accounting standards and International Accounting Standards with high-quality solutions.

The IASC is governed by a board of 19 individuals, with geographic representation from North America, Europe, and Asia/Pacific.

13.4.2 Structure of the IASB

The IASC trustees appoint the 14 members of the IASB, 12 of which are full-time positions. Funding is supplied by the IASC. There are no geographic requirements for IASB members. However, different constituencies are represented. At least five members must have an auditing background. Other constituencies include financial statement preparers, users, and academe. A majority of 8 of 14 votes is required to pass new standards. In designing and implementing standards, the IASB follows due process, similar to the AcSB and FASB.

13.4.3 Authority of the IASB

Unlike the AcSB and FASB, compliance with IASB standards is not mandatory. Compliance is up to the individual countries and firms involved. While many countries do require various degrees of conformance with IASB standards, other countries, such as the United States, have not gone this far. However, the European Union plans to require public companies within its jurisdiction to comply with IASB standards in 2005.

The International Organization of Securities Commissions (IOSCO) represents the world's securities regulators, including Canadian regulators and the SEC in the United States. It recommends to its members that they use IASB standards, although individual member countries may require reconciliation of IASB standards with their own GAAP. For example, foreign firms that wish to trade their securities in the United States or Canada must currently meet SEC or OSC requirements. These include filing financial statements either in accordance with local GAAP or, if the statements are prepared under GAAP of some other jurisdiction, with a reconciliation of net income and balance sheet line items with local GAAP.[1]

A concern relating to international accounting standards is the *enforcement* of standards. Lack of enforcement increases the exposure of the market to adverse selection and moral hazard problems, regardless of the quality of the underlying standards. In this regard, the IASB is in a different situation than the FASB. While IOSCO endorses the use of IASB standards, it does not have the enforcement authority of the SEC and OSC. Enforcement is up to the authorities in the respective jurisdictions that adopt IASB standards. Even if IASB GAAP becomes acceptable, securities regulators would have to be assured that enforcement is adequate before removing requirements for reconciliation. Possibly, IOSCO and/or large international accounting firms could provide this assurance.

13.4.4 International Convergence of Accounting Standards

The establishment of the IASC was part of the increased globalization and integration of economic activity that has taken place in recent years. In particular, this globalization includes securities markets, with many corporations listed on stock exchanges in two or more countries. Consequently, large, multinational corporations bear the costs of preparing reports to satisfy the securities legislation of more than one jurisdiction. These requirements also raise investors' costs to interpret and analyze financial statements of non-domestic firms.

This raises the question of international convergence of accounting standards. To the extent that international accounting standards become acceptable to securities regulators as a substitute for local GAAP, costs of multiple exchange listings will fall. This should lower firms' financial statement preparation costs. It should also lower their costs of capital, as they are better able to tap more liquid sources of financing. Investors' costs of interpretation and analysis should also be lowered. In this regard, the 2002 Norwalk Agreement between the FASB and IASB commits the two bodies to work towards a common set of high-quality standards. In Canada, the AcSB announced in March 2005 a proposal to align its standards for public companies with IASB standards by 2010, abandoning its previous policy of moving Canadian standards into alignment with those of the FASB. Of course, as FASB and IASB standards converge under the Norwalk Agreement, the effect will be to converge all three sets of standards.

Some progress has been made towards convergence. For example, the provisions of IAS 39,[2] dealing with the recognition and measurement of financial instruments, are substantially similar to those of FASB 115 and FASB 133 discussed in Section 7.3, although IAS 39 applies to financial liabilities as well as financial assets. As in Canada (see Section 8.3), IFRS 2 requires expensing of ESOs. In December 2004 the FASB announced implementation of a similar standard effective in June, 2005. IFRS 3 requires the purchase method of accounting for purchased goodwill. Goodwill is not amortized but is subject to a ceiling test. These requirements are similar to SFAS 142 and Section 3062 of the *CICA Handbook* discussed in Section 7.4.2.

Yet, differences remain. The IASB does not at present have a standard for comprehensive income. Instead, unrealized items such as gains and losses resulting from fair valuing available-for-sale securities are included directly in shareholders' equity. IAS 16 allows upwards revaluation of property, plant, and equipment, whereas historical cost is generally used in the United States and Canada. Development costs may be capitalised under IAS 38, similar to Section 3450 of the *CICA Handbook*. In the United States, almost all R&D is expensed.

Perhaps the main hurdle faced by the IASB is securing acceptance of its standards, without reconciliation, by the SEC. As mentioned, the SEC currently requires reconciliation with FASB standards if U.S.-listed firms' financial statements are prepared under IASB standards. In addition to issues of standards enforcement, the SEC's willingness to accept IASB standards depends on the quality of those standards and their consistency with those of the FASB.

Given the differences that remain, full standards convergences may take some time. In addition to technical matters, convergence faces issues of culture, nationalism, and different institutional and regulatory frameworks. It should be noted, however, that convergence does not mean that standards are necessarily identical. Rather, convergence results from a process of negotiation that may take these issues into account, thereby allowing for some differences.

It is interesting to consider what might happen if the SEC did accept financial statements prepared under IASB standards. Specifically, suppose that the SEC allowed all firms under its jurisdiction to report, without reconciliation, using either FASB or IASB standards. This proposal, which would introduce a measure of competition to the standard-setting process, was discussed by Dye and Sunder (2001). One possible effect, they suggest, is a "race to the bottom," whereby each standard setter lowers its standards so as to attract firms and their managers away from the other. As a result, the potential for bad earnings management is increased. This outcome is analogous to the Nash equilibrium outcome of the game discussed in Example 9.1.

However, as Dye and Sunder discuss, there are forces to control such a tendency. For example, there would be investor reaction to a firm that chooses low-quality accounting standards. As pointed out in Section 12.3.3, market forces reward managers who release full and timely information. Furthermore, a race to the bottom is inconsistent with the objectives of the IASB and FASB, which include high-quality accounting standards and efforts to promote their convergence.

Indeed, a benefit of competition in standard setting derives from the impossibility of calculating the socially correct extent of regulation as concluded in Chapter 12. A monopolistic standard setter may attempt to maximize its influence by imposing more and more standards, as predicted by the interest group theory of regulation. As a result, the extent of regulation may go beyond its socially optimal level. Competition among standard setters would help to control this tendency since firms that did not like one set of standards could simply adopt the other, thereby causing the over-zealous standard setter to "lose customers." In addition, firms could signal their commitment to full disclosure by means of the set of standards they adopt.

A potential cost of competition is to reduce **network externalities**. That is, investors would bear costs of having to learn more than one set of accounting standards. Lack of comparability does impose costs. However, Dye and Sunder suggest that these costs would be relatively low. For example, analysts and other experts could specialize in interpreting a particular set of standards. The results of their analyses would quickly be incorporated into share market values, thereby price-protecting ordinary investors. Indeed, as mentioned, the very fact that a firm chooses a particular set of accounting standards has information content.

While the question of competition between standard setters is complex, these arguments suggest that greater acceptance by national standard setters of IASB standards may have social benefits.

13.5 Relationship to Theories of Regulation

Our description of the standard-setting process shows that it is characterized by due process. For example, in Canada, the United States, and internationally, major constituencies with an interest in financial reporting are represented on the standard-setting bodies. Also, there are provisions for public hearings, exposure drafts, and, generally, for openness, as well as requirements for super-majority votes in favour before new standards are issued.

This due process characteristic is consistent with conflict-based theories of constituency interaction. The sources of market failure in the production of information discussed in Chapter 12 imply that market forces cannot always be relied upon to generate the right accounting standards and procedures. Yet, the complexities arising from the diverse information needs and interests of investors and managers make it effectively impossible for standard setters to calculate the right accounting standards either. We simply do not know how to calculate the best tradeoff between the conflicting uses of information by investors and managers that is required by the public interest theory of regulation. This is why the choice of accounting standards is better regarded as a conflict between constituencies than as a process of calculation. The AcSB, the FASB, and the IASB are players in a complex game where affected constituencies choose strategies of lobbying for or against a proposed new standard.

If the players of the game are to accept the outcome (that is, the issuance or non-issuance of a new standard and, if issued, its specific reporting requirements) they must feel that the process was fair, and that their strategy at least had a chance of working. In terms of the game theoretic Example 9.1, the players must know the strategies available to the other parties. The willingness of players to accept a new standard is enhanced if they feel that their views were heard. This explains the attention to due process as a way of moderating the inherent constituency conflict in standard setting.

These considerations suggest that the interest group theory of regulation may be a better predictor of new standards than the public interest theory, since the interest group theory formally recognizes the existence of conflicting constituencies. To pursue this question further, we next consider some of the conflict leading up to a specific FASB standard.

13.6 Conflict and Compromise

13.6.1 An Example of Constituency Conflict

We described SFAS 115, "Accounting for Certain Investments in Debt and Equity Securities," in Section 7.3.2. However, we did not consider the process that led up to SFAS 115. Here, we consider aspects of this process, which provide an interesting and important example of the problems of developing a new standard. Exhibit 13.1 reproduces an article by Robin Goldwyn Blumenthal that appeared in *The Wall Street Journal*, September 11, 1992, following the release of an exposure draft by the FASB. The exposure draft specified that at least some securities held by firms be valued at fair value. Recall that this implies market value if reliably available. Otherwise, fair value can be determined by present value, use of models, or other appropriate techniques. The problems of gains trading, and of volatility of reported net income under the new proposed standard, were considered in Section 7.3.2. Here, our main interest is in the constituency conflicts leading up to SFAS 115.

Exhibit 13.1 FASB Moves Closer to Forcing Banks to Value Securities Near Market Prices

New York—The Financial Accounting Standards Board moved a step closer to implementing controversial rules that would require banks to value many of their securities closer to market prices.

In issuing its exposure draft, the FASB formally proposed rules on accounting for securities held as investments; the proposal is similar to a compromise approach outlined in July. Although there appears to be solid support for the proposal by six of the seven members on FASB's board, there is likely to be continuing strong opposition to the proposal during the comment period by banks, which in the past year have bought record amounts of securities.

"It's a huge change in accounting," said Donna Fisher, manager of accounting policy at the American Bankers Association. In effect, the proposal would make it more difficult for banks to classify securities as long-term investments, and thus account for them at original cost rather than market value. Although the proposal would affect any company that invests in marketable equity securities and debt securities, it would have the greatest effect on financial institutions such as banks, whose investments in those securities represent about 30% of their total assets, Ms. Fisher said.

Gains Trading

The proposal, which is intended to standardize accounting methods on investments in securities for various industries, also attempts to address a practice by banks called gains trading, in which securities that have appreciated in value are sold to recognize gains while those that have fallen in value are held as long-term investments and thus recorded at original cost.

continued →

Under existing accounting rules, "there was a perception that people were inappropriately reporting something at cost when in fact they were not holding on to [the securities] for the long term," said Robert C. Wilkins, an FASB project manager.

The FASB, the chief rule-making body for accountants that is based in Norwalk, Conn., has been under pressure for several years from the Securities and Exchange Commission to hold investment securities at more up-to-date values, known as marking to market. SEC Chairman Richard Breeden began voicing his support for marking to market all investment securities two years ago.

Although the FASB had at one point considered eliminating the current three categories of investment securities and forcing companies to mark all of them to market, it abandoned that approach because it couldn't figure out how to mark related liabilities to market, Mr. Wilkins said. In July, the FASB also eased its approach to declines in value of debt securities held as "available for sale." These would be booked to shareholders' equity on the balance sheet, rather than reducing profits on the income statement.

Pluses and Minuses

Walter Schuetze, the SEC's chief accountant, said the proposal had pluses and minuses. "The plus is that more marketable securities will be accounted for at market in the balance sheet," Mr. Schuetze said. However, he pointed out that under this proposal, there is room for "so-called psychoanalytic accounting," which allows management to classify three different ways the same securities at the time they are purchased.

Mr. Schuetze also said the proposal didn't adequately address gains trading, and that it failed to give enough guidance on when to write down stocks and bonds when the decline in market price is deemed to be "other than temporary."

Banking representatives, however, had other views on the proposal. "They don't come out and say you must mark securities to market but the net effect we think will be very close," said Ms. Fisher of the American Bankers Association. She said that if the proposal is adopted, banks would need to try to reduce volatility in their capital accounts, possibly by investing in shorter-term securities.

Bankers say that for the most part they purchase intermediate-term securities with a maturity of two to five years. "Most of our securities are short term," said William J. Rossman, chief executive officer of Mid-State Bank in Altoona, Pa., and president of Robert Morris Associates, a trade group of commercial lenders. "You're not going to find too many banks taking short-term funds and investing in 30-year bonds."

The proposed rules must now go through a public comment period, in which the FASB undoubtedly will be hearing from opponents. The exposure draft could take effect as early as 1994 if it is approved.

Treasury Undersecretary Jerome Powell, in remarks to a mortgage bankers group, warned that market value accounting would make bank earnings very volatile and add to the credit crunch.

continued ➔

Before considering constituency conflicts, consider the effects of full marking-to-market, which Exhibit 13.1 mentions the FASB had considered at one point. Full marking-to-market would not only involve fair valuation of all of a firm's financial instruments, both assets and liabilities, but also involve including the unrealized gains and losses in reported net income, with consequent volatility. (This volatility would be reduced to the extent that it was hedged.) Note also that full marking-to-market would eliminate the ability of firms to engage in gains trading. If securities were valued at market, with gains and losses included in net income as they occurred, management would not control the timing of these gains and losses. Also, there would be no effect on the bottom line upon sale, so that gains trading would be eliminated.

As might be expected, full marking-to-market would be objected to by banks' managers, since banks hold large amounts of financial assets and liabilities. Banks would see both the volatility of their earnings increase (to the extent this was not hedged) and their ability to engage in earnings management severely reduced. Exhibit 13.1 describes the objections of the American Bankers Association, Robert Morris Associates, and the Independent Bankers Association of America, all representing management.

In addition, the U.S. Treasury was concerned about economic consequences. It felt that marking-to-market would affect banks' operating and financial strategies, to the point where they would be unwilling to lend long-term, which would affect the availability of credit in the economy. This concern arises because as interest rates vary so does the market value of fixed-term securities. Since the longer the term the greater the market value variation in response to a given change in interest rates, banks would cut down on long-term lending in order to reduce volatility of earnings. Consequently, the Treasury strongly opposed the proposed standard.

Also, the original proposal for full marking-to-market accounting faced technical difficulties. Certain financial liabilities, such as banks' deposit liabilities, were difficult to value, because of core deposit intangibles. Models to provide reliable values in the face of these difficulties are not available.

As suggested in the case of ESOs (Section 8.3), if a standard has technical difficulties, it can be even more strongly attacked by its opponents. Here, inability to value core deposit intangibles was a major technical difficulty. To make matters worse, if financial liabilities were excused from the standard, then they could not hedge gains or losses on financial assets, thereby making concerns about volatility even greater.

However, Exhibit 13.1 also describes the support of another powerful constituency, the SEC, for full marking-to-market. This support is not hard to understand. As an agency whose role is to protect investors and encourage the proper operation of securities markets, the SEC would be expected to favour the conveying of fair values to investors.

Also, the SEC favoured the recording of these fair values in the accounts (as opposed to footnote presentation), since, with such recording, gains trading would be eliminated.

Obviously, the FASB was in a difficult position as it tried to produce a standard that would be generally acceptable. Nevertheless, SFAS 115 passed in 1993, along the lines discussed in Section 7.3.2. The standard took effect for fiscal years beginning after December 15, 1993.

It is interesting to note again some of the compromises that were made in the standard, relative to the original goal of full mark-to-market accounting. First, liabilities are excluded, due to measurement difficulties. Second, to reduce volatility, some debt securities continue to be valued at cost under SFAS 115. Recall that these are securities for which the firm "has the positive intent and ability" to hold them to maturity. Marking-to-market is required for trading securities and for available-for-sale securities. Third, to further reduce volatility, unrealized gains and losses on available-for-sale securities are excluded from reported net income and reported in other comprehensive income.

Presumably, the above compromises were made to reduce the objections of management. However, as a result, gains trading is not eliminated, and may even be encouraged since firms could realize gains merely by transferring securities from held-to-maturity to trading.[3] However, by placing severe constraints on the ability both to classify securities as held-to-maturity in the first place and to reclassify, the FASB hoped to minimize the incidence of gains trading. Furthermore, expanded disclosure requirements under SFAS 115 would be more likely to reveal gains trading profits than before. In addition, if a firm were to sell part of its held-to-maturity securities before maturity, this would be inconsistent with intent to hold and would likely result in the remaining securities being reclassified to trading or available-for-sale.

These constraints on gains trading were apparently made to satisfy the SEC. Had the SEC decided not to go along, this would have put the FASB in a very difficult position. It would have been caught between the demands of the SEC for more fair value accounting and the financial institutions for less.

13.6.2 Comprehensive Income

In 1997, SFAS 130, **Comprehensive Income**, was issued by the FASB. While a comparable Canadian standard is now in place, it is not scheduled for implementation until October 2006. Consequently, we discuss SFAS 130 here. Comprehensive income is defined as all changes in equity during the period except those resulting from investments by or distributions to owners. Thus, in addition to net income as calculated under GAAP, comprehensive income includes other items such as unrealized translation gains and losses resulting from consolidation of foreign subsidiaries under SFAS 52, unrealized gains and losses on marking-to-market available-for-sale securities under SFAS 115 (Section 7.3.2), and unrealized gains and losses on cash flow hedges of forecasted transactions under SFAS 133 (Section 7.3.4). In each of these cases, management objects to the inclusion of these items in net income, on the grounds that they are volatile, uncontrollable, and uninformative about their effort. Our study of contracting theory suggests reasons for management's concerns.

SFAS 130 requires that items such as these be included in a statement entitled **Other Comprehensive Income**, which can be presented either along with the income statement or in a separate statement of changes in shareholders' equity. Once unrealized gains and losses are realized, for example by selling available-for-sale securities, the now-realized gain or loss is transferred from other comprehensive income to net income.

Comprehensive income is thus the sum of net income and other comprehensive income. To illustrate, we extend the hierarchy of earnings numbers given in Section 5.5 (again, ignoring income taxes) as follows:

Core earnings	xx
Unusual and non-recurring items	xx
Income from continuing operations	xx
Extraordinary items	xx
Net income	xx
Other comprehensive income	xx
Comprehensive income	xx

This dichotomization between realized (net income) and unrealized (other comprehensive income) earnings components emphasizes the two roles of financial reporting—providing useful information to investors and enabling the managerial labour market to evaluate manager performance. Since current market value is the best indicator of future value when markets work reasonably well, unrealized gains and losses provide relevant information to investors about future firm performance. However, to the extent that unrealized gains and losses are less informative about manager effort than realized gains and losses, net income is a more informative measure of performance for contracting. This contracting efficiency could perhaps be enhanced by moving additional items from net income to other comprehensive income, such as ceiling test writedowns where these are deemed to be uninformative about effort (recall BCE's writeoff of stranded costs in Section 10.6). Of course, such an approach would need standards to control a manager's temptation to avoid responsibility for losses by shuffling informative loss items out of net income, or shuffling uninformative gains the other way. Given such controls, the dichotomization approach has some potential to relieve the fundamental problem of financial accounting theory.

Despite this potential, SFAS 130 ignores any mention of the role of net income in motivating manager performance. Nevertheless, this role seems implicit. For example, the standard states (paragraph 66) that other comprehensive income is not a measure of financial performance, implying that net income is.

Theory in Practice 13.1

Under SFAS 130, unrealized gains and losses on available-for-sale securities are included in other comprehensive income (OCI). As these unrealized gains and losses are realized through sale of the securities, they are transferred to net income.

continued →

Thus, despite SFAS 115, firms can still engage in a form of gains trading—they can manage reported net income by selling available-for-sale securities. For example, to increase reported net income, it is only necessary to sell available-for-sale securities that have unrealized gains attached. Of course, this also reduces OCI, since the gain is now realized, and comprehensive income (the sum of net income and OCI) is unaffected. Nevertheless, managers may feel that investors will concentrate on net income for evaluation of firm performance.

An interesting characteristic of SFAS 130 is that it allows the firm to report OCI either below net income or as part of a statement of changes to shareholders' equity. This latter option shows OCI *apart* from net income—for example, as note information or as part of an expanded statement of retained earnings. The significance of including OCI apart from net income is that gains trading may be less noticeable—the investor has to study the OCI statement to realize that the realized gain or loss in net income is merely the result of realizing gains and losses that have already occurred and are thus of little economic significance.

This behaviour was studied by Lee, Petroni, and Shen (2004) (LPS). They obtained a sample of 82 U.S. insurance companies. Such firms hold large amounts of available-for-sale securities, typically about 40% of total assets. Consequently, the potential to manage net income by gains trading is great.

LPS classified their 82 firms into "cherry pickers" (firms that appeared to gains trade so as to manage reported net income) and firms that did not exhibit this behaviour. For example, if a firm followed a pattern over time of reporting realized gains on securities when its net income before such gains was unusually low, it was classified as a cherry picker. The implication is that the firm was managing its reported net income upwards, perhaps to meet analysts' and investors' earnings expectations. There were 23 cherry pickers in their sample.

Then, LPS looked at the reporting option used by the 23 cherry picking firms. They found that 75% of them used the option of reporting apart from net income. Of the 59 firms not classed as cherry pickers, only 38% used this option.

LPS' evidence suggests that cherry pickers feel they have something to hide and, accordingly, choose the less transparent reporting option. Another interpretation, however, is that managers may feel that since realized gains and losses are not subject to the volatility of unrealized gains and losses, they are more informative about their efforts in running the firm.

The reporting of comprehensive income raises the question of whether it is decision useful for investors. The above vignette suggests some potential, since a careful examination of other comprehensive income may reveal earnings management. The usefulness issue was investigated by Dhaliwal, Subramanyam, and Trezevant (1999). For a large sample of U.S. firms, they calculated the association between share returns and comprehensive income, and compared the result with the association between share returns and net income. They found no clear evidence that other comprehensive income is more highly correlated with share returns than net income, implying no additional decision usefulness. Skinner (1999) points out that this result is what we would expect given securities market efficiency. Much of the information about the components of other comprehensive income would have been available to the market from other sources, such as supplementary information in financial statement notes.

Given a lack of decision usefulness, what is the purpose of SFAS 130? It seems that the standard represents a political compromise between investors' and managers' interests. Investors benefit from the decision usefulness of fair value accounting. Managers seem willing to accept fair value accounting providing that resulting unrealized gains and losses are excluded from net income.

13.6.3 Summary

There seems little doubt that a standard such as SFAS 115 is decision useful to investors—for example, recall our reference to the studies of Barth, Beaver, and Landsman (1996), and Barth (1994) in Section 7.5.2 that found a securities market response to fair values of banks' loans and investments portfolios. Furthermore, the reduction in information asymmetry between management and investors that results from investors' enhanced knowledge of security values, and from reductions in gains trading, will improve the working of securities markets, with consequent social benefits. However, while these are valuable improvements, it should be clear that much more is required if a standard is to succeed. An acceptable compromise between the interests of affected constituencies is also essential. With respect to SFAS 130, the compromise is to exclude from net income unrealized gains and losses over which management has relatively little control and which are uninformative about manager effort.

13.7 Rules-Based Versus Principles-Based Accounting Standards

The practice versus theory vignette above leads to the distinction between **rules-based** and **principles-based accounting standards**. Rules-based standards, of which SFAS 115 is an example, attempt to lay down detailed rules for how to account. For example, an objective of SFAS 115 was to eliminate gains trading. However, as the vignette illustrates, it is difficult to lay down detailed rules to deal with every possible situation (for another illustration, see Chapter 7, Problem 7). An alternative to detailed rules is for accounting standards to lay down general principles only, and rely on auditor professional judgement to ensure that application of the standards is not misleading. Thus, if the general rule is that gains trading should be eliminated, the auditor will object if the manager appears to use gains trading for opportunistic purposes.

In this regard, the SEC, in a 2003 study, "Study Pursuant to Section 108(d) of the Sarbanes-Oxley Act . . . ," recommends that the FASB adopt a principles-based approach to accounting standards. Note that such an approach puts more weight on the Conceptual Framework (see Section 3.8) to provide a framework for professional judgement. The SEC study is in broad agreement with the FASB's own 2002 "Proposal for a Principles-Based Approach to U.S. Standard-Setting." The FASB is currently working on ways to implement this approach.

Principles-based accounting standards also raise the important ethical issues discussed in Section 1.3, since there is increased emphasis on the accountant/auditor's judgement. Professional accounting bodies must strive to ensure that their members put longer-run public interests (e.g., securities and managerial labour markets should work well) ahead of shorter-run interests of clients (e.g., opportunistic earnings management). Of course, professional accounting bodies already do this, through codes of professional conduct, discipline committees, and due process in standard setting. Nevertheless, in view of recent reporting failures as described in Section 1.2, even greater efforts to increase the transparency of the accounting profession are warranted, since enforcement becomes more critical and delicate in a judgement-based system.

In this regard, the organization of the standard-setting body itself has ethical implications. In Canada, the standard setting body (AcSB) and the discipline-enforcing body are both wings of the same professional organization (CICA). This creates at least the appearance of a moral hazard problem, since the body responsible for financial accounting standards is associated through the professional organization with the body responsible for enforcement. In contrast, the FASB and IASB are distinct from a professional accounting body.

13.8 Criteria for Standard Setting

We have seen that there are a number of factors that affect the process of standard setting. Standards should be decision useful, but they should also be acceptable to other constituencies—in particular, management. This puts the standard setter in a conflict situation and it is difficult to predict what an acceptable resolution of this conflict will be. Nevertheless, we now suggest some criteria that should be kept in mind when trying to understand standard setting.

13.8.1 Decision Usefulness

The criterion of decision usefulness underlies the information and measurement perspectives on financial reporting, and the empirical capital market studies. Recall that the more informative about future firm performance, that is, the less noisy, is an information system the stronger will be investor reaction to information produced by the system, other things equal. Thus, empirical evidence that security prices respond to accounting information suggests that investors find that information useful.

This suggests that a necessary condition for the success of a new standard is that it be decision useful. Of course, this can be hard to assess beforehand, since the market has not yet had a chance to respond to the standard. Nevertheless, the theory of rational investor decision-making can be used to predict decision usefulness. For example, Bandyopadhyay (1994) predicted that oil and gas companies' earnings reported under successful efforts were more informative than under full cost accounting, and provided evidence to this effect. Also, as argued in Chapter 6, the incorporation of fair values into financial reporting will increase investor decision usefulness to the extent that this tightens up the linkage between current and future performance.

However, while decision usefulness may be a necessary criterion for a successful standard, it is not sufficient to ensure success. We saw in Section 5.6 that, because of certain public good characteristics of accounting information, we cannot be sure that the standard that has the greatest decision usefulness is best for society. Since investors do not directly pay for accounting information, they may "overuse" it. Thus, a standard could appear to be decision useful, yet society would be worse off because the costs of producing the information were not taken into account. Furthermore, changes in standards can impose contracting costs on firms and their managers. In effect, as implied by the fundamental problem of financial accounting theory, standard setters must consider other criteria than decision usefulness.

13.8.2 Reduction of Information Asymmetry

We saw in Section 12.3.3 that market forces operate to motivate management and investors to generate information. Standard setters should be aware of these forces and take advantage of them, to the extent possible, to reduce the need for standards. Unfortunately, market forces alone cannot ensure that the right amount of information is produced. As we saw in Section 12.4, one of the reasons for this is information asymmetry. Consequently, as suggested by Lev (1988), standard setters should use reduction of information asymmetry in capital and managerial labour markets as a criterion for new standards.

While the public good characteristics of accounting information complicate the ability of decision usefulness to guide standard setters, as just pointed out, these same characteristics mean that standards can be quite effective in reducing information asymmetry. That is, since the use of financial accounting information by one individual does not destroy it for use by another, expanding disclosure by means of standards works towards a fair distribution of the benefits of information to all investors. These benefits are available *directly* to those who are willing and able to use the expanded information (as in the case of Bill Cautious in Example 3.1), or *indirectly* to other investors through the price protection mechanism of efficient securities markets (Section 4.3.1). Consequently, reduction of information asymmetry improves the operation of markets, since investors will perceive investing as more of a level playing field. This will expand market liquidity, reduce the "lemons" phenomenon, and generally produce social benefits from better-working markets.

Standard setters should be aware of the informativeness of market price itself as a conveyor of information. As discussed in Section 4.4, the efficient market price of a firm's shares reflects, with noise, what is publicly known about that firm. Furthermore, more is publicly known about large firms than small firms to the extent they are in the public eye and have analyst and media following. Consequently, we would expect the extent of information asymmetry between managers and investors to be greater for small firms, suggesting that standard setters should require at least as high disclosure standards for small firms as for large firms. In this regard, it is interesting that while the *CICA Handbook* applies to all profit-oriented enterprises, certain disclosure exemptions for small firms are allowed, for example, with respect to earnings per share for firms whose shares are not publicly traded (paragraph 3500.02).

However, it should be noted that reduction of information asymmetry as a criterion is again a necessary condition for a successful standard but not a sufficient one. Just as decision useful information has a cost, so does reduction of information asymmetry. Consequently, it is hard to know when standards to reduce information asymmetry cease to be cost-effective.

13.8.3 Economic Consequences of New Standards

As mentioned above, one of the costs of a new standard is the cost imposed on firms and managers to meet that standard. This goes beyond the out-of-pocket costs of producing the newly mandated information. Costs are also created by contract rigidities, as in an increased probability of violating debt covenants, and effects on the level and volatility of managers' future bonus streams. These costs can affect operating and financial policies. Furthermore, to the extent that new standards require the release of proprietary information, firms' future profitability can be unfavourably or favourably affected by the reduction of competitive advantage.

The reduction in managers' freedom to choose from different accounting policies that frequently results when a new standard is implemented is also a source of economic consequences. We argued in Section 12.3.5 that firms can signal inside information by accounting policy choice. Also, earnings management can reveal inside information, as discussed in Section 11.5. Obviously, if accounting policy choice is constrained, there is a reduction in the extent to which these private forces for information production can operate.

Finally, the Darrough and Stoughton model in Section 9.3 suggests that the greater the degree of competition in an industry the better the disclosure, other things equal. As a result, there may be less need for accounting standards in some industries than in others.

These considerations suggest that standard setters should weigh the possible economic consequences of new standards as an important source of cost that will affect both the need for the standard and the willingness of constituencies to accept it. Of course, it may be that the economic consequences of a new standard will be overstated during the debate leading to the standard. For example, would banks really stop long-term lending if their long-term investments have to be fully marked-to-market? Probably not, but the costs to banks of long-term lending would increase and, as a result, the charges to borrowers would likely rise.

13.8.4 The Political Aspects of Standard Setting

Economic consequences leads directly to our last criterion, namely the political aspects of standard setting. Standard setters, in effect, must engineer a consensus sufficiently strong that even a constituency that does not like a new standard will nevertheless go along with it. This is the "delicate balancing" act that Zeff referred to (see Section 8.2). As should be apparent from Sections 13.3 and 13.4, the structure and due process of standard setting bodies, both nationally and internationally, is designed to encourage such a consensus.

We conclude that the standard setting process seems most consistent with the interest group theory of regulation. Certainly, technical, and even theoretical, correctness is not sufficient to ensure the success of a standard. As we argued in Section 8.3, failure to record an expense for ESOs overstates net income and reduces the comparability of reported earnings across firms. Yet the FASB's 1993 exposure draft proposing fair value accounting for ESOs met with such resistance that it had to be withdrawn, and its 2005 expensing standard encountered similar resistance (see problem 4). While careful attention to due process may be time-consuming, such attention seems essential if costly and embarrassing retractions are to be minimized. Too many of these will threaten the existence of the standard-setting body itself.

13.8.5 Summary

Accounting standard setters can be guided by decision usefulness and reduction of information asymmetry. However, these criteria are not sufficient to ensure successful standard setting. The legitimate interests of management and other constituencies also need to be considered, as does careful attention to due process. Because of the fundamental problem of financial accounting theory, it seems that the actual process of standard setting is better described by the interest group theory of regulation than by the public interest theory.

13.9 Conclusions and Summing Up

In a sense, this whole book comes to a focus on standard setting. We saw, in Chapter 2, that under ideal conditions accounting and reporting standards are not needed, since there is only one way to account, on the basis of the present values of firms' future cash flows. Indeed, under ideal conditions one can question whether financial accounting is needed at all.

Fortunately, in view of our conclusion in Section 2.6 that accountants would not be needed under ideal conditions, such conditions do not exist. As a result, financial accounting becomes much more challenging. Information asymmetry is a major source of this challenge.

We have seen two major types of information asymmetry. The first is adverse selection. That is, managers and other insiders typically know more than outside investors about the state and prospects of the firm. Here, the accounting challenge is to convey information from inside to outside the firm, thereby improving investor decision-making, limiting the ability of insiders to exploit their information advantage, and enhancing the operation of capital markets.

The second type of information asymmetry is moral hazard. That is, the effort exerted by a manager is unobservable to shareholders and lenders in all but the smallest firms. Here, the accounting challenge is to provide an informative measure of managerial performance. This enables incentive contracts to motivate manager effort, protect lenders, and inform the managerial labour market.

It is important to realize that the accounting system that best meets the first challenge is unlikely to best meet the second, so that actual financial reporting represents a compromise between the two. Specifically, investors need decision-relevant information to help them predict future firm performance. This implies fair value-based information since current fair values are generally the best predictors of future values. However, problems of volatility and possible subjectivity of fair values reduce the informativeness of net income about manager performance. To the extent that historical cost accounting or, more generally, conservative accounting is less subject to these problems, it can be argued that it better meets the challenge of enabling efficient contracts. Consequently, fair value- and historical cost-based accounting must be traded off.

It is this need for financial reporting to fulfill a dual role of meeting investors' information needs and the needs of efficient contracting that creates the fundamental problem of financial accounting theory. Investors, including securities commissions acting on their behalf, push for additional information, including fair value information. Management pushes the other way when they perceive that proposed standards will affect their flexibility under the contracts they have entered into, inhibit their ability to credibly communicate with the market through accounting policy choice, reduce their ability to hide poor performance through opportunistic earnings management, or choose a tradeoff between full disclosure to investors and the agency costs that are thus created. As mentioned, the standard setter must then seek a compromise between these conflicting interests. The structure of standard-setting bodies is designed to facilitate such a compromise.

With the increasing globalization of commerce, including securities markets, the need for international accounting standards will expand. However, the difficulties of standard setting will also increase. In addition to investor-manager conflict, new constituencies will arise representing different levels of economic development, different business practices, and different cultures. Standard-setting bodies will have to adapt to take these additional challenges into account.

Questions and Problems

1. Contrast the public interest and interest group theories of regulation with respect to:
   a. The role of the regulatory body.
   b. Their implications for the amount of the regulated commodity or service to be supplied. (CGA-Canada)

2. Refer to the article "FASB Moves Closer to Forcing Banks to Value Securities Near Market Prices" (*The Wall Street Journal*, September 11, 1992), reproduced in Section 13.6.1.

   Required
   a. Describe how the structure of standard setting is designed to facilitate the resolution of constituency conflicts such as those described in the article.
   b. Explain why a more-than-majority vote by FASB members is required to pass a new standard.

3. The Australian Accounting Standards Board (AASB) has decided to adopt IASB accounting standards, effective January 1, 2005. What are some of the costs and benefits to a country such as Australia of adopting IASB standards? Should Canada do the same thing?

4. In March 2004, the FASB issued an exposure draft of a standard proposing the expensing of ESOs. However, the proposal faced powerful opponents. These include large corporations such as Texas Instruments, Cisco Systems Inc., Intel Corporation, and Sun Microsystems, Inc., all of which are heavy ESO users. Also, bills have been introduced in the U.S. Congress to override or water down the expensing requirement. For example, one such bill would limit ESO expensing to the firm's top five officers. The outcome of these bills remains to be seen, since Congress has the power to override the FASB.

   Objections to the proposed standard are similar to those raised when the FASB attempted to implement a similar standard in 1994. These include the confusing of investors, damage to job creation and innovation, damage to the competitive position of U.S. industry, and unreliability of fair value ESO measures.

The proposed standard also has powerful proponents, including some congressional leaders and Chairman Greenspan of the Federal Reserve. Also, despite the opposing arguments, by early 2004 almost 500 U.S. corporations had voluntarily decided to expense their ESOs.

Required
a. In theory, what are the advantages of ESOs as a compensation device?
b. In practice, during the boom of the late 1900s, what were the negative effects of ESOs on some managers' incentives and actions?
c. Are ESOs an expense? Explain why or why not.
d. With what theory of regulation are the claims of opponents of the proposed standard most consistent? With what theory are the FASB's actions in implementing the new standard most consistent? Explain your answers.
e. Suppose that you are a member of the FASB. Evaluate a proposal to expense ESOs in relation to the four criteria suggested in Section 13.8.

5. The article here reproduced from *The New York Times* (October 12, 1997), describes pressures to "kill" the FASB, and hand its duties over to the SEC. The reason for the pressure seems to be due to SFAS 133 (see Sections 7.3.3 and 7.3.4), which requires firms to mark derivative instruments to market.

Politicians Threaten Accounting Integrity

Sixty years ago, an intense battle was waged inside the young Securities and Exchange Commission. There was no consensus about how to fix what all agreed was the deplorable accounting that was showing up in corporate financial reports.

On one side was the commission's new chairman, William O. Douglas, who thought the commission should promulgate its own standards. On the other was the S.E.C.'s chief accountant, Carman C. Blough, who thought the Government could not do a good job and wanted it left to the private sector, with S.E.C. oversight. On a 3–2 vote of the commission in 1938, Douglas lost.

Blough then persuaded the American Institute of Certified Public Accountants that it needed to get moving. After hearing Blough give a harsh speech noting more than 30 questionable accounting practices that had been approved by accountants, the institute set up a Committee on Accounting Procedure to make rules. That body was replaced by the Accounting Principles Board in 1959 and by the Financial Accounting Standards Board in 1973, as the rule makers gained more power and independence.

The arrangements have sometimes been cumbersome and slow. It has been more than a decade since the board took up the question of accounting for derivatives, and only now is it poised to issue a rule. But the process has produced the best accounting anywhere and helped to make New York the financial capital of the world. It would be hard for the S.E.C. to match the detailed expertise of the F.A.S.B. and its staff.

Nonetheless, a campaign is on to kill the F.A.S.B. The banks are furious over the new derivatives rule, which would force users of derivatives to record the market value of those instruments in their financial reports. The banks say the rule will confuse

continued ➔

investors and scare off some companies that would benefit from using derivatives. They have lobbied hard in Congress, and both the House and Senate have held hearings to bash the F.A.S.B. on the issue. Last week, John Reed, the chairman of Citicorp, called for abolishing the F.A.S.B. and transferring its duties to the S.E.C.

Mr. Reed's suggestion, as it happened, was published in a letter to the editor of the *Wall Street Journal* on the same day that the Senate killed campaign finance reform. The sad reality today is that injecting politics into accounting carries with it a real risk regarding accounting integrity. It is not hard to imagine a future S.E.C. budget being held up by a Congressman, or confirmation of a future S.E.C. chairman delayed by a senator, amid quiet negotiations regarding the need to change an accounting rule that threatens—quite unfairly, of course—to penalize the profits, and perhaps hurt investors and employees, of a company that has been a substantial supporter of the legislator.

The F.A.S.B.'s new derivatives rule is not perfect, but it is an improvement over current practice. If need be, it can be changed later. But the wisdom of that rule is much less important than the preservation of a process that has worked well without a hint of impropriety. If the politicians succeed in killing this rule, as they did with an earlier proposal to change accounting for employee stock options, it is hard to see how the F.A.S.B. will survive. And that would pose a real threat to continued investor confidence.

It is time for businesses, even those that don't like the derivatives proposal, to tell the politicians to leave accounting alone.

ALREADY THE OLDEST

Rule makers for American accounting:

Committee on Accounting Procedure

1938–1959	*21 years*

Accounting Principles Board

1959–1973	*14 years*

Financial Accounting Standard Board

1973–present	*24 years*

Source: Copyright © 1997 by the New York Times Co. Reprinted by permission.

Required

a. Use the interest group theory of regulation to explain the reasons for the campaign to kill the FASB. Why would certain bank executives prefer accounting standards to be set by the SEC?

b. Use the public interest theory of regulation to evaluate the costs and benefits of moving financial accounting standard setting to the SEC. Include in your answer an evaluation of the structure of the FASB. Also consider the effects of such a move on investor confidence in capital markets.

6. IAS 39, *Financial Instruments: Recognition and Measurement*, requires companies using IASB standards to fair-value many financial instruments including derivatives, effective January 1, 2005. This standard moves the accounting for financial instruments into substantial agreement with SFAS 115 and 133, and pending standards in Canada. It is an example of the ongoing movement towards international harmonization of accounting standards. However, this movement is not complete. For example, the IASB does not as yet have a standard on other comprehensive income. Instead, unrealized gains and losses from fair valuing available-for-sale financial instruments and cash flow hedges are reported in a separate section of shareholders' equity.

IAS 39 has met substantial opposition from the European Union (EU), which has required its members to adopt IASB standards effective in 2005. The opposition arises from concerns of European banks and insurance companies, who claim that fair value accounting will introduce volatility into their financial statements. The EU has threatened to exempt banks and insurance companies from IAS 39, but has held off while encouraging the IASB and the EU banks and insurance companies to discuss a possible compromise. Subsequently, the EU approved a watered-down version of IAS 39. However, this version is controversial, and efforts continue to find a compromise more in line with the original standard.

Required
   a. Why would banks and insurance companies be concerned about financial statement volatility introduced by IAS 39? Consider both the balance sheet and income statement in your answer.
   b. As international harmonization of accounting standards progresses, there will be increasing pressure on the SEC to accept either FASB or IASB standards for firms under its jurisdiction. At present, EU firms with shares traded in the Unites States must present a reconciliation between their financial statements and financial statements prepared under FASB standards. For example, they must show what their net income would be under FASB rules. What would the costs and benefits to firms and investors be if the SEC was to drop its requirements for reconciliation, and accept either FASB or IASB standards? In your answer, consider the possibility of a "race to the bottom."

7. El Paso Electric Company is a U.S. electric power generating company incorporated in the state of Texas. In its December 31, 2003 annual report, El Paso reported net income for the year of $60,251 (thousand). To this, it added Other Comprehensive Income of $4,808, which included $6,647 unrealized gains, net of tax, for the year on marketable securities. The company's comprehensive income for the year was $65,059.

Required
   a. Explain the nature of the $6,647 unrealized gains on marketable securities. Why is it not included in net income for the year?

b. As an investor, which earnings measure, net income or comprehensive income, is most useful to you in deciding whether to buy, hold, or sell El Paso shares? Explain.

c. As a member of the Compensation Committee of El Paso's Board of Directors, which performance measure, net income or comprehensive income, is most useful to you in deciding on the amount of cash bonuses for senior officers for 2003? Explain.

d. A former member of the FASB stated that if unrealized gains and losses on available-for-sale marketable securities had to be included in net income, rather than in other comprehensive income, SFAS 115 would not have been a viable accounting standard. Use the four criteria for standard setting given in Section 13.8 to explain this statement. Consider both the interests of investors and managers in your answer.

8. In its 1999 *Annual Report*, Scotiabank's auditors qualified their audit report. The problem was with the bank's provision for credit losses. During 1999, Scotiabank decided to increase its general provision for credit losses on loans receivable by $700 million. This was in addition to a specific provision for loan losses on identified problem loans. The general provision applies to loans that have not as yet been specifically identified as in arrears.

Under GAAP, the $700 increase in the general provision should be charged as an expense of the year. However, Scotiabank obtained permission from the Superintendent of Financial Institutions of Canada (OSFI) to charge $550 million of this amount ($314 million after tax) directly to retained earnings.

As a result, Scotiabank reported net income for 1999 of $1,551 million. Net incomes for 1998 and 1997 were $1,394 million and $1, 514 million, respectively.

This direct charge to retained earnings was criticized in the financial media. For example, Eric Reguly, in *The Globe and Mail*, December 7, 1999, called it "an accounting sleight-of-hand that has never been used by the Big Five Canadian banks." Reguly describes the objections of the OSC which, however, could do nothing because the federal Bank Act (administered by OSFI) overrides the Ontario Securities Act. OSFI permitted the direct charge, according to Reguly, because it wanted banks to have a "thicker safety cushion."

Required

a. Use the public interest theory of regulation to justify OSFI's permission for the direct charge to retained earnings.

b. Use the interest group theory of regulation to explain OSFI's permission for the direct charge.

c. Given that the treatment was fully disclosed in the Notes to Scotiabank's *Annual Report*, in the auditors' report, and in the media, how do you think the securities market would respond to this treatment?

9. Refer to Theory in Practice 13.1 concerning SFASs 130 and 115 in Section 13.6.2.

Required

a. Why does SFAS 115 require unrealized gains and losses on available-for-sale securities to be included in OCI rather than in net income?

b. If securities markets are fully efficient, would a strategy of trying to disguise gains trading by reporting OCI in a statement of changes in shareholders' equity rather than below net income work? Explain why or why not.

c. If securities markets are not fully efficient, would such a strategy work? Explain.

d. You are the auditor of a firm using this strategy. You object to it, and management responds that the strategy is clearly in accordance with GAAP since SFAS 130 allows OCI to be included in a separate statement apart from net income. Furthermore, if you do not accept it you will be forced to resign as auditor. This will also result in your loss of systems and tax consulting work for the client. Would you resign? Explain your decision.

Notes

1. The need for reconciliation is reduced somewhat for large Canadian firms that report to the SEC due to the Multi-jurisdictional Disclosure System, which allows firms to file SEC reports using the documents they file in Canada, and vice versa.

2. For "International Accounting Standard." Such standards are now called International Financial Reporting Standards (IFRS).

3. For another gains trading strategy, which exploits the fact that realized gains on available-for-sale securities are transferred from other comprehensive income to net income under SFAS 130, see problem 9 of this chapter.

Bibliography

ABARBANELL, J.S. and B.J. BUSHEE, "Fundamental Analysis, Future Earnings, and Stock Prices," *Journal of Accounting Research* (Spring 1997), pp. 1–24.

ABARBANELL, J.S., W.N. LANEN, and R.E. VERRECCHIA, "Analysts' Forecasts as Proxies for Investor Beliefs in Empirical Research," *Journal of Accounting and Economics* (July 1995), pp. 31–60.

ABARBANELL, J. and R. LEHAVY, "Can Stock Recommendations Predict Earnings Management and Analysts' Earnings Forecast Errors?" *Journal of Accounting Research* (March 2003), pp. 1–31.

ABOODY, D., M. BARTH, and R. KASZNIK, "SFAS 123 Stock-Based Compensation Expense and Equity Market Values," *The Accounting Review* (April 2004), pp. 251–275.

ABOODY, D. and R. KASZNIK, "CEO Stock Option Awards and the Timing of Corporate Voluntary Disclosures," *Journal of Accounting and Economics* (February 2000), pp. 73–100.

ACKERT, L.F., and B.F. SMITH, "Stock Price Volatility, Ordinary Dividends, and Other Cash Flows to Shareholders," *The Journal of Finance* (September 1993), pp. 1147–1160.

AGGARWAL, R. K., and A. A. SAMWICK, "Executive Compensation, Strategic Competition, and Relative Performance Evaluation: Theory and Evidence," *The Journal of Finance* (December 1999), pp. 1999–2043.

AHMED, A. S., B. BILLINGS, M.S. HARRIS, and R. M. MORTON, "Accounting Conservatism and Cost of Debt," working paper, School of Management, Syracuse University (March 2000).

AKERLOF, G.A., "The Market for 'Lemons': Quality Uncertainty and the Market Mechanism," *Quarterly Journal of Economics* (August 1970), pp. 488–500.

ALCHIAN, A., "Uncertainty, Evolution and Economic Theory," *Journal of Political Economy* (June 1950), pp. 211–221.

AMERICAN ACCOUNTING ASSOCIATION COMMITTEE TO PREPARE A STATEMENT OF BASIC ACCOUNTING THEORY, "*A Statement of Basic Accounting Theory*" (American Accounting Association, 1966).

AMERICAN ACCOUNTING ASSOCIATION FINANCIAL ACCOUNTING STANDARDS COMMITTEE, "Equity Valuation Models and Measuring Goodwill Impairment" *Accounting Horizons* (June 2001), pp. 161–170.

AMERICAN INSTITUTE OF CERTIFIED PUBLIC ACCOUNTANTS STUDY GROUP ON THE OBJECTIVES OF FINANCIAL STATEMENTS, *Objectives of Financial Statements* (New York, NY: AICPA, 1973).

AMIR, E., "The Market Valuation of Accounting Information: The Case of Postretirement Benefits Other Than Pensions," *The Accounting Review* (October 1993), pp. 703–724.

ANTLE, R. and A. SMITH, "An Empirical Examination of the Relative Performance Evaluation of Corporate Executives," *Journal of Accounting Research* (Spring 1986), pp. 1–39.

ARROW, K. J., *Social Choice and Individual Values*, Cowles Foundation Monograph (New York, NY: John Wiley, 1963).

ARYA, A., J. FELLINGHAM, and J. GLOVER, "Teams, Repeated Tasks and Implicit Incentives," *Journal of Accounting and Economics* (May 1997), pp. 7–30.

ARYA, A., J. GLOVER, and S. SUNDER, "Earnings Management and the Revelation Principle," *Review of Accounting Studies* (1998), pp. 7–34.

BABER, W.R., S. JANAKIRAMAN, and S-H. KANG, "Investment Opportunities and the Structure of Executive Compensation," *Journal of Accounting and Economics* (June 1996), pp. 297–318.

BABER, W.R., S-H. KANG, and K.R. KUMAR, "The Explanatory Power of Earnings Levels vs. Earnings Changes in the Context of Executive Compensation," *The Accounting Review* (October 1999), pp. 459–472.

BAIMAN, S. and R. E. VERRECCHIA, "The Relation Among Capital Markets, Financial Disclosure, Production Efficiency, and Insider Trading," *Journal of Accounting Research* (Spring 1996), pp. 1–22.

BALL, R. and E. BARTOV, "How Naive Is the Stock Market's Use of Earnings Information?" *Journal of Accounting and Economics* (June 1996), pp. 319–337.

BALL, R. and P. BROWN, "An Empirical Evaluation of Accounting Income Numbers," *Journal of Accounting Research* (Autumn 1968), pp. 159–178.

BALL, R. and S.P. KOTHARI, "Nonstationary Expected Returns: Implications for Tests of Market Efficiency and Serial Correlation in Returns," *Journal of Financial Economics* (1989), pp. 51–74.

BANDYOPADHYAY, S., "Market Reaction to Earnings Announcements of SE and FC Firms in the Oil and Gas Industry," *The Accounting Review* (October 1994), pp. 657–674.

BANKER, R.D. and S. DATAR, "Sensitivity, Precision, and Linear Aggregation of Signals for Performance Evaluation," *Journal of Accounting Research* (Spring 1989), pp. 21–39.

BARNEA, A., J. RONEN, and S. SADAN, "Classificatory Smoothing of Income with Extraordinary Items," *The Accounting Review* (January 1976), pp. 110–122.

BARRON, O., J. PRATT, and J.D. STICE, "Misstatement Direction, Litigation Risk, and Planned Audit Investment," *Journal of Accounting Research* (December 2001), pp. 449–462.

BARTH, M.E., "Fair Value Accounting: Evidence from Investment Securities and the Market Value of Banks," *The Accounting Review* (January 1994), pp. 1–25.

BARTH, M.E., G. CLINCH, and T. SHIBANO, "Market Effects of Recognition and Disclosure," *Journal of Accounting Research* (September 2003), pp. 581–609.

BARTH, M.E., J.A.ELLIOTT, and M.W. FINN, "Market Rewards Associated with Patterns of Increasing

Earnings," *Journal of Accounting Research* (Autumn 1999), pp. 387–413.

BARTH, M.E., W.H. BEAVER, and W.R. LANDSMAN, "Value-Relevance of Banks' Fair Value Disclosures under SFAS 107," *The Accounting Review* (October 1996), pp. 513–537.

BARTON, J., "Does the Use of Financial Derivatives Affect Earnings Management Decisions?" *The Accounting Review* (January 2001), pp. 1–26.

BARTOV, E., D. GIVOLY and C. HAYN, "The Rewards to Meeting or Beating Earnings Expectations," *Journal of Accounting and Economics* (June 2002), pp. 173–204.

BARTOV, E. and P. MOHANRAM, "Private Information, Earnings Manipulation, and Executive Stock Option Exercise," *The Accounting Review* (October 2004), pp. 889–920.

BARTOV, E., S. RADHAKRISHNAN, and S. KRINSKY, "Investor Sophistication and Patterns in Stock Returns after Earnings Announcements," *The Accounting Review* (January 2000), pp. 43–63.

BASU, S., "The Conservation Principle and the Asymmetric Timeliness of Earnings," *Journal of Accounting and Economics* (December 1997), pp. 3–37.

BCE INC., *1997 Annual Report* (Montreal, QC: BCE Inc., 1997).

BEAVER, W.H. and J. DEMSKI, "The Nature of Income Measurement," *The Accounting Review* (January 1979), pp. 38–46.

BEAVER, W.H. and W.R. LANDS-MAN, *The Incremental Information Content of FAS 33 Disclosures* (Stamford, CT: FASB, 1983).

BEAVER, W.H., *Financial Reporting: An Accounting Revolution*, Second Edition (Englewood Cliffs, NJ: Prentice Hall, 1989).

BEAVER, W.H., P. KETTLER, and M. SCHOLES, "The Association Between Market-Determined and Accounting-Determined Risk Measures," *The Accounting Review* (October 1970), pp. 654–682.

BEAVER, W.H., R. CLARKE, and W.F. WRIGHT, "The Association Between Unsystematic Security Returns and the Magnitude of Earnings Forecast Errors," *Journal of Accounting Research* (Autumn 1979), pp. 316–340.

BEAVER, W.H., "The Information Content of Annual Earnings Announcements," *Journal of Accounting Research* (Supplement 1968), pp. 67–92.

BEAVER, W.H., "What Should Be the FASB's Objectives?" *The Journal of Accountancy* (August 1973), pp. 49–56.

BEGLEY, J., and G.A. FELTHAM, "The Relation between Market Values, Earnings Forecasts, and Reported Earnings," *Contemporary Accounting Research* (Spring 2002), pp. 1–48.

BENSTON, G.J., "Required Disclosure and the Stock Market: An Evaluation of the Securities Exchange Act of 1934," *American Economic Review* (March 1973), pp. 132–155.

BERGER, P.G. and R. HANN, "The Impact of SFAS 131 on Information and Monitoring," *Journal of Accounting Research* (May 2003), pp. 163–223.

BERNARD, V.L. and D.J. SKINNER, "What Motivates Managers' Choice of Discretionary Accruals?" *Journal of Accounting and Economics* (August-December 1996), pp. 313–325.

BERNARD, V.L. and J. THOMAS, "Post-Earnings Announcement Drift: Delayed Price Reaction or Risk Premium?" *Journal of Accounting Research* (Supplement 1989), pp. 1–36.

BERNARD, V.L. and R.G. RULAND, "The Incremental Information Content of Historical Cost and Current Cost Income Numbers: Time Series Analysis for 1962–1980," *The Accounting Review* (October 1987), pp. 707–722.

BERNARD, V.L., "Capital Markets Research in Accounting During the 1980s: A Critical Review," working paper, University of Michigan, 1989.

BERNARD, V.L., "Cross-Sectional Dependance and Problems in Inference in Market-Based Accounting Research," *Journal of Accounting Research* (Spring 1987), pp. 1–48.

BLACK, F. and M. SCHOLES, "The Pricing of Options and Corporate Liabilities," *Journal of Political Economy* (May/June 1973), pp. 637–654.

BLAZENKO, G. and W.R. SCOTT, "A Model of Standard Setting in Auditing," *Contemporary Accounting Research* (Fall 1986), pp. 68–92.

BOLAND, L.A. and I.M. GORDON, "Criticizing Positive Accounting Theory," *Contemporary Accounting Research* (Fall 1992), pp. 147–170.

BOTOSAN, C.A. and M.A. PLUM-LEE, "A Re-examination of Disclosure Level and the Expected Cost of Equity Capital," *Journal of Accounting Research* (March 2002), pp. 21–40.

BOTOSAN, C.A. and M.A. PLUM-LEE, "Stock Option Expense: The Sword of Damocles Revealed," *The Accounting Review* (December 2001), pp. 311–327.

BOWEN, R.M., L. DuCHARME, and D. SHORES, "Stakeholders' Implicit Claims and Accounting Method Choice," *Journal of Accounting and Economics* (December 1995), pp. 255–295.

BOYLE, P. and P. BOYLE, *Derivatives: The Tools That Changed Finance* (London: Risk Books, 2001).

BROWN, L.D., and J.C.Y. HAN, "Do Stock Prices Fully Reflect the Implications of Current Earnings for Future Earnings for *ARI* Firms?" *Journal of Accounting Research* (Spring 2000), pp. 149–164.

BROWN, L.D., R.L. HAGERMAN, P.A. GRIFFIN, and M. ZMIJEWSKI, "Security Analyst Superiority Relative to Univariate Time-Series Models in Forecasting Quarterly Earnings," *Journal of Accounting and Economics* (April 1987), pp. 61–87.

BROWN, R.G. and K.S. JOHNSTON, *Paciolo on Accounting* (New York, NY: McGraw-Hill, 1963).

BROWN, S., K. LO, and T. LYS, "Use of R^2 in Accounting Research: Measuring Changes in Value Relevance Over the Last Four Decades," *Journal of Accounting and Economics* (December 1999), pp. 83–115.

BROWN, S.J. and J.B. WARNER, "Measuring Security Price Performance," *Journal of Financial Economics* (September 1980), pp. 205–258.

BURGSTAHLER, D. and I. DICHEV, "Earnings Management to Avoid Earnings Decreases and Losses," *Journal of Accounting and Economics* (December 1997), pp. 99–126.

BUSHMAN, R.M. and R.J. INDJE-JIKIAN, "Accounting Income, Stock

Price and Managerial Compensation," *Journal of Accounting and Economics* (January/April/July 1993), pp. 3–23.

BUSHMAN, R.M., R.J. INDJEJIKIAN, and A. SMITH, "CEO Compensation: The Role of Individual Performance Evaluation," *Journal of Accounting and Economics* (April 1996), pp. 161–193.

CALLEN, J.J. and D. SEGAL, "Do Accruals Drive Firm-Level Stock Returns? A Variance Decomposition Analysis," *Journal of Accounting Research* (June 2004), pp. 527–560.

CANADIAN INSTITUTE OF CHARTERED ACCOUNTANTS, *CICA Handbook* (Toronto, ON: CICA, 1998).

CHIEFTAIN INTERNATIONAL, INC., *2000 Annual Report* (Edmonton, AB: Chieftain International, Inc., 2000)

CHRISTENSEN, J., "Communication in Agencies," *The Bell Journal of Economics* (Autumn 1981), pp. 661–674.

CHRISTENSEN, P.O., J.S. DEMSKI, and H. FRIMOR, "Accounting Policies in Agencies with Moral Hazard," *Journal of Accounting Research* (September 2002), pp. 1071–1090.

CHRISTIE, A.A. and J. ZIMMER-MAN, "Efficient and Opportunistic Choices of Accounting Procedures: Corporate Control Contests," *The Accounting Review* (October 1994), pp. 539–566.

CLARKSON, P., A. DONTOH, G.D. RICHARDSON, and S. SEFCIK, "The Voluntary Inclusion of Earnings Forecasts in IPO Prospectuses," *Contemporary Accounting Research* (Spring 1992), pp. 601–626.

COLLINS, D.W. and S.P. KOTHARI, "An Analysis of the Intertemporal and Cross-Sectional Determinants of Earnings Response Coefficients," *Journal of Accounting and Economics* (July 1989), pp. 143–181.

COURTEAU, L., J. KAO, and G.D. RICHARDSON, "Equity Valuation Employing the Ideal versus Ad Hoc Terminal Value Expression," *Contemporary Accounting Research* (Winter 2001), pp. 625–661.

CRAWFORD, V.P. and J. SOBEL, "Strategic Information Transmission," *Econometrica* (November 1982), pp. 1431–1451.

DANIEL, K.D. and S. TITMAN, "Market Efficiency in an Irrational World," *Financial Analysts' Journal* (1999), pp. 28–40.

DANIEL, K.D., D. HIRSHLEIFER, and A. SUBRAHMANYAM, "Investor Psychology and Security Market Investor Under- and Over-Reactions," *Journal of Finance* (December 1998), pp. 1839–1885.

DANIEL, K.D., D. HIRSHLEIFER, and A. SUBRAHMANYAM, "Overconfidence, Arbitrage, and Equilibrium Asset Pricing," *The Journal of Finance* (2001), pp. 921–965.

DARROUGH, M.N., "Disclosure Policy and Competition: Cournot vs. Bertrand," *The Accounting Review* (July 1993), pp. 534–561.

DARROUGH, M.N. and N.M. STOUGHTON, "Financial Disclosure Policy in an Entry Game," *Journal of Accounting and Economics* (January 1990), pp. 219–243.

DATAR, S.M., G.A. FELTHAM, and J.S. HUGHES, "The Role of Audits and

Audit Quality in Valuing New Issues," *Journal of Accounting and Economics* (March 1991), pp. 3–49.

DATAR, S.M., S.C. KULP, and R.A. LAMBERT, "Balancing Performance Measures," *Journal of Accounting Research* (June 2001), pp. 75–92.

DeANGELO, H., L.E. DeANGELO, and D.J. SKINNER, "Accounting Choice in Troubled Companies," *Journal of Accounting and Economics* (January 1994), pp. 113–143.

DeANGELO, L.E., "Auditor Size and Auditor Quality," *Journal of Accounting and Economics* (December 1981), pp. 183–199.

DECHOW, P.M., "Accounting Earnings and Cash Flows as Measures of Firm Performance: The Role of Accounting Accruals," *Journal of Accounting and Economics* (July 1994), pp. 3–42.

DECHOW, P.M. and I. DICHEV, "The Quality of Accruals and Earnings: The Role of Accrual Estimation Errors," *The Accounting Review* (Supplement 2002), pp. 35–59.

DECHOW, P.M., A.P. HUTTON, and R.G. SLOAN, "An Empirical Assessment of the Residual Income Valuation Model," *Journal of Accounting and Economics* (January 1999), pp. 1–34.

DECHOW, P.M., R.G. SLOAN, and A.P. SWEENEY, "Causes and Consequences of Earnings Manipulation: An Analysis of Firms Subject to Enforcement Actions by the SEC," *Contemporary Accounting Research* (Spring 1996), pp. 1–36.

DECHOW, P.M., R.G. SLOAN, and A.P. SWEENEY, "Detecting Earnings Management," *The Accounting Review* (April 1995), pp. 193–225.

DEFOND, M.L. and J. JIAMBALVO, "Debt Covenant Violation and Manipulation of Accruals," *Journal of Accounting and Economics* (January 1994), pp. 145–176.

DeLONG, J.B., A. SHLEIFER, L. SUMMERS, and R.J. WALDMANN, "Positive Feedback Investment Strategies and Destabilizing Rational Speculation," *Journal of Finance* (June 1990), pp. 375–395.

DEMSKI, J. and D.E.M. SAPPING-TON, "Delegated Expertise," *Journal of Accounting Research* (Spring 1987), pp. 68–89.

DEMSKI, J. and D.E.M. SAPPING-TON, "Fully Revealing Income Measurement," *The Accounting Review* (April 1990), pp. 363–383.

DEMSKI, J., *Information Analysis* (Reading, MA: Addison-Wesley, 1972).

DEMSKI, J., "Positive Accounting Theory: A Review," *Accounting, Organizations and Society* (October 1988), pp. 623–629.

DEMSKI, J., "The General Impossibility of Normative Accounting Standards," *The Accounting Review* (1973), pp. 718–723.

DHALIWAL, D.S., K.J. LEE, and N.L. FARGHER, "The Association Between Unexpected Earnings and Abnormal Security Returns in the Presence of Financial Leverage," *Contemporary Accounting Research* (Fall 1991), pp. 20–41.

DHALIWAL, D.S., K.R. SUBRA-MANYAM, and R. TREZEVANT, "Is Comprehensive Income Superior to Net Income as a Measure of Firm Performance?" *Journal of Accounting and Economics* (January 1999), pp. 43–67.

DIAMOND, D.W. and R.E. VERREC-CHIA, "Disclosure, Liquidity, and the Cost of Capital," *The Journal of Finance* (September 1991), pp. 1325–1359.

DICHEV, I.D. and D.J. SKINNER, "Large-Sample Evidence on the Debt Covenant Hypothesis," *Journal of Accounting Research* (September 2002), pp. 1091–1123.

DOMTAR, *Annual Report 1996* (Montreal, QC: Domtar Inc., 1997).

DORAN, B.M., D.W. COLLINS, and D.S. DHALIWAL, "The Information Content of Historical Cost Earnings Relative to Supplemental Reserve-Based Accounting Data in the Extractive Petroleum Industry," *The Accounting Review* (July 1988), pp. 389–413.

DOYLE, J.T., R. J. LUNDHOLM, and M.T. SOLIMAN, "The Predictive Value of Expenses Excluded from Pro Forma Earnings," *Review of Accounting Studies* (2003), pp. 145–174.

DURNEV, A., R. MORCK, B. YEUNG, and P. ZAROWIN, "Does Greater Firm-Specific Return Variation Mean More or Less Informed Stock Pricing?" *Journal of Accounting Research* (December 2003), pp.797–836.

DYCKMAN, T.R. and A.J. SMITH, "Financial Accounting and Reporting by Oil and Gas Producing Companies: A Study of Information Effects," *Journal of Accounting and Economics* (March 1979), pp. 45–76.

DYE, R.A. and S. SUNDER, "Why Not Allow FASB and IASB Standards to Compete in the U.S.?" *Accounting Horizons* (September 2001), pp. 257–271.

DYE, R.A., "Disclosure of Nonproprietary Information," *Journal of Accounting Research* (Spring 1985), pp. 123–145.

DYE, R.A., "Earnings Management in an Overlapping Generations Model," *Journal of Accounting Research* (Autumn 1988), pp. 195–235.

DYE, R.A., "Proprietary and Nonproprietary Disclosures," *Journal of Business* (April 1986), pp. 331–366.

EASLEY, D. and M. O'HARA, "Information and the Cost of Capital," *The Journal of Finance* (August 2004), pp. 1553–1583.

EASTON, P.D. and M.E. ZMIJEWS-KI, "Cross-Sectional Variation in the Stock-Market Response to Accounting Earnings Announcements," *Journal of Accounting and Economics* (July 1989), pp. 117–141.

EASTON, P.D. and T.S. HARRIS, "Earnings as an Explanatory Variable for Returns," *Journal of Accounting Research* (Spring 1991), pp. 19–36.

EASTON, P.D., T.S. HARRIS, and J.A. OHLSON, "Aggregate Accounting Earnings Can Explain Most of Security Returns," *Journal of Accounting and Economics* (June/September 1992), pp. 119–142.

ECKERN, S. and R. WILSON, "On the Theory of the Firm in an Economy with Incomplete Markets," *The Bell Journal of Economics and Management Science* (Spring 1974), pp. 171–180.

ELLIOTT, J.A. and J.D. HANNA, "Repeated Accounting Write-Offs and the Information Content of Earnings," *Journal of Accounting Research* (Supplement 1996), pp. 135–169.

ELLIOTT, J.A., J.D. HANNA, and W.H. SHAW, "The Evaluation by the

Financial Markets of Changes in Bank Loan Loss Reserve Levels," *The Accounting Review* (October 1991), pp. 847–861.

ELY K. and G. WAYMIRE, "Accounting Standard-Setting Organizations and Earnings Relevance: Longitudinal Evidence from *NYSE* Common Stocks, 1927–93," *Journal of Accounting Research* (Autum 1999), pp. 293–317.

EVANS, J.H. and S.S. SRIDHAR, "Multiple Control Systems, Accrual Accounting, and Earnings Management," *Journal of Accounting Research* (Spring 1996), pp. 45–65.

FAMA, E.F., "Agency Problems and the Theory of the Firm," *Journal of Political Economy* (April 1980), pp. 288–307.

FAMA, E.F. and K.R. FRENCH, "The Cross-Section of Expected Stock Returns," *The Journal of Finance* (1992), pp. 427–465.

FAMA, E.F., "Efficient Capital Markets: A Review of Theory and Empirical Work," *Journal of Finance* (May 1970), pp. 383–417.

FAMA, E.F., "Market Efficiency, Long-Term Returns and Behavioral Finance," *Journal of Financial Economics* (September 1998), pp. 283–306.

"Fat Cats Feeding," *The Economist* (October 9, 2003), pp. 64–66.

FELTHAM, G.A. and J.A. OHLSON, "Uncertainty Resolution and the Theory of Depreciation Measurement," *Journal of Accounting Research* (Autumn 1996), pp. 209–234.

FELTHAM, G.A. and J.A. OHLSON, "Valuation and Clean Surplus Accounting for Operating and Financial Activities," *Contemporary Accounting Research* (Spring 1995), pp. 689–731.

FELTHAM, G.A. and J. XIE, "Performance Measure Congruity and Diversity in Multi-Task Principal/Agent Relations," *The Accounting Review* (July 1994), pp. 429–453.

FINANCIAL ACOUNTING STANDARDS BOARD, *Proposal for a Principles-based Approach to U.S. Standard-setting* (Norwalk, CT: FASB, 2002).

FINANCIAL ACCOUNTING STANDARDS BOARD, *Statement of Financial Accounting Concepts No. 1, Objectives of Financial Reporting by Business Enterprises* (Norwalk, CT: FASB, 1978).

FINANCIAL ACCOUNTING STANDARDS BOARD, *Statement of Financial Accounting Concepts No. 2, Qualitative Characteristics of Accounting Information* (Norwalk, CT: FASB, 1980).

FINANCIAL ACCOUNTING STANDARDS BOARD, *Statement of Financial Accounting Standards No. 2, Accounting for Research and Development Costs* (Norwalk, CT: FASB, 1974).

FINANCIAL ACCOUNTING STANDARDS BOARD, *Statement of Financial Accounting Standards No. 19, Financial Accounting and Reporting by Oil and Gas Producing Companies* (Norwalk, CT: FASB, 1977).

FINANCIAL ACCOUNTING STANDARDS BOARD, *Statement of Financial Accounting Standards No. 25, Suspension of Certain Accounting Requirements for Oil and Gas Producing Companies* (Norwalk, CT: FASB, 1979).

FINANCIAL ACCOUNTING STANDARDS BOARD, *Statement of Financial Accounting Standards No. 33, Financial*

Reporting and Changing Prices (Norwalk, CT: FASB, 1979).

FINANCIAL ACCOUNTING STANDARDS BOARD, *Statement of Financial Accounting Standards No. 52, Foreign Currency Translation* (Norwalk, CT: FASB, 1981).

FINANCIAL ACCOUNTING STANDARDS BOARD, *Statement of Financial Accounting Standards No. 69, Disclosures about Oil and Gas Producing Activities* (Norwalk, CT: FASB, 1982).

FINANCIAL ACCOUNTING STANDARDS BOARD, *Statement of Financial Accounting Standards No. 87, Employers' Accounting for Pensions* (Norwalk, CT: FASB, 1985).

FINANCIAL ACCOUNTING STANDARDS BOARD, *Statement of Financial Accounting Standards No. 106, Employers' Accounting for Postretirement Benefits Other Than Pensions* (Norwalk, CT: FASB, 1990).

FINANCIAL ACCOUNTING STANDARDS BOARD, *Statement of Financial Accounting Standards No. 107, Disclosures about Fair Value of Financial Instruments* (Norwalk, CT: FASB, 1991).

FINANCIAL ACCOUNTING STANDARDS BOARD, *Statement of Financial Accounting Standards No. 115, Accounting for Certain Investments in Debt and Equity Securities* (Norwalk, CT: FASB, 1993).

FINANCIAL ACCOUNTING STANDARDS BOARD, *Statement of Financial Accounting Standards No.123, Accounting for Stock-based Compensation* (Norwalk, CT: FASB, 1995).

FINANCIAL ACCOUNTING STANDARDS BOARD, *Statement of Financial Accounting Standards No. 130, Reporting Comprehensive Income* (Norwalk, CT: FASB, 1997).

FINANCIAL ACCOUNTING STANDARDS BOARD, *Statement of Financial Accounting Standards No. 131, Financial Reporting for Segments of a Business Enterprise* (Norwalk, CT: FASB, 1997).

FINANCIAL ACCOUNTING STANDARDS BOARD, *Statement of Financial Accounting Standards No. 133, Accounting for Derivative Instruments and Hedging Activities* (Norwalk, CT: FASB, 1998).

FINANCIAL ACCOUNTING STANDARDS BOARD, *Statement of Financial Accounting Standards No. 141, Business Combinations* (Norwalk, CT: FASB, 2001).

FINANCIAL ACOUNTING STANDARDS BOARD, *Statement of Financial Accounting Standards No. 142, Goodwill and Other Intangible Assets* (Norwalk, CT: FASB, 2001).

FOSTER, G., C. OLSEN, and T. SHEVLIN, "Earnings Releases, Anomalies, and the Behavior of Security Returns," *The Accounting Review* (January 1984), pp. 574–603.

FRANCIS, J., K. SCHIPPER, and L. VINCENT, "Expanded Disclosures and the Increased Usefulness of Earnings Announcements," *The Accounting Review* (July 2002), pp. 515–546.

FRANCIS, J., R. LAFOND, P. OLSSON, AND K. SCHIPPER, "Costs of Equity and Earnings Attributes," *The Accounting Review* (October 2004), pp. 967–1010.

FRANKEL, R. and C.M.C. LEE, "Accounting Valuation, Market Expectation, and Cross-Sectional Stock Returns," *Journal of Accounting and Economics* (June 1998), pp. 283–319.

FRIEDLAN, J.M., "Accounting Choices of Issuers of Initial Public Offerings," *Contemporary Accounting Research* (Summer 1994), pp. 1–31.

GAVER, J.J. and K.M. GAVER, "The Relation Between Nonrecurring Accounting Transactions and CEO Cash Compensation," *The Accounting Review* (April 1998), pp. 235–253.

GHICAS, D. and V. PASTENA, "The Acquisition Value of Oil and Gas Firms: The Role of Historical Costs, Reserve Recognition Accounting, and Analysts' Appraisals," *Contemporary Accounting Research* (Fall 1989), pp. 125–142.

GINTSCHEL, A. and S. MARKOV, 'The Effectiveness of Regulation FD," *Journal of Accounting and Economics* (September 2004), pp. 293–314.

GJESDAL, F., "Accounting for Stewardship," *Journal of Accounting Research* (Spring 1981), pp. 208–231.

GONEDES, N. and N. DOPUCH, "Capital Market Equilibrium, Information Production, and Selected Accounting Techniques: Theoretical Framework and Review of Empirical Work," *Journal of Accounting Research* (Supplement 1974), pp. 48–129.

GROSSMAN, S., "On the Efficiency of Competitive Stock Markets Where Traders Have Diverse Information," *The Journal of Finance* (May 1976), pp. 573–585.

GROSSMAN, S., "The Informational Role of Warranties and Private Disclosure about Product Quality," *Journal of Law and Economics* (December 1981), pp. 461–484.

GUAY, W.R., "The Impact of Derivatives on Firm Risk: An Empirical Examination of New Derivatives Users,"

Journal of Accounting and Economics (January 1999), pp. 319–351.

HALL, B.J. AND K.J. MURPHY, "Stock Options for Diversified Executives," *Journal of Accounting and Economics* (February 2002), pp. 3–42.

HAMADA, R., "The Effect of the Firm's Capital Structure on the Systematic Risk of Common Stocks," *Journal of Finance* (May 1972), pp. 435–452.

HANNA, J.D., "Never Say Never," *CA Magazine* (August 1999), pp. 35–39.

HANNA, J.R., D.B. KENNEDY, and G.D. RICHARDSON, *Reporting the Effects of Changing Prices: A Review of the Experience with Section 4510* (Toronto, ON: CICA, 1990).

HARRIS, T.S. and J.A. OHLSON, "Accounting Disclosures and the Market's Evaluation of Oil and Gas Properties," *The Accounting Review* (October 1987), pp. 651–670.

HARRIS, T.S. and J.A. OHLSON, "Accounting Disclosures and the Market's Valuation of Oil and Gas Properties: Evaluation of Market Efficiency and Functional Fixation," *The Accounting Review* (October 1990), pp. 764–780.

HATFIELD, H.R., *Accounting* (New York, NY: Appleton-Century-Crofts, Inc., 1927).

HEALY, P.M. and K.G. PALEPU, "The Effect of Firms' Financial Disclosure Strategies on Stock Prices," *Accounting Horizons* (March 1993), pp. 1–11.

HEALY, P. M. and K. G. PALEPU, "The Fall of Enron," *Journal of Economic Perspectives* (Spring 2003), pp. 3–26.

HEALY, P.M., A.P. HUTTON, and K.G. PALEPU, "Stock Performance and Intermediation Changes Surrounding Sustained Increases in Disclosure," *Contemporary Accounting Research* (Fall 1999), pp. 485–520.

HEALY, P.M., "The Effect of Bonus Schemes on Accounting Decisions," *Journal of Accounting and Economics* (April 1985), pp. 85–107.

HEMMER, T.S., S. MATSUNAGA, and T. SHEVLIN, "Estimating the 'Fair Value' of Employee Stock Options with Expected Early Exercise," *Accounting Horizons* (December 1994), pp. 23–42.

HIRSHLEIFER, D. and S.H. TEOH, "Limited Attention, Information Disclosure, and Financial Reporting," *Journal of Accounting and Economics* (December 2003), pp. 337–386.

HIRSHLEIFER, D., "Investor Psychology and Asset Pricing," *Journal of Finance* (2001).

HIRSHLEIFER, J., "The Private and Social Value of Information and the Reward to Inventive Activity," *American Economic Review* (September 1971), pp. 561–573.

HOLMSTRÖM, B., "Moral Hazard and Observability," *The Bell Journal of Economics* (Spring 1979), pp. 74–91.

HOLMSTRÖM, B., "Moral Hazard in Teams," *The Bell Journal of Economics* (Autumn 1982), pp. 324–340.

HOLTHAUSEN, R.W., D.F. LARCKER, and R.G. SLOAN, "Annual Bonus Schemes and the Manipulation of Earnings," *Journal of Accounting and Economics* (February 1995), pp. 29–74.

HOLTHAUSEN, R.W. and D.F. LARCKER, "The Prediction of Stock Returns Using Financial Statement Information," *Journal of Accounting and Economics* (June/September 1992), pp. 373–411.

HRIBAR, P. and D. W. COLLINS, "Errors in Estimating Accruals," *Journal of Accounting Research* (March 2002), pp. 105–134.

HUDDART, S. and M. LANG, "Employee Stock Option Exercises: An Empirical Analysis," *Journal of Accounting and Economics* (February 1996), pp. 5–43.

HUDDART, S., "Employee Stock Options," *Journal of Accounting and Economics* (September 1994), pp. 207–231.

HUGHES, P.J., "Signalling by Direct Disclosure Under Asymmetric Information," *Journal of Accounting and Economics* (June 1986), pp. 119–142.

INDJEJIKIAN, R. J. and D. NANDA, "Executive Bonuses and What They Imply about Performance Standards," *The Accounting Review* (October 2002), pp. 793–819.

INTERNATIONAL ACCOUNTING STANDARDS BOARD, *International Accounting Standard IAS 22, Business Combinations (Revised 1998)* (London: IASB, 1998).

INTERNATIONAL ACCOUNTING STANDARDS BOARD, *International Accounting Standard IAS 39, Financial Instruments: Recognition and Measurement* (London: IASB, 1999).

ITTNER, C.D., D.F. LARCKER, and M.V. RAJAN, "The Choice of Performance Measures in Annual Bonus Contracts," *The Accounting Review* (April 1997), pp. 231–255.

JAMAL, K., M. MAIER, and S. SUNDER, "Privacy in E-Commerce:

Development of Reporting Standards, Disclosure, and Assurance Services in an Unregulated Market," *Journal of Accounting Research* (May 2003), pp. 285–309.

JENSEN, M.C. and K.J. MURPHY, "CEO Incentives—It's Not How Much You Pay, But How," *Harvard Business Review* (May/June 1990), pp. 138–149.

JENSEN, M.C. and W.H. MECK-LING, "Theory of the Firm: Managerial Behavior, Agency Costs and Ownership Structure," *Journal of Financial Economics* (October 1976), pp. 305–360.

JONES, J., "Earnings Management During Import Relief Investigations," *Journal of Accounting Research* (Autumn 1991), pp. 193–228.

KAHNEMAN, D. and A. TVERSKY, "Prospect Theory: An Analysis of Decision Under Risk," *Econometrica* (March 1979), pp. 263–291.

KAPLAN, R.S., "Comments on Paul Healy," *Journal of Accounting and Economics* (April 1985), pp. 109–113.

KIM, O. and R.E. VERRECCHIA, "Pre-announcement and Event-period Private Information," *Journal of Accounting and Economics* (1997), pp. 395–419.

KIM, O. and Y. SUH, "Incentive Efficiency of Compensation Based on Accounting and Market Performance," *Journal of Accounting and Economics* (January/April/July 1993), pp. 25–53.

KNETSCH, J. L., "The Endowment Effect and Evidence of Nonreversible Indifference Curves," *The American Economic Review* (December 1989), pp. 1277–1284.

KORMENDI, R.C. and R. LIPE, "Earnings Innovations, Earnings Persistence, and Stock Returns," *Journal of Business* (July 1987), pp. 323–346.

KOTHARI, S.P., "Capital Markets Research in Accounting," *Journal of Accounting and Economics* (September 2001), pp. 105–231.

KOTHARI, S.P., J. SHANKEN, and R. SLOAN, "Another Look at the Cross-Section of Expected Returns," *Journal of Finance* (March 1995), pp. 185–224.

KROSS, W., "Stock Returns and Oil and Gas Pronouncements: Replications and Extensions," *Journal of Accounting Research* (Autumn 1982), pp. 459–471.

KURZ, M., ed., *Endogenous Economic Fluctuations* (New York, NY: Springer-Verlag, 1997).

KURZ, M., "Endogenous Uncertainty: A Unified View of Market Volatility," working paper, Stanford University, September 1997.

LAFFONT, J.J., *The Economics of Uncertainty and Information* (Cambridge, MA: MIT Press, 1989).

LAMBERT, R.A. and D.F. LARCKER, "An Analysis of the Use of Accounting and Market Measures of Performance in Executive Compensation Contracts," *Journal of Accounting Research* (Supplement 1987), pp. 85–125.

LAMBERT, R.A. and D.F. LARCKER, "Firm Performance and the Compensation of Chief Executive Officers," working paper (January 1993).

LAMBERT, R.A., D.F. LARCKER, and R.E. VERRECCHIA, "Portfolio Considerations in Valuing Executive Compensation," *Journal of Accounting Research* (Spring 1991), pp. 129–149.

LANDSMAN, W. R. and E. L. MAY-DEW, "Has the Information Content of Quarterly Earnings Announcements Declined in the Past Three Decades?" *Journal of Accounting Research* (June 2002), pp. 797–808.

LANG, M.H. and R.J. LUNDHOLM, "Corporate Disclosure Policy and Analyst Behavior," *The Accounting Review* (October 1996), pp. 467–492.

LANG, M.H., K.V. LINS and D.P. MILLER, "ADRs, Analysts, and Accuracy: Does Cross Listing in the United States Improve a Firm's Information Environment and Increase Market Value? *Journal of Accounting Research* (May 2003), pp. 317–345.

LEE, C.M.C., B. MUCKLOW, and M.J. READY, "Spreads, Depths, and the Impact of Earnings Information: An Intraday Analysis," *The Review of Financial Studies* (1993), pp. 345–374.

LEE, C.M.C., "Market Efficiency and Accounting Research: A Discussion of 'Capital Market Research in Accounting' by S.P. Kothari," *Journal of Accounting and Economics (*September 2001), pp. 233–253.

LEE, C.M.C., "Measuring Wealth," *C.A. Magazine* (April 1996), pp. 32–37.

LEE, Y-J, K. PETRONI, and M. SHEN, "Cherry Picking, Financial Reporting Quality, and Comprehensive Income Reporting Choices: The Case of Property-Liability Insurers," (September 21, 2004). Forthcoming in *Contemporary Accounting Research*.

LELAND, H.E. and D.H. PYLE, "Information Asymmetries, Financial Structure, and Financial Intermediation," *The Journal of Finance* (May 1977), pp. 371–387.

LEV, B. and S.R. THIAGARAJAN, "Fundamental Information Analysis," *Journal of Accounting Research* (Autumn 1993), pp. 190–215.

LEV, B. and P. ZAROWIN, "The Boundaries of Financial Reporting and How to Extend Them," *Journal of Accounting Research* (Autumn 1999), pp. 353–385.

LEV, B., "On the Association Between Operating Leverage and Risk," *Journal of Financial and Quantitative Analysis* (September 1974), pp. 627–640.

LEV, B., "On the Usefulness of Earnings: Lessons and Directions from Two Decades of Empirical Research," *Journal of Accounting Research* (Supplement, 1989), pp. 153–192.

LEV, B., "Toward a Theory of Equitable and Efficient Accounting Policy," *The Accounting Review* (January 1988), pp. 1–22.

LEV, B., "The Impact of Accounting Regulation on the Stock Market: The Case of Oil and Gas Companies," *The Accounting Review* (July 1979), pp. 485–503.

LINSMEIER, T.J., and N.D. PEARSON, "Quantitative Disclosure of Market Risk in the SEC Release," *Accounting Horizons* (1997), pp. 107–135.

LINTNER, J., "The Valuation of Risky Assets and the Selection of Risky Investments in Stock Portfolios and Capital Budgets," *Review of Economics and Statistics* (February 1965), pp. 13–37.

LIST, J.A., "Does Market Experience Eliminate Market Anomalies?" *The Quarterly Journal of Economics* (February 2003), pp. 41–71.

LIU, C-C., S.G. RYAN, and J.M. WAHLEN, "Differential Valuation Implications of Loan Loss Provisions Across Banks and Fiscal Quarters," *The Accounting Review* (January 1997), pp. 133–146.

LO, K., "Economic Consequences of Regulated Changes in Disclosure: The Case of Executive Compensation," *Journal of Accounting and Economics* (August 2003), pp. 285–314.

LYS, T., "Mandated Accounting Changes and Debt Covenants: The Case of Oil and Gas Companies," *Journal of Accounting and Economics* (April 1984), pp. 39–65.

MAGLIOLO, J., "Capital Market Analysis of Reserve Recognition Accounting," *Journal of Accounting Research* (Supplement 1986), pp. 69-108.

MARQUARDT, C.A., "The Cost of Employee Stock Option Grants: An Empirical Analysis," *Journal of Accounting Research* (September 2002), pp. 1191–1217.

MATSUMOTO, D.A., "Management's Incentives to Avoid Negative Earnings Surprises," *The Accounting Review* (July 2002), pp. 483–514.

McNICHOLS, M. and G.P. WILSON, "Evidence of Earnings Management from the Provision for Bad Debts," *Journal of Accounting Research* (Supplement 1988), pp. 1–31.

MERINO, D.B. and M.D. NEIMARK, "Disclosure Regulation and Public Policy: A Sociohistorical Reappraisal," *Journal of Accounting and Public Policy* (Fall 1982), pp. 33–57.

MERTON, R.C., "A Simple Model of Capital Market Equilibrium with Incomplete Markets," *The Journal of Finance* (July 1987), pp. 483–510.

MERTON, R.C., "Theory of Rational Option Pricing," *Bell Journal of Economics and Management Science* (Spring 1973), pp. 141–183.

MIAN, S.L. and C.W. SMITH, JR., "Incentives for Unconsolidated Financial Reporting," *Journal of Accounting and Economics* (January 1990), pp. 141–171.

"Microsoft to Award Stock, Not Options to Employees," *The Globe and Mail* (July 9, 2003), p. B9 (Reprinted from an article in *The Wall Street Journal* by Don Clark).

MILGROM, P., "Good News and Bad News: Representation Theorems and Applications," *Bell Journal of Economics* (Autumn 1981), pp. 380–391.

MYERS, J.N., "Implementing Residual Income Valuation with Linear Information Dynamics," *The Accounting Review* (January 1999), pp. 1–28.

MYERSON, R.B., "Incentive Compatability and the Bargaining Problem," *Econometrica* (1979), pp. 61–74.

NEWMAN, P. and R. SANSING, "Disclosure Policies with Multiple Users," *Journal of Accounting Research* (Spring 1993), pp. 92–112.

O'BRIEN, P.C., "Analysts' Forecasts as Earnings Expectations," *Journal of Accounting and Economics* (January 1988), pp. 53–83.

ODEAN, T., "Volume, Volatility, Price and Profit When All Traders Are Above Average," *Journal of Finance* (December 1998), pp. 1887–1934.

OHLSON, J.A., "On the Nature of Income Measurement: The Basic

Results," *Contemporary Accounting Research* (Fall 1987), pp. 1–15.

ONTARIO SECURITIES COMMISSION, National Instrument 51–102, "Continuous Disclosure Obligations" (Ontario Securities Commission: March, 2004).

ONTARIO SECURITIES COMMISSION, "OSC National Policy Statement No. 27," *OSC Bulletin* (December 18, 1992), pp. 6055–6144.

ONTARIO SECURITIES COMMISSION, "Statement of Executive Compensation," Form 40, Securities Act, Regulation 638/93, *The Ontario Gazette*, Vol. 126-39 (September 25, 1993), pp. 1203–1216.

PAE, S., "Optimal Disclosure Policy in Oligopoly Markets," *Journal of Accounting Research* (June 2002), pp. 901–932.

PALEPU, K.G., P.M. HEALY, and V.L. BERNARD, *Business Analysis and Valuation*: (South-Western College Publishing, Cincinnati, OH: 2000).

PALMROSE, Z-V and S. SCHOLZ, "The Circumstances and Legal Consequences of Non-GAAP Reporting: Evidence from Restatements," *Contemporary Accounting Research* (Spring 2004), pp. 139–180.

PATON, W.A. and A.C. LITTLETON, *An Introduction to Corporate Accounting Standards* (Ubana, IL: American Accounting Association, 1940).

PAVLIK, E.L., T.W. SCOTT, and P. TIESSEN, "Executive Compensation: Issues and Research," *Journal of Accounting Literature* (1993), pp. 131–189.

PELTZMAN, SAM, "Toward a More General Theory of Regulation," *The Journal of Law and Economics* (August 1976), pp. 21–240.

PENNO, M.C., "Information Quality and Voluntary Disclosure," *The Accounting Review* (April 1997), pp. 275–284.

POSNER, R.A., "Theories of Economic Regulation," *Bell Journal of Economics and Management Science* (Autumn 1974), pp. 335–358.

PRATT, J.W., "Risk Aversion In the Small and In the Large," *Econometrica* (January–April 1964), pp. 122–136.

RAIFFA, H., *Decision Analysis: Introductory Lectures on Choices Under Uncertainty* (Reading, MA: Addison-Wesley, 1968).

RAJGOPAL, S. and T. SHEVLIN, "Empirical Evidence on the Relation Between Stock Option Compensation and Risk Taking," *Journal of Accounting and Economics* (June 2002), pp. 145–171.

RAMAKRISHNAN, R.T.S. and J.K. THOMAS, "Valuation of Permanent, Transitory and Price-Irrelevant Components of Reported Earnings," working paper, Columbia University Business School, July 1991.

ROLL, R., "R^2," *Journal of Finance* (July 1988), pp. 541–566.

RYAN, S.G., "A Survey of Research Relating Accounting Numbers to Systematic Equity Risk, with Implications for Risk Disclosure Policy and Future Research," *Accounting Horizons* (June 1997), pp. 82–95.

SALY, P.J., "Repricing Executive Stock Options in a Down Market," *Journal of Accounting and Economics* (November 1994), pp. 325–356.

SAVAGE, L.J., *The Foundations of Statistics* (NY: Wiley, 1954).

SCHIPPER, K., "Commentary on Earnings Management," *Accounting Horizons* (December 1989), pp. 91–102.

SCHRAND, C.M. and B.R. WALTHER, "Strategic Benchmarks in Earnings Announcements: The Selective Disclosure of Prior-Period Earnings Components," *The Accounting Review* (April 2000), pp. 151–177.

SCHRAND, C.M., "The Association Between Stock-Price Interest Rate Sensitivity and Disclosures about Derivative Instruments," *The Accounting Review* (January 1997), pp. 87–109.

SCOTT, W.R., "Auditor's Loss Functions Implicit in Consumption-Investment Models," *Journal of Accounting Research* (Supplement 1975), pp. 98–117.

SCOTT, W.R., "Group Preference Orderings for Audit and Valuation Alternatives," *Journal of Accounting Research* (Spring 1977), pp. 120–138.

SECURITIES ACT, *Revised Statutes of Ontario, 1990*, Vol. 11, Chapter 5.5 (Toronto, ON: Queen's Printer for Ontario, 1991).

SECURITIES AND EXCHANGE COMMISSION, *Accounting Series Release No. 150* (Washington, DC: SEC, 1973).

SECURITIES AND EXCHANGE COMMISSION, *Accounting Series Release No. 253* (Washington, DC: SEC, 1978).

SECURITIES AND EXCHANGE COMMISSION, *Disclosure of Accounting Policies for Derivative Financial Instruments and Derivative Commodity Instruments and Disclosure of Quantitative and Qualitative Information About Market Risk Inherent in Derivative Financial Instruments, Other Financial Instruments, and Derivative Commodity Instruments* (Washington, DC: SEC, 1997).

SECURITIES AND EXCHANGE COMMISSION, *Study Pursuant to Section 108(d) of the Sarbanes-Oxley Act of 2002 on the Adoption by the United States Financial Reporting System of a Principles-Based Accounting System* (Washington, DC: SEC, 2003).

SENGUPTA, P., "Corporate Disclosure Quality and the Cost of Debt," *The Accounting Review* (October 1998), pp. 459–474.

SHARPE, W.F., "Capital Asset Prices: A Theory of Market Equilibrium Under Conditions of Risk," *The Journal of Finance* (September 1964), pp. 425–442.

SHEFRIN, H. and M. STATMAN, "The Disposition to Sell Winners Too Early and Ride Losers Too Long," *Journal of Finance* (July 1985), pp. 777–790.

SHILLER, R.J., "Do Stock Prices Move Too Much to Be Justified by Subsequent Changes in Dividends?" *The American Economic Review* (June 1981), pp. 421–436.

SHILLER, R.J., *Irrational Exuberance* (New York, NY: Broadway Books, 2000).

SKINNER, D.J. and R.G.SLOAN, "Earnings Surprises, Growth Expectations, and Stock Returns or Don't Let an Earnings Torpedo Sink Your Portfolio," *Review of Accounting Studies* (2002), pp. 289–312.

SKINNER, D.J., "How Well Does Net Income Measure Firm Performance? A Discussion of Two Studies," *Journal of*

Accounting and Economics (January 1999), pp. 105–111.

SLOAN, R.G., "Accounting Earnings and Top Executive Compensation," *Journal of Accounting and Economics* (January/April/July 1993), pp. 55–100.

SLOAN, R.G., "Do Stock Prices Fully Reflect Information in Accruals and Cash Flows About Future Earnings?" *The Accounting Review* (July 1996), pp. 289–315.

SMITH, A., "Earnings and Management Incentives: Comments," *Journal of Accounting and Economics* (January/April/July 1993), pp. 337–347.

SPENCE, M., "Job Market Signalling," *Quarterly Journal of Economics* (August 1973), pp. 355–374.

STIGLER, G.J., "The Theory of Economic Regulation," *The Bell Journal of Economics and Management Science* (Spring 1971), pp. 3–21.

STOCKEN, P.C. and R.E. VERREC-CHIA, "Financial Reporting System Choice and Disclosure Management," *The Accounting Review* (October 2004), pp. 1181–1203.

STOREY, R.K. and S. STOREY, *The Framework of Financial Accounting Concepts and Standards* (Norwalk, CT: Financial Accounting Standards Board, 1998).

STUDY GROUP ON THE OBJEC-TIVES OF FINANCIAL STATE-MENTS, *Objectives of Financial Statements* (New York, NY: American Institute of Certified Public Accountants, 1973). (Also called the Trueblood committee report).

SUBRAMANYAM, K.R., "The Pricing of Discretionary Accruals," *Journal of*

Accounting and Economics (August-December 1996), pp. 249–281.

SUROWIECKI, JAMES, *The Wisdom of Crowds* (New York, NY: Doubleday Division of Random House Inc., 2004).

SWEENEY, A.P., "Debt-covenant Violations and Managers' Accounting Responses," *Journal of Accounting and Economics* (May 1994), pp. 281–308.

TITMAN, S. and B. TRUEMAN, "Information Quality and the Valuation of New Issues," *Journal of Accounting and Economics* (June 1986), pp. 159–172.

VERRECCHIA, R.E., "Discretionary Disclosure," *Journal of Accounting and Economics* (December 1983), pp. 179–194.

WARFIELD, T.D. and J.J. WILD, "Accounting Recognition and the Relevance of Earnings as an Explanatory Variable for Returns," *The Accounting Review* (October 1992), pp. 821–842.

WATTS, R.L. and J.L. ZIMMERMAN, "Positive Accounting Theory: A Ten Year Perspective," *The Accounting Review* (January 1990), pp. 131–156.

WATTS, R.L. and J.L. ZIMMERMAN, *Positive Accounting Theory* (Englewood Cliffs, NJ: Prentice-Hall, 1986).

WATTS, R.L., "Conservatism in Accounting Part I: Explanations and Implications" *Accounting Horizons* (September 2003), pp. 207–221.

WATTS, R. L., "Conservatism in Accounting Part II: Evidence and Research Opportunities," *Accounting Horizons* (December 2003), pp. 287–301.

WEIL, R.L., "Role of the Time Value of Money in Financial Reporting," *Accounting Horizons* (December 1990), pp. 47–67.

WELKER, M., "Disclosure Policy, Information Asymmetry, and Liquidity in Equity Markets," *Contemporary Accounting Research* (Spring 1995), pp. 801–827.

WOLFSON, M.A., "Empirical Evidence of Incentive Problems and Their Mitigation in Oil and Gas Tax Shelter Programs," in J.W. Pratt and R.J. Zeckhauser, eds., *Principals and Agents: The Structure of Business* (Boston, MA: The President and Fellows of Harvard College, 1985), pp. 101–125.

WONG, M.H.F., "The Association Between SFAS 119 Derivative Disclosures and the Foreign Exchange Risk Exposure of Manufacturing Firms," working paper, Haas School of Business, University of California at Berkeley, July 1998.

WURGLER, J., "Financial Markets and the Allocation of Capital," *Journal of Financial Economics*, Vol. 58 (2000), pp. 187–214.

XIE, H., "The Mispricing of Abnormal Accruals," *The Accounting Review* (July 2001), pp. 357–373.

YERMACK, D., "Good Timing: CEO Stock Option Awards and Company News Announcements," *Journal of Finance* (1997), pp. 449–476.

ZEFF, S.A., "How the U.S. Accounting Profession Got Where It Is Today: Part II," *Accounting Horizons* (December 2003), pp. 267–286.

ZEFF, S.A., "The Rise of Economic Consequences," *The Journal of Accountancy* (December 1978), pp. 56–63.

Index